ARCTIC
OCEAN
GREENLAND
U.S.S.R.
Balmoral
Preswick
Goose Bay
Bonn
London
Paris
Harmon AFB
SPAIN
Rome
Toulon
Ankara
Lisbon
Madrid
PORTUGAL
Athens
Tunis
Teheran
Kabul
New Delhi
Casablanca
MOROCCO
IRAN
ATLANTIC
SAUDI ARABIA
Karachi
Agra
INDIA
Ramey AFB
San Juan
PUERTO RICO
Paramaribo
SURINAM
OCEAN
INDIAN
OCEAN
BRAZIL
Brasilia
São Paulo
Rio de Janeiro
Santiago
Montevideo
Buenos Aires
Mar del Plata
S. Carlos de Bariloche
ARGENTINA
Feb. 22 – Mar. 7, 1960
Washington, Ramey AFB, San Juan, Brasilia, Rio de Janeiro, São Paulo, Rio de Janeiro, Buenos Aires, Mar del Plata, San Carlos de Bariloche, Santiago, Montevideo, Buenos Aires, Paramaribo, Ramey AFB, San Juan
May 14 – May 19, 1960
Washington, Paris, Lisbon, Washington
June 12 – June 27, 1960
Washington, Anchorage, Wake, Manila, Taipei, Naha, Seoul, Wake, Honolulu, Washington
Oct. 24. 1960
Washington, Diablos Dam, Washington

WAGING PEACE

The White House Years

WAGING PEACE

1956–1961

Dwight D. Eisenhower

DOUBLEDAY & COMPANY, INC., GARDEN CITY, NEW YORK

Printed in the United States of America

To my grandchildren:

DWIGHT DAVID
BARBARA ANNE
SUSAN ELAINE
MARY JEAN

In the faith that when they become interested in the history of the period in which they spent their childhood they will enjoy no less freedom, opportunity, and liberty of action than are now possessed by all American citizens.

Preface

THIS volume, like the one preceding it, is an account of my presidential years as I see them, based on memory and on voluminous records, public and private. The first volume, *Mandate for Change,* covers generally the period from January 1953 to February 1956, the time of my decision to run for re-election, with occasional departures from these time limits to permit fuller development of certain issues.

The second volume, *Waging Peace,* details major developments from the national elections of 1956 until just after Inauguration Day 1961, or the four years of my second term. Again, there are a few glimpses into the time before and beyond those years.

The episodes told herein, and in the preceding volume, involve certain conditions, problems, and actions of eight years. Time and circumstances affect all decision-making. Our case was no exception. Consequently, this work does not pretend to be, nor should it be taken, as an index or guide to the specific current or future policies of the United States of America. However, if anything here—the story of a lesson learned, a principle proved, or an old truth emphasized—should be found of value by those who in years to come will bear responsibilities in the federal government, all of us who served this nation in my administration will be deeply rewarded.

—D.E.

Gettysburg, Pennsylvania, 1965

Contents

Preface vii

BOOK ONE

I *The Political Campaign, 1956* 3

Announcement of intention to run again. Nixon as running mate. Ileitis attack. Panama Conference. The convention in San Francisco: renomination, platform, celebration. Goals of the Republican party. The campaign: flying trips, the "truth squad." Stevenson's attacks on Milton Eisenhower, nuclear testing, and the draft. Election results.

II *Build-up to Suez* 20

The historical background. Tensions between Israel and her neighbors. Military alliances in Suez. The rise of Nasser. Czech arms deal. The Baghdad Pact. Crises in Jordan and Cyprus, clashes along the Gaza Strip. Offers of assistance for the Aswan Dam. Missions of Eric Johnston and Foster Dulles. Egyptian seizure of the Canal. Exchanges of British and American views. Meetings with bipartisan congressional leadership. 22-nation conference in London. The Menzies mission. Canal Users Association. The Second London Conference. British and French appeal to the UN, and a result—"Six Principles." Evidence of Israeli mobilization.

III *Twenty Busy Days* 58

Khrushchev confronts Gomulka. Riots in Wroclaw and Poznan. Soviet tanks in Budapest. Disquieting reports from the

VII *Renewed Tension in the Middle East* 177

The "Eisenhower Doctrine." Ben-Gurion and the resolution for the withdrawal of Israeli troops from Egypt. UN Emergency Force along the Gaza Strip. A plea from King Saud. Suez Canal Authority begins operations. Crisis in Jordan. Liquidation of Oman rebellion. The Syrian problem.

VIII *Sputnik and a Sputtering Economy* 205

Soviet Union orbits first manmade satellite. Apprehension in the Free World. "Shocked" politicians and concerned parents. A brief history of missile development. Initiation of Project Vanguard. Scientists urge acceleration in science and engineering. Interlude: the visit of Queen Elizabeth and Prince Philip. Second Sputnik and Laika. The Gaither Report. Speeches on the "right to confidence."

IX *A Drastic Personal Test* 227

Third illness. Difficulties with speech. A personal test at a NATO summit. Nostalgic visits in Paris. Agreement on the question of arms for Europe. A plan to deal with presidential disability.

BOOK THREE

X *Science and Defense* 239

State of the Union message on scientific and military strength. Drive for the National Defense Education Act. Reorganization of the Department of Defense. Resistance in the Congress. Polaris. Changes of military advisers. Explorer I launched. Creation of National Aeronautics and Space Administration. Human benefits and space exploration through satellites. Selection of astronauts and launching of Project Mercury. *Nautilus* cruise under Arctic ice cap. Effect of scientific and technological change on man and his institutions.

XI *Landing in Lebanon* 262

President Nasser announces formation of United Arab Republic. Iraq and Jordan merge. Abdication of King Saud. Christians vs. Moslems in Lebanese politics. Armed uprising

BOOK FIVE

Illustrations

BOOK ONE

Our resources are too many, our principles too dynamic, our purposes too worthy, and the issues at stake too immense for us to entertain doubt or fear. But our responsibilities require that we approach this year's business with a sober humility.

—State of the Union message,
January 5, 1956

CHAPTER I

The Political Campaign, 1956

When an election is past, it is altogether fitting a free people . . . that until the next election they should be one people.

—*Abraham Lincoln*

ON the evening of Wednesday, February 29, 1956, I walked in the crisp winter air from the Executive Mansion toward the presidential offices in the West Wing of the White House. The brilliant ceiling lights shining on the whitewashed colonnade, and the brightly lighted offices in that wing, formed a striking contrast to the blackness of the South Grounds, silhouetting two or three large television vans parked on the drive. As was my custom on such occasions, I went directly to the Cabinet Room, where my secretary, Mrs. Ann Whitman, was standing by, and spoke with Robert Montgomery, who handled the technical preparations for telecasts. A soft-spoken, gentle man, Montgomery always took pains to make certain that the lights were right, that I wore nonreflecting reading glasses, that the furniture and cameras were positioned correctly.

Shielded from the noise and confusion of the cameras, cables, and microphones that had completely taken over my oval office, I again went over the address sentence by sentence, and then relaxed for a moment. About five minutes before time to go on the air, I went to my desk. Then, at 10 P.M., sitting alone in front of a bank of busy, shadowy people, humming equipment, and blinding lights, I spoke as simply as I knew how to millions of Americans.

I had gone through this ritual many times before and would go through it many times again. But this occasion was unique in one respect: it was the only address I was to give as President in which the single subject to be dealt with was myself—my health, my plans, and the reasons for my decision to run for a second term.

This announcement came as a surprise to no one that night. I had given my basic decision earlier in the day at a press conference. But I had also said that I would not think of running for office again without giving the people full, frank information about my health, my future method of campaigning, and my plans for running the presidential office if re-elected.

First I reiterated the decision to accept the Republican nomination (should it be tendered to me). Then, because five months earlier I had suffered a heart attack, I explained the latest findings of the doctors—optimistic findings, by and large. There was no denying that in view of my illness I was more of a risk than a normal person of my age, but I reported the doctors' assurances that the increased percentage of risk was not great.[1] I would have to try to maintain an orderly schedule of work, with a rest at midday (the doctors had told me that out of every twenty-four hours, I was to spend ten resting, or as they put it, "flat on your back"). I would have to keep my weight at the right level and retire at a reasonable hour. Regular exercise and recreation were required. I planned to eliminate some of the less important social and ceremonial activities of the office. "But let me make one thing clear," I said. "As of this moment, there is not the slightest doubt that I can perform as well as I ever have, all of the important duties of the Presidency." I had in fact been doing so for many weeks.

I described consultations with "multitudes of friends and associates," but told the audience that the decision was my own. Finally, to avoid any misunderstanding, I announced how I intended to conduct the campaign:

> ". . . every delegate attending the Republican convention next August is entitled to know now that . . . . I shall, in general, wage no political campaign in the customary pattern.
>
> "Instead, my principal purpose, if renominated, will be to inform the American people accurately, through means of mass communication, of the foreign and domestic program this administration has designed and has pressed for the benefit of all our people; to show them how much of that program has been accomplished or enacted into law; to point out what remains to be done, and to show how we intend to do it. . . ."

The work we had set out to do four years before was not yet finished.

With full disclosure of the facts concerning my personal condition and the way I was then managing the affairs of the office, I felt that when the citizens went to the polls in November they could "do so with a full

[1] Their reports said that my heart was not enlarged, pulse and blood pressure were normal, blood analysis excellent, weight satisfactory, and that I showed no signs of undue fatigue after periods of normal mental and physical activity.

understanding of both the record of this administration and of how I propose to conduct myself now and in the future."

My campaign would be the record.

Doctors' orders or no, I would not have conducted the same sort of campaign in 1956 as I had in 1952. Because I was the President I was determined not to go "whistle-stopping" or "barnstorming." But the limitations I had placed on myself for physical reasons were later to give way—slightly in the case of the campaign, and more than slightly in the course of conducting the affairs of state through the next four years.

The address completed, I returned to the second floor of the White House, talked casually for a while with members of my family who were gathered for the occasion, and then excused myself to go to bed. The decision made and announced, I slept soundly.

* * *

This done, I could continue to concentrate exclusively on the never-ending domestic and foreign challenges of the Presidency. President Giovanni Gronchi of Italy was then in Washington for a State visit which commanded much of my time for several days. Soon thereafter I wrote to Russian Premier Nikolai Bulganin on the subject of disarmament and made new recommendations concerning that difficult subject. I sent a memorandum to all branches of government describing a plan for establishing a Federal Council on the problems of the aged, and issued a statement setting up a national committee to encourage the development of scientists and engineers.

The Congress was in session—a circumstance, needless to say, that always commands the close attention of a President. At the same time the campaign, for me, had already begun. It meant playing a vital role in another of the three-months-long, quadrennial American political spectacles, some aspects of which have caused them to be called The World's Greatest Circus. Certainly they have their share of clowns and daredevils, gymnastic fence-straddling, and parades of elephants and mules. The national conventions of the two major parties were the official curtain-raisers.

The campaign would inevitably revolve around the administration's record of the past four years. Democrats would view it with disdain. Republicans would strive to embellish it with gilt and garland. Actually, that record had many important positive items in the ledger, but here and there some had to be recorded in red ink.

My nomination by the Republicans was at the moment a virtual certainty, save for an unforeseen circumstance or physical collapse, but the identity of my opponent would be unknown until the Democratic convention acted. Early primary contests involved, principally, former Governor Adlai E. Stevenson of Illinois and Senator Estes Kefauver of Tennessee.

One of the more publicized pre-convention political developments involved Vice President Nixon. There was much speculation about the identity of the individual to be named as my running mate. President Franklin Delano Roosevelt had conducted his four political campaigns with three different vice presidential nominees, Garner, Wallace, and Truman, and the curious had a right to assume, I suppose, that if political expediency should so indicate, I might jettison Richard Nixon for someone who might "strengthen the ticket."

Even before my own decision on a second term had been announced, I had invited the Vice President to my office to discuss the prospects. When he arrived, I set out certain hypotheses pertaining to the coming years that, I thought, he should examine carefully. He knew of my high regard for him and thus I could discuss alternatives without fear of offense or misunderstanding.

I began with the obvious: If we assumed I would decide to run again, I could not, prior to the decision of the convention, presume to name him as the party's nominee for the vice presidential post. Of course, both of us knew that if I decided to run and were nominated, my choice of a running mate would be accepted by the delegates. In this private meeting I wanted to talk over, in particular, the paths he might take to his own political future—hopefully, the Presidency in 1960.

I then told him unequivocally that if he wanted to continue in his present post I would gladly and, indeed, gratefully accept him as the party's nominee. "I deeply appreciate all the effective work you've done at my request during the past four years," I said. Some of these tasks had been crucially important; all had been onerous. In undertaking them Mr. Nixon had been working voluntarily, for the Vice President of the United States, with the constitutional duty of presiding over the Senate, is not legally a part of the Executive branch and is not subject to direction by the President.

It was on such a volunteer basis that early in my administration I had first sent him as a personal representative on a seventy-two-day trip to Australia, Indonesia, Thailand, Japan, India, Pakistan, Afghanistan, and Iran—a rugged itinerary by plane, car, helicopter, and oxcart. His task had been to help convince our Asian friends that the United States was as fully concerned about their needs and dangers as we were about Europe. It had been a highly successful mission. The Vice President and his wife had been greeted everywhere with enthusiasm and good will. Through his observations and conferences, the Vice President had acquired knowledge and understanding of the areas visited, valuable to us in the formulation of our policies.

Since 1953 the Vice President had served as Chairman of a committee which sought to eliminate discrimination on the basis of race or color in the employment practices of government contractors. In addition, he regularly attended all meetings of the Cabinet, the National Security Council, and the legislative leaders. He had been a troubleshooter in politics and in civil rights, and he had a special talent for understanding and summing up the views of others.

Through this unprecedented association—the Vice Presidency had not historically afforded an opportunity for an extensive use of a man's abilities—I had been able to keep in close touch with the Vice President and to evaluate his growing skills. Consequently my readiness to accept him as running mate in 1956 was evident, or should have been; at any rate it was a fact that I tried to make plain several times in press conferences and elsewhere. So in this conversation in the early days of 1956, I emphasized to him that the decision to seek the Vice Presidency again would be exclusively his own.

"You should," I suggested, "make a searching survey of the probable advantages and disadvantages to yourself and to the party before you give me an answer." Mr. Nixon well knew that for the entire four years of my first administration I had been searching everywhere for men of promise and had done my best to give them political visibility. There was no difficulty in finding able administrators and leaders,[2] but the problem of making them better known and appreciated by the public proved troublesome. Indeed, except for Dick Nixon, there was no young Republican who, as the 1956 conventions approached, was both experienced in the responsibilities of government at the White House level and so well known nationally that the public would consider him a reasonable candidate for the Presidency in 1960. That fact worked to Dick's advantage. But he had a disadvantage, I pointed out. Since the election of Martin Van Buren as the successor to Andrew Jackson in 1836 no incumbent Vice President had been elected President. Would he, I wondered, increase his acceptability to the party and the American public as a presidential candidate in 1960 if he should decline to run again for the Vice Presidency and instead accept another post in which he would have, in his own right, obviously important responsibilities?

[2] Among the best—men whom I considered, along with others, to have the necessary qualities for successful administration and leadership—were Robert Anderson, Herbert Brownell, Cabot Lodge, Alfred Gruenther, Gabriel Hauge, Lucius Clay, and my brother, Milton S. Eisenhower.

During my first administration, Mr. Nixon had become well acquainted with the duties of the Departments. In the event he decided to withdraw from the vice presidential race, I was quite ready to appoint him to one for which his talents would be well suited. Already I knew that two or three Cabinet officers desired to return to private life and were remaining in Washington only at my request; Defense Secretary Charles Wilson was among them. The Vice President's participation in National Security Council meetings, his legal background, and his interest in national defense would have made reasonable his appointment as Wilson's successor. I advised him to talk over this and other possibilities with his wife, Pat, and with any other person he trusted implicitly, and to give me an answer at his convenience. He agreed.

I was not alone in my view about Mr. Nixon's future. For example, early in March, George Whitney, an old and respected friend, had written me: "The fact is obvious that the age element among practically all of those [Republicans] in prominent positions is pretty high and, four or five years from now, will be much higher. There are very few younger men who have really peeked over the horizon as yet. Nixon is one of them and it seems to me that, in fairness to him, as well as with ordinary prudence for the future, he should be pushed out in the open in a job of his own where he can demonstrate that he has administrative ability and other qualities of leadership that are so essential in the top job; in other words, make a career in his own name rather than as No. 2. . . . To sum it all up in one sentence, I think it is fairer to Nixon, and better for the future of the country, that he spend the next four years in some position where publicly he can demonstrate how good he is in his own right, rather than stay in a position which, though it carries many important duties, including most valuable service to you personally, has the outward appearance to the public of a secondary job."

His opinions were typical of many expressed to me during the period.

On the other hand, one strong consideration that I had mentioned to Dick would point toward his remaining in his present post. This was the undeniable truth that, in view of my recent illness, the chances of my demise or complete disability within a span of four years were, if not much greater according to the doctors, were certainly more so than they would be for one who had no such notations on his medical record. As of that moment, because of his unique service in the Vice Presidency, I believed Nixon to be the best prepared man in government to take over my duties in any emergency.

As the weeks went by, questions involving his future were often posed at press conferences. My answer always included an expression of satisfaction with his work and an assertion that the matter was in Mr. Nixon's hands. He would let me know his own decision in his own good time. I pointed out that there need be no hurry about this since the question would not become decisive until the convention might once again nominate me for the Presidency.

During this time I did not press the Vice President for a decision, respecting his right to work the matter out himself. Years later I learned from a book of his (*Six Crises*) that he regarded that period as one of agonizing uncertainty, apparently believing that I might be thinking of dropping him and hoping that I would personally make the final decision. To do so did not occur to me. I had placed the question completely in his hands, where I thought it properly should be. "If you want the post it's yours," I had told him, "so far as it is in my power to make it so."

Many weeks after our first conversation on the subject, he came into my office to say that he had decided to stand again for the Vice Presidency. I sent for Jim Hagerty, my Press Secretary, and said, "Jim, let's get an announcement out right away." The Vice President accompanied Jim to his office where it was made. This was on April 26, 1956. Some six weeks later, on June 7, I was stricken with an ileitis attack and had to undergo a serious emergency operation.

* * *

This was my second illness in a year. This time, the doctors said from the moment I rallied from the operation that my condition was excellent, that I could expect a rapid and complete recovery and that I could leave the hospital in about two weeks. However, since the operation received tremendous emphasis in the press, many persons became justifiably doubtful once more of the soundness of my decision to run again for the Presidency. In this their fears were heightened by the medical dissertations of several columnists who, for one reason or another, took it upon themselves to publish their disagreements with the doctors' optimistic prognosis.[3] Strangely enough, although I was truly miserable for several days I was never disturbed, in this instance, by the doubts that beset so many others. My current ailment was something acute which was corrected by immediate surgery; and once I was conscious again and in possession of my faculties, I did not bother with the question of full re-

[3] One columnist, for example, announced the discovery that ileitis recurs in one out of three cases within two years. The doctors explained their prognosis (to those who chose to listen) by citing the demonstrated truth that ileitis, a young man's disease, almost never recurs in *anyone of my age group*, a fact that a responsible reporter could easily have found out in advance.

covery. Nevertheless I was, for a brief time, largely isolated from politics and from rumor.

When I left the hospital I was greeted by the story that opposition was developing within the party to the inclusion of Mr. Nixon on the Republican national ticket for 1956. This rumor seemed at first to have little substance, and I gave it no concern until one day Harold Stassen, who was then serving as Special Assistant on Disarmament, came to my office to talk about the matter. He said his own personal surveys indicated a considerable dissatisfaction with Nixon; to renominate him as Vice President would weaken the ticket and would be a bad political mistake.

Mr. Stassen's attitude was astonishing to me, but because I was at that moment hurrying to leave Washington for Panama,[4] I said, "You are an American citizen, Harold, and free to follow your own judgment in such matters."

While in Panama I received the news that Mr. Stassen had publicly announced his opposition to Mr. Nixon and the name of his own candidate for the post, Christian A. Herter, then Governor of Massachusetts. Jim Hagerty immediately issued a statement that I had told Governor Stassen that despite his acknowledged right to follow his own judgment as a private citizen—a point I had emphasized to him—he obviously could not undertake independent political activity of this kind as a member of my "official family." Upon my return I therefore saw him in Gettysburg and granted him a leave of absence without pay until after the convention.

For a short time the affair stirred excitement. At least it looked to some, hoping for diversion, that it might prevent the convention from turning out to be a "coronation." But the move died aborning; Governor Herter announced his lack of interest in running and later formally nominated Dick Nixon at the convention; and Harold Stassen, himself, made one of the seconding speeches.

One week before the Republican convention opened, the Democratic party met in Chicago and again nominated Governor Stevenson as its candidate for President, this time naming Senator Kefauver for the second spot.

Adlai Stevenson had been the first Democrat to announce his candidacy. Afterward, he had traveled a rocky road toward renomination. Through-

[4] The meeting of the Presidents of the Americas, the result of a casual chat with the newly elected Secretary General of the Organization of American States (OAS), Ambassador José A. Mora, was to me a compromise with my long-cherished desire to visit every one of the Latin American states while in office. The original date had been set for June 25–26, 1956, but was rescheduled after my ileitis operation with the consent of the sixteen other heads of state who were to attend, to July 21.

out the spring he and his principal opponent, Senator Kefauver, had slugged at each other through a series of bitter party primaries. By early April Kefauver was accusing Stevenson of "mud-slinging and character assassination." On the other hand, soon after the convention opened former President Truman, backing New York's Governor Averell Harriman, was alleging that Stevenson could not win because he was a tame campaigner—"too defeatist."

My view, at the time, was that a Democratic team of Senator Lyndon Johnson for President and Senator Hubert Humphrey or Senator John F. Kennedy for Vice President would have had better vote-getting power than the one named. Such a ticket would have appealed to both wings of their party while, in addition, Lyndon Johnson's experience in the national legislature—especially his acknowledged skill in legislative maneuver and negotiation—would have had considerable appeal to voters.

Most Republican leaders were convinced that the team finally selected by the Democrats was probably the weakest they could have named; confidence as the Republican convention opened was consequently brimming over. While overconfidence is always a mistake in a person or organization, nonetheless in this case I shared the feeling of optimism; barring some crisis, I was confident the campaign could scarcely fail to result in victory for us.

I was in Washington when the Republican convention began and remained there while its preliminary work was going on. Well in advance of the meeting I had let it be known that I hoped the platform would be a short, emphatic document—one that avoided the long and dreary listing of items to which we "pointed with pride," the reciting of reasons for "viewing with alarm," and the drawn-out "pledging for the future"—all characteristic of most political platforms. But the authors of the 1956 platform, proud of Republican accomplishments in the preceding four years, could not control their desire to describe them in detail. Their enthusiasm resulted in a document of some twelve thousand words.

In important points of substance, if not in length, I had my way. On August 18, for instance, I telephoned Under Secretary of State Herbert Hoover, Jr., who was keeping close watch on the drafting of the foreign policy plank, to tell him that the draft of the section on the tariff was so negative and so contrary to my insistence that international trade should expand, as to cause me to contemplate sending word that I would not accept the nomination, and that the delegates "could find themselves another candidate."

Faced with this gentle admonition, the platform drafters wrote a section that I could approve.

On the convention itself I also had definite ideas. The 1952 convention had reinforced my aversion to endless oratory. Further, I felt we would have difficulty in making this convention interesting to the public. So I wrote to Republican National Committee Chairman Leonard Hall suggesting a directive from him to the delegates which would urge (1) no long speeches (2) solid intellectual content for every talk (3) frequent change of pace (4) an appearance by at least one bona fide independent (5) a warm welcome to independents and Democrats (6) strict adherence to the time schedule (7) no "steam roller" tactics and (8) no—repeat no—long, dreary speeches. Chairman Hall emphatically agreed but after listening to the proceedings, we concluded that the letter had achieved little and that little in the wrong direction.

I reached San Francisco on the evening of August 21, to be met by the Vice President, California Governor Goodwin Knight, and numbers of well wishers. It was nearly dusk as we drove into the handsome city and we encountered huge crowds in which everyone seemed intent on outdoing everyone else in noise and laughter. Outside the hotel many thousands filled Union Square; refusing to leave the scene, they fairly shook the windows with their shouts. The St. Francis Hotel was a madhouse. My wife, son, and daughter-in-law, as well as two brothers and their wives, in all the joyous confusion of a rollicking, cheerful political traffic jam, were buffeted about, pulled and pounded and offered every kind of gift—from miniature medallions in the form of elephants to homes for our use during the week.

In the ensuing days I was practically overwhelmed with conferences. The first morning I had ten appointments and a press conference; at noon I succeeded in getting a little rest and a quick lunch. During the afternoon and evening I had eleven more engagements.

One that I especially enjoyed was with Frank Leahy, the legendary football coach at Notre Dame. For years we had been good friends, but it was not until 1952 that I learned of Frank's conviction that I ought to be President. He had worked hard in the first campaign. Now, in San Francisco, he came to assure me that his convictions had not changed. He was ready to undertake any chore to assist in my re-election. In all this his complete unselfishness was obvious; a rare man in politics, he wanted nothing.

Before Mamie and I departed that evening for the Civic Auditorium, we received distressing news. The Communists had attacked a Navy patrol plane off the coast of Red China and the plane was now missing. At the moment, I could do little more than direct an immediate investigation.[5]

[5] Wreckage was later sighted and a few bodies recovered in the water; there were no survivors. Red China refused to pay compensation, claiming the plane had flown over its territory.

The following morning was even more hectic, but again I did have a bite of lunch at about midday, and then my wife and I met with a group of teen-agers. Afterwards we left for the famous Cow Palace, the site of the convention.

The convention had made my renomination unanimous. Dick Nixon's was also; but before that, one delegate from Nebraska, apparently in protest against conformity, put into nomination a fictitious "Joe Smith." Reporters, sensing and needing a story, vigorously tried to make something of the incident. Of course the Democrats hoped to build Joe Smith into a symbol of "steamrolling" Nixon's nomination. They eventually gave up the attempt.

At my request, the traditional nominating speech was made by Charles Halleck, a man who had been a faithful, hard-driving, and effective leader in the House of Representatives, helping to enact into law the proposals the administration laid before the Congress. With the renomination of the Vice President the procedural formalities were completed, and on the evening of August 23 I mounted the platform.

The convention marked the hundredth anniversary of the first one held by my party. Hence it was natural that many speakers had dwelled on the party's history. Nostalgia was pleasant, and I, too, recalled aspects of an inspiring past, but emphasized that we should look to a demanding future. In addition to asking ourselves what would happen in the coming election, we should consider especially what might happen to the nation and the world in the next hundred years.

To support this argument I quoted first the great Norwegian, Henrik Ibsen, who once wrote, "I hold that man is in the right who is most clearly in league with the future."

To be in league with the future, a political party, first, had to be guided by long-range principle, not short-term expediency. Government, of course, affects profoundly the daily lives and plans for every person in the country, and if governmental action is without the solid guideline of enduring principles, national policies are bound to flounder in confusion. Change based on principle is progress; constant change without principle becomes chaos. I cited free collective bargaining without governmental interference as one long-range principle to be observed and as a cornerstone of Republican philosophy in labor-management relations. And I rejected the expediency that, in all labor disputes, would have the federal government "do something—anything—" to settle the matter. It was this kind of thinking that constantly, and futilely, demanded getting an injunction or seizing the steel mills or, in general, "knocking their heads together."

A second reason for saying the Republican party looked to the future was that ever since the 1930s our opponents had been citing the depression of that period to condemn all Republican effort and action. This obsession, I argued, was silly because the present and future were bringing *new* problems and possibilities to federal and local governments: in water supply, highways, health, housing, power development, and peaceful uses of atomic energy. Problems of urban organization and of education were also domestic situations to which the Republican party proposed to give major interest.

I went on to cite other reasons for calling ours the party of the future: it tried to unite the country, not divide it; the phrase *E pluribus unum* we thought should still be the watchword of our nation.

Our party held up the free and creative individual citizen as the ultimate source of our country's prosperity and progress. We had little faith in giving a monopoly on problem-solving to bureaucrats and a few political leaders in Washington.

Finally, I said that a party of the future must be completely dedicated to peace, as indeed must all Americans, for without peace there would *be* no future. I pointed out how diligently we had worked to modernize our security establishment, to buttress it with a powerfully producing economy, and to strengthen our partnership for peace with our allies around the globe.

"We live in a shrunken world," I said, "a world in which oceans are crossed in hours, a world in which a single-minded despotism menaces the scattered freedoms of scores of struggling independent nations." There could be no enduring peace while other nations suffered privation and injustice. "We are in the era of the thermonuclear bomb that can obliterate cities and can be delivered across continents. With such weapons, war has become, not just tragic, but preposterous. With such weapons, there can be no victory for anyone."

In the conviction that my party's principles were in league with the demands of this kind of world and this kind of future, I accepted the nomination of the convention.

* * *

For me, the campaign started off at a leisurely pace. I still had a little recovering to do from the ileitis operation, for I had not fully regained my strength. So, after the convention, my wife and I went to the

Monterey Peninsula and stayed at the Cypress Point Golf Club for several days.

On the 12th of September a Republican picnic was held at our family farm at Gettysburg. Some of the guests were uneasy, for that morning the newspapers had given us a shock: elections in Maine, which fortunately did not involve the national ticket, had in an unprecedented turnabout gone Democratic. Though there were many explanations, the incident impelled me to warn against complacency. I recalled the battle of the Kasserine Pass in World War II, where inexperienced troops had learned to their stunned surprise that the enemy could attack at two o'clock in the morning, a lesson which had surely eliminated any complacency in our ranks.

Early in the campaign Party Chairman Leonard Hall decided to repeat a tactic that had proved useful in 1952; it had been born out of necessity that year. A "Truth Squad," usually including about four senators and congressmen, was to follow the principal Democratic speakers around the country. Wherever they stopped, a Truth Squad would stop, hold a news conference, and as quickly and emphatically as possible publicize data and explanations that refuted Democratic allegations not based on fact.

In the 1956 campaign, I urged the squad to repeat the truth tirelessly and forcefully on every issue, large or small. Again the tactic worked well, psychologically as well as factually. Truth on the trail of a candidate who is careless in his statements and charges is always menacing. (Governor Stevenson quipped once amusingly that the squad bore the same relationship to truth as a fire department did to a fire: "It will," he said, "extinguish it if it can.")

Though still expecting to avoid a strenuous campaign of interminable motorcades and speeches, I insisted on making a few short visits about the country, primarily to get a personal sense of public attitudes and reactions. My first trip was to Iowa for two speeches on September 21.

I took note of proposals put forward by the Democratic nominees for the ills of farming. Senator Kefauver, for example, speaking at a Minnesota meeting during the primary campaign, had proposed governmental price supports of 100 per cent of parity for farmers whose income was under $7500 a year, with sliding supports up to 90 per cent, depending on income, for all others. This I considered to be pure political claptrap and said so. To all such "forensic farmers," I said, farming looks easy "when your plow is a pencil and you're a thousand miles from the cornfield."

At that time, low agricultural prices were continuing to cause much unhappiness in the farm belt. This condition was considered a political liability. Even so, I was determined not to abandon the struggle to obtain sensible laws which would gradually eliminate price-depressing surpluses, would be in harmony with the basic principles of private, competitive enterprise, and would benefit the agricultural community over the long pull. We were unwilling to return to a program of increased governmental bribes designed to create a false and fleeting prosperity—and to purchase votes. Throughout the campaign, I referred repeatedly to the farm problem, never ceasing to urge that we depend less upon high, rigid price supports and more upon a free market, unregimented farming, and broadened demands at home and abroad in order to achieve fair returns for farm products.

A presidential campaign conducted by an incumbent is of course subject to interruptions, some planned, some not. Non-partisan talks and meetings have to be interspersed with political ones. Thus my campaigning was interrupted by addresses before a conference of the World Bank and the International Monetary Fund, a bi-partisan meeting of the Sales Executives Club and the Chamber of Commerce of Cleveland, and the Civil Service Assembly of Canada and the United States.

My personal attitude toward the campaign did undergo a significant change at one point. This was when the Democratic presidential candidate charged on September 25 that my administration had appeased Argentine dictator Juan Perón. "A member of the President's personal family," Governor Stevenson said, "assumed special, if informal, responsibilities for our relations with Argentina. . . . During these same years we made loans to Perón, and Perón . . . piled up balances of more than $100 million in Switzerland for the use and benefit not of the Argentine people, but of Perón." This accusation suddenly became a prominent feature of a campaign which had promised the electorate a sophisticated, intellectual exploration of "new ideas" on foreign policy.

But he was never to follow up on the charge. Within twenty-four hours after his talk, I exposed its falsity in a news conference: "It is true the government loaned Mr. Perón's government $130 million," I said, "but it wasn't a *Republican* government. It was the Democratic government in 1950 and 1951; and from the time I came in until Perón went out, *the government did not sign one single loan agreement with Mr. Perón.*" If he had received $100 million from the United States to place in his personal account in Switzerland, I said, reporters should go to the Democrats for the necessary explanation.

The unjustified attack on the administration, and on my brother Milton in particular—a distinguished educator and administrator, who had selflessly served the country in several capacities on a temporary and unpaid basis during my administration (and who had served in government before)—made me angry. Thereafter, I kept reminding the public of the charge. Our opponents had made the mistake of peering into the barrel of their own gun when they pulled the trigger.

As all indications seemed increasingly to favor a victory for the Republican national ticket, the opposition searched for any issue that seemed capable of exploitation. They had a hard time of it, and for good reason. The country was prosperous. In spite of continuous international tension, we were at peace. Vital accomplishments could not be talked away: a gigantic interstate highway program, sound hydropower development, the launching of the St. Lawrence Seaway project, the extension of social security coverage to an additional ten million people, a huge tax reduction in 1954, the government conducted with integrity, and the economy freed of many repressive controls were widely known achievements.

The national budget, so badly out of balance when we took office in 1953, showed a modest surplus in 1956. Personal income had risen from $273 billion in 1952 to $331 billion in 1956, while in the same years the Gross National Product had risen from $347 billion to $419 billion. The United States defense establishment had been remodeled and revised after the conclusion of the Korean War, and was growing rapidly in strength and efficiency. The Trieste problem had been solved, while Iran and Guatemala had been saved from almost certain domination by the Communists. In the four years of my administration the cost of living had been held to an increase of about 2.8 per cent while the real wages of factory workers had increased by 8.6 per cent. In the summer of 1956, the United States was prosperous, confident, and relatively untroubled by either domestic or foreign crisis of major proportions. Many polls continued to suggest that the Republican national ticket stood high in public esteem. The opposing candidates, then, could only assert that they could conduct the government better.

Throughout the campaign, my confidence in the outcome did not waver. My son John was astonished one day to discover this attitude. Many months earlier he had urged me to refuse renomination, but once my affirmative decision was made, he became intensely, though privately, interested in a favorable outcome. So, when he came to my office one day in early October to call my attention to unfavorable judgments in the press concerning Republican chances, I looked up and laughed. "Pay no attention to such stuff," I remarked. "Stevenson has lost. And what's more, he knows it." John was momentarily shocked and not completely convinced. He later said that he left my office that morning hoping that I had real evidence to back up my sunny outlook.

Part of the evidence was in the quality of the issues our opponents began using, possibly discouraged by the quick collapse of the baseless charges against Milton. One was to put an end to nuclear testing by the United States; the other to end the draft.

The issue of American policy on nuclear testing, resting as it did on scientific as well as security considerations, was scarcely a subject to be debated in a political campaign. Politically, I was convinced that Adlai Stevenson's arguments would do his cause little good, particularly since he confused his hearers by apparently advocating initially a unilateral suspension of American tests, in the hope others would follow, and then shifting to the view that we should "take the lead in promoting curtailment" of such tests. But I was anxious to avoid causing undue anxiety on this important subject.

To set the record straight I released statements[6] that summarized our position: Continued testing would remain essential to our security until we could obtain a Soviet agreement, one in which we could have complete faith, that the Communists would likewise cease testing. The best scientific information available, that of the independent National Academy of Sciences, indicated that the present level of testing did not imperil the health of humanity, while our latest tests were enabling scientists to learn better methods for reducing fallout.

To the end-the-draft notion I responded by saying that to call the draft "wasteful" under the conditions then prevailing evidenced either ignorance of our military needs or a willingness to take undue chances with our nation's security.

As the tempo of the campaigning increased, accusations were bandied back and forth by speakers for both parties. Some were complete distortions, others were witty. They did little to inform the nation but sometimes they amused it. One story was that a Republican asked a friend whom he was going to vote for. The man said he planned to vote for Adlai Stevenson. The Republican, upset, asked why. "Because," the man said, "I voted for Stevenson four years ago, and everything's been fine ever since."

The campaign rocked along into its waning days. Spokesmen on both sides racked their brains to find new telling arguments and succeeded mainly in spreading hundreds of thousands of fairly fruitless words in the mass media. I came to believe that most election campaigns could well be of thirty days' duration, without changing the result decisively. I believe this today.[7] I feel certain that candidates, parties, and the nation—

[6] For October 6 statement see *Public Papers of the Presidents,* 1956, pp. 863–66. For October 24 statement, *ibid.,* pp. 997–1002.

[7] An exception to this generality may have been the 1960 election; it was won, perhaps, partly because of the length of the campaign.

and our pocketbooks—would benefit if we shortened the campaign period.

During the later stages of the 1956 campaign, my interest was drawn farther and farther from politics as crises in Suez and in Hungary, detailed in the next chapters, became acute and foreboding. The immediate outcome of these developments could not be foreseen, but they would claim the interest of the entire world for weeks to come.

* * *

"What are you going to do for a living if the President loses?" a reporter asked Jim Hagerty.

"The question," Jim answered, "is academic."

That is the way it turned out. On the evening of November 6 the results were tabulated. Though the Republicans failed to regain control of either House of Congress, the national ticket swamped the Democratic nominees by 457 electoral votes to 73 and by a margin of more than nine million popular votes.[8]

We carried forty-one states—all but Alabama, Arkansas, Georgia, Mississippi, Missouri, and North and South Carolina. For the first time in eighty years, Louisiana went Republican. For the first time since 1928, the Republican ticket carried the city of Chicago.

With this response I was naturally pleased. The United States had obviously approved the administration's policies and the performance of the past four years.

[8] Map, "Presidential Election, 1956," appears following page 360.

CHAPTER II

Build-up to Suez

Yon foaming flood seems motionless as ice;
Its dizzy turbulence eludes the eye,
Frozen by distance.

—*Wordsworth*

BEGINNING in the latter months of my first term and for several years thereafter, no region of the world received as much of my close attention and that of my colleagues as did the Middle East. There, against a background of new nations emerging from colonialism, in the face of constant thrusts of new Communist imperialism, and complicated by the old implacable hatred between Israeli and Arab, the world faced a series of crises. These crises, which at times threatened to touch off World War III, posed a constant test to United States will, principle, patience, and resolve.

* * *

The Middle East is a land bridge connecting Europe, Asia, and Africa. Its soil has borne the travelers, merchants, and conquering armies of the centuries. Three of the world's religions were founded there —Judaism, Christianity, and Islam—and under its surface lie the world's largest-known oil reserves, the "black gold" of our machine age. The Middle East is, with good reason, often called the crossroads of the world.

Before World War I much of the territory of the Middle East—Iraq, Saudi Arabia, Jordan, Israel, Syria, and Lebanon—was under the control of the Ottoman Turks. Between the two World Wars the entire region from the eastern shore of the Mediterranean to the Iranian border was comprised of protectorates and partially independent nations. Some were pacified and dominated by Britain and France, the former in Jordan and Iraq and the latter in Syria and Lebanon. Thus there was relatively little overt unrest during those two decades. But in the years following the close of the Second World War the region, responding to an awakened and intense spirit of nationalism, became transformed into a number of independent but unstable governments, jealous of each other, and sitting precariously atop volatile, impoverished populations. Tragically low standards of living made human life a cheap commodity. The inevitable result was such a seething cauldron of political unrest and incessant "border" warfare that the formation of a steady and comprehensive American policy toward the region as a whole was difficult to develop and maintain. Even direct relations between the United States and each individual nation were subject to every kind of disturbing fluctuation, for antagonisms among neighbors were often so strong that friendship with one brought the automatic hostility of another.

Jewish-Arab tensions, dormant for many years, broke out explosively after World War II and became inflamed by the war in 1949, during which the Arabs converged on Israel in an attempt to drive the new settlers into the sea. The Israeli, who had better-organized, -disciplined, and -equipped units, defeated their neighbors in a series of limited actions by skillfully concentrating their main forces against the Arabs one at a time. The resulting truce did nothing to lessen local antagonisms. Israel, to the acute and lasting resentment of the Arabs, gained territory considerably in excess of that prescribed by the United Nations when the independence of Israel had been recognized in 1947—a recognition that no Arab state had ever accepted. From 1949 onward, peace in the region has never become complete. Border incidents are common and boundaries, to this day, are lined with pillboxes, machine guns, and watchful border guards.

Quite apart from this turmoil, the instability of the Arab nations immediately surrounding Israel was marked. On the north of Israel was Lebanon, a nation half Christian and half Moslem, republican in government and pro-Western in orientation. To the east of Lebanon, Syria, governed by the French between the World Wars and still harboring resentments against its former masters, had the strongest Communist Party of any nation in the Middle East. The two Hashemite[1] Kingdoms of Jordan and Iraq were closely akin yet different. Jordan lacked the oil that made Iraq an economically viable nation. Saudi Arabia was the location of many of the "Holy Places of Islam" and another nation rich

[1] So named because their rulers, second cousins, belonged to a royal dynasty of that name.

with oil, but one that saw much of its income unwisely dissipated by the selfish indulgences of the Royal Family. Egypt, Israel's most powerful and bitterest enemy, was a kingdom until 1952 and since then a dictatorship.[2] Egypt occupied a position of pivotal importance to the politics of the area, partly because the personality and views of Gamal Abdel Nasser appealed to Arabs everywhere who desired to unite in one great Arab nation. Moreover, Egypt had within its borders one invaluable tangible asset: the Suez Canal, Western Europe's lifeline to the East.

This canal was the most important waterway in the world and a highly profitable one. In 1955 more than 100 million tons transited it, more than twice the amount that went through the Panama Canal. It was utilized by ships of more than forty nations, with British shipping in first place and United States shipping in second. The Canal's gross revenues of some $100 million produced annually about $30 million net profit.

In the uneasy Middle Eastern situation, after World War II, American policy had been one of neutrality. Our hope was to prevent armed conflict between the Israeli and the Arabs and gradually to help bring about normal relations among the nations of the region. In an early attempt to establish peace and preserve the status quo, three Western nations, Britain, France, and the United States, signed in May 1950 an agreement to act together to defeat any seizure of Middle East territory by force. If either side attained marked military superiority, there could be no stability. To this end the three Western powers agreed to consult each other to ensure that arms shipped to the Arabs and Israelis were adequate for the maintenance of internal order but limited—and, so far as possible, balanced. We hoped that, while trying to prevent either side from achieving a decisive edge in weapons of Western production, we would at the same time be discouraging them from approaching the Communists for arms.

Britain had long been the principal arms supplier to the Middle East but the United States had agreements under which it could sell small quantities of weapons to Egypt, Israel, Iraq, Lebanon, and Saudi Arabia as needed. By no means did we desire to become a main source of arms supply for the region; even less did we want to damage British influence there, though at times the British seemed suspicious that we did. The fact was that, despite United States and some French interest in the

[2] The Egyptian military coup that deposed King Farouk and replaced him with General Mohammed Naguib took place in July 1952. General Naguib, a popular hero of the Egyptian populace, was in fact, merely a figurehead. However, he retained the appearance of power until October of 1954, at which time he was displaced by Lieutenant Colonel Nasser, who by that time had been serving for some months as Premier. The latter was, and is, a dynamic, personable individual who was said to have been the Egyptian strong man from the time of the 1952 coup.

region, we felt that the British should continue to carry a major responsibility for its stability and security. The British were intimately familiar with the history, traditions, and peoples of the Middle East; we, on the other hand, were heavily involved in Korea, Formosa, Vietnam, Iran, and in this hemisphere. At the same time, France had heavy commitments in North Africa west of Tripoli.

As an objective friend, our government attempted to help in settling outstanding problems. One example was a series of missions undertaken by one of my personal representatives, Mr. Eric Johnston, who in 1955 and 1956 endeavored to settle a heated controversy that had developed between Israel on one side and Jordan and Syria on the other, over the division of the waters of the Jordan Valley.[3] At times the effort seemed promising, but prejudice and resentments on both sides caused rejection of the plan which had achieved agreement among the engineers; no progress was made.

King Farouk's abrupt departure from Egypt in 1952 marked the beginning of long and difficult diplomatic negotiations between Egypt and Britain regarding the Suez Base, occupied ever since World War II by the British Army. The Egyptians resented its presence and made their displeasure evident by clandestine depredations including arson and raids, as well as by governmental protest.

I believed that it would be undesirable and impracticable for the British to retain sizable forces permanently in the territory of a jealous and resentful government amid an openly hostile population. Therefore, Secretary Dulles and I encouraged the British (who had already expressed their willingness eventually to cede the base to Egypt) gradually to evacuate the eighty thousand troops still stationed there. Protracted negotiations were finally brought to a successful conclusion in 1954; the last soldier was scheduled to leave the base area in June of 1956.

During the early months of Colonel Nasser's Premiership (beginning in April of 1954) the nations of the West tended to look hopefully toward him because he appeared to favor a pro-Western alignment. His group had come into power allegedly intent on reform and on elimination of corruption. But as time went by it became apparent that Nasser had ambitions transcending a reformer's role.

[3] Mr. Johnston met with some success, and at one time actually obtained the private assurance of the technical and professional advisers representing the two sides that his proposals were satisfactory. However, the mission finally came to naught because of the refusal of political leaders to let their respective peoples learn of any project involving cooperative effort among the opposing camps. Apparently they believed that to do so would bring on revolution and the loss of their personal positions of power.

His vision and, before long, his activities ranged far outside the borders of Egypt. France accused him of fomenting troubles among the Arabs in Algeria; the British alleged that he was working covertly to generate discontent in Cyprus to embarrass them. In addition, Nasser early made it plain that the supplies of arms which had been provided to Egypt previously would no longer suffice for his needs, creating a feeling in the British government, privately expressed, that he was trying to become "an Egyptian Mussolini." The United States tried to abstain from these and other quarrels, feeling that as a "neutral" we might be helpful in composing differences.

Militarily, Egypt was weak. In early 1955 there was no question that, should war break out between Israel and Egypt, the latter would be decisively defeated. However, the Israelis were surrounded on land by avowed enemies. Their security problem had to take into account the probability of a conflict along their entire national border, with the Arab forces possibly concentrated and acting under a single command. With a population of somewhat less than two million, the Israeli maintained a standing army of some fifty thousand plus two hundred thousand ready reserves who could be mobilized within forty-eight hours. This army, though small, was probably almost equal in sheer numbers to the total the surrounding governments could muster and supply. It was certainly better motivated, better trained, and more effective as a fighting force.

* * *

The first evidence of serious Communist penetration in the Middle East occurred in the fall of 1955 (when I was in the hospital recovering from the heart attack) in what has since become called the notorious Nasser "arms deal."

As early as February of that year Nasser had attempted to obtain arms from the United States. Apparently alarmed over the ferocity of an Israeli reprisal raid in the Gaza Strip,[4] Nasser requested arms—$27 million worth. Our State Department, confident that he was short of money, informed him that payment would be expected in cash rather than barter. He dropped the matter temporarily, but his threats to begin negotiations with the Soviets sounded suspiciously like blackmail. Our attitude may, with the advantage of hindsight, appear to have been unrealistic, but even if we had been able to predict Nasser's later actions we still would have been on the horns of a dilemma. We were obliged to abide by our

[4] Border incidents were occasioned at least partly by Egyptian commando, or *fedayeen* raids into Israel. Israel often retaliated with what seemed merciless severity.

standing agreement with the French and British to maintain a rough balance between the military strength of Israel and the neighboring Arab states, a balance that this arms sale would have drastically disturbed.

President Nasser did nothing further for a time but when, in September, the Israelis jarred him by executing another strong and successful raid on an Egyptian outpost, he made good his threat of the previous June and took steps to obtain arms from Communist nations.

In an attempt to dissuade Colonel Nasser from closing the deal with the Communists, the State Department dispatched to Cairo an able American career diplomat, Mr. George V. Allen. His mission was unsuccessful and an arms deal between Egypt and Czechoslovakia was signed in October. The value of the consignment was variously estimated between $90 million and $200 million, an amount so much larger than the $27 million we had been discussing as to excite suspicion of its purpose. Such an acquisition would have been far beyond the financial capabilities of Egypt except for the fact that the Czechs agreed on a barter arrangement, Egyptian cotton for Czech arms. (Incidentally, the cotton was later sold in Western Europe and depressed Egypt's cotton prices in the world market.)

About a week after the contract was signed it was reported that the Russians had offered arms to Israel, an offer that was quickly spurned. But the Israeli countered by calling on the United States to furnish arms to restore the military balance. After considerable deliberation, we concluded that in the circumstances a United States shipment of arms would only speed a Middle East arms race; therefore we decided against it for the moment.

These Communist efforts to foment difficulties were of course completely consistent with their avowed and continuing design to cause global confusion. At the moment the Reds apparently believed that the Middle East provided an unusually bright opportunity to make inroads into the Free World and to disrupt the normally close cooperation among the nations of the West. The United States could not afford to let such action go unnoticed. Under normal circumstances we were quite content for the experienced British to take the Western initiative in promoting stability in the Middle East, but when the Soviet Union threatened to become actively involved, the United States could no longer remain a silent partner. We had to step in to counter the weight of Soviet power.

Accordingly, in the second week of October, Foster Dulles had a talk with V. M. Molotov, Soviet foreign minister, warning that the Czech shipment of arms to Egypt was making war more and more likely in the Middle East and was creating a new wave of bitter anti-Communist feeling in the United States. In a note to Premier Nikolai Bulganin I wrote: "I received on October 22nd your message regarding the sale of arms to Egypt. I note that you feel that there are no grounds whatever for concern. However, on the basis of all my information, this large transaction has created a greatly increased danger of a major outbreak of violence in the area.

"I am asking Secretary Dulles to discuss the situation further with Foreign Minister Molotov at Geneva."

Bulganin's reply was soothing, but noncommittal. The arms deal went through and our attitude toward Soviet penetration naturally hardened. But we did not cease our efforts to make Nasser see the benefits of strengthening his ties with the West.

* * *

While these events were occurring, the British, with our support and encouragement, were in the process of completing negotiations for what came to be known as the Baghdad Pact, a defensive alliance among Britain, Turkey, Pakistan, and the Arab nation of Iraq, to strengthen these countries near the Soviet Union's southwestern boundary. I hoped that this arrangement might quickly be approved by all the nations involved. As military commander in NATO, some four years before, I had visited Turkey and inspected its military establishment. This visit, even more than a knowledge of modern Turkish history, persuaded me that the Turks were good fighting men, while Pakistanian hostility to Communism was traditional. Thus I was delighted when, during the second week of October 1955, this pact was joined by Iran, whose geographical location made it indispensable in filling the gap in the area of the Soviet border.

But in this fluid situation trouble was always brewing. The Pact, unfortunately, was viewed by most Arabs—particularly pro-Nasserites—not as a measure to protect the region against Soviet encroachment, but as a device to perpetuate unpopular British influence. Iraq, being the only Arab member in the Baghdad Pact, immediately became a target of criticism by other Arab governments.[5]

Britain's efforts to induce Jordan to join the Pact caused even more trouble. Britain had always exerted considerable influence in Jordan, and contributed $20 million annually to the support of that country's elite fighting force known as the Arab Legion. With a British military mission

[5] As an obvious retaliatory action against the formation of the Baghdad Pact and to establish a coalition against Israel, Egypt created a military alliance with Syria and Saudi Arabia, and later with Yemen, called the "Southern Tier." The name, obviously, was selected to indicate a balance against the "Northern Tier," the original name for the Baghdad Pact.

and this financial help, Jordan possessed the strongest military force in any of the Arab nations, except for Egypt. But when in late 1955 Britain asked Jordan to join the Baghdad Pact, a large part of the Jordanian population violently objected. Riots, stimulated partly by inflammatory broadcasts from Cairo, broke out. Three successive Jordanian governments fell in one month-long crisis. Resentment was directed against all Western nations, not only Britain. During the weekend of January 8, 1956, mobs set fire to the United States Technical Air Center in Amman and stoned the American Consulate in the Arab sector of Jerusalem.

Finally a man named Samir el Rifai was named Premier of Jordan. He pledged to keep the nation out of the Baghdad Pact, which pledge created hope that he might continue in office for a reasonable period.

A new aspect of the growing Middle East free-for-all was an intensification of propaganda activity, largely Nasser's, against weaker and pro-Western Arab governments. A propaganda station, called the "Voice of the Arabs," had been established in Cairo. This station and its provocative broadcasts brought official protests to the Egyptian government from the U. S. State Department, from British and French Foreign Offices, and even from Jordan. Indeed, the tenor of the broadcasts was so inflammatory against all nations even vaguely friendly to the West that Jordan's Premier Rifai, though known to be friendly to Nasser, finally found it necessary to jam the Arab "Voice."

Western—particularly British—influence in the Middle East seemed to be crumbling in the face of this new force, Pan-Arabism, with Nasser as its symbol. On March 2, 1956, apparently as a slap at the British, King Hussein of Jordan summarily dismissed his long-time British adviser, Lieutenant General John Bagot Glubb, Commander of the Arab Legion, on whom the West had counted as a bulwark of stability in that country.[6] King Hussein has, in a book called *Uneasy Lies the Head,* insisted that his act was a purely internal matter involving his own authority. Nevertheless, reaction in Britain to Glubb's dismissal was militant. The British government urgently renewed a request it had previously made that the United States join the Baghdad Pact. We seriously considered this move, but while it seemed wise to increase our material and moral support for the Pact, it did not appear feasible to join it formally without at the same time giving assurances of protection to Israel, which in turn might drive Iraq out.

Hussein weathered the storms. For us the episode was a fairly rep-

[6] The Jordanian Army contained many members of the pro-Nasser "Free Officers' Movement." The Arab Legion, on the other hand, composed largely of Bedouins, was the only military unit on whose loyalty Hussein could depend.

resentative example of a Middle Eastern tangle of conflicting considerations, one with so few possibilities of being resolved that it had to be lived with rather than settled.

* * *

Late in 1955 riots broke out on the island of Cyprus between the four hundred thousand Cypriots of Greek and the one hundred thousand of Turkish descent. Acts of violence became common, one of which involved the British governor himself. He found a bomb in his bed, and he could scarcely be criticized for discharging all of his Greek Cypriot servants.

It was characteristic of the complex diplomacy of the 1950s that the nations involved, Greece, Turkey, and Britain, were all allies of ours. Furthermore, as clashes continued, much of the Middle East security force that Britain maintained on the island would be tied down keeping order in its own base.[7]

Most portentously, perhaps, this aggravation, though not directly related to the Arab-Israeli-British turmoil, had indirect effects. When Cyprus—Britain's major base in the Mediterranean—turned into a powder keg, it surely contributed to the British mood of "Enough!" They had agreed in 1954 to leave their Suez Base, an act of incalculable significance for the British end-of-empire feeling; they were being subjected to taunts and insults in Cairo; and now their last important bastion in that part of the world was quaking.

* * *

Throughout 1955 and early 1956 border fights between the Israeli and the Arabs continued. Late in 1955 outbreaks occurred almost daily, primarily in the Gaza Strip. On January 22, 1956, the Security Council of the United Nations censured Israel for the size and intensity of her invariable retaliatory attacks against Arab border violations. Israel was warned against endangering the truce in the area. Further, Israel was placed on notice that if she launched preventive war against the Arabs, the UN would adopt sanctions against her. In March Secretary-General Dag Hammarskjold was dispatched (after some debate in which the So-

[7] The island provided a base from which British forces could support any military action in the eastern Mediterranean. We were anxious that an arrangement acceptable to all would quickly be achieved. But our hopes were by no means strengthened when on March 9, 1956, Greek Cypriot Archbishop Makarios was arrested and deported to the Seychelles Islands.

viets supported Arab opposition) to survey the situation and take any measures he deemed necessary to reduce the intensity of the Arab-Israel conflict. Little came of this trip, but at least his presence caused a *de facto* cease-fire for a month.

Through all this, the efforts of the West to maintain a rough balance in armaments between Israeli and Arabs caused anguish, it seemed, whenever arms were sent to either.[8] One typical flurry illustrates the sensitivity of all concerned: On Wednesday, February 15, the press reported that an American shipment of eighteen M-41 light tanks was loaded in Brooklyn and was ready to sail for Saudi Arabia. Almost simultaneously came a protest from the Israeli, who were not then receiving arms.

This was the kind of thing that can seldom be resolved before it has been blown up from a minor into a major incident. To get time to study the matter I ordered the State Department to delay the shipment temporarily. Quickly it became obvious that there was nothing amiss in the transaction. The quantity and kinds of arms—actually a relatively insignificant shipment—conformed to the U.S.-British-French agreement of 1950 and the request, nearly a year old, had been carefully studied by both State and Defense and approved as routine. The Saudis had paid cash for the tanks nearly three months in advance of the scheduled sailing date. Accordingly, on February 18 I directed that the movement proceed as planned.

Soon after this incident Under Secretary Hoover came to see me with a request that we agree to France's sending twelve Mystère jet fighter planes to Israel. I replied that our position should be one of "no objection." I was pleased, however, that the French had queried us; their doing so seemed to prove they shared my conviction that such coordination between us was desirable and necessary. (Later, these "twelve" Mystère fighters would display a rabbitlike capacity for multiplication.)

At about this time a new idea was suggested for dealing promptly with any foreseeable need of American arms in the Middle East. I thought "arms in escrow" had real merit. The plan was to store appreciable quantities of military equipment aboard a United States vessel located in the Mediterranean, ready for instant dispatch to any nation in the Middle East which might be a victim of an aggression. The Department of De-

[8] The Israeli had been, for several months, clamoring for more arms for themselves. Late in October 1955 the Israeli Cabinet had decided to expand its arms procurement program, subject only to a reservation by the Finance Minister that money had to be found first. According to one source the program had totaled $50 million, with a heavy concentration on French jet planes and tanks.

fense was doubtful about the value of the project, but I thought it would have important advantages in its demonstration of complete impartiality between the Arabs (primarily Egypt) and the Israeli. We pushed the plan through, and by the middle of July 1956, a vessel, so supplied, was on station in the Mediterranean.[9]

By this time Secretary-General Hammarskjold's mission was completed, with no truce, although the situation seemed to quiet down on the Arab-Israeli border for the time being.

Meanwhile a once small, threatening cloud was becoming larger and darkening the entire region; it was the growing closeness of relations between the ambitious Nasser and the Soviets. This development colored the negotiations that had been under way for some months between Nasser on the one side and the World Bank, Britain, and ourselves regarding plans for financing a huge dam on the Nile.

The prospective Aswan High Dam was a long-term pet of President Nasser, a gigantic power and irrigation project that would take nearly twenty years to construct and would cost over a billion dollars. If agreement could be reached among the countries with interests in the waters of the Nile (Egypt, Ethiopia, Sudan, and Uganda) and if the Egyptian economy could stand the strain over the years—with outside help, of course—the result would be a tremendous boost to the poor population of Egypt.

The problems involved in this were many, and Egypt had been trying to solve them when Secretary Dulles went to Cairo back in 1953. Since that time, the World Bank had been working on the financing.

One of the attractive aspects of seeking a sensible way to help the Egyptians with the dam was that for once, perhaps, our contributions and other forms of aid to a Middle Eastern country would be more constructive than the ticklish business of trying to keep arms in balance.

Direct participation by the United States began, to all intents and purposes, in December 1955, when Under Secretary of State Herbert Hoover, Jr., the British Ambassador to the United States (Sir Roger Makins), and Mr. Eugene Black (President of the World Bank) met with Mr. Abdel Moneim el Kaissouni, Egyptian Minister of Finance, to discuss the extent to which the two Western powers and the World Bank would be able to assist. In essence, aid by the United States and Britain

[9] It remained there only a short time. Aggressive acts by Nasser a few days later minimized the likelihood that we would be supplying him with any arms for some time. The scheme serves, however, as an example of the lengths we were prepared to go to show impartiality and to deter aggression.

was to defray the "foreign exchange costs" (the initial purchases of tools, materials, etc., from sources outside Egypt) of the first stages of the work, then estimated to take four or five years. We all but committed ourselves to further support at the completion of the first stage.[10]

President Nasser's reaction to this offer was anything but encouraging. Having completed his arms deal with the Communists only a few weeks before, he now gave the impression of a man who was convinced that he could play off East against West by blackmailing both. He said almost as much to an American newspaper reporter in early April 1956, when he asserted that he was still considering a Soviet offer to build the dam.[11]

This threat of blackmail was a sensitive matter. The Aswan Dam was not a popular project in this country, especially in the Congress, particularly in view of Nasser's apparent tendency to move closer to the Soviets; it would take all the pressure Foster and I could bring to bear to obtain congressional approval for our contribution, and we had little zest for an all-out legislative fight in behalf of a nation that thought it could do as well by dealing with the Soviets. Nasser added to our annoyance in late May when he announced his recognition of Red China.

By the middle of June my associates and I were becoming doubtful of the wisdom of United States participation in the Aswan Dam project. Secretary of the Treasury George Humphrey, for one, had concluded that the Egyptians were holding an option on our offer of assistance while they were shopping around to see if they could get a better offer from the Soviets.[12] He also began to doubt that the Egyptians could support the extensive arms purchases they were trying to make, do their share on the dam, and also meet the payments on the Aswan loans when they came due.

[10] Since the financing was to be spread out over a period of time, we expected that our annual cost would approximate only about $20 million. Eventually our offer was defined as follows: a grant of $70 million ($56 million from the United States; $14 million from Britain) and a loan between us of $200 million. Later the two countries would give "sympathetic attention"—which really meant approval, given legislative authority—to a further loan of $130 million. Egypt should contribute approximately $900 million in local materials and services over a period of fifteen years.

[11] Secretary Dulles told a press conference on that occasion that "some of the preconditions to a start are still under discussion."

[12] This feeling was enhanced at the time by reports from Cairo, where the new Soviet Foreign Minister, Dmitri T. Shepilov, was helping Nasser celebrate the departure of the last British soldier from the Suez Base. Amidst displays of Communist weapons Shepilov was said to have offered Nasser a loan of $400 million—with no interest and sixty years to pay.

Foster, also, was having serious second thoughts. In view of the burdens the project would impose on the Egyptian people, he was beginning to think that any nation associated with construction of the dam would eventually wind up very unpopular among the Egyptians.

However, the United States considered itself obligated as a result of the meeting six months before, and on June 20 Eugene Black went to Cairo to brief Nasser on a final offer, still with United States support. At this meeting Nasser gave Black a series of counterproposals, some of which would be totally unacceptable to all three of the financing authorities. Thereafter, negotiations halted.

When Foster described the extraordinary counterproposals that Nasser had given to Eugene Black, the two of us concluded that Nasser was not really interested in serious negotiation on the project, and we considered the matter dead for all practical purposes. When weeks went by without a further word from Nasser, we became convinced that the rumor of a vast offer, made by Soviet Foreign Minister Shepilov during his visit to Cairo in the middle of June, was probably true. Other reports of an agreement by Nasser to purchase an additional $200 million in arms from the Communists (mortgaging Egypt's stockpile of cotton) made it obvious that Egypt could never fulfill her part of the financing on terms we could accept.

On July 13 Foster reported to me that he had warned the Egyptians we were not now in a position to deal with this matter because we could not predict what action our Congress might take[13] and our views on the merits of the matter had somewhat altered. He told the Egyptians that we would consult with them the next week.

President Nasser, however, now brought the matter to a head. On July 19 his ambassador called on Foster to issue a new demand for a huge commitment over a period of ten years.[14] Foster informed the

[13] A couple of days later the Senate Appropriations Committee included in its report the language that the "Committee directs that none of the funds provided in this [Mutual Security] Act shall be used for assistance in connection with the Construction of the Aswan Dam nor shall any of the funds heretofore provided under the Mutual Security Act as amended, be used on this Dam without prior approval of the Committee on Appropriations." I would not admit that the Committee's announcement could have any real effect on negotiations because if such a report could have the standing of law, it would render the Executive powerless in his conduct of foreign relations. Nevertheless the Committee's report did reflect the existence of an anti-Dam coalition in Congress. It included Senators with pro-Israeli sympathies, Southerners concerned over the cotton market, and those who were opposed to any kind of assistance to foreign nations other than our own loyal allies.

[14] For an account of this meeting, see Robert Murphy, *Diplomat Among Warriors*, p. 376.

Egyptian ambassador that the Western Powers had long since interpreted Egyptian silence and their unacceptable counterproposals as a lack of interest in our offer and considered it withdrawn.[15]

I have never doubted the wisdom of canceling our offer [see Appendix A], but I was concerned, in view of the events of the following weeks, that we might have been undiplomatic in the way the cancellation was handled. A short time after the cancellation I said as much to Foster. He answered in writing:

September 15, 1956

Dear Mr. President:

You asked whether our withdrawal from the Aswan Dam project could properly be deemed "abrupt."

I think not, at least so far as Egypt was concerned. For several months we had left unanswered an Egyptian memorandum on this subject, and the Egyptians knew full well the reasons why. Telephone conversations of which we learned indicated that the Egyptian Government knew that when they came, as they did, to get a definitive reply it would be negative.

There had for some time been mounting Congressional opposition. The Senate Appropriations Committee had already passed a resolution directing that there should be no support for the Aswan Dam without the approval of the Committee—an action which, while it was probably not Constitutional, indicated a Congressional attitude, in the face of which it would have been impossible to finance the Dam. If I had not announced our withdrawal when I did, the Congress would certainly have imposed it on us, almost unanimously. As it was, we retained some flexibility.

Of course Egypt, in its flirtations with the Soviet Union, had itself consciously jeopardized our sharing in this project, and they had tried to bluff us by pretending to [accept] Soviet "offers."

The outcome was not in fact anything in the nature of a "shock" or "surprise" to the Egyptians.

Faithfully yours,

John Foster Dulles

Perhaps Nasser was not surprised, but he put on a convincing act for the world. According to the newspapers, when Nasser received the news of cancellation of our aid offer, he went into a rage. He made a vitriolic public attack on the United States on July 24. And on the 26th he proclaimed, in a three-hour harangue, the nationalization of the Suez Canal with all its properties and assets, ostensibly as a means of financing the Aswan Dam.

He announced that a new Suez Canal Company would be formed, to

[15] The Russians late in 1958 agreed to loan Egypt $100 million for the dam. Construction began in early 1960.

be run by Egyptians, and that Egypt would pay for the seized property if all Suez Company assets (the Canal represented probably less than a half of the company's assets) were surrendered. He assumed control over the Canal Company's offices in Egypt, and on the next day, imposed military law in the Canal Zone. He forbade all employees of the Suez Canal Company, including foreigners, to leave their jobs, threatening long-term imprisonment for any disobedience.[16]

The fat was now really in the fire. Nasser had moved to take over in total the world's foremost public utility. Its loss—if it were to cease functioning—would seriously cripple Western Europe. To permit such an eventuality to occur was unthinkable.

Deeply suspicious of Nasser's motives, France and Britain considered Suez as something of a symbol, a symbol of their position in the entire Middle East and Arab world; their reaction was not immediately predictable but it would require all we could do to keep the lid from blowing off.

* * *

The Suez Canal, completed in 1869 by the French engineer De Lesseps and an international stock company, has an interesting history. A convention to provide for its protection was signed at Constantinople in 1888, the nine signatory nations being Great Britain, Germany, Aus-

[16] Regardless of the refusal of the United States to participate on the Aswan Dam project Nasser would, I suspect, have nationalized the Suez Canal sooner or later anyway. It is interesting to speculate, however, whether we might have done better to have allowed the matter to drag until Nasser himself reached the point of exasperation. Had we thus avoided a showdown on the issue, we would probably have deprived Nasser of a dramatic and plausible excuse for his subsequent actions affecting the Canal.

Over a year later I apparently mentioned the subject again and touched a sensitive spot with Foster Dulles. This time he wrote as follows:

"Dear Mr. President:

"In view of your reference the other day as to the 'way' in which the Aswan Dam decision was handled, I thought you might like to recall the actual terms of the statement we issued. This was shown to the Egyptian Ambassador in advance and he made no comments. Also, it is to be recalled that President Nasser has since said that he planned for nearly two years to seize the Suez Canal Company, but was waiting for a good occasion.

"He knew that if he pressed for a decision from us when he did the result would be negative because the Congressional action had been announced. Nevertheless, he pressed for a definitive answer, and I suspect did so in order to create the 'occasion' for which he said he was looking. . . .

"Faithfully yours,
"John Foster Dulles"

tria-Hungary, Spain, France, Italy, the Netherlands, Russia, and Turkey.[17] In 1875 Prime Minister Benjamin Disraeli of Britain had bought the stock in the Canal Company then owned by Egypt, which brought Britain's share to about 44 per cent of the holdings. Thus, while neither the Company itself nor the Canal ever belonged completely to England, that nation was by far the largest single shareholder.

Contrary to popular belief, the Suez Canal had never at any time been under organized international political control. The Canal Company performed housekeeping functions only, with no power of decision over who might use the waterway. In the Russo-Japanese War, for example, the Russian fleet used the Canal although Britain was an ally of Japan. During the Italian invasion of Ethiopia the Canal remained open to Italy in spite of the effort of the League of Nations to prevent that war.

With only Canal profits, it would take Nasser thirty-seven years to finance the Aswan Dam through this source without raising tolls. Obviously outside help was still vital to him.

* * *

The Canal seizure caused consternation in Britain and France. On the morning of Friday, July 27, I received a message from our chargé d'affaires in London. He had attended a British Cabinet meeting held in a somber atmosphere. Some concern for the legalities of the situation were expressed, he reported, but it was obvious that the British did not intend to be governed by technicalities.

They felt that the West must begin at once an examination of possible economic, political, and military countermeasures. Any immediate recourse to the United Nations seemed to them to be risking delay, thus allowing a situation to exist long enough to imply world acceptance of its permanence. Prime Minister Anthony Eden was reported to favor an immediate meeting between the United States, the United Kingdom, and France at the "ministerial level." In the meantime the British were alerting their commanders in the Mediterranean, an indication that the government was already contemplating the possibility of military action.

Foster Dulles was in Latin America. When I discussed this report with Under Secretary Herbert Hoover, Jr., he thought that the British might feel compelled to move drastically, fearing that delay would have an unfavorable worldwide impact on their relations with other restless countries.

[17] Egypt at the time was occupied by the Turks. (See State Department Bulletin XXV, page 612.) Decades later, in 1954, Egypt had announced its adherence to the treaty.

It was clear that Nasser's seizure of the international waterway would produce widespread legal, political, and economic problems for a number of nations because the Canal was, in effect, a global public utility. Almost any affected government could find some justifiable reasons for taking whatever action it might choose. For example, if the British should decide at once to move forcefully, justification might be found in a British refusal to allow its nationals, including the Suez Canal Company pilots, to be held in slavery, as the imprisonment Nasser had brandished seemed to imply.

As our first move, I instructed Mr. Hoover to challenge the distorted charges Nasser had hurled against the United States and to make clear our interest in the efficient functioning of the Canal. Accordingly, Hoover summoned the Egyptian ambassador the next morning and expressed in no uncertain terms our displeasure at the language used by the Egyptians concerning the United States role in the whole affair.

On the same day, July 27, I received a report from Ambassador Douglas Dillon in Paris transmitting the French government's opinions. As might be expected, that government took an even more emotional view than the British. Foreign Minister Pineau compared Nasser's action to the seizure of the Rhineland by Hitler two decades earlier. He argued that the West should react promptly and in strength, or else Europe would soon find itself "totally dependent on the good will of the Arab powers." Pineau planned to go to London and said that the British and French were jointly studying the military problem involved in reoccupying the Canal. He thought that the Soviet Union would not take any effective counteraction.

Prime Minister Eden's views were amplified in a cable to me. He argued that we could not afford to allow Nasser to seize control of the Canal in complete defiance of international agreements. United States interests were, he felt, identical with Britain's, and if both of us would take a stand we would have the support of all the maritime powers. If we did not do so at once, he added, the influence of Britain and the United States throughout the Middle East would be "irretrievably undermined."

Anthony's greatest concern was with the long-term outlook: he was insistent that we not allow Egypt to expropriate the Canal and use its revenues for internal purposes. Also, the British government emphasized that it had no faith in Egyptian technical qualifications for operating it.

Anthony's pessimism regarding the possibility of obtaining our objectives by negotiation was disturbing. He thought we should bring heavy political pressure to bear on Egypt and said that we must be ready, as a last resort, to "bring Nasser to his senses" by force. The British, he said, were prepared to do so. He had that morning instructed the British Chiefs of Staff to prepare a contingency plan for a military movement. Anthony proposed an immediate conference between our three foreign ministers in London.

That afternoon I discussed the Prime Minister's cable with Under Secretary Hoover and my Staff Secretary, Colonel Andrew Goodpaster. On the matter of the meeting in London there was little problem. Although I would not permit Secretary Hoover to be absent from Washington for an indefinite period while Foster Dulles was in South America, I approved the dispatch of Deputy Under Secretary Robert Murphy to London.

The moment was tense, but Anthony had assured me that the British would not intervene with force or make drastic moves in that direction until our representative arrived. In fact, I did not view the situation as seriously as did the Prime Minister; at least there was no reason to panic.

Under the Constitution our government could not, of course, except in an unforeseen emergency, employ military forces against another nation unless so authorized by Congress. As a precautionary measure, I asked Mr. Hoover to notify, confidentially, the top leaders of both parties of Congress of the situation's dangerous potentialities. Furthermore, he was to warn them I might be required to call a special congressional session. Upon the conclusion of the meeting I telephoned Vice President Nixon to ask him also to mention this possibility to his colleagues in the Senate, Majority Leader Lyndon Johnson and Minority Leader William Knowland, and to offer to keep them abreast of developments. At the end of the day I sent a message to Anthony Eden:

> "Your cable just received. To meet immediate situation we are sending Robert Murphy to London to arrive there Sunday or very early Monday. . . .
>
> "We are of the earnest opinion that the maximum number of maritime nations affected by the Nasser action should be consulted quickly in the hope of obtaining an agreed basis of understanding."

Basically Bob Murphy was to urge calm consideration of the affair and to discourage impulsive armed action. While I agreed that it would not be difficult to seize and operate the Canal at the time, the real question would be whether such action would not outrage world opinion and whether it could achieve permanent, soundly based stability. Should nationals of Western countries be seized or mistreated, of course, such an event would change the complexion of the problem and warrant any action that might be necessary. But in the situation as it then stood Murphy was to represent my conviction that any sweeping action to be taken regarding Nasser and the Canal should not be an act of the "Big Three Club"; it would have to be taken on the responsibility of practically all the maritime powers. In addition, I wished to avoid any effort by our allies, the French in particular, to relate Nasser's action to the Arab-Israeli quarrel.[18]

Murphy departed later that day. The next day, July 29, after five hours of talks with British Foreign Secretary Selwyn Lloyd and French Foreign Minister Christian Pineau, he was able to report some moderation in the attitudes of most of the British officials. The follow-up cable was also initially encouraging. Murphy had been successful, for the time, in inducing both British and French leaders to relegate the idea of immediate use of force to the background, pending the outcome of a conference of affected nations.

In contrast to this moderation in the tone of official utterances, however, the public in both France and Britain showed accelerating anger and resentment. Cheering in the House of Commons greeted the Prime Minister when he announced on Monday, July 30, that Britain had cut off all aid to Egypt. Additionally he declared that no arrangements for the future of this international waterway were acceptable that "would leave it in the unfettered control of a single power." In this heated atmosphere, responsible French and British officials began to show impatience with the restraining influence of the United States.

Obviously we were anxious to sustain our continuing relations with our old and traditional friends, Britain and France. But to us the situation was not quite so simple as those two governments portrayed it. The basic premise of their case was that Egypt, with no authority under international law, had unilaterally flouted a solemn treaty. Next they asserted that the seizure by the Egyptians of the Canal Company would seriously damage the interests of the West, particularly France and Britain, because the efficient operation of the Canal required trained and professional personnel that the Egyptians could not supply. Entirely aside from any political, financial, and legal injustice of the seizure, the technical difficulties of operation would be, they claimed, practically insurmountable. A final consideration, which I suspected was the overriding one, was obvious fear of the great increase in Nasser's prestige if he were able to carry out his design successfully. His influence would be-

[18] A new French request had arrived the day before for United States concurrence with the idea of sending more jet fighters to Israel, apparently because of the Canal situation. While the immediate dispatch of an additional twenty-four *Mystère* fighters to Israel might possibly have merit for other reasons, I thought it would be a mistake to link the two problems of the Canal and the Arab-Israeli borders.

come so immense, in their view, that he would eventually become, in effect, an Arab dictator controlling the Mediterranean.

My opinions in this matter, with which the Secretary of State was in full agreement, were no different from those of the French and British insofar as they revolved around the consequences to the world, particularly the Western world, of any closing of the Canal. Moreover, fundamental to our thought, as well as to that of our allies, was the need for sustaining close cooperation in all of our common problems and basic policies. But in this case our reasons for differing with our allies were roughly as follows:

We doubted the validity of the legal position that Britain and France were using as justification for talk of resorting to force. The weight of world opinion seemed to be that Nasser was within his rights in nationalizing the Canal Company. All considered the Canal to be a utility essential to global welfare rather than a piece of property to be operated at the whim of a single government; nevertheless, the waterway, although a property of the Canal Company, lay completely within Egyptian territory *and under Egyptian sovereignty*. The inherent right of any sovereign nation to exercise the power of eminent domain within its own territory could scarcely be doubted, provided that just compensation were paid to the owners of the property so expropriated. The main issue at stake, therefore, was whether or not Nasser would and could keep the waterway open for the traffic of all nations, in accordance with the Constantinople Convention of 1888. This question could not be answered except through test.

Next, we believed that a resort to force, in settling questions such as this one, at such a stage, would be unjustified and would automatically weaken, perhaps even destroy, the United Nations. There was no naïve belief on our part that the United Nations could, by administering a slap on the wrist to Nasser, restore the status quo in the Canal Zone. But we were convinced that until every possible resource of the United Nations had been exhausted in reaching a solution satisfactory to all, the use of arms by the West was not a sensible course of action.

In my telephonic and other communications with Prime Minister Eden I frequently expressed the opinion that the case as it stood did not warrant resort to military force.

I told Anthony that I doubted the validity of his argument that no one except the European technicians, then operating the Canal, were capable of doing so. Thirty years earlier I had been personally acquainted with the daily operations of the Panama Canal, a much more complex mechanism, and I could not wholly accept the contention that an exceedingly high level of technical competence was required throughout the operating organization at Suez. In this I was backed up by Admiral Arleigh Burke, the Chief of Naval Operations, who advised that passage through the Suez Canal was not nearly so difficult as had been imagined in some quarters. This view was reinforced by the insurance companies which announced that they would not cancel insurance merely because Western pilots might leave the Canal. I repeated that this point could be proved only by testing and told Anthony that even if the British were correct, this would never be considered by friendly nations, much less by others, as a legitimate cause for immediate occupation by force.

It seemed appropriate also to suggest to our British friends that their own unfortunate experiences from 1952 onward in attempting to maintain indefinitely the Canal Base should provide proof of the futility of any effort to establish and sustain a permanent foreign domination of an important sector of Egypt. Experiences in India, Indochina, and Algeria, too, had demonstrated that since the founding of the United Nations in 1945, the use of occupying troops in foreign territories to sustain policy was a costly and difficult business. Unless the occupying power was ready to employ the brutalities of dictatorship, local unrest would soon grow into guerrilla resistance, then open revolt, and possibly, wide-scale conflict. We of the West, who believed in freedom and human dignity, could not descend to use of Communist methods.

Although Murphy had apparently convinced our allies to hold off military action pending a conference of maritime nations, he soon began to experience difficulty in convincing the Prime Minister that the conference should not be held as early as August 1 or 2.[19]

On Tuesday morning, July 31, Foster Dulles, who had just returned from South America, came to my office along with a number of others to discuss a message from London of even more serious implications. In essence it stated that the British government had taken a firm decision to "break Nasser" and to initiate hostilities at an early date for this purpose.

They estimated that six weeks would be required for setting up the operation. Such a decision—contradictory to what we had understood—was, I thought, based far more on emotion than on fact and logic. It

[19] Our State Department thought that it would take about two weeks for adequate diplomatic preparation. As we saw it at the moment, the first nations to be invited should be the signatories to the Constantinople Convention of 1888, plus twelve non-signatory powers representing those nations with the largest tonnages transiting the Canal. With this much agreed upon we concurred with the British that referring the problem to the UN Security Council or General Assembly would be unwise until after the projected conference could meet and act.

contemplated an action that, under existing circumstances, we would not support.

I can scarcely describe the depth of the regret I felt in the need to take a view so diametrically opposed to that held by the British. Some in the British Cabinet were old friends of mine; indeed, several were comrades in the dramatic days of World War II and of the less exacting but still momentous times at NATO. I admired these men and knew that no totally narrow or selfish motivation could be blamed for their decision. Yet I felt that in taking our own position we were standing firmly on principle and on the realities of the twentieth century.

In spite of my convictions, I could well sympathize with the British and the intensity of their reaction, specifically their feeling that they had been making accommodations and concessions to unappreciative and ungrateful governments in the Middle East until they had reached a point where they felt they must assert themselves and their rights in unmistakable language. Foster, whom I dispatched to London, was well aware of my sympathy in this aspect and, I think, shared it.

Nevertheless I felt it essential to let the British know how gravely we viewed their intentions and how erroneous we thought their proposed action would be. I wrote Anthony of my misgivings. If implemented, I said, their plan would antagonize the American people despite all that could be done by the top officials of our government.

So, as Foster departed for London on July 31, I handed him the letter to deliver to the Prime Minister. Although there was nothing new in its argument, I wanted to give him a written record of the main factors in our conclusions [see Appendix B].

On the same day, Nasser announced in Cairo that normal trade would go on with Britain unless outside intervention occurred. He stated further that the freedom of navigation in the Canal would not be affected by nationalization—but he warned that if the West attempted military intervention the Egyptians would fight. Khrushchev made a statement in Moscow supporting Nasser, to which we replied that if the Soviets moved into the troubled scene they would find us at the side of our allies.

The Soviets, doubtless, had a legitimate interest in the uninterrupted use of the Canal, but indications were strong that such interest was far overshadowed by the historic Russian ambition to gain a foothold in the Middle East. Their activities in promoting antagonism and confusion among the Arabs, in particular, were well known to us; part of this scheme was to pose as the champion of the underdog, giving support to the newly emerging nations against onetime colonial powers. One role of the United States in this crisis (as in others to come, such as Lebanon and Berlin) was to counter Soviet rumblings and to ensure that they would become nothing more. Without this kind of confrontation it is more than doubtful that Soviet participation could have been limited to diplomatic maneuver.

Nasser's statement, on the other hand, had strong elements of the mock heroic. The military power with which he could resist an invasion was puny. But the spectacle of Nasser's defiance of the big powers of Western Europe undoubtedly struck a responsive chord in the hearts of Arabs from Dakar to Kuwait. This I could understand; and yet I could not help being a little annoyed. As I wrote to my friend Swede Hazlett:

> Nasser and the Suez Canal are foremost in my thoughts. Whether or not we can get a satisfactory solution for this problem and one that tends to restore rather than further to damage the prestige of the Western powers, particularly of Britain and France, is something that is not yet resolved. In the kind of world that we are trying to establish, we frequently find ourselves victims of the tyrannies of the weak.
>
> In the effort to promote the rights of all, and observe the equality of sovereignty as between the great and the small, we unavoidably give to the little nations opportunities to embarrass us greatly. Faithfulness to the underlying concepts of freedom is frequently costly. Yet there can be no doubt that in the long run faithfulness will produce real rewards.

Soon after reaching London Foster Dulles cabled me to say that things were going well for the moment. France and Britain were still determined to move into the Canal with force unless Nasser retreated, but Foster thought he had persuaded them that they should first make a genuine effort to mobilize world opinion in favor of an international solution of the problem.

The talks came to an end with an agreement to propose a twenty-four-nation conference to meet in London on August 16 for the purpose of restoring international authority over Suez.[20]

Secretary Dulles came back to Washington and reported to the nation by radio and television. He outlined our position with precision and emphasized our hope for a peaceful solution with justice for all parties. At the same time, however, the press was reporting military preparations by the British. Most significant were a Royal Proclamation authorizing the call-up of reserves, orders preparing the way for requisitioning of merchant shipping, the loading of three aircraft carriers with ammunition and fuel in the Portsmouth Naval Yard, and the dispatch of several

[20] Countries invited were Egypt, France, Italy, Holland, Spain, Turkey, Britain, the Soviet Union, Australia, Ceylon, Denmark, Ethiopia, West Germany, Greece, India, Indonesia, Iran, New Zealand, Japan, Norway, Pakistan, Portugal, Sweden, and the United States.

squadrons of Canberra bombers to Malta. The French fleet in Toulon also was made ready for action. These things did nothing to stop the boiling of the pot.

Unfortunately Egypt declined to attend the forthcoming conference on the basis that the invitation had come under a threat of armed force and of economic pressure. Nasser now moved reserves into the former Suez Base area and branded the forthcoming meeting as a "conference of aggression." The response from other nations, however, was good; the total number of countries accepting invitations was twenty-two. Except for Egypt, only Greece, where public opinion was inflamed against Britain over the Cyprus issue, refused to attend.

On the morning of August 8, before a regularly scheduled press conference, I had a call from Foster, which under less trying circumstances might have provided some comic relief. Foster had talked with the British ambassador, Sir Roger Makins, who was horrified by a remark made by Defense Secretary Charles Wilson the day before, to the effect that the Suez thing was a relatively small matter—a "ripple." To the British, French, and other maritime nations, including the United States, this Suez thing was anything but a ripple, and I had to tell my Defense Secretary he shouldn't deride its seriousness.[21]

If the British and French governments were concerned that we viewed the situation lightly, their fears were groundless. At a meeting in my office on the 9th, the Secretary of State explained in detail the plan we had carefully prepared for proposal in the coming conference. The objective of the United States would not be to reinstate the Suez Canal Company, but to establish a public international authority to operate the Canal in accordance with the Treaty of 1888. Such an authority would have control of Canal finances and would set up an operating body. Egypt would be fully represented in both organizations but would control neither, and would participate generously in Canal revenues.

Foster recognized that the acceptance of this program was open to serious question; he said that "If the only issue were the Canal itself, there would probably be no problem."

My view was that if Nasser was wholly arrogant, the United States would have to support any reasonable countermeasures. The fate of Western Europe must never be placed at the whim of a dictator and it was conceivable that the use of force under *extreme* circumstances might become necessary. In this unhappy event, quick military action

[21] Secretary Wilson was, as usual, colorfully quotable. He was trying to show that in military programing, we cannot, in his words, afford to "flip up and down" with every international incident.

must be so strong as to be completed successfully without delay—any other course would create new problems.

I emphasized, however, that if Nasser were to prove (1) that Egypt could operate the Canal and (2) would indicate an intention to abide by the Treaty of 1888, then it would be nearly impossible for the United States ever to find real justification, legally or morally, for use of force. "The situation would change radically," I repeated, "in the unlikely case that innocent United States citizens should be held prisoner or their lives endangered."

At this point I sent a message to leaders of both parties asking them to return to Washington to meet with me on Sunday the 12th. In addition, because future negotiations with Nasser might possibly result in a treaty, I felt it desirable that Foster be accompanied to the forthcoming London conference by a senatorial representative from each party. Senator H. Alexander Smith of New Jersey, senior Republican on the Foreign Relations Committee, expressed willingness to attend. In an attempt to secure the cooperation of a senatorial Democrat, Mike Mansfield of Montana was invited to accompany Foster's party.

On Sunday I met with the bipartisan group of legislative leaders who had flown back to Washington as I had requested. On the Democratic side this caused some inconvenience because their national convention was then in its preliminary stages. Present at the meeting were eleven senators, headed by Senators Johnson, Knowland, George, Russell, and H. Alexander Smith, and eleven Congressmen headed by Sam Rayburn, Joe Martin, Charlie Halleck, and Les Arends.

I discussed Suez in general terms and our hopes for the coming twenty-two-nation London Conference. Arthur Flemming, Director of the Office of Defense Mobilization, gave an extensive briefing on the world petroleum situation, with particular reference to the crisis that would develop in the European economy if the Canal were blocked and the Middle East pipelines cut. Rapid American help would then be mandatory.

The Secretary of State outlined our general view of the current circumstances and prospects for the future. He called attention to our warning to the British and French that we were not willing to support them in any precipitous or unjustified action. The next step for us, Foster said, would be governed largely by the attitude taken by the various nations at London. If the Conference should present a reasonable and proper proposal to Nasser—and he then rejected it—it would seem clear that we would be in a position to support the British and French in more forceful measures. All present understood that our meeting was for briefing purposes only.

Soon after that meeting, however, the idea of senatorial representation at the London Conference had to be discarded because none of the appropriate Democrats found it convenient to attend.[22]

* * *

The London Conference that opened on August 16 had all the aspects of an unfriendly poker game. On the first day Foster outlined the Western plan for international operation of the Canal. That evening he reported to me that the Soviet and Indian delegations had not shown their hands.

By the next day our conjectures were confirmed: the Soviets would follow a line designed primarily to appeal to Asian countries. Their answer to the Western presentation stressed the right of nationalization, sanctity of sovereignty, and elimination of the remnants of colonialism. One device Dmitri Shepilov employed was to support the Egyptian viewpoint in public while implying, in private conversation with Foster, that the Soviets were willing to negotiate some kind of mutually satisfactory arrangement with the United States. The impression he tried to give was that the Soviets would be agreeable to imposing international controls upon Egypt, provided that the plan was so devised and worded as not to alienate the Arabs from the Soviets. A second proviso, Shepilov hinted: Whatever we agreed must bear the appearance of a dual action on their part and ours. This was an obvious and infantile attempt to split the United States from its allies.

As the meeting was in session a more conciliatory tone in British public statements developed. The military movements ordered days earlier, which had contributed to the crisis atmosphere, were now described as precautionary only.

By the evening of Saturday the 18th, Foster was able to report to me that the Conference had finished its general debate, except for Krishna Menon of India, who had refused to speak, even though ample time had been provided him.

In the meantime, Foster worked out with the British and French a draft of a concrete proposal. He sent me the text. The preamble specified "that an adequate solution must, on the one hand, respect the

[22] Senator Walter George was physically unable to go; Lyndon Johnson and Mike Mansfield declined. Senator Fulbright was then invited; he not only replied in the negative but also informed Secretary Dulles that the question of Democratic participation had been studied by the party's leadership and nobody was available. As a substitute for actual senatorial representation, Senator George planned to remain in Washington and keep in daily touch with the State Department. As a result of this, the Republican senator, H. Alexander Smith, reverted to his plan to attend the Republican convention in San Francisco.

sovereign rights of Egypt, including its rights to just and fair compensation for the use of the Canal, and on the other hand, safeguard the Suez Canal Convention of October 29, 1888." The text then quoted from the 1888 Convention that there should be established "a definite system designed to guarantee at all times and for all the Powers the free use of the Suez Maritime Canal." A system should be adopted to assure maintenance of the Canal as an open and secure international waterway; insulation of the Canal from the politics of any one nation; respect for the sovereignty of Egypt; greater financial return to Egypt for the use of the Suez Canal; compensation to the Suez Canal Company; and maintenance of Canal tolls as low as consistent with the foregoing requirements, and except for a fair return to Egypt, no profit for any other nations.

The purpose of other details was to assure justice for all concerned, especially Egypt, and to provide for effective sanctions to deal with any violation of the Convention.

I undertook a thorough study of the proposed plan and concluded that if Nasser had any disposition whatsoever to negotiate the problem he would find the paper acceptable as a basis. The principal stumbling block to his concurrence would be, I thought, that part of the implementing paragraph describing the duties of the "Board." It was specified that the Board should do the "operating, maintaining and developing of the Canal," wording which I thought might be difficult for Nasser to accept. From the point of view of the United States, I would be satisfied to have the Board occupy a *supervisory* rather than an *operating* role, similar to that of a corporate Board of Directors, with day-to-day operating responsibility residing in an executive appointed by Nasser, subject to the Board's agreement.

I notified Foster of my general approval subject to this one reservation, and hoped "that the results of the conference will not be wrecked on the rigidity of the positions of the two sides on this particular point." Otherwise, I told him his document looked extraordinarily good to me.

I received Foster's answer before seven o'clock in the morning of August 20. Apparently much disturbed, he cabled:

> . . . It is felt very strongly here by most of the countries that if all the hiring and firing of pilots, traffic directors and other technicians and engineers is made by the Egyptians without some right of appeal, then in fact Egypt will be able to use the Canal as an instrument of its national policy.
>
> It would be very difficult and perhaps impossible from the standpoint of the British and French, to get agreement now to take a position which would seem to involve abandonment of this principle.

Upon receipt of Foster's message I said again that I was concerned only that we not permit future negotiations with Egypt to come to an eventual point of collapse over details of a proposed operating arrangement. But clearly recognizing the difficult role Foster was filling, I assured him I would approve whatever decision he might have to make on this point, minor to us but apparently very important to our allies.

As it turned out, Foster decided that, to obtain French and British agreement, he would be forced to adhere to the original text of the proposal.[23]

He placed the full proposal before the London Conference. Shepilov said that the Soviet Union would not be able to accept it. Response among the Asian nations, however, appeard to be better than we might have hoped, save for India, whose Krishna Menon now took the opportunity to submit his own proposal. In this impractical document, which was largely ignored, references to international bodies were, in Foster's words, "pure scenery."

The voting on the United States proposal turned out to be surprisingly good. By the next day the Conference was drawing to a close, with Foster's acuity evidenced by the support of four Asian-African countries, Ethiopia, Iran, Pakistan, and Turkey. Indeed, with nominal amendments, these four nations agreed to introduce our proposal as their own. As a result, eighteen nations—all of those present with the exception of the Soviet Union, India, Indonesia, and Ceylon—supported the position. In its final form the text of the agreement stood essentially as proposed, revised only by elimination of reference to compensation of the Suez Canal Company and a few other items.

Faced with this impressive diplomatic accomplishment, Shepilov went into action in the habitual, and boring, Communist style. He made an inflammatory speech calling the eighteen-nation proposal "a tool of maneuver of colonialism" designed to "reimpose Western rule upon Egypt." The speech was beamed for consumption in the Arab world and was calculated to make it difficult for Nasser to accept the program, even if heavily disguised. This uncalled-for and scornful rejection by the Soviets of a reasonable proposal provided, for me, one more link in a growing chain of evidence that the Soviets wanted no just resolution of any kind of the issues and problems facing mankind. Instead, they sought to create new ones.

[23] With this I cannot argue, even though I feel it is possible that the insistence of our allies that the "Board" operate rather than supervise might have had an influence on Nasser's later rejection of the proposal.

The "eighteen" of the London Conference appointed a committee to take the proposal to Nasser. The committee comprised representatives from Australia, Ethiopia, Iran, Sweden, and the United States, with Prime Minister Robert G. Menzies of Australia as chairman.

The next day, on August 24, Foster reported to the National Security Council at the White House. He was hopeful, although there were ominous overtones in his report, when he commented that the British and French had gone along with our plan only reluctantly, possibly hoping that Nasser would not accept it. His suspicions were aroused by the contention of the British and French that the Menzies Committee should state our position and thereafter refuse to participate in negotiations. This take-it-or-leave-it attitude boded no good for the forthcoming conversations.

Another discouraging indication was Nasser's attitude. Although he did, on August 27, agree to confer with the Menzies Committee, he repeatedly stated in public that he had no intention of accepting international control over the Canal.

Nasser seemed to exhibit an extraordinary and almost inexplicable sensitivity to any matter pertaining to the Canal. One morning I learned that the Egyptians were most unhappy over certain phrases I had used in a press conference in expressing friendship for Egypt and optimism over the results of the London Conference and of Nasser's acceptance of the Menzies visit. The words that the Egyptians objected to were, in referring to the Canal, "internationalized by the Treaty of 1888."

In the meantime we kept on receiving bits of information concerning British military preparations. One puzzling report was the announcement that the British had granted the French permission to station French troops on Cyprus.[24] By now I was wondering at times whether the British and French governments were really concerned over the success or failure of the Menzies mission. For example, at the very time that Prime Minister Menzies and his Committee were to begin their journey to Egypt, we heard the disturbing news that the French and British had given orders to begin evacuation of their nationals from Egypt, Jordan, Syria, and even Lebanon. Our government promptly instructed our ambassadors in both London and Paris to approach the British and French foreign officers and express concern. Such evacuation hardly showed an

[24] Ironically enough, while Britain and France were both moving troops to Cyprus, new violence broke out on that island itself. Two bombings were aimed at the homes of British soldiers, and a tank landing craft in the island's main fort was damaged by guerrillas.

intent to work for a peaceful solution. Apparently the British ambassador in Lebanon shared the same concern, and requested permission from his foreign office to ignore the instructions, at least in that country. The result was a cancellation of the evacuation orders, but the news of the cancellation became known only after Prime Minister Menzies had held his first meeting with Nasser. Whatever psychological damage was to be feared had already been accomplished.

The apparent divergence between the British government and our own was becoming serious enough that I thought I should write to Prime Minister Eden once more. Accordingly I dispatched a message to him on September 2 [see Appendix C]. My purpose was to remove from Anthony's mind any possible misapprehension as to the convictions of the American government and people.

When Prime Minister Menzies and his committee arrived in Cairo on that same Sunday, it was at once apparent that despite the cordial atmosphere they encountered, the position of the Egyptians was unchanged. Nasser was moderate in his attitude, and his foreign minister, a professional diplomat named Mahmoud Fawzi, went well out of his way to be friendly. However, Nasser first requested that his meetings with the group be held to one day because, he claimed, he was involved with other things. Colonel Nasser lost no time in disclosing that the "other things" were the economic sanctions against Egypt which had been threatened and the military preparations on the part of the French and British.

The Menzies mission remained in Cairo a week, during which time they conferred off and on with Nasser and exchanged memoranda. While Nasser promised that he would assure freedom of passage of the Canal, provide for its future navigational requirements, and establish equitable controls, he made no concessions on the main proviso of the eighteen-nation proposal: some form of international control of the Canal. The Canal would remain exclusively and entirely in Egyptian hands.

* * *

It had become increasingly evident in London and Washington that Nasser would reject our proposals. Anthony Eden had written me to this effect several days before the Menzies mission ended. Anthony's letter went to some length to elaborate on the anxiety of his government about Nasser's ultimate ambitions, and the British conviction that his seizure of the Canal constituted only the first step of a planned program. He compared Nasser's tactics to those of the Soviets. He equated any exercise of allied restraint and patience to the arguments which had prevailed during the rise of Hitler during the years prior to 1939. His letter concluded on a disturbing note. The British, he wrote, believed that Nasser's plan included the expansion of his power until he could, in effect, hold the Western world for ransom. If this were so, then Britain's duty would be plain: "We have many times led Europe in the fight for freedom. It would be an ignoble end to our long history if we tamely accepted to perish by degrees."

On Friday morning, September 7, I called Foster to discuss this communication. Foster felt that Anthony's fears of being wholly deprived of Middle East oil were exaggerated. For my part, while I agreed with much that Anthony had said, I disagreed with his tendency to present Western Europe with only two dire alternatives: the immediate use of force on one hand or an inevitable demise on the other.

My conviction was that the Western world had gotten into a lot of difficulty by selecting the wrong issue about which to be tough. To choose a situation in which Nasser had legal and sovereign rights and in which world opinion was largely on his side, was not in my opinion a good one on which to make a stand. Accordingly, I drafted a reply to this effect.

The next evening, Saturday, Foster and I met in the Oval Room on the second floor of the White House to discuss the draft of my letter. Foster's suggestions were helpful and one was, in addition, amusing. In the letter I had included a paragraph which read:

> "It took your nation some eighteen years to put the original Napoleon in his proper place, but you did it. You have dealt more rapidly with his modern imitators."

This example, Foster pointed out, smiling, might have an effect opposite to that for which I was striving, since Napoleon was put out of commission *not* by peaceful means but by force. I deleted the paragraph but sent the letter [see Appendix D].

That evening, I discussed with Foster a plan for a "Users Association," an idea we were then considering and which I had briefly mentioned in my communication to Anthony. In essence the Users Association was conceived to be a formal extension of the group of eighteen nations which, at the August London Conference, had agreed on a formula for international control of the Canal (the formula which Nasser at that moment was in the process of rejecting). The "User" plan was based upon the contingency, feared by the British, that when the Western pilots, some one hundred in all, should leave their posts, the loss of these highly skilled people would result in a breakdown of traffic and a paralysis of the Canal, whether Nasser willed so or not.

The plan proposed to organize the using nations for collective bargaining with Nasser, for mobilization of world opinion, and for mutual assistance if the Canal and the Middle East pipeline should become wholly or partially blocked. In the event that such an interregnum developed, we hoped to avoid open hostilities by placing responsibility for the Canal's operation on technicians rather than politicians.

The plan was finally put forward officially and thoroughly discussed at a second London Conference. Nasser, however, rejected it as a device for "aggression," and it was never tested.

* * *

On September 14, 1956, the Western pilots walked off their jobs at the Suez Canal. The very next day Egyptian pilots brought through the Canal a convoy of thirteen ships. As it soon turned out, not only were the Egyptian officials and workmen competent to operate the Canal, but they soon proved that they could do so under conditions of increased traffic and with increased efficiency. By the end of the week 254 ships passed through without a break in traffic. The assumption upon which the Users Association[25] was largely basćd proved groundless. Furthermore, any thought of using force, under these circumstances, was almost ridiculous.

While everybody was seeking some acceptable solution to the Canal controversy, the opposing military forces on Israel's borders continued their senseless skirmishing. On September 23, a severe clash occurred along the Jordan-Israeli boundary. Apparently the Jordanians fired first, killing four Israeli archeologists digging in a no-man's land. The Israeli responded with a raid on a Jordanian Army unit, killing fifty Jordanian soldiers in Husan.

At this point the British and French governments decided to take the Suez case to the United Nations. They asked for a United Nations study of the Egyptian government's acts in "bringing to an end the system of international operation of the Suez Canal." The next day, Egypt filed a cross petition asking the Council to take action "against some powers, particularly Britain and France, whose actions constitute danger to international peace and security." Both measures were put on the agenda on September 23, the debate to begin on October 5. The French and the British measure was approved for the agenda by a vote of 11 to 0, and

[25] However, a fuller description of its objectives and composition as well as the discussion it provoked, can be found in Appendix E.

the Egyptian by a vote of 7 to 0, the United States voting for approval of both. Our vote on the Egyptian proposal I later came to think was a mistake; but at the time I agreed with the State Department's opinion that to vote favorably on both would be evidence of impartiality. In addition it was general United States practice to approve the inclusion of items on the United Nations Security Council agenda rather than block debate by procedural means.

As the time approached for the opening of the debates our relations with our two closest allies showed further signs of strain. Difficulties compounded as the result of the emotional fear the French privately but constantly expressed of Nasser's influence in North Africa. They continued to drum on the argument that since we were allies in Europe we were bound to "stand by" them in any situation they might encounter or create anywhere on the globe. While as a matter of sentiment, and in many cases as a matter of practicality, this was so, it could not apply in every conceivable circumstance. In the instant case, much as we valued our friendship with France, and much as we desired solidarity with our principal allies, we could not encourage the unjustified domination of a small nation by foreign armies.

One evidence of this growing rift had been the French and British decision to take the Canal issue to the United Nations. The decision was made without our knowledge. While Selwyn Lloyd and Christian Pineau had discussed this possibility with Foster during the Second London Conference, the latter had no inkling at the time that a decision had been made or would be made without further consultation.

Thus in early October, there was one immediate question in our minds. What was the true purpose of the French and British in going to the United Nations? Was it, we wondered, a sincere desire to negotiate a satisfactory peaceful settlement (as the British insisted) or was this merely a setting of the stage for eventual use of force in Suez? We were apprehensive; many other traditional friends of the two nations were even more disturbed.

Our concern was heightened on the morning of October 5 when Foster met with Lloyd and Pineau in New York. Foster had taken the initiative and, pointing out the lack of real understanding existing between their two governments and ours, he asked why they were bringing the Suez to the United Nations at this time. Was it for war or peace?

Pineau and Lloyd replied in effect that they did not believe that any peaceful way existed. They urged the use of force, arguing that only through capitulation by Nasser could the Western standing in Africa and the Middle East be restored.

Foster disagreed vehemently, referring to my recent letters to Eden and setting forth our conviction that Africa, the Middle East, and Asia would be inflamed against the West if we resorted *unnecessarily* to force. After this meeting, M. Paul Henri-Spaak, the Belgian foreign minister, came to see Foster to say he thought it would be disastrous to fail to give the United Nations a real chance. The whole world, he said, would condemn the British and French if it became apparent that they were to be branded as aggressors.

Shepilov, of course, professed a desire to work out a solution. Egyptian Foreign Minister Fawzi seemed sincere in thinking that there might be some hope for international participation in the Canal's operation if a means could be found to provide more money to the Egyptians in order to develop the Canal.

In spite of the doubts in these private conversations, the resolution submitted by the British and French on the afternoon of October 5 was one which we could readily support, since it espoused the principles of the First London Conference. Therefore, after his meeting with Selwyn Lloyd and Christian Pineau, Foster announced that the United States intended to vote for the resolution. The resolution was a sixteen-paragraph statement of the Western case. It provided that the Security Council would recommend that the government of Egypt cooperate in working out a solution to the Canal problem on the basis of the eighteen-nation proposal.

Almost as soon as debate opened, a stalemate appeared practically certain. Fawzi rejected the Anglo-French proposal outright and Shepilov backed him up. The proposal, as such, never came to a vote.

With this rejection looming, Foster began to work through other channels. During the first week of October he persuaded the French and British to negotiate privately with the Egyptians. On Tuesday afternoon, the 9th, the French, British, and Egyptians got together but nothing productive resulted.

About this time I received a note from Anthony Eden, written in longhand, a heartwarming note that I valued highly. Feelings between the Western allies, even in these troubled times, held no personal rancor. After sending me birthday greetings from him and his wife he wrote:

"Our friendship remains one of my greatest rewards. Public life makes one value such a relationship more than ever in these anxious times."

Anthony had, in the meantime, sent a copy of a recent letter he had received from Bulganin and a copy of his own reply. I made this comment:

October 11, 1956

Dear Anthony:

Let me acknowledge the note from you which transmitted a copy of Bulganin's letter to you. Truly, this is a rather forbidding letter, and it is scarcely couched in the terms which one would expect in a communication from one Head of Government to another. Also, Foster tells me that Shepilov made a quite nasty speech at the United Nations Council last Monday.

It is clear that the Soviets are playing hard to gain a dominant position in the Near East area, and it is likely they have developed quite a hold on Nasser. This problem will probably remain with us whatever may be the results of the talks in New York. . . .

With warm regard,

As ever,

/s/ Ike E.

P.S. I got a chance, at this morning's Press Conference, to say something on how much Britain and the British mean to us.

By the end of a week of work in the United Nations, Secretary-General Hammarskjold revealed the fruits of his behind-the-scenes efforts in the form of a paper which had been discussed and approved informally by all, including the Egyptians. This important paper came to be known as the "Six Principles." These, which were soon formally agreed to by the foreign ministers, represented a solid starting point on which to base further negotiation. The diplomats had made progress.

(1) There should be free and open transit through the Canal without discrimination, overt or covert . . . ;

(2) The sovereignty of Egypt should be respected;

(3) The operation of the Canal should be insulated from the politics of any country;

(4) The manner of fixing tolls and charges should be decided by agreement between Egypt and the users;

(5) A fair proportion of the dues should be allotted to development;

(6) In case of disputes, unresolved affairs between the Suez Canal Company and the Egyptian Government should be settled by arbitration with suitable terms of reference and suitable provisions for the payment of sums found to be due.

The French and British supported these basic Six Principles but insisted that the main problem was still before us: implementation. How to make the principles work? Who would ensure these principles? Who would arbitrate disputes? What should the dues and tolls be? As a result, they produced a new U.K.-French proposal to replace that of September

26 which had not yet come to a vote. This paper listed the Six Principles, but a note of belligerence crept in when it observed that the Principles corresponded to the conclusions of the First London Conference that Nasser had rejected at the time of the Menzies visit to Cairo. The paper proposed that, pending a definite settlement, the Users Association, "which has been qualified to receive the dues payable by ships belonging to its members," should cooperate with the Egyptian authorities—and vice versa—to "ensure the satisfactory operation of the Canal and free and open transit through the Canal in accordance with the 1888 Convention."

The principles contained in this proposal of the French and British we could support gladly, and Foster made an eloquent presentation on its behalf the day it was submitted, October 13.

That day stands out in my mind as one typical of the infusion—or confusion—of politics and personal and world affairs. On the day when the United Nations vote was being taken on the U.K.-French proposal for the Suez Canal, we were in the midst of our national political campaign. I went to the South Grounds of the White House at 2 P.M. to greet a birthday parade of well-wishers, primarily Republicans and "Citizens" groups. That evening I left the White House and motored to the Sheraton-Park Hotel to participate in an impromptu televised question-and-answer program with persons of both parties entitled, "People Ask the President." Afterward I went to another hall in the same hotel where a birthday banquet was being given for me by "Citizens for Eisenhower and Nixon." Here I spoke for a few moments to six hundred guests and then departed. At the White House I went on television with my wife, our son, daughter-in-law, and grandchildren in another feature of the birthday celebration. At the end of the program I went to our living quarters and turned on the television to pick up news comments on the day's proceedings at the United Nations. Here, to cast a gloomy pall over the end of a busy day, I was informed by a hyperbolic commentator that the entire United Nations debate was in a state of collapse.

Foster soon informed me, however, that he thought negotiations would continue directly among the British, French, and Egyptians under the auspices of the Secretary-General, probably to be resumed within about ten days. He believed there might even be further talks at the United Nations in New York on Monday, since Dag Hammarskjold, Selwyn Lloyd, and Mahmoud Fawzi would all be there. Foster's news was encouraging.

Thus as we entered the latter half of October the diplomatic situation seemed to be improving. Ensuing negotiations, although often burdensome and difficult, had produced some results and had brought us to a point where an "Implementing Council" with an "Executive Administration" had been agreed to under the Users Association.

But there were troubling clouds on the horizon. Disturbing was the apparently growing instability in Jordan at a moment when Jordan's young King Hussein was hard put to hold his kingdom together.

On October 15, Foster and several assistants came to see me about a new situation. The Israeli, for some reason we could not fathom, were mobilizing. High-flying reconnaissance planes revealed that the Israeli had *sixty* French Mystère airplanes, not twelve, as the French had reported to us. Obviously a blackout of communications had been imposed. From about this time on, we had the uneasy feeling that we were cut off from our allies.

We guessed that Prime Minister Ben-Gurion was planning to seize some of Jordan's territory, probably the land west of the Jordan, if, as many suspected, that country were in the process of disintegrating. Furthermore we had learned that the Israeli ambassador, Abba Eban, was departing for a visit to Israel. This gave me the opportunity to transmit a personal message that I wanted Ben-Gurion to receive directly from his own ambassador.

Both Foster and I suspected that Ben-Gurion might be contemplating military action during these pre-election days in the United States because of his possible overestimate of my desire to avoid offending the many voters who might have either sentimental or blood relations with Israel. I emphatically corrected any misapprehension of this kind he might have.

Upon Foster's departure I made a few notes [see Appendix F]. Today they remind me that, although the Suez Canal issue and its diplomatic activities were foremost in the headlines, the problem of the Arab-Israeli border was never far from our minds, and all this was happening at a time when the entire United States would have been, normally, standing on tiptoe as it prepared to make its quadrennial selection of political leaders.

A week later Foster confessed that he was baffled in trying to understand the real objectives of the British and French, and he suspected that they were not too sure themselves. It was possible, he thought, that our friends were nursing the hope that our pursuit of a peaceful solution of the Suez Canal problem was primarily for election purposes, after which we might back them in a war or "police action."

I considered the possibility of inviting both Anthony Eden and Premier Guy Mollet to come to Washington shortly after the election. This invitation, if accepted, would give an opportunity for a frank exchange of views at highest levels without danger of being interpreted either at home or abroad as an election "gimmick." This we decided might be best scheduled for late November, if done at all.

Here matters stood as the world approached the fateful days of the latter part of October 1956.

CHAPTER III

Twenty Busy Days

All hell broke loose.
—*John Milton*

OCTOBER 20, 1956 was the start of the most crowded and demanding three weeks of my entire Presidency. The drama of those weeks is still so fresh in my memory that I can recite its principal events and our decisions with scarcely a pause—but the best way to see them is as they happened, simultaneously, the major mixed with the minor. It requires a day-by-day, at times hour-by-hour, account to bring the dramatic period alive. Actually, several stories unfold at once, which I shall attempt to keep distinct as best I can. The Presidency seldom affords the luxury of dealing with one problem at a time.

SATURDAY, OCTOBER 20

On October 20 I left Los Angeles routed to Washington, D.C., with a short stop in Colorado. I was finishing up a campaign tour through the Western states. The preceding evening I had delivered a political address to a large crowd in the Hollywood Bowl. Now I was scheduled to meet with well-wishers at Stapleton Airport, Denver.

Background, Polish Crisis

Shortly after two o'clock on the morning of that same day,[1] Khrushchev, Molotov, Mikoyan, and Deputy Premier Lazar M. Kaganovich,

[1] All times in the text are local times. At seven o'clock in the evening in Moscow and Cairo, it is six o'clock in Warsaw and Budapest, five o'clock in Paris and London, and noon in Washington.

then in Poland, boarded a plane at the Warsaw airport and flew home to Moscow. They had flown to Poland the day before reportedly to pressure the heads of the Polish Communist Party (the United Workers' Party) into retaining in the party leadership the Russian Marshal Konstantin Rokossovsky—Minister of Defense in the Polish government and a symbol of Soviet control. They had failed.

That failure marked a turning point in a long case history. After World War II Wladyslaw Gomulka, formerly a trade union official, became Secretary General of the Polish Communist Party and Vice Premier in the Polish government. In 1948–49, he was accused of Titoist sympathies and ousted from both posts. In 1949, the Russian Rokossovsky became Poland's Minister of Defense; two years later Gomulka was arrested and imprisoned. With the apparent post-Stalin softening of the Soviet attitude toward Poland, Gomulka was "rehabilitated"; released from prison in April of 1956, he was subsequently invited to enter the government. For this re-entry Gomulka laid down his price: a post in the Party Secretariat and the dismissal of Rokossovsky.

On October 19 the Central Committee of the Polish United Workers' Party was ready to pay this price. At ten o'clock in the morning it opened its meeting in the building of the Council of Ministers. Gomulka was at once elected to Central Committee membership. But just as the Committee was about to proceed with the next order of business—the ousting of Rokossovsky—Edward Ochab, the Party's First Secretary, exploded a bombshell: at that very moment Khrushchev and his three colleagues were touching down at the Warsaw airport. The Central Committee members drove at once to the Belvedere Palace. There, through the next six hours, they held a face-to-face debate with the world's top Communist command. The Russians demanded that Rokossovsky remain. The anti-Stalinist Poles said no. Khrushchev informed the Poles that as he spoke, a Soviet division was on the move toward Warsaw. A *putsch,* Ochab countered, would mean war.

Khrushchev was furious: He is reported to have burst out: "If you don't obey we will crush you. . . ." And he leveled the standard Communist charge: *"We will never permit this country to be sold to the American imperialists."*

The Poles refused to knuckle under, Khrushchev flew home, and in a historic speech to the Central Committee that day (now Saturday, October 20) Gomulka declared: "There is more than one road to Socialism. There is the Soviet way, there is the Yugoslav way, and there are other ways." The Polish people, he affirmed, will "defend themselves with all means; they will not be pushed off the road of democratization."

That day, newspaper reports said, Soviet troops crossing the Polish border from East Germany ran into Polish gunfire.

Fragmentary intelligence reports reached me by teletype on the *Columbine* as we approached the airport in Denver.[2] I delayed leaving the plane until I discussed these developments by telephone on the *Columbine* with Foster Dulles back in Washington. These reports so filled my mind that to a political talk at the Denver airport I added this comment:

"We read about Poland in our papers, we read about these captive peoples that are still keeping alive the burning desire to live in freedom, a freedom that we [here] have come to take almost for granted, but which they have found is the most difficult thing to sustain in the world. Our hearts go out to them, [we trust] that they at last may have that opportunity to live under governments of their own choosing."

* * *

SUNDAY, OCTOBER 21

The next morning I read in the Sunday newspapers that Adlai Stevenson was mapping a sweeping attack on the Eisenhower-Dulles foreign policy. In the course of the day the Polish Communist Central Committee elected a new party Politburo with Rokossovsky eliminated and with Gomulka named First Secretary. In Jordan, a national election returned a large anti-Western majority to the Parliament.

Bulganin Dips into U. S. Politics

From the Soviet Union, Bulganin had sent me a letter on ceasing atomic testing. I had studied the gist of it on the *Columbine* during my return flight from the West Coast. But before I had a chance to get a full translation, Radio Moscow broadcast the text. It said in part:

[2] These reports, sent in daily, come through in approximately the following style (the language and order are rearranged for security reasons):

(3) Radio Warsaw has just broadcast a report of a clash of troops on Poznan Highway between Rokossovsky forces and Gomulka security group forces.

(4) Former Party official and Polish Communist Executive Gomulka, released recently from prison, bitter about Khrushchev interference, forced Khrushchev to halt Soviet division moving to Warsaw by warning he would "break off all contact with USSR leaders."

(5) Polish delegation returned with Khrushchev and associates to Moscow. No names but they do know Gomulka did not go because he is now speaking in Warsaw.

> We realize, of course, that an election campaign is being conducted in the United States in the course of which the discussion of various questions of international significance, among them the question of disarmament, acquires the form of a polemic. However, we cannot fail to note the fact that in a number of cases, in speeches by persons in an official capacity, there has been obvious distortion of the policy of the Soviet Union concerning the above-mentioned questions. Unfortunately, this applies particularly to the statements by Mr. Dulles, who does not hesitate to make direct attacks against the Soviet Union and its peace-loving foreign policy. . . .
>
> We fully share the opinion recently expressed by certain prominent public figures in the United States concerning the necessity and the possibility of concluding an agreement on the matter of prohibiting atomic weapon tests and concerning the positive influence which this would have on the entire international situation.

In the White House that Sunday, I drafted the following reply:

> I have the letter which your Embassy handed me through Secretary Dulles on October nineteenth. I regret to find that this letter departs from accepted international practice in a number of respects.
>
> First, the sending of your note in the midst of a national election campaign of which you take cognizance, expressing your support of the opinions of "certain prominent public figures in the United States" constitutes an interference by a foreign nation in our internal affairs of a kind which, if indulged in by an Ambassador would lead to his being declared persona non grata in accordance with long-established custom.
>
> Second, having delivered a lengthy communication in the Russian language, you have published it before it could be carefully translated and delivered to me. Because of this, and of the necessity of placing the facts accurately before the public, I am compelled to release this reply immediately.
>
> Third, your statement with respect to the Secretary of State is not only unwarranted, but is personally offensive to me.
>
> Fourth, you seem to impugn my own sincerity.
>
> However, I am not instructing the Department of State to return your letter to your Embassy. That is not because I am tolerant of these departures from accepted international practice, but because I still entertain the hope that direct communications between us may serve the cause of peace. . . .
>
> The United States has for a long time been intensively examining, evaluating and planning dependable means of stopping the arms race and reducing and controlling armaments. These explorations include the constant examination and evaluation of nuclear tests. To be effective, and not simply a mirage, all these plans require systems of inspection and control, both of which your Government has steadfastly refused to accept. Even

my "Open Skies" proposal of mutual aerial inspection, suggested as a first step, you rejected. . . .

We shall entertain and seriously evaluate all proposals from any source which seem to have merit, and we shall constantly seek for ourselves formulations which might dependably remove the atomic menace.

In reading today the words of that message I find nothing that I would change.

* * *

MONDAY, OCTOBER 22

The Polish unrest spread like a prairie fire. In Wroclaw, thousands of students paraded through the streets shouting, "Long live free Poland!" In Lodz, six thousand textile workers threatened to go on strike unless the Russian troops stationed in Poland were withdrawn. In Warsaw, students rallied under a banner reading "Long live friendship with the Soviet Union on the principles of equality!"

* * *

Rumblings in Hungary

The fire ignited in Poland brought a holocaust to Hungary.[3] Against their Soviet masters, the Hungarian people had a long list of grievances. These included the Russian occupation troops, the Security Police, the attacks on the Roman Catholic Church, the trial and imprisonment of Cardinal Mindszenty, the collectivization of the land, the quotas for the production of crops, the forced crop collections, and the forced industrialization, which had cut living standards. In the three years following the death of Stalin the Hungarian Communist Party had been the arena for a running intramural battle between the Stalinist Matyas Rakosi and the milder Imre Nagy. In 1953 Nagy became Premier. In 1955 Rakosi succeeded him. In 1956 Rakosi was ousted, but his replacement was another Stalinist, Erno Gero.

On October 22 the news of the Poles' successful defiance touched off one public meeting after another in the streets of Budapest: students and intellectuals called for the election of Nagy, the punishment of Rakosi, and the departure of the Russian army.

[3] Map, "Hungary," appears following page 360.

That day in Washington, from 8:36 in the morning until 6:17 at night, I held conference after conference—in fact there were twenty-three of these, several involving identical personnel.

Practically all had to do with subjects directly or indirectly related to the developing Hungarian crisis.

TUESDAY, OCTOBER 23

Revolution in Budapest

The next day excitement grew. Young Communist demonstrators marched through the streets of Budapest shouting: "Down with Gero!" "We want Nagy!" "Out with the Russians!" They headed for Radio Budapest. There they paused outside and sent in a delegation asking the radio to broadcast their demands. Police put the delegates under arrest. The crowd, angered, moved in force to storm the station doors. The police fired. When the smoke cleared several demonstrators lay wounded, one dead.

After this incident the government *invited* Soviet forces into Budapest to restore order. The Central Committee, while retaining Gero as Party Chief, installed Nagy as Premier. Over Radio Budapest, Nagy promised "democratization and improved living standards"; he urged the mobs in the streets to disperse. But the riots went on.

* * *

Politics at Home

A few hours later that same evening Governor Stevenson, at Madison Square Garden in Manhattan, called for a "new U.S. foreign policy." The gist of his talk was that Israel must have the arms necessary to guarantee her territorial integrity.

At the same time, in Washington, after a full day of appointments and conferences, I drove to the Sheraton-Park Hotel to address the anniversary dinner of the Brotherhood of Carpenters and Joiners. Because Poland was so much on my mind, I spoke of "the fruits of Communistic imperialism, now daily become evident in the satellite world.

"The day of liberation," I said, "may be postponed where armed forces for a time make protest suicidal. But all history testifies that the memory of freedom is not erased by the fear of guns, and the love of freedom is more enduring than the power of tyrants. . . ."

WEDNESDAY, OCTOBER 24

Street Fighting in Budapest

On this day, bit by bit, we began to receive word of new conflict in Hungary. We could not get through to our Legation in Budapest and therefore had to rely on news ticker reports based on radio broadcasts from Budapest. When the picture became clear, we could see what had happened: Ten thousand Soviet troops, with eighty tanks, artillery, and armored cars rolled into Budapest to crush the "counter-revolutionary uprising." That afternoon, Budapest time, several hundred workers and students demonstrated peacefully in Parliament Square, demanding the ouster of Gero. The political police and Soviet tanks opened fire. The dead littered the square. Inflamed, mobs raced through the city, tore down Soviet flags, and smashed Soviet monuments.

Radio Budapest announced Gero was through as Party Chief; Janos Kadar had replaced him. But now the rebels wanted more. Helped by Hungarian troops, they fought on into the night, hurling homemade hand grenades (called, ironically, Molotov cocktails), and facing the fire of Soviet tanks.

* * *

Meanwhile, at 4:27 in the morning, the State Department had received a cable from Winthrop Aldrich, the United States Ambassador to Great Britain. At a small cocktail party the previous afternoon, the ambassador wrote, a former member of the British Cabinet said he had resigned his post not only because of physical exhaustion, as he had announced to the public, but also because he believed that Britain's *use of force* against Egypt would be a "great blunder."

By 11:30 that morning, Secretary Dulles was in my office to discuss this piece of intelligence with me. We considered again inviting Eden and Mollet to Washington toward the end of November. But, I emphasized, such an invitation would not stand if the British and French took military action against Egypt.

At the same meeting the Secretary and I reviewed the developments in Hungary and events in Poland and agreed that the United States should quietly let the Polish ambassador know that we would be glad to have the views of that government on the subject of economc aid for Poland. Encouraged by this sample of Polish dissatisfaction with Communist rule, we wanted to explore the chances of helping to assist centrifugal, disruptive currents in the Iron Curtain countries.

Meanwhile in Warsaw, Gomulka, trying to calm unrest, addressed a crowd carrying the flags of Poland and of Hungary. Soviet troops—on maneuvers near major Polish cities—were going back to their barracks, he said on Khrushchev's assurance, and eventually they would leave altogether. "Thank you for your devotion. Now go home."

Most of them did. "Warsaw," a newspaper correspondent wrote, "began to take on a lonely air." The Polish revolution was coming to rest on a high plateau.

In the midst of these concerns, between 2:40 and 3:30 in the afternoon in a studio at Broadcast House in Northwest Washington, I answered, for a radio and television audience, a series of questions from a group of Republican women on a variety of subjects—the bomb, inflation, recessions, and small business.

THURSDAY, OCTOBER 25

More Politics

At 8:35 A.M. on the 25th, after early meetings with Colonel Andrew Goodpaster and Governor Sherman Adams, Mrs. Eisenhower and I took a train for New York City; during the journey I worked on a campaign speech to be delivered at Madison Square Garden that evening.

When the train reached New York, we were met by large and enthusiastic crowds, shouting "I Like Ike!" It was a good time to be "liked," and the warmth of their cheering was encouraging, but I had an uneasy feeling that they might have been thinking exclusively of the political campaign, while my mind was absorbed with the international contests that had broken out in several parts of the earth.

* * *

That day I issued this statement on Hungary:

> The United States considers the development in Hungary as being a renewed expression of the intense desire for freedom long held by the Hungarian people. . . .
>
> The United States deplores the intervention of Soviet military forces which under the Treaty of Peace[4] should have been withdrawn and the presence of which in Hungary, as is now demonstrated, is not to protect

[4] Signed in Paris in February of 1947.

Hungary against armed aggression from without, but rather to continue an occupation of Hungary by the forces of an alien government for its own purposes.

On that date, we had a report from an Austrian businessman who had fled from Budapest to Vienna, that already as many as five thousand were dead, and that "the whole town echoes with artillery fire."

As I rode the train to New York, Premier Imre Nagy was announcing over Radio Budapest that he would open negotiations with the Russians for withdrawal of Soviet troops as soon as order returned. He promised amnesty for rebels who would quickly surrender. The rebels refused and called a general strike.

* * *

Accord in the Middle East

That day Jordan, Egypt, and Syria announced the signing of the "Pact of Amman," which provided that (1) they would increase their military cooperation and (2) in the event of a war with Israel, would place their armed forces under an Egyptian commander. This pact, Ben-Gurion said later, put Israel in "direct and immediate danger."

* * *

At four o'clock in New York, I greeted a number of groups representing Americans of various extraction—Negro, Italian, Puerto Rican, Armenian, Chinese, Lithuanian, Polish, Slavic, Greek, Hungarian—and then at eight-thirty my wife and I left the Commodore Hotel for Madison Square Garden for a major speech in the '56 campaign. Crowds thronged the streets and filled the Garden to the rafters.

At 9:35 that evening I left Madison Square Garden for La Guardia Airport and shortly after ten was back aboard the presidential plane for the return trip to Washington.

FRIDAY, OCTOBER 26

Hungarian Fighting Continues

On the 26th, Belgian diplomats who had fled from Budapest to Vienna were reporting that the rebels controlled all of western Hungary; that Hungarian soldiers, who had torn the red stars from their caps, controlled the roads out of Budapest, and that "freedom stations" had begun broadcasting.

"Lay down your arms!" Imre Nagy urged over Radio Budapest, promising to establish a popular front government. The rebels refused.

"Soldiers remain loyal to your government," Radio Budapest pleaded, almost in frenzy. "Please help us . . . Gero is gone. Nagy is back. He will create a new order!"

* * *

From nine o'clock to 10:42 A.M. in Washington, I presided over the 201st meeting of the National Security Council.

That morning we had a scattering of reports from around the globe, all disquieting. There were rumors—which turned out to be false—of the assassination of the King of Jordan; news of riots in Singapore and of serious unrest in Morocco, Tunisia, and Algeria. But the compelling news continued to be Hungary.

Allen Dulles reported on the entry of Soviet troops before dawn the preceding Wednesday, the desertion of Hungarian troops, the alleged desertion of some Russian tanks, the fighting in the streets of Budapest. This information, Mr. Dulles said, came in a cable from Budapest which the author wrote lying on the floor to keep from getting shot.

Whereas Tito—and the Red Chinese also—approved of the Polish stand, Mr. Dulles went on, both had kept silent on the subject of Hungary. "The Chinese Communists," he said, "may not be unhappy over what's happening in Hungary. If so, we might at this moment be seeing the beginning of the first rift between China and the U.S.S.R."

"What was the Czech reaction?" I asked, and Mr. Dulles replied, "We have very little information out of Czechoslovakia. Chip Bohlen recently saw Bulganin and Khrushchev together at a reception in Moscow. Khrushchev, he said, had never looked so grim. His days may well be numbered."

Allen Dulles speculated. "Possibly it will fall to Zhukov to choose his successor; in fact, Zhukov himself may succeed Khrushchev."

We knew this was a dangerous moment—that the Communist leaders in Moscow were doubtless searching their souls for answers to painful questions:

Could they permit a Gomulka to rule in Poland after what happened in Hungary? Could they permit a loosening of control in the satellites, or had the time come to return to the iron-fisted techniques of Stalinist rule?

"I doubt that the Russian leaders genuinely fear an invasion by the West," I told the members of the Council. "But with the deterioration of the Soviet Union's hold over its satellites might not the Soviet Union be tempted to resort to extreme measures, even to start a world war? This possibility we must watch with the utmost care."

I then directed the preparation of an immediate, comprehensive analysis of the events in both Poland and Hungary, with the possible types of American action considered.[5]

Turning to the Middle East, the Secretary of State reminded the Council of the "very worrisome" events in Jordan; a clear danger existed, he said, that the present nation there might disintegrate. The result, he thought, would inevitably be war between Israel and the Arabs. If Hussein had in fact been assassinated, the Iraqis, Admiral Arthur Radford felt, would march into Jordan. He added the conjecture that Britain might well increase its forces in Jordan; and Israel would want to secure the west bank of the Jordan River.

* * *

Shortly thereafter I met five representatives of the Pennsylvania Council of Republican Women, who presented a scroll welcoming Mrs. Eisenhower and me to Pennsylvania. (We had definitely established our permanent home at Gettysburg.) Though the heavens fall, I thought ruefully, a President's planned schedules must be kept or public interest might well turn into alarm.

At four o'clock that afternoon I walked with Jim Hagerty to the Broadcast Room in the basement of the Mansion to record a message to Texas farmers, who were suffering one of the worst droughts in years. But in the back of the minds of all of us was the possibility that Russia might start a military movement to put down her rebellious satellites which could develop to the proportions of a major war. They had lost what hold they had on Yugoslavia, and now there were chains breaking in Poland and Hungary. Though the situation was cloudy, we put the Defense Department and other security agencies on special alert.

SATURDAY, OCTOBER 27

The beginnings of this day had nothing to do with fighting and bloodshed. At ten o'clock I met Mr. and Mrs. Jackson Wheeler of Los Angeles, their daughter, Judy, and their son, Charles Jackson, the youngest Eagle Scout in the history of Scouting.

[5] To respond to this directive, a position paper was developed on Hungary and Poland, reaffirming our reassurances to the Soviet Union that we had no intention of making these countries our allies; and declaring that if the U.S.S.R. used force to suppress the Gomulka regime or any further move toward Polish independence, the United States would be prepared to support UN action—including the use of force—to prevent the U.S.S.R. from reinforcing its control.

Then I met Senator Charles Potter of Michigan and seven Michigan Minutemen and Women of 1956, and was photographed with them. These pleasantries over, real work began.

* * *

Hungarian Revolt Spreads

Shortly after eleven, Secretary Dulles came in to report: "Within Hungary itself," he said, "the revolt has become widespread. Large sections of the Hungarian armed forces have gone over to the dissidents, and throughout the countryside there are large areas in opposition to the regime. Also, signs of condemnation of the Communists are arising all over Europe. In Italy, Spain, and France there are strong demonstrations for the Hungarians. The Nagy government in Hungary includes a number of 'bad' people, associated with the Molotov school, and will have difficulty in attracting support."

Israeli Arms Build-up

The subject then turned to recent reports that had come in of a considerable mobilizing of the military in Israel. Foster suggested that I communicate directly to the Israeli government. At 12:25 P.M. the State Department forwarded my cable to Ben-Gurion, expressing my "concern at reports of heavy mobilization on your side. . . . I renew the plea . . . that there be no forceable initiative on the part of your Government which would endanger the peace. . . ."

* * *

Meanwhile, fighting had been raging on through the city streets and countryside of Hungary; the revolutionaries faced fifty thousand to seventy-five thousand Soviet troops and political police. On the Austrian border, even some of the political police abandoned their posts. Late in the afternoon, Budapest time, Nagy announced the formation of a new government which included the non-Communist postwar leaders Zoltan Tildy and Bela Kovacs. But the rebels fought on.

* * *

At two o'clock in the afternoon, accompanied by my doctor, General Snyder, I left the White House for Walter Reed Army Hospital for an overnight head-to-toe examination, the last before the election, now only ten days away.

That evening in Dallas, Secretary Dulles delivered a speech which I had, as usual, previously reviewed carefully. It declared that "the weakness of Soviet imperialism is being made manifest." He added that East European nations, dissociating themselves from exclusive dependence on the U.S.S.R., could "draw upon our abundance" during their "economic adjustment." The United States would not demand that they renounce Communism.

Suez he called "an unfinished drama of suspense, which illustrates the kind of an effort, often called 'waging peace,' which will be required, day in and day out, for many years. . . ." in finding acceptable answers to critical international problems.

SUNDAY, OCTOBER 28

Returning to Washington National Airport from Dallas, Secretary Dulles met reporters who asked his opinion of the Soviet charge that American agents had fomented the Hungarian uprising. The Secretary answered with one word, "Tommyrot." He added that he didn't know how tommyrot would translate into Russian.

Later that day the UN Security Council voted to consider the question of Soviet oppression in Hungary.

Israel ordered a general mobilization of its reserves. Ambassador Abba Eban was still telling the State Department that this mobilization was purely defensive. But at that very moment we were getting reports of a sizable increase in diplomatic radio traffic between the Israeli and the French. We believed this had real significance.

While I was still at Walter Reed, at 3:30 in the afternoon I sent a second cable to Ben-Gurion, the gist of which I made public: "This morning I have received additional reports which indicate that mobilization of Israel's armed forces is continuing and has become almost complete. . . ." I again urged Israel "to do nothing which would endanger the peace." Influenced by the Israeli mobilization, the State Department announced that "as a matter of prudence, . . . measures are being instituted to reduce the numbers of Americans, particularly dependents, in several of the Middle Eastern countries . . . persons who are not performing essential functions will be asked to depart until conditions improve." This action shows how far the Middle East situation had deteriorated, in our opinion, for only a week earlier we had opposed a similar decision by the British government.

When the physical examination was completed, the doctors told me my condition was excellent. On returning to the White House I dictated two new, stronger paragraphs on civil rights to be included in speeches to be made in the South the next day. I wanted my position on this subject understood with equal clarity in all sections of the country. These passages reiterated my 1952 pledge to "use every proper influence of my office to promote for all citizens that equality before the law and of opportunity visualized by our Founding Fathers."

MONDAY, OCTOBER 29

By 7:30 A.M. I was in my office. At eight o'clock Secretary Dulles telephoned to suggest that we bring to the attention of the Russian hierarchy one paragraph from his Dallas speech, stressing to the Kremlin that every word in it had my approval.

I agreed. Later in the day the Secretary cabled Ambassador Bohlen in Moscow instructing him to convey to Khrushchev and his associates, including Zhukov, these words:

> "The U.S. has no ulterior purpose in desiring the independence of the satellite countries. Our unadulterated wish is that these peoples, from whom so much of our own national life derives, should have sovereignty restored to them, and that they should have governments of their own free choosing. We do not look upon these nations as potential military allies. We see them as friends and as part of a new and friendly and no longer divided Europe. We are confident that their independence, if promptly accorded, will contribute immensely to stabilize peace throughout all of Europe, West and East."

Politics and Plane Rides

At 8:20 A.M. Mrs. Eisenhower and I left the White House for a political trip to Miami, Jacksonville, and Richmond. We arrived at the first stop, Miami, at 11:56 A.M. An hour later we were in the air again. I was beginning to campaign more than I had planned.

At 2:24 in the afternoon the *Columbine* touched down in Jacksonville. One part of my talk referred directly to the Hungarian crisis and to the Democrats' call for a unilateral reduction in American military power:

> ". . . at this particular stage of the world's history," I said, "where we see a once proud people being trampled down by marching regiments, this is no time to stop the draft—this is no time to stop perfecting our weapons."

In another hour I was airborne again, and at 5:49 P.M. arrived at Byrd Field in Richmond to make the third address of the day. But throughout the day, using the communications facilities on the *Columbine,* I kept in touch with Washington.

* * *

In the course of the day the French government complained to the UN Security Council that a vessel intercepted off the coast of Algeria contained arms and munitions for more than fifteen hundred men, loaded onto the ship by Egyptian troops at Alexandria, and accompanied by six French-Algerians "who had studied terrorist tactics in Cairo." The French protested that nearly a quarter of the Algerian rebels' arms had come from Egypt. The French thought they had a clear culprit for the cause of much of their Algerian struggle: Gamal Abdel Nasser.

* * *

Meanwhile, all non-essential American citizens were being evacuated from Jordan, Syria, Egypt, and Israel, in accordance with the State Department's directive. At the American Embassy at Amman, Ambassador Lester Mallory and a skeleton force of Foreign Service people waited for what they thought was an imminent Israeli attack on Jordan.

An attack did come, but in the Sinai Desert—not in Jordan, but in Egypt.[6] The Israelis dropped a parachute battalion in the Mitla Mountain passes forty miles east of Suez. Other Israeli troops driving through the Sinai Desert reinforced them. Still another Israeli force advanced through the Desert toward Ismailia. A fourth element struck at the Egyptian bases of Rafu and El Raish near the Mediterranean Coast and sealed off the Gaza Strip. Finally, a force went down the west coast of the Gulf of Aqaba and headed for Sharm el Sheikh, in a maneuver to unblock the Egyptian obstruction to Israeli shipping through the Gulf. In the course of the night, the Israeli had knifed seventy-five miles into Egypt, arriving at a point only twenty-five miles east of Suez. Against an estimated Israeli army of fifty thousand troops, with two hundred thousand ready reserves, some heavy artillery and jet fighters, and no bombers, the Egyptian Army could muster seventy-five thousand troops, with ninety MIGs and fifty twin-jet Ilyushin bombers.

Word of all this reached me late in the day as the *Columbine* touched down at Richmond. Deciding not to cancel my scheduled appearance there, by 7 P.M. I arrived back in Washington, where I received further details from Secretary Dulles, Under Secretary Hoover, Secretary Wilson, Admiral Radford, Allen Dulles, and others.

[6] Map, "Crisis in Suez, October 29, 1956," appears following page 360.

Some of them saw the Israeli attack as a probing action, while others believed it would be a rapid move which would take the Israeli forces to Suez within three days at the most, and this would be the end of the whole affair. Foster disagreed with both.

"It is far more serious than that," he said. "The Canal is likely to be disrupted and the oil pipelines through the Middle East broken. If these things happen, we must expect British and French intervention. In fact, they appear to be ready for it and may even have concerted their action with the Israelis," recalling that for the past ten days we had received no news at all from the British and French.

Some at the meeting speculated that the British and French might be counting on the hope that when the chips were down, the United States would have to go along with them, however much we disapproved. But we did not consider that course. Under the 1950 agreement the United States was pledged to support the victim of an aggression in the Middle East. The only honorable course was to carry out that pledge, and I approved a White House statement of the United States' determination to do so.

In the course of the meeting, I decided that we should telephone Mr. J. E. Coulson, who, in the absence of the British ambassador, was serving as chargé d'affaires, ask him to come to the White House, and tell him what we planned to do.

At the close of this meeting I met with him, Secretary Dulles, and Colonel Goodpaster.

". . . The prestige of the United States and the British is involved in the developments in the Middle East," I said. "I feel it is incumbent upon both of us to redeem our word about supporting any victim of aggression. Last spring, when we declined to give arms to Israel and to Egypt, we said that our word was enough. . . .

"In my opinion, the United States and the United Kingdom must stand by what we said. In view of information that has reached us concerning *Mystères* and the number of messages between Paris and Israel in the last few days, I can only conclude that I do not understand what the French are doing."

"I do not know about the messages," Mr. Coulson interposed.

"If I have to call Congress in order to redeem our pledge," I went on, "I will do so. We will stick to our undertaking."

"Would the United States not first go to the Security Council?" Mr. Coulson asked.

"We plan to get to the United Nations the first thing in the morning—when the doors open," I replied, "before the U.S.S.R. gets there."

* * *

Backwash

Simultaneously up in Boston, Governor Stevenson, on a political tour, charged that the administration had given the American people reassurances on the Near East which were "tragically less than the truth." He "assumed" that I was unaware of what Foster Dulles was doing and of his "incredible blunders." Happily for my disposition, the details of this allegation were not called to my attention for days.

In Cairo the American ambassador delivered my note to Nasser urging him to refrain from any action which would lead to full-scale war.

And the British Mediterranean Fleet was moving from Malta toward Cyprus.

This night of October 29 some prominent Republicans called on me to say that for the only time in the political campaign they thought I might not win the election. Their reasoning was simple: the Israeli had committed aggression that could not be condoned. Perhaps it would be necessary for the United States, as a member of the United Nations, to employ our armed force in strength to drive them back within their borders. If this turned out to be the case, much of the responsibility would be laid at my door. With many of our citizens of the eastern seaboard emotionally involved in the Zionist cause, this, it was believed, could possibly bring political defeat. None of them, however, urged me to abandon my position.

I thought and said that emotion was beclouding their good judgment. In any event, their uncertainty would be temporary; the next few days would give us a definite answer.

TUESDAY, OCTOBER 30

The Ben-Gurion Position

At 4:39 the next morning, a cable from David Ben-Gurion answered my messages. Nasser had "created a ring of steel" around Israel, Ben-Gurion said:

> "With Iraqi troops poised in great numbers on the Iraq-Jordan frontier, with creation of joint command of Egypt, Syria and Jordan, with decisive increase of Egyptian influence in Jordan, and with renewal of incursions into Israel territory by Egyptian gangs, my government would be failing its essential duty if it were not to take all necessary measures to ensure

that declared Arab whim of eliminating Israel by force should not come about. My government has appealed to people of Israel to combine alertness with calm. I feel confident that with your vast military experience you appreciate to the full the crucial danger in which we find ourselves."

State Department reports arriving that day were still referring, somewhat anachronistically, to the difficulties in working out agreements concerning the Canal among Britain, France, and Egypt. Selwyn Lloyd had reportedly tried to convince Pineau of the need for further negotiations toward a peaceful Suez settlement; the French Cabinet, however, had been reluctant to negotiate, preferring "stronger measures, presumably economic." Furthermore, Egyptian Foreign Minister Fawzi had told our ambassador in Cairo, Raymond A. Hare, that Egypt would have been willing to meet with the British and French in Geneva, were it not for the unreasonable British and French demands, including in his statement the charge that the British and French wanted to make the Users Association an "instrument of coercion or economic warfare."

Shortly after ten o'clock that morning I met with Secretary Dulles and other advisers. One thing the conference reflected: our lack of clear understanding as to exactly what was happening in the Suez area, due to the break in our communications with the French and British. We were in the dark about what they planned to do.

Before the meeting ended, therefore, at exactly 10:15 A.M., I sent Anthony Eden a long cable (the text hitherto unpublished), asking his help in "clearing up my understanding" about what was happening between the United States and its European allies. After mentioning the Israeli build-up with illegal French help, I said:

> Last evening our Ambassador to the United Nations met with your Ambassador, Pierson Dixon, to request him to join us in presenting the case to the United Nations this morning. We were astonished to find that he was completely unsympathetic, stating frankly that his government would not agree to any action whatsoever to be taken against Israel. He further argued that the tri-partite statement of May, 1950, was ancient history and without current validity.
>
> Without arguing the point as to whether or not the tri-partite statement is or should be outmoded, I feel very seriously that whenever any agreement or pact of this kind is in spirit renounced by one of its signatories, it is only fair that the other signatories should be notified. Since the United States has continued to look upon that statement as representing the policies and determination of our three governments, I have not only publicly announced several times that it represents our policy, but many of our actions in the Mid East have been based upon it. . . . We have had no thought of repudiating that statement and we have none now.
>
> All of this development, with its possible consequences, including the possible involvement of you and the French in a general Arab war, seems

to me to leave your government and ours in a very sad state of confusion, so far as any possibility of unified understanding and action are concerned. It is true that Egypt has not yet formally asked this government for aid. But the fact is that if the United Nations finds Israel to be an aggressor, Egypt could very well ask the Soviets for help—and then the Mid East fat would really be in the fire. . . .

Because of all these possibilities, it seems to me of first importance that the UK and the US quickly and clearly lay out their present views and intentions before each other, and that, come what may, we find some way of concerting our ideas and plans so that we may not, in any real crisis, be powerless to act in concert because of misunderstanding of each other. . . [see Appendix G for the complete text of this letter].

This cable crossed one from Anthony which argued: "Egypt has to a large extent brought this attack on herself . . . we cannot afford to see the Canal closed or to lose the shipping which is daily on passage through it." He felt "decisive action should be taken at once to stop the hostilities." As he wrote later, he believed Israel justified in its invasion: "The marked victim of the garrotter is not to be condemned if he strikes before the noose is around his throat." Eden believed Israel could probably defeat Egypt. The chief peril, as he saw it, was the extension of war by the intervention of other Arab states.

At 12:09 P.M. I replied, reiterating that our two governments differed on the Tri-Partite Declaration.

But by that time the British and French—Mollet and Pineau had flown to London—had made their decision: they would issue Egypt and Israel an ultimatum demanding that, within twelve hours, both sides withdraw ten miles from the Suez Canal and permit Anglo-French occupation of the key points along it. The United Kingdom decided against any consultation before taking this action, Eden argued later, because only swift Israel military success and Anglo-French action within twenty-four, or at the most forty-eight, hours could prevent the spread of the war to Syria, Jordan, and Iraq.

Yet another cable, this time from Mollet, said that in agreement with the British Government the French had decided to address to the Israeli and Egyptian governments a "solemn appeal" for them to end hostilities and for them both to withdraw their troops from the Canal Zone. To guarantee the effectiveness of the cease-fire, he said the French and British were also asking to assume "temporarily control" of the key positions of the Canal. He said that this demand "is but too well justified by a long experience with failures to honor international agreements and with provocations by Arab States in the Near East. . . ."

Somewhat backhandedly, I thought, he added the hope I would endorse the ultimatum: "I entertain the firm hope that the measures jointly decided on by the French and British Governments will receive your approval and that you will support them with your high authority."

Far more candidly Mollet admitted afterward: "If your government was not informed of the final developments, the reason . . . *was our fear that if we had consulted it, it would have prevented us from acting.*"[7]

In his second cable Sir Anthony, after the delivery of notes to the Israeli and Egyptian ambassadors, also told me of the ultimatum. At the end he expressed hope that "when the dust settles, there may well be a chance for our doing a constructive piece of work together." He did not support or condone Israel, Eden protested; he simply wanted to stop the fighting.

In New York City the UN Security Council was considering a resolution, drafted by the United States, asking all members of the United Nations to refrain from using force in the Middle East. When the vote came, the Soviet Union supported it; the British and French used their veto. They used it also to defeat a Soviet resolution calling on Israel to pull back behind the armistice line.

At 4:45 that afternoon, I telephoned Foster Dulles to say that I felt I owed Eden an answer after Eden's second explanatory cable had crossed the American message. This exercise, I said, was getting to be "a sort of transatlantic essay contest."

To both Eden and Mollet I sent a warning:

> I have just learned from the press of the 12-hour ultimatum which you and the French Government have delivered to the Government of Egypt requiring, under threat of forceful intervention, the temporary occupation by Anglo-French forces of key positions at Port Said, Ismailia and Suez in the Suez Canal Zone. I feel I must urgently express to you my deep concern at the prospect of this drastic action even at the very time when the matter is under consideration as it is today by the United Nations Security Council. It is my sincere belief that peaceful processes can and should prevail to secure a solution which will restore the armistice con-

[7] Though the British government was the largest single shareholder in the Suez Canal Company—44 per cent—private French citizens held more than 50 per cent of the shares. Incidentally, it is to be remembered that, although the British-Egyptian Pact which empowered the British to re-enter the Canal Zone in the event of an attack, specifically excluded an attack by Israel, the tri-partite Declaration of 1950 pledged the British, French, and Americans to take action to prevent any violation of the Egyptian-Israeli frontiers and armistice lines. The present trouble was that the British and French demanded not that both sides withdraw *behind their frontiers, but rather that they withdraw only ten miles from the Canal.* In the circumstances the Israelis accepted the ultimatum—on condition Egypt accept it. Nasser scornfully ignored it; if the British and French tried to seize Suez, he promised them a fight.

dition as between Israel and Egypt and also justly settle the controversy with Egypt about the Suez Canal.

Then Jim Hagerty released to the press a statement, somewhat milder, on the United States reaction to the ultimatum and on our intention to work out a cease-fire through the United Nations.

When Eden heard that the substance of my final message had been released, he cabled me that in view of the publicity, he "must be free to make public the substance" of his two earlier messages.

In longhand I wrote out at the bottom of his cable: "My answer is, by all means use any part you see fit."

Some hours earlier Eden had broken the news of the ultimatum to the House of Commons:

> "Unless hostilities can be stopped," he said, "free passage through the Canal will be jeopardized. . . . Her Majesty's Government and the French Government have called upon [Israel and Egypt] to stop all warlike action . . . forthwith and to withdraw their military forces to a distance of ten miles from the Canal. . . . We have asked the Egyptian Government to agree that Anglo-French forces should move temporarily into key positions. . . . If at the expiration of [twelve hours] one or both have not undertaken to comply . . . British and French forces will intervene in whatever strength may be necessary."

The Labor Party went through the roof. Labor MPs charged that the government was using the Israeli invasion as a pretext for reoccupying the Canal Zone. Late that evening, after two hours of debate, the House (despite Eden's Conservative Party majority) gave Anthony only a shaky vote of support, 270 to 218.

* * *

Meanwhile the American political campaign went on. I heard that Jacob Javits, running for the Senate, had made a courageous speech in New York City defending the administration, refusing to condone the Israeli attack, and urging bipartisanship.

WEDNESDAY, OCTOBER 31

Conciliatory Statement from Moscow

On October 31 *Pravda* published an astonishing and seemingly contrite "Declaration by the Soviet Government on the Principles of Development and Further Strengthening of Friendship and Cooperation between the Soviet Union and Other Socialist States."

It affirmed that Russia and its satellites could "build their mutual relations only on the principles of complete equality . . . and of non-interference in one another's internal affairs." It admitted "downright mistakes, including mistakes in mutual relations among socialist countries." It declared that the Soviet Union stood ready to discuss the further presence of Soviet "technical advisers" in satellite countries. And it affirmed the general principle that troops should be stationed in other countries "only with the consent" of the host state.

Though the statement alleged that Soviet military units had gone into Budapest only to bring order to the city, at the Hungarian Government's request, it promised that the Soviet Government would withdraw its troops as soon as the Hungarian Government considered that withdrawal necessary.

"This utterance," Allen Dulles declared, "is one of the most significant to come out of the Soviet Union since the end of World War II." "Yes," I replied, "if it is honest."

The Hungarian revolution was, at that moment, at its high-water mark. How cynical would their statement appear within a matter of days.

* * *

Israel Moves On

At dawn that Wednesday morning, the Israeli forces were still driving westward across the Sinai Peninsula.

At 9:47, Washington time, Senator Knowland telephoned me from California.

"Will it be safe," he asked, "for me to get on a plane, away from the telephone for three to four hours, in case you decide to call Congress back?"

"Yes," I told him. "But keep in touch."

"I'm shocked by the actions of our allies," he went on.

"I understand your feeling," I answered, "but I don't think it will do any good to be bitter toward the British."

At 11:45 Ambassador Lodge telephoned from the United Nations that there was enthusiastic and well-nigh unanimous approval of the policy we had adopted before that body—calling upon Israel and Egypt to cease fire, upon Israel to withdraw behind the armistice line, and upon all UN members to refrain from the use of force and from military, economic, and financial aid to Israel until it complied with this UN resolution.

Meanwhile, in the British House of Commons, the Laborites continued their onslaught against the government. Hugh Gaitskell called the

Suez venture "disastrous folly"; Philip Noel-Baker censured the government for failing to inform the United States in advance. Against these attacks Eden countered that the government wanted the military action to be "temporary"; but he insisted it was his intention "that our action to protect the Canal and separate the combatants should result in a settlement which will prevent such a situation arising in the future."

In Washington I dictated still another cable to Anthony. It was never sent because the next event overtook it, but the draft is worth quoting, perhaps, as evidence of my thoughts at the time.

The most pertinent passage was, "I must say that it is hard for me to see any good final result emerging from a scheme that seems to antagonize the entire Moslem world. Indeed I have difficulty seeing any end whatsoever if all the Arabs should begin reacting somewhat as the North Africans have been operating against the French."

Then, as dusk fell over Egypt, British planes based on Cyprus launched a bombing raid against Cairo, Alexandria, Port Said, and Ismailia, striking airfields, ports, railways, communication centers, and the radio towers of the "Voice of the Arabs" at Abu Zabel near Cairo.

The British reported no resistance in the air and only weak and erratic anti-aircraft fire from the ground. But in the Suez Canal near Lake Timsah, the Egyptians quickly sunk a 320-foot-long ship, the *Akka,* which more than two months before had been loaded with cement and rocks and towed to the spot for a voyage to the bottom should events so require. The Suez Canal was blocked. In the next few days, the Egyptians were to send thirty-two ships to the floor of the Canal and blame all of the sinkings on the British.

* * *

To the People

In Washington I spent the day preparing for a broadcast that night. Because of my preoccupation with the developing situation, it was not until ten minutes before the program began, at 7 o'clock, that the last page was typed. Beginning with Poland and Hungary, the address described our readiness to give economic help to new and independent governments in Eastern Europe without demanding any particular form of society. It further assured the Soviets once more that we wished to be friends with these new nations but did not regard them as potential allies.

Turning to the Middle East, I reiterated our fundamental policy of friendship for Israeli and Arab alike. And then I focused on the current attack against Egypt, pointing out first that "the United States was not consulted in any way" about the military actions.

It was the right of those nations to make such decisions, I said, and our right to dissent. We recognized the grave anxieties of Britain and Israel and France, we knew that they had been subjected to grave provocations, and we believed, without minimizing our friendship, that they were in error.

"We are forced to doubt that resort to. . . . war will for long serve the permanent interest of the attacking nations," I added. There would be no U.S. involvement in the hostilities, I would not call the Congress into special session, and though we had been rebuffed the day before in the UN—because of a veto by Great Britain and France—we did not believe that organization's processes were exhausted. (We would take our request that Israel withdraw and hostilities end before the General Assembly, where no veto operated.)

I then stated my belief in the United Nations as the soundest hope for peace. Though the society of nations had been slow to accept it, the truth was that:

> The peace we seek and need means much more than mere absence of war. It means the acceptance of law, and the fostering of justice, in all the world.

* * *

But politics still had its moment in the day. Adlai Stevenson sent me a wire cautioning against hasty use of our armed forces. Such incidents one could expect at the climax of a presidential campaign.

THURSDAY, NOVEMBER 1

Hungarian Appeal to the UN

On Thursday, November 1, an eventful day, Imre Nagy informed the Soviet ambassador that Hungary was renouncing the Warsaw Pact,[8] declaring its neutrality, and appealing to the United Nations for help in defense of that neutrality.

[8] A mutual defense treaty signed in 1955 by the Soviet Union, Albania, Bulgaria, Czechoslovakia, East Germany, Hungary, Poland, and Rumania. It set up the Warsaw Treaty Organization—the Communist parallel to NATO.

Egypt Regroups

Egypt broke its diplomatic ties with Britain and France; Nasser ordered the bulk of Egyptian forces withdrawn from the Sinai Peninsula to fight the British and French in defense of the Canal.

In the House of Commons Anthony Eden pleaded that Britain and France would welcome eventual United Nations control of the Suez area, but only after Israeli and Egyptian forces had been separated and peace had been restored. The Laborites called for a vote of censure. Bitter debate followed, with Gaitskell and Bevan heading the attack. The censure motion failed 324 to 255.

* * *

At nine o'clock that morning a meeting in my office began with an intelligence review by Allen Dulles. "The occurrences in Hungary," he said, "are a miracle. They have disproved that a popular revolt can't occur in the face of modern weapons. Eighty per cent of the Hungarian Army has defected. Except in Budapest, even the Soviet troops have shown no stomach for shooting down Hungarians."

The problem in Hungary, he concluded, was the lack of a strong guiding authority for the rebels; Imre Nagy was failing, and the rebels were demanding that he resign. Cardinal Mindszenty, if supported by the Roman Catholic ardor of the Hungarian people, was a possible leader; newspapers that morning were reporting his release from house arrest and his return to Budapest.

Turning to the Middle East, Foster Dulles reviewed the history of recent weeks. Much of what he said was an estimate only because of our having been practically cut off from normal diplomatic connections with Britain and France, except for my personal communications with Eden.

He referred to the vast increase in diplomatic traffic between France and Israel. Then, he said, "Israel mobilized and struck. We believed that Israel would attack Jordan, not Egypt," he said. "The Anglo-Jordanian treaty probably prevented that attack and caused Britain, France, and Israel to agree on an Israeli strike against Egypt and on the British and French use of this strike as a pretext to protect the Canal. In all probability," the Secretary went on, "these moves were concerted; the French did the planning, the British acquiesced, and the French, in violation of the 1950 agreement, covertly supplied the Israelis with arms."

Under the rules of the United Nations, he continued, if a veto prevents action by the Security Council, the General Assembly can be convened within twenty-four hours. The Assembly could therefore meet that afternoon at five.

". . . It is nothing less than tragic," he concluded, reminding us all of a somber fact, "that at this very time, when we are on the point of winning an immense and long-hoped-for victory over Soviet colonialism in Eastern Europe, we should be forced to choose between following in the footsteps of Anglo-French colonialism in Asia and Africa, or splitting our course away from their course. Yet this decision must be made in a mere matter of hours—before five o'clock this afternoon."

We could not permit the Soviet Union to seize the leadership in the struggle against the use of force in the Middle East and thus win the confidence of the new independent nations of the world. But on the other hand I by no means wanted the British and French to be branded as naked aggressors without provocation. I therefore instructed Foster to draft two statements: an announcement of our suspension of all military and some governmental economic aid to Israel; and a moderate resolution for submission to the General Assembly in an effort to block a resolution—certain to be an objectionable one—by the Soviet Union.

At 11:10 Foster telephoned me to read the draft text of our statement on mild sanctions against Israel. It seemed satisfactory to me. I then told him to send the text of our proposed United Nations resolution to Cabot Lodge at once so that he could rally support for it before Secretary Dulles would personally present it to the General Assembly later that day. The resolution called for an immediate cease-fire, withdrawal of all troops behind the armistice lines, a ban on all military shipments into the area of hostilities, and action to open the Canal.

That night, with a feeling of relief, I delivered my final platform speech of the campaign in Philadelphia. I canceled the rallies still on my calendar.

Speaking about the tangled situation that had developed out of Middle East difficulties, I said:

> We cannot—in the world, any more than in our own nation—subscribe to one law for the weak, another law for the strong; . . .
>
> There can be only one law—or there will be no peace. . . .
>
> We value—deeply and lastingly—the bonds with those great nations [Britain and France], those great friends, with whom we now so plainly disagree. And I, for one, am confident that those bonds will do more than survive. They can—my friends, they must—grow to new and greater strength.
>
> But this we know above all: there are some firm principles that cannot bend—they can only break. And we shall not break ours.

FRIDAY, NOVEMBER 2

UN Results on Suez

Early Friday morning the UN General Assembly approved the United States cease-fire resolution 64 to 5. Britain, France, Australia, New Zealand, and Israel opposed it; Canada, South Africa, Belgium, Laos, the Netherlands, and Portugal abstained. Then Lester Pearson of Canada introduced a key proposal—for a United Nations police force—that eventually helped the UN turn a corner toward a solution.

By this date, the Egyptan air force had been put out of action. Britain reported one hundred Egyptian planes destroyed. Israel reported the conquest of the Sinai Peninsula and the Gaza Strip, with thirty thousand Egyptians killed, captured, or put to flight.

Food for Hungary

I issued a statement authorizing food and other relief to the Hungarian people—an initial allocation of $20 million from the funds appropriated by the Congress for emergency use.

* * *

Cable from Paris

That afternoon I met with Secretary Dulles and Under Secretary Hoover. During the meeting we received a report from Assistant Secretary William Rountree in the State Department recounting a conversation between Ambassador Douglas Dillon and French Foreign Minister Pineau in which Pineau outlined step by step the whole history of French collusion in the Suez crisis.

"Were the British involved?" Secretary Dulles asked.

"Oh yes," Rountree assured him.

* * *

Letters at the End of Day

That evening I sent personal letters to two of my close friends—Swede Hazlett and Al Gruenther. While these letters dealt mainly with the Middle East, a few paragraphs were definitely descriptive of my feelings about the election, then only days away.

November 2, 1956

Dear Swede:

. . . in my last evening's talk, in Philadelphia, I confined myself to laying out the approach I have employed since 1952 to the whole problem of foreign relations and how I would approach it in the future if the American people want me to continue.

Actually, unless I win by a comfortable majority (one that could not be significantly increased or decreased in the next few days by any amount of speaking on either side), I would not want to be elected at all.

This is for a few simple reasons. . . .

My first reason. Since by the Constitution this is my final term, my influence in these next four years with my own party is going to be determined by their feeling as to how popular I am with the multitudes. If they feel that my support will be a real asset in the next election they, individually and as a party, will be disposed to go in the direction that I advocate. . . .

My second reason is that in any event, whether or not we win control of one or both Houses of the Congress, the division is certain to be very close. In almost every project some Democratic help will be absolutely necessary to get it accomplished. Again this strength can be marshalled, on both sides of the aisle, *only* if it is generally believed that I am in a position to go to the people over the heads of the Congressmen. . . .

For these two reasons I think that my only opportunity for doing anything really worthwhile is to win by a comfortable majority. This belief, incidentally, was an additional reason for my deciding to do a bit of travelling in the campaign. It also offered me a chance to prove to the American people that I am a rather healthy individual.

November 2, 1956

Dear Al:

. . . I am not going to bore you with reciting all of our Mid East troubles . . .

Strangely enough, I have seen some of my old British friends in the last few days and most of them are truly bitter about the action taken by their Government. . . . I believe that Eden and his associates have become convinced that this [Canal seizure] is the last straw and Britain simply *had* to react in the manner of the Victorian period.

If one has to have a fight, then that is that. But I don't see the point in getting into a fight to which there can be no satisfactory end, and in which the whole world believes you are playing the part of the bully and you do not even have the firm backing of your entire people.

SATURDAY, NOVEMBER 3

On this date Syrian saboteurs blew up the British oil pipelines running through their country from Iraq to the Mediterranean, except for a small one which we thought would likely be put out of action soon.

In Britain, Anthony Eden rejected the UN cease-fire proposal, but added that the British and French would stop firing as soon as (1) Egypt and Israel agreed to accept a UN force to keep the peace; (2) the UN decided to maintain such a force until an Arab-Israeli peace settlement could be reached, along with an agreement on "satisfactory arrangements" for the Suez Canal; and (3) Israel and Egypt agreed to accept a limited number of French and British troops on Egyptian soil until the UN force came into being.

Democratic Views on the Crisis

Still campaigning, Estes Kefauver claimed he saw the origin of the whole crisis in the United States' "preoccupation with oil." Mrs. Eleanor Roosevelt voiced her opinion that Israel had acted in self-defense, and that the administration had favored the Arabs. After American policy failed, she asked, what else could Britain and France do but march in?

All commentary lost any importance to me when the news arrived that Secretary Dulles had just entered Walter Reed Army Hospital for an emergency operation.

SUNDAY, NOVEMBER 4

At 3:13 in the morning in the UN Security Council, began a meeting in which the Soviet Union, using its veto for the seventy-ninth time,[9] torpedoed an American resolution calling upon the Russian government at once to withdraw its forces from Hungary.

At about four that morning the State Department received from our legation in Budapest a cable saying that the "British Military Attaché called and stated that he had heard officially that the Soviets had given the Hungarian Government an ultimatum of 0800 to the effect that if the Government did not capitulate within four hours, the Soviets would bomb Budapest."

[9] By the time of this writing (November 1964) the Soviet Union had used its veto 102 times, the United States never.

The Revolt Crushed

The Soviet Union promptly launched a major assault on Hungary: two hundred thousand troops and four thousand tanks reportedly moved into Budapest "to help the Hungarian people crush the black forces of reaction and counter-revolution." Imre Nagy took refuge in the Yugoslav Embassy; Cardinal Mindszenty fled to the American Legation. A new Communist government—the Hungarian Revolutionary Workers and Peasants Government—under the command of Janos Kadar came into existence. That one day, it was reported, there were fifty thousand Hungarians dead and wounded in the streets of Budapest.

At once I wrote to Bulganin:

> I have noted with profound distress the reports which have reached me today from Hungary.

The Soviet's declaration of October 30, 1956, which restated the policy of "non-intervention in internal affairs of other states," was generally understood, I said, to promise the early withdrawal of Soviet forces from Hungary:

> Indeed, in that statement, the Soviet Union said that "it considered the further presence of Soviet Army units in Hungary can serve as a cause for an even greater deterioration of the situation."

This statement we regarded as an "act of high statesmanship," I added, and consequently we were inexpressibly shocked by the reversal of this policy—all the more so because their renewed use of force against the Hungarians took place while negotiations were going on between the Soviets and the Hungarian government for the removal of Soviet military units. "I urge in the name of humanity and in the cause of peace," my letter ended, "that the Soviet Union take action to withdraw Soviet forces from Hungary immediately. . . ."

* * *

Operations in Sinai

By November 4 Israel had occupied nearly all the Sinai Peninsula and all the Gaza Strip. It had captured Tiran and Sanifar, two islands in the Gulf of Aqaba used by Egypt to blockade the Israel port of Eilat. It had taken more than five thousand Egyptian prisoners and quantities of Soviet-manufactured arms.

The British and French ground forces, however, had not yet entered the fight. The British and French armada from Cyprus—one hundred warships and troop transports—approached the Egyptian coast. Though the United Nations had adopted both the Canadian resolution calling for the creation of a UN force, with a six-thousand-man ceiling, within forty-eight hours, and an Afro-Asian resolution calling upon the Secretary-General to arrange a cease-fire within twelve hours, and though Egypt announced its acceptance of the cease-fire resolution of November 2, Anthony Eden refused to postpone his invasion: "If we draw back now," he said to me in the second of two cables, "everything will go up in flames in the Middle East. . . . We cannot have a military vacuum while a UN force is being constituted."

That evening, in Trafalgar Square, the British Labor Party put on a giant rally demanding that Prime Minister Eden resign.

* * *

At 4:31 in the afternoon the UN General Assembly approved the United States resolution calling on the Soviet Union to withdraw its troops from Hungary, 50 to 8 (the Soviet bloc, including Poland, opposed; fifteen abstentions).

The Problem of the Use of Force

The twin problems of Hungary and Suez now became more acute and, in addition, created an anomalous situation. In Europe we were aligned with Britain and France in our opposition to the brutal Soviet invasion of Hungary; in the Middle East we were against the entry of British-French armed forces in Egypt.

The launching of the Soviet offensive against Hungary almost automatically had posed to us the question of employing force to oppose this barbaric invasion.

The Hungarian uprising, from its beginning to its bloody suppression, was an occurrence that inspired in our nation feelings of sympathy and admiration for the rebels, anger and disgust for their Soviet oppressors. No one shared these feelings more keenly than I; indeed, I still wonder what would have been my recommendation to the Congress and the American people had Hungary been accessible by sea or through the territory of allies who might have agreed to react positively to the tragic fate of the Hungarian people. As it was, however, Britain and France could not possibly have moved with us into Hungary. An expedition combining West German or Italian forces with our own, and moving across neutral Austria, Titoist Yugoslavia, or Communist Czechoslovakia, was out of the question. The fact was that Hungary could not be reached by any United Nations or United States units without traversing such territory. [See map, "Hungary."] Unless the major nations of Europe would, without delay, ally themselves spontaneously with us (an unimaginable prospect), we could do nothing. Sending United States troops alone into Hungary through hostile or neutral territory would have involved us in general war. And too, if the United Nations, overriding a certain Soviet veto, decided that all the military and other resources of member nations should be used to drive the Soviets from Hungary, we would inevitably have a major conflict. Though the General Assembly passed a resolution calling upon the Soviets to withdraw their troops, it was obvious that no mandate for military action could or would be forthcoming. I realized that there was no use going further into this possibility.

So, as a single nation the United States did the only thing it could: We readied ourselves in every way possible to help the refugees fleeing from the criminal action of the Soviets, and did everything possible to condemn the aggression.

MONDAY, NOVEMBER 5

At eight o'clock in the morning, six hundred British paratroopers jumped on Gamil Airfield, to the west of Port Said on the Suez Canal. Five hundred French paratroopers dropped to the south of Port Said.

During the afternoon the British and French continued landings. By 7 P.M. the Egyptian commander at Port Said had agreed to surrender.

In the next hour or so, however, the Soviet Union broke silence. Loudspeaker vans in Port Said blared out the news that Russian help was on the way. In that hour and a half Bulganin released messages to Eden, Mollet, and Ben-Gurion. He told them the Soviet Union was prepared to use force to crush the aggressors and restore the peace. And he warned them that a spread of the fighting could lead to World War III.

By 8:30 the Egyptian Governor of Port Said had reversed his earlier decision: the fighting, he said, must go on.

At the same time Bulganin wrote to me proposing that the United States and the Soviet Union join forces, march into Egypt, and put an end to the fighting. "If this war is not stopped, it is fraught with danger and can grow into a Third World War," he added.

At five o'clock I met with Under Secretary Hoover, State Department legal adviser Herman Phleger, Governor Adams, and members of the

White House staff. We discussed a proposed White House statement in reply to the Bulganin note.

"This statement," I said, "ought to include a clear warning—a passage that would make it unmistakably clear that the United Nations, including the United States, would oppose with force any attempt to violate the UN plan for getting a cease-fire. The Soviets," I went on, "seeing their failure in the satellites, might be ready to undertake any wild adventure . . . . [they] are as scared and furious as Hitler was in his last days. There's nothing more dangerous than a dictatorship in that frame of mind."

Accordingly, the White House statement called the Soviet plan for joint American-Soviet action "unthinkable," and warned that the entry of any new troops into the Middle East would oblige all members of the United Nations, *including the United States,* to take effective countermeasures.

In England, Eden also rejected Bulganin's threats, asked him to support the proposal for a United Nations police force, and proceeded to deliver a scathing attack on the hypocrisy of the Soviet Union's coming as a peacemaker into the Middle East while its hands were still stained with Hungarian blood.

* * *

Throughout the campaign Governor Stevenson had declined to touch what he must have considered a politically powerful argument in his favor: my health. On election eve, reportedly against the advice of some of his aides, he raised the issue, pointing out the "scientific evidence" that I couldn't last another four years, and declaring that he "recoiled" at the thought of Richard Nixon's directing the destiny of America and serving as guardian of the hydrogen bomb.

TUESDAY, NOVEMBER 6

Increased Fighting

It was Election Day. Israel's part in the fighting had ended. But in the early morning hours, additional British assault forces from Malta were landing at Port Said, and running into heavy Egyptian fire. French commandos landed at Port Fuad, meeting no resistance.

In Washington at a meeting which began at 8:37 A.M., Allen Dulles gave me late intelligence reports. The Soviet Union had told the Egyptians, he believed, that they would "do something" in the Middle East.

We speculated that they might try to stage fighter planes into Egypt. I told Allen Dulles to order high-altitude reconnaissance flights over Israel and Syria to see whether Soviet planes and pilots had landed at Syrian bases. "Our people should be alert in trying to determine Soviet intentions," I said. "If the Soviets should attack Britain and France directly, we would of course be in a major war."

Later in the morning, my wife and I drove the eighty miles to Gettysburg to vote.

I returned to Washington at about noon by helicopter. Andy Goodpaster met me at the airfield and reviewed the major developments on the way in to the White House—particularly the prospects for a cease-fire, and intelligence reports received during the morning of jet aircraft of unknown nationality overflying Turkey. (Later reports had not confirmed these overflights, although all intelligence agencies continued to be particularly watchful.)

In an immediate meeting in the White House Cabinet Room, Admiral Radford said the Joint Chiefs had been reviewing our military state of readiness and had concluded that measures for its improvement, as I had directed, were indicated. He read off a list of twenty or thirty steps of this character.

"These," I said, "should be put into effect by degrees—not all at once, in order to avoid creating a stir. Units can be put on alert, and the number of ships and aircraft on ready status should be increased."

Though I questioned whether movements should be started to the Persian Gulf and other areas, and though many of the measures were simply precautionary, I believed that we should progressively achieve an advanced state of readiness, starting the next morning. Many precautionary items would escape notice but I suggested that the military services might soon call back personnel from leave, an action impossible to conceal which would let the Russians know—without being provocative—that we could not be taken by surprise.

In the course of the meeting, Admiral Radford remarked, "It is very hard to figure out the Russian thinking in connection with their proposal. For them to attempt any operations in the Middle East would be extremely difficult, militarily. The only reasonable form of intervention would be long-range air strikes with nuclear weapons—which seems unlikely."

His reasoning proved sound.

Meanwhile British forces were reaching El Cap, twenty-three miles south of Port Said, and they and the French were claiming control of the Canal area. At the very moment we were meeting in the White

House the British government was ordering a cease-fire, to take effect at midnight unless the Allied forces should be attacked by the Egyptians.[10]

During the noon meeting I telephoned Anthony Eden. I told him of our satisfaction that he found it possible to order the cease-fire. He replied that the decision involved some risk, but felt that the situation justified it.

"I hope that you will now go along with the United Nations resolutions without imposing any conditions," I said. "This I think would be highly advisable so as to deny Russia any opportunity to create trouble. The United Nations is making preparation for the concentration of a caretaking force."

Anthony felt that the size of that force would have to be considerable. "I hope you [the Americans] will be there," he said. "Are we all going to go?"

"What I want to do is this," I replied. "I would like to see none of the great nations in it." My thought was that if any of the large nations provided troop contingents the Soviets would try to provide the largest. I told Anthony we should put the matter in Mr. Hammarskjold's hands and say to him, "When we see you coming in with enough troops to take over, we'll leave."

If anyone then made an aggressive move, I said, the attack would be a challenge to the whole United Nations. This, I felt, no one would want to make.

The Prime Minister asked time to think this suggestion over and then said, "If I survive here [remain as Prime Minister] tonight I will call you tomorrow." Referring to our election he asked: "How are things going with you?"

We had been giving all our thought to Hungary and the Middle East, I said. "I don't give a darn about the election, I guess it will be all right."

Later that afternoon Prime Minister St. Laurent of Canada called. "Things are pretty encouraging," I told him. "Never have I seen action on the part of a government that excited me more than the rapid way

[10] Eden later announced that he arrived at the cease-fire decision because he had accomplished the British purpose: to separate the combatants and prevent the spread of the war. He also mentioned a great drain in British gold and dollar reserves, which had fallen by $57 million in September, 84 million in October, and 279 million in November—an amount equal to 15 per cent of the British reserves' total. This cost of war was not irrelevant.

you and your government moved into the breech with your proposal for a United Nations force to go to Suez. You did a magnificent job, and we admire it."

WEDNESDAY, NOVEMBER 7

War Ends

At two o'clock in the morning, Cairo time, fighting ended in the Middle East.

Politics Come to an End

A few hours later I was standing before a shouting audience of elated Republicans; the national Republican ticket had won another landslide victory.

* * *

Prospects of a Big Three Conference

Several hours later, at 8:43 A.M. Washington time, Prime Minister Eden telephoned: in the course of the conversation we discussed the possibility of some dangerous Soviet moves. In reply to a suggestion I said I would be delighted to have Eden and Mollet come to the United States. In spite of our long insistence against the use of force without exhausting every possibility of settling the Suez difficulty by peaceful means, I added, "After all, it [our disagreement over Suez] is like a family spat." I asked Eden to call Mollet to let him know. After hanging up, I telephoned Acting Secretary Hoover to say that Eden and Mollet planned to "fly over that evening."

In the meantime my staff had become concerned that an immediate meeting of the British, French, and American heads of government would have a bad effect on Hammarskjold's efforts to restore peace to the Middle East, to which we were so definitely committed. Mr. Hoover also felt that the Arabs might, as a unit, turn against us if it should appear that we now appeared to be supporting the British-French actions in the Canal Zone. Almost unanimously my principal assistants recommended that the meeting be postponed. Though I was disappointed in losing this opportunity to talk frankly with Eden and Mollet, I decided to accept the recommendation.

In any event, I again telephoned Eden at 10:27, to say that we should have to postpone our meeting. I gave him the gist of my advisers' conclusions, and then mentioned one further point which had persuaded me of the wisdom of a postponement:

> "Although I had a landslide victory last night, we are not like you, and we have lost both Houses of Congress. Therefore, I have to have the Senate and House leaders in right now. We have already issued the invitation [to them]. They are to be here Friday and Saturday, and I have to be meeting with them. . . . I have got to get them to back up whatever we agree to. My Congress won't be back in session until January 6."

Obviously the congressional leaders should be advised and consulted before we could commit ourselves to any kind of program requiring later congressional action.

I ended by saying, "I am very anxious to talk to you and Mollet about our future. But I believe, in view of what my people say, that we'll have to postpone a little bit. I am sorry . . ."

After the phone calls Anthony cabled, "I do hope it will be possible for us to meet in the very near future." I agreed, on the condition that first the United Nations Resolution be carried out.

At 11:10 I went to Walter Reed Army Hospital to confer with Secretary Dulles, who was recuperating from his operation. I remarked on the postponement of the Eden trip.

"When Eden comes," I said, "he will want to talk about what the Bear will do and what we should do in the face of the Russians' acts. There's no point now in making any recriminations against the British; what we need now is to prepare for whatever action we will take if Russia should enter the Middle East while British, French, and Israeli forces remain there. We also need a coordinated Anglo-American intelligence effort in the region."

Israeli Refuse to Budge

That day I received reports that Ben-Gurion had rejected the United Nations order to withdraw Israeli forces from the Sinai Peninsula and the Gaza Strip and to permit the UN force to enter. I cabled Ben-Gurion at once telling him the United Nations forces were being dispatched to Egypt, urging him to comply with the United Nations resolution, and letting him know the United States viewed Israel's refusal to withdraw "with deep concern."

* * *

Hungary

That day also Bulganin replied to my November 4 letter on Hungary. He said, "I feel urged to state that the problem of the withdrawal of Soviet troops from Hungary touched therein comes completely and entirely under the competence of the Hungarian and Soviet governments."

This note from Bulganin, written of course in the knowledge that Hungary was, in the circumstances, as inaccessible to us as Tibet, was almost the last provocation that my temper could stand.

THURSDAY, NOVEMBER 8

Israel Agrees to Withdraw

After conferring with his Cabinet for nine hours, Ben-Gurion announced that Israel would withdraw from Egypt immediately after the United Nations force arrived. Ambassador Eban transmitted a message to me from Ben-Gurion saying that Israel welcomed my statement that a United Nations force was on its way. "We have never planned to annex the Sinai Desert," he said, adding that "upon conclusion of satisfactory arrangements with the United Nations in connection with this international force entering the Suez Canal area," Israel would willingly withdraw her forces.

Results of the Suez Battle

Anthony Eden later wrote that the British and French together had landed twenty-two thousand troops in Egypt, that the British had sixteen killed, ninety-six wounded; the French ten killed, thirty-three wounded. By November 8 a thousand Egyptians and fewer than two hundred Israeli reportedly had died in the fight. The Suez Canal was completely blocked by sunken ships. The British pipeline from Iraq had been sabotaged, and three of its pumping stations destroyed. (The Arabian-American Oil Company tapline, running from Saudi Arabia through Syria to the Mediterranean, was at the moment still unaccountably intact.) This destruction meant that as soon as a cease-fire could be arranged and the United Nations force stationed, the United States would have to consider putting into effect a crash plan, drawn up months earlier, for shipping more oil to Europe.

Now all of us were looking ahead. That day I dictated two pages of ideas on actions we might take after the cease-fire in the Middle East.

November 8, 1956

(1) Information, not yet official, indicates that both Israel and Egypt have now fully accepted the terms of the United Nations cease-fire plan, and that peaceful conditions should prevail soon in the Mid East.

(2) If the above hope is borne out by events of the next day or so, we should be promptly ready to take any kind of action that will minimize the effects of the recent difficulties and will exclude from the area Soviet influence.

(3) Measures to be taken under these elements would be:

(a) Rapid restoration of pipeline and Canal operation. This might have to be done almost wholly by American technical groups, but I should think that we might also mobilize some people from Germany and Italy. This work should begin instantly.

(b) Push negotiations under the United Nations so as to prevent renewed outbreak of [Mid-East] difficulty.

(c) Provide to the area, wherever necessary, surplus foods, and so on, to prevent suffering.

(4) Simultaneously we must lay before the several governments information and proposals that will establish real peace in the area and, above all, exclude Communist influence from making any headway therein. There are a number of things to do [in this particular pupose]. . . .

We must make certain that every weak country understands what can be in store for it once it falls under the domination of the Soviets.

And beyond this, however, are the constructive things that we can do once these nations understand the truth of the immediately preceding paragraph.

For example, we can provide Egypt with an agreed-upon amount of arms—sufficient to maintain internal order and a reasonable defense of its borders, in return for an agreement that it will never accept any Soviet offer.

We should likewise provide training missions. . . .

We could assist with technicians in the repair of damage done in Egypt . . . and could even make an economic loan to help out.

In Israel we could renew the Jordan compact (Eric Johnston plan) and take up again the $75 million economic loan that they desire.

We could possibly translate the tri-partite statement of May 1950 into bilateral treaty with each of the countries in this area.

We could make some kind of arms agreement—particularly maintenance and training—with Israel of exactly the same type we could make with Egypt.

We could explore other means of assisting the Arab States of Iraq,

Jordan, Saudi Arabia, and Lebanon, and develop ways and means of strengthening our economic and friendly ties with each of these countries, either on a bilateral or group basis.

These notes pointed toward a Mid-East doctrine we would formally evolve in early 1957.

The Middle East crisis was now starting downhill. Gomulka and his government in Poland were hanging in midair with their revolution. And the Soviet Union had murderously throttled the Hungarian drive for freedom. On the morning of November 8, two hundred thousand Russian troops were still inside Hungary; Hungarian refugees were fleeing to Austria at the rate of three thousand to four thousand a day; the fighting there would leave forty thousand Hungarian families homeless and twenty-five thousand Hungarian patriots dead. It was not going to be easy to pick up the pieces of those twenty days.

* * *

AFTERMATH

In the days immediately following the cease-fire the Soviet Union threatened to send "volunteers" into Egypt. We had, of course, already warned about the consequences of any such move.

On November 11, I wrote in formal reply to Bulganin's letter of November 5, which suggested Soviet-American intervention in Egypt: "Any such action would be directly contrary to resolutions of the General Assembly of the United Nations which have called for the withdrawal of those foreign forces which are now in Egypt. The introduction of new forces under these circumstances would violate the United Nations Charter, and it would be the duty of all United Nations members, including the United States, to oppose any such effort."

Two days later, in his final press conference at SHAPE, General Alfred M. Gruenther issued the same warning without diplomatic varnish: If the Communists attacked the West, he said, the Soviet Union and the Soviet Bloc would be "destroyed . . . as sure as day follows night."

The Soviet threat proved to be nothing but words. Indeed Nasser himself seemed to want no important Soviet help, for he said to Ambassador Hare as early as November 8, "Don't worry about these Soviet moves: I don't trust *any* big power."

Late in November, in violation of a pledge of safe conduct, the Soviets seized Imre Nagy. In an exhibition of pure, barbaric vengeance, he was later tried in secret and executed. On December 1, I announced that the

United States, under existing law, would offer asylum, as a start, to more than twenty-one thousand Hungarian refugees—that we would bring to the United States with all possible speed refugees who sought asylum here; and that I would request emergency legislation to permit qualified refugees who accept asylum to obtain permanent residence in the United States. By the end of the year 150,000 Hungarians had left their homeland.

By the end of November we were satisfied that the British and French would rapidly and unconditionally withdraw their troops from Egypt. Accordingly I approved a "Middle East Plan of Action," which had been prepared by the Department of the Interior, the Office of Defense Mobilization, and the Department of Justice in August. It was a plan to add two hundred thousand barrels of oil a day to the quota of three hundred thousand then being shipped to Western Europe from ports on the Gulf of Mexico and in South America.

Private industry cooperated to the full with the Government to make a success of this effort in the face of enormous difficulties, including tanker shortages, the long haul around the Cape of Good Hope, the dislocation of North and South America petroleum outlets, and the need to reroute tankers and reverse pipeline flows.

We now began financial help to the British.

By December 22 the British and French were completing their withdrawal, and a week thereafter the Egyptian government agreed to an immediate start on a full-scale clearance of the Suez Canal.

* * *

Looking backward to those days, it is easy to see that the British and French won battles but nothing else. Israel, also winning battles, succeeded in unblocking the Gulf of Aqaba and temporarily halting the *fedayeen* raids across her borders.

There are a number of fascinating "might have beens" which will, of course, probably never be answered. If the British and French had not intervened, could the Israeli alone have completed the defeat of the Egyptians? If so, what would have happened under the terms of the Three-Power Declaration of 1950? My belief is that we would have taken such action as would have induced withdrawal, possibly initiating a blockade.

Did the British and French actions provide an excuse for the Russians to move with massive force into Hungary? If the Russians had moved into Hungary with no Suez problem preoccupying all Western Europe, would the reaction of the West have been more intense? To both of these questions my own answer has always been negative.

Some critics have said that the United States should have sided with the British and French in the Middle East, that it was fatuous to lean so heavily on the United Nations. If we had taken this advice, where would it have led us? Would we now be, with them, an occupying power in a seething Arab world? If so, I am sure we would regret it.

During the campaign, some political figures kept talking of our failure to "back Israel." If the administration had been incapable of withstanding this kind of advice in an election year, could the United Nations thereafter have retained any influence whatsoever? This, I definitely doubt.

* * *

On November 23 Winston Churchill wrote me a long letter urging that we leave to historians the arguments over recent events in the Middle East and that we take action in harmony to forestall a Soviet triumph there; it would be folly, he said, to let the great essentials be lost in bickerings, and to let misunderstanding make a gulf in the Anglo-American alliance.

I replied at once in a letter [contained in Appendix H] which I closed: "I hope that this one may be washed off the slate as soon as possible and that we can then together adopt other means of achieving our legitimate objectives in the Mid-East. Nothing saddens me more than the thought that I and my old friends of years have met a problem concerning which we do not see eye to eye. I shall never be happy until our old time closeness has been restored."

[illegible] [illegible] [illegible] [illegible] [illegible] [illegible] [illegible] [illegible] in the Middle [illegible] [illegible] [illegible] [illegible] [illegible] [illegible] Soviet [illegible] [illegible] would [illegible]

[illegible] [illegible] [illegible] [illegible] [illegible] [illegible] which I [illegible]

I hope [illegible]

BOOK TWO

. . . New forces and new nations stir and strive across the earth, with power to bring, by their fate, great good or great evil to the free world's future. From the deserts of North Africa to the islands of the South Pacific one-third of all mankind has entered upon an historic struggle for a new freedom: freedom from grinding poverty. Across all continents, nearly a billion people seek, sometimes almost in desperation, for the skills and knowledge and assistance by which they may satisfy from their own resources, the material wants common to all mankind. . . .

We look upon this shaken earth, and we declare our firm and fixed purpose—the building of a peace with justice in a world where moral law prevails.

—*Second Inaugural Address,*
January 21, 1957

CHAPTER IV

A Sequence of Summits

Observe good faith and justice towards all Nations. Cultivate peace and harmony with all.

—*Washington, Farewell Address*

At noon on a January day in 1957, I stood on a platform in front of the United States Capitol and said, among other things, that all across the globe "there harshly blow the winds of change." We, in our good fortune, could never turn our backs to those winds or the peoples they touched.

For one truth had to rule everything we thought and did—the unity of all who dwell in freedom is their only sure defense. No nation could any longer be a fortress, lone and strong and safe. And any people, seeking such a shelter, could only build their own prison.

To proclaim the pursuit of peace was easy; to serve it would be hard. Yet this peace we sought could not be born of fear; it had to be rooted in the lives of nations.

Against the backdrop of such thoughts expressed in my second Inaugural Address, a number of heads of government came to Washington in the winter of 1956–57 and the following spring. Invariably, these conversations were arranged because of the mutually expressed desire to see each other. They were long, friendly, face-to-face talks, designed to fortify the Atlantic Alliance, to buttress the Free World's resistance to Communism in the Middle East, and to explore the purposes and aspirations of the world's underdeveloped countries.

* * *

On November 21, 1956, Habib Bourguiba, Premier of Tunisia, came to the White House, accompanied by Mongi Slim, the Tunisian Ambassador to the United States, and Robert Murphy, Deputy Under Secretary of State.

Bourguiba, leader of the revolutionary Néo-Déstour Party, had for long years led his country's fight for freedom from France, a fight which came to a victorious end on March 20, 1956, when France and Tunisia signed an agreement recognizing Tunisia's independence. A highly intelligent and dynamic Moslem, Bourguiba was dedicated to agricultural and industrial development in his nation and to raising the living standards of his people. He did not recognize the leadership of Gamal Abdel Nasser who, in the name of Arab nationalism, seemed to be striving for the unification of the Islamic world, with Nasser as its head. Moreover, Bourguiba did not hesitate to challenge the most cherished customs of the Moslems.[1]

Bourguiba had publicly attacked the "brutal and inhuman" Soviet intervention in Hungary and in other ways had shown warmth toward the West. But he was, after all, Moslem, and in the struggle of Algerians for independence from France his sympathies were naturally with his own co-religionists. Just a few weeks before his visit to Washington, the French had intercepted five rebellious Algerian leaders, flying to Tunisia to confer with Bourguiba and the Sultan of Morocco. This event had stalled the pending negotiations between France and Tunisia on military and financial cooperation, a development that was disappointing to the United States because of our hope for an agreement between the two.

Since 1943 I had been well acquainted with Tunisia and its people. After Allied forces had driven Rommel from Africa in May of that year, I had established my forward headquarters in a small cottage near the site of Carthage, the ancient city destroyed by the Romans. Here President Roosevelt, on his way to the Cairo and Teheran Conferences late in 1943, had, to the unhidden concern of the Secret Service men, insisted on touring the Tunisian battlefield with me. As a diversion in this otherwise serious business, we enjoyed trying to guess the exact location of the decisive Roman-Carthaginian Battle of Zama in 202 B.C.[2]

As Bourguiba and I met in the Oval Room of the White House, it was only natural that we should speak of those days when I was Com-

[1] Once, as the month of Ramadan approached—a time of strict fasting for orthodox Moslems—Bourguiba told the faithful that such fasting was harmful, that it tired people and incapacitated them for physical labor and for the hard work of economic development.

[2] It was while the President, on his return trip from Teheran, was visiting my Tunisian headquarters late in 1943 that he informed me I was to command OVERLORD, the cross-channel invasion of Europe, later launched on D-Day, June 6, 1944.

Vhat are you going to do for a living if the
esident loses?' a reporter asked Jim Hagerty.
ne question,' Jim answered, 'is academic.'
at is the way it turned out."

ection victory celebration in Wash-
gton, early morning, November 7

"Beginning in the latter months of my first term and for several years thereafter, no other region of the world received so much of [our] close attention... as did the Middle East.

"The Middle East is a land bridge connecting Europe, Asia, and Africa. Its soil has borne the travelers, merchants, and conquering armies of the centuries. Three of the world's religions were founded there, Judaism, Christianity, and Islam—and under its surface lie the world's largest known oil reserves, the 'black gold' of our machine age. The Middle East is, with good reason, often called the crossroads of the world."

Caravan of camels travel road paralleling pipelines to the oil tanks seen on the horizon

TWENT

"October 20, 1956 was the start of the most crowded and demanding three weeks of my entire Presidency. The drama of those weeks is still so fresh in my memory....The best way to see them is as they happened, simultaneously, the major mixed with the minor....The Presidency seldom affords the luxury of dealing with one problem at a time."

Hollywood, California,
October 19

"A presidential campaign conducted by an incumbent is of course subject to interruptions, some planned, some not. Non-partisan talks and meetings have to be interspersed with political ones..." Here, a political address to a large crowd in the Hollywood Bowl.

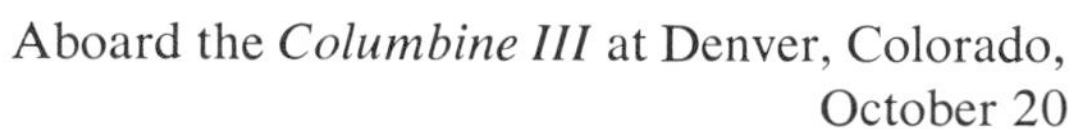

Aboard the *Columbine III* at Denver, Colorado,
October 20

"Fragmentary intelligence reports [on the Polish revolution] reached me by teletype...I delayed leaving the plane until I discussed these developments by telephone on the *Columbine* with Foster Dulles back in Washington."

Polish Communist Party leader Wladyslav Gomulka tells huge rally in Warsaw that Russian troops will be pulled back after the people's angry demonstrations

"'The Polish people,' he affirmed, will 'defend themselves with all means; they will not be pushed off the road of democratization.'"

USY DAYS

Democratic candidate Adlai Stevenson in New York City, October 23

"Governor Stevenson, at Madison Square Garden in Manhattan, called for a 'new U.S. foreign policy.'"

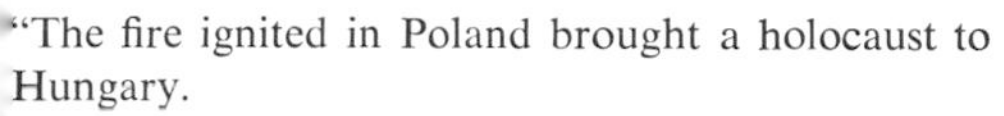

Huge statue of Joseph Stalin pulled down and defaced in Budapest, October 24

"The fire ignited in Poland brought a holocaust to Hungary.

"Inflamed, mobs raced through the city, tore down Soviet flags, and smashed Soviet monuments.... they fought on into the night, hurling homemade hand grenades (called, ironically, Molotov cocktails), and facing the fire of Soviet tanks."

Midnight memorial for the dead rebels

Israeli drive westward across the Sinai Peninsula, October 29, 1956

"In the course of the night, the Israeli had knifed seventy-five miles into Egypt, arriving at a point only twenty-five miles east of Suez."

British troops advance through Port Said, November 5

"Anthony Eden refused to postpone his invasion: 'If we draw back now . . . everything will go up in flames in the Middle East.' "

JSY DAYS

ime Minister David Ben-Gurion stud-
. map of battle area in a plane over the
nai Peninsula, November 13. Around
m: Mrs. Paula Ben-Gurion, left,
ughter Renana, and Major General
oshe Dayan

received reports that Ben-Gurion had re-
ted the United Nations order to withdraw
aeli forces from the Sinai Peninsula and
e Gaza Strip and to permit the UN force
enter."

A United States vessel carries 1750 refugees into New York City, January 1, 1957

"On December 1, I announced that the United States, under existing law, would offer asylum, as a start, to more than twenty-one thousand Hungarian refugees."

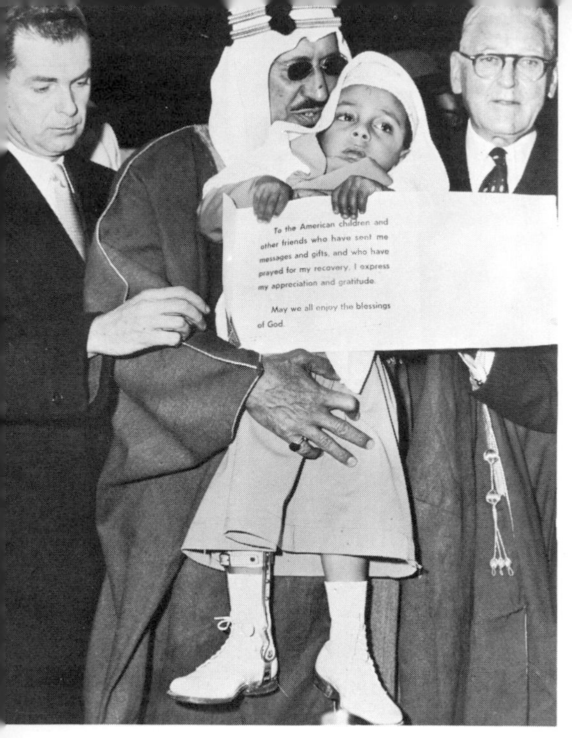

"The King's concern for his little son, wh
had suffered since birth from a partial par
alysis of his right arm and leg, for whic
no cure had been found in his country, wa
touching. I offered to send the boy to Wal
ter Reed Army Hospital for examinatio
and treatment."

King Saud holds Prince Masshur dis
playing his thank-you note as h
leaves the hospital on February 4
1957. Left, Victor Purse, assistan
U.S. protocol chief; right, Majo
General Howard Snyder, the Presi
dent's physician

"With vessels of two navies present, to say nothing of a garrison ashore, an extraordinary amount of saluting took place; I was later told that eighty-four rounds were fired, which seems a lot of explosions in the cause of peace."

Prime Minister Harold Macmillan, Bermuda Governor Lieutenant General Sir John Woodall, President Eisenhower, British Foreign Secretary Selwyn Lloyd at Albuoys Point, Bermuda

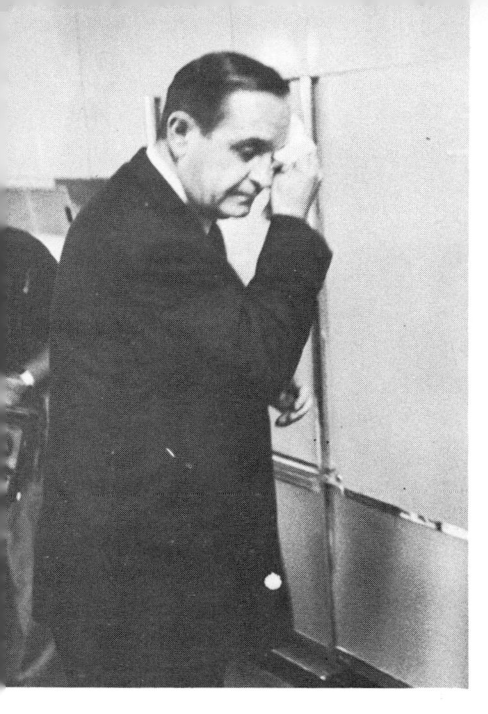

"The United States government and the Governor of Arkansas were now heading toward a collision."

Governor Orval Faubus after a television address protesting the use of federal troops

"There was only one justification for the use of troops: to uphold the law. Though Faubus denied it, I, as President of the United States, now had that justification and the clear obligation to act."

Federal troops escort Negro students into Central High School, Little Rock

-5-

country are united in their respect for observance of the law -- even in those cases where they may disagree with that law. They deplore the call to violence of extremists.

I ~~have confidence~~ that the overwhelming majority of the people in the South are of good will, united in their efforts to preserve and respect the law even ~~if~~ they disagree with it. They ~~will reject the call to violence of extremists~~. ~~They~~ recognize ~~their~~ moral and public responsibilities. ~~They~~ are keenly aware of the tremendous disservice that has been done to the people of Arkansas in the eyes of the nation, and that has been done to the nation in the eyes of the world.

I call upon ~~all~~ citizens of the State of Arkansas to ~~bring~~ to an immediate end all interference with the law and its processes. If resistance to the Federal Court orders ~~is brought to an immediate end~~, the further presence of Federal troops will be unnecessary. ~~It is my hope that proper order will soon prevail.~~

The preparation of an address: page of televised speech on Little Rock, with President Eisenhower's latest revisions

mander-in-Chief of the Allied forces in Tunisia and when he, a leader of his people, was constantly under the surveillance of the French. He was a visibly energetic man, his eyes bright, and a smile frequently lighting his face.

I asked M. Bourguiba about his nation's work in repairing the World War II destruction of the port of Bizerte and the city of Tunis. He said that considerable progress had been made, but much remained to be done. "We need help," he said, and he took the occasion to thank America for a contribution of forty-five thousand tons of wheat made to Tunisia by our people some weeks earlier to prevent a possible famine.

He described the efforts he had made over the years to achieve the independence of his country while remaining in friendly association with the French. "The French are a century behind the time," he said, "particularly in the way they want to retain control over their formerly extensive empire."

"Well," I said, "France's relationships with her colonies have advanced considerably, and there is much evidence that traditional French ideas are changing." We talked for a long time on the theories and history of colonization—especially about the French and British experiences in dealing with underdeveloped areas. We agreed that the British had, on the whole, been fairly successful in dealing with the problems arising out of the growing restlessness of the twentieth century. When Britain had found, for example, that it was difficult to retain colonies in a subordinate status, the idea of a commonwealth had been developed. This had led to independence for most of her former colonies, but many of these, because of self-interest, chose to hold to Britain as associates for trade and other reasons. M. Bourguiba thought that something similar would be entirely possible in French North Africa if the Algerian question could be settled and if the French would do their part. The French must, he felt, initiate reasonable proposals leading toward eventual Algerian independence; otherwise the tempers of the remaining dependent people would become frayed and real enmities spring up between colonies and the former "mother country."

This lead gave me the opportunity to inquire about Bourguiba's specific ideas on a settlement for Algeria. He answered without hesitation: "The French should immediately agree in principle to confer independence on Algeria; independence could then be implemented in successive stages." He firmly believed that this type of settlement was possible and would produce a result which in the end would be beneficial to France. "The fighting in Algeria," he said, "holds back Tunisia's economic and social progress. I want to do everything I can to promote a happy solution of the Algerian problem."

I mentioned Israel, expressing the hope that our interest in the existence of this postwar state in the Middle East would not poison American relations with the Moslem nations, whether with the older states or new ones, like Tunisia. Bourguiba replied, "My attitude regarding Israel will never, in any way, adversely affect Tunisian relations with the United States." Throughout the conversation I took pains to assure our visitor of America's genuine interest in the Moslem world and our desire to improve our understanding of Moslem culture, religion, education, and customs. I was struck by his sincerity, his broad knowledge, and his amicable spirit.

One valuable opportunity of the Presidency is the chance to learn of directly conflicting points of view on important questions. These are often volunteered by friendly people who may be on opposite sides of a particular issue. An interesting contrast to the tone of President Bourguiba's observations on the French-Algerian differences was the conclusion expressed in a letter to me datelined *Lambarene 27 January 1957*. It spoke of grave consequences that would follow if the French government did not have the support of the United States in a forthcoming United Nations vote on an Afro-Asian resolution—subsequently voted down—asking France to permit Algeria self-determination and to let the UN assist with cease-fire talks with the Algerian rebels. The situation would become so difficult, the letter said, that it did not seem likely that the French government could continue in office. The defeat of France in the vote could compromise the cause of Europe, it went on, adding that: "It is anguish that dictates these lines to me." The letter was signed Albert Schweitzer.

* * *

The next head of government to visit Washington was Prime Minister Nehru of India.

India had been a source of fascination to me for many years, even though I had never been there. I had read about the modern development and government of India and frequently had expressed a hope of paying a visit to that subcontinent.[3]

But Mr. Nehru was no stranger to me. He had visited Columbia University while I was its President, and on that visit I had been privileged

[3] This hope, repeated casually during the 1956 campaign, inspired one of those single-minded partisan comments common in the heat of elections. One of my political associates, under the impression that I was planning such a trip and was about to start off without delay, exploded, *"India?* We need him more in *Ohio!"*

to hold an extensive conversation with him. Over the years Mr. Nehru had been to many Americans a somewhat inexplicable and occasionally exasperating personality. Early in his career he had leaned to Marxism; later as a lieutenant of Gandhi's in the independence movement he spent a number of years in British jails; as Prime Minister he seemed to some observers to be treading the Communist line at times, and he was often Delphic in the ambiguity of his statements.

He seemed to believe—most unrealistically, I thought—that peace in the dawn of the nuclear age could be brought about by voluntary, unilateral disarmament on the part of the West. In this, perhaps, he had been bemused by India's success in the use of passive resistance in achieving independence from the British. As I said one day to a visitor, "Gandhi used passive resistance against Britain. But the British, with their advanced stage of civilization and their deep respect for human life, refrained from the use of force in India because of the moral brake they put on themselves. Should Nehru try passive resistance against the Communists, I'm sure he would get a rude awakening."

One thing about Mr. Nehru that was difficult for most Americans in government to understand was his evident confidence in his ambassador to the United Nations, V. K. Krishna Menon. To many of us, Mr. Menon appeared to have more respect for Communist doctrine than for Western culture, government, or leaders. Under a cloak of humility and modesty, he never hesitated to take upon himself the role of consultant, adviser, and authority on every kind of difficult international situation. By July of 1955 Mr. Menon had visited me twice in company with Secretary Dulles to talk about establishing a basis of mediation between Red China and ourselves. Both times I had told him bluntly that there was no use of ever mentioning the subject as long as Americans were unjustly held as prisoners by the Communists in Red China, to be used as pawns in bargaining.

About six weeks before Mr. Nehru was scheduled to come to Washington he wrote me about the Israeli invasion of Egypt. This he labeled as "naked aggression" and the Anglo-French action an affront to the United Nations. He urged that I use every means at my disposal to halt the drive toward general war. A week later he wrote to me again, this time on Hungary. The tone of the two letters was markedly different. In the latter, he said, "I have indeed been greatly troubled by what has happened there and I drew the attention of Mr. Bulganin to it. He has briefly replied and has promised to send a fuller reply later."

Mr. Nehru wrote that he had been informed by the Soviets that they had previously decided to withdraw their troops from Hungary, but subsequent events compelled them to intervene "temporarily to protect the lives of their own people as governmental authority appeared to have vanished and mutual killing was taking place." He seemed quite ready to accept this explanation of a most hideous crime. Yet, in the same letter in which he rationalized Russian conduct, he went back once again to the hateful "aggression" in Egypt, which he said "has powerfully moved the countries of Asia and Africa." This drove home to me the fact that most neutralist nations tended to criticize armed intervention in Suez while almost ignoring it in Hungary or to equate Hungary and Suez, though the dead in Hungary exceeded those in Suez by 25 to 1.

Prime Minister Nehru arrived in Washington on December 16, 1956. On the following morning I called for him at Blair House and together we drove to my farm at Gettysburg, where we spent that day and part of the next in some fourteen hours of conversation.

Returning to Washington on the 18th, Mr. Nehru came to the White House the next morning and we continued private talks in my office. Following our conversations I made fourteen pages of notes on them.

Of immediate concern, of course, was Egypt and the Middle East. "Nasser, in my opinion," said Nehru, "is the best of the group of Egyptians—mostly military—for whom he is the spokesman. If Nasser were to be removed, his successor would be someone far more inimical to the West and more unreasonable in his actions."

The Prime Minister was obviously interested in the diplomatic negotiations the previous year leading to the cancellation of the Aswan Dam offer. I gave him the facts of the negotiations that were finally used by Nasser as an excuse for seizing the Canal Company in late July. Mr. Nehru seemed astonished to learn that our original offer had to all intents and purposes been rejected by Egypt before we had publicly withdrawn it and that Nasser was scarcely justified in pretending to be surprised when our own loss of interest in the project was announced.

"Arab leaders tend to get excited when they address a crowd," Mr. Nehru commented, "and they can be counted on to talk in extravagant terms under such circumstances; more attention should be paid to their studied, written statements," he maintained, "than to their oratory." He had a low opinion of the pro-Western Premier Nuri as-Said of Iraq, but did not mention the Baghdad Pact as such.

In contrast to the mild letter he had previously sent me, Mr. Nehru described his horrified reactions to the Hungarian affair. India, he said, had sent at least token help by shipping certain cargoes of food and other supplies to the Hungarian refugees. He did venture a guess that Soviet action in Hungary spelled the eventual death knell of international Communism. His explanation ran something like this: "In spite of the fact that Hungary has been under the complete domination of the international Communists for a period of ten years, the Communist bosses have made so little progress in converting the people to their ideology that the world has witnessed the spectacle of an uprising in which people were perfectly ready to be killed rather than submit again to their Communist overlords." He concluded that the demonstration of this fact to the world must have given a terrible shock to the men in the Kremlin, so shocking that they would likely have to make a reappraisal of their plans. Perhaps, he said, the Communist appeal from now on would be couched in language more likely to cater to the dissatisfied and needy of the world, while threats and the effort to dominate by force would become less blatant. This would bc a propitious moment, he suggested, because of the blunder of the Soviets in Hungary, for the Free World to move to strengthen the faith and hope of those who would like to live in independence but who have been misled, at least partly, by Communist doctrine. "Nationalism is stronger than Communism," he added.

Of Communist China, he said, "I feel it is only logical that any government controlling six hundred million people will sooner or later have to be brought into the council of nations." This contention became more valid with each passing year, he said, because Chiang Kai-shek and his army on Formosa were showing the ravages of time and eventually Formosa would be a weakened area which, almost by force of circumstances, would fall into the hands of the Communists.

The Prime Minister outlined the reasons why India had, since independence, pursued a policy of neutrality. First he insisted that he used the word "neutrality" in its traditional sense, to mean simply a position of aloofness from power combinations, particularly power combinations at war or threatening war between themselves. He made clear that he did not use the word to distinguish between concepts of government based on the dignity of man and those based on dictatorship.

He said that India might, logically, fear major attack from two countries only—the U.S.S.R. and China. Either one, however, would experience difficulty in conducting large conventional military operations against India because of the fortunate location of the Himalayan mountain chain. Furthermore, he felt that both these countries had vast internal problems and would probably confine their aggressive intentions to nations that posed a threat or supplied a tempting prize to the Communists. India fulfilled neither condition. If ever a world war should come about, he felt, the Communists would be too much interested in other areas to attack India.

"Neutrality has another advantage," he said. "India and China have eighteen hundred miles of common border. Any attempt to maintain a defense of this long border would be such an expensive proposition as to render India completely unable to raise the standards of living of her people. Starvation and disease would make the nation even more susceptible to Communist penetration."

The Prime Minister suggested one final reason for India's continuance as a neutral. Any nation giving up neutrality to enter into a defensive organization should be able to do its part. India was in no position whatsoever to arm in proportion to its population and geographical size. Any definite alignment by India with the Free World would serve to weaken rather than to strengthen the combination.

Our conversation then turned to socialism. According to my notes Mr. Nehru expressed his thoughts in this fashion: All countries are a "little bit socialistic"—there is no such thing as pure free enterprise practiced anywhere. The extreme of Communism is practiced in the Soviet Union and Iron Curtain countries, all others having some form of incentive enterprise.

The appropriate level of state management is often determined by the conditions prevailing; it differs, for example, according to the stage of development within a nation. In less-developed nations, capital must be acquired for industrial progress and at times only the government can do this job. In India they refer to these two phases of economic development as the public and private sectors, not as socialism or free enterprise.

On the subject of Pakistan the Prime Minister was less detached. He reviewed the historical developments that led to the 1947 partition. He felt that the British had made an egregious blunder in dividing the subcontinent of India between two nations, India and Pakistan. The Pakistani, he insisted, had not obtained independence by their own efforts; they had obtained it through the success of Indian nationalism. He went on to describe the difficult administrative job brought about by partition and emphasized the difficulties that arose out of the forced migrations of people between the two countries—Hindus moving from Pakistan into India, and Moslems from India into Pakistan. Furthermore, India did not accept the theory of organization of states along religious lines. As a proof of this, Mr. Nehru cited the presence of forty million Moslems remaining in India and the fact that Moslems were represented in his own Cabinet. The huge migrations of peoples, he said, had ceased for a while, but now had been renewed, not by any movement of people from India into Pakistan, but rather by the determination of Indians in East Pakistan to leave that part of the country. India, he claimed, was forced to absorb these people at the rate of one thousand a day.

Mr. Nehru said that among the several outstanding problems between India and Pakistan he would consider none insuperable. Three of them were:

(1) the division of the waters of the Indus River Basin between Pakistan and India;

(2) the settlement of property claims arising out of the migrations back and forth across the border;

(3) Kashmir.

"Of these, the only one I think will cause real difficulty in settling is the last," he said. He asserted that the people of Kashmir wanted to belong to India, but he did not explain why he had always opposed a vote on that question in the region. He reviewed in detail Kashmir's tribal invasions after the partition, the employment of Indian troops to stop the invasions, and the establishment of armistice lines. "Economic and political life," he pointed out, "has now become crystallized around the existence of this armistice line," which gave Pakistan one-third the territory and one-fourth the population of Kashmir. If the United Nations would approve of this status quo as a basis for permanent settlement, Mr. Nehru believed, both sides would eventually agree, although there would be some grumbling.

One thorn in the side of India at the moment was the existence of the small enclave of Goa on its west coast, in Portuguese hands since the early sixteenth century. Despite recent disputes, Mr. Nehru said that India harbored no intention of using force to settle this matter.[4] According to him Goa was of no economic value to Portugal and existed merely to satisfy the Portuguese feeling that it helped to make them an "empire."

The Prime Minister thought the United States could be of help in both the Goa and Pakistan problems. He thought we should urge Portugal to release Indian prisoners they held, one of whom was a member of the Indian Parliament. This he said would be only a gesture, but it would at least show respect for India. In the Pakistan problem we might help by urging Pakistan to cease using its newspapers, which he said were really state-controlled, to incite the fears of the Indians. He said that if Pakistan's newspaper propaganda would talk peace instead of war, the whole situation would be much ameliorated.

The Prime Minister believed that the wide gulf dividing the Soviets

[4] Apparently he later changed his mind; Goa was taken over forcibly by India in December of 1961.

and the United States was partially created by each side. Although he did not attempt a judgment as to the degree of guilt, he was clearly of the opinion that if one of the two parties should make an honest effort toward conciliation the other would go along.

Speaking of Europe, Mr. Nehru seemed sympathetic with Russian fears of a rejuvenated Germany. He had concluded that the problem of a divided Germany would be settled only if a European organization could be set up that to the Russian mind would be a guarantee of their own safety. As a possibility he talked about the establishment of a neutral belt reaching down from Northern Europe into the Mediterranean, the belt to include all the present satellite states, as well as Germany. When I voiced grave doubts that a people as dynamic as the Germans could ever be successfully treated as neutrals, he agreed.

I tried to underscore the difference between our objectives and those of the Soviets. "In every public statement and expression of purpose," I pointed out, "we seek only the right of every people to determine for themselves their form of government and status in the family of nations. The Soviets, on the other hand, both by announced purpose and by action, have demonstrated their determination to dominate the world." I cited the fate of the captive nations of Eastern Europe as a type of colonialism that was far more serious and cruel than that practiced in the past by some of the Western nations—the latter a dying practice that still excited the resentment and even hatred of the Afro-Asian bloc.

"Moreover," I went on, "there has been, in recent years, a tremendous change in the relations of former colonies and their former mother countries." New nations were springing up rapidly. "I fail to understand," I said, "why all Asians are not far more alarmed by the forceful domination of Eastern Europe by Russia than you are by the few vestiges of Western colonialism. Despite colonial histories and our recent troubles in the Middle East, the Western nations are primarily interested in the progress of humanity. By contrast the Hungarian revolution has provided convincing proof the Soviets are interested only in its domination, no matter by what means, including forceful suppression."

I was disappointed to find that none of this seemed wholly convincing to the Prime Minister; at least he gave no expression of emphatic concurrence.

But I kept trying. "One of the world's troubles is that no one can put any real trust in the pledged word of the Russians," I said. "Time and again they have violated promises, understanding, and even written agreements. In these circumstances, we have found it impossible as yet to make any cooperative progress with the Russians in the problems of stopping nuclear testing, working toward mutual disarmament, or solving the difficulties of a divided Germany." We had come to the conclusion that only agreements that carried within themselves the *certainty* of enforcement would be useful in dealing with the Soviets. I argued that if there was any sincerity in the Soviets' professed desire for peace and general disarmament they would willingly agree to a kind of mutual inspection that would assure justice to both sides and inspire confidence. Finally I commented that the flat refusal of the Soviets to agree to some kind of reasonable arrangement should alarm the uncommitted nations of the world, just as it made the United States and her Western associates determined to protect themselves and their rights, by force, if necessary.

The Prime Minister did not in any way deny the logic of such beliefs; he merely expressed the opinion that because the natural attitude of the Soviets was a suspicious one and because they felt themselves "looked down upon" by the Western world, the West might be well advised to initiate conciliatory moves on a unilateral basis and thereafter examine the Soviets' reaction. If these moves should prove successful, the way would be open for further progress.

I pointed out that in Korea, Indochina, Formosa, Greece, and elsewhere, the Communists had been stopped in aggressive action only by the interposition of Western resolution and force, and that until there could be convincing proof that the Russians were genuinely dedicated to peace, and ready to meet us halfway, there was no hope of inducing the West to go into unwise ventures which would be interpreted by the Soviets only as weakness and invitation to further aggression.

The Prime Minister again remarked that in the long run Communism would defeat itself. With this I agreed, but observed that it was rather cold comfort to realize that the historically inevitable doom of dictatorships often occurred only after the passage of much time, the loss of life, the postponement of peace. This fact could make the matter purely academic so far as any single generation was concerned.

I liked Prime Minister Nehru. I deeply sympathize with the agonizing problems that the Chinese aggression later caused his nation. He sincerely wanted to help his people and lead them to higher levels of living and opportunity; I think it only fair to conclude that he was essential to his nation. Pandit Jawaharlal Nehru was not easy to understand; few people are, but his was a personality of unusual contradictions.

On a trip to India several years later, I came to see a small example of the fact that this distinguished man of non-violence could, on occasion, swing a mighty stick to clear his way through a crowd. More curious was his apparent tolerance, relatively speaking, of Soviet attitudes—of their determination for world domination, their refusal to enter into meaningful disarmament agreements, and their brutal suppression of the Hungarian revolt. One explanation, of course, was the fact that his own country had lived so long under foreign domination. But I think the answer goes deeper than that; as an Asian from a less-developed nation, it is possible that Mr. Nehru felt more resentment of an intangible Western condescension toward his people than he felt toward any specific act of violence that either East or West might commit. Life, after all, is cheaper in the Orient, or so it would appear; recognition as equals by the "white" race is not. Perhaps Mr. Nehru, despite his excellent Western education and flawless English, was able to identify with the Soviets at times as "fellow Asians," a point that came out continually in his hope that the West could do something to make the Soviets feel they "were not being looked down upon." Intellectually he could never support Communist aggression, but his condemnation of such policies was tempered with sympathy. This feeling—if my conclusion is valid in his case—is shared by millions upon millions in Africa and Asia. It will be years, probably generations, despite the best efforts of the West, before this will no longer be so.

* * *

My next visitor was the King of Saudi Arabia, who came to Washington on the 30th of January 1957.

This visit inevitably brought a flare-up of opposition from part of the Jewish community in the United States. The sympathies of many of our Jews were naturally given to their co-religionists in Israel; their view of the Arab-Israeli troubles in the Middle East was influenced by the instinctive reaction that, in every instance of difficulty, the fault was wholly on the side of the Arabs.

It cannot be denied that many of the Arab actions, irritating to the Israeli, seemed to be inspired by nothing more than hatred of every Jew, merely because he was a Jew. In our government's negotiations for landing rights in Saudi Arabia for American military personnel, one of the conditions imposed by the Saudi government was that no Jew would be allowed on the field. No Arab government would recognize Israel; the Egyptian government would allow no Israeli ship to go through the Suez Canal. The Arabs found many ways to infuriate citizens of Israel and Jews throughout the world, and as a result, the King of Saudi Arabia—who as the Keeper of the Holy Places of Islam was the nominal head of the Moslem world—was, in Jewish eyes, a symbol of Arab injustice and cruelty.

However, I was convinced of the truth of the adage that in most quarrels of this type neither side is either wholly at fault and neither entirely blameless. In any event, regardless of the merits of the many contentions, I felt it necessary for us to take the lead in trying to find solutions to the difficult problems involved.

From time to time, during all the postwar years, I had been visited by advocates of both Arab and Jewsh causes. I had listened to complaints from all quarters, and one was no less eloquent than another. Arabs were particularly enraged because the world at large, so they claimed, had encouraged and assisted the Jews in tearing out of traditional Arab territory a sizable and critical area to make the new State of Israel a "home" for Jews on the eastern shore of the Mediterranean. Arabs were dispossessed in that region, they said, robbed of their property, cruelly treated, and finally crowded into camps in neighboring Arab states. By 1957 Arab refugees under United Nations care numbered nearly a million. And frequently, when completing impassioned presentations of their case, visiting Arabs had said to me, "But of course, the Western nations will do nothing to correct the wrongs we have endured; only a few Arabs vote in your countries."

When the public was informed of the King's impending visit, I was urged to cancel the invitation. The Mayor of New York, sensitive to the heavy Jewish population in his area, announced that the traditional reception tendered by the city to visiting heads of state would be omitted. In many quarters the King was called by unflattering names. There was much other evidence to indicate that the visiting monarch might suffer embarrassment.

For my part, I had no intention of changing the plans to bring King Saud to Washington. I did direct that fully adequate measures be taken to protect the King and his party from annoyance and humiliation.

We were hopeful that much good might result from his visit. From the beginning of my first administration I had sought means of ameliorating the mutual prejudices and hatreds between the Arabs and Israeli, in the hope of bringing about a *modus vivendi* out of which genuine cooperation might develop. Working together, the nations of the region, I believed, could form a sturdy and permanent bulwark against Communist encroachment; but if they spent their time, effort, and substance fighting each other, the over-all effect would be to make the Middle East nothing but a happy hunting ground for Communist oppression—with disastrous results for the Free World.

There was another purpose in issuing the invitation. At the time, as the Suez experience showed, Colonel Nasser of Egypt was not only trying to improve his own position by working with the Kremlin, he was striving to get himself recognized in the Arab world as its political leader—the virtual head of an enormous Moslem confederation which, he hoped, would unite behind him to achieve his further ambitions. To check any movement in this direction, we wanted to explore the possibilities of building up King Saud as a counterweight to Nasser. The King was a logical choice in this regard; he at least professed anti-Communism, and he enjoyed, on religious grounds, a high standing among all Arab nations.

So my invitation to the King did not spring solely out of a desire to pay him a courtesy; it had serious and important objectives, which I was determined to pursue.

Then at the last moment we had another annoying, indeed a silly, incident that threatened to wreck the entire arrangement.

Because of my heart attack and ileitis operation, it had been agreed among all of us in government that unimportant activities and ceremonies would be eliminated, as much as possible, from my routine schedules. All departments cooperated in this purpose. For example, the State Department had suggested a change in my practice—which had by no means as yet become traditional—of going to the Washington airport to meet visiting heads of state. Washington was not the usual point of entry for a head of state coming to the United States; since I obviously could not go to San Francisco, Miami, or New York to meet an arriving dignitary, it seemed that the White House—where the grounds provided an ideal site for a ceremonial reception—would be the logical place to greet such visitors.

The State Department went to unusual lengths to explain to foreign governments and their ambassadors in Washington the reasons for the change, emphasizing that in this way my health and well-being would be safeguarded.

When these explanations eventually reached the Saudi Arabian Court, the King apparently interpreted the move as a personal affront, as an effort to belittle him, his position, and his nation. He said that he would not, in these circumstances, go to Washington. When Foster reported this development to me I told him that the purpose we wanted to accomplish was far more important than any risk to my health caused by going out, in bad weather, for a ceremony at the airport. I added: "Of course, this means that we will abandon all thought of changing the welcoming procedure for heads of state; I will not make any distinctions or exceptions among such visitors. As long as it seems necessary—as it does to me—that I meet King Saud in this fashion I'll do the same in all succeeding cases."

The King, after the usual ceremonial greetings, came to my office for a rather secluded conference. He seemed to be somewhat introspective and shy. Saud definitely preferred to talk tête-à-tête rather than in a larger group. His eyesight was bad. Behind his thick glasses his manner was pleasant and courteous, his speech courtly. He made a reference to Allah in almost every passage of a conversation.

Our principal talk was a long one with no one else present except the King's interpreter. There were few points made that could be considered as new or highly important. Most had already been discussed interminably through our respective emissaries.

The King talked about the history of British-Arab relations and the unsatisfactory state into which they had then fallen. The gist of his theory was that dating back into his father's reign, the Arab policy had been to trust the British and to work with them for the advancement of Saudi Arabia. This policy had been practically forced upon them because the only alternative would have been to seek help from the Soviet government. Long before his father died, however, relationships between Arabia and Britain had become strained. Therefore the British had developed a deliberate policy of keeping the Arabs weak, of denying them any weapons, at least in amounts that would be satisfactory to any self-respecting nation. Because of this weakness the Arabs had suffered many indignities, to say nothing of encroachments upon their borders by the British.

For the same reason, he said, the Arabs had undergone the belligerencies of the Israelis and had been helpless to reply. The situation had grown steadily worse over the years. His military impotence seemed to be the most galling of all the complaints he voiced to me. Because of this shameful weakness, the King went on, his people had become more and more restless, more and more demanding that he do something. A strong element in his country had arisen who urged him to deal with the Soviets. Russia had often offered to give them arms, in generous amounts. The offers, he said, he had thus far spurned.

Now, he said, he simply must act. He referred repeatedly to the "demands of his people" and the "strength of public opinion." He talked about such matters far more than one would expect from a ruler who is universally assumed to be an absolute monarch.

I suggested that this matter of armaments was not so simple as it appeared. He should proceed cautiously in making up his mind how much he wanted and could support. I told him that in helping to arm certain other nations we had found that in some cases they had requested and received far too much. As a result their economies were showing strains because the nations had proved unequal to the task of maintaining their forces. The best military policy for any nation that had critical problems of economic development, I went on, was to seek only such arms as would assure the maintenance of internal order and freedom from subversive activities, together with a small reserve that would give it reasonable protection against raiding attacks against its borders. To meet major military threats, I argued, a nation should depend largely upon its alliances with other free nations of the world. I maintained that the United Nations was set up to preserve weak nations from unjustified and unprovoked aggression and that he could always count upon help in such a case.

The King remarked that his country had nine hundred thousand square miles and at least twelve million people. The British, he said, were nibbling at Arabian borders at some points and had been particularly aggressive in the case of Buraimi[5]; the Israeli had sent raiding parties into Arabia a number of times and now even Iran had committed an aggression against him, having seized the islands of Farasan and Aribi in the Persian Gulf. "I know that Britain would oppose our acquisition of armaments from you," he said, adding that the United States would long ago have agreed to let him have arms except for British opposition.

Continuing his plea for more arms, the King said that his military program would take up half of his national budget. This meant that he would need considerable economic help. To this I rejoined that we had often encountered similar situations in which, almost invariably, the real need was technical assistance, to enable our friends to put their resources to intelligent use.

The King told me he had been working hard at building new schools, hospitals, roads, and communications. Their five-year progress had been excellent but it was, nevertheless, still far too meager. All his public expenditures had gone into these activities. "The money I have received has been wisely spent and for these good purposes," he said. The Bedouins were in a particularly deplorable state economically and had so little in the way of resources that they were practically living on the dole. This dole, he said, came from his private purse. (He did not explain the distinction between private and public purses in Saudi Arabia.) Now he could do no more. His nation needed desperately to obtain economic assistance.

Again I emphasized that money alone could neither make a country prosperous nor raise its level of industrialization. It took, in addition to investment, the brains, experience, and wisdom to strive for balance

[5] An oasis area, potentially rich in oil, in southeastern Arabia. In October of 1955 British-directed forces seized Buraimi, thus "recovering" it for Britain's ally, the Sultan of Muscat and Oman.

among the various segments of an economy. I pointed out that purchasing power had to accompany the production of goods. People had to be able to buy if the products of the factory were to be sold. The problem was basically one of raising the living standards of a whole people, which could not be accomplished simply by passing a certain amount of money from one government to the other.

The King referred to his meeting with other Arab chieftains at Cairo. Reports of the leanings of Nasser and the President of Syria toward the Soviets, he felt, had been exaggerated. Each of these men had told the King that if the Soviets should make any attempt to interfere in their internal affairs, they would instantly cease all dealings with the Soviets. The King seemed to believe that these rulers could take from the Soviets anything they pleased without danger of losing exclusive power of decision and control over all internal affairs, a type of naïveté that was alarming. He said that he had told Arab colleagues flatly, "I am with you in Arab cooperation and in opposition to Israel, but I will not go one step with you in working with the Soviet Union—I shall have nothing to do with the Soviets."

At the time of our talks the Israeli had largely withdrawn from the Sinai Peninsula following the Suez operation, but they still remained in the Gaza Strip and along the coast of the Gulf of Aqaba. This fact, naturally, provoked discussion. The King argued that the Israeli should retire immediately from all these points and stop their border raids. He repeated that in the relatively quiet state that would result from such Israeli movements, the Middle East could begin to hope to find the solution of bigger and broader problems. He went on to repeat the one-sided Arab interpretation of every annoying incident occurring in the region.

To this kind of warped presentation I had listened often; after he had finished, I summarized the opposite argument, to which I had listened just as often.

The King's concern for his little son, who had suffered since birth from a partial paralysis of his right arm and leg, for which no cure had been found in his country, was touching. I offered to send the boy to Walter Reed Army Hospital for examination and treatment; the doctors there prescribed special leg braces and shoes. The King's gratitude was fully and sincerely expressed. I was told by nurses and orderlies at the hospital that his thanks to them was conveyed in valuable gifts, including a donation to the hospital of $2000 a year "in perpetuity" to be used for the treatment of child patients.[6]

No political advances were realized in the talks.[7] But I think the King did come to believe that the United States was as ready to be a friend to the Arabs as we were to the Israeli; he expressed satisfaction that with this knowledge he could be a stronger influence in helping to produce a solution for many problems constantly arising among the nations of the Middle East. He ended by saying that he hoped I would take the trouble to meet with more of the Arab leaders, especially those of Syria and Egypt.

* * *

In January Anthony Eden had resigned as Prime Minister of Britain. On the 10th of that month I had written:

> I cannot tell you how deeply I regret that the strains and stresses of these times finally wore you down physically until you felt it necessary to retire. To me it seems only yesterday that you and I and others were meeting with Winston almost daily—or nightly—to discuss the next logical move of our forces in the war.
>
> Now you have retired, I have had a heart attack as well as a major operation, and many others of our colleagues of that era are either gone or no longer active. The only reason for recalling those days is to assure you that my admiration and affection for you has never diminished; I am truly sorry that you had to quit the office of Her Majesty's First Minister.

Anthony was succeeded by another old friend, Harold Macmillan. I had first become acquainted with Macmillan in Algiers in 1943, where he was assigned as my British political adviser. From the start I found him more than competent; my high opinion of him had been frequently expressed in later years, publicly and privately. When in January I had

[6] American children by the hundreds, hearing of the little Prince's malady, sent him during his hospitalization coloring books, cowboy suits, teddy bears, toys, and "get well" letters.

[7] The U.S. within the following month did increase military and economic aid to Saudi Arabia by approximately $180 million. In return Saudi Arabia agreed, as announced at the end of our conference, to a five-year extension of our lease on the Dhahran Air Base.

learned of his appointment, I wrote to congratulate him, adding these words:

> . . . welcome . . . to your new headaches. Of course you have had your share in the past, but I assure you that the new ones will be to the old [as] a broken leg is to a scratched finger . . .
>
> Knowing you so long and well I predict that your journey will be a great one. But you must remember the old adage, "Now abideth faith, hope and charity—and greater than these is a sense of humor."

The change of Prime Ministers in the government of our closest ally, Britain, would itself have justified an early meeting between us; in addition there were serious matters to discuss. We made plans to meet in Bermuda in late March. Before the conference, however, we became concerned over word that Britain intended to reduce its NATO forces materially, for reasons both strategic and financial. I telephoned Prime Minister Macmillan at once, asking him not to make the reduction until after we could talk the matter over at Bermuda. Harold, however, could not go along; the condition of the British exchequer dictated immediate economies.

* * *

I decided to go to Bermuda by naval vessel, taking a leisurely course to our destination in order to get some rest and possibly a day of fishing. We left Norfolk on March 14, on the cruiser *Canberra,* commanded by Captain C. T. Mauro. Jim Hagerty, General Howard Snyder, and Captain Pete Aurand joined me for a six-day cruise to end at Bermuda, first visiting the Bahamas for three good days in the sun.

As we debarked off Bermuda on March 20, 1957, we offered Captain Mauro our congratulations on the care and skill of his crew and our thanks for his hospitality. He started us away on a Navy barge. Our destination was Hamilton pier. The barge had been painted, repainted, and beautifully shined up, and it boasted at least one Presidential Seal. It was not just good-looking; its appearance gave persuasive evidence of its high state of efficiency. Unfortunately, for efficiency and naval morale, the barge had been on its way toward the pier for only minutes when a small pin was lost out of the steering mechanism, and the boat went out of action.

My party and I quickly transferred to the Captain's gig, which had been following. We knew that Captain Mauro would be intensely embarrassed after all the care he had lavished for almost a week on our comfort and enjoyment; furthermore, such a breakdown of equipment within sight of hundreds of members of the Royal Navy must have seemed no less than the hand of a diabolical fate. Nothing was lost, except a little pride, perhaps, and as soon as possible we sent him a message to assure him we appreciated the gift of prophecy that had caused him to send along an additional barge, to meet the accident he must have foreseen. How much the message assuaged his feelings I do not know.

With vessels of two navies present, to say nothing of a garrison ashore, an extraordinary amount of saluting took place; I was later told that eighty-four rounds were fired, which seems a lot of explosions in the cause of peace. *The Star-Spangled Banner* was played twice—once in error—but finally Harold and I set off in a car for the Mid-Ocean Club.

The first session of the conference was held the following day, March 21, and lasted until noon.

As we entered the conference Harold happened to call attention to the date, saying it was coincidence that we were meeting at the time of the spring equinox. Aloud, but scarcely consciously, I said, "Yes, eight years ago today I stopped smoking." He looked at me and exclaimed, "Now how on earth did you remember that?" I think I was almost as astonished as he: at least all I could manage by way of explanation was "It just popped out." Actually it was only another example of how frequently the memory is stimulated to bring up the most inconsequential matters simply because of association of ideas.

We discussed all phases of the Middle East problem, and it was apparent from the start that a large measure of agreement existed on most of the matters that had filled the pages of the public press for the past many weeks. Among the items that came in for special and searching investigation was the question of our future relationships with the Middle East and a satisfactory arrangement for the use of the Suez Canal. Still, Foster and I at first found it difficult to talk constructively with our British colleagues about Suez because of the blinding bitterness they felt toward Nasser. Prime Minister Harold Macmillan and Foreign Minister Selwyn Lloyd were so obsessed with the possibilities of getting rid of Nasser that they were handicapped in searching, objectively, for any realistic method of operating the Canal.

Early in the conversation, Lloyd launched into a denunciation of Nasser, condemning his motives, plans, and trustworthiness. He feared that Nasser, in pursuing his soaring ambitions, would probably become the stooge of the Kremlin, just as Mussolini had become the stooge of Hitler.

Despite this feeling, the British told us of their urgent need for reasonable terms in the use of the Canal. If we should fail to get such an arrangement (which would include a suitable toll rate) we should not dodge the issue, they said, and pretend that it was at least a half-victory and one with which we could live.

"There seems to be some inconsistency in these two attitudes," I said. "If we are at this moment to begin an attack on Nasser, and do everything in our power overtly and covertly to get rid of him, there will be little or no hope of getting an early and satisfactory settlement on the Canal."

Reluctantly, they concurred. While still looking upon Nasser as a troublemaker, they finally agreed that the task at hand was to negotiate on the Canal operation.

From the specific question of the Suez Canal we went to the general problem of maintaining oil production in the Middle East and access to it through pipelines and otherwise. This brought out some very plain talk, and I think much was done to clarify the issues involved. Harold Macmillan felt that Kuwait was really the key to the over-all Middle East oil production problem. Even in a region where many areas produce huge amounts of oil, he pointed out, Kuwait's production was by far the largest. By itself it could produce oil enough for all Western Europe for years to come. The problem, then, would become that of retaining access to Kuwait and an adequate flow of oil therefrom. One of the requirements for success in this would be to achieve better relationships with the surrounding nations, most importantly Saudi Arabia. Yet a second British objective involved their determination to support their ally, the Sultan of Muscat and Oman, in his claim to the Buraimi oasis. This had occasioned a sharp dispute between the British and Saudis. Here again, the pursuit of both these objectives simultaneously, I remarked, could well endanger the attainment of the first. The British gave a number of reasons, some of which I thought reasonable, for retaining their hold upon Buraimi, but as a result of the day's conversation they implied that they were going to take a second look at their activities in the region.

The Prime Minister outlined the major factors in the complex problems of Cyprus. While Britain wanted nothing more in the island except to keep an adequate base, any political solution that the British could suggest antagonized either the Greeks or the Turks. The British believed that the struggle that would be created by dropping British responsibility in the island might even lead to war between the Turks and the Greeks.

I told Harold of messages I had received, particularly from the Greeks, asking me to urge upon him the importance of freeing Archbishop Makarios, the Greek Cypriot leader and advocate of the island's independence, whom the British had deported the year before to the Seychelles in the Indian Ocean because of his defiance of British authority. I told the Prime Minister that in my opinion I thought they were not gaining much by keeping him prisoner. As I saw it, they would gain most by releasing him even though they might not, for the moment, allow him to return to Cyprus. At the very least this gesture would serve as an indication of good faith as the British were trying, with Greece and Turkey, to reach a solution to this problem. The British delegation gave me the impression that this suggestion would be seriously considered.[8]

On March 22, Secretary Dulles, Lewis Strauss, Chairman of the Atomic Energy Commission, and I met with Prime Minister Macmillan and Foreign Minister Lloyd on another type of problem and made a commitment of signal importance to the security of the Free World for the next several years. Under detailed arrangements to be agreed upon later, the United States would turn over to the British a number of intermediate-range ballistic missiles, as soon as they were fully developed.[9] This agreement would put missiles of intermediate range within striking distance of the heartland of the Soviet Union.

In later days of concern over Soviet ICBM development, these missiles would serve as a powerful deterrent to any atomic transgression by the Communists.

The meeting was by far the most successful international conference that I had attended since the close of World War II. For this there were several reasons. One was the importance of the problems we faced and the need for reaching definite answers. It was not possible to refer them to a study group for later consideration as is so often the solution agreed upon in international conferences.

Next there was a noticeable atmosphere of frankness and confidence throughout the meeting. Our determination to rebuild our close understanding was aided, in part, by the fact that Harold and I were old comrades.

Finally we found that each side was well informed on the several subjects taken up; so conversations were far more definite and to the point than is normally the case; generalizations and protestations of good

[8] On March 28 the British freed Archbishop Makarios from detention, with permission to go anywhere but Cyprus. In 1960, under an agreement reached in 1959, Cyprus became independent, with the Archbishop its first elected President and with British bases still under British control.

[9] The atomic warheads for these missiles, as always, would remain under United States' official control until released by mutual agreement in event of emergency.

will are too often expected to take the place of clear exchanges of information and opinion.

The conference, I believe, did much to restore Anglo-American understanding and thus to strengthen the North Atlantic community of nations.

* * *

I had long urged a step-by-step progress toward unity within the North Atlantic Community. I was therefore delighted not only with the outcome of this Bermuda conference but with the outcome of another, held two days later in Rome. There the nations of the Western world made a new and significant commitment. On March 25, representatives of Belgium, France, the Netherlands, Luxembourg, Italy, and West Germany met in Rome to sign the treaties establishing a European Atomic Energy Community (EURATOM) and the European Economic Community.

I heartily favored both these steps. Through EURATOM the member nations would cooperate—by setting up reactors and research centers, for example—in putting atomic energy to constructive use on their continent. Through the EEC, the Common Market, they would work toward the gradual elimination of tariff barriers among themselves. Though some provisions of the Rome treaty might serve to restrain trade between Europe and the outside world, the possible building of a powerful United States of Europe was a dream, that some day, I hoped to see realized.

Several weeks earlier I had visitors at the White House: Franz Etzel, Vice President of the European Coal and Steel Community; Louis Armand, the President of the French National Railroad, and Francesco Giordiani, President of the Italian Research Council—the "three wise men" of EURATOM. It was their task to set up plans for the installation of the first nuclear electric power stations on European soil. EURATOM, I said, would be a blessing for the Free World. I observed that European countries might find one Biblical passage that applied to their problem. To save their lives, perhaps they must first lose them. I meant, of course, that to reinforce their life as nations, they might have to yield a little as independent nations. Later that month, I had an opportunity to talk in the same vein to the French Premier, Guy Mollet; I also told Heinrich von Brentano, the German Foreign Minister, that nothing was more important to Europe than close relations, historically unprecedented, between France and Germany.

EURATOM was one step; then would come the effort toward economic union.

The drive toward a union which was economic surely might some day spark a drive toward a union which was political. Six years earlier, speaking in London,[10] I had said that it would be difficult to overstate the benefits that would accrue if the free nations of Europe ever became a unit. But instead,

> . . . history, custom, language, and prejudice have combined to hamper integration. Progress has been and is hobbled by a web of customs barriers interlaced with bilateral agreements, multilateral cartels, local shortages, and economic monstrosities. How tragic! . . .

Here was a task to challenge the efforts of the wisest statesmen, the best economists, the most brilliant diplomats, I said. Europe could not attain the towering material stature possible to its peoples' skills and spirit so long as it was divided by patchwork territorial fences.

> But with unity achieved, Europe could build adequate security and, at the same time, continue the march of human betterment that has characterized Western civilization. Once united, the farms and factories of France and Belgium, the foundries of Germany, the rich farmlands of Holland, Denmark, the skilled labor of Italy will produce miracles for the common good.

Now, in the spring of 1957, statesmen and economists and diplomats were taking one important step in response to that challenge. These men were making history.

[10] At a dinner of the English-Speaking Union, July 3, 1951.

CHAPTER V

A Family of Controversies

To a stranger all the domestic controversies of the Americans at first appear to be incomprehensible or puerile, and he is at a loss whether to pity a people who take such arrant trifles in good earnest or to envy that happiness which enables a community to discuss them.

—*Alexis de Tocqueville,*
Democracy in America

"I WOULD deplore the day," Secretary of the Treasury George M. Humphrey said, answering a question at a news conference on January 15, 1957, "that we thought we couldn't ever reduce expenditures of this terrific amount, [and] the terrific tax we are taking out of this country." Then he added: "If we don't, over a long period of time, I will predict that you will have a depression that will curl your hair."

"Could we have the stenotypist read that back to us?" a reporter asked eagerly. "That is a good quote."

It was indeed. It reverberated from coast to coast, though in the excitement Secretary Humphrey's "forecast" tended to lose his qualifying words "over a long period of time."

The federal budget—which had been reduced from the $80.2 billion of President Truman's budget for fiscal 1953—a Korean War year—had now climbed from $57.1 billion in appropriations in fiscal 1955 to $63.2 billion in 1956, to $70.5 billion in 1957, to a projected $73.3 billion for 1958.

This trend concerned the Secretary as it did all of us. But, speculative interpretations to the contrary, he was neither criticizing the administration to which he belonged nor suggesting that the budget we had just submitted to the Congress was all wrong. "I think this budget as now drawn," Secretary Humphrey told the reporters, "has been prepared with the very greatest care, and I think there are a lot of economies and a lot of savings that we ought to be able to make if we pay strict attention to our business and work at them hard enough during the [next] eighteen months."

If this program is adopted and resolutely followed, he concluded, we could, a year hence, give consideration not only to some further payment on the public debt but also to further tax reductions. This hope, of course, was conditioned upon continuation of our present prosperity.

The Secretary then summarized his suggested line of attack against unnecessary federal spending and potential inflation: (a) an attempt to get the general public to reduce its demands for Federal services; (b) an effort to get the Congress to make no appropriations above the figures in the administration's budget; (c) a requirement that every government agency take vigorous measures, without harm to either security or service to the public, to see that actual expenditures are kept well within the present budgeted figures between now and the end of the next fiscal year and to "search out additional ways to save money and manpower"; and (d) an attempt to make further cuts in the budget for fiscal year 1959.

George and I had discussed the problem of high governmental expenditure time and again and had kept up an active correspondence and dialogue on the subject.[1] At a meeting of the Cabinet on January 9, 1957, I had personally edited the formal statement he read at the quoted press conference, but its basic purport was completely forgotten in the wake of his highly quotable, extemporaneous "hair curling" phrase.

Actually there were two major concerns that the Secretary felt regarding this high level of governmental expenditures. One was the possibility that high taxes would take too much money out of the economy—money needed to make jobs as time went on. Increasingly high taxes could take money that might otherwise go into new plants, new products, new research. The other danger in high expenditures, as we saw it, was the possibility of increased inflation resulting from a long series of deficits.[2]

[1] In the month just past, for example, he had sent a memorandum which is representative of his ideas and expression of them:

"We are reaching the point where continued increases in interest rates are becoming less and less effective in restraining increases in costs and prices. . . .

"Our most powerful weapon to combat price increases would be a reduction in Government expenditures. This would increase available manpower outside the Government as manpower is reduced by the Government."

[2] The administration's 1958 budget foresaw a slight surplus, of $1.8 billion. But this surplus assumed a tax intake of nearly $74 billion. To provide a tax revenue of $74

It was a point I had stressed—together with a plea for business and labor restraint in price and wage increases—in my State of the Union message:

> This danger requires a firm resolution that the Federal Government shall utilize only a prudent share of the Nation's resources, that it shall live within its means, carefully measuring against need alternative proposals for expenditures.

Unsound, inflationary fiscal policies, George believed, would bring on a loss of confidence (a key word in the Secretary's lexicon—something he treated almost as a commodity, as real as goods, services, equipment, buildings, and roads).

On the need for cutting expenditures to—but not beyond—the bone, I agreed completely with the Secretary and told reporters so at a news conference on January 23. But we also agreed on one other central fact, namely, that the size of the national budget largely reflected the size of the national danger.[3]

But now an unexpected phenomenon occurred. The Democrats inexplicably became economy-minded. The administration had assumed that the Congress, under Democratic control, would try to pile up appropriations and thus increase my budget. This year there was a difference. Members of the Senate and House began to sense, possibly, an economy mood in their states and districts. Whether the legislators were influenced by George Humphrey's press conference remark or merely desirous of exploiting it, I do not know. But they tried to turn to their own advantage my reference, in the January 23 news conference, to George Humphrey's statement that Congress should make responsible cuts in the budget.

I told reporters that I had already instructed all members of the administration to find every place where there might be a chance to save a

---

billion, the economy would have to continue its steady growth. Such uninterrupted growth for a very long period of time seemed possibly too much to expect.

Moreover, we were concerned about the beginning of a decrease in the buying power of the dollar. When I took office in 1953, the "1939 dollar" was worth 51.9 cents; it was worth the same in 1955. But between April 1956 and January 1957, its value dropped from 51.7 cents to 50.3 cents. We were determined to arrest this trend.

[3] For fiscal year 1955 the Congress had appropriated for major national security $32.5 billion; for 1956, $34.9 billion; for 1957, $38.3 billion. For 1958 I would ask $41.1 billion—again, a peacetime record figure.

A large part of this almost nine-billion-dollar increase in military spending reflected the costs of the new and urgent missile programs, developments that were born out of exhaustive studies by our scientists and the work of our intelligence services in the early stages of my administration.

dollar, even if already budgeted. If Congress could find such opportunities, I would be delighted, I added. Indeed, it was their duty to look for legitimate opportunities to do so.

Considering in retrospect the political realities of the nation's capital, where even such a truism as this can be twisted for partisan exploitation, perhaps this invitation to Congress to do its Constitutional duty had better been left unsaid. But in the long pull candor and bare-bones talk in public affairs are, whenever possible, best for the nation and, indeed, the best politics. I might very well say the same thing over again, exactly the same way, vexing though the consequences were for a short time.

The members of Congress were in their own view equal to the challenges of cutting; they took up their axes and prepared to begin. Their announced goals were drastic. The Republican Minority Leader in the Senate, William Knowland, predicted a cut in the budget of at least two billion dollars; Senator Styles Bridges of New Hampshire foresaw a cut of 2.5 billion, and Senator Harry Byrd of Virginia, the Chairman of the Senate Finance Committee, a cut of 6.5 billion.

On March 12, the House of Representatives passed Resolution 190 requesting me to "indicate the places and amounts in his [the President's] budget where he thinks substantial reductions may best be made." Republicans on the House floor, in fighting the Resolution, called it an abdication of House and Senate authority.

Asked about this by reporters the next day, I commented: "Of course, the Congress has the constitutional power of appropriating money . . .

"I have no objection whatsoever to re-examining our own budget. In fact, the last Cabinet meeting was given over wholly to that subject . . . how we could cut out useless positions, how we could save money." But, I added, *substantial* cuts in the budget could be made only at the expense of reducing, eliminating, or slowing down great programs. Otherwise, there did not appear to be any huge amounts to be saved.

For the next six weeks budget-cutting talk intensified, with statements by congressmen and private citizens alike. Even my brother Edgar joined in, citing our youngest brother, Milton, and Sherman Adams as culprits. "Edgar has been criticizing me since I was five years old," I told a questioner; I was sure he would continue to do so. Responding to the House Resolution, I offered Speaker Sam Rayburn recommendations on how the House might help the situation.[4] But I also sent along a list of ten steps

[4] The Congress could save $1.342 billion by cutting contingent expenses by $300 million, and by postponing the appropriation of five hundred million dollars for military assistance under the Mutual Security Program, $200 million for military

they had not asked for—how the House might improve the budgetary situation for the future.[5]

On the evening of May 14, I reported by television to the American people on the cost of their government. I explained that 35 per cent of the budget, mostly fixed by law, included more than $7 billion interest on the national debt; $5 billion for veterans' pension, education, medical care, and similar benefits; $5 billion for agriculture price supports and related items, and $3.5 billion for grants and loans to the states for unemployment compensation and welfare works. The next major part of the budget, $5 billion, was earmarked for domestic programs, which, in the administration's view, were both needed and efficiently administered.

Then I turned to the lion's share, the amount earmarked for the United States' security, and spoke of the folly of gutting this part of the budget:

> . . . The national defense item is by far the largest in our budget, but let us see just how large it is. The estimate just for our own military forces and our atomic development, together with a small amount for stockpiling critical and strategic materials, is almost $40 billion. This does not, by any means, equal the full amount first recommended by our uniformed services. They wanted some $10 billion more.
>
> But I earnestly believe that this defense budget represents, in today's world, the proper dividing line between national danger on the one hand and excessive expenditure on the other. If it is materially cut, I believe the country would be taking a needless gamble. For myself, I have seen unwise military cuts before. I have more than once seen their terrible consequences. I am determined to do all I can to see that we do not follow that foolhardy road again.

I concluded with the one overriding, incontrovertible fact about the United States government budget in 1957 (applicable, too, in the years before and after). "As we look at the whole range of the budget there is only one hope of making the really great savings that we all want so much. That hope is to achieve an effective disarmament agreement with an easing of world tensions, so that the enormous sums we have to spend for our defense can be drastically reduced."

---

public works, $254 million for the Soil Bank, $50 million for the Federal National Mortgage Association, $25 million for college housing, and $13 million for the Corps of Engineers.

[5] These included such proposals as adjustment of postal rates, state and local participation in water resource projects, and enactment of the item veto (the right of a President to veto single items in a money bill sent to him for signing, enabling him to defeat pork-barrel projects tacked onto valuable legislation).

* * *

Though the talk seemed to have some effect, many members of Congress still apparently wanted to show their cost-cutting powers.

In particular, they took aim at mutual security and the United States Information Agency, less than massive but vital programs with no political appeal, in which the benefits to the United States, dollar for dollar, were incalculable. As the session ground on, the 85th Congress seemed to lose all sense of direction. While it worked to establish a record for economy, it also worked to increase expenditures for pet projects and pressure groups.[6]

In the search for any proposal that seemed popular, statesmanship was forgotten. Before the session was over, we found not only mutual security and United States Information Agency funds cut, but our important overseas status-of-forces treaties attacked and a much-needed school construction bill rejected.

* * *

The mutual security system had been devised and put into operation by a Democratic Administration and a Republican Congress soon after World War II. In the years since, it had been the means by which the United States gave military and economic help to friendly governments abroad. We believed in the necessity of sustaining the program at a reasonable level, but because it had restricted vote appeal there was a constant and determined campaign waged within the Congress either to cut the amounts needed or even to discontinue the program.

To defend the Mutual Security Program to the general public I knew would be a nearly impossible task. On one occasion toward the end of April, I had a long talk with a number of successful, usually well-informed people who urged me to make a speech—or even two—to show,

[6] By late July, I was writing to a friend of my exasperation. In the field of housing, I said, Congress had insisted upon putting a billion dollars *more* in the authorization bill than the administration had requested. On top of that, Congress was then trying to raise the pay of mailmen that would give them a 12 per cent increase even though Congress was well aware of the fact that this would practically compel raises for the entire classified civil service. This would vastly increase federal expenditures. Worse, there could be little doubt that the industrial wage-price spiral would get a terrific upward jolt from any such action on the part of the federal government. But in voting for special expenditures even while he made speeches on general economy the congressman felt that he was winning votes for himself. So out the window went whatever concern he might have felt about the effect of government expenditures on inflation.

among other things, that mutual security funds were essential and that to slash them would be far worse than cutting off a like amount in any other category. I wrote George Humphrey at once about this suggestion, adding:

> Some of this gives me almost a sense of frustration. It would appear that enough had been said to allow any man of intelligence who is interested in governmental affairs, to understand exactly what our individual and collective opinions are. But the point that impresses me is that if these people, admittedly well-educated and generally informed in business matters, and supposedly well-read, are so confused as to the true state of affairs, then it must be clear that the taxicab driver, the farmer, the miner, the carpenter, the barber, and all their wives, must be in a state of utter bewilderment.

No one had succeeded in having the public understand that mutual security was not philanthropy; it was defense. Three-fourths of the mutual security budget went into two essential programs: 50 per cent into direct military assistance, including funds for military "hardware"; and about 25 per cent provided money to friendly nations in which United States bases were located or enabled them to raise and support military forces for the common defense.

Many persons did not understand that while we in 1957 had approximately a million ground troops for collective defense, those with whom we were allied had nearly five million; that our two thousand combat ships were supplemented by twenty-five hundred of our allies; that United States aircraft made up only a little more than half the Free World total. Our allies' contributions came from leaner purses: Our per capita income was about $2400, Spain's $300, Turkey's $110, Taiwan's $99, Thailand's $65, Vietnam's $50. Candidly our share of security costs was a bargain. Moreover, and highly important, while it cost $3515 to maintain an American soldier for a year, to maintain a Pakistani the price was $485, for a Greek, $424.

Our entire annual budget for mutual security equaled only one-fourth our expenditures for cigarettes, cigars, pipe tobacco, and liquor.

It was a widespread popular view that our mutual security effort consisted of Uncle Sam's bundling up billions of green American dollars and shipping them to the far corners of the earth in a futile attempt to buy friends. Actually, however, more than three-fourths of mutual security funds were spent in the United States and thus made jobs for half a million men and women.

There were, to be sure, understandable reasons why, in nearly a decade since the launching of the Marshall Plan and, later, the Mutual

Security Program, the American people had not arrived at a more accurate appraisal of this national undertaking. Part of the problem was that many of the facts in support of mutual security had to be guarded as national secrets. Who receives the money? What is done with it? How many soldiers does it support? What important bases of ours—air, naval, missile—are located in the countries we assist? How many airplanes on each base? How many missiles? What exactly would happen if we pulled out?

To provide detailed answers to these questions would, in many instances, have worried our friends and comforted our enemies. Therefore, an advocate of mutual security found himself constantly fending off the "giveaway" attack with one hand tied behind him and his best ammunition unusable. I naturally recognized these restraints but bridled against the impediments they imposed on understanding. One day in chatting with a friend as we flew from Augusta to Washington I likened Mutual Security to the hypothetical case of mutual ownership of the airplane. We might agree that to cut costs we would give up a few creature comforts and do without one of the stewards. Then, we might decide that we no longer wanted to be able to fly in all kinds of weather, and so we could reduce personnel in the forward compartment, making the co-pilot serve as navigator. We could also get rid of splendid but expensive radar equipment. But sooner or later, the too-economy-minded would suggest that we cut out one or more of the engines. The result for all of us would be unpleasant.

The point that I tried to impress upon the Congress and the public was that we should confine budget-cutting to programs that represented some greater convenience, comfort, or protection against the normal vicissitudes of living; we could not logically apply them against systems that kept our national "air liner" safe and sound in this turbulent world.

One day Jim Hagerty brought me a teletype quotation from a speech by Senator Styles Bridges, ranking Republican on the Senate Appropriations Committee, labeling mutual security advocates "do-gooders." I asked Senator Bridges to visit me. "It is pretty hard," I told him, "when not only as President, but as the titular head of the party, I have to hear that one of the principal people in the party has said that mutual security is nothing but a do-gooder act . . . I think nothing could be further from the truth. I realize that as of this moment it is a very popular thing to talk about saving a dollar. Frankly, I would rather see the Congress cut a *billion* off the defense part—as much as I think it would be a mistake."

Bridges read the ticker story and said that he had always been a supporter of mutual security; his recent statement meant that we should exclude such countries as India, Yugoslavia, and Indonesia from the list of beneficiaries.

I disagreed and told him that the Mutual Security Program served our own enlightened self-interest. Those interests were long-term. While an immediate cut might have been popular then, in the long run it could prove to be the most costly move we had ever made.

As we talked it became apparent that only part of the Senator's statement had been quoted. He made it clear that he would not be a party to sabotaging the Mutual Security Program; rather he hoped only that my pledge to cut half a billion from the budget's request for mutual security might be made larger.

I thanked him for his explanation and said I would count on his help in saving the item from destruction. And I added: "I want to wage the cold war in a militant, but reasonable, style whereby we appeal to the people of the world as a better group to stay with than the Communists. I'm not concerned about 'buying friends' or purchasing satellite countries or any other thing—that is all false. As a free country, the only ally we can have is a *free* ally, one who wants to be with us—that is what we are trying to develop."

Soon thereafter I sent a special message to Congress and carried the mutual security message to the nation, again by television. I said that it had helped Iran stay free in 1953, Guatemala to regain freedom in 1954, and at that very moment in 1957, it was helping sustain the freedom of the Kingdom of Jordan, threatened by the growth of Communist subversion and infiltration. The work of combating Communism in Jordan, I reported, would have been impossible without economic aid from outside Jordan, including help from the United States. And:

> When our young men were dying in the Argonne in 1918 and on the beaches of Normandy and in the Western Pacific in 1944 and at Pusan in 1950—and when the battlefields of Europe and Africa and Asia were strewn with billions of dollars worth of American military equipment, representing the toil and the skills of millions of workers—no one for an instant doubted the need and the rightness of this sacrifice of blood and labor and treasure.
>
> Precisely the same needs and purposes are served by our Mutual Security programs today—whether these operate on a military or an economic front. For on both fronts they are truly defense programs.

The whole design of the defense against Communism could not be completed with guns alone, I added. For freedom was menaced by the poverty that Communism exploits. We could not fight poverty with guns.

The day after the broadcast, I telephoned Secretary Dulles that White House mail was now running 9 to 1 in the administration's favor. The

Secretary reported that he had just returned from congressional hearings, which he said were wonderful, full of praise; indeed, one senator had said he would vote for mutual security for the first time in ten years. The attack against the Mutual Security Administration was fended for the moment, to be renewed in fury a little later.

* * *

Another item in the budget that I was anxious to preserve in spite of my determination to minimize over-all expenditures was the appropriation for the United States Information Agency. The director of the agency, newly appointed, was Dr. Arthur Larson, a scholar whose political philosophy was similar to my own.

In some respects our government's informational program abroad had achieved even less public understanding and support than had the Mutual Security Program. During World War II, as the Office of War Information (OWI), it could tell the public little of its work: To keep our allies informed of vital developments, to persuade neutrals to join us or at least not to help the enemy, to encourage peoples in occupied areas to maintain hope but not to rise until the crucial times arrived, and to frighten and discourage enemy populations. When the war ended, this organization might have been dismantled had it not at once become evident that the Kremlin was initiating a worldwide program of propaganda, twenty-four hours a day in some forty languages, and composed of monumental lies, often repeated, designed to win the minds of men everywhere away from a philosophy of freedom and for the acceptance of Communist imperialism. In self-defense our government was compelled to transform the Office of War Information into a permanent United States Information Agency whose sole and essential purpose was to let all the world know the truth and only the truth about our policies, plans, actions, and purposes. "Wars begin in the minds of men and in the minds of men the foundations of peace must be constructed."

To my associates and me, the Agency was a non-military arm of defense and a voice of our foreign policy, both of which would be helped by achieving genuine understanding among the peoples of the world. Unfortunately, however, the Agency had never been popular with the Congress. This persistent unpopularity was of no help to Arthur Larson when it became his duty to appear before the Congress.

Moreover, early in the 1956 campaign a book of his had been published, *A Republican Looks at His Party,* advocating a method of presenting Republicanism to the public in such fashion as to appeal particularly to independents and "switch" voters. The popularity of this book and its argument made him a particularly tempting partisan target on Capitol Hill.

In the January budget I had asked for $144 million for the USIA—$31 million more than the year before. Despite my urgent support of the Agency's important work, the House on April 17 refused. Now Arthur Larson, on May 2, was preparing to ask the Senate to put back at least some of the reduction.

He faced an appropriations subcommittee under the chairmanship of Senator Lyndon Johnson.

From the tone of Senator Johnson's opening statement Larson might well have guessed what was going to happen:

> You appear before us under conditions which guarantee a considerable amount of distinction. Of all the Agency heads . . . you are asking for the most money to be restored to the funds cut by the House . . . we look to you as the distinguished author and spokesman for your party to enlighten us.

The most significant barb in this statement was in the word "spokesman." On April 16, the day before the House voted its cut, Mr. Larson had been in Hawaii addressing an enthusiastic crowd of Republicans. One sentence was to make him a rich target for Democratic ire:

> "Throughout the New and Fair Deals, this country was in the grip of a somewhat alien philosophy, imported from Europe."

The subcommittee knew of the speech.

From the ominous beginning, things grew steadily worse. Larson endured day after day of carping and badgering. On May 14, the Republican legislative leaders told me it was going to be difficult even to hold the line at the House's low figure of $105 million: Johnson already was talking about slicing that to $91 million, Mansfield to $70 million, and Fulbright to $55 million.

When the Senate subcommittee brought out its report, the USIA got about what Senator Johnson had said: $90.2 million; it also got the acid advice that it "should concentrate on improving its personnel" and the recommendation that the Agency should return, as before 1953, to the State Department. Lyndon Johnson left no doubt about his views: "there is not one scintilla of evidence in the more than twelve hundred pages of hearings which would justify the assertion by a judicious, prudent man that the $90 million we have recommended will be wisely spent."[7]

[7] The appropriation for USIA for the current fiscal year (1965) totals more than $154 million.

The Senate did not quarrel with the recommendation of Johnson's subcommittee, though two weeks later Senate conferees did agree to raise the final figure to $96 million—$10 million less than the House had voted and nearly $50 million less than I thought necessary. I was disappointed by this irresponsible diminution of an agency on the front line in the cold war.

Although even some Republicans opposed USIA, I found myself, in this instance, wishing profoundly that I could have a Congress controlled by my own party. In this way I could have employed the influence of patronage and its withholding, and other means normally available to a President in getting affirmative action in Congress on his proposals.

I discussed the USIA with Secretary Dulles and the mounting congressional pressure to have it transferred to the State Department. I was somewhat inclined toward approving such a transfer because it seemed to be the only way to get sufficient money to support the Agency's necessary functions. Foster, however, did not think any such radical move was necessary. The State Department, he felt, should not become a collection of operating agencies. It should confine itself to foreign policy formulation, advice, and execution. I authorized the Secretary to hold to his position.

Senator Johnson's attack on the USIA program was followed in the middle of June by his suggestion to Secretary Dulles that Congress adopt a resolution encouraging me to "make every effort" to increase the international exchange of information. Secretary Dulles emphatically told Johnson that I would disapprove such a resolution for the simple reason that I had initiated the idea myself at the 1955 Summit Conference and had been working hard on it ever since.

A battle that enlivened and marred Executive-Legislative relations during the first session of the 85th Congress involved school construction.

At that time, the United States, according to the calculations of the Department of Health, Education, and Welfare, had a shortage of approximately 159,000 classrooms. The states were building about sixty-nine thousand classrooms a year, enough to stay one jump ahead of the increase needed every year but not to cut materially into the shortage.

Since 1955 I had striven for a bill that would stimulate local construction. I believed that the federal government should help make up the deficiencies, most of them attributable to a long depression and two wars. But the federal government should under no circumstances become involved in school operating costs, for to assume this responsibility would, I was convinced, give it permanent and constantly increasing power in the field of education. The result would be to induce every state to look more and more to Washington, D.C., for help and thus to minimize its own costs. Such a practice could inevitably lead to an unwarranted measure of federal control. National control of curricula or supervision of teachers, for instance, would be, to my mind, a calamity of the first order.

The Congress had done nothing about classroom shortages. Early in 1957, therefore, I again sent to Capitol Hill a Special Message on Education, including a request for a four-year, $1.3 billion total program of federal grants to the states for school construction. This was to be an "emergency measure," to stimulate greater state and local efforts to meet needs.

At once the bill ran into crossfire.

In favor of a school construction bill were the American Association of University Professors, the American Association of University Women, the National Education Association, the American Veterans Committee, and the AFL-CIO. The Americans for Democratic Action were in favor of a bill but not ours. On February 12 its national director called the administration's school construction bill "a penny pinching half-starved bill, with the marks of the budget-wringer still fresh upon it." To get schools built, he proposed federal expenditures of a billion dollars a year.

Against federal participation in school construction, in that year of economy, stood the Chamber of Commerce of the United States, the American Farm Bureau Federation, the American Legion, the American Medical Association, and the National Association of Manufacturers. The states, they insisted, could do the job without any help from Washington. Federal aid, they said, would be the thin end of the wedge for federal domination and a contributor to the unconscionable size of the federal budget and federal taxes.

I disagreed—this was becoming normal—with both extremes. On May 23 I had a long talk with Congressman Samuel K. McConnell, Jr., of Pennsylvania, the ranking Republican member of the House Committee on Education and Labor, who recently had completed a tour to see for himself whether in fact the United States at that moment was suffering from a shortage of classrooms. He brought with him to the White House photographs he had taken of buildings that were crowded, unsanitary, and unsafe—an eloquent answer to all who denied a need existed or that the states could or were meeting the need. Later to Representative Clarence J. Brown of Ohio, who thought my proposal too radical (and who always claimed to be an ardent supporter of the late Senator Taft), I sent the following letter:

June 12, 1957

Dear Clarence:

This morning you said that you could not go home if you stood for a school program. Here is what Bob Taft said on the radio in Ohio on June 2, 1949:

> "One of the most important jobs the Senate did in the month of May was the passage of this Aid to Education Bill. This Bill provides 270 million dollars a year (meaning a continuous, never-ending program) to the 48 States to enable them to improve their grade schools and high schools so that at least 55 dollars per child will be available to every school in the United States, including colored schools where there are separate schools. The purpose is to make available to every child minimum educational opportunities, no matter how poor the State or the district in which he may live. I was one of the sponsors of the Bill, and I believe that it is absolutely necessary if there is to be anything like equality of opportunity for children in many of the poorer States. No boy can possibly have equality of opportunity if he does not have enough education to understand at least what his opportunities are."

The next year he was elected by the largest majority he ever got in his State.

Sincerely,

D.D.E.

P.S. I supplied the underlining . . ."

I continued to urge the need for emergency action and for establishing a grant formula that would provide adequately for federal aid in accordance with the states' actual need for help. I insisted that any bill be based upon the principle of need, and limited as to time.

On July 25 the House killed the educational bill, which as in 1956 carried an anti-segregation rider. This rider again consolidated the opposition. Ninety-seven Democrats and 111 Republicans had voted "aye"; 126 Democrats and 77 Republicans voted "no."

* * *

One difference of opinion began, not on Capitol Hill but on a hilltop in Japan. There, on the afternoon of January 30, 1957, Army Specialist 3/C William S. Girard and another soldier were guarding a machine gun overlooking a maneuver area made available by the Japanese government for the part-time use of the United States Army.

Red flags dotted the area, warning off Japanese civilians. These warnings had not been effective. Japanese people continued to comb the ground for empty brass cartridge cases which could be sold locally. The risk of accident was such that the American officer in charge withdrew all live ammunition from the troops when the morning's exercises ended. Girard had been issued blank ammunition.

A Japanese man approached. Placing a brass shell case in his rifle grenade launcher, Girard fired a blank cartridge in the man's vicinity. The man fled. Then a Japanese woman approached and Girard, using the same makeshift equipment, fired again. The woman, Mrs. Naha Sakai, fell dead. The empty shell case had hit her in the back not more than thirty yards from where Girard stood.

After a long disagreement with Japanese authorities over whether Girard had acted "in the performance of official duty," the American authorities surrendered him in accordance with the "Status of Forces" provisions to the Japanese for trial. (Under these agreements, which make it possible for foreign nations to accept the stationing of United States troops on their soil, the host nation has jurisdiction over crimes charged against American servicemen off duty, while the United States has jurisdiction if committed on duty. The agreements also provide that either government can waive its jurisdiction.)

Between 1953 and 1957, more than thirty-eight thousand cases had come up in which American personnel were subject to trial in foreign courts. The Girard case provoked loud protest. "Why did the Army turn Girard over for trial?" the Republican legislative leaders wanted to know. At a White House meeting on May 21, Secretary of the Army Wilber Brucker explained the legal dispute in the Pentagon and in Japan preceding the decision and then added that he wanted to reverse it. Senator Knowland spoke strongly for American jurisdiction over its own servicemen. I told Secretary Brucker to bring the matter back to me before a decision was made.

After the meeting I telephoned Secretary Dulles. This episode had illustrated once more the frictions that are inevitable when troops of one country are quartered on another's soil. The logical thing to do, I told Foster, was to remove our forces from Japan. I saw no strategic need for combat divisions to remain there; perhaps it would soon be wise, I suggested, to start a progressive withdrawal. In a later meeting I emphasized again the need to reduce the number of United States forces in foreign territory—forces which cannot escape being regarded as occupation troops. Plans for the withdrawal were immediately launched. But the Girard case was still to be settled.

On May 29, Secretary Dulles, Defense Secretary Charles Wilson, and others discussed the alternatives with me: allow jurisdiction to remain with Japan or do an about-face and demand jurisdiction. But I now had new information provided by Secretary Brucker. Out of fourteen thousand cases since 1953 in which Americans were subject to trial in Japanese courts, the Japanese had voluntarily relinquished jurisdiction in 13,642—or 97 per cent. Japanese sentences were generally lighter than those of American military authorities. The United States had not been required to forego jurisdiction over Girard but instead had followed Treaty procedures in voluntarily relinquishing it. In my view we could not go back on that agreement. "The decision will stand," I said. "We will not demand Girard's return to our jurisdiction."

In a meeting soon afterward with the Republican legislative leaders, Senator Knowland admitted that the administration had little alternative but, he said, repercussions would follow.

By coincidence, Prime Minister Nobusuke Kishi of Japan was due to arrive in Washington later that month. Secretary Dulles reported to me that House Speaker Sam Rayburn wanted us to cancel the visit. I refused. We were entering a new phase in our relations with Japan. In the past eighteen months the Japanese had restored political relations with seventy-two countries. Japan had regained its economic health. Because of changing conditions its government was requesting a readjustment in its dealings with the United States. The far-left Socialist Party was gaining strength and Japanese newspapers were printing quantities of leftist editorials. If the United States did not "work with Japan," Ambassador Douglas MacArthur II told me, it was his judgment that within five years the Japanese could "be headed in the wrong direction."[8]

In any event, I was determined that the Kishi visit would proceed as planned.

Although I wrote to Mrs. Girard, assuring her that her son's "every right will be fully protected," the United States Congress was far from finished with its fixation on Girard and on our Status of Forces Agreements. On July 1 the House Foreign Affairs Committee reported out a House Joint Resolution, introduced by Republican Congressman Frank T. Bow of Ohio, to revise our Status of Forces Agreements to provide that foreign countries would have no criminal jurisdiction over United States servicemen stationed within their boundaries. In a letter to the committee, Secretary Wilson said that the "practical effect" of this measure "would be the withdrawal of the United States forces from all over the world." On a previous occasion the Bow bill had died in committee; the Girard case had brought it back to life.

We met again. Congressman Joseph W. Martin, Jr., of Massachusetts,

[8] On March 14 Secretary Dulles had sent me a cable suggesting a long-range study of developing Australia as a defense production base for the Far East; there were "some risks," the Secretary thought, "in depending wholly upon Japan."

Minority Leader in the House, reported that to embarrass the administration many Democrats were pushing the Bow bill on the Hill. Moreover, he added, in a straight vote its proponents would likely win. Should the administration and its supporters try to modify it?

Senator Knowland favored an Executive Order asserting that any soldier accused of a crime when on military duty would get an American trial. Robert Dechert, General Counsel of the Department of Defense, disagreed. If we said "no waivers of jurisdiction," a "foreign government like Japan would cut out the 97 per cent waivers we are now getting from them."

"Any young man drafted in peacetime, sent overseas against his will and assigned to duty," Knowland argued, "should not be turned over to any other government for trial; he's wearing the uniform of the United States."

Mr. Dechert went back to the Girard case in particular: it was well understood in Japan, before the Army's decision, that the Japanese would charge him with the minimum offense and would, at worst, give him a very light sentence. To enact the Bow Amendment, he insisted, would be to negate any of our treaties which included a provision for United States waiver of jurisdiction.

Senator Dirksen feared that the issue was so hot that the Congress might even override a presidential veto. I told him that we would fight it all the way.[9] We succeeded.

On July 22, I wrote to my friend Swede Hazlett:

> . . . right at this moment lack of understanding of America's international position and obligations accounts for the fact that we seem to be trying to make a national hero out of a man who shot a woman—in the back at something like ten to fifteen yards distance.
>
> As quickly as this incident became a popular one in some parts of the isolationist press, it was taken up by dozens of Congressmen who "viewed with alarm" and were "shocked and distressed" . . .
>
> We have even had a serious attempt made to force me to denounce our Status of Forces treaties. These treaties, as you know, are fair and just to Americans serving abroad and are the only means by which we retain jurisdiction in most offenses committed. Because they establish a reasonable jurisdictional balance between ourselves and the host country, they are at the very foundation of our defensive alliances. To denounce them would make us completely isolationist and force us to abandon practically every base we have abroad.

[9] Two days later the United States Supreme Court unanimously held the government's right to surrender Girard to the Japanese.

Girard was later tried by a Japanese court and given a three-year *suspended* sentence. The abortive and unwarranted attack on our "Status of Forces" Agreements was forgotten.

* * *

The Girard case, the school construction bill, and manifold other matters had obscured the dreary and sometimes acrimonious struggle over the Mutual Security Program for a time, but actually we were never wholly free of it. Too many members of Congress, Democrats and Republicans alike, were so sensitive to the appeal of the cry "giveaway" and so well aware of the fleeting popularity to be gained by its repetition that intelligent discussion between proponents and opponents of the program became all but impossible.

With Congress controlled by the Democratic party, I could employ only persuasion to gain approval of programs that, in my view, were virtually necessary to the welfare of the United States. But, obviously, many others did not agree with me. My disposition, as I renewed my attempts at persuasion, became anything but sunny. One day I dashed off a note to General Persons, then head of my liaison group with the Congress, that included this quotation from the fifth chapter of St. Paul's First Epistle to the Thessalonians:

> "Now we exhort you, brethren, warn them that
> are unruly, comfort the feebleminded, support
> the weak, be patient toward all men."

He had the note framed and hung on the wall of his office.

Involved first was authorization and, second, the appropriation.[10] Conferences on these subjects were never pleasant; frequently they brought forth bitter exchanges.

One senator alleged that support of "foreign aid" had driven Senators George and Connally out of the Senate and added that he himself "could well be defeated if I should continue to support the program at its present high levels."

[10] The difference between "authorization" and "appropriation" can be confusing. Providing money for any project is at least a two-part process. The authorization, among other things, sets a ceiling on the funds for a specific program. The appropriation, handled by a committee different from the one which passes on the authorization, grants the exact amount of money that the Executive branch can spend on it.

In this case I requested $3.865 billion, half a billion less than originally requested in the 1958 budget. In addition, I wanted a Development Loan Fund with a $500 million appropriation for 1958, to help less-developed free countries start on long-term economic growth.

At another point, talking to my old friend Sam Rayburn, who was telling me of the political risk run by any congressman supporting my recommendations, I asked, "Do you think the country is turning isolationist?"

"Yes," he replied.

I wanted his help in resisting cuts in the program. "I don't have much room in which to work," he replied.

Republican Congressman Alvin M. Bentley of Michigan, completely indifferent to any consideration of national good or party loyalty, proposed on the floor of the House additional cuts in a program that had already been slashed heavily in committee. I exploded. I told a staff assistant who brought me this information that I hoped the congressman would never seek political support from me. If he did so, the answer would be far from satisfactory to him.

Incidents of this kind occurred daily. The final authorization for fiscal 1958 was $3.3 billion—nearly a half billion dollars less than I had asked.

Now the drive to obtain appropriations began. It was in effect the same siege all over again.

The operation aways started in a subcommittee of the Appropriations Committee of the House, headed by Congressman Otto Passman of Louisiana.

Passman's subcommittee set appropriations below the authorization and the House agreed to the cut, allowing only $2.5 billion, some $1.3 billion below my request. In doing so, it rejected motions by several Republican congressmen—Walter Judd, John Taber, Richard Wigglesworth, and Edward J. Miller—to restore more than $700 million. I appreciated their loyalty and their readiness to fight for the good of the nation but the opposition was too strong.

To reinforce my arguments I pointed again and again, in meeting after meeting, phone call after phone call, to some of the problems then besetting various areas in which we had important interests and in which our aid could become vital in producing a satisfactory result.

The Defense Support Program, for example, which the House had already cut by nearly $300 million, covered fifteen countries. Five of them had highly important American bases: Ethiopia, Libya, Morocco, the Philippines, and Spain. Three others had military forces of significance and also American military facilities: Nationalist China on Taiwan, Turkey, and Greece. Five countries had forces totaling two million strong: Vietnam, Korea, Turkey, Taiwan, and Pakistan.

At that moment Syria was in a crisis. The leaders of Israel, Lebanon, Jordan, Turkey, and Iraq were fearful of the possibility of a Communist takeover in that country. Indeed, because of the possibility of conflict in the Middle East, I would shortly order a speedup in the shipment of military hardware to Iraq, Jordan, Saudi Arabia, Iran, Turkey, Ethiopia, Pakistan, and Lebanon. Here was an excellent example of the proper use and the exceptional value of mutual security money, and I urged Foster Dulles to use it to try winning support in Congress.

On August 21, I met with a number of staff members for a briefing. "What might you say," one asked, "about the accomplishments of the Congress so far in this session?"

"Nothing printable" was my reply—"disappointing" was the word I used in a news conference later that day.

By August 26, I was writing to Harold Macmillan:

> Although I have brought every possible personal influence to bear, the Congress, motivated by a belief that our people are getting weary of very high taxes and convinced that most of our citizens do not understand the aims and purposes of mutual security, has consistently refused to allow the amounts needed. I hope the situation can be partially corrected in the Senate, but in any event, we are going to be hard pushed this year to carry on all the activities which the Administration believes to be in the best interests of the free world . . .

At 5:10 that afternoon I met off-the-record with Senator Richard Russell of Georgia. Among other things, Russell questioned the value of Taiwan to the United States. I tried to explain what would happen if the Communists got it. After a long talk Russell agreed that, although he would have to vote against the mutual security appropriations, he would make no speeches against it.

I continued to urge the Congress to provide funds to build up military strength around Syria, and said that, if necessary, I would come down to the Congress for still more money in January. I told the Republican legislative leaders that if congressmen were going to ignore my earnest convictions in the security field and fail to support the modified mutual security bill, I would not be able to understand them should they ever request my help in the future.

The Senate voted to restore a portion of the cuts, but in the Senate-House conference, which Senator Knowland told me was the "nastiest" in which he had ever participated, the Senate conferees largely surrendered to the House, and reported out an appropriation that was smaller than my recommendation by more than a billion dollars.

* * *

On mutual security the Congress had written this record: In response to the administration's total request of 3.8 billion dollars, it had authorized 3.3 billion dollars and appropriated 2.7 billion.

There were similar actions which I deemed to be irresponsible: The Congress had, by adjournment day, chopped nearly five billion from the budget I had sent up in January. (The Bureau of the Budget at once announced that later supplemental appropriations would of necessity put much of this money back.) The biggest reductions were in defense: for the entire military budget, I had requested 36.1 billion dollars; the Congress appropriated 33.7 billion dollars. Few congressmen who voted for these cuts were anxious to recall them one month later when the first Russian Sputnik was launched.

At the close of the session, I received the traditional phone call from the Majority and Minority Leaders. "Mr. President," said Senator Johnson, "I'll bet you're just as happy to see us go as we are to go."

In fervent assent, I wished them all a speedy trip home.

As the congressional members scattered, I did not trust myself to make further comment. The 1957 session marked the low point in effective cooperation between the administration and the Congress.

CHAPTER VI

Civil Rights

The highest test of civilization of a race is its willingness to extend a helping hand to the less fortunate.

—*Booker T. Washington*

As the first session of the 85th Congress passed into history unmourned by me, it could, however, point to one real accomplishment: enactment of the first piece of civil rights legislation since 1875.

Since my boyhood I had accepted without qualification the right to equality before the law of all citizens of this country, whatever their race or color or creed. In World War II I had affirmed my belief in this principle through orders desegregating many Red Cross clubs, while, during some stages of the fighting, I had sent into previous all-white units Negro replacements who not only fought well but also encountered little or no resentment from their comrades.

In my first State of the Union message,[1] in 1953, I had affirmed my loyalty to this principle once again. I followed that affirmation by ordering in some cases and encouraging in others certain specific acts of desegregation within the federal government and within the nation's capital—a city which I hoped could become a showplace of peaceful civil rights progress. In that year segregation ended in the District of Columbia's hotels, restaurants, motion picture theaters, and Capital Housing Authority projects. The door to this accomplishment had been opened when the Attorney General, as one of the first acts of the administration, had successfully argued in court that the local anti-discrimination laws of the District of Columbia (the so-called "lost laws") were valid and in force. The District government ended discrimination by its contractors and in

[1] Quotations from this message are found in *Mandate for Change,* pp. 120–24, 235.

its own personnel practices. Segregation came to an end in schools on military posts, among civilian employees at naval bases, throughout the armed forces, and in Veterans Administration hospitals. I established a committee, with Vice President Nixon as chairman, to combat racial discrimination in employment in work performed under government contract.[2]

Late in 1952 I had asked Governor Adams to look for qualified Negroes to serve in the Executive branch. Among the outstanding people we brought into the government were E. Frederic Morrow, the first Negro ever to serve as an administrative officer on a President's personal staff; and Lois Lippman, who became the first Negro ever to work as a member of the secretarial staff in the White House office; J. Ernest Wilkins, Assistant Secretary of Labor, representing his department, became the first Negro in United States history ever to sit officially at the President's Cabinet table.

While in that first State of the Union message I had made clear my commitment to the cause of civil rights, I did not agree with those who believed that legislation alone could institute instant morality, who believed that coercion could cure all civil rights problems, and who were so eager to denounce discrimination that they habitually tacked anti-segregation amendments onto critically needed legislation, such as for school construction, and thus insured its death.

* * *

On May 17, 1954, the United States Supreme Court, in a unanimous opinion, made one of the most historic judgments of its existence. It reversed the 1896 Plessy *v.* Ferguson decision, which had put the Court's approval on "separate but equal" public educational facilities for children of the white and Negro races.

The 14th Amendment to the Constitution, the Court said in 1954, guarantees equal protection of the laws to all citizens. Can separate facilities, it asked, be in fact equal? It decided not: segregating children, the Court concluded, "generates a feeling of inferiority as to their status in the community that may affect their hearts and minds in a way unlikely ever to be undone. A sense of inferiority affects the motivation of a child to learn. Segregation . . . therefore, has a tendency to retard the educa-

[2] On August 14, 1953, I wrote to Governor James F. Byrnes of South Carolina on this subject—continuing a discussion we had had at a recent luncheon—in an effort to find a path through the thorny field of civil rights that nearly all sections of the country could agree on. [Text in Appendix I.]

tional and mental development of Negro children . . . separate educational facilities," the Court concluded, "are inherently unequal."

In a later ruling the Court decreed the pace and the method for compliance with its 1954 decision. It left principal responsibility with the local school authorities. Recognizing "varied local school problems," it called for a "prompt and reasonable start" and left to the federal district courts responsibility in any case brought before them for assuring children the right to enter unsegregated schools "with all deliberate speed."

The legal action leading to the basic decision had begun long before I took office. On June 8, 1953, the Supreme Court invited the Attorney General, although the United States was not a formal party to the school segregation cases, to appear at oral argument, and file a brief which would discuss five specific questions that had been left unanswered to the Court's satisfaction in early stages of the litigation. On August 19, 1953, I wrote a memorandum for the record inquiring about the propriety of the Attorney General's giving his opinion, when filing his brief in answer to the request of the Supreme Court, *for or against* the constitutionality of segregation in the public schools. Of course I acknowledged that he should give the Court full answers to the five specific questions posed by the Court. I was informed by the Attorney General that in his capacity as an officer of the Court it was his duty to be prepared to state his opinion, which settled the matter. The Court did ask his opinion at the oral argument and the response was that he believed segregation in the public schools was unconstitutional.

After the Supreme Court's 1954 ruling, I refused to say whether I either approved or disapproved of it. The Court's judgment was law, I said, and I would abide by it. This determination was one of principle. I believed that if I should express, publicly, either approval or disapproval of a Supreme Court decision in one case, I would be obliged to do so in many, if not all, cases. Inevitably I would eventually be drawn into a public statement of disagreement with some decision, creating a suspicion that my vigor of enforcement would, in such cases, be in doubt. Moreover, to indulge in a practice of approving or criticizing Court decisions could tend to lower the dignity of government, and would, in the long run, be hurtful. In this case I definitely agreed with the unanimous decision.

As soon as the decision was handed down, I called the District of Columbia Commissioners to my office and told them that the District should take the lead in desegregating its schools as an example to the entire country. By the opening of the fall term in September of that same year, the policy of nonsegregation had gone into effect in Washington, with no violence.

Again and again I urged restraint and forbearance. On March 14, 1956, a reporter asked me about a manifesto in which about a hundred Southern members of the Senate and the House had committed themselves to use every legal means to overturn the 1954 Supreme Court ruling. I answered by saying that:

> . . . the first thing about the manifesto is this: that they say they are going to use every *legal* means. No one in any responsible position anywhere has talked nullification; there would be a place where we [would] get into a very bad spot for the simple reason that I am sworn to defend and uphold the Constitution of the United States and, of course, I can never abandon or refuse to carry out my own duty.

I went on to point out that the decision of the Court clearly recognized the need for implementation through successive steps, since there were highly charged emotions to be considered on all sides of the question.

The Supreme Court decision of 1896 had upheld as legal the doctrine of "equal but separate" facilities for the races; that doctrine had thus helped form the customs and convictions of at least two generations of Americans. To expect a complete reversal in these habits and thinking in a matter of months was unrealistic; time, I said, would be needed, as well as a readiness of both sides to use good sense and forbearance.

The recent record of the South seemed to imply a steady though painfully slow improvement in some areas of race relations. For example, in 1953, before the Supreme Court decision, state-owned universities in twelve border and southern states had admitted Negroes. By 1956 in these states thirty-six state-financed colleges—previously all-white—had desegregated without violence. So had ten southern medical schools and thirty southern nursing schools. By early 1956 more than five hundred Negro men and women were studying in formerly all-white state-supported southern colleges and universities.[3]

Later in March of 1956 I wrote to the evangelist Dr. Billy Graham urging him to influence southern ministers to strive to calm rather than to inflame popular opinion—to stress the progress already made, even before the 1954 Court decision. And I added that "I shall always, as a

[3] In an effort to find a way to achieve a gradual school desegregation, I considered a scheme that would work down from the top grades. It would begin with graduate school where, with mature and relatively purposeful students, instantaneous, across-the-board integration on the basis of merit could be effected. Then, working down, one more grade per year, starting from the senior year of college, could be integrated. Perhaps when we reached the lower grades, the rate could be accelerated.

I admit that my scheme would be a slow one—in fact, probably too slow to fit the aspirations of many Negroes. But it would, I was convinced, effect real progress and would insure an orderly integration process.

matter of conviction and as a champion of real, as opposed to spurious, progress, remain a moderate in this regard."

Civil rights supporters, I told the legislative leaders on April 17, 1956, seemed never to consider that although the federal government had, in the past, used troops on a number of occasions to enforce the laws, troops could not force local officials to operate the schools; private schools could be set up, and Negroes, as well as many others, would get no education at all. These words proved grimly prophetic.

Nevertheless in early 1956, Director J. Edgar Hoover of the FBI had to report to me, in a Cabinet meeting, that racial tensions in the South were continuing to heighten. "Rock more boats and create more storms," a Memphis National Association for the Advancement of Colored People leader had said. "If it is necessary for us to stir up more tension and more unrest to win our fight, I am willing to do it."

The Communist Party of the United States, doing its best to twist this movement for its own purposes, was urging its members to infiltrate the NAACP (which had declared itself militantly anti-Communist), and had launched a program to drive a wedge between the administration and its friends in the South in that election year of 1956. If necessary, the Communist Party declared, the federal government should send troops into Mississippi to avenge the murder in 1955 of a fourteen-year-old Negro boy, Emmett Till.

In December of the preceding year, 1955, Negroes in Montgomery, Alabama, had begun a citywide boycott of buses to force an end to the city transit company's Jim Crow practices: people were shot, bombs were set off on the front porches and in the front yards of boycott leaders, and the Montgomery police had to convoy buses through the Negro sections of town to prevent bloodshed. These acts were indefensible and the administration, as well as all other sensible people, was outraged.

Throughout the South opponents of integration predicted that bloodshed would come anyway if the Negroes should push the whites too far. The segregationists dug in. "The Anglo-Saxon people," a leading southern senator told a screaming audience in Montgomery while the bus boycotts were still going on, "have held steadfast to the belief that resistance to tyranny is obedience to God." That resistance was, however, to be non-violent, the same senator urging "a just and legal fight to preserve the South's traditional way of life."

One instrument of that fight was a set of widely scattered organizations called Citizens Councils, said to have a total membership of 116,000 (a majority of whom lived in Mississippi). The purpose of the Councils—and there was no secret about it—was to put economic pressure on anybody, particularly on any Negro, who did anything to further desegregation. "We won't gin their cotton, we won't allow them credit, and we won't rent them houses," one Council leader proclaimed, "if they try to break down segregation." A Negro dentist and a Negro filling station operator stepped over the line; their credit was canceled. A Negro doctor joined the NAACP; his colored patients soon discovered that their white employers refused to pay the doctor's bills, as they had before. A group of Negroes signed a petition for school desegregation; they got fired from their jobs.

A second device for the maintenance of segregation was the use of intimidation to keep Negroes from registering and voting. The 1950 census reported 5.7 million non-white citizens in the South over the age of twenty-one, but two years before only 1.3 million, fewer than one in four, had registered to vote.

Faced with these allegations and facts—most of them brought to me by my Secretary to the Cabinet, Maxwell M. Rabb—I determined to seek an effective method for separating truth from falsehood in the whole troubled area. So, in my 1956 State of the Union message, I said that it was disturbing that in some localities there is evidence

> that Negro citizens are being deprived of their right to vote and are likewisc bcing subjected to unwarranted economic pressures. I recommend that the substance of these charges be thoroughly examined by a bipartisan commission created by the Congress.

In a press conference on March 14, I announced that I wanted a legally constituted commission because it would have the power to subpoena witnesses and compel them to testify. Director Hoover had told me that Negro witnesses to acts of violence in the South usually were fearful of talking to FBI agents. In Georgia, South Carolina, and Florida, the FBI was not permitted to interview a prisoner complaining of a civil rights violation without the presence of a prison official—in South Carolina, without the written permission of the governor himself. It was time, I thought, to establish such an investigative body.

After considerable discussion, in which the entire Cabinet participated, my civil rights recommendations went to the Congress. These were a four-point program, calling for a new bipartisan civil rights commission, a civil rights division under a new Assistant Attorney General in the Department of Justice, new laws to aid in enforcing voting rights, and amendments to existing laws to permit the federal government to seek in civil courts preventive relief in civil rights cases. At the time, these proposals were little less than revolutionary. Attorney General Brownell, in particular, was under no illusion as to the character of the opposition to be encountered, but he argued that to do less would not be in keeping with Republican tradition. I supported this conviction, but we were under no illusion as to the difficulties to be overcome. For more than eighty years no civil rights legislation had been passed by the Congress.

The opposition massed. On July 13, eighty-three southern representatives—four of them were Republicans—signed a manifesto against the administration bill, urging all members of the Senate and House "to join with us in the employment of every available legal and parliamentary weapon to defeat this sinister and iniquitous proposal."

Nonetheless, ten days later a bill including provisions for the Commission and Civil Rights Division passed the House 279 to 126. One hundred sixty-eight Republicans and 111 Democrats voted for it; twenty-four Republicans and 102 Democrats voted against it. And then it died: that same day it went on to the Senate Judiciary Committee, where it never again saw the light of day.

The administration had steered a difficult course between extremist firebrands and extremist diehards. This was due to conviction, not politics. But it is interesting that in the election of 1956, according to a *Congressional Quarterly,* I enlarged the sizable vote I had received four years earlier among Negroes of the North and throughout the South. In the South the Republican national ticket picked up Kentucky, West Virginia, and Louisiana, but lost Missouri. And in thirty-five congressional districts outside the South with a Negro population of 10 per cent or more, we increased the Republican vote from an average of 42 per cent in 1952 to 47 per cent in 1956.

The policy of steady progress without rashness was evidently winning support from people in the vital and massive American Center.

In the State of the Union message on January 10, 1957, I submitted to the Congress a succinct and uncomplicated civil rights request: enact the program proposed for 1956.

In conference after conference with the Republican legislative leaders, I urged them to do what they could to get action on this legislation in the House of Representatives before the Easter recess. House Minority Leader Martin reported that already Democrats were trying to delay action. Senator Knowland reported that opposition senators had told him that if the Republicans insisted on pushing ahead with the civil rights bill, they would have to pay for it by losing some other pieces of legislation they wanted. By June 18, however, the House passed the administration bill, 286 to 126; 118 Democrats and 168 Republicans voted for it; 107 Democrats and only 19 Republicans voted against it. The House Republicans therefore had gone on record for racial equality before the law by a ratio of nearly 9 to 1, the Democrats by a ratio of about 13 to 12.

From the House, the bill headed down the slope once again toward the Senate Judiciary Committee, presided over by Senator James O. Eastland of Mississippi. But this year there was a difference. On the Senate floor Senator Knowland objected to consigning the bill to the Judiciary Committee and certain death. Senator Russell of Georgia immediately rose and offered a point of order against the Knowland motion. The moment had arrived for the first crucial Senate vote of 1957 on civil rights.

The Senate rejected Russell's point of order and thus upheld Knowland by a vote of 45 to 39, 34 Republicans and only 11 Democrats favoring Knowland's position. Against them stood the 39, of whom 5 were Republican. It struck me as rather odd that the 34 Democrats should include a number who normally proclaimed themselves champions of "liberalism," and the "little people." Among them were Clinton Anderson, J. William Fulbright, Albert Gore, Lyndon B. Johnson, Estes Kefauver, John F. Kennedy, Robert Kerr, Mike Mansfield, and Wayne Morse.[4]

One is impelled to ask why these senators should have aligned themselves on the negative side of this key issue. One might speculate that they were devoted to the parliamentary process—that they stood firmly for the conservative notion that no piece of legislation should ever get out of its habitual legislative channels, that order and tradition must prevail at all costs, even if following the rules should result in a denial of the rights of American citizens. Such reasoning would seem somewhat stodgy and out of character for these men.

There is possibly another reason, suggested in a curious relationship between the voting on civil rights and one on power development the next day. This second vote involved one of the biggest, and in my opinion the most unjustified, federal reclamation projects of the twentieth century; the bill proposed more than one-half billion dollars for a monster Hell's Canyon Dam on the Snake River in Idaho, a dream of those who championed complete federal domination in electric power production. The Senate, that day, authorized the dam by vote of 45 ayes to 38 nays. The proponents of the dam included 40 Democrats.

And who were the Democrats?

Voting "aye" were not only champions of liberalism and devotees of an ever-expanding network of federal power projects. Just as in the

[4] On this vote they sided with Republicans Barry Goldwater, George Malone, Karl Mundt, John Williams, and Milton Young.

previous day's voting a number of liberals joined conservative southerners to oppose civil rights legislation, so now a number of well-known southern fiscal conservatives joined the liberal forces to put over a half-billion-dollar incursion into the federal treasury. Among them, for example, were Senators John Sparkman, John McClellan, George Smathers, Richard Russell, Herman Talmadge, Allen Ellender, Russell Long, Kerr Scott, Samuel Ervin, John Stennis, and James Eastland.

Of the inconsistencies in the voting pattern of these two succeeding days in June, no explanation was ever offered by the principals.

Anyway, the chips were down on civil rights. On July 2 Senator Russell, in a new maneuver, called for a national referendum on the civil rights bill, which he said was "cunningly designed to vest in the Attorney General unprecedented power." I publicly opposed the idea of a referendum, and on July 8 debate began on Knowland's motion to consider the House bill. In the following eight days the senators delivered sixty-six speeches.

Senator Dirksen reported to me on Senator Russell's sharp objections to Section III of the bill, which would empower the Attorney General to seek injunctions against violations of any civil right, voting or non-voting. This provision, Russell argued, would permit the Justice Department to use "the whole might of the federal government, including the Armed Forces if necessary, to force a co-mingling of white and Negro children" in the public schools of the South.

Senator Dirksen predicted—accurately, it turned out—that a great many liberals would once again come to the southerners' support for an amendment to assure anyone who was cited for contempt of court in a civil rights case the right to trial by jury. The basic purpose here would be to put into the hands of a local jury, who might be prejudiced, the determination of contempt of court. Attorney General Brownell argued, with my support, that this one amendment would in effect nullify the other provisions, however meritorious, of any new civil rights law.

The next day I had a long talk with Senator Russell. I assured him of my understanding of the enormity of the problems facing the South and of my anxiety to be helpful in solving them, but told him I could not yield in my purpose of protecting the citizen's right to vote. This was the overriding provision of the bill that I wanted set down in law; *with his right to vote assured, the American Negro could use it to help secure his other rights.*

Incidentally, a few southerners in the Congress, some of them my personal friends, privately told me that in the matter of voting rights they agreed on the justice of and the need for my stand. But this declaration would be accompanied by the statement, "officially and publicly, I must be, in my state, against every kind of proposal on civil rights of whatever nature."

On July 16 the Senate agreed to take up the House bill. Senator Russell announced that the southern forces were "prepared to expend the greatest effort ever made in history to prevent passage of this bill in its present form." That same day I issued a statement approving the purposes of the bill as it came from the House and urging the Senate, "in whatever clarification it may determine to make," to "keep the measure an effective piece of legislation to carry out these . . . objectives."

As the senators in interminable speeches expressed their opinions on civil rights legislation, I wrote a letter to Captain Hazlett:

> The plan of the Supreme Court to accomplish integration gradually and sensibly seems to me to provide the only possible answer if we are to consider on the one hand the customs and fears of a great section of our population, and on the other the binding effect that Supreme Court decisions must have on all of us if our form of government is to survive and prosper . . .
>
> . . . . I hold to the basic purpose. There must be respect for the Constitution—which means the Supreme Court's interpretation of the Constitution—or we shall have chaos. We cannot possibly imagine a successful form of government in which every individual citizen would have the right to interpret the Constitution according to his own convictions, beliefs and prejudices. Chaos would develop. This I believe with all my heart—and shall always act accordingly."

The next day, July 23, it became necessary to write to another friend, Governor Byrnes, expressing my feelings on what appeared to be another side of the issue:

> I note you expressed hope that I should show confidence in the people of the South. I am compelled to wonder why you have to express such a thought as nothing more than a *hope*. Many of my dearest friends are in that region. I spent a not inconsiderable part of my life in the South or in border states, and, moreover, this question of assuring the civil rights of all citizens does *not* apply exclusively to the southern areas.
>
> I do not feel that I need yield to anyone in my respect for the sentiments, convictions, and character of the average American, no matter where he may happen to dwell.

The following day the Senate by a vote of 52 to 38 amended Section III of the administration's bill. This amendment eliminated the authority of the

Attorney General to bring civil action against violators of civil rights other than voting rights.[5] This was a blow.

The Attorney General was bitterly disappointed over this development. When the bill was initially written he was aware of doubts on my part as to the constitutionality of this particular provision, but he soon convinced me; thereafter I favored its enactment into law and on July 16th, 1957, I released a statement calling upon the Senate, in addition to protecting voting rights, to enact ". . . a reasonable program of assistance in efforts to protect other . . . constitutional rights of our citizens." Now, however, we were warned by our own legislative leaders that if we tried to restore all the provisions of Section III there would be no legislation whatsoever. So convincing was their testimony on this point that, in hope of securing the remainder of the bill, I agreed to push no farther during the current session for the original text. The situation was tense but I was determined, above all else, to do all I could to assure the right of Negroes to vote on the same basis as all others, and to protect them in doing so. For this purpose I was prepared to call, if necessary, a special session of the Congress.

Then the coalition move began to weaken the bill further with a jury trial amendment, sponsored by three liberal Democrats—Joseph O'Mahoney of Wyoming, Estes Kefauver of Tennessee, and Frank Church of Idaho. At a news conference on July 31, I emphasized my opposition to this amendment, citing thirty-six different laws in which contempt cases require no jury trial.

A vote for the jury trial amendment, Knowland said on the Senate floor the next day (August 1), "will be a vote to kill for this session . . . an effective voting rights bill." He appealed to Republicans to stand with the administration.

But Lyndon Johnson declared that "by adopting this amendment, we can strengthen and preserve . . . the right to a trial by jury." "The people," he declared, "will never accept a concept that a man can be publicly branded as a criminal without a jury trial."

Late at night on August 2 the vote came: the Senate accepted the amendment. The vote was close, 51 to 42; 33 Republicans and 9 Democrats voted to kill the amendment; 12 Republicans and 39 Democrats[6]

[5] Thirty-four Democrats, led by Senator Johnson, and 18 Republicans voted for this Aiken-Anderson amendment; 25 Republicans, led by Senator Knowland, and 13 Democrats voted against it.

[6] Those 39 included Anderson, Church, Fulbright, Gore, Johnson, Kefauver, Kennedy, Kerr, Mansfield, McClellan, Murray, and Yarborough. The 12 Republicans were Butler, Capehart, Case (S.D.), Curtis, Goldwater, Malone, Mundt, Revercomb, Schoeppel, Smith (Me.), Williams, and Young.

voted to keep it. These men had gone on record for a law which guaranteed a jury trial to anyone accused of criminal contempt in an injunction suit brought by the United States. The jury trial amendment covered criminal contempts committed not only under the civil rights bill but under the entire body of federal law. It therefore affected the courts' power to enforce effectively a whole group of statutes, including the Sherman Act, the Clayton Act, the Securities Act of 1933, the Interstate Commerce Act, the Natural Gas Act, the Federal Power Act, and the orders of the National Labor Relations Board. In thus interposing a jury trial between a federal judge and his legal orders, the bill not only failed to protect the citizen's right to vote, it threatened to weaken our whole judicial system. Deputy Attorney General William P. Rogers called the bill as it now stood "a monstrosity—the most irresponsible I have seen in Washington." The next morning a statement went out which left no doubt about my disappointment.

But on August 7 the Senate passed the bill, with its deletions and amendment, 72 to 18.

As the bill now stood, Bill Rogers said, it gave the policemen a gun with no bullets. It contained these provisions:

(1) The Civil Rights Commission, as requested.

(2) The new assistant secretary, to head a Civil Rights Division in the Department of Justice, as requested.

(3) A provision making unlawful the use of threats, intimidation, or coercion to prevent the exercise of the right to vote in federal elections, and giving the Attorney General the power to bring injunction proceedings to combat such threats.

(4) A "window-dressing" provision purporting to give Negroes a right they already had—the right to serve on federal juries. (Section 1863 of Title 28, U. S. Code, already provided that no citizen should be excluded from jury service in any federal court of the United States because of race or color.)

(5) The jury-trial provision. Among other defects, this provision would hamstring the Civil Rights Commission by necessitating a jury trial for any violation of a District Court order enforcing the Commission's power to subpoena.

I wrote of my disappointment to a southern friend Robert M. Woodruff in Atlanta:

> The week has been a depressing one. I think the country took an awful beating in the second defeat that the civil rights bill took in the Senate. . . . The distorted pictures that were presented concerning jury trials in actions rising out of injunctions to prevent interference with

voting right—particularly distortions by some of the so-called liberals—were such as to confuse both the people and some members of the Congress. Add to this a lot of political log rolling, and it is no wonder that confusion and misunderstanding resulted.

Wires and letters poured into the White House urging me not to sign a "phony" civil rights bill. Ralph Bunche wrote: "It would be better to have no bill than one as emasculated as that which has come out of the Senate. The President's fine and forthright stand on the issue, however, is both encouraging and heartwarming." From Jackie Robinson: "Am opposed to civil rights bill in its present form. Have been in touch with a number of my friends. We disagree that half loaf better than none. Have waited this long for bill with meaning—can wait a little longer." From the Reverend W. H. Jernagin, Chairman, Executive Board of the National Fraternal Council: "National Fraternal Council of Churches of 14 denominations and ten million members in its annual session endorsed your Civil Rights Bill. Ninety per cent of colored Americans favor the bill passed by the House. Personally I would rather have no bill passed at this Congress than the one passed by the Senate." From A. Philip Randolph, President of the Brotherhood of Sleeping Car Porters: "In the name of the officials and members of the Brotherhood of Sleeping Car Porters, urge veto of Civil Rights Bill. It is worse than no bill at all." Many more messages were in the same vein.

For the moment the only possible action for the administration was to get out of the ensuing Senate-House Conference as much of the House bill as possible. Together with Jerry Morgan, my congressional liaison staff—Jerry Persons, Bryce Harlow, Jack Martin, Ed McCabe, Jack Anderson, Earle Chesney, Homer Gruenther—phoned and visited, pleaded and persuaded, night and day with key members of the Congress.

After the Senate action, the House refused on August 13 to send the bill to the Conference Committee and to concur in the Senate amendments. The result was that the bill went for further action, if any, to the House Rules Committee, under the chairmanship of Judge Howard Smith of Virginia, who was content to keep it there.

In the face of such repeated obstructionism, I thought it ironic that the Democrats were attempting to make it appear that any civil rights legislation that might be enacted would be theirs, and that any Republican who did not go along would appear to be a Horatius standing at the bridge in a fight to the death to block it.

On the Republican side, work began on a new proposal affecting jury trial in criminal contempt cases. It included the provision that the judge had the right to decide whether the defendant should receive a jury trial in a criminal contempt action resulting from an infringement of the right to vote. If there were no jury trial, the maximum penalty could total no more than ninety days and three hundred dollars; if there were a jury trial, the maximum penalty could total no more than six months and one thousand dollars.

On August 22 Sam Rayburn said the Democrats were willing to talk it over.

Knowland, Johnson, Rayburn, and Martin carried on extended negotiations. Late on the afternoon of August 23 my telephone rang. Lyndon Johnson was on the line: "I can get Ervin and the others to agree to a compromise of three hundred dollars and forty-five days." He then asked me whether the administration would accept this.

After a quick call to Knowland and Martin, I told Senator Johnson that the compromise was acceptable. I was quick to compliment him on his successful negotiation of this compromise.

From this moment, events moved swiftly. Senator Russell understandably announced that he and his southern associates were "unalterably opposed" to the compromise. This was anticipated and discounted. Now, with the support of Johnson and Rayburn, the House approved the compromise bill 279 to 97.

On the Senate side the next day, Strom Thurmond of South Carolina made a one-man stand against the bill, speaking twenty-four hours and eighteen minutes in an effort to get his views across. By twelve minutes past nine on the evening of August 29, he had broken an old record set in April 1953, when for twenty-two hours and twenty-six minutes a senator had held the floor. Thurmond collapsed. The Senate adopted the compromise, 60 to 15. I signed it into law on September 9.

As passed, the Civil Rights Act of 1957: (1) created, with a two-year life, the six-member Civil Rights Commission; (2) set up a Civil Rights Division in the Justice Department; (3) extended the jurisdiction of the district courts to include any civil action begun to secure relief under any act of Congress providing for the protection of civil rights, including the right to vote; (4) empowered the Attorney General to seek an injunction when an individual had been deprived of the right to vote; and (5) included the jury trial compromise to which the Republican and Democratic leaders had agreed.

Within two months I had appointed the members of the Civil Rights Commission, headed by former Supreme Court Justice Stanley F. Reed, and including John A. Hannah, President of Michigan State University; John S. Battle, former Governor of Virginia; the Reverend Theodore M. Hesburgh, President of Notre Dame; Robert G. Storey, Dean of Southern Methodist University Law School; and J. Ernest Wilkins, Assistant Secretary of Labor.

The new Civil Rights Division in the Department of Justice would, in the ensuing years of my administration, bring into court more than one hundred cases and investigate more than four thousand complaints of civil rights violation.[7] Many cases were settled by the mere fact of investigation. Thus the United States had its first Civil Rights Act in eighty-two years.

* * *

But there was little time for rejoicing or relaxation. Four days after the Senate approved the compromise, the Governor of Arkansas, Orval Faubus, called out units of the Arkansas National Guard and ordered them to take up positions outside Central High School in Little Rock to "preserve peace and good order" and, incidentally, to keep Negro students from passing through the doors to take their seats on their first day of school in classrooms formerly all white.

This outrageous action called to my mind the first act of the Rodgers and Hammerstein musical *South Pacific* in which the hero, a Frenchman, mistakenly calls the heroine's American hometown "Small Rock." Before September 1957, that line was meaningless to foreign audiences. Thereafter, no one anywhere would miss the point: the name of Little Rock, Arkansas, would become known around the world. But the world's disapproval should not have been for a city, only for a man and a handful of its population.

In Little Rock that fall, integration was to begin in the high schools, which then had 2740 white students and 811 Negroes. Public high school integration was to begin with just nine Negro boys and girls who were planning to walk through the doors of Central High School on the morning of September 3.[8]

[7] On May 6, 1960, I signed into law Public Law 86-449—the Civil Rights Act of 1960, an administration measure which, by authorizing federal judges to appoint referees to help Negroes register and vote and by setting new criminal penalties against bombings and violence used to obstruct a federal court's order, strengthened the provisions of the 1957 law.

[8] When schools opened in the fall of 1957, the Southern Educational Reporting Service announced that 350,000 Negro children in the South were attending classes in "integrated situations"—50,000 more than in the fall of 1956. Two million white children were also in school "under integrated conditions." These students went to school in 751 school districts—67 more than had desegregated by the fall of 1956.

In Washington, D.C., 75,000 Negro children were going to class that fall with white children; 32,000 Negroes were in integrated classes in St. Louis, and 12,000 in Louisville.

Seven million white students and nearly 2½ million Negroes, however, in more

In accordance with the Supreme Court's direction, the school board of the Little Rock school district had announced in 1955 a plan for a gradual transition to a system of racially desegregated schools. The senior high schools were to integrate by the fall of 1957, the junior high schools by 1959 or 1960, the elementary schools by 1962 and 1963. On August 28, 1956, the United States District Court, Eastern District of Arkansas, handed down its decision that this desegregation plan was, in the circumstances, adequate; the court denied the contention of certain litigants who complained that the process would take too long. On April 26, 1957, the Court of Appeals for the Eighth Judicial Circuit upheld this judgment.

As the desegregation day approached, however, opponents tried another tactic. A group of white mothers filed a petition in the Arkansas State Chancery Court to keep the plan from taking effect. On August 29, Governor Orval Faubus appeared before that court to express his concern that desegregation in Little Rock might lead to violence. Later that day the court entered a restraining order to keep the desegregation plan from going into effect.

The next day, however, *on the petition of the Little Rock school board,* the United States District Court issued an order to prevent anyone's interfering "with the opening of the integrated high school in the Little Rock School District on September 3."

The judge who had delivered this ruling was Ronald N. Davies of Fargo, North Dakota, who had been assigned in regular course by his superiors in the federal court system to sit temporarily in the Arkansas district where the case arose.

This was the situation when Governor Faubus ordered the Arkansas National Guard to stop Negro children from entering the high school. Arkansas State Police units were mobilized to act "as an arm" of the state militia. The mission of the Guard, Faubus said, "was to maintain or restore the peace and good order of this community"; the mission of the state militia was "to maintain or restore order and to protect the lives and property of citizens." The state militia, Faubus contended, "will not act as segregationists or integrationists, but as soldiers called to active

---

than 2200 school districts throughout the South, still went to classes separately. Moreover, the statistics on "integrated situations" reflected often only token, not total, integration. In Nashville, for example, 1920 white children and 1300 Negroes in the first grade were all considered "integrated"; but the fact was that only 13 Negroes actually went to classes in formerly all-white schools.

duty to carry out their assigned tasks." But *"it will not be possible,"* he continued, to maintain order *"if forcible integration is carried out tomorrow . . . therefore . . . the schools in Pulaski County, for the time being, must be operated on the same basis as they have been operated through the past."*

The Little Rock school board, seeing the Governor's statement and the stationing of the troops, asked that "no Negro students attempt to enter Central or any white high school until this dilemma is legally resolved."

The next morning, however, several Negro students approached Central High. Guardsmen turned them back. "You are directed to place off-limits to colored students those schools heretofore operated and recently set up for white students," Faubus had ordered.

This directly and flagrantly defied the order of the federal court.

The school board filed a petition with the district court citing these events and asking the court to exempt them from a charge of contempt and to "instruct them as to whether they should recall the request" that no Negro student should try to enter a white high school.

After listening to evidence on both sides, Judge Davies decided that it revealed no reason for discarding the original plan of integration approved by the district court. He ordered the school board to integrate the schools forthwith.

I asked Attorney General Brownell's opinion on whether the United States courts had the power to review the action of the Governor in preventing the execution of the orders of the federal court by the use of military force. He said that federal courts could rule on the legality of the action of a state governor which contravenes a federal court order, even though the Governor seeks to justify his action by claiming it is necessary to keep the peace. The Governor of Arkansas, the Attorney General said, had made no effort to uphold the jurisdiction of the federal court. "The propriety of his action should be judicially determined" by the district court.

Accordingly, the federal court the next day began its inquiry. In doing so, it requested the assistance of the local United States Attorney, who in turn called in the FBI. Faubus immediately wired to me saying that he was being investigated by federal authorities; that his telephone wires were being tapped; that he had heard of plans to take him "into custody by force." I replied to Faubus saying that both the charges of a plot to take him into custody and of wire-tapping had "no basis of fact."

In response to his request for my assurance of understanding and cooperation, I said, "The only assurance I can give you is that the Federal

Constitution will be upheld by me by every legal means at my command."

In the succeeding days the Little Rock school board, apparently growing fearful of an impending crisis, asked Judge Davies to set aside his order for immediate integration. The Judge refused.

On September 9 the district court asked the United States to enter the case as an *amicus curiae*[9] and to file a petition for an injunction against the Arkansas Governor. The court set September 20 as the date for its hearing on the legality of his action.

The United States government and the Governor of Arkansas were now heading toward a collision. Seeing this coming, the Democratic congressman who represented the Little Rock district, Brooks Hays, telephoned his friend Sherman Adams and made a courageous offer (which, in the 1958 election, was to cost him his position in the Congress); he would, if the President wanted, serve as an intermediary between the President and the Governor.

"The President might agree to such an arrangement," Adams said, "but Faubus will first have to declare his willingness to comply with the Constitution, Federal law, and the 1954 decision of the Supreme Court."

After the fights over the rights bill and budget, I had gone to Newport, Rhode Island, for a rest. On September 11 Governor Adams telephoned from Washington. He described the talks that Brooks Hays had been having with Governor Faubus. The Governor, Hays reported, would like to find a way out of the situation—would like to ask for a meeting with me.

I said that if Governor Faubus wanted to have an honest discussion, I would see him.

Brooks Hays had told Adams that Faubus was not essentially a segregationist—that his son attended an integrated college. He also said that Faubus believed that the beginning of integration should be made in the first grades, as in some other areas.

I then called the Attorney General saying that while the federal government should not usurp the responsibility of a state for the preservation of law and order, under the law we could not tolerate defiance of the proper orders of a federal court.

Brownell agreed but doubted the value of a meeting with Faubus.

Brooks Hays had, at my insistence, persuaded Faubus to agree that in wording his wire requesting a meeting he would say, "It is certainly my intention to comply with the order . . . by the District Court." But

[9] "Friend of the Court," a person who states some matter of law for the court's assistance.

when the wire arrived, it read, "It is certainly my desire to comply with the order . . . *consistent with my responsibilities under the Constitution of the United States and that of Arkansas.*" This significant change made by Faubus supported the Attorney General's skepticism that any good could come out of a meeting with him.

On the morning of Saturday, September 14, Faubus arrived at Newport. He talked alone with me for about twenty minutes. Then he and I were joined by Brownell, Gerald D. Morgan, my special counsel, Governor Adams, and Brooks Hays for a further discussion.

Again and again Governor Faubus said that he was a loyal citizen; that he recognized the supremacy of federal law and courts; that he was going to make this attitude clear to the public.

"I believe," I told him, "that when you go home, you should not necessarily withdraw the National Guard troops. Just change their orders to say that since you have been assured that the federal government is not trying to do anything that has not been already agreed to by the school board and directed by the courts, the Guard should continue to preserve order but allow the Negro children to attend Central High School." He was due to appear the following Friday, the 20th, before the Court to determine whether an injunction was to be issued.

"In any event," I said, "you should take this action promptly. Then the Justice Department can go to the court and ask that you not be brought into court."

Finally I told him that I did not believe it was beneficial to anybody to have a trial of strength between the President and a governor.

"In any area where the federal government has assumed jurisdiction and this is upheld by the Supreme Court," I said, "there can be only one outcome: the state will lose. I don't want to see any governor humiliated."

He seemed to be very appreciative of this attitude. I definitely got the understanding that, upon returning to Arkansas, he would within a matter of hours revoke his orders to the Guard to prevent re-entry of the Negro children into the school.

After the meeting, Faubus and Hays went to Providence. At Newport, Brownell, Adams, and Hagerty worked over the draft of a statement for me to issue. Within a short time, Brooks Hays telephoned us from that point. He said that Faubus was refusing to make the clear commitment he had promised. After a long discussion on wording, Adams and Hays (with Faubus in the background answering questions) finally agreed on this exact wording:

> I have assured the President of my desire to cooperate with him in carrying out the duties resting upon both of us under the Federal Constitution. In addition, I must harmonize my actions under the Constitution of Arkansas with the requirements of the Constitution of the United States.

That day a reporter in Providence asked Faubus: "Will the National Guard troops still be on duty at Central High Monday morning?"

"That problem," Faubus answered, "I will have to take care of when I return to Little Rock."

The troops stayed at Central High all the following week.

Congressman Hays continued to confer with Faubus. On September 18, after the seventh meeting in three days, Hays said that "the situation was not getting any worse or any better."

The next day, Faubus's attorney filed an affidavit in the federal court asking Judge Davies to disqualify himself because of "prejudice." The next morning Judge Davies refused. When he thus denied their motions, Faubus's lawyers walked out of the hearing. Judge Davies announced that the hearing would go on without them.

The witnesses of the Department of Justice then proceeded to testify. The Mayor of Little Rock, its Chief of Police, and the authorities of the local school board described the peaceful race relations in the city over the past quarter century. They recounted the end of Jim Crow seating on city buses in January of that very year, without violence. They told of the absence of any sign of evidence that desegregation would produce disorder. And the Mayor and the Chief of Police told the court that Faubus had asked for no police report on the possibility of danger before he moved in the Guard; in their view, the local police could keep the peace.

When the witnesses had finished, Judge Davies declared: "It is very clear to this court . . . that the plan of integration adopted by the Little Rock school board and approved by this court and the Court of Appeals for the Eighth Circuit has been thwarted by the Governor of Arkansas . . .

"It is equally demonstrable from the testimony here today that there would have been no violence in carrying out the plan of integration and that there has been no violence."

Thereupon the court handed down an injunction against further interference with the orders of the court by Faubus and the Commander of the National Guard.

In a broadcast that night Faubus announced that he would comply with the injunction and order the removal of the Guard. He said, however, that he would appeal the court's ruling and that he would ask Negro parents to keep their children away from the high school during a "cooling-off period."

The next day Faubus left Little Rock for Sea Island, Georgia, for a meeting with members of the Conference of Southern Governors. I called Faubus's withdrawal of the Guard a "necessary step in the right direction," and expressed confidence that the citizens of Little Rock would "vigorously oppose any violence by extremists and welcome the opportunity to demonstrate that in their city and in their state proper orders of the United States court will be executed promptly and without disorder."

Little Rock Mayor Woodrow Wilson Mann announced that the local police would keep order at the school when it opened the following week.

In succeeding days the administration was not free of partisan criticism. One Governor, G. Mennen Williams, of Michigan, cried, "Seldom has the nation seen a comparable spectacle of hesitation and confusion." Governor Williams apparently wanted to invade Arkansas at once.

Overseas, the mouthpieces of Soviet propaganda in Russia and Europe were blaring out that "anti-Negro violence" in Little Rock was being "committed with the clear connivance of the United States government . . ."

The morning of Monday, September 23, arrived. From all over the city, a mob of more than a thousand angry and determined whites, stirred up by recent events and Governor Faubus, converged on Central High School, determined to keep out the Negro students who were due to enter. Eight Negro children arrived, however, and somehow slipped in unseen through a side door. For three hours the mob rioted outside. They brushed aside the local police. Then, on an order from Mayor Mann, the police removed the Negro children from the school.

The issue had now become clear both in fact and in law.

Cruel mob force had frustrated the execution of an order of a United States court, and the Governor of the state was sitting by, refusing to lift a finger to support the local authorities. Under the law, the Attorney General advised me, the Governor had a "mandatory duty" to suppress violence and "remove any obstruction to the orderly enforcement of law."

"This Constitution," Article VI reads, "and the laws of the United States which shall be made in pursuance thereof . . . shall be the supreme law of the land . . . all executive . . . officers . . . of the . . . States, shall be bound by oath or affirmation to support this Constitution . . ."

This particular governor, however, saw in the mobs not his duty but rather his vindication for having called out the National Guard in the first place. But here again he was on the wrong side of the law: "A state government," a Minnesota district court decision of 1936 read, "cannot suppress disorder the object of which is to deprive citizens of their lawful rights, by using its forces to assist in carrying out the unlawful purposes of those who create the disorders . . . the use of troops or police for such purposes would . . . constitute an assurance to those who resort to violence . . . that, if they gathered in sufficient numbers to constitute a menace to life, the forces of law would . . . actually assist them in accomplishing their objective." The result would be anarchy.

There was only one justification for the use of troops: to uphold the law. Though Faubus denied it, I, as President of the United States, now had that justification[10] and the clear obligation to act.

On that same day, September 23, I issued the required proclamation (Number 3024) and with it the following statement.

> I want to make several things very clear in connection with the disgraceful occurrences of today at Central High School in the City of Little Rock. They are:
>
> (1) The Federal law and orders of a United States District Court implementing that law cannot be flouted with impunity by any individual or any mob of extremists.
>
> (2) I will use the full power of the United States including whatever force may be necessary to prevent any obstruction of the law and to carry out the orders of the Federal Court.
>
> (3) Of course, every right-thinking citizen will hope that the American sense of justice and fair play will prevail in this case. It will be a sad day for this country—both at home and abroad—if school children can safely attend their classes only under the protection of armed guards.
>
> (4) I repeat my expressed confidence that the citizens of Little Rock and of Arkansas will respect the law and will not countenance violations of law and order by extremists.

[10] It rested on the Constitution and on federal laws going back to 1792, when George Washington signed a bill authorizing the use of the state militia to curb "combinations too powerful to be suppressed by the ordinary course of judicial proceedings," and 1807, when the Congress gave the President the power to use federal troops for the same purpose. "If the emergency arises," the Supreme Court had ruled in 1894, "the army of the nation and all its militia are at the service of the nation to compel obedience to its laws."

Specifically, the law says that if unlawful obstructions ". . . make it impracticable to enforce laws of the United States in any state by the ordinary course of judicial proceedings, the President has the authority to use the state militia and the armed forces of the United States to put down the insurrection." Under another section of the United States Code, the President can suppress any insurrection, domestic violence, or conspiracy which (a) so hinders the execution of the laws that people are deprived of their lawful rights and state authorities "are unable, fail, or refuse to protect" those rights; or (b) obstructs the execution of United States laws or impedes the course of justice under those laws. Still another section requires the President to issue a proclamation before invoking the authority of either of these preceding sections.

The next morning, Tuesday, September 24, the mob choked the streets again.

A frantic wire arrived from Mayor Mann, who had been in close touch by telephone with Max Rabb in the White House:

> The immediate need for federal troops is urgent. The mob is much larger in numbers at 8 A.M. than at any time yesterday. People are converging on the scene from all directions and engaging in fisticuffs and other acts of violence. Situation is out of control and police cannot disperse the mob . . . :

Even before the Mayor's telegram arrived, of course, the question had become not whether to act, but what force I should use to insure execution of the court's order, on the assumption that the situation would not improve markedly. The local United States Marshal could not enforce the court order, and in the circumstances could not enlist citizens to help him. Brownell and I discussed several possibilities. We rejected suggestions that I use the FBI to keep the peace. General Maxwell D. Taylor, Army Chief of Staff wanted to try the Arkansas National Guard before ordering out federal troops. If this were done, I said, the Guardsmen should come from other parts of Arkansas, not Little Rock, to prevent sending brother against brother.

This conversation took place shortly before Mayor Mann's wire arrived. After reflecting on the kind of troops to use, I decided to dispatch regular federal troops. Shortly after twelve noon, I telephoned the Attorney General that I was about to sign an Executive Order (10730) which would federalize the Arkansas National Guard and send regular federal troops into Little Rock. At 12:15 I called General Taylor and gave him this decision.

Taylor acted promptly.

That afternoon five hundred paratroopers of the 101st Airborne Division, from nearby Fort Campbell, Kentucky, arrived in Little Rock; another five hundred moved in later the same day.

* * *

"I can't imagine any set of circumstances that would ever induce me to send Federal troops . . . into any area to enforce the orders of a federal court," I had told a July news conference, but in just two months that set of circumstances had arrived.

Thirteen of my predecessors in office, beginning with President Washington, had used troops to put down domestic civil disorders. Over the objection of the Governor of Illinois, Grover Cleveland in 1894 sent federal troops and National Guardsmen into Chicago to uphold a federal district court injunction against Pullman Company strikers. And sixteen years earlier President Rutherford B. Hayes had written a penetrating analysis:

> Without passion or haste, the enforcement of the laws must go on. If the sheriffs or other state officers resist the laws, and by the aid of state militia do it successfully, that is a case of rebellion to be dealt with under the laws framed to enable the Executive to subdue combinations or conspiracies too powerful to be suppressed by the ordinary civil officers of the United States. This involves proclamations, the movement of United States land and naval forces, and possibly the calling out of volunteers. . . . Good citizens who wish to avoid such a result must see to it that neither their State Governments nor mobs undertake to prevent United States officers from enforcing the laws. My duty is plain. The laws must be enforced.

Over many decades citizens of this country have suffered intolerable acts of injustice in every state of the union. But however serious the injustice and the provocation, the federal government under our system can intervene only to correct particular wrongs specified by law. The Little Rock situation—rebellion, the breaking of a federal law, and the flouting of federal court orders by some who were sworn to uphold the law—was obviously in the authorized category. That situation, if a successful defiance of federal court orders continued, could lead to a breakdown of law and order in a widening area. And around the world it could continue to feed the mill of Soviet propagandists who by word and picture were telling the world of the "racial terror" in the United States.

Despite these facts, my action caused, as expected, loud protests, mostly politically inspired, throughout the south. Governor Faubus, returning from Sea Island to Little Rock, was perhaps the most restrained: "I believe he showed bad judgment." Senator Lyndon Johnson contributed: "There should be no troops from either side patrolling our school campuses." Senator Eastland was perhaps the most doom-laden: "The President's move," he said, "was an attempt to destroy the social order of the South"; and Senator Olin Johnston's was surely the bravest: "If I were a governor and he came in, I'd give him a fight such as he's never been in before."

That morning in Newport, I had written to General Gruenther:

> . . . I do not want (by rushing back to Washington) to exaggerate the significance of the admittedly serious situation in Arkansas. I do not want to give a picture of a Cabinet in constant session, of fretting and worrying about the actions of a misguided governor who, in my opinion, has been motivated entirely by what he believes to be political advantage in a particular locality.

> The Federal government has ample resources with which to cope with this kind of thing. The great need is to act calmly, deliberately, and giving every offender opportunity to cease his defiance of Federal Law and to peaceably obey the proper orders of the Federal court. In this way the actions of the Executive in enforcing the law—even if it becomes necessary to employ considerable force—are understood by all, and the individuals who have offended are not falsely transformed into martyrs.
>
> On the other hand, for a number of reasons I wish I were back there. My work would be a lot easier to do.

Later in the day, however, I decided to return to Washington, mainly because I wanted to give the people a radio-television report, and doing so from Newport was difficult. That evening I spoke to the nation:

> . . . To make this talk I have come to the President's office in the White House. I could have spoken from Rhode Island, where I have been staying recently, but I felt that, in speaking from the house of Lincoln, of Jackson and of Wilson, my words would better convey both the sadness I feel in the action I was compelled today to take and the firmness with which I intend to pursue this course until the orders of the federal court at Little Rock can be executed without unlawful interference. . . .

The very basis of our individual rights rest, I said, on the certainty that the President and the Executive branch ensure that the decisions of federal courts are carried out with all the means at the President's command.

> Unless the President did so, anarchy would result. . . .
>
> Mob rule cannot be allowed to override the decisions of our courts.
>
> Now, let me make it very clear that federal troops are not being used to relieve local and state authorities of their primary duty to preserve the peace and order of the community.

The troops were not there to take over the responsibility of the School Board and "other responsible local officials" in running Central High School. The running of schools and keeping the peace were strictly local affairs, I emphasized; the government does not interfere except when requested by one of the states. These troops were there to see to it that the court's orders suffered no interference.

> . . . with deep confidence, I call upon the citizens of the State of Arkansas to assist in bringing to an immediate end all interference with the law and its processes. If resistance to the federal court orders ceases at once, the further presence of federal troops will be unnecessary and the City of Little Rock will return to its normal habits of peace and order and a blot upon the fair name and high honor of our nation in the world will be removed.

By the next morning violence had ended. Two men tried to keep the troops from dispersing spectators around Central High School; one was clubbed, and another was struck in the arm by the point of a bayonet. (Neither was more than superficially injured.) But nine Negro students entered the high school doors, and, under Army guard, sat through a full day of classes.

At Sea Island the Southern Governors Conference adopted a resolution proposing that a committee, with Governor Luther Hodges of North Carolina as chairman, meet with me to seek withdrawal of the troops. I said to my associates that while I should like to confer with such a committee in the hope of preventing recurrences of the Little Rock incident, my own responsibilities under the Constitution were not subject to negotiation.

The same day the Attorney General reported that Bishop Robert R. Brown of Little Rock, the Episcopal Bishop of Arkansas, had telephoned to say that the church leaders of Little Rock supported my action, and offered to do anything they could to help. Accordingly, I wrote Bishop Brown of my gratitude.

On September 26 I received a telegram from Senator Russell of Georgia protesting the "highhanded and illegal methods" used by the armed forces "carrying out your orders to mix the races" in the public schools of Little Rock. On a sheet of White House stationery I composed a reply, which bluntly defended my decision:

> . . . the obligations of my office required me to order the use of force within a state to carry out the decisions of a federal court. . . . The Arkansas National Guard could have handled the situation with ease had it been instructed to do so. As a matter of fact, had the integration of Central High School been permitted to take place without the intervention of the National Guard, there is little doubt that the process would have gone along quite as smoothly and quietly as it has in other Arkansas communities. . . .
>
> I must say that I completely fail to comprehend your comparison of our troops to Hitler's storm troopers. In one case military power was used to further the ambitions and purposes of a ruthless dictator; in the other to preserve the institutions of free government.

The afternoon of October 1, I met in the White House with the committee from the Southern Governors Conference: Governors Luther Hodges of North Carolina, Frank G. Clement of Tennessee, Leroy Collins of Florida, and Theodore R. McKeldin of Maryland.

If these governors could persuade Faubus to do so, I told them, I was ready to join in issuing a statement that Faubus had promised to assume full responsibility for law and order in Little Rock and promised to help carry out the order of the court, and that therefore I would direct the withdrawal of the troops and the defederalization of the National Guard.

The governors then adjourned to the conference room. From there Governor Clement telephoned Faubus and as strongly as he could tried to impress upon him the necessity of the Negro children's getting an equal chance at a good education. Finally, Faubus agreed: "The orders of the federal court," he said he would announce, "will not be obstructed."

His wire arrived. But, as before, he equivocated in his wording: "I now declare," the wire said, "that upon withdrawal of federal troops I will again assume full responsibility, in cooperation with local authorities, for the maintenance of law and order, and the orders of the federal court will not be obstructed by me."

This wire was worthless: the word "again" gave Faubus an escape route to his earlier means of "keeping the peace," namely, stationing the National Guard around the school to keep the Negroes out; the words "by me" suggested that he might willingly let others do the obstructing.

That evening, when my wife and I came back to the Mansion from the home of Secretary Dulles, I issued a statement on my refusal to remove the troops. The statement of the Governor of Arkansas, I said, did not constitute the assurance that he intended to use his full powers as Governor to prevent the obstruction of the orders of the United States district court. Under the circumstances, I had no choice.

The next day Faubus held a press conference. The essence of his statements was that he refused to budge. A representative of the Governors Conference urgently requested him to do so, with no result. Governors McKeldin, Clement, and Collins telephoned the White House to express their approval of my readiness to withdraw the troops promptly upon receipt of assurance from the Arkansas governor that he would carry out the law, and to voice their disappointment with that individual.

At my news conference on October 3 I made my stand unmistakable. Robert E. Clark of INS asked:

> Mr. President, the Little Rock situation seems to have reached an impasse with the refusal of Governor Faubus to give the guarantees you asked before withdrawing federal troops. What prospects do you see for working out an agreement with Faubus at this stage, and what do you think the next step in this direction should be?

> "Well," I replied, ". . . There are two different situations [that] could justify the withdrawal of federal troops: one, the satisfactory and unequivocal assurances that the orders of the federal court would not be obstructed, and that peace and order would be maintained in connection therewith. The second would be an actual factual development of peaceful conditions to the extent where the local city police would say, 'There will be no difficulty that we can't control in the carrying out of this court's orders.'"

One of the significant things about this conference was the unusual number of reporters who afterwards went out of their way to express, directly or indirectly, approval of my position and my forbearance in expression.

On October 14 I approved Secretary Brucker's order to withdraw half the Army troops and to defederalize four-fifths of the National Guardsmen. On October 23, Negro students left Central High for the first time without a military escort. By November 15 the National Guard took over the control of the school area. By November 27 the last of the 101st Airborne Divison left Little Rock. Of 10,500 National Guardsmen who had been federalized, nine hundred were still on duty at nearby Camp Robertson, and at Central High School only twenty-one remained. On May 8, 1958, I announced that when school ended, the Guard would leave.

The Arkansas Governor remained adamant. The Legislature passed a new law giving him sweeping powers, and when September came again, in 1958, he closed all the high schools in Little Rock. In June of 1959 the federal court declared the Arkansas schools reopened. Two Negroes entered Central High the following fall, and police and firemen dispersed a mob of 250. Three Negroes entered Hall High School without incident.

* * *

Long after the Little Rock crisis simmered down, it remained a tempting target for political propagandists. But it is doubtful that the accusations and the spate of partisan criticism so freely poured out in the autumn of 1957 made much impression on the common-sense attitude of the vast majority of Americans.

My personal conviction as to the need for and the correctness of the action we took was summarized in a single sentence of a letter I later wrote to a friend.

"If the day comes when we can obey the orders of our courts only *when we personally approve of them,* the end of the American system, as we know it, will not be far off."

And if the day ever comes when the nations of the world will obey the mandates of international law, whether they approve of them or not, the end of international conflicts, as we know them, will also not be far off.

What Little Rock was to law in the United States, Suez was to law among the nations: an example of the United States government's staking its majesty and its power on a principle of justice—a principle greater and higher than the particular interests of the individuals who clashed in the crisis. Both events, however tragic and unnecessary they may have been, have left to history a demonstration of a profound regard for that supreme law whose voice is the "harmony of the world"—a law to which, in the words of Richard Hooker, all men owe "homage, the very least as feeling her care, and the greatest as not exempted from her power."

CHAPTER VII

Renewed Tension in the Middle East

The end of the fight is a tombstone white, with the name of the late deceased,
And the epitaph drear: "A Fool lies here, who tried to hustle the East."

—*Kipling*

FOLLOWING the Suez Canal difficulties of late 1956 and the withdrawal of French and British forces from Egypt in December of that year, the Middle East remained highly unstable.[1] The Israeli were emotional in their insistence on holding some of the territorial gains they had made in the fighting of 1956; they retained garrisons in the Gaza Strip, and along the coast of the Gulf of Aqaba. Trouble could break out at any moment because of the British determination that their vital lifeline not be cut by the volatile and unpredictable Nasser. Once again Egyptian commandos were making forays into Israel by night. Moreover, the Egyptian government was shaky, according to some intelligence reports, and dissidents, it was said, were darkly plotting to destroy Nasser. The value of the Egyptian pound had dropped from $2.80 to about $1.60—scarcely more than half its former value. As Secretary Wilson observed, Egypt was "now as flat broke as it could possibly be."

In this confusion, one danger loomed above all others: The leaders of the Soviet Union, like the Czars before them, had their eyes on the Middle East. The Soviet goal was by no means merely the right to move ships through the Suez Canal, for less than 1 per cent of the Canal

[1] Map, "The Middle Eastern Situation, 1957," appears following page 360.

traffic was Russian. Neither was the goal Middle Eastern oil; the Soviet Union had no need for it and, indeed, exported oil itself. The Soviet objective, was, in plain fact, power politics: to seize the oil, to cut the Canal and pipelines of the Middle East, and thus seriously to weaken Western civilization.

* * *

On the afternoon of New Year's Day, 1957, the Secretary of State and I met with leaders of both parties in the new Congress to ask their support for a new declaration of American policy in the Middle East. We felt that a declaration making clear the American view of the current situation and our intentions respecting it was necessary so that all, including the Soviets, would understand that despite our disagreement in 1956 with our major European allies over a logical course of action respecting the Suez Canal, we were fully determined to sustain Western rights in the region.

"The existing vacuum in the Middle East," I told the leaders, "must be filled by the United States before it is filled by Russia." Time was of the essence: I believed the first session of the 85th Congress, as its first order of business, should authorize a special economic fund and the use of military force if necessary in the Middle East.

"Should there be a Soviet attack there," I said, "I can see no alternative to an immediate United States move to stop it."

I reaffirmed my regard for constitutional procedures but pointed out that modern war might be a matter of hours or even of minutes.

If the administration were given this kind of authority, it might never have to be used. Concerning the possibility of indirect assault by the Soviets, I said that the situation required that the United States negotiate agreements to help the Middle East countries economically and militarily.

The senators and representatives—Knowland and Johnson, Martin and Rayburn, Leverett Saltonstall and J. William Fulbright and their colleagues—listened in silence. Then the questioning began.

Senator H. Alexander Smith of New Jersey questioned the possibility of an adverse reaction to this proposed military approach outside of United Nations channels. Secretary Dulles assured him that the United States, if given this authority, would act only on request of an attacked country in the same manner as provided by arrangements in other areas of the world.

Senator Knowland asked, "Should the concept be broadened to cover a situation where a country invites the entry of Russian divisions, which would certainly be against our national interest? "In such a case," I replied, "there will be time to consult with Congress again."

Representative John McCormack of Massachusetts asked whether the President, as Commander-in-Chief, did not already have power to carry out these proposals without seeking congressional authorization. My answer was that greater effect could be had from a consensus of Executive and Legislative opinion, and I spoke earnestly of the desire of the Middle East countries to have reassurance now that the United States would stand ready to help.

Congressman Leo Allen[2] suggested that this measure would be like the one on Quemoy and Matsu. I agreed, commenting that in modern war there might not be time for orderly procedures; it was necessary to make our intent clear in advance.

If the United States should adopt this proposal for the Middle East, Senator Russell warned, we should not let it appear that only a "small war" might follow.

"If Russia moves there will be no such thing as a 'small war,'" I said.

The meeting that New Year's afternoon ran nearly four hours, until after nightfall. I appreciated the forbearance of my colleagues from the Congress and their willingness to set politics aside while we examined together the situation that faced the nation in the Middle East. Near the end of the meeting I reminded the legislators that the Constitution assumes that our two branches of government should get along together. I gave my heartfelt assurances that I would do my best to get along with the Congress and that in the matters we had discussed this afternoon, no question of partisanship would move me one inch—although I had, of course, to remind all that I hoped my own party, by its excellence of performance, would command the favor of the American people.

Turning to the Democratic leaders in particular, I added:

". . . You know you are as welcome in this house—in this office—as anyone. Naturally, I work . . . normally and properly with my own party leaders in the Congress. But the Congress is under Democratic control, and you as the official leaders have the right and you have the duty to call on me when you think something necessary, just as I have the duty to call it to your attention when I think something is needed.

"And if anyone in this administration violates this principle and I am told about it, he will promptly hear from me. . . .

"When I say Happy New Year to you I mean it from the bottom of my heart, even though we belong to different clubs. . . ."

[2] Ranking Republican member of the House Rules Committee.

At 7:50 on the morning of Saturday, January 5, I arrived at my White House office. It was still dark outside. I dictated an insert for the Special Message to the Congress on the Middle East. At noon, I went up to Capitol Hill to deliver it in person before the legislators assembled in a Joint Session.

> Weaknesses in the present situation and the increased danger from International Communism, convince me that basic United States policy should now find expression in joint action by the Congress and the Executive. Furthermore, our joint resolve should be so couched as to make it apparent that if need be our words will be backed by action. . . .
>
> The action which I propose would, . . . first of all, authorize the United States to cooperate with and assist any nation or group of nations in the general area of the Middle East in the development of economic strength dedicated to the maintenance of national independence.

A further purpose was to authorize the President to undertake programs of military assistance and cooperation with any nation desiring them, such programs to include United States military aid when requested, against armed aggression from any nation controlled by international Communism.

The message recommended financial support in reasonable amounts and pledged, "These measures would have to be consonant with the treaty obligations of the United States, including the Charter of the United Nations."

That same day the administration bill, House Joint Resolution 117, was introduced into the Congress.[3]

The members of the Congress did not move as one man to endorse the administration's proposal. Far from it. Some thought it would confer on the President constitutional authority belonging to the Legislative branch. Others, friends of Israel, did not like helping any Arab nation. Still others feared it would weaken our ties with either Western Europe or the United Nations or both. One suggested the far-fetched possibility that if the Soviet Union did some minor meddling in the Middle East, the Resolution would authorize "an all-out attack" on the Soviet Union.

Speaker Rayburn circulated among his colleagues on Capitol Hill a substitute—a thirty-four-word declaration, "The United States regards as vital to her interest the preservation of the independence and integrity of the states of the Middle East and, if necessary, will use her armed force to that end."

When asked, "would the administration accept this substitute?" Secre-

[3] As in the Formosa Strait, the administration refused to draw a hard, thin line around the countries of the Middle East it stood ready to defend: such a definition, we believed, could encourage an aggressor to seize any area outside the boundary.

tary Dulles, with my approval, gave a flat "No." A resolution in these words, he said, would look like an effort to establish an American protectorate over the countries of the Middle East with no thought for the wishes of the peoples of the Middle East; it would call for a guarantee, by the United States alone, of existing Middle East boundaries; it would violate the UN Charter by calling for military action to overthrow any regime which comes under Communist control by peaceful means; and it would ignore the importance of economic aid.

From around the world reports came in of varying responses to the suggested new policy.

Britain and France generally favored the plan. Communist China and the Soviet Union condemned it as a "substitution for British and French imperialism." The Moslem countries divided: Syria was hostile, Iraq and Saudi Arabia were cautiously critical, while Turkey, Pakistan, Lebanon, and Iran saw the doctrine as the best possible guarantee of peace.

Prime Minister Nehru wrote to me of his dislike of a "military approach to these problems"—an approach which, he thought, might excite ". . . passions and create divisions among the Arab countries and thus add to the tension. . . .

"I do not think that, in existing circumstances," Nehru continued, "there is any danger of aggression in the Middle East from the Soviet Union. The Soviet Union is too much tied up with its difficulties in the Eastern European countries. Even otherwise, nationalism is a far stronger force in the Middle East than any other."

The next day I dictated a reply, assuring him that the United States' purpose was to help stabilize the area and promote the rise of living standards.

> We have no thought that any country in the group would want, or indeed could afford, great armaments. When we speak of assisting in a military way, we mean only to help each nation achieve that degree of strength that can give it reasonable assurance of protection against any internal rebellion or subversion and make certain that any external aggression would meet resistance. . . .
>
> . . . it is my belief that this announcement will tend to diminish, if not eliminate, any chance of this kind of aggression. . . .
>
> But we are far more interested in bringing about conditions that will tend to lessen tensions and provide a climate that will bring about the possibility for conciliation even among the Israeli and the Arabs. We stand ready to make considerable sacrifices to bring this about, and in return we want nothing whatsoever except the confidence that these nations are gradually developing their economic strength and living standards and are achieving the ability to live more happily and peacefully among themselves and with the world.

At the first news conference of my second term on the morning of January 23, I was asked whether I had any comment on the Democratic criticism that in asking for advance approval to use the armed forces, I was creating a tradition which might restrict and embarrass future Presidents.

"What we want now," I said, "is an expression of the convictions of the vast portion of the American people without regard to party. . . .

". . . I would like the nations to know that America is largely one in our readiness to assume burdens and, where necessary, to assume risks to preserve the peace, because this peace is not going to be obtained in any cheap way and it is not going to be maintained in any cheap way."[4]

On January 30 the House passed the Middle East Resolution 355 to 61.

After extensive consideration of the Joint Resolution the Senate, on March 2, voted down 58 to 28 a proposal by Senator Richard Russell to eliminate any funds for economic and military assistance. This rejection came after Senator Knowland read on the floor of the Senate a letter from me opposing this cut and deploring any suggestion that "our country wants only to wage peace in terms of war." For the Russell amendment, which would have cut the heart out of the Resolution, only five Republicans lined up with twenty-three Democrats.[5]

Three days later, the Senate passed the Joint Resolution by a vote of 72 to 19 and on March 9 the Resolution was signed into law. As in similar cases in the past, the doctrine acquired the name of the President who proposed it and came to be known as the "Eisenhower Doctrine."

With the help of statesmen of both parties, against the grumbling of some opposing congressmen and senators, and against the well-intentioned counter-suggestions of some leading Democratic foreign policy thinkers, we had effectively obtained the consent of the Congress in proclaiming the administration's resolve to block the Soviet Union's march

[4] The next day Senator J. William Fulbright of Arkansas demanded that Secretary Dulles submit a white paper justifying in detail the conduct of American foreign policy in the Middle East since 1952.

Secretary Dulles made the obvious response: nothing he could think of would do more damage to our relations with England and France than such a rehearsal of events now past, dredging up the painful memories of recent division, and "reopening all the old wounds" in the Atlantic Alliance. After modifying his original proposal to take the policy review back to 1946, Fulbright finally abandoned it.

[5] In the course of the Senate's deliberations, I wrote a letter of thanks to former President Truman in appreciation for a syndicated newspaper column urging prompt passage of the Resolution. "I feel that your attitude," I said, "is in the high tradition of non-partisanship on foreign policy matters of grave national concern."

to the Mediterranean, to the Suez Canal and the pipelines, and to the underground lakes of oil which fuel the homes and factories of Western Europe.

* * *

Early in 1957 the Egyptians, with some outside help, had begun the laborious task of removing from the Canal the ships Nasser had sunk the previous autumn to block use of the waterway. But as yet the interested parties had worked out no satisfactory formula for the operation of the Canal. In particular they could not agree on payment of tolls and provisions for Canal maintenance and improvement.

The first problem facing Western diplomats was inducing the Israeli to withdraw their armies from Egyptian territory.

The 1956 Israeli attack against Egypt had not been made without serious provocation. The Suez Canal had been closed to Israeli shipping since 1950, as had the Gulf of Aqaba. Furthermore, the Gaza Strip had long been a base for the *fedayeen* raids into Israeli territory. Now, having exposed the relative weakness of Egypt's military establishment, the Israeli were reluctant to give up these positions which, in their eyes, did much to guarantee the rights and safety of their people.

But if Israel did not desire to defy the United Nations, it was first necessary that her forces withdraw unconditionally behind the borders fixed by the truce of 1949. Only then could the nation expect the support of the rest of the Free World in securing, by peaceful means, her legal rights.

At times some progress toward peaceful solutions seemed assured, but at the end of January the Israeli were still refusing to quit the Gaza Strip without strong guarantees against Egyptian aggression; the Egyptians were threatening to stop clearing the Canal until the Israeli in fact withdrew.[6]

[6] Part of the difficulty arose, as Foster Dulles pointed out, from the differing interpretations that Egypt and Israel placed upon the terms of the 1949 Armistice. In effect each supported those clauses that served its own interests and rejected those that favored its opponent. Israel, for example, claimed that under the Armistice agreement Egypt had no rights of belligerency in the Gulf of Aqaba. The Strait of Tiran, the narrowest point of the Gulf of Aqaba, between Saudi Arabia on one side and Egypt on the other, was only six miles wide. This meant that, under the three-mile limit, it actually did not constitute international waters. However, since the Gulf widens to twelve to nineteen miles farther north (and touches the national territories of Israel and Jordan) it does, in this area, become international waters. International law does not prohibit passage of other vessels through territorial waters of a nation if they are destined for international waters so long as belligerency does

With progress practically stalemated and the Secretary-General unable to achieve any improvement, Cabot Lodge, on February 2, made a statement in the United Nations in support of two resolutions. The purpose of one was to get the Israeli forces to withdraw behind the 1949 armistice line; the other called upon Egypt and Israel to observe the provisions of the 1949 Armistice, and directed the Secretary-General to place the United Nations Emergency Force on the 1949 demarcation line to keep the peace in the area. Both resolutions were passed.

On February 3 I backed up these resolutions with a direct cable to Ben-Gurion:

> It is my earnest hope that this withdrawal will be completed without further delay.
>
> You know how greatly our nation values close and friendly relations with yours, and we wish to continue the friendly cooperation which has contributed to Israel's national development. . . . Such continued ignoring of the judgment of the nations, as expressed in the United Nations Resolutions, would almost surely lead to the invoking of further United Nations procedures which could seriously disturb the relations between Israel and other member nations including the United States.

A week later Ben-Gurion cabled a refusal: Israel would not evacuate the Gaza Strip unless (a) Israel retained civil administration and police power in the Gaza Strip, and (b) Israel had assurance of freedom of passage through the Gulf of Aqaba.

The next day, February 11, the State Department sent the government of Israel a secret *aide-mémoire* [see Appendix J]. While neither the United States nor the United Nations, it said, had the authority to impose upon Israel and Egypt a change in substance of their armistice agreement, if Israel would withdraw its forces, the United States as a member of the United Nations would seek a disposition of the United Nations Expeditionary Force which would assure that the Gaza Strip would no longer be used as a base for armed infiltration and attack. Moreover the United States was willing to do its part to help assure all nations the right of passage through the international waters of Aqaba.

---

not exist. The term is called "innocent passage," a condition which does not permit search of the vessels passing through.

At the same time, Israel argued that Egypt, to which country administration of the Gaza Strip had been allocated under the same Armistice, no longer had any rights whatsoever in that area. In flat denial of these arguments, Egypt claimed a right to the Gaza Strip under the Armistice of 1949, and threatened to defend her territorial waters in the Gulf of Aqaba by military action.

Basically we were attempting to avoid taking sides in the Arab-Israeli quarrel in the belief that thus we might be useful in helping to compose the current crisis with fairness. Because France and Britain now had the status of Israel's allies, while Western Germany, because of war-created prejudices, could scarcely fit the role of mediator, it seemed doubly important that the United States do everything possible to maintain contacts, and if possible, friendships, with both sides.

Consequently, when the Arab nations prepared to submit to the United Nations a resolution to force Israeli withdrawal, we instructed Cabot Lodge to use every means possible to delay submission of the resolution in the hope that the Israeli would, in the meantime, voluntarily comply with the resolutions earlier passed.

But on February 15 the government of Israel sent the government of the United States an *aide-mémoire,* again refusing to move. Early the next morning, at George Humphrey's place near Thomasville, Georgia, I talked for nearly an hour and a half with Secretary Dulles, Ambassador Lodge, and Secretary Humphrey. Further delay on the Arab resolution in the United Nations, Cabot said, would not be obtainable after this weekend.

Secretary Dulles strongly expressed the view that we had gone as far as possible to try to make it easy for the Israelis to withdraw. To go further, he said, would surely jeopardize the entire Western influence in the Middle East, and the nations of that region would conclude that United States policy toward the area was, in the last analysis, controlled by Jewish influence in the United States. In such event the only hope of the Arab countries would be found in a firm association with the Soviet Union. Should this occur, it would spell the failure of the "Eisenhower Doctrine" even before it got under way. Ambassador Lodge indicated that on the basis of his assessment of the situation at the United Nations, failure of the Doctrine would likely open the way to war.

In considering various possible courses of action, I rejected, from the outset, any more United Nations resolutions designed merely to condemn Israel's conduct. Once more, I rejected also any new resolution like that of October 30, 1956, which had called only for a suspension of governmental support of Israel. Indeed, such a suspension against both Israel and Egypt was already in effect by the United States.

To prevent an outbreak of hostilities I preferred a resolution which would call on all United Nations members to suspend not just governmental but *private* assistance to Israel. Such a move would be no hollow gesture. As we discussed it, George Humphrey put in a call to W. Randolph Burgess, Under Secretary of the Treasury for Monetary Affairs, who gave a rough estimate that American private gifts to Israel were about $40 million a year and sales of Israel's bonds in our country between $50 and $60 million a year. (His information was in part based on Treasury figures on income tax deductions.)

I asked Foster to make public the text of our confidential message to Israel of February 11.

Time was getting short. As Ambassador Lodge said, most nations in the United Nations were restlessly getting ready to call for sweeping economic sanctions against Israel to force its withdrawal.

On February 18, Ben-Gurion cabled to me appealing once again for postponement of the United Nations' discussion of the subject. "Withdrawal under present circumstances will spell disaster for us. . . . For the UN to take this course is to adopt [a] double standard of morality."

In a special White House conference with congressional leaders of both parties two days later, politics was in the back of many of the conferees' minds. In 1956 the Republican national ticket had carried New York by more than one and one-half million votes—the largest margin in the history of the Empire State. But faced with the possibility of having to take a stand for strong American action against Israel, some of those present were more than a little nervous.

I opened the conference that morning by stressing the importance of stability in the Middle East, which would open the way for urgently needed financial assistance to Israel through the Export-Import Bank. Even more important was the need to develop solutions to the basic problems of the region: Who was to use the Suez Canal? How could Israeli-Arab feuding be stopped? Noncompliance with the United Nations resolution, I explained, would mean that none of these things could be accomplished. Economic stagnation would increase. In turn, these developments, along with increased influence of Russia in the Arab states, could lead to interruption of the flow of oil through the remaining pipeline, continued blocking of the Canal, possibly a serious crash in the French and United Kingdom economies and, finally, an increased possibility of general war.

Secretary Dulles said, "My opinion is that Israel will soon withdraw the last of her troops if her government is convinced that the United States would insist on such action." He felt that the United States position was the crucial factor in the current situation. "Should the Arab nations see any confirmation of this belief," he said, "they would feel compelled to turn to Russia." He added that the United States had no intention of adopting an anti-Israel policy, only that it was determined to oppose Israel's refusal to conform to United Nations decisions.

Both Senator Lyndon Johnson and Senator William Knowland argued that in "cracking down" on Israel we were using a double standard—following one policy for the strong and one for the weak.

"Why doesn't the United Nations vote sanctions against Russia for non-compliance with the outstanding United Nations resolution on Hungary?" Knowland wanted to know. Ambassador Lodge replied that the United Nations would never attempt to apply sanctions against either Russia or the United States. This, he said, was just one of the facts of diplomatic life, because the territories and economies of each were so strong as to make them practically immune.

I suggested that the group agree to a statement setting forth our convictions and intentions. Senator Johnson had reservations about a statement and recommended that Secretary Dulles first attempt to find whether a substantial Senate and House vote pledging support of the administration's policy would cause Israel to withdraw. The Congress would move quickly, Johnson said, if it could be assured that its action would have this result. But Speaker Rayburn flatly refused to take any part in a congressional resolution, and Mr. McCormack said he would not be a party even to the statement I had suggested.

When the meeting broke up at eleven o'clock, a White House staff member called the discussion, in which both minority and majority leaders had opposed the administration, "a can of worms." As I reflected on the pettiness of much of the discussion of the morning, I found it somewhat dismaying that partisan considerations could enter so much into life-or-death, peace-or-war decisions.

After the meeting I told Secretary Dulles, Ambassador Lodge, and Jim Hagerty that I would now, by television and radio, take my case to the country.

First, however, I cabled Ben-Gurion, warning that without his immediate and favorable decision, there could be no assurance that the next UN moves would not be quite serious:

> I would greatly deplore the necessity of the United States' taking positions in the United Nations, and of the United Nations itself having to adopt measures, which might have far-reaching effects upon Israel's relations throughout the world.

In the Cabinet Room, while technicians readied my regular office, I began writing my talk which was delivered at nine o'clock that night.

I spoke of the "grave and repeated provocations" that had led to

Israel's invasion of Egypt before turning to the United Nations resolutions and to Israel's adamant attitude. Focusing on the Israeli argument that it should have "firm guarantees as a condition to withdrawing its forces of invasion," I asked a question of principle:

> Should a nation which attacks and occupies foreign territory in the face of United Nations disapproval be allowed to impose conditions on its own withdrawal?
>
> If we agree that armed attack can properly achieve the purposes of the assailant, then I fear we will have turned back the clock of international order.

Then I took up the question Lyndon Johnson and William Knowland had raised—that of following a double standard by agreeing to punish little Israel while permitting big Russia to go free. No one deplored more than I did the fact that the Soviets ignored UN resolutions—and no nation was more vigorous than we were in exerting moral pressure against the Soviet Union. But it was relatively impervious to other types of sanction.

> It would indeed be a sad day if the United States ever felt that it had to subject Israel to the same type of moral pressure as is being applied to the Soviet Union.

I concluded my broadcast with the expression of one plain conviction: "The United Nations must not fail."

I believed that the UN had no choice but to exert pressure upon Israel, I said. We hoped that the Israelis would see that their best immediate and long-term interests would be served by trusting in the world organization and in our own declaration that we would attempt to see the Gaza Strip, the base from which the Egyptians launched their attacks, secured by a UN expeditionary force.

The next move was up to the government in Tel Aviv. The next day Prime Minister Ben-Gurion cabled me. The Israeli Cabinet, he said, had been in extraordinary session all day. Ambassador Eban would leave tomorrow morning for New York and Washington. Ben-Gurion hoped that I would use the influence of our government to get the General Assembly to suspend its discussion until Monday, after Eban had had a chance to talk with Dulles. "It is our most ardent wish to cooperate in the fullest in seeking a solution."

Events, however, were gaining momentum. In the General Assembly the next day, February 22, Middle Eastern and other states broke their silence. Lebanon, Iraq, the Sudan, Pakistan, Afghanistan, and Indonesia introduced their own resolution calling for the end of military, economic, and financial assistance to Israel. Cabot Lodge delayed taking a stand until the end of the talks between Eban and Dulles.

It was clear that a sanctions resolution, in one form or another, was moving toward a vote. But the vote never came. On March 1, Mrs. Golda Meir, the Israeli foreign minister, went before the General Assembly to announce Israel's plans for a "full and complete withdrawal" of military forces.

I cabled Ben-Gurion:

> I was indeed deeply gratified at the decision of your Government to withdraw promptly and fully behind the Armistice lines as set out by your Foreign Minister in her address of yesterday to the General Assembly. I venture to express the hope that the carrying out of these withdrawals will go forward with the utmost speed.
>
> I know that this decision was not an easy one. I believe, however, that Israel will have no cause to regret having thus conformed to the strong sentiment of the world community as expressed in the various United Nations Resolutions relating to withdrawal.

I informed Ben-Gurion of our intention to act swiftly in carrying out the pledges we had made to him and his nation.

To prevent further border clashes, a United Nations Emergency Force consisting of Danish and Norwegian troops, under the command of Canadian Major General E. L. M. Burns, immediately moved into the Gaza Strip. Secretary-General Hammarskjold had obtained from Nasser an informal commitment that the Gaza Strip would not be reoccupied, even by officials. Soon thereafter Colonel Nasser, regrettably but within his rights according to the Armistice of 1949, sent certain administrators back into the territory, thus creating consternation anew in Israel. His action represented not only a violation of an understanding between him and Secretary-General Hammarskjold, but evidenced a lack of concern for the good will of those powers which had so recently come to his aid. When, after weeks of highly confused report from the area, it became apparent that the Egyptians had gone back on their word, the Secretary-General became quite discouraged.

Despite Prime Minister Ben-Gurion's misgivings, there was no question that Israel had gained by her unconditional withdrawal from the Gaza Strip. By acceding to world opinion and by retiring from territory previously seized by military force, Ben-Gurion had increased Israel's standing among the nations of the world. Colonel Nasser, who had remained in power only through the restraint of the West, failed to seize this opportunity for true statesmanship, thereby depriving his country of the assistance and cooperation of all self-respecting governments.

* * *

The Gaza Strip having been evacuated, attention immediately turned to the matter of Israeli shipping on the Gulf of Aqaba. In this instance the *de facto* situation worked to the advantage of Israel. With their armies withdrawn, the Israeli could justly claim that no belligerency in the Gulf existed. At a press conference on March 7 I said that we, together with other principal maritime nations, were prepared to declare the Gulf of Aqaba an open international waterway and to use it as such. To make clear our support of the right of "innocent passage" we directed an American tanker chartered by an Israeli company to proceed through the Gulf early in April and dock at the head of the Gulf in Israeli territory.

King Saud protested our stand passionately and persistently. He wrote to me alleging that Israel had adopted a policy of provocation against Moslem people all over the world. For example, he said that an Israeli destroyer had sailed from Eilat headed on a threatening course toward the Arab town of Sheikhameed, turning away only after it had reached a point only a kilometer from the town, well within his waters. He cited further examples, including naval air maneuvers over the Gulf, all of which, he said, had caused considerable uneasiness among his people along the coastline. He interpreted all these movements as clear evidence of Israeli hostile intentions.

I again assured the King of our readiness to prevent aggression against his country, but reminded him that, so far as the legalities in the Gulf of Aqaba were concerned, "the views of the United States, which were explained by Secretary Dulles and myself when you were here . . . differ from those of Your Majesty." We would uphold the international character of the Gulf.

King Saud had always expressed a grave concern over the fate of the Holy Places of Islam in the Arabian Peninsula. One of his fears was that if Israeli shipping should be allowed to use the Gulf, Arab pilgrims would be blocked from visiting those places. I had given assurances that the United States would support the principle of "innocent passage" of the Gulf for the Arabs as for the Israelis. Apparently this had been satisfactory to the King, although he would have preferred recognition of the Gulf as an Arab "possession."

Upon returning to his own country after his February trip to the United States, King Saud was active in efforts to induce some of the Arab states, notably Syria and Jordan, to join him in opposing both Communism and Nasser's ambition to head the Arab community. At a "summit meeting" of Arab heads of state in Cairo, attended also by President Shukri al Kuwatly of Syria and King Hussein of Jordan, Saud apparently clashed with President Nasser over the latter's insistent probing into the details of the King's "agreements" with me, and at one time reportedly threatened to abandon the conference.

As time went on, the King's pro-Western position caused him more and more difficulty with some Arab governments. Nasser began a whispering campaign, charging that Saud was little more than a tool of the United States. The King, however, manfully persisted in his anti-Communism. At the same time, we were gratified to have a report that King Saud was working out his problems with Iraq and had advised King Hussein to do the same.[7]

All these clashes, added to the never-ending quarrels between Arabs and Jews, forced us to realize anew that though the role of the peacemaker may be blessed, it can likewise be exceedingly hard.

* * *

During the spring of 1957 the Suez Canal was steadily cleared of obstacles, but not of the problem of its operations. Early in the year it had appeared that the Canal might be open by the first of March and in full operation by the end of that month. Unless some agreement on how it should be operated could be reached in the interim, all the advantages of possession would lie with President Nasser. He was now arguing that the French-British-Israeli invasion had relieved him of responsibility to abide by any agreements to which he had previously been a party. His was the aggrieved nation, and he was determined to make the most of the advantage that he believed world opinion had given him.

In the negotiations that ensued, the concern of the Western powers, particularly of the British, was twofold. Many in the West, particularly in England, still doubted the ability of the Egyptians to operate the Canal and questioned their readiness and capacity to make necessary periodic improvements and repairs. There was likewise a fear, heightened by British and French mistrust of Colonel Nasser and his ambitions, that the Canal, under Nasser's control, would become an instrument of Egyptian politics.

By the first week of March the channel still contained two large sunken vessels. The Egyptians said these had high explosives as cargo. Removing the ships, they said, would be a slow process. This concern over the two

[7] Intelligence reached both Saud and Hussein of plots to assassinate them. They were said to be, in diplomatic understatement, "highly irritated by these reports."

vessels, I decided, stemmed partly from a determination to delay the clearing operation until the Israeli should have completed their withdrawal from the Sinai Peninsula.

British opinion, meanwhile, was reported to be simmering and likely to explode if the Egyptians were able to enforce the direct collection of tolls.

But on March 18 Nasser once again declared that the Canal would be operated and managed by an autonomous Suez Canal Authority, established by the government of Egypt. He added that Egypt would feel bound by the Convention of 1888 and listed restrictions that it promised unilaterally to observe in the raising of tolls.

Finally the last sunken ship was cleared out of the Canal, and on the 29th of March the first convoy of nine freighters went through. Within a few days, Cairo announced, vessels of twelve different nations were transiting the Canal. Coincidentally, Secretary-General Hammarskjold gave up trying to negotiate with the Egyptians, and the burden fell on the United States to seek, in secret talks in Cairo, an operational agreement acceptable to the West.[8]

After these had dragged on profitlessly for several weeks, Egyptian Foreign Minister Mahmoud Fawzi sent Dag Hammarskjold a letter in which he declared Egypt's position on the operation of the Suez Canal. It was a far cry from what the West, and particularly the British, wanted, but did contain concessions. The Egyptians refused to negotiate on fixing tolls, but agreed that 25 per cent of the gross receipts would be set aside for development of the Canal, and that disputes over compensation of the former owners would be settled by arbitration. The declaration again asserted Egypt's intention to respect the terms and spirit of the Constantinople Convention of 1888, and provided for an Arbitration Tribunal to make binding decision on disputes over Canal regulations.

Because the Canal lay within Egyptian territory, it appeared that this stand could scarcely be questioned legally. Nasser's plan and his good faith could be tested only by actual operations. We decided to do so immediately. Therefore, we announced in the Security Council of the United Nations that the United States would tentatively accept the Egyptian arrangements and that our future attitude would depend on the man-

[8] Responsibility for negotiating with Egypt fell logically on the United Nations and on the Secretary-General in particular. There was no real legal basis for any single nation to conduct negotiations. Nevertheless, it early became apparent that the Secretary-General was going to encounter immense difficulties in approaching Nasser since the United Nations of itself possessed no incentives to offer a shrewd and materialistic dictator. As Foster Dulles said, all the "carrots" were actually in the hands of the United States.

ner in which Egypt carried them out. For a period the British continued skeptical and as late as the third of May, Selwyn Lloyd told Foster that he still hoped for a Security Council meeting on the subject. "This," as Foster wrote, seemed "like keeping the bidding open when you hold a Yarborough."[9]

Before many weeks had passed it became abundantly clear that the Egyptians could run the Canal as well as had the old Suez Canal Company. This cut the ground from under the British argument that Egyptians did not have the technical skill to operate the waterway. Moreover, since Nasser gave no indication of repudiating the pledges made in his declaration, antagonism, even in Britain, gradually subsided. This improvement in relations was abetted by an apparent effort in Egypt's controlled press to paint Britain in a better light, and to cease, temporarily at least, the virulent attacks against the British that for months had been continuous and strident.

Thus finally ended one of the most difficult episodes in recent American diplomatic history, one in which we had been forced, for a period, to oppose three of our friends—two of which were our closest traditional allies—in a quarrel against a country suspected of acting under the influence of the Kremlin. Little or nothing had been gained by the attacking powers in their military operations. On the other hand, British and French relations with the Middle East soon began to improve. Regardless of our views as to the wisdom of the invasion of Egypt, Britain and France showed the world the difference between their own regard for the resolutions of the United Nations and that manifested by the Soviets in Hungary and elsewhere.

* * *

The conclusion of the Suez incident, did not, however, conclude our current intense interest in the Middle East. In early January, some months before the reopening of the Canal, I had asked James P. Richards, a Democrat from South Carolina, who had formerly been chairman of the House Committee on Foreign Affairs, to perform a mission for me under the Middle East Doctrine. He was to devise effective methods of cooperating with interested nations for the improvement of their security and for their economic progress. Richards was authorized to determine what countries wished to cooperate in this effort, and to make commitments for assistance within the limitation of funds appropriated by the

[9] Bridge players need no explanation of this term. For the benefit of others, a Yarborough is a worthless hand, which contains no card higher than a nine.

Congress, which for the current year amounted to $200 million. It was understood, of course, that he would not make commitments without authorization from Washington, but it was also understood that we would act promptly on his recommendations.

At the time of his departure in March, Ambassador Richards, with a small staff of experts, was scheduled to visit only Lebanon, Libya, and Turkey, but in the end he went to fifteen countries.[10] Of the countries visited, twelve soon declared their support of the purposes of the Doctrine. Israel also subsequently endorsed it.

* * *

We had other problems in the region. Rumblings of internal difficulties in Jordan had been reported by Allen Dulles in the first week of February, when King Hussein made a courageous but unsuccessful attempt to reform his Cabinet. The trouble was apparently instigated by Communists. Hussein's next crisis came in early April when he removed a pro-Soviet Premier and replaced him, unfortunately perhaps, with an old-fashioned conservative. Colonel Nasser reportedly became irritated by the change and directed a propaganda barrage against King Hussein. The new Jordanian government lasted less than three weeks. Our observers believed the King's life to be in danger.

Hussein struck back at once. Assured of the loyalty of his army, he took to the radio to denounce Egypt, Syria, and the dissidents in his own country.[11] He imposed martial law and a tight curfew and formed a new government under the leadership of Premier Ibrahim Hashim. Nevertheless, the weakness of Jordan encouraged a belief that it was about to disintegrate. Her neighbors were animated by a single thought —how to gain the lion's share of the spoils. Such an outcome would almost certainly mean general war in the region.

On April 24, President Chamoun of Lebanon sent me a message urging me to take swift and decisive action to save Jordan at almost any cost. I answered that we had conveyed to Hussein our encouragement and political support. Moreover, going on Israel's promise to refrain from any attempt to take advantage of the situation, I informed President Chamoun also that units of the United States Sixth Fleet were even then

[10] Afghanistan, Ethiopia, Greece, Iran, Iraq, Israel, Lebanon, Libya, Morocco, Pakistan, Saudi Arabia, Sudan, Tunisia, Turkey, and Yemen. In the entire Middle East he missed only Syria, Egypt, and Jordan. In the case of the first two the political climate was far from favorable, in the third an internal crisis precluded a visit.

[11] King Hussein has written a moving account of this whole episode, including the plot against his life and his direct appeal to the army, bypassing his Army Chief of Staff, in his book, *Uneasy Lies the Head.*

moving into the eastern Mediterranean and called his attention to the help that Hussein had received from King Saud and from the Iraqi.

At the same time, I authorized Jim Hagerty to say that both the Secretary of State and I regarded the "independence and integrity of Jordan as vital," purposely using language which was akin to that in the Joint Resolution itself.

With these actions the situation in Jordan seemed to stabilize and on April 29 we announced an economic aid grant of $10 million to that country. On the first of May we recalled the Sixth Fleet to the western Mediterranean.[12]

* * *

A period of quiet now apparently settled over the Middle East. But it was apparent only. Toward the end of July this interlude was disturbed by a sudden uprising headed by the Imam of Oman against the Sultanate of Muscat and Oman, a British protectorate on the eastern side of the Arabian Peninsula.

The history of United States relations with this Sultanate goes back as far as 1832, when the United States signed a treaty with the Sultan of Oman, one of the first that the United States signed with any Asian country.

What made this revolt of potential importance was the strong suspicion that it was fomented from without. It was scarcely practicable for the subordinate sheikdom of Oman, unless given assistance from elsewhere, to carry on a military operation against the British-supported Sultan. Further, while the situation remained vague, we knew that some of the Oman forces had been trained in Saudi Arabia by Egyptian and Saudi officers, apparently without Saud's approval. Nevertheless the British, in a chronic state of anxiety over the fate of their oil-rich protectorates in the region, simply assumed that King Saud would have to be behind such activity.

We were, of course, striving to develop closer relations with King Saud and doing everything we could to improve the atmosphere between him and the British. So, because our friendship with Saud had become widely known in Britain, it was perhaps not surprising that we should share in

[12] The Soviets seemed particularly sensitive to movements of Western fleets within the Mediterranean. On April 26 when the Sixth Fleet was steaming eastward, the Soviet delegate to the United Nations formally made the ridiculous proposal to the Security Council that it stop the Sixth Fleet from going to the eastern Mediterranean. Since, obviously, the Security Council had no vestige of authority to control the movements of any nation's naval units in international waters, his words were greeted with a silence that must have been embarrassing.

any resentments and suspicions directed toward him. Indeed, a press survey in Britain during the last week of July 1957, showed an astonishing amount of public belief that the American oil companies were indirectly behind the rebellion. This was absurd, but the belief was slow to die.

Toward the end of July the British decided it was necessary to use ground forces to suppress the rebellion. The operation itself was conducted by a handful of troops and was completed in several days, during which little actual fighting took place. King Saud sent a message assuring me that he was not supplying the arms to the rebels; these, he claimed, were obtained under an agreement between Nasser and Nehru. The King cited no proof of this claim but, immediately, I notified Harold Macmillan, who was highly gratified by this indication that King Saud did not wish to build the incident into a major quarrel between Saudi Arabia and Britain. Assuring Harold of the falsity of any rumors involving United States oil companies I wrote, "If we were willing to tolerate this kind of thing, we would never have been so ready to do our best to help solve the oil problems that were generated for you by the Suez crisis of last fall."

Finally the Sultan of Muscat and Oman who, like the British, had been deeply suspicious of King Saud, agreed to meet with the latter. There the incident ended, but it has always remained in my mind as an example of the inflammatory possibilities of even the smallest clash in that combustible part of the world.

* * *

As one ended, another crisis promptly made its appearance. On August 13, 1957, the Syrian radio blared forth an accusation that the United States was engaged in a plot to overthrow the Kuwatly regime there, and that three United States embassy and attaché officials in Damascus were to be expelled for alleged subversive activities. A few days later the Syrian Army Chief of Staff, a political moderate, resigned his position and his important post was taken over by an officer known to be pro-Moscow in sympathies.

The entire action was shrouded in mystery but the suspicion was strong that the Communists had taken control of the government. Moreover, we had fresh reports that arms were being sent into Syria from the Soviet bloc.[13]

[13] These events did not come as a complete surprise. As early as the previous January, Allen Dulles had submitted reports indicating that the new Syrian Cabinet was oriented to the left, with the strong man of the Cabinet appearing to be Khaled el

In the days following the revolt and the propaganda attack on the United States, we tried, through the heavy cordon of censorship (which even included a Syrian security detachment surrounding the United States Embassy), to find out how far toward Communism the Syrian government had swung. If the government comprised only radical Arab nationalists and pro-Nasserites, that was one thing; if they were to go completely Communist, that could call for action.

Syria's neighbors believed that the pendulum had swung far toward the danger point. Almost immediately the Middle East broke into a diplomatic furor approaching panic. There were meetings between the Turks and Iraqis; the Iraqis and Jordanians; the Jordanians and the Turks. Lebanon, already overrun with Syrian agents, asked the United States for formal assurances of support in the event that Lebanon were attacked by Syria. Even President Kuwatly of Syria seemed shaken by the rapidity of the events in his own land; apparently fearful of his own future, he hurried off to Egypt to consult with President Nasser. Although the suddenness of the Syrian action had apparently startled Nasser (it was reported that he regarded the chief of staff of the Syrian army as an out-and-out Communist), he still found it necessary to join publicly with Syria in denouncing the alleged "U.S. plot to overthrow the Syrian regime."

In the United States we were determined not to make premature public commitments on insufficient information. One clear fact was emerging, however. Syria's neighbors, including her fellow Arab nations, had come to the conclusion that the present regime in Syria had to go: otherwise the takeover by the Communists would soon be complete. A strong Soviet outpost would be in existence amidst this formerly neutral region.[14]

In these circumstances most Middle East countries seemed to believe that direct military action would be necessary. This would have to take place, they said, before the Syrians and Soviets had a chance to sign and make public a mutual defense treaty or before Syria was recognized officially as a Communist satellite. No military action should be initiated,

---

Azm, the Minister of State, who was known to be anti-Western and pro-Egyptian. In July the Syrians, busy at fomenting trouble with Israel and Lebanon, had been assured of $500 million in long-term military and economic aid from Soviet Russia.

[14] Syria was far more vulnerable to Communist penetration than was Egypt. In Egypt, where one strong man prevailed, Colonel Nasser was able to deal with Communists and accept their aid with some degree of safety simply because he demanded that all Soviet operations be conducted through himself. In Syria, where a weak man was in charge of the government, the Soviet penetration bypassed the government and dealt directly with the various agencies, the army, the foreign ministry, and the political parties. Syria was considered ripe to be plucked at any time.

they agreed, until Syria had actually committed aggression against her neighbors and thus provoked retaliation. If the government went as far left as her neighbors surmised, such provocation would be forthcoming in a short time, and concerted action would be necessary.

Of the nations of the region, it seemed that Iraq was the logical Arab power to take the initiative in retaliation, being the strongest and most stable of those that had a common boundary with Syria. Turkey could not be expected to initiate action because, while a Moslem country, her domination of the region before World War I was too unfavorably remembered by the Arabs for them to accept her leadership. But there was considerable doubt as to Iraq's capabilities, alone, to carry out a successful military operation, if this should become necessary. It was thought that if on the west, south and north of Syria, Lebanon, Jordan, and Turkey should each mass its own troops along the Syrian boundary, that country would be required so to disperse its own forces as to facilitate successful Iraqi military operations from the east. The Arabs' question was simple: What would the United States do to help them?

To give a simple answer was not easy. Less than a year before, supporting the principle that military force was not a justifiable means for settling of disputes, the United States had taken drastic action in the United Nations. Now we were being asked to give our tacit approval to an invasion of one sovereign nation by another.

The circumstances were, however, quite different. In this instance the Arabs, who considered themselves one great confederation, took the attitude that one of their states had been invaded from without even though only by infiltration and subversion. They genuinely felt that action to restore Syria to Syrian rule would be basically defensive in nature, particularly because they intended to react to anticipated aggression, rather than to commit a naked aggression. Although they believed that Colonel Nasser had been acting the year before within his legal rights in nationalizing the Suez Canal, in the case of Syria they were convinced that an outside power, the Soviet Union, had moved in, clandestinely, to take over the rights of another.

The consequences of inaction, the Arabs believed, would be almost catastrophic to them and to all the West. With Syria firmly in Communist hands, the other Arab nations could scarcely avoid a similar fate. Such a development would confront Western Europe with difficulties that in the long run could lead to a calamity. And in the end this chain of events would spell so much danger to the United States that we could not afford to ignore its possible beginning.

We decided upon several interim actions. First, a message was to be sent to Premier Menderes of Turkey, one that he could communicate to his neighbors. (We knew that the leaders of Iraq and Jordan were, at the time, in Istanbul.) The message would give assurances that if Syria's Moslem neighbors felt it necessary to take action against aggression by the Syrian government, the United States would undertake to expedite shipments of arms already committed to the Middle Eastern countries and, further, would replace losses as quickly as possible.

Next, we would make it our business to see that no outside countries—for example, Israel or the U.S.S.R.—would interfere with the measures taken by these Moslem nations to protect themselves from Syrian attack and to assure restoration of Syria to the Syrians.

Our assistance would be forthcoming only if the actions taken were confined to these logical and reasonable objectives and contained no purpose of permanently occupying Syrian territory.

In addition to the message dispatched to Premier Menderes, we at once sought assurances from the Israeli that they would abstain from using the current confusion as a chance of seizing territory for themselves. (In spite of all the furor, the Arab nations were not yet convinced that Israel was not their principal enemy.) If Israel should act indiscreetly, total chaos could result; what set out to be an action against the new Syrian government might very well turn into a concerted Arab action against Israel.

As a preliminary move United States aircraft were sent from Western Europe to the United States base at Adana, Turkey, to be available in case of need, and the Sixth Fleet was ordered again to the eastern end of the Mediterranean.

I realized that Middle East tensions and the preparatory moves we were making could snowball into a real risk of war. If Syrian aggression should provoke military reaction by Iraq, and a difficult campaign should bring the Turks to Iraq's aid, the Soviets might very well take this occasion to move against Turkey. Should that happen, a much larger war would be almost upon us. The alternative, however—to do nothing and lose the whole Middle East to Communism—would be worse. In view of these potentialities I asked that key members of Congress be notified the next day of the impending movements. Our "ready" forces, particularly the Strategic Air Command, were alerted.

With these preliminary actions taken, I dispatched Ambassador Loy W. Henderson, Deputy Under Secretary of State for Administration, to Ankara where King Hussein of Jordan, the Crown Prince of Iraq, and King Faisal were present. Ambassador Henderson would therefore have an excellent opportunity to obtain a consensus from these several heads of state.

The responses to our various messages reflected a common recognition of the gravity of the situation, but otherwise varied widely. Premier Menderes of Turkey seemed optimistic. Premier Ben-Gurion of Israel quickly recognized the necessity of Israel's abstention from any participation but he urged strongly that the United States take swift and direct action against Syria. He was convinced that Syria had already turned Communist, saying in his first message, "It is impossible to distinguish between Syria and Russia." The Prime Minister was also concerned by the recent step-up in anti-Israel propaganda in the Russian press, a development, he pointed out, that is never without purpose. He concluded that Israel was the ultimate target of the weapons that the U.S.S.R. was pouring into Syria. He said, "The establishment of Syria as a base for international Communism is one of the most dangerous events which has befallen the Free World in our time."

Foster's message to the British Foreign Minister calling attention to the risks which we were taking, received a somewhat different response. In Selwyn Lloyd's absence Mr. Macmillan himself had temporarily taken over the duties of Foreign Minister and likened the developments in Syria to the Soviet takeover in Czechoslovakia in 1949. Remembering that the response of Western Europe had been the formation of NATO, Harold was apparently thinking of some method of creating or improving Middle Eastern defense structures among friendly nations.[15] More hopeful in one respect than any other of my correspondents, Harold felt that this crisis might be the beginning of a realization among the Arabs that their number one enemy was Communism, not Israel.

The situation, which initially had seemed to be relatively clear, soon became confused. Messages were arriving in Washington daily, almost hourly, and their purport was far from consistent. Whereas early information had indicated the possibility of prompt Iraqi military action with the Turks abstaining, there were now hints of a reversal of this arrangement. A deterrent to Iraqi action was the threat to her oil income that would result from Syrian interruption of the pipelines crossing that country. Half of Iraq's total $400 million annual governmental income was involved.

King Hussein of Jordan unexpectedly left on vacation to Italy, thus giving a clear indication that Jordan, contrary to what we had been led

[15] The Prime Minister did not contemplate any countermoves involving a military defense structure so formal as NATO, but he suggested a coordinated Moslem defense alignment, possibly a "Southern Tier" to supplement the Baghdad Pact, or simply a rearrangement of the Baghdad Pact.

to believe a few days earlier, did not want to join in any move against Syria. We were next astonished to find that King Saud, rather than addressing himself to the dangers of a Communist Syria in the Middle East, was still preoccupied with Israel, the Gulf of Aqaba, and the slowness of our arms deliveries to his government.

In all this tangle, I could see two things: First, because of the reaction among the Arabs, the Turks should be restrained from taking any initiative against Syria.[16] While I recognized that the United States had no power to forbid the Turks to act as they might see fit, we could and would use every possible influence to prevent a Turkish attack. Second, all of our arms commitments to our friends in the area should be filled quickly.

For the next few days we awaited the results of Ambassador Henderson's discussions in the Middle East. An unsettling report from Lebanon alleged extensive infiltration of the Lebanese border by Syrians carrying explosives, rifles, and ammunition. On the encouraging side, the Lebanese were confident that the majority of the Syrian people disliked the nature of what was believed to be their new government regime.

The unpredictable King Saud now seemed prepared to accuse the United States of creating much of the difficulty, although we could not understand why. The King, of course, continued to differ with the United States over Aqaba, and to subordinate concern about Syria to his fervent hope that the Israeli should be prohibited from any use of that body of water. Neither the fact that nearly all maritime nations took the same position as the United States, nor our proposal to take the matter to the World Court, seemed to mollify him.

(Another explanation for the attitude of the King came in a message from President Chamoun of Lebanon. Chamoun had said that Saud was afraid of Radio Cairo which, if it attacked him, could easily provoke trouble and might even stir up a revolution. The many Egyptian officers, teachers, and technicians present in Saudi Arabia gave them great influence.)

Loy Henderson returned to Washington on September 4. His story was intriguing. His broad conclusion was that there was a fear in all Middle East countries that the Soviets might be able to topple the regimes in each of their countries through exploiting the crisis in Syria. He found that while the Lebanese were doing an effective job in picking up infiltrators, they doubted that they could survive as an ally of the West

[16] Foster told me of a document, reportedly held by the Turks, which promised that the Soviets would undertake to back Syrian territorial expansion at the expense of Turkey, Iraq, and Jordan.

more than three to six months if something were not done to remove a Soviet-dominated Syrian regime.

Nonetheless, Henderson reported a surprising amount of rivalry among the Arabs. Considerable mutual animosity existed, for example, between the royal houses of Jordan and Iraq, both of which belonged to the Hashemite dynasty. Moreover, it was clear that Iraq would want to avoid any loss of her oil revenues through the breaking up of the pipelines across Syria. All-in-all, Loy Henderson concluded, the capability and the readiness of the Arabs to take military action in the event of border difficulties with Syria seemed to be slight.

But the Turks, he went on, were still determined to eliminate the Syrian regime. If nothing was done, the Turks feared rebellion or internal trouble at home. Menderes was disposed to act, even if this meant that he might be going counter to United States advice and objectives.

In the meantime the political and propaganda moves of the Soviets were such as to presage, in Foster Dulles' judgment, an intensification of the cold war. He cited several facts: they had penetrated Syria seriously; they were conducting naval maneuvers in the Mediterranean; the Soviets had dropped any interest in cultural exchanges; their latest boasts concerning Soviet ICBMs had included threatening overtones; a recent note to us on the Middle East situation was couched in the rudest and most provocative terms.

In any event, by the summer of 1957, the United States had done everything we felt it possible to do. We had restrained Israel; we had assured the Arabs of our support against Communist penetration; we had airlifted arms to Turkey and vastly expedited delivery to the other nations; we had moved the Sixth Fleet to positions where it could wield the weight of United States naval power, if necessary. We had kept the British informed and had assured them of our aid in the event the Mid-East pipelines were cut off. All we could do now was to watch the situation closely for the next sign of a move—either a major aggression on the part of the Syrians or some evidence that the situation was relaxing.

Neither happened.

By mid-September 1957, all the Arab governments save that of Lebanon had seemingly abandoned any thought of collective action. An Arab summit meeting was held at Damascus between King Saud, Iraqi Premier Ali Jawdat, and Syrian President Kuwatly. After the meeting King Saud declared publicly that he would deplore any aggression against any Arab country, including Syria.[17] But, as this meeting was breaking up, Saud

[17] Sometime later in reporting on this incident, Allen Dulles discounted the belief that King Saud had shifted to support of the current Syrian regime. Mr. Dulles

called to the American chargé d'affaires and asked him to transmit his friendly greetings to me, saying he was looking forward to our continuing friendship and close cooperation and that he hoped to see me soon. Our chargé noted that King Saud had made this statement in front of the Syrians, a gesture which was possibly designed to impress them as well as to send his reassurances to me.

The Turks, however, were far from complacent. Despite a reluctance of their military, the Turkish government was maintaining a readiness to act. Turkish forces on the Syrian border had been increased from thirty-two thousand to fifty thousand, a fact that Soviet intelligence had noted and seemed to be using as a pretext for increased truculence.

On October 5 Foster Dulles took advantage of the fact that Foreign Minister Andrei Gromyko was in the United States to hold a personal conference with him. The result was an extended dreary repetition of all the accusations and half-truths that by this time had become so familiar. In sending over his notes of the meeting, Foster wrote: "You may be interested in looking over the typed notes of the talk I had with Mr. Gromyko on Saturday. It was rather lengthy. All I can say is that to read it will not be as tedious as to have listened!"

On October 8 Mr. Khrushchev, in an interview with a well-known American correspondent, James Reston, accused the United States of trying to stir up war over Syria. Khrushchev asserted that Loy Henderson had been given specific instructions to this effect, and having failed to obtain cooperation of the Arab states, the United States was now engaged in an effort to get Turkey to launch an attack. In a sentence obviously designed for Turkish consumption, he said, "If the rifles fire, the rockets will start flying."

To refute the accusation that the United States was trying to start a war, we put out a statement telling the truth. We reminded Khrushchev that Turkey was an independent nation, capable of creating its own foreign policy. We warned him that "he should be under no illusion that the United States, Turkey's friend and ally, takes lightly its obligations under the North Atlantic Treaty or is not determined to carry out the national policy expressed in the Joint Congressional Resolution on the Middle East." At a press conference Foster Dulles re-emphasized that "if there is an attack on Turkey by the Soviet Union, it would not mean a purely

believed in fact that King Saud was trying to bolster the prestige of Kuwatly in order to prevent the creation in Syria of a revoltionary command counsel type of regime such as Nasser had created in Egypt.

defensive operation by the United States, with the Soviet Union a privileged sanctuary from which to attack Turkey."[18]

In October, Cabot Lodge made an eloquent presentation in the United Nations of the entire Middle East affair. The favorable reaction of the assemblage was a tribute to Cabot's abilities and to the general esteem in which the United States was held, viz-à-viz the Soviet Union.

At the end of 1957, though tensions continued, the Suez Canal was operating efficiently and carrying the traffic of nearly all the maritime nations of the world; the Gulf of Aqaba was open to Israeli shipping; United Nations forces maintained an uneasy peace in the Gaza Strip. On the other hand the threat of Soviet penetration of the Middle East remained, and a left-wing regime seemed strongly entrenched in Syria.

One fact was especially encouraging. Throughout 1957, relations between the British and American governments had been a model of harmony and mutual confidence. Our British friends had several times expressed their gratification at this development. On my part, I could not have been more satisfied with the closeness created between Macmillan's government and ours.

[18] Secretary Dulles had been made the villain of American foreign policy by Khrushchev. At this press conference Foster reminded the group of the dark threats hurled at Turkey when it joined NATO in 1952, and recalled that Dulles himself had been charged by the Communists with having started the Korean War; the Soviets had passed photographs of the Secretary in Korea around the UN Security Council, presumably designed to prove that he had begun everything with an attack on North Korea by South Korea.

CHAPTER VIII

Sputnik and a Sputtering Economy

Fear cannot be banished, but it can be calm and without panic; and it can be mitigated by reason and evaluation.

—*Vannevar Bush*

AT 7:30 on the evening of Friday, October 4, 1957, at the Tyuratam Range in Kazakhstan, the Soviet Union fired into orbit the world's first manmade satellite. It carried a new name into the language—"Sputnik," Russian for "traveling companion." Two hours after Sputnik had successfully completed its first orbit of the earth, the Soviet news agency, Tass, began broadcasting details to the world. Sputnik, Tass said, was circling the earth in a ninety-five-minute orbit about 560 miles up, traveling at approximately eighteen thousand miles an hour. The satellite itself had a diameter of twenty-two inches, a weight of 184 pounds. From two transmitters, it was sending continuous radio signals to the earth.

This feat precipitated a wave of apprehension throughout the Free World. Newspaper, magazine, radio, and television commentators joined the man in the street in expressions of dismay over this proof that the Russians could no longer be regarded as "backward," and had even "beaten" the United States in a spectacular scientific competition. People now recalled with concern that only a few weeks earlier the Soviet Union had claimed the world's first successful test of a multi-stage ICBM—a shot which, the Russians said, demonstrated that they could fire a missile "into any part of the world."

The Soviet scientific achievement was impressive. The size of the thrust required to propel a satellite of this weight came as a distinct surprise to us. There was no point in trying to minimize the accomplishment or the warning it gave that we must take added efforts to ensure maximum progress in missile and other scientific programs.

Most surprising of all, however, was the intensity of the public concern. Soviet space ambitions had been no secret. In April of 1955 the Soviet Union had named publicly a commission of scientists who would seek to launch a satellite. (They had in fact been at work for a year or more.) In June 1957, for example, Soviet scientists at an International Geophysical Year meeting,[1] reminded the world of their intention.[2] In September they reiterated it, this time announcing estimates of the satellite's approximate weight. Nonetheless, the possibility of Soviet success had either been accepted, or ignored, by our own people. As a matter of fact, the *New York Times,* on October 1, 1957, carried on its front page an article headlined "Light May Flash in Soviet's 'Moon'"; the story caused little stir. Yet three days later, when the "moon" became a fact, its light was blinding. Politicians declared themselves "shocked." Alleging inexcusable delay in our own space program, Senators Stuart Symington and Henry Jackson charged, on the day after the Russians' Sputnik announcement, that our government's policy of economy had caused this country's satellite program to fall behind. They purported to read in the Sputnik success alarming evidence that the Soviet Union was now not only first in space, but far ahead in guided missiles.

Why, such critics demanded, were we not the first to place a satellite in space?

One answer, which the political opposition soon realized and understandably soft-pedaled, was supplied by one of America's foremost missile experts. "The United States," Dr. Wernher von Braun said, "had no ballistic missile program worth mentioning between 1945 and 1951. Those six years, during which the Russians obviously laid the groundwork for their large rocket program, are irretrievably lost. . . . our present dilemma is not due to the fact that we are not working hard enough now, but that we did not work hard enough during the first six to ten years after the war."

* * *

To understand the meaning of Dr. von Braun's statement, it is necessary to retrace the story of the missile program, for the satellite vehicle is dependent upon the same "booster" (first-stage rocket) as the one

[1] An international cooperative scientific study project involving scientists from forty nations. The "Year" actually spanned eighteen months, from July 1, 1957, through December 1958.

[2] As early as November of 1956 our intelligence people had estimated the U.S.S.R. would probably have the ability to launch an earth satellite after November of 1957.

which launches a long-range missile.[3] It was in this effort—the development of large-thrust boosters—that the Soviets had achieved a spectacular head start.

Warnings had not been lacking, immediately following the war, that missile development should be accorded high priority. In 1948, for example, a Presidential Air Policy Commission had said: "It would be unwise to assume . . . that other nations will not have . . . missiles capable of delivering an attack on the United States mainland . . . by the end of 1952. . . . the United States must press most energetically and immediately its basic and applied research and development program . . . with a view toward the development at the earliest possible date of the most effective piloted aircraft and guided missiles and the defense against them." In February of 1947, when I was serving as Chief of Staff of the Army, I had reported at a hearing before the House Military Appropriations Subcommittee that "in the field of guided missiles, electronics, and supersonic aircraft we have no more than scratched the surface of possibilities which we must explore in order to keep abreast of the rest of the world. Neglect to do so could bring our country to ruin and defeat in an appallingly few hours."

However, the responsible political authorities, preoccupied in those years with the reduction of military force and expenditures, failed to put more than token effort into the development of the ballistic missile. In the seven years between fiscal years 1947 and 1953, the United States programed less than seven million dollars for long-range ballistic missiles. Twice, once in 1947 and again in 1950, the Executive refused to spend

[3] The satellite and the missile do have many different requirements. The satellite, for example, requires instruments of considerable power and yet light weight so that it can send messages back to earth affording information on the nature of outer space. Without this instrumentation the launching of a satellite is a completely useless stunt. It requires, furthermore, a system for firing the second- and third-stage rockets at such time as to give the satellite its maximum impetus at a point in its trajectory when it has assumed the intended altitude.

The missile, on the other hand, faces problems of re-entry into the earth's atmosphere, a problem not shared with these first satellites which were not designed for recovery. This proved to be a metallurgical problem of no mean proportions because of the high temperatures generated on the surface of the re-entering nose cones. Furthermore, to launch a satellite the size of the Soviet Sputniks, a booster was required of far greater thrust than that necessary for any of our own missiles, even the intercontinental type. (This was due partly to the efficiency we had obtained in yield per pound of warhead.)

While a successful satellite program is related to a successful missile program, the achievement of superiority in one does not necessarily indicate superiority in the other.

money which Congress had appropriated to the Air Force for this purpose, thus cutting back on the Air Force's work on missile research and development.

Deeply concerned in 1953 at the previous lack of attention given to missile development, my administration quickly turned to outstanding scientists and engineers to determine the feasibility of developing effective weapons of this character. On February 10, 1954, one of those scientific groups, headed by Dr. John von Neumann, reported the possibility of a major breakthrough—as the result of AEC research—in reducing the size of missile warheads and recommended development of a correspondingly designed intercontinental ballistic missile (ICBM). Because it takes about two hundred pounds of launching weight to put one pound of warhead on target several thousand miles away, and because the first atomic warheads weighed nine thousand pounds, this reduction was a requisite to the development of an effective ICBM. By May the Castle bomb tests in the Pacific had substantiated the von Neumann findings. In accordance with this report, the Air Force reshaped its program and began to accelerate work on an ICBM. By early 1955 its Atlas project was mushrooming: from the fiscal year 1953 figure of $3 million, in 1954 it went to $14 million and in 1955 to $161 million.

In February of 1955 a second scientific committee, headed by Dr. James R. Killian, recommended that we develop, along with the ICBM, an intermediate-range ballistic missile (IRBM) with a range of fifteen hundred miles. By the summer of 1955 the Air Force research and development ICBM program had been given the highest priority, and by December we concluded it wise to assign highest priority to programs for two ICBMs, Atlas and Titan, and two IRBMs, Jupiter and Thor. To these programs we devoted all the resources that they could usefully absorb at any given time.[4]

The earth satellite program was, on the other hand, unrelated to missile development in the beginning. My first intimation that the orbiting of an earth satellite was either feasible or desirable came in 1954, the year when world scientists, meeting in Rome, urged the construction of satellites for the International Geophysical Year. In 1955 we agreed to undertake such a project, and Jim Hagerty, in company with Dr. Alan T. Waterman and Dr. Detlev W. Bronk, director and chairman, respectively, of the National Science Foundation, made an appropriate announcement from the White House. The American space program thus in no way began as a race or contest with any other nation. Instead, the under-

[4] We programmed $515 million for fiscal year 1956; $1.3 billion for 1957.

taking and all information gained from it were something of a gift to the scientific community of the entire world.

In the United States we were careful to keep the earth satellite program separated from the Defense Department's work on long-range ballistic missiles. Though the Navy would supply the launching facilities for the satellite, it was to go into orbit strictly as a peaceful scientific experiment, and was not to interfere with our top priority work on missiles. No secret missile information would be involved in the satellite program; our scientists deliberately planned to share all information acquired with participating scientists all over the world.

This separation of the earth satellite program ("Project Vanguard") from the military missile program had disadvantages, to be sure, the principal one being that the satellite program could not make full use of all the advances made in our experimentation with military missiles. The Army, in particular, had a group of scientists and engineers at the Redstone Arsenal who, as it turned out, could undoubtedly have placed a satellite in orbit sometime late in 1956, considerably before the Soviets.[5] However, when this capability was discovered in the middle of 1956, the Defense Department and the National Science Foundation showed little inclination either to drop Vanguard, already well under way, or to divert the Redstone group from missiles to satellite work. Since no obvious requirement for a crash satellite program was apparent, there was no reason for interfering with the scientists and their projected time schedule.

Much vital work on both the missile and satellite programs was going on during the spring of 1957, but that was the period when the opposition Congress was engaged in reducing my legislative program, making cuts which, in their effect upon mutual security and defense, were serious and, to me, frustrating. At one meeting I told Republican legislative leaders that our security demanded that we be the first nation to produce operational long-range ballistic missiles, and that we should fight with all our resources against the opponents in the House of Representatives who had threatened to reduce the Defense Department budget by $2 billion, principally in appropriations for missiles and aircraft.

At another meeting Charlie Wilson reported that some members of the Congress had criticized the Defense Department for using some of its emergency funds to help tide over the earth satellite program. The costs of Vanguard had mushroomed, and he felt he had allocated to it about all he could, particularly at a time when he was having difficulty

[5] By use of the Jupiter-C booster, a by-product of their developing the Army Redstone.

in finding funds necessary for essential missile projects. Both he and Dr. Waterman hesitated to try to wring more money needed for satellites out of the Congress, bent as it was at that moment on "economy."

The funds for Vanguard were eventually found,[6] and the program continued as rapidly as, in the scientists' opinions, the money could be usefully spent. But its progress was not without delays and difficulties —some created by the same legislators who were later so quickly converted to impatience with our efforts.

* * *

On the morning of Tuesday, October 8, I met with a group of my principal military and scientific advisers to discuss the Soviet satellite and the reaction to it. I was particularly annoyed by a complaint made publicly by two Army officers over the earlier decision to continue the Navy's Vanguard as the United States satellite program, when, according to them, a booster developed by the Army could have long since done the job. I asked Donald A. Quarles, Deputy Secretary of Defense, about this report.

"There is no doubt," he replied, "that the Army Redstone, had it been used, could have orbited a satellite a year or more earlier." But he reviewed and defended the reasons for the separation of the satellite and missile programs. Basically the reasons were simple. In the satellite program, a part of the International Geophysical Year project, it was expected that all information gained would be freely given to all nations. Observers would be welcome. On the other hand, in a missile program, many defense secrets would be jealously guarded. In order to be successful in both purposes—and to keep the satellite effort from interfering with the high-priority work on ballistic missiles—it seemed mandatory to separate the programs.

Then Secretary Quarles brought up an additional point: "The Russians have in fact done us a good turn, unintentionally, in establishing the concept of freedom of international space." By orbiting Sputnik, which had gone into flight over the airspace of country after country, they themselves had confirmed this principle. We felt certain that we could get a great deal more information of all kinds out of the free use of space than they could. Later that same morning I met with Secretary

[6] In a supplemental appropriation bill which I signed late in August of 1957, the Congress, at my request, authorized the transfer of an additional $34.2 million for Vanguard out of the Defense Department's 1958 appropriation.

Wilson. I directed him to have the Army prepare its Redstone at once as a backup for the Navy Vanguard.

That afternoon we conferred with Dr. Bronk of the National Science Foundation.

"Is there anything in the Soviet achievement," Governor Adams asked, "to make us alter our research and development program, particularly in the missile field?"

Dr. Bronk's answer was instantaneous: "No, in my opinion, there is not. We can't always go changing our program in reaction to everything the Russians do."

The next morning at a news conference I congratulated Soviet scientists on putting a satellite into orbit. I reminded the reporters that merging our scientific satellite effort with our military programs "could have produced an orbiting United States satellite before now, but to the detriment of scientific goals and military progress." Therefore, I concluded, though Sputnik proved that the Russians have a "very powerful thrust in their rocketry," so far as security was concerned, the new satellite did "not raise my apprehensions."

* * *

Nonetheless there were two problems created by the Soviet Sputnik. The first, a short-term one, was to find ways of affording perspective to our people and so relieve the current wave of near-hysteria; the second, to take all feasible measures to accelerate missile and satellite programs.

To discuss these matters I asked the members of the Science Advisory Committee of the Office of Defense Mobilization, a group of distinguished scientists, to meet with me. As the group gathered in mid-October, I said that I had invited them in order to learn what ideas and proposals they might like to advance. The question before us was plain: How could all the many governmental and government-connected scientific activities be best supported so as to achieve the best kind of progress? I was curious, of course, to find out whether this group really thought that American science was being truly outdistanced.

Dr. Isidor Rabi, of Columbia University, was the first to reply.

"Today," he said, "we can see a number of advantages on our side. But the Russians have picked up a tremendous momentum. Unless we take vigorous action, they could pass us swiftly, just as in a period of twenty to thirty years we caught up with Western Europe and then left it far behind."

Dr. E. H. Land, president of the Polaroid Corporation, went even further. He was concerned primarily with a difference in attitude between ourselves and the Soviets regarding science. In the United States these days, he said, we were not great builders for the future but rather we seemed more preoccupied with stressing mass production of things we had already achieved; the Soviets, on the other hand, are in a pioneering frame of mind, regarding science as an essential tool and as a way of life. In Russia, Dr. Land concluded, science was being pursued, almost universally, both for enjoyment and for the strength of the country.

The country, Dr. Land thought, would reap a tremendous return if I could find ways of inspiring our youth to pursue a whole variety of scientific adventures. There must be some way, he said, to give science the popular appeal in this country that it held in the Soviet Union. We had, of course, done a number of things to give such encouragement [see Appendix K].

I questioned the assumption that the Russians were trying to inspire all their people to enter scientific pursuits. I thought instead, from watching their record over the years, that they had adopted a practice of culling out the best minds and ruthlessly spurning the rest, so far as higher education was concerned. I said I would seek out every possibility for kindling more enthusiasm for science among young Americans, but I told the scientists that it was fatuous to think that one speech—or any one man—could do the job. There would be a need for an unlimited follow-through. People were alarmed and were thinking about science and education; perhaps this reaction could be turned to good effect.

Dr. Rabi had another suggestion. Many policy matters coming to the President, he said, include a strong scientific component. He therefore recommended the appointment of an outstanding full-time scientific adviser to the White House staff. This I thought a fine idea and remarked that an adviser in that position would also be helpful in stimulating interest in science.[7]

* * *

Coincidentally with all these preoccupations, we had, for some time, been intently scanning indicators of the nation's economy because of developing signs of weakness—signs which did nothing to cheer up the country after Sputnik.

[7] Later in the meeting one member of the group, Dr. Jerome B. Wiesner of MIT, reminded everyone that much of the problem in missiles and satellites came from our late start, rather than from delays after they were initiated by the current administration.

"I have avoided bringing up this fact," I said, "because it tends to make the question a political football." Not all my scientific advisers were Republicans.

Throughout my Presidency I made it a practice to keep in close touch with the nation's business health by means of weekly reports, in capsule form, from various Departments. A typical summary from Secretary of Commerce Lewis Strauss, for example, would cover steel mill operations, automobile output and sales, crude oil and coal production, electric power consumption, railroad car loadings, department store sales, stock indices, and employment figures. When I noted what might appear as a change in trend in any of the areas, I would ask for a detailed report. The Council of Economic Advisers alerted me to broad movements in the economy, giving me a weather map of the climate of business, a map which continuously improved in its promptness and accuracy.

On October 14 I had a major conference with a group of economic experts, including among others, Secretary of the Treasury Robert B. Anderson, who had succeeded George Humphrey; Professor Raymond J. Saulnier, who had succeeded Arthur F. Burns as Chairman of the Council of Economic Advisers; and William McChesney Martin, Jr., Chairman of the Board of Governors of the Federal Reserve System. After a long discussion, all present concurred with Martin, who said, "The economy is making a sidewise movement with a slight tendency to decline." In layman's terms, a recession could be in the offing.

"We must watch several dangers," Dr. Saulnier added. "Federal revenues, instead of totaling $76 billion this year, might come to only $72 billion. Unemployment might go up—by a half million or even as much as a million and a half. We must take every measure to prevent a sharp decline in the economy."

The group agreed to meet periodically and to keep me informed on government measures that might be advantageous in combating tendencies toward recession.

* * *

In the midst of problems came a welcome interlude—a long-planned state visit from Queen Elizabeth of England and Prince Philip. They arrived in Washington on Thursday morning, October 17. Enthusiastic crowds, standing in a drizzling rain, lined the streets to greet them. My son John and daughter-in-law Barbara joined us for luncheon, and at eight o'clock that night came the first of a lengthy series of engagements. The British Embassy had set up for the royal couple a four-day schedule so crowded that it would have killed anybody but two people as young and vigorous as they. I later told Prime Minister Macmillan that I would have fired any aide who dared to set up for me a program like theirs.

In toasting the Queen at the state dinner that evening I recalled our association with her countrymen back in the days of World War II: "To me was given the great privilege of serving with the people of that nation for almost four years. From the Royal Family to the humblest citizen, they so conducted themselves that they enlisted the admiration, the liking, and the respect of every American who came in contact with them."

Then I reaffirmed a conviction that had been made even stronger, if possible, during the events of the weeks just past:

"Those great days are not over. The Free World is engaged in a struggle and the total of the Free World's assets are so much greater than those of our potential enemy, . . . that it is ridiculous to compare their brains, their abilities in science, in philosophical thought, or in any phase of culture or of the arts with the combined total of the Free World.

"But I say 'combined total' advisedly. We are too much separated by things that concern us locally. This is a struggle of ideologies, of a religious way of life against atheism, of freedom against dictatorship.

"But we have the power. The only thing to do is to put it together.

"Our scientists must work together. NATO should not be thought of merely as a military alliance. NATO is a way of grouping ability—of our manhood, our resources, of our industries and our factories.

"At the heart and foundation of all of this, the English-speaking people march forward together, to stand steadfast behind the principles that have made the two nations great—of the same faith in their God, and in themselves—a belief in the rights of man.

"That is the way we will go forward. That courage—the respect we have for Britain—is epitomized in the affection we have for the Royal Family. . . .

"Ladies and gentlemen, will you please rise with me and drink a Toast to the Queen."

For the entire period of their stay, the Queen and Prince lived with us in the White House, giving us a most pleasant change of pace amidst our day-to-day space and budgetary concerns. We renewed friendships that went back to 1942, when the Queen was a very young Crown Princess.

The couple found time to visit the Upperville area in Virginia, where the Queen was anxious to see the horses so popular in that region. On Sunday the four of us together went to two religious services, first to Episcopal services at the Washington Cathedral and immediately thereafter to the Presbyterian church where my wife and I were parishioners. The route we were to follow from and to the White House had been previously published, with the result that gaily dressed crowds greeted the couple all along the way. It was a beautiful autumn day; Washington was looking its very best, and the Queen and her husband seemed to enjoy it to the full.

Among her most enthusiastic greeters were our four grandchildren. The Queen, a mother herself, brought them handsomely bound books, appropriate to the age of each—Kipling, *Alice in Wonderland,* and the like. By agreement we reserved an hour where she could receive all four—the eldest was then nine years of age, the youngest, two. The children, particularly the older ones, were impressed. Still, having learned something about queens and kings, I am sure they were expecting to meet two persons dressed in brilliant robes, jewels, and crowns. To find that the Queen of England, the young woman talking to them, wore only a dress, however lovely, seemed to perplex them at first but the beautiful and charming lady soon captivated them by her graciousness.

At the time of the Queen's visit, Sputnik had been orbiting the earth for some two weeks and I was anxious to learn of the British reaction. Strangely enough the Prince implied that the British people, on the whole, were far less apprehensive about the satellite than was our population. Like ourselves they had long since heard of the Soviet intention to put a satellite in space, but they seemed to take its successful orbiting as an expected development.

This was one ceremonial visit that we were sorry to see end. However, I think our visitors could have scarcely shared this feeling; they had spent days crowded with so much activity and so many people that they must have looked forward to a period of rest and quiet.

* * *

The Queen's visit, as pleasant an interlude as it was, could not interrupt for long the need for attention to less pleasant subjects and people.

The Democratic Advisory Council, for example—a body, incidentally, that was almost as objectionable to the Democratic leadership in the Congress as it was amusing to us—was, as usual, excessively verbal in this hour of difficulty. I was not too much surprised when, on October 21, I read that it had issued a statement of alarm about the economy, charging that the administration's "negative" policies had thwarted growth, favored big business, and failed to halt inflation. "We cannot," it declared in familiar phrases, "afford to wait until Republican policy gets us into a full-scale depression."

On the 22nd of October I went to New York to speak on medical education. I had completed preparation of the talk three weeks earlier, the day before Sputnik went up, but the headlines after my speech took note of two last-minute additions.

The first was "I shall seek opportunities to talk with the American people, telling them of my beliefs and my determinations in these matters." The "matters" were the methods of raising the level of our achievements in science, the character and power of our defense and economy, and our responsibilities abroad. "I have unshakable faith in the capacity of informed, free citizens to solve every problem involved," I said, adding that if in my forthcoming series of speeches I could offer perspective and truth, they would be worth any amount of time and effort.

The second insertion was also impromptu, made on the rostrum as I was speaking against morbid pessimism about the capacity of our private enterprise system to generate and maintain high levels of employment, production, and income.

I was delighted, I said, in a short talk with the guest of honor, Alfred P. Sloan, to hear him ask why people were so pessimistic about our economy, one of the great things that man had produced. There were a good many people in the room that night, I added, who had served in the war and I didn't believe that any one of them ever saw a victory won by a man with his chin lowered to his chest. "You have to get it up!" I said, and this one sentence gave the ensuing talks the light-hearted label, "chins-up speeches." But before the speeches could be drafted, there were other developments.

* * *

In the weeks and months after Sputnik many Americans seemed to be seized not only with a sudden worry that our defenses had crumbled, but also with an equally unjustified alarm that our entire educational system was defective. The Soviets, some suspected, would soon surpass us intellectually, if indeed they had not already done so.

Acting on such an assumption, many argued for a broad-gauge crash federal outlay to finance higher education. In answer to such suggestions, I could only remind people to think the problem through: "There are very grave dangers that would accompany any initiation of *general* federal support for these institutions," I wrote to one educator. "In this statement I do not mean, of course, to be opposed to support . . . in special areas to meet special and pressing needs of the government." But I was convinced that my objections to the concept of generalized and direct federal help for all higher education were sound. I enumerated several:[8]

[8] Several years later the Association of American Universities issued a comprehensive document in which it opposed general federal assistance to higher education but favored "categorical aid" in areas of greatest national concern.

(a). The United States government can obtain no money for this purpose that is not already in the hands of its citizens, corporations, states and localities. Consequently, the process of taking the money away from citizens to return it to localities for special purposes implies a centralization of wisdom in Washington that certainly does not necessarily exist.

(b). The more that our institutions, in general practice, lean on the federal government for this kind of help, the more they invite a kind of federal influence and domination that could have very bad effects. These I do not need to elaborate. . . .

Geographic as well as functional distribution of power has benefited this nation enormously. I hope that this concept may always continue to rule our thinking.

Having said this, I do assure you that I frequently approve federal aid for special educational purposes as indicated above. Moreover, I am heartily in favor of liberal support of public institutions by the states themselves, believing that there is no more necessary function in the country than the proper education of our youth. This means that opportunity must be open to the poor as well as to those who can defray the costs of their own education. . . .

Other persons recommended astronomical amounts of direct defense spending. Again and again I reiterated my philosophy on the defense budget: Excessive spending helps cause deficits, which cause inflation, which in turn cuts the amount of equipment and manpower the defense dollar can buy. The process is circular and self-defeating.

Every addition to defense expenditures does not automatically increase military security. Because security is based upon moral and economic, as well as purely military strength, a point can be reached at which additional funds for arms, far from bolstering security, weaken it.[9]

But I also rejected advice which urged that I submit a balanced budget for the next fiscal year, no matter how impelling the reasons for additional expenditures. In November, for example, I received a letter on this subject from George Humphrey:

[9] Moreover, when a science and engineering program is going ahead flat-out at 100 per cent capacity, more money cannot speed it up, any more than all the water in the Mississippi can speed the growth of a tree. When Dr. Wernher von Braun was asked a question about increasing defense spending, for example, he replied that "some additional funds for basic and applied research and development for future growth potential would help tremendously in the long run." But he also said, by and large, our five key ballistic missile programs could not be speeded up appreciably by an increase in funds. ". . . We don't need excessive amounts of extra money—we certainly don't have to double our present missile budget."

> I believe the Budget for next year must be reduced below the amount of this year's Budget in a significant amount. Adjustments between departments can be made both throughout the government and in the Pentagon itself. It is the total that is of first importance. . . .
>
> I realize that the total defense budget cannot properly be decreased at this time, but I think our country would respond tremendously to some reduction in other departments.

I replied at once:

> . . . My instant reaction is that if confidence in this country will be won only if we have a significant reduction in the budget, and damaged or even destroyed if the budget goes up, then there better be some looking for storm cellars. . . .
>
> Over the past five years it seems to me that I have put in two-thirds of my time fighting increased expenditures in government [see Appendix L].

George was now out of government, but wanting to draw him out on matters affecting the economy, I reviewed for him some of the work I had done to reduce costs and achieve a sound pay-as-you-go budgetary position. He already knew that the administration had cut the roster of federal civil positions by a quarter of a million. We had carefully prepared every military budget so as to support only the essential, shifting the emphasis from traditional or conventional defense to the development of powerful deterrent forces; had tried (unsuccessfully) to make the interest rates for borrowings from the federal Treasury at least equal to the cost to the government of getting the money; had so far as practicable taken the government out of business that properly pertained to private industry. In appropriate welfare programs, we had striven to limit federal participation to that of leadership or partnership with individual states. By every practical means we had sought to decentralize governmental activities to states and communities except where obviously the federal government had to assume primary responsibility.

Counteracting efforts toward cost reduction were several important influences or developments. First, the reports of the scientific-military committees in 1954–55 had led us to large and increasing expenditures for missiles, satellites, and improved military weaponry of all kinds. Polaris had become one of our most useful and most expensive programs. Another upward spiraling influence was political—the conviction held by so many politicians that more rather than less federal participation in education, health preservation, and housing was mandatory. Increased federal spending, they argued, was "good for the country."

* * *

One approach to increased security was to pool brainpower. Our defenses were cooperative—why could not our research be cooperative also? When Prime Minister Macmillan came to Washington in late October, he and I announced that our representatives to NATO would urge an enlarged Atlantic effort in scientific research and development. I would ask Congress to amend the Atomic Energy Act to permit close collaboration in atomic research between our scientists and engineers and those of the Great Britain and other friendly countries.

Our atomic energy laws had been written when we thought we had a monopoly in this branch of science. Now, when many of our former secrets were known to our enemies, it made no sense to keep them from our friends. I wanted the law changed, and I told my principal associates, as they studied the prospect of sharing nuclear information with others, "Don't be too lawyer-like. A great alliance requires, above all, faith and trust on both sides."

Harold and I agreed that in the absence of the disarmament we both sought there should be increased assurance that nuclear weapons would in fact be available for the common security when needed. By the end of the month, the Defense Department was developing a plan for a NATO stockpile of atomic weapons.

* * *

Then on November 2 the world received word that the Soviet Union had launched its second satellite—an eleven-hundred-pound vehicle with an air-conditioned compartment containing a dog, named "Laika" or "Limonchek" ("Little Lemon"). This time there was no hysteria. By a strange but compassionate turn, public opinion seemed to resent the sending of a dog to certain death—a resentment that the Soviet propagandists tried to assuage, after its death, by announcing that it had been comfortable to the end.

* * *

The public, however, became bewildered and upset when word got out that a far from optimistic secret report had been made to me in the National Security Council. The report was prepared by a group of private citizens who operated under a lengthy title: The Security Resources Panel of the Office of Defense Mobilization Science Advisory Committee.

Their findings soon came to be called "the Gaither Report."[10] The committee was originally organized to investigate the "relative value of the various active and passive measures to protect the civil population in case of nuclear attack and its aftermath"—or civil defense—the group later agreed to expand the study. It finally included an examination of the deterrent value of our retaliatory forces, and the economic and political consequences of any significant change in our defense programs.

This panel, like others, had been formed to bring new minds and background experience to bear on major problems of government. It was empowered to receive information from government agencies and departments and to come up with an independent appraisal. With no vested interest in a particular department, and no federal jobs to protect, the panel was a means of obtaining independent judgments.

The Gaither Report contained voluminous background studies, based on both classified and public information. It included some sobering observations: (1) that the Soviet Gross National Product, though no more than one-third that of the United States, was increasing at a much faster rate than ours; (2) that the Soviet Union was spending on its armed forces and heavy industry an amount about *equal* to that of the United States; (3) that the Soviet Union had enough fissionable material for at least 1500 nuclear weapons in 4500 long- and short-range jet bombers, 250–300 long-range submarines, and an extensive air defense system; (4) that for more than a year, the Soviet Union had been producing ballistic missiles with a 700-mile range; (5) that the Soviet Union could, by late 1959, possibly launch an attack against the United States with 100 intercontinental ballistic missiles carrying megaton nuclear warheads; and (6) that if such an attack should come, our civilian population would be unprotected, and the planes in our Strategic Air Command (SAC), except for a small fraction of them on "alert status," would be vulnerable.

From these observations the panel went to a sweeping set of recommendations: on the need to build fallout shelters on a massive scale, to improve our air defense capability, to pool technological resources with our allies, to increase the Strategic Air Command's offensive power, to increase our forces for limited warfare, to step up our anti-submarine activities, and to reorganize the Pentagon and end interservice rivalries.

[10] It had been established in April of 1957 under the chairmanship of Mr. H. Rowan Gaither, Jr., then Chairman of the Board of the Ford Foundation. In the course of its study, Mr. Gaither had become ill, and Robert C. Sprague, chairman of the Sprague Electric Company, became the panel's director, with William C. Foster of the Olin Mathieson Chemical Corporation as co-director. Robert Lovett, John J. McCloy, Frank Stanton, Jerome B. Wiesner, and others served on the board.

When my associates and I considered and discussed the report, I remarked, "It will be interesting to find out how long it can be kept secret." A roughly accurate account soon appeared in a local publication.

In the weeks following, opposition politicians clamored for the release of the official text. Senator Lyndon Johnson asked for a version with classified information deleted. In a subsequent meeting, those who supported publication argued that rumor respecting the report was painting a much worse picture than the report itself justified; its release, they argued, would therefore have a calming effect. Moreover, as Vice President Nixon observed, "Most of the recommendations are already in the papers anyway. Making the document public should give us no great problem."

A second group, however, argued that release of the report would have "catastrophic results." It would violate a long-standing practice, they said, never to make public a report made to the President in the confidence of the National Security Council. What our political opponents wanted, this group contended, was the set of tables estimating the relative strength of the United States and the Soviet Union year by year, over the next several years.

I did not agree with all of the panel's hypothetical figures; moreover, the panel had failed to take into account certain vital information and other considerations. For example, I reminded Mr. Gaither and his associates that our overseas bases gave us a great capacity for dispersion and that the Free World, holding the periphery, could pose a threat to the Soviet Union from a multitude of points. I recognized that any good, critically minded panel could, by concentrating on one aspect of a total situation, find that there is more to do. The reactions of the members of the National Security Council were roughly the same as my own: the Gaither Report contained certain useful distillations of data and some interesting suggestions, but the entire report could not be accepted as a master blueprint for action. The President, unlike a panel which concentrates on a single problem, must always strive to see the totality of the national and international situation. He must take into account conflicting purposes, responding to legitimate needs but assigning priorities and keeping plans and costs within bounds. I could see no national advantage in broadcasting the opinions and suppositions in the report with the attendant risks to security.

Foster Dulles expressed similar objections. The panel, he observed, had confined itself to military problems. "But the international struggle," he said, "is not just military. The Soviet Union made its greatest gains—its greatest seizures of territory and people—in 1945–50, when it had the ravages of war to repair and when only the United States had the atomic bomb." He felt that if the United States should embark on a massive shelter program to protect itself, despite the fact that our allies could not afford such protection, we could "just write off our friends in Europe." Furthermore, he said, the United States should not overdevote resources to defense, only to lose the world economic competition.

In spite of all the fury and conflicting advice, the decision on releasing the text was quite easy to make. The answer was "no." I informed Senator Lyndon Johnson of my decision, pointing out that "throughout our history the President has withheld confidential advisory opinions and information whenever he found that its disclosure would be inimical to the nation's security. . . . Only by preserving the confidential nature of such advice is it possible to assemble such [advisory] groups or for the President to avail himself of such advice."

As I continued to consider the report, I noted it remarked on the $38 billion ceiling on defense expenditures. I reminded the members of the panel that I had urgently recommended a figure of $39.5 billion, but the Congress had seen fit to reduce it by $1.5 billion.

The problem remained, however, of what to do about the panel's specific recommendations. I recognized they were sincerely made. We would study them earnestly, taking up proposals one by one, and decide whether to accept, modify, or reject them. Given the atmosphere of the time, "We must neither panic nor become complacent," I told my associates. "We should decide what needs to be done, and do it—avoiding extremes." The problem was not unfamiliar. Our security depended on a set of associated and difficult objectives: to maintain a defense posture of unparalleled magnitude and yet to do so without a breakdown of the American economy.

"We must get people to understand that we confront a tough problem," I said, "but one that we can lick." We could not turn the nation into a garrison state.

Accordingly, in the early months of 1958, the Department of Defense, the Department of State, and other security agencies thoroughly explored the panel's recommendations. Some of them we accepted. (I was personally interested most in the measures to put more SAC bombers on an alert status and to disperse our SAC bases.)[11] Other recommendations were accepted with modifications, such as the recommendation to increase the number of ICBMs by the end of fiscal '63. One recom-

[11] The SAC bases were located, by and large, where our old Air Force bases had been before—and many of those had simply been appendages to old Army posts. The SAC establishment had, to this extent at least, grown somewhat like Topsy. The Gaither Report suggested making use of other air facilities.

mendation we rejected out of hand—a proposal to build blast shelters to protect SAC runways by tunneling them into mountains.

A massive program for fallout shelters had often been considered, but the panel's recommendations brought it up again for lively debate. Former Governor Leo A. Hoegh of Iowa, now Civil Defense Administrator, argued that $22.5 billion for fallout shelters would be a good investment—one which might save fifty million American lives. But Foster Dulles disagreed, emphatically. "If a wave of a hand could create those shelters," he said, "we'd of course be better off with them than without them. But it's hard to sustain simultaneously an offensive and defensive mood in a population. For our security, we have been relying above all on our capacity for retaliation. From this policy we should not deviate now. To do so would imply we are turning to a 'fortress America' concept."

"You *are* a militant Presbyterian, aren't you?" I remarked. A little laughter around the table helped to lighten the air.

I decided that we would not embark on an all-out shelter program. But on August 8, 1958, I signed legislation, advocated by the administration for more than two years, to give the federal government and the states a joint responsibility for civil defense and to authorize federal financial help for state civil defense projects.

In the final result the Gaither Report was useful; it acted as a gadfly on any in the administration given to complacency, and it listed a number of facts, conclusions, and opinions that provided a checklist for searching examination.

On the morning of November 7 newspapers carried Khrushchev's boastful prediction of a Soviet victory over the United States in the building of heavy industry and the production of consumer goods. That evening, from my office in the White House, I delivered the first of a series of nationwide talks on science and defense. This was no exercise in positive thinking based on hopes alone. We had much about which to be confident. The talk bristled with specifics.

The United States, I said, could practically annihilate the war-making cabability of any other nation. Ever since our adoption of the so-called "New Look" in military preparation, and especially after the 1954–55 reports of our scientific panels, soaring imagination, skill, and energy had gone into our missile programs. American submarines were carrying missiles with nuclear warheads. One of our submarines had cruised under the Arctic ice cap for more than five days. We had dispersed our stock of nuclear weapons to assure that, if we were attacked, ample quantities would be available for instant retaliation.

"We are well ahead of the Soviets," I said, "in the nuclear field both in quantity and in quality. We intend to stay ahead."

Already we could fire large ballistic missiles more than a thousand miles; test missiles had traveled successfully more than thirty-five hundred miles, I said. Our many forward positions, ringing the Soviet Union, made an intermediate-range missile, for some purposes, as good as an intercontinental missile.

We had a continental warning system "reaching from far out in the Pacific around the northern edge of this continent and across the Atlantic approaches . . . a complex system of early warning radars, communication lines, electronic computers, supersonic aircraft, and ground-to-air missiles, some with atomic warheads." And I spoke of the strong ground and naval forces which we and our allies had stationed abroad.

There were the facts—as many as could be disclosed—as hard and clearly as I could state them. On them rested this conclusion: "It is my conviction, supported by trusted scientific and military advisers, that, although the Soviets are quite likely ahead in some missile and special areas, and are obviously ahead of us in satellite development, as of today the over-all military strength of the Free World is distinctly greater than that of the Communist countries."

But such facts, formidable as they were, were no reason for self-congratulation. Unless we moved further, I said, we could fall behind. As spurs to action I announced a number of specific decisions, among them:

(1) I was appointing Dr. James R. Killian, president of the Massachusetts Institute of Technology, as Special Assistant to the President for Science and Technology, a new post. He would be aided by a staff of scientists and by an advisory group—the existing Science Advisory Committee of the Office of Defense Mobilization, now enlarged, reorganized, and elevated to the White House.[12]

(2) I had directed Secretary of Defense Neil McElroy "to make certain that the Guided Missile Director is clothed with all the authority that the Secretary himself possesses" in the field of missile development, so that no administrative or interservice block would occur.

[12] The appointment of Dr. Killian, and later Dr. George B. Kistiakowsky of Harvard, worked out wonderfully. In character and accomplishment they could have had no superiors. Whatever the task—to build an airframe for the enormous B-70, or solve the metallurgical problem of ways to dissipate heat for nose cone re-entries into the earth's atmosphere—the scientific adviser kept me enlightened. My "wizard" helped me to keep the subject of space away from becoming a "race" and from deteriorating into a series of stunts. He helped to make certain that the government was supporting both basic and applied research. Without such distinguished help, any President in our time would be, to a certain extent, disabled.

(3) Any new missile program would be, when practicable, put under a single manager and administered without regard to the separate services.

Certainly we needed to feel a sense of urgency, I continued in the talk. But this did not mean that we should mount our charger and try to ride off in all directions at once. We had to clearly identify the exact and critical needs to be met, then apply our resources at that point. This meant selectivity in national expenditures of all kinds. We could not have, on an unlimited scale, both what we must have and what we would like to have. We *could* have both a sound defense and a sound economy—*if we set our priorities* and stayed with them, and if each of us was ready to carry his share of the burden.

Concluding, I said that although for that night's purposes I was stressing science and defense, we were not forgetting that there was more to science than its function in defense. The peaceful contributions of science, to healing, to enriching life, to freeing the spirit—these "are the most important products of the conquest of nature's secrets." And the spiritual powers of a nation—its religious faith, its capacity for intelligent sacrifice—these were the most important stones in any defense structure.

* * *

I had made as strong a case for confidence and sane direction as I could. I was hampered, of course, by the fact that I could not reveal secrets which in themselves would have reassured our people. For example, shortly before this address Foster Dulles, in a meeting with Allen Dulles, General Goodpaster, and me, had asked, "Should we disclose tonight that the United States has the capability of photographing the Soviet Union from very high altitudes without interference?"

Reluctantly, I decided I could not make such a revelation. It was not to become public for another two and a half years when an airplane called the U-2 fell in Soviet territory.

* * *

Six days later I flew to Oklahoma City and spoke again of deterrent and defense. I included short discussions on scientific education and greater concentration on research. We had tough choices to make, I said. Some civilian programs were desirable but not essential. Some savings would be squeezed out through the wringer. "And pressure groups will wail in anguish," I said. But we would not sacrifice security to worship a balanced budget. We would never be an aggressor—we wanted adequate security—we wanted no more than adequacy. But we would accept nothing less.

* * *

This was a period of anxiety. Sputnik had revealed the psychological vulnerability of our people. The Communists were steadily fomenting trouble and rattling sabers; our economy was sputtering somewhat, and the ceaseless and usually healthy self-criticism in which we of the United States indulge had brought a measure of genuine self-doubt. Added to these and other factors was the failure of our first satellite launching attempt in the full glare of publicity, and the alleged missile "gaps" which political observers claimed they had detected. There was ample stimulus for public uncertainty.

The Soviet satellites were a genuine technological triumph, but this was exceeded by their propaganda value. To uninformed peoples in the world, Soviet success in one area led to the belief that Soviet Communism was surging ahead in all types of activity.

One beneficial effect to us was that the Soviet achievement jarred us out of what might have been a gradually solidifying complacency in technology. It caused us to give increased attention to scientific education in this country and ultimately to all phases of education.

Their most harmful effects were to cause those people who had manifold reasons to be proud to be temporarily fearful, and to add fuel to the fire of demand for larger appropriations as the answer to everything.

The older I grow, the more I come to respect balance—not only in budgets but in people.

As we began to overcome the psychological crisis, I felt a degree of satisfaction. I could not know then that Sputnik would color events of the next three years, including the 1960 election, or that the third confidence speech on which I was working would never be delivered. Another blow to come—a personal one, just one week away—involved a sudden illness, my third in three years. As I wrote a friend on November 18:

"Since July 25th of 1956, when Nasser announced the nationalization of the Suez, I cannot remember a day that has not brought its major or minor crisis." Crisis had now become "normalcy."

CHAPTER IX

A Drastic Personal Test

It is part of the cure to wish to be cured.

—Seneca

AFTER my last office engagement on the morning of Monday, November 25, I went to Washington National Airport to extend a ceremonial greeting to the Moroccan King, Mohammed V, who was arriving for a state visit. When we had accepted the traditional salutes, reviewed the troops, and delivered the customary expressions of welcome and response, we rode together through the noontime crowds to the Guest House (formerly Blair House) where the King was to reside. There we parted to meet again at dinner that evening. I went back to the White House for a short midday rest.

Following the rest and a light lunch, I walked to my office to resume work for the afternoon.

At my desk I found papers waiting for signature. As I picked up a pen to begin, I experienced a strange although not alarming feeling of dizziness. Since the sensation lasted only a moment, I reached for another paper. Suddenly I became frustrated. It was difficult for me to take hold of the first paper on the pile. This finally accomplished, I found that the words on it seemed literally to run off the top of the page.

Now more than a little bewildered, I dropped the pen. Failing in two or three attempts to pick it up, I decided to get to my feet, and at once found I had to catch hold of my chair for stability.

I sat down quickly and rang for my secretary. As Mrs. Whitman came to my desk I tried to explain my difficulty—and then came another puzzling experience: I could not express what I wanted to say. Words—but not the ones I wanted—came to my tongue. It was impossible for me to express any coherent thought whatsoever. I began to feel truly helpless.

Actually my performance must have been worse than I suspected, for

Mrs. Whitman, after urging me to go home and unable to make any sense out of my words—which I was fully aware were nothing but gibberish—became thoroughly alarmed and called for General Goodpaster.

Andy Goodpaster wasted no time asking questions or making any attempt to diagnose the difficulty. He knew something was wrong and concentrated on getting me to my room in the Mansion. Though I was not yet convinced that I was the victim of anything more than a temporary dizzy spell, I was so puzzled by my futile efforts to communicate with my assistants that I responded without protest to Goodpaster's grasp of my arm and his urgent, "Mr. President, I think we should get you to bed."

I had no difficulty in walking and felt no pain or discomfort. In my room, Goodpaster helped me to undress and lie down. The doctor soon arrived. Having resigned myself to bed I spent no time worrying about the source of my trouble; I just turned over to take a nap.

Sometime later there arrived the inevitable medical consultants, two very gifted and (I was later to learn) well-known neurological surgeons. By this time I could communicate a little, but only a little. The doctors, following a lengthy examination, including questioning, arrived at a tentative conclusion.

I had suffered, they said, a minor "spasm"—I am not sure whether they referred to a nerve or a small blood vessel. In any event the result was, according to their explanation, a temporary interruption in communication between my mental "dictionary" and the thought I wished to express. Thus, when I sought for a word there was no way of finding the right one; so far as vocabulary was concerned I had a loss of memory. The doctors said I had improved even during the period of their visit, and predicted a full recovery in a matter of days, possibly of hours.

When the doctors left, I thought about the remainder of my day's schedule and recalled that I was to be host at a dinner that evening for King Mohammed. Encouraged by the doctors' findings, I got up about 6:00 P.M., put on a robe, and shuffled into Mamie's room adjoining. My son and my doctor were with her and all seemed less than happy—they were appalled—to see me. I was going to be present I told them at the evening festivities as planned. This started an argument, all three providing spirited opposition. They told me that Vice President Nixon had already agreed to act in my stead while Mamie asserted that if I insisted on going then she would not! It soon appeared to me that a retirement in good order was called for; I went back to bed.

There was still some apprehension in the household. Later I learned that Dr. Snyder and John shared the night watch, each sitting in my room for half the night.

When morning came I quickly learned that I was not fully recovered. My eyes happened to be attracted to a favorite picture of mine, done by Turner, the noted British water colorist. It was called "The Smugglers," a scene of smuggling a century ago on the River Clyde in Scotland. On a cliff in the background was Culzean Castle, where my wife and I had been given a life tenancy by the Scottish Trust and where we had spent pleasant days amidst some of the hospitable Scots. The picture was a favorite, not only because of the subject but because of the skill of the artist.

With the doctors once more in my room, I tried to tell them about the picture. I could remember neither its name nor that of the castle. In every way I could, I tried to give hints and clues to the assembled company, which again included my wife and son. I persisted in the effort until I began to feel annoyed (I was told later that I showed some temper). I had sense enough by then, however, to cease trying to force myself and I gave up any thought of going to the office. Indeed, the doctors kept urging me to rest—the best cure for my ailment, they said.

Gradually, memory of words returned; the doctors pronounced me 95 per cent recovered and said that before long I should be completely cured.

In this prediction they were not wholly accurate. From that time onward I have frequently experienced difficulty in prompt utterance of the word I seek. Even today, occasionally, I reverse syllables in a long word and at times am compelled to speak slowly and cautiously if I am to enunciate correctly. This is not, I am told, particularly noticeable to anyone else but it certainly is to me.

In any event I was finally pronounced fit for light duty after two days' confinement to my room, and I attended church with Mamie on Thanksgiving, about seventy-two hours after experiencing the first symptoms.

However, the doctors had one more test for me. It was one I had never heard of before; to take it I had to go to the hospital. The test itself was described to me as a charting of the electronic impulses in the head—something similar to the electrocardiogram for the heart. All over my head electrodes were held in place by small mudballs so that the operator could find whether or not any part of my brain was damaged. The verdict was that I was normal—but I still knew that my memory for words was not what it had been.

By the time I came back to work a new argument broke out over my health and planned activities. Sometime earlier I had decided to go to the NATO meeting scheduled for December only a matter of days after my illness. Doctors, friends, family, and associates protested but now, able to talk, I was determined to have my way—and for a good reason.

This particular illness was of a kind that could, if it became severe, create a situation in which the patient might be partially incapable of analyzing difficult problems and making reasonable decisions concerning them. Possibly he could become unable to express his thoughts—in the case of the President, be unable even to express a decision to resign. Some believed that a situation of this sort may have happened during the Wilson Administration. I was going to make sure it would not happen in my case.

The test I now set for myself was that of going through with my plan of proceeding to Paris and participating in the NATO conference and in all the attendant activities, some of them presumably strenuous. If I could carry out this program successfully and without noticeable damage to myself, then I would continue in my duties. If I felt the results to be less than satisfactory, then I would resign.

I do not mean to imply that there was anything dramatic in my plan; it was a simple, logical test to see whether I was physically and mentally capable of serving as President. Had I indulged myself and declined to go to Paris I would have, from then on, lost some confidence in myself.

* * *

The forthcoming conference in Paris was an important one, a NATO "summit." For the first time the several member nations were being represented by their heads of government rather than by their foreign ministers. The purpose of this unusual arrangement was the conviction, almost universally held among the NATO members, that the organization needed review and a renewed sense of its own importance which such a meeting could be expected to impart. It was to be the first NATO meeting since the Suez crisis in 1956 and the first after Sputnik went up. Furthermore, the West was beginning to sense that the nature of the Communist threat was changing. The danger of Communist military aggression and of a general war was being somewhat discounted, while more subtle infiltration and subversion under the cloak of promises of Communist aid to uncommitted countries were becoming more noticeable. These reasons were persuasive to the heads of government who were now going to Paris to take a new, hard look at the objectives and capacities of the organization.[1]

[1] To insure a bipartisan viewpoint we invited Adlai Stevenson to aid in the preparation of the United States position and to accompany us to Paris. Governor Stevenson at first accepted, but later declined to go. He did, however, work with Foster Dulles in the preparatory phase.

My departure on December 13 took place under a pall. The West was tense and uneasy because of Soviet successes in orbiting two satellites; our own first successful launching was yet a month and a half away. The American economy was showing further signs of uncertainty and slippage. And of course in my mind was the question of my future fitness to meet the rigorous demands of the Presidency.

With a small party I boarded the *Columbine* late in the evening and reached Paris at three o'clock in the afternoon. Ceremonies were held under leaden skies, with a damp and biting wind adding to everyone's discomfort. The formalities with French Premier Felix Gaillard soon over, I began my trip from Orly Airport to the U. S. Embassy.

In contrast to the cold reception I expected under the circumstances, the streets to and through Paris were thronged with thousands upon thousands of people. Apparently willing to forget their resentments against America's stand during the Suez crisis the year before, they turned out in a gesture of good will to give a warm welcome to a temporarily ailing head of an ally. I was touched and heartened. Unwilling to appear to ignore their kindness, I stood up in the open car nearly all the way into Paris. Fortunately, the automobile was going at a rapid pace and my exposure to the elements was for less than an hour.

That night, at the U. S. Embassy, I was treated to the hospitality of my gracious host and hostess, Ambassador and and Mrs. Amory Houghton. Their ability to make me feel completely relaxed and at home did much to help in the days ahead.

The next day was one of preparation. On Monday, December 16, the thirteenth anniversary of the opening of the Battle of the Bulge, the first sessions of the conference began at the Palais de Chaillot. The opening phases of the meeting were routine, with each nation's representatives delivering prepared statements. To my relief, reading a presentation caused me no distress or embarrassment; the first stage of my self-imposed test was passed.

Between plenary sessions I held conferences with various heads of government and foreign ministers, including Prime Minister Macmillan, Chancellor Adenauer, Foreign Minister Zoli of Italy, Premier Felix Gaillard, and others.

On Tuesday morning I seized an opportunity to make a nostalgic visit to my former headquarters at Marly, the Supreme Headquarters of NATO Forces that I had left five and a half years earlier. Of my former associates, only a few top ones such as General Lauris Norstad and General Courtlandt Schuyler were still there. Nevertheless, my feeling of comradeship for these military people of many nationalities was strong. But what had been represented as a quiet, informal visit turned out to be a reception. After visiting my old office I found myself on the front steps in front of a microphone, addressing a large crowd of men and their families. Ignoring the horrified looks of my staff, I removed my hat and spoke extemporaneously in public for the first time since my illness. I talked of my feeling for these people, my respect for the job they were doing, and of my occasional nostalgia for the military service. The talk was short; it could not have lasted more than a few minutes. It was easy to make, for it flowed naturally from a depth of sentiment. But to me it represented another milestone. Though I found myself thinking ahead in my sentences to pick up synonyms for words I might have trouble commanding, no one seemed to detect difficulty in my effort. I felt that my recovery was progressing satisfactorily.

The NATO meeting was a success. Its most notable characteristic was the feeling of optimism and mutual trust increased with each session. Specific proposals were adopted for the establishment of stocks of nuclear warheads in Europe and the provision of intermediate-range ballistic missiles to SACEUR (Supreme Allied Commander, Europe). Agreement was reached that European members should produce modern weapons to a larger degree and a resolution adopted that the NATO countries would accept any properly inspected procedure proposed by the Soviets that might lead to a *controlled* reduction of armaments. We agreed to a foreign minister's meeting with the Soviets to try to break the procedural deadlock on disarmament; we approved a greater pooling of scientific facilities; and greater cooperation in rendering aid to capital-hungry nations of the Free World. But the real satisfaction came from the benefits of meeting again, face to face, the heads of government with whom such close cooperation is necessary and often inspiring.

And so, feeling a sense of relief and optimism, on Thursday evening, December 19, I took leave of Ambassador and Mrs. Houghton and departed for Orly Airport.[2] I left with the conviction that the French people still held deep sentiments of friendship for the United States and of satisfaction that NATO was showing new evidence of vitality and determination.

[2] On this occasion, incidentally, in anticipation of heavy crowds again, the Secret Service came up with a device where I could, without fatigue on my part, be seen by the crowds lining the streets in the darkness. With a strong light focused on me, I sat in the back seat of a "bubble-top" car, safe from bad weather conditions but able to respond to the farewells of the crowd.

"Early in 1957, the Egyptians, with some outside help, had begun the laborious task of removing from the Canal the fifty or more ships Nasser had sunk the previous autumn."

Secretary-General of the United Nations Dag Hammarskjold watches vessel being raised in Suez Canal

SPUTNIK AND SPUTTERIN ECONOM

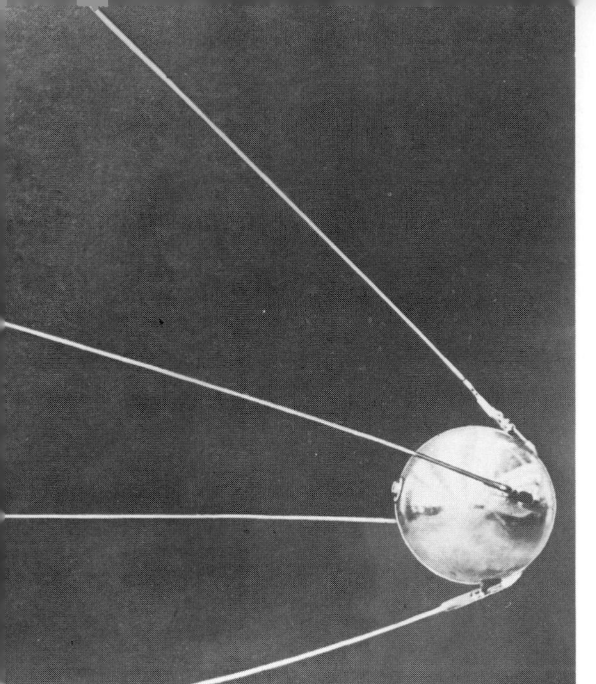

Sputnik I

"The *New York Times,* on October 1, 1957, carried on its front page an article headlined 'Light May Flash in Soviet's "Moon"'; the story caused little stir. Yet three days later, when the 'moon' became a fact, its light was blinding."

President Eisenhower (in sports shirt) watches Terrier guided missile fired from U.S.S. *Canberra*

"Ever since our adoption of the so-called 'New Look' in military preparation...soaring imagination, skill, and energy had gone into our missile programs. American submarines were carrying missiles with nuclear warheads. One of our submarines had cruised under the Arctic ice cap for more than five days."

ecretary of Defense Neil McElroy scusses Jupiter and Thor missile oduction before Senate preparedss subcommittee. Deputy Secretary onald Quarles is in the background

Thor missile unloaded from a Globemaster

en on bridge of U.S.S. *Nautilus* look place to pass under the North e during a period of low visibility

Polaris IRBM launched from a submarine under the Atlantic.

"By the end of my administration the Polaris gave the United States an extremely mobile, practically invulnerable retaliatory capability."

"This particular illness was of a kind that could, if it became severe, create a situation in which the patient could be partially incapable of analyzing difficult problems. . . . The test I now set for myself was that of going through with my plan of proceeding to Paris and participating in the NATO conference."

Opening session of the NATO conference in Paris. First row, facing the camera: Turkish Premier Adnan Menderes, Prime Minister Harold Macmillan, President Eisenhower, NATO Secretary-General Paul-Henri Spaak of Belgium, Luxembourg

Explorer I on exhibition at the National Museum of Science in Milan

"On the night of January 31, 1958, the Army was to launch Explorer I, which we hoped would be the United States' first orbiting earth satellite."

Seated: Virgil I. Grissom, Malcolm Scott Carpenter, Donald K. Slayton, Leroy Gordon Cooper, Jr. Standing: Alan B. Shepard, Jr., Walter M. Schirra, Jr., John H. Glenn, Jr.

"NASA's third purpose [was] Project Mercury. The first seven 'astronauts' to undergo rigid training for this program were selected and their names announced on April 9, 1959."

Assembly of Project Mercury space capsules in a "superclean" (sterilized) room

"Through the two and a half years following its inception, NASA made a splendid record in three fields: the practical use of earth satellites for human benefit; the scientific study of space and celestial bodies; and progress toward the exploration of outer space by man in flight."

LANDING II LEBANOI

"King Faisal of Iraq [left] and King Hussein of Jordan [right] were second cousins, and personally courageous men. Their federation, called the Arab Union, was announced on February 14, just two weeks after the formation of the U.A.R."

Iraqi soldiers patrol the gutted palace in Baghdad

"On Monday morning, July 14, 1958, I wa shocked to receive news of a coup in Baghda against the Hashemite monarchy. . . . The army apparently with mob participation, had move upon the royal palace and had murdere Crown Prince Emir Abdul Illah. The fate c King Faisal and Premier Nuri as Said . . . wa in serious doubt."

Iraqi General Kassem is followed downstairs by his chief aide, Colonel Wasfi Tahir, hours after the revolt

'he time was rapidly ap-
oaching, I believed, when
: had to move into the
iddle East, and specifi-
lly into Lebanon, to stop
: trend toward chaos."

U. S. Marines
entering Lebanon,
July 15, 1958

Unloading men
of the
U. S. Army Task Force

"When Ambassador Murphy reached Beirut on July 19, he immediately called on President Chamoun and found him nervous and depressed.... The arrival of American troops, however, seemed to increase his confidence, and he talked of issuing a peremptory order to General Chehab to attack the rebels."

mbassador Robert Murphy talks with General Chehab, commander-in-
ief of the Lebanese Army

THE TROUBLED ISLANDS AGAIN

Chinese Nationalist sentry looks to the mainland, less than two miles away

"The Chinese Communists initiated a massive artillery bombardment of both the offshore islands, firing twenty thousand rounds."

The ruins of a home in Nan Shan village, Quem

"Quemoy was strafed and the Reds sent out fighter planes in strength."

Fuel drums pushed onto Quemoy Beach, October 11

"Communist guns would cease firing for a week on Quemoy supply convoys if United States destroyers would cease to escort....

"The Nationalists took full advantage of the respite and on a single day unloaded nearly a twenty-day supply."

When we were back in Washington General Snyder turned to me to say, "You are much better than when we set out on the journey."

As he spoke, I realized that I already had abandoned any doubt concerning my physical capacity to continue my duties; during the remaining three years of my Presidency no question of the kind again occurred to me.

But three illnesses in three successive years, any one of which could have been completely disabling if not fatal, convinced me that I should make some specific arrangements for the Vice President to succeed to my office if I should incur a disability that precluded proper performance of duty over any period of significant length. I had often discussed this possibility, mostly with the Attorney General.

The problem was not simple; but in these days when even a short delay in making vital decisions might be disastrous, some satisfactory arrangement to cover the problem was necessary for the nation's safety.

As one approach we had considered the possibility of a constitutional amendment, a solution that I favored in principle. If the matter could be settled properly in an amendment, the various provisions would become a part of our basic law and thus be less susceptible to whimsical partisan interpretation or manipulation. The difficulty, however, was to find terminology to suit every case and still avoid making of the Constitution an instrument of overly detailed legalisms and instruction.[3] Any congressional enactment would, however, have the same difficulty in terminology and would moreover be susceptible to change any time that a sufficient majority in the Congress might so desire.

I felt that I should not wait for legislative or amendatory action. So I decided at once to set up a plan that, for my case, would be satisfactory. The plan is best described by quoting a hitherto unpublished letter to the Vice President.

My letter began by adverting, first, to the variety of conditions under which a "disability" of the President might occur. It then noted that even if a law should be enacted one day, or an amendment adopted to clarify the meaning of the Constitution, a considerable time would elapse before this could be accomplished. In addition, I wrote that even though he and I had

[3] The number of contingencies that can be visualized is almost limitless. Here is a sample posed to me one day: Suppose a President remains disabled and the Vice President succeeds; then the Vice President dies and is succeeded under present law by the Speaker of the House who is of another party. Then the President believes himself free of his disability and under the conditions is supposed to resume his office. Who decides? There are two or three variations, at least, to this single situation.

reached rough agreements as to the methods and procedures that we would observe between ourselves, whenever circumstances might indicate a need for him to act temporarily for me, it was still desirable to have a written record.

I continued:

> In any instance in which I could clearly recognize my own inability to discharge the powers and duties of the Presidency I would, of course, so inform you and you would act accordingly.
>
> With the exception of this one kind of case you will be the individual explicitly and exclusively responsible for determining whether there is any inability of mine that makes it necessary for you to discharge the powers and duties of the Presidency, and you will decide the exact timing of the devolution of this responsibility on you. I would hope that you would consult with the Secretary of State, Governor Adams and General Heaton, and if feasible, with medical experts assembled by him, but the decision will be yours only.
>
> I will be the one to determine if and when it is proper for me to resume the powers and duties of the Presidency.
>
> I know, of course, that you would make any decision for taking over the Presidential powers and duties only when you feel it necessary. I have no fear that you, for any fleeting or inconsequential purpose, would do so and thereby create confusion in the government. Circumstances would have to guide you, and if the imminence or occurrence of any world or domestic emergency demanded, you would have to act promptly. . . .
>
> There is only one final thought I would like to add. If any disability of mine should, in the judgment of any group of distinguished medical authorities that you might assemble, finally become of a permanent character, I would, of course, accept their decision and promptly resign my position. But if I were not able to do so, and the same group of consultants would so state, then you would take over not only the powers and duties but the perquisites of the Presidency, including the White House itself. In temporary cases of my "inability," we agree that you should act for the necessary period in your capacity as Vice President and, additionally, as "acting President."
>
> With warm regard,
>
> *As ever,*
>
> D.E.

I had been assured by the Attorney General that nothing in this letter contravened the spirit or letter of the Constitution or any of the laws of the United States.

The Vice President replied:

February 10, 1958

Dear Mr. President:

It seems to me that the procedure outlined in your letter of February 5 is in complete accord with both the intent and the letter of the disability provisions of the Constitution. I agree completely with your interpretation of the responsibilities of the Vice President in such cases.

With every good wish,

Sincerely,
/s/ Richard Nixon

Such a plan, of course, presupposed that the President and his Vice President were mutually trustful; it would scarcely work if for any reason they were personally unfriendly to, or distrustful of, each other. In this case I was confident that Dick Nixon was highly qualified to take over the duties of the Presidency on a moment's notice; so for the remainder of my term I had no reasons to worry about the continuity of Executive responsibility.

BOOK THREE

The world that is being remade on our planet is going to be a world of many mature nations. As one after another of these new nations moves through the difficult transition to modernization and learns the methods of growth, from this travail new levels of prosperity and productivity will emerge.

This world of individual nations is not going to be controlled by any one power or group of powers. This world is not going to be committed to any one ideology.

Please believe me when I say that the dream of world domination by one power or of world conformity is an impossible dream.

—Address to the Third
Special Emergency Session
of the General Assembly of
the United Nations,
August 13, 1958

CHAPTER X

Science and Defense

Let all things be done decently and in order.
—*I Corinthians 14:40*

THE startling technological developments of the mid- and late fifties—ballistic missiles, atomic-powered submarines, electronics, satellites—inevitably raised the question: could current organization and institutions cope with the problems brought on by technological progress?

The nation's security and scientific advance had always commanded the intense interest of the administration and its technical advisers, and in November of 1957 I had brought into the White House for the first time a Science Advisory Committee and a Special Assistant for Science and Technology. But by early 1958 the time had clearly arrived for another step in streamlining our military establishment and moving forward in science with speed, not haste. During the ensuing congressional session these efforts produced gratifying results:

(1) To strengthen American education, particularly in science, mathematics, and foreign languages, the Congress passed the administration's National Defense Education Bill.

(2) Despite entrenched opposition on Capitol Hill, we recommended and obtained new legislation to reduce interservice rivalries and to strengthen the control of the President and the Secretary of Defense over strategic planning and operations.

(3) Obtaining needed laws for intensifying research and development for both peaceful and military purposes, we established a new space agency under civilian authority, and orbited a succession of satellites.

* * *

Our attack in these three areas was outlined in my State of the Union message, delivered on January 9, 1958.

As I met with legislative leaders to discuss it two days before delivery, several commented on the defeatism evident in many newspaper columns. Though the legislators recognized that the actual strength of the United States was far superior to that suggested by complainers who alleged the Soviet Union had passed us in many important military fields, they also recognized the necessity for a tone and attitude in the State of the Union message which would help rekindle the trust and confidence of the American people. The two Sputniks in orbit had not, as 1958 opened, been matched by successful United States launchings. Instead, a month earlier, in a glare of publicity, a Vanguard had failed a scheduled test two seconds after takeoff. It had caught fire, fallen back to earth, and was totally lost.

Normally the State of the Union message adverts to the President's plans for the major activities of the Executive branch in the year ahead. But this was no ordinary year. To improve public confidence through specific plans of action, I decided to confine the annual message—probably for the first time in history—to just two subjects: the strength of our nation, particularly its scientific and military strength, and the pursuit of peace.

I reviewed our current military posture. Our defensive shield comprehended a vast complex of ground, sea, and air units, superbly equipped and strategically deployed around the world. We had, I explained, a powerful deterrent to war in the retaliatory power of our Strategic Air Command and naval aircraft. Even assuming a surprise attack on our bases, with a marked reduction in our striking power, our bombers would immediately be on their way in sufficient strength to accomplish their mission of devastating retaliation. This was no secret, I said; every informed government recognized this fact.

As all of us knew, at that moment the Soviets were somewhat ahead of us in the production of satellite boosters of extraordinary power. But, I assured the Congress, the progress of our programs, together with a close study of all relevant intelligence, demonstrated that we would have the missiles in the needed quantity and in ample time to sustain and strengthen the deterrent power of our increasingly efficient bombers.

Among specific measures for improving security, I first listed defense reorganization. Pointing out that some of the important new military systems which technology had produced did not fit into any existing service pattern, I said that the resulting uncertainties and the jurisdictional disputes attending them tended to bewilder and confuse the public.

I did not develop in full the charge of harmful interservice rivalries, but, "Whatever they are, America wants them stopped."[1] As one way of helping to stop bickering, I would present specific recommendations, in a separate message, for some reorganization of the Defense Department.

With respect to other facets of a comprehensive security program, I wanted a strengthened Mutual Security Program, a five-year extension of the Trade Agreements Act, and an increase in scientific cooperation with our allies.

For education and research, I recommended "a balanced program to improve our resources, involving an investment of about a billion dollars over a four-year period," and an increase in federal appropriations for basic research.

* * *

In the furor immediately following Sputnik, some alarmed citizens, who knew little of the orderly processes of education, were urging vastly increased spending and wholesale revision of our schools so as to turn nearly every student into a scientist or engineer as quickly as possible. They echoed the curious assumption, widely held in Washington, that money alone, and almost overnight, could produce trained minds. On this subject I had received from Dr. James Conant, former Ambassador to the Federal Republic of Germany, a thoughtful telegram—a message particularly impressive because of his twenty years as President of Harvard University, and his intimate knowledge of and analytical observations on our secondary school system.

Proposals for "crash programs put forward in recent days," he wrote, "may cause damage to schools by confusing school boards and undermining confidence of communities." He outlined several specific measures for improvements and then concluded: "Those now in college will before long be living in the age of intercontinental ballistic missiles. What will be then needed is not more engineers and scientists, but a people who will not panic and political leaders of wisdom, courage, and

[1] Here, as at many other points during the address, the congressmen and senators, aware of their constituents' concern and clamor for action, broke in with hearty applause. In fact, one observer commented that the speech's reception on Capitol Hill that day reminded him of the time a politician got up to address a fanatically partisan outdoor audience somewhere down in Texas. As soon as the speaker began with "Ladies and Gentlemen," a cowboy leaped from his seat, slapped his knee with his ten-gallon hat, and hollered, "He's talkin' my language!"

devotion, with capacity for solving intricate human problems, not more Einsteins but more Washingtons and Madisons." Here, succinctly put, were views with which I was in sympathy and which I had often expressed to associates.

On January 27 I sent Congress a special message on education. Its recommendations included a fivefold increase in the programs of the National Science Foundation for research, for furthering science education, and for accelerating the training of science teachers.

For the Office of Education of the Department of Health, Education, and Welfare, the most important proposal was to set up ten thousand federal scholarships a year for needy and able high school graduates, with preference given to those strong in science and mathematics. I proposed federal matching grants to states to help them employ additional science and mathematics teachers, purchase laboratory equipment, and improve testing and guidance programs. I urged the establishment of graduate fellowships to encourage able students to go into college teaching, and proposed a system of matching grants to help colleges and universities expand their graduate schools.[2]

Despite general concern about alleged deficiencies in American education, the measures recommended were certain to encounter opposition. (It should be emphasized for the sake of perspective that the United States has long had and has today the most effective system of mass education in the world. Further, some of our preparatory, collegiate, and graduate institutions have attained unmatched levels of quality.) Indeed, in formulating the recommendations to the Congress, I had given way to the experts among my advisers. I disliked the use of federal funds to pay for the normal operation of schools. I favored better salaries for teachers, but I believed that the sources of their income should be state and local. I finally agreed with the recommendations of the experts, but for a fixed period only.

After reading my message on education, Speaker Sam Rayburn called it "controversial." In both 1956 and 1957, as all of us remembered, the House had voted down much-needed legislation for schoolroom construction. Moreover, opinion was divided on specific remedies for current defects.[3]

[2] The message also recommended federal support for a number of activities designed gradually to remedy our students' glaring deficiency in foreign languages.

[3] My brother, Milton, President of the Johns Hopkins University, for example, came to see me early in January urging several changes in the administration program suggested by Marion B. Folsom, who in August 1955 had succeeded Oveta Culp Hobby as Secretary of the Department of Health, Education, and Welfare.

Despite the difficulties of arriving at a formula which would produce a satisfactory solution, the administration drove ahead to get a new education law on the books. In June, as the House committee considered the legislation, I met with Secretary Folsom, Dr. Killian, and other advisers to consider strategy. I insisted that we stick to the main points of the administration bill, resisting in particular an increase in scholarships above ten thousand and the elimination of a "needs" test. "Our purpose," I said, "is to help the good student who otherwise wouldn't get an education." I opposed a provision, proposed in the House, which would assure every scholarship student a minimum federal payment of $500 whether he needed it or not.

When the measure reached the House floor, the members eliminated all scholarships and wrote in a provision substituting 3 per cent federal loans. This amendment, sponsored by Congressman Walter Judd was, I thought, a good one. It provided for repayment of each loan by the recipient within ten years of his leaving school. In essence its purpose was to make an education available to the able student while encouraging self-reliance.

The bill as enacted kept the student loan program and authorized total loans and grants of about $1 billion over the following seven years. Specifically, it authorized, for the next four years, grants to improve public school instruction in science, mathematics, and modern foreign languages; 5550 graduate fellowships for future college and university teachers; grants for testing and guidance and for the training of public school guidance counselors. It included one thing I had neither requested nor wanted—grants to the states of $60 million for vocational programs for students not going to college.

I signed the National Defense Education Act into law on September 2, confident it would do much to strengthen American education still further.

During the spring, Marion Folsom had told me of his desire to resign as Secretary of HEW in order to return to private business. He had been a member of the administration since 1953, serving first as Under Secretary of the Treasury. He was a devoted public servant and I regretted his decision to resign. In March I offered the position to Dr. Arthur S. Flemming, who had served in my first term as Director of the Office of Defense Mobilization and who was then President of Ohio Wesleyan University.

Milton recommended, for example, increasing the number of scholarships to thirty thousand a year and giving preference to students who were good not only in science and mathematics but also in foreign languages and English.

Though the University trustees were reluctant to let him go, they agreed to do so, and on August 1, 1958, he took over the post which he was to hold with distinction until my final day in the White House.

* * *

The most spectacular legislative battle of that year involved the reorganization of the Department of Defense.

When, in my State of the Union message, I had said America wanted interservice rivalries stopped, the line had drawn enthusiastic approval. Yet reorganization was to be neither easy nor automatic. Between November of 1957 and April of 1958 I spent many hours working on details of a reorganization plan. Nelson Rockefeller, Chairman of the Advisory Committee on Government Organization, which I had established before taking office in 1953, had sent to me in November his Committee's recommendations for organizing operational forces as truly unified commands and running the chain of control from the President through the Secretary of Defense (and Joint Chiefs of Staff) directly to commanders of each unified force, rather than through the service Secretaries. His Committee also urged strengthening the role of the Chairman of the Joint Chiefs of Staff and conferring on the Secretary of Defense statutory authority for all research and development within the Department.

In the Pentagon the new Secretary of Defense, Neil H. McElroy,[4] set up a distinguished advisory group, headed by Charles A. Coolidge of Boston, to study the detailed reform needed within the Defense Department. The panel included Admiral Radford, General Bradley, General Twining, General Gruenther, Nelson Rockefeller, former Deputy Secretary of Defense William C. Foster, and former Defense Secretary Robert Lovett.

Military organization was a subject I had long lived with; while I had definite ideas of the corrective measures that needed to be taken, I heartily approved of an objective exploration of the widest possible scope, in the hope—which proved vain—that with a report from such a distinguished body of broadly experienced individuals a bill could be

[4] Charlie Wilson had informed me during the summer of his desire to retire. Much as I hated to lose him I could not, of course, argue; after almost five years in a grueling position he deserved a rest. His letter of resignation was made public on October 2, 1957, and on October 9, Mr. McElroy, the dynamic president of The Procter & Gamble Company, was sworn in as his successor.

drawn that would command my approval and overwhelming support in the Congress.

On January 25, accompanied by General Goodpaster and Bryce Harlow, I went to the Pentagon to meet with Secretary McElroy, Deputy Secretary Quarles, other interested officials, and the members of the Advisory Committee. We had a spirited round-table discussion on the entire subject.

It seemed to me that some of the participants were too eager to prove that things were perfect as they were; so I remarked, "We can't laugh off present criticism; it won't do simply to justify everything now being done." I urged less attention to details and more to basic concepts.

"The armed services today," I said, "have some 130 liaison officers assigned to congressional work. Each separate service tends to permit and in fact to urge its own quota of this liaison army to engage in specialized propaganda. The same thing is true in public relations. Secretary Wilson once told me that each service has a public relations office larger than that of the Secretary of Defense." These matters were far more serious than merely the cost of maintaining the numbers involved; the real defect was in the rivalries and divisive influences inherent in any such fragmented organization.

I told the Joint Chiefs of Staff to increase their value as a corporate body; to this end they should better integrate their staff—the Joint Staff. "The Joint Chief system as it now exists," I said, "is too complicated to work in warfare when minutes will be as precious as months have been in the past. Readiness for anticipated emergency demands that the peacetime organization be made so simple and clear that decision and control are free of delays and obstructions."

Most of those present wanted to avoid any radical change, feeling that the best chance of getting some improvement rested on cautious attempts to change a number of small things. But I was determined not to gloss over the problem.

Three days later I told the Republican legislative leaders, "I want the Pentagon people to develop an effective plan so that they can subsequently go to the Congress and give it their enthusiastic support; only free and thorough debate can bring about a plan to which the vast majority of experienced service people can adhere. But if something good doesn't come out of the Pentagon study, I will just have to take the bull by the horns—call in the leaders of the Senate and the House, including Democrats, in an effort to try to get their support directly."

In Congress we knew we would find pockets of resistance to any fundamental change. This resistance was headed primarily by Representative Carl Vinson of Georgia, who first went to Congress in 1914, became Chairman of the Naval Affairs Committee in 1931, and had served as Chairman of the House Armed Services Committee in every Congress controlled by the Democrats since 1949. For years he had been "Uncle Carl" to many of us; but he viewed with suspicion any proposal which might diminish the degree of control which he and his committee and the Congress exercised over military activities, many of which were matters of detail only. Recognizing my determination to bring about a modernization of Defense organization, he let it be known that he was going to try to defeat the effort.

Toward the end of February, before I gave out the details of the administration's plan, he introduced his own "reorganization" bill. Among other things it included a questionable provision limiting civilian employees in the Department of Defense to six hundred and a provision making the service Secretaries statutory members of the National Security Council.[5] On the morning of March 28 I invited Mr. Vinson, along with two other influential members of the House Armed Services Committee, Republican Les Arends and Democrat Paul Kilday, to the White House for breakfast. We discussed the changes which I was about to propose.

"All we're trying to do," I told them, "is to set up an establishment that will function in peacetime, as it necessarily must in wartime, under the Secretary of Defense." But Mr. Vinson was unconverted. "We're going to have trouble," I told an associate after the breakfast meeting ended, because he obviously thought that the Congress should and could control in detail every Defense activity.

On April 3 I sent to Congress a special message on the reorganization. ". . . separate ground, sea, and air warfare," I said at the outset, "is gone forever. If ever again we should be involved in war, we will fight it in all elements, with all services, as one single concentrated effort. Peacetime preparatory and organizational activity must conform to this fact."

[5] This second proposal was meaningless unless its sole purpose was to raise the "prestige" of service Secretaries. Even to this day I become alarmed by the many misconceptions about the National Security Council. These are found even among officers of the Executive branch, all of whom have every opportunity to obtain an understanding of its purpose and its functioning. These misapprehensions seem to be most noticeable in the Congress, whose members are used to the "committee" system of making decisions. Assuming that the NSC acts by committee vote, Congress is frequently impelled to add to, or subtract from, its "statutory" membership. While the NSC is authorized by law and is, when correctly employed, a vitally important body, it is only advisory in action. Its duty is to advise the President but he can use it, ignore it, meet with it personally or not in whole or in part, and can add, as he sees fit, any number of people to its membership. So Mr. Vinson's proposal of this item was of no significance whatsoever.

I included specific recommendations.

The first was the organization of all our deployed troops into *truly* unified commands, all directly responsive to their designated commander, regardless of the service from which the troops might come. The establishment of unified commands and the selection of the commanders would be under the direction of the Commander-in-Chief and with his approval.[6]

Second, I recommended that we "clear command channels so that orders will proceed directly to the unified commander from the Commander-in-Chief and the Secretary of Defense," whose operational command post would be the Joint Chiefs of Staff. At that time the channel of command ran from the President to the Secretary of Defense,[7] to a service Secretary designated as the executive agent for the theater, then to the service Chief of Staff, and finally to the commander in the field—a chain "cumbersome and unreliable in time of peace and not usable in time of war." In addition to recommending its elimination, I asked also repeal of any statutory authority "which vests responsibilities for military operations in any official other than the Secretary of Defense." The Chief of Naval Operations, for example, by law commanded naval operating forces directly. The confusion between his authority and that of the commanders-in-chief of unified commands charged with combat involving forces of several services was obvious.

Third, I recommended that, as a matter of law, the Joint Chiefs of Staff could serve as a unit in assisting the Secretary of Defense to control the new unified commands, acting only under his authority. To strengthen the Joint Staff I recommended the addition to it of an integrated operations division and, to this end, the raising or removing of the statutory limit—then 210 officers—on the Joint Staff's size. I wanted it

[6] Our overseas forces had operated under so-called "unified commands" since the early days of World War II. But the component units, divisions, carriers, and wings were normally assigned to the specified commander for tactical operations only; for other functions the separate services were in a controlling position. In some respects the authority sought for unified commanders was even more sweeping than that I exercised over all the American Forces assigned to OVERLORD in World War II.

In my own experience in the European Theater I had found little difficulty with a loose theater organization, partly because of the spirit of cooperation existing in wartime and partly because I was also the administrative commander of by far the largest single component force in Europe, the United States Army, which included the Air Force. At SHAPE in 1951, likewise, President Truman had been careful to spell out that the Sixth Fleet operating in the Mediterranean was directly under my command. But my experiences, I well realized, were not universal.

[7] In every instance where the term "Secretary of Defense" was used in this message, it was understood to include "with the advice of the Joint Chiefs of Staff."

made clear that the *principal* duty of each Chief of Staff was to serve as a member of the Joint Chiefs; to this end, I urged authority for each chief to delegate major portions of his service responsibilities to his deputy.

Fourth, I pointed out that the service Secretaries, if relieved of direct responsibilities for military operations, could devote themselves primarily to managing the administrative, training, and logistics functions of their services. I was by no means recommending the abolition of the military departments or their merger into a single service, but their concentration upon the tasks they could and should do.

Fifth, I insisted that we should reorganize Defense research and development to strengthen the Defense Secretary's control over it. To this end, I recommended the establishment of a new position of Director of Defense Research and Engineering at a salary equal to those of the service Secretaries. This new official, who would be a nationally recognized leader in science and technology, would advise the Secretary on scientific and technical questions; supervise all research and engineering activities in the Department; and direct all research and development requiring centralized management. He would thus minimize duplication and rivalry among the three services in their work in science and engineering.

Finally, to strengthen the authority of the Secretary of Defense, I recommended that Defense funds be appropriated not to the military departments but directly to him; that the National Security Act of 1947 be amended to eliminate the provision that the military departments are to be "separately administered," and that the Secretary strengthen his supervision over public affairs and legislative liaison work within the Department.

These recommendations, so briefly outlined here, I believed would bring about reasonable and attainable improvements in our current Defense establishment, a step in a necessary evolution. As far back as 1945, for example, I told the cadets at West Point that I would like to see all the services, one day, in one uniform.[8] However, I well recognized that the feeling of the individual soldier, sailor, marine, or airman for his own service was very real, that much of his morale was based on this service loyalty. Therefore, a complete amalgamation of the services in

[8] I have always believed that a nation's defense would be most efficiently conducted by a single administrative service, comprising elements of land, sea, and air. I did not (and do not) join those who insist that a system of "checks and balances" among services contributes to a nation's security. Successful defense cannot be conducted under a debating society.

1958, I felt, would be unwise and extreme; the best we could do would be to eliminate those elements in the law that promoted service rivalries. On this point my message said:

> While at times human failure and misdirected zeal have been responsible for duplications, inefficiencies, and publicized disputes, the truth is that most of the service rivalries that have troubled us in recent years have been made inevitable by the laws that govern our defense organization.

I recommended the abolition of the system of using individual services as "executive agents"[9] in the chain of command between the Secretary of Defense and the unified commanders. The executive agent system had been set up in 1953 for peacetime use in order to clarify a single channel of reporting through one rather than through three departments to the Secretary of Defense.

By this time, five years later, it seemed possible to take another step forward—by expanding the communication facilities and authorizing direct control of unified commands through the Joint Chiefs of Staff under the Secretary of Defense. The cutting out of all other links between unified commanders and the staff of the Secretary of Defense was also a step in raising the status of the unified commanders. This change I effected on a *de facto* basis by a simple directive to the Secretary of Defense. However, I asked for congressional cooperation to repeal any authority which vested legal responsibility for combat operations in any officials other than the Secretary of Defense.

Also important was the abolition of the "committee system" of planning, another measure I was able to take by Executive action. Previously the pick and shovel work of strategic planning had been done by subordinate committees, each composed of four coequal services representatives, functioning somewhat as junior sets of Joint Chiefs. In submitting their recommendations to the Joint Chiefs, these committees were expected, if possible, to produce agreed conclusions. But because each member was acting strictly as a representative of his own service, the resulting "plan" was little more than a worthless scheme to balance

[9] The selection of an executive agent for a specific theater was based largely on the sizes of the forces involved and on the communications available. Thus the Army had been designated the executive agent for Europe and the Navy for the Pacific. This system had been an improvement over that previously in operation; but as it turned out, it had constituted a source of controversy among the services, each executive agent feeling a proprietary interest toward its own theaters. The number and size of theaters for which a given service was executive agent seemed somehow to be of some importance to that service's prestige.

various service considerations and prejudices. Under the new system, such strategic planning would be conducted within the Joint Staff itself. Plans would be sent to the various service staffs for comment, but the disapproval of one service could not embarrass the work of the Joint Staff.

I knew it would be more than troublesome to secure these changes. When I outlined them to the legislative leaders on April 1, Senator Knowland pointed out that the Congress would not surrender lightly its prized power of making detailed appropriations directly to each of the military services. As soon as the plan became public, Congressman Vinson brought out the old charge that I was seeking to set up a "Prussian-style" general staff. Other critics argued that the plan would make the Secretary of Defense a czar; still others said it would work to the advantage of the Air Force, which was reputed to have more influence than the other services with the professionals in the Secretary of Defense's office.

Shortly before I sent my message to Congress, I invited Secretary of the Navy Thomas Gates and Admiral Arleigh Burke, Chief of Naval Operations, to the White House one evening. We had an excellent talk. But though they completely accepted the administration's plan for unified strategic planning and direction and for strengthening the control of the Secretary of Defense, they warned of "emotionalism" over the effects of the plan among officers at lower levels in the Navy.

"Since good organization must conform to the conditions of the time, reorganization will always be indicated when new ideas, weapons, facilities, or political facts change sufficiently as to outmode old customs," I remarked.

To support the plan I took advantage of a scheduled appearance before the American Society of Newspaper Editors in the middle of April.

"The fact is," I told the editors, "modern weapons and methods of war have scrambled traditional service functions . . . our military weapons and techniques and certain provisions of the law just do not mesh. . . . I have simply asked the Congress to accept and apply these facts of military life."

Summarizing my recommendations, I turned to the criticisms—which, I said, "will probably be loudest and most bitter not from responsible service leaders but rather from outside sources. These sources often resist military change far more vigorously than the services themselves." I was thinking, for example, about one of the service (civilian) "Leagues," the officials of which were stirring up so much trouble that some of my friends in the organization threatened to resign.

I went on:

It will also be said that [it sets up] a monstrous general staff—usually called "Prussian." I am always amused when I hear that word, because I nearly always ask the individual to explain it to me by telling me what he thinks a Prussian general staff was. Few can do it. In any event, they fear that this monstrous staff will be set up to dominate our armed forces and in due course will threaten our liberty.

This is nonsense.

Thinking of some of the publicly expressed, but unjustified, objection to the bill, I summarized what it would not do:

"There will be:

"—no single chief of staff;

"—no Prussian staff;

"—no czar;

"—no forty-billion-dollar blank check;

"—no swallowing up of the traditional services;

"—no undermining of the constitutional powers of Congress."

So strong were my convictions on the need for this reform, that I resorted to a means I had not used before—at least on such scale. I began to write directly to influential citizens all across the nation to explain the issues at stake and to ask them to make their own conclusions known to the members of Congress, especially to its military committees. Quickly some members charged me with the heinous offense of "going over the head of Congress." The criticism was most welcome; it gave evidence that effects of my efforts were being felt in the proper places. So I continued—writing altogether to hundreds of friends urging them to throw their support behind the administration's bill.

The result was a flood of messages. It was reported that one of my friends in the business world sent twenty thousand letters of his own to inform his friends and employees and to ask their help. My congressional supporters said their offices were deluged with messages favoring the bill. Several of the more outspoken early critics of the plan suddenly began to see many virtues in it.

As the House Armed Services Committee continued to deliberate, support came from unexpected quarters. For example, Congressman Clarence Cannon of Missouri, Chairman of the House Appropriations Committee, made a statesmanlike speech for reorganization; I telephoned him my warm thanks. I was also grateful to learn that former President Truman had spoken out for Defense reorganization, as well as for the mutual security and international trade bills, which we were trying to get through.

On May 22 the House Armed Services Committee reported out a military bill which, though it reflected constructive action on most of my proposals, included several objectionable features. Among other things, it kept individual service Secretaries in the chain of command—a point which I had not originally considered overly objectionable (and so stated) inasmuch as the Secretaries, as Presidential appointees, would in normal course function in full harmony with Presidential will, but which, on reflection, I concluded would be at basic variance with the general concept of reorganization being sought.[10] The reported bill also gave the Congress sixty days in which to vote down any proposal to transfer, merge, reassign, or abolish a "major combatant function." It empowered any member of the Joint Chiefs to define such a "major function" and thus to throw any proposed change to the Congress for decision. It gave the service Secretaries and the military chiefs the right on their own motion to go directly to Congress with "any recommendations relating to the Department of Defense that they might deem proper." This provision I termed "legalized insubordination."

Again I had suggestions from the Pentagon to "go along" with these provisions. Instead, I issued a statement emphasizing my objections.

On the evening of May 27, I met with Representative John McCormack in my White House study, and went over my objections one by one; he indicated his sympathy with them. When the vote came on June 11, however, the House, on straight party lines, concentrating on the service Secretary item and eager in this respect to display independence of presidential desires, voted through the bill as it came out of the Armed Services Committee.

The bill then went on the Senate, where, it was amended to my satisfaction. Within a few days the House and Senate conferees agreed on a final compromise.

The compromise included only two of the features I had opposed—the "legalized insubordination" and the power of Congress to veto the transfer of a major combatant function. As to the first of these, I felt somewhat as President Grant did when he said, "I cannot make the Comptroller General change his mind, but I can get a new Comptroller General." The other was less important. They made a small hole in the doughnut.[11]

[10] It was interesting that this provision, one of the less important ones, became the *cause célèbre* in House consideration of the bill; it served, though quite unintentionally, as a sort of "red herring," drawing the ire and fire of disconsolate members, while allowing the whole major undertaking to proceed virtually unscathed.

[11] In making a "substantial transfer" of a major combatant function, the Secretary of Defense had to report it to the House and Senate Committees, which then had thirty days to report out a resolution against the transfer. If either committee did so, the Senate or House had another forty days to approve the resolution. If either house approved it, the transfer could not take place. Regardless of this provision,

The bill, on the other hand, gave the Secretary of Defense power to transfer, reassign, abolish, or consolidate functions in order to increase efficiency. It enlarged the Joint Staff, and gave the chairman of the Joint Chiefs of Staff the responsibility of selecting the staff director. It gave the President, through the Secretary of Defense, the power to establish and control "unified or specified combatant commands for . . . military missions," and to determine the forces which the Army, Navy, and Air Force would then assign to such commands. Locally all units would be under the operational control of the commander of the unified forces. It also established a Director of Defense Research and Engineering, to supervise all such work within the Department.

On August 6 I signed the Defense Reorganization Bill into law.

I reminded my associates, however, that the law was just another step toward what the majority of experienced military men knew was necessary. Not only would new developments demand further revision, but it was quite clear that the members of the Congress, only a few of whom are knowledgeable in the principles of military organization and operations, normally display too much concern for the old, even the obsolete.

In the Indian wars of the second half of the nineteenth century our skeletonized Army stationed throughout the prairie and desert areas of the West was fighting with single shot weapons long after the Indians had succeeded in acquiring effective repeating rifles. In the light of such traditional inertia we had, I felt, now achieved remarkable results. We had in fact placed the Defense Department on a foundation of organization and procedure that would make a reality of civilian control by the President and Secretary of Defense, and make it possible for the Joint Chiefs of Staff to fulfill the vast responsibilities which only they were qualified to discharge.

* * *

Neil McElroy was able to absent himself from his private duties only for a period of two years. I had realized and accepted this fact in order to obtain a man of his qualifications when I had requested him to take the position of Secretary of Defense.

His period as Secretary, from October 1957 to December 1959, was a significant one. The success of the Defense Reorganization Bill was due in

---

the Secretary of Defense had the authority to assign to any Department the development and operational use of any new weapons system, and during an emergency the President could transfer major combatant functions without going to Congress.

large measure to his efforts. During his time in office the missile and space programs were reorganized and given added emphasis. We deployed our first operational ballistic missiles overseas, the Jupiter and Thor, both of about fifteen hundred miles range. While vulnerable to surprise attack, moving these two weapons forward gave the Free World a strong missile capability while the longer-range ICBMs were being devised.

Before the development of the Atlas ICBM was complete, work was begun on its second-generation sister, the Titan. The latter, a more sophisticated device, had the advantage of operating from underground, "hardened" sites, which much enhanced its value as a retaliatory weapon in general war. We had already concluded, however, that the future of ballistic missiles lay with solid fuel propellants which permitted far more rapid firing and greater convenience and safety in fuel storage. In 1958 we began developing the Minuteman, a solid-propellant ICBM incorporating the advantages of the others.

In much of this work Secretary McElroy was assisted by his outstanding Deputy Secretary, Donald A. Quarles. With an engineering background and long involvement in defense work, Don Quarles had an unusual understanding of the problems of the uniformed services and the scientists alike. His sudden death in May of 1959 was a shock to his friends and a grievous loss to the United States.

To replace Neil McElroy as Secretary of Defense I prevailed on Secretary of the Navy Tom Gates to delay his return to private life. He first took the post of Deputy Secretary for the duration of Mr. McElroy's term and then in December assumed the post of Secretary of Defense. During his term as Secretary he had the satisfaction of seeing the Polaris, developed by the Navy under his leadership, make its first successful firings and join America's growing missile arsenal. By the end of my administration the Polaris gave the United States an extremely mobile, practically invulnerable retaliatory capability.

The advent of Polaris created a problem in command relationships. Up to this point the nuclear retaliatory power of the United States had been concentrated almost exclusively in the Strategic Air Command. It now became necessary to insure that all potential worldwide targets be covered and that confusion and unnecessary duplication between naval and Air Force targeting be eliminated.

Secretary Gates therefore proposed a new concept, that of an Integrated Field Operations Center, in which representatives of all services, particularly the Air Force and Navy, would coordinate their targeting plans. Many professionals were initially opposed to using the facilities of the Strategic Air Command to house the Center. Nevertheless I approved

Secretary Gates' recommendation, and within a short time he reported that the Center was operating successfully, with members of all services quite satisfied with the results.

* * *

In August 1957 the four-year tour of Admiral Arthur W. Radford as Chairman of the Joint Chiefs of Staff came to an end. Radford had been a tower of strength in struggling for better teamwork among the services. He was nearly unique among professional military men in his understanding of the relationships between national military and economic strength.

Radford's successor was General Nathan F. Twining, the former Chief of Staff of the Air Force and a man of integrity and great common sense. Fortunately, while our revolutionary changes were taking place in weapons and their control, Nate Twining had a thorough understanding of the problems involved. His unusual human qualities did much to achieve the necessary interservice cooperation. Unfortunately, he underwent a serious operation in 1959, and requested that he be permitted to retire the following year, before his second two-year term would expire. I regretted the loss of the services of such a professional, but I could not refuse.

With General Twining's retirement in 1960, General Lyman L. Lemnitzer, formerly Army Chief of Staff, was appointed to the position of chairman of the Joint Chiefs. I had not felt any strong obligation to adhere to any unwritten understanding that the position of chairman be rotated among the services—Army, Navy, Air—but I thought that such rotation, all other things being equal, was desirable. Happily, I felt that each individual appointed during my administrations to the chairman's position—Radford, Twining, and Lemnitzer—was the best qualified man available in any of the services.

* * *

On the night of January 31, 1958, the Army was to launch Explorer I, which we hoped would be the United States' first orbiting earth satellite. I was at the Augusta National Golf Club at the time, and late that afternoon Jim Hagerty came to see me. We discussed the launching, and agreed that when he had been assured that the attempted shot was not to be postponed he would come to tell me. Should it be "scrubbed out," he was to call Sergeant Moaney, asking him to give me just a two-word message: "Nothing doing."

At 8:30 General Goodpaster called Jim from Washington. The launching was on, and Jim, staying in Augusta, drove out to my cottage to bring me the news. Somewhat later Goodpaster called again to say that from his office in the White House he would keep two telephone lines open: one to Jim's office at the Bon Air Hotel in Augusta, another into the telecommunications center at the Pentagon. Three minutes later he told Jim, "I've just got word that X minus 7 was 10:41."

Goodpaster gave Hagerty the countdown. "The firing command was given at 10:48. It takes sixteen seconds to start the rocket lifting off the ground. Here's the report:

"The main stage lifted off at 10:48:16.

"The program is starting O.K.

"They are putting it in the right attitude.

"It is still going.

"It is still going at fifty-five seconds.

"It is still going and looks good at ninety seconds.

"Jupiter is on the way!

"It is through the jet stream—they were worried about that jet stream.

"One hundred fifteen seconds, it is going higher and higher.

"Everything is going all right at 145 seconds."

At 10:56 I had the news from Goodpaster directly. "The second stage ignition has gone off O.K.," he reported.

"When will the announcement come that the satellite is in orbit?" I asked.

"It will be an hour and a half or two hours before they're definitely sure."

In less than an hour Goodpaster told Jim: "The first analysis that we've received is that the satellite has passed over the first station, Antigua, on time. This fact tends to show that the third and fourth stages went off O.K."

At midnight I called Jim. He had left the phone to talk to the reporters. One of his secretaries answered, and I began asking her questions about the launching. She had taken extensive notes on all the conversations between Jim and Andy but, unhappily, her notebook was in the next room where she could not reach it. Then, at the same moment, Goodpaster called in again.

"Everything's going well," he said.

At 12:44 Jim was on my telephone again, saying, "It's in orbit. Andy has just received the official word."

"That's wonderful," I replied. "I surely feel a lot better now." But I warned, "Let's not make too great a hullabaloo over this." I did not want this success to result in any boastful pronouncements; primarily it marked a big step, but only a step, in a gigantic undertaking of space exploration.

I asked that my congratulations and deep appreciation be conveyed to all who had taken part in this splendid achievement.

With the January 31 launching, a long and difficult period had ended. Within the next eight weeks we made two other successful shots: the Navy's Vanguard, launched March 17, and Explorer III, which went into orbit on March 26.

* * *

The exploration of outer space, a comprehensive and costly venture, demanded new controlling and operating mechanisms within the government.

On February 7, 1958, Secretary McElroy announced the establishment of a new Advanced Research Projects Agency, headed by Roy W. Johnson, an executive vice president of General Electric, to work on space projects of military value. The following month Dr. Herbert F. York, Director of the Livermore Laboratory of the AEC and associate director of the Physics Department at the University of California, became the Agency's chief scientist. (He later became director of Scientific Research and Engineering for the entire Department.)

After extensive consultation and deliberation, however, I decided that non-military research in outer space could best be conducted by a new civilian agency. Information acquired by purely scientific exploration could and should, I thought, be made available to all the world. But military research would naturally demand secrecy. The highest priority should go of course to space research with a military application, but because national morale, and to some extent national prestige, could be affected by the results of peaceful space research, this should likewise be pushed, but through a separate agency.

On April 2, I requested Congress to establish a National Aeronautics and Space Agency (NASA). The legislation encountered the usual delays in the Congress, but when it appeared that the legislation might be amended undesirably, I met with Senate Majority Leader Lyndon Johnson, who agreed to work for the changes I thought necessary. The result was that the bill went through the Senate in the form that the administration approved.[12]

[12] The National Aeronautics and Space Act of 1958 required that all aeronautics and space activities be controlled by the civilian agency, *except those that the President determined were primarily associated with national defense*. Along with the new National Aeronautics and Space Administration, it established the Aeronautics and Space Council, the membership of which included the President, Secretary of State, Secretary of Defense, the head of the National Aeronautics

On August 8 I named Dr. T. Keith Glennan, President of Case Institute of Technology in Cleveland, as the new Agency's first administrator. Through the two and a half years following its inception, NASA made a splendid record in three fields: the practical use of earth satellites for human benefit; the scientific study of space and celestial bodies; and progress toward the exploration of outer space by man in flight.

In its search for practical applications of earth satellites, the Agency on April 1, 1960, sent up Tiros I, a meteorological satellite. It carried two television cameras, each the size of a water glass. By January of 1961 it had produced more than twenty two thousand photographs of cloud formations, and had given scientists comprehensive information on storm centers over such vast untracked areas as the southern seas, formerly observed only by scattered ships. Then in November of 1960 NASA launched Tiros II, an advanced version of Tiros I which included an apparatus for measuring radiation from the sun and earth and thus for gaining new information about the circulation, temperature, and composition of the earth's atmosphere.

Another practical application of earth satellites was in communications. On the night of December 18, 1958, an Atlas ICBM earth satellite (Score) was fired into orbit with a recording of my voice. This satellite then rebroadcast a Christmas message from space to all those over whose home it passed. On August 12, 1960, Echo number one went into orbit—a 136-pound spherical balloon one hundred feet in diameter flying at an average altitude of about one thousand miles and reflecting radio messages back to earth. During its first orbit, NASA scientists at the Jet Propulsion Laboratory in Gladstone, California, transmitted a recorded message from me to the Bell Telephone Laboratories station in Holmdel, New Jersey:

> The satellite balloon which has reflected these words may be used freely by any nation for similar experiments in its own interests. Information necessary to prepare for such participation was widely distributed some weeks ago.
>
> The United States will continue to make freely available to the world the scientific information acquired from this and other experiments in its program of space exploration.

Later Echo transmitted photographs and telephone calls, foreshadowing a new system of global communications through television, radio, and telephone.

---

and Space Administration, the chairman of the Atomic Energy Commission, and four other members, including three from private life. It permitted the President, for four years, to transfer to NASA related functions of other agencies.

In the exploration of outer space, NASA launched five deep probes between October 1958 and January 1961. Pioneer V, a satellite with a life expectancy of one hundred thousand years, was shot into orbit about the sun. Equipped with two radio transmitters, it carried instruments to measure radiation from the sun, the spatial distribution of energy particles, the number and density of meteoric dust particles striking its surface, and the strength of outer space magnetic fields. When Pioneer V had reached a point about 22½ million miles from the earth, NASA reported that this was the farthest range "over which man has tracked, received telemetry from, and maintained control over an instrumented vehicle." Pioneer VIII, an earth satellite, developed new information on the composition of the upper atmosphere.

The first phase of NASA's other purpose—to put a man into orbit and bring him back safely—acquired the identifying label of Project Mercury. On April 9, 1959, the names of the first seven "astronauts" selected to undergo rigid training for this program were announced, although it would be many months before manned flights could begin.[13] At Cape Canaveral, Florida, on the morning of December 19, 1960, a Redstone rocket boosted an unmanned Mercury capsule into flight. The capsule soared to an altitude of 135 miles above the earth. Fifteen minutes later, 235 miles away, it plunged into the Atlantic Ocean within five miles of the aircraft carrier *Valley Forge,* one of the recovery vessels, and a helicopter picked up the capsule. Less than twenty minutes afterward it was on deck. All systems had worked perfectly. With this test flight, the United States was approaching the day when the first of our Mercury astronauts would orbit the earth, in preparation for flight to the moon and other ventures into space.[14]

Pursuing all these purposes, NASA scientists were working on launch vehicles of colossal thrust: the Atlas-Centaur, for example, capable of launching a fifteen-hundred-pound planetary probe or a four-ton earth satellite; or Saturn, a vehicle capable of launching a space craft to circumnavigate the moon and return to earth. Toward the end of the 1960s, Dr. Glennan informed me, the United States hoped to have a launch vehicle even more powerful than Saturn—Nova, consisting of a cluster of engines with a total thrust of six to twelve million pounds. With this vehicle, he

[13] The men selected were Navy Lieutenant Malcolm S. Carpenter, Air Force Captain Leroy G. Cooper, Jr., Marine Lieutenant Colonel John H. Glenn, Jr., Air Force Captain Virgil I. Grissom, Navy Lieutenant Commander Walter M. Schirra, Jr., Navy Lieutenant Commander Alan B. Shepard, Jr., and Air Force Captain Donald K. Slayton. These names, in varying degrees, have since become household words.
[14] The first recovery of a satellite occurred on August 11, 1960. For a comprehensive discussion of the flight of Discoverer XIII, see Appendix M.

said, the United States would have the power to carry a fifty-ton payload to the moon or put into earth orbit a space laboratory weighing 150 tons.

In cooperation with the Atomic Energy Commission, NASA scientists had begun work on a nuclear rocket engine and on a nuclear-generated auxiliary power system for future spacecraft.

Within its first two and one-half years NASA had expanded its annual rate of spending from an initial $335 million to $915 million, and had taken on eighteen thousand employees. Our objective was ambitious but sought only constructive progress. We deliberately avoided hysterically devised crash programs and propaganda stunts.

Within the Pentagon, scientists were working on satellites for military purposes, including navigation, communications, reconnaissance, and the detection of nuclear explosions. By the end of 1960, the United States had successfully launched thirty-one earth satellites; of these, sixteen were still in orbit about the earth. We had launched four deep space probes; two were still in orbit about the sun. In contrast, by that date the Soviet Union had one vehicle moving in orbit about the earth, one about the sun. Though we had not yet matched the Soviet Union's achievement in building rocket engines of powerful thrust, a development they began in 1945, we had narrowed their lead and in other sectors had gone far ahead.

In another kind of scientific adventure, the atomic submarine *Nautilus* on August 3, 1958, first cruised under the Arctic ice cap to the North Pole. It was followed a week later by the atomic submarine *Skate*.

* * *

No one can contemplate the rapidity of scientific advance during recent decades and the consequent vast changes in our social order without pausing to speculate on the actual and as yet unimagined accomplishments, and their several effects, certain to confront mankind in the next half-century.

For three thousand years—from the time of Rameses II to that of Napoleon—man's means of transportation and communication changed little. By land, he depended upon the horse as his most useful aid in moving from place to place, and for transmitting messages. Sea routes were utilized only by the sailing ship. Air travel was unknown.

But within 150 years after Napoleon's Waterloo, the sailing ship, except for sport, has practically disappeared and the horse in all civilized countries is experiencing the same fate. Their places have been filled with luxury liners, jet planes, electronics, and atomic power.

Today the guided missile is, gradually, supplanting the airplane as an engine of war, and manned satellites about the earth will soon be commonplace.

The curve of change bends ever-steeply upward; almost every day brings us news of a new scientific advance in pure research, in engineering, in medicine, in the products and services presented to man for his use.

One is inclined to question whether changes of this kind will cause, or at least be accompanied by, comparable revolutions in national structures and political forms.

The ancient civilizations of China, Egypt, and Rome lived for centuries, for long eras, practically unaltered, just as their means of production, scientific practices, and social customs showed little radical change from century to century.

But now, in an affluent society and with scientific advances rushing forward at an incredible speed, what is going to be the effect on humans?

One plausible conclusion is that we—especially of the Western world—will lose something of our spirit of nationalism, possibly too rapidly for our own good. We must realize that few of us, because of our sketchy information about others, can think globally. Our outlook on the times in which we live is certain to be colored by national history, traditions, customs, and aspirations.

Yet if political and social change should tend to keep pace with scientific advance—as one small example, automation is already posing social problems that could become extremely unsettling—we must contemporaneously examine and explore thoroughly the organisms and institutions that we have established to sustain the concepts of liberty and human dignity.

We must constantly study ourselves, both individually and as a society, and do so with as much care and thoughtfulness as we do when bringing into man's service every significant invention or discovery. As we achieve new understandings of elements and forces that for ages past have been believed impervious to change, we must be watchful lest we weaken the vitality of the human spirit and the devotion to moral principle that are mankind's most priceless possessions.

CHAPTER XI

Landing in Lebanon

Even peace may be purchased at too high a price.

—*Benjamin Franklin*

WESTERN concern about the apparently inexorable drift of Syria toward the Communist orbit during late 1957 was by no means lessened when in late January 1958 President Nasser—whose exact political leanings were still something of a mystery—announced that Egypt and Syria planned to unite, forming a new nation, the United Arab Republic.

Foster Dulles was attending a meeting of the Baghdad Pact nations in Ankara as the news broke, and the conference drew to a close in a troubled and confused atmosphere. At the start, it was unclear whether this union was prompted by Communist influence or whether the Communists were merely going along with Nasser's ambition eventually to unify the Arab world. The other Arab nations viewed the development with real anxiety.

On February 1 Nasser and President al Kuwatly of Syria signed the merger documents.

Under the arrangement, we learned, the Syrian army was to be removed from politics, Syrian political parties would be dissolved, and Communism allegedly would be suppressed.[1] All key appointments would be controlled from Cairo. The deputy director of our Central Intelligence Agency, General Charles P. Cabell, reported that the Syrian army, fearful of growing Communist influence in the country, had been a prime mover in engineering the union.

Reportedly, Nasser had at first been reluctant to enter the Syrian picture,

[1] The Communist Party, active in Syria, was outlawed in Egypt.

largely because of his worry over Soviet attitude. He had apparently acceded to the union because he felt he could not refuse, but he well knew that the new United Arab Republic would face serious economic difficulties and would have to find new jobs for many newly unemployed Syrian army officers. Furthermore, the combined nation would come into existence with the handicap of being split, geographically, by Israel.

Middle East reactions to the formation of the U.A.R. varied. Though the Arab populations, as a whole, seemed to view the event as a first step toward the long-sought goal of Arab unity, their governments were generally fearful of this obvious elevation of Nasser's influence and prestige. King Saud was reportedly angry in finding a hostile combination on his flanks, and the Lebanese government was frightened. Ben-Gurion was suspicious. Of the Arab nations, only Yemen seemed to show any degree of enthusiasm, and its Prince made a trip in the first week of February to discuss some sort of loose federation between his country and the new "two-in-one."

In obvious response to this development, Jordan and Iraq decided to form a federation.[2] King Faisal of Iraq and King Hussein of Jordan were second cousins, and personally courageous men. Their federation, called the Arab Union, was announced on February 14, just two weeks after the formation of the U.A.R. King Faisal, the elder of the two kings (and the ruler of the more powerful nation), was to head the federation, but in all other respects the two nations would be equals. The Cabinet was to be split evenly between the two nationalities and was to alternate its place of business every six months between Amman and Baghdad. Both Kings were to retain their thrones.

This Arab Union caused considerable annoyance to Colonel Nasser, who almost immediately went to Damascus for a series of mass rallies in which he launched public tirades against it. Ominously, crowds of Nasser's supporters streamed across the border from the small country of Lebanon to join the rallies.

* * *

On the morning of March 6, 1958, I had word that King Saud of Saudi Arabia, the man who we had hoped might eventually rival Nasser as an Arab leader, was in grave trouble. The King had been cautious

[2] This movement had received some State Department encouragement. At the Baghdad Pact meeting in Ankara, Foster Dulles had promised Premier Nuri as Said of Iraq that he would approach Saud in an effort to achieve closer cooperation between Saudi Arabia, Jordan, and Iraq. Saud had, however, been unenthusiastic.

in his official and outward dealings with Egypt and Syria, but behind the scenes had apparently been engaged in intrigues against the leaders of both countries. His activities were now unmasked by Lieutenant Colonel Abdel Hamid Seraj, the new Interior Minister for Syria, and Nasser in Egypt.[3] The result was what might be expected. Nasser declared an all-out propaganda battle against the King and withdrew the sizable military mission which he normally maintained in Saudi Arabia. There was a threat of a complete break in relations between the two countries.

To weaken further King Saud's precarious position, many of his people developed strong pro-Nasser sympathies, and some ten thousand Egyptians resided in Saudi Arabia. Moreover, the King did not have the complete loyalty of his several brothers and of other members of his own household.

Not a strong individual, he finally was forced to a virtual abdication. On March 24 he granted his pro-Nasserite brother, Crown Prince Faisal, full powers over the state's foreign, internal, and financial policies. By this surrender of power, which reduced him to a figurehead, the King saved his titular claim to the throne. But as a potential bulwark against Communist expansion efforts in the Middle East, King Saud's usefulness was temporarily, at least, at an end.

* * *

In that same spring serious trouble began to break out in Lebanon. This tiny republic, with a population of only about a million and a half, was officially an Arab nation, with some 90 per cent of its people speaking Arabic. Until recently, a little more than half of the citizenry had been Christian; however, the influx of Moslem refugees from Palestine had now tipped the balance slightly in the other direction.[4] The Lebanese President, Camille Chamoun, and Foreign Minister, Dr. Charles Malik, were definitely pro-Western. Lebanon's policies had long since begun to irritate other Arabs, particularly those of the pan-Arab, pro-Nasserite groups. In 1956, for example, President Chamoun had incurred Arab displeasure by refusing to break relations with Britain and France at the time of the invasion of Egypt. In 1957, because of Lebanon's acceptance of the Middle East Doctrine, Egypt and Syria refused to import twenty

[3] Apparently the plots that the King was involved in were so badly managed that many outsiders had learned of them. Our intelligence people had, I was told, tried to warn King Saud that he was falling into a trap. But the warnings either fell on deaf ears or came too late.

[4] A large percentage of these refugees were militant pan-Arabists, who blamed the United States for the existence of Israel, the cause of their exile.

thousand tons of Lebanese apples. However, the Lebanese Prime Minister, Sami es Sohl, was a sound link between the Christian and Moslem groups; he was one Moslem official known to be strongly pro-Western.

On the personal side, President Chamoun had been unusually solicitous for my health and welfare after my heart attack in 1955. In 1957 I had been able to repay his concern by asking Dr. Paul Dudley White, on a trip to the Middle East, to examine the Lebanese Prime Minister, who had recently been stricken with a similar affliction. In other personal and official ways our relationships had become increasingly strong.

The pro-Western orientation of President Chamoun's government, while gratifying and helpful, had its dangers in that it accented the cleavage within his own country. In the summer of 1957, for example, Foster Dulles, in reporting on the parliamentary elections which had just been held, expressed concern that the elections had gone so completely our way as to create internal tension. Excellent moderates among the Arab nationalists had been thrown out of office, and the government's conduct of the election had been attacked by the opposition. Nasser worked hard to aggravate these internal difficulties. If he was not a Communist, he certainly succeeded in making us very suspicious of him.

Since the establishment of the U.A.R. in February there had been increasing numbers of border crossings between Lebanon and Syria by Arab nationalists, and it seemed likely that Lebanon occupied a place on Colonel Nasser's timetable as a nation to be brought under his influence.

Then in late April matters came to a head. The trigger for the crisis was a rumor, well-substantiated, that President Chamoun had given his assent to a movement to amend the Lebanese constitution, with the purpose of achieving for himself an unprecedented second term in office. Dissidents, who were forming into armed bands, were almost completely Moslem.

When the news first came to me, I was convinced that President Chamoun had made a political error. If he had not actually favored the constitutional amendment, he should have quickly dispelled all rumors by a public announcement. He did not do so, however, and because of Arab-Christian rivalries in Lebanon, this news stirred up renewed resentment. Rebellion, smoldering for some weeks, finally broke out in early May in an armed uprising in Beirut.

The forces available to the government in Lebanon were quite small, consisting of nine thousand men in the Army and twenty-five hundred in the gendarmerie. Though the picture was far from in focus, the Lebanese army seemed to have the weapons and the strength to put down the rebels, except for one fact—the Chief of Staff, General Fuad

Chehab, appeared to have little enthusiasm for prosecuting the battle.[5] It was soon rumored that he was biding his time to see which side would gain the upper hand—the government or the rebels. Nevertheless, President Chamoun would not relieve him.

Behind everything was our deep-seated conviction that the Communists were principally responsible for the trouble, and that President Chamoun was motivated only by a strong feeling of patriotism. He was the ablest of the Lebanese politicians and would undoubtedly agree not to be a candidate again for the Presidency if only he could be assured of a strong and sincere pro-Western successor.

On the morning of May 13 I met with Secretary Foster Dulles and others to discuss a communication from President Chamoun inquiring as to "what our actions would be if he were to request our assistance." We met in a climate of impatience because of our belief that Chamoun's uneasiness was the result of one more Communist provocation. Although temporarily pursuing a "soft" propaganda line, the Soviets were pushing everywhere, stirring up trouble in Venezuela, Indonesia, and Burma, not to mention the Middle East. Radio Cairo, which was blasting forth its encouragement to the Lebanese rebels, was an additional annoyance. Against similar provocations in the past the United States had for one reason or another often been unable to lend a hand. But here was one case where it appeared, if the Lebanese government should call upon us for help, we might move firmly and in full accord with the local government and the principles of the United Nations.

Of course, if we did intervene, the consequences could easily become drastic. Foster Dulles felt that if we should send troops into Lebanon there would be a major adverse reaction in the Middle East. He suspected that the pipelines across Syria would probably be blown, the Suez Canal might be blocked, and the wave of resentment among the Arab populations could become so strong that it might be impracticable for the governments of Iraq and Jordan to cooperate no matter how much they might desire to do so. Possible Soviet reaction was another item to consider. This point did not worry me excessively; I believed the Soviets would not take action if the United States movement were decisive and strong, particularly if other parts of the Middle East were not involved in the operations.

As the discussion went on, it became clear that Foster Dulles favored direct action but his brother Allen, the Director of the Central Intel-

[5] Robert Murphy believed that one reason for his caution was concern over the loyalties in an army half Moslem in composition.

ligence Agency, took a more cautious attitude, urging a delay of at least twenty-four hours.

Indeed, unless something radical should happen during the day, Allen Dulles' concern was largely academic, because the only problem immediately at hand was to inform President Chamoun of the kind of help he could expect upon our receipt of an appropriate request from Lebanon's duly constituted government.

Our reply was that, under these circumstances, we would respond favorably and strongly but with certain conditions, which were set forth in the reply I directed the Secretary of State to send to President Chamoun. First, we would not send United States troops to Lebanon for the purpose of achieving an additional term for the President. Second, the request should have the concurrence of some other Arab nation. Third, the mission of United States troops in Lebanon would be twofold: protection of the life and property of Americans, and assistance to the legal Lebanese government.

We promptly agreed upon certain preliminary actions. Once again we would move amphibious elements of the Sixth Fleet to the eastern Mediterranean. We would alert those Army airborne battle groups in Europe which had been earmarked for possible air transport to this region, and would airlift to Beirut already promised police equipment, small arms, ammunition, and tear gas.

For the moment we planned to make no report to the United Nations, assuming that it would be better for the Lebanese to submit their own statement to the Security Council. In addition I insisted that we emphasize to President Chamoun the value of his maintaining the independence of Lebanon without outside tactical help if this were possible; our intervention should be a last resort.

As it turned out there was no immediate need for intervention. The Lebanese army got the principal outbreak under control. But it seemed to lack the aggressiveness to stop the trouble completely. As May progressed, Beirut became quiet, though possession of the city of Tripoli was in contention between the armies and the rebels. The Lebanon-Syrian border was open to a steady influx of Syrians who meant no good to Chamoun's government.

On the 22nd of May President Chamoun requested an urgent meeting of the United Nations Security Council to consider his complaint that Egypt and Syria had been instigating the revolt and arming the rebels. There was no doubt in our minds of the truth of the charge. Arrogant and aggressive, the rebels seemed to be trying to cut the northern half of Lebanon from the southern half, as a preliminary to gaining control of the whole.

Dr. Charles Malik presented on June 6 a lengthy indictment of the United Arab Republic to the Council. Four days later the Council voted 10 to 1 (with Russia abstaining) for the Secretary-General to send a military observation team to Lebanon. The U.A.R. voiced no objection. The first members of the team arrived in the area two days later.

The failure of President Nasser to object to a United Nations observation team in Lebanon was puzzling. However, it did seem to fit in with certain new indications that he would be just as happy to see a temporary end to the struggle. Almost simultaneously with the passing of the Security Council resolution he contacted our government and offered to attempt to use his own influence to end the trouble. His conditions were not wholly unreasonable. They were that President Chamoun should finish out his term; that General Chehab, who many of our specialists felt was the strongest Lebanese politician outside of Chamoun, should succeed him; and that the rebels within Lebanon should be accorded amnesty. This message we passed on to President Chamoun through diplomatic channels, making certain he understood that our government was only a messenger in this regard and that we were not joining hands with the United Arab Republic against him. Apparently mistrusting President Nasser's motives, President Chamoun did nothing to follow up this lead.

The UN's Dag Hammarskjold arrived in Lebanon on June 18, at which time an undeclared forty-eight-hour truce set in. He concluded that infiltration from Syria was not so heavy as President Chamoun claimed.

That same day, in press conference, I was asked, "Under what conditions would we be prepared to take military action in connection with the Lebanese crisis?" I had determined previously that I would say nothing to hinder the United Nations observation team; so I said, "Secretary-General Hammarskjold is taking this whole matter under his earnest and personal view. I should say that it would be dependent somewhat upon the judgments of the armistice team and the Secretary-General as to what we might have to do. But I would not want at this time to make predictions."

Upon receiving word of this press conference President Chamoun seemed to become excited, even though he had been assured previously that our intentions had not changed basically as a result of the entrance of a United Nations observation team. (He had reportedly been on the verge of panic two days earlier, and had secured from his Cabinet written permission to call for the intervention of United States and British troops.) Nevertheless, after the press conference, I found it necessary to assure him that my remarks should be read within the context of the clear understanding between us. I pointed out that since Lebanon itself had invoked and received the support of the United Nations, the United States would find it awkward to act with military force unless the United Nations should confess failure in preserving the peace. Manifestly, if we should act prematurely we would have to bear the brunt of the responsibility for the collapse of the United Nations effort. I assured President Chamoun, however, that in a crisis we would not require the concurrence or the recommendations of the Secretary-General before providing military assistance, but pending the occurrence of such a crisis the efforts of the United Nations should not be impeded. I assured the President, again, of our confidence in him. But I also repeated that the introduction of Western forces in his country would create additional resentment in the Arab world, thus playing into Nasser's hands. Therefore I urged President Chamoun to do everything in his power to solve the problem with his own forces.

In early July it appeared that the Lebanon crisis would pass without Western military assistance. President Chamoun announced for the first time in public—although this was more or less a foregone conclusion—that he would leave office when his term expired on September 23. We doubted that his announcement would be sufficient to satisfy the Arab extremists who wanted him to leave officc immediately, but this pledge did rob them of their original excuse for rebelling. A search then began for a compromise candidate acceptable to both Christians and Arab nationalists.

* * *

The situation in Lebanon, which had seemed to be quieting, was now made critical by events in another land—Iraq. On Monday morning, July 14, 1958, I was shocked to receive news of a coup in Baghdad against the Hashemite monarchy. This was the country that we were counting on heavily as a bulwark of stability and progress in the region. The army, apparently with mob participation, had moved upon the royal palace and had murdered Crown Prince Emir Abdul Illah. The fate of King Faisal and Premier Nuri as Said, both of whom were friendly to the West, was in serious doubt. We feared the worst. This somber turn of events could, without vigorous response on our part, result in a complete elimination of Western influence in the Middle East. Overnight our objective changed from quieting a troubled situation to facing up to a crisis of formidable proportions. Lebanon again came into our conscious concern because of the internal conflicts in that country and the pressures exerted by Syria.

That morning I gathered in my office a group of advisers to make sure that no facet of the situation was overlooked. Because of my long study of the problem, this was one meeting in which my mind was practically made up regarding the general line of action we should take, even before we met. The time was rapidly approaching, I believed, when we had to move into the Middle East, and specifically into Lebanon, to stop the trend toward chaos. An additional factor in my deep concern was the presence in Lebanon of a relatively large number of American citizens whose lives might be endangered.

In reviewing the situation, C.I.A. Director Allen Dulles first reported on facts as he knew them. "The coup," he said, "was executed by pro-Nasser elements of the Iraqi army, and a 'Republican' government has been set up that includes pro-Nasser people. We have no information as yet that Nasser himself is behind the coup. A strict curfew has been instituted in Iraq and almost fifty officers of the Iraqi army have already been 'retired,' including a large proportion of pro-West officers. We have no reports on Iraqi forces outside Baghdad, and there is still just a possibility that the brigades in or near Jordan might prove loyal to the monarchy. King Faisal and Prime Minister Nuri as Said have disappeared but are presumed dead."

(We soon learned that both Faisal and Said had been killed, and that the army brigades supported the new regime.)

"In Jordan," he continued, "King Hussein has also been the target of a plot, but the King seems to be all right for the moment. He has reacted boldly, declaring himself the new head of the Arab Union and its armed forces. We don't really see how he expects to make it stick. Israel is reportedly alarmed. Prime Minister Ben-Gurion might possibly be prodded by extremists into seizing that portion of Jordan west of the Jordan River. Kuwait could also be in the balance.

"In Lebanon," Allen Dulles said, "the government of President Chamoun is alarmed and has officially requested through our ambassador that the United States and Britain intervene within forty-eight hours. President Chamoun is reported to be very bitter because we have not sent United States troops to support him. He has pledged to go down fighting, and has told General Chehab to obey orders or leave his position."

Allen Dulles reported King Saud to be worried and secretly demanding that the Baghdad Pact powers intervene in Iraq, on pain of Saudi Arabia's having to "go along" with the United Arab Republic.

The time had come to act. But first there were some preliminary chores to perform within our own family. I then turned to Secretary Dulles, saying: "Foster, give us your analysis of an American intervention in Lebanon. What would the Russians do?"

He replied, "The Russians will probably make threatening gestures—toward Turkey and Iran especially—but will not act unless they believe the results of a general war would be favorable to them." Foster did not believe the Soviets would put this to the test because of their respect for our power—especially overwhelming in bombers.

However, the case for intervention was far from one-sided. "If the United States went into Lebanon," Foster said, "we could expect a very bad reaction from most Arab countries." He repeated his previous statement that the pipeline across Syria would probably be cut and our use of the Suez Canal impeded or denied. King Saud, despite his personal desire for us to move, could probably do nothing to help. The British would have to move into Kuwait to protect their oil, and the United States would have to substantially increase strength at Dhahran U. S. Air Force Base in Saudi Arabia.

As to the *coup d'état* in Iraq, Foster continued, we lacked hard evidence implicating Nasser. On the possibilities of counterrevolution, these were largely dependent on the leadership of Nauri as Said, who for all we knew might be dead. If he were gone, the direct counteraction in Iraq would be out of the picture.

The Iraqi crisis was just another flare-up in the tinderbox of the entire Middle East. As I told my colleagues, "We must all realize that a single move can of itself produce no permanent settlement. Any intervention in Lebanon will put out one fire only; until stable governments are set up and supported locally, the Middle East will never calm down." As a consequence, the situation had to be studied carefully, and anything we did should conform with our over-all policy of friendship with all nations of the region, with the Charter of the United Nations, and with due regard for world opinion.

Foster estimated that public opinion in Western Europe and probably in Latin America would support a move into Lebanon. Most of Asia, India, Ceylon, and vocal Africa would oppose us. Many leaders in these latter areas would secretly applaud but would be afraid to talk.

The present case, from a legal viewpoint, was far different from that of the British-French attack on Egypt. Our intervention would be a response to a proper request from a legally constituted government and in accordance with the principles stated in the Middle East Doctrine. But, Foster warned, many people would not get the distinction and some domestic opposition could be anticipated.

Following this protracted conference I arranged to meet with a bipartisan group of legislators for a full briefing. At 2:30 that same afternoon (July 14) twenty-two leaders of both houses of Congress filed into my office. The mood was anything but cheerful as Allen and Foster Dulles gave their analyses. The purpose of this meeting was, of course, only exploratory. On my part, I wanted to probe the thinking of the leaders of Congress and to give them our latest intelligence and the lines of action under consideration. My guests were somber, but their attitudes, for the moment, reflected nothing of partisanship. All of the conversation was remarkably constructive. One area of discussion was the role of the United Nations and the timing of our notification to that organization. Here Foster had to explain Article 51 of the United Nations Charter, which permitted a country to act on an emergency basis pending the first opportunity to turn the problem over as soon as the United Nations was able to act.

Some members of Congress recalled the favorable effect of our Suez policies in 1956 and felt that intervention in Lebanon would be followed by an opposition reaction. I pointed out the basic differences in the two situations. In the first case intervention involved an attack against Egypt and its government—what we were considering was an entry into Lebanon to defend a people upon the request of their government.

Speaker Sam Rayburn was fearful that we might be getting into something that was strictly a civil war. Most skeptical of all was Senator Fulbright, who seemed to doubt seriously that this crisis was Communist-inspired. He felt that Secretary-General Hammarskjold's previous lack of success in identifying rebel support across the Syrian border should preclude our moving. However, I pointed out that Hammarskjold had reported only that the traffic was light during the time the United Nations team had been on station, and some of our own observers definitely doubted the competence of the team.

Congressman Robert B. Chiperfield of Illinois and Carl Vinson felt we had no choice but to move. Congressman Vinson had, in fact, thought we must make up our minds to "go the distance." Congressman John M. Vorys of Ohio reminded the group that the Soviets had claimed back in 1947 that the Greek conflict, to which the United States had committed so much material and advisory help, was also nothing but a civil war.

At the end of the meeting I felt sure that Congress, while not attempting to impede our intervention in Lebanon, would not, in the absence of some greater emergency, support any more extensive action than had been discussed at the meeting. Except for a very few, like Vinson, Vorys, and Chiperfield, none of the leaders was outspoken in his support of intervention in Lebanon; but authority for such an operation lay so clearly within the responsibility of the Executive that no direct objection was voiced. In any event, the issue was clear to me—we had to go in.[6]

[6] Map, "The Lebanon Landings, July 15, 1958" appears following page 360.

With the meeting adjourned, my associates and I discussed the likelihood of British participation in the landing. This I opposed because I felt that United States forces would be adequate, and with the thirty-seven hundred British troops intact on Cyprus, a reserve would be available for use for purposes beyond the limits of the Middle East Resolution.

As to tactics and availability of forces for the Lebanon landing, General Twining advised that three Marine battalions were afloat in the eastern Mediterranean, ready to move in at any time. Time and distance factors dictated that the first battalion would have to be ashore alone for something like twelve hours. I directed that the landing take place the next afternoon, at 3 P.M. Lebanon time.[7]

Elements of the Sixth Fleet would move eastward at once, and the two Army battle groups in Europe earmarked for movement to the Middle East should receive their orders at approximately the same time as the first landings in Lebanon. In the meantime we were to call for an emergency meeting of the United Nations Security Council as early as possible, that is, the next morning, July 15. I would avoid making any statement until the landing was actually taking place.

The meeting over, everyone except the Secretary of State departed rapidly to carry out his own individual task. Foster Dulles stayed with me while I telephoned Prime Minister Macmillan. I found Harold completely in accord with my decision, almost eager. He accepted without murmur my feeling that British forces should remain in reserve while United States forces made the landings. He said that he had received a request for support from King Hussein. (I had to smile at Harold's efforts at a code over the telephone—"We have had a request from the two little chaps," meaning Hussein and Chamoun.) He was anxious, however, that we realize the extent to which this situation might grow; he wanted my assurances that we were in this together, all the way. This I gave him with the understanding that I could take action only one phase at a time. The government was moving in accord with the provisions of the Middle East Resolution, but if the conflict expanded into something that the Resolution did not cover, I would, given time, go to the Congress for additional authorization.

Obviously the decision to send troops to Lebanon was not one to be taken lightly. In review, as is normal in decisions involving operations of

[7] This would be 9 A.M. Eastern Daylight time. Vice Admiral James L. Holloway, Jr., Commander-in-Chief Naval Forces Eastern Atlantic and Mediterranean, was designated as the commander of the over-all operation. On July 23, Major General Paul D. Adams, U.S.A., was designated Commander of Land Forces in Lebanon under Admiral Holloway.

war, the problem was to select the least objectionable of several possible courses of action. For example, to initiate the D-Day invasion of Normandy in 1944 the decision was whether to attack under threat of unfavorable weather conditions or to immobilize for at least two weeks the powerful forces poised for action. Neither alternative was attractive. In Lebanon the question was whether it would be better to incur the deep resentment of nearly all of the Arab world (and some of the rest of the Free World) and in doing so to risk general war with the Soviet Union or to do something worse—which was to do nothing. In both D-Day and Lebanon, there was little doubt in my own mind as to the correctness of the decisions. Despite the vast disparity in the size of the two operations, the possible consequences in each case, if things went wrong, were chilling.

Of course the decision to intervene represented only one step in our efforts to restore reasonable stability to the Middle East. We had also to explain to the American people and to the world the reasons for such action. Therefore I wrote an announcement for Mr. Hagerty to issue on the morning of July 15. The timing of the release was to coincide as closely as possible with the landings, half a world away. The statement noted the request of President Chamoun that United States forces be sent to Lebanon, and emphasized that his appeal had been made with the concurrence of all members of his Cabinet.

> In response to this appeal from the government of Lebanon, the United States has dispatched a contingent of United States forces to Lebanon to protect American lives and by their presence there to encourage the Lebanese government in defense of Lebanese sovereignty and integrity. These forces have not been sent as any act of war. They will demonstrate the concern of the United States for the independence and integrity of Lebanon, which we deem vital to the national interest and world peace. Our concern will also be shown by economic assistance. We shall act in accordance with these legitimate concerns.

It declared our intention of reporting our action to an emergency meeting of the United Nations Security Council and to explain that we had acted under the inherent right of collective self-defense as defined in the United Nations Charter.

During the day essentially the same information was given out three more times: in a message to Congress, in Cabot Lodge's announcement in the United Nations, and finally by a radio-television address which I delivered that evening at 6:30 P.M. In that talk I drew a parallel between the Lebanon situation and that which had faced us in Greece in 1947. I called attention also to the Communist takeover of Czechoslovakia in

1948, the Communist conquest of the Chinese mainland in 1949, and their attempts to take over Korea and Indochina, beginning in 1950.

To correct any misunderstandings as to our attitude, I emphasized once again that the United States had no intention of replacing the United Nations in its primary responsibility of maintaining international peace and security. Rather, we had felt forced to react quickly because only swift action would suffice. I expressed the hope that measures taken by the United Nations would preserve Lebanon's independence and "permit the early withdrawal of United States forces."

Determined that the American people would understand the situation fully, I said, "I am well aware of the fact that landing of United States troops in Lebanon could have some serious consequences. That is why this step was taken only after the most serious consideration and broad consultation. I have, however, come to the sober and clear conclusion that the action taken was essential to the welfare of the United States. It was required to support the principles of justice and international law upon which peace and a stable international order depend."

The basic mission of United States forces in Lebanon was not primarily to fight. Every effort was made to have our landing be as much of a garrison move as possible. In my address I had been careful to use the term "stationed in" Lebanon rather than "invading." If it had been prudent, I would have preferred that the first battalion ashore disembark at a dock rather than across the beaches. However, the attitude of the Lebanese army was at that moment unknown, and it was obviously wise to disembark in deployed formations ready for any emergency. As it turned out, there was no resistance; in fact, the Lebanese along the beaches welcomed our troops. The geographic objectives of the landings included only the city of Beirut and the adjoining airfield. Occupation of the hinterland was not contemplated.[8]

On the military side, the news during the day of July 15 was good. General Twining came to see me late in the morning to tell me that the landing operations had gone well. A landing team consisting of the 2nd Battalion of the 2nd Marine Regiment (seventeen hundred men) had landed exactly on schedule. General Chehab, Admiral Holloway, and U. S. Ambassador Robert M. McClintock had met the troops on the road from the airport and after a short delay had led them into Beirut. A

[8] The decision to occupy only the airfield and capital was a political one which I adhered to over the recommendations of some of the military. If the Lebanese army were unable to subdue the rebels when we had secured their capital and protected their government, I felt, we were backing up a government with so little popular support that we probably should not be there.

second battalion (the 3rd Battalion, 6th Marine Regiment) would land beginning at dawn the next day, and a third one (the 1st Battalion, 8th Marine Regiment) by nightfall.[9] The two Army battle groups in Germany (the 187th Airborne Battle Group and the 503rd Airborne Battle Group) could land in twelve hours on call from Admiral Holloway. This would give us a very respectable force in the area.

General Twining said that the Joint Chiefs of Staff recommended the deployment of Air Force tankers into forward positions, and an increased level of alertness for the Strategic Air Command, with more than eleven hundred aircraft armed and their crews ready. Because the tanker deployment would be a move of considerable size and impossible of concealment, Twining remarked that it might create some misinterpretation of our intentions. But, far from objecting to the tanker aircraft deployment's becoming known, I felt this knowledge would be desirable, as showing readiness and determination without implying any threat of aggression. The move was arranged.

In addition to the three Marine battalions and the two Army battle groups immediately earmarked for the operation, several other preparatory and supporting moves were ordered. General Twining said that two divisions, the 101st Airborne Division and the Second Marine Division, were available for movement overseas, but shipping was short. For the moment, at least, I foresaw no need for these additional forces and, rather than chartering additional vessels, instructed the General merely to keep a roster of available shipping. In the meantime a part of the 82nd Airborne Division was held ready for quick airlift to Europe.

Reactions to the landings, both at home and abroad, were much as predicted. The *New York Times* reported, on July 15:

> Arkady A. Sobolev of Russia said that U.S. had committed an "act of aggression against the Arab world."
>
> The crucial question, however, was whether Moscow would confine its response to the U.S. move to words rather than deeds. A wave of anxiety over that question swept through world capitals.
>
> In Washington . . . Republicans generally supported the decision firmly; many Democrats expressed grave misgivings, but said that once American soldiers had been committed they had to go along with the decision in the interests of national security. . . . Former Presidents Hoover and Truman both said Mr. Eisenhower had no choice but to act to save Lebanon. . . .[10]

[9] The third battalion landing team actually landed in the objective area at 9:00 A.M. July 18, local time.

[10] On July 17 I wrote Mr. Truman thanking him for his forthright support.

> Abroad, the reaction of the "neutrals" was, as expected, bitterly critical of the U.S. But there also were signs of deep uneasiness over the American decision in some pro-Western circles. West Germany, which stands on the front line of Western defense in Europe, was plainly disturbed over the danger of a general war. . . . leaders of the Laborite opposition cried "shame!" when Foreign Secretary Selwyn Lloyd defended the U.S.
>
> . . . there were rumors that King Hussein of Jordan planned to move into Iraq to bring it back into the pro-Western camp. . . .

A few days later, in Moscow, a large crowd gathered outside the United States Embassy and inflicted some damage, and Nasser flew to that city to confer with Khrushchev.

Confidential reports on governmental attitudes—which rarely reach the press—were pouring in from our embassies and other sources. General Goodpaster kept a running note of the intelligence material which he furnished me on a day-to-day basis. Reactions ranged all the way from gratification in Turkey and Pakistan to loud condemnation from the Soviets.

Excerpts from the reports sent to me on July 18 and 19 give a sample of intelligence coming in:

> July 18—. . . Chamoun will try to clean out disloyal elements from Lebanese Army; NATO reactions to UK help to Jordan were generally favorable, with strong support by most delegates; . . . Israel welcomes US and UK intervention—will move if Hussein falls; situation in Jordan has quieted and stabilized; Egyptians profess fear of Soviet involvement, and view US warning against attack on US forces as an ultimatum; Chamoun lacks power to remove treasonable elements from his army. Reports that Soviets are reacting with intensified political and propaganda measures, but without taking commitments or without significant military moves; growing evidence that Lebanese military forces and rebels may clash with US Marines; in Iraq rebel forces seem to be in control and are consolidating their position; . . . information that Lebanese army initially intended to resist US Marines but backed down at last moment.
>
> July 19—USSR continues political attack against Western intervention in Jordan and Lebanon; but without commitments and with very cautious statements as to action; . . . attitude of Lebanese army remains equivocal, with growing probability of terrorist attacks against American troops together with Fedayeen from Syria; Nehru appears to seek a mediatory role as in Suez and Korean crises; Turks desire to move into Iraq, and say they have decided to do so, asking US material and moral support (notably against USSR); UAR has reacted strongly against the US warning, particularly our warning against attack by forces known to be under UAR control; Yemeni reaction to the coup is mixed with ruling family showing fear of attack against themselves; Faisal stresses neutrality in Saudi Arabia,

in contrast to Saud who frantically urges pro-Western action against Iraq; Britain has moved a battalion to Aden and authorized British agent in Kuwait to call for troops in event of disturbances, but concern remains in Kuwait due to ineptness of regime; in Iraq high governmental officials express desire to protect commercial and other commitments and to establish good terms with US and UK; Interior Minister Arif is appearing as the real organizer of the [recent] coup.

Along with the landings in Lebanon we moved energetically to consolidate our political position in other parts of the Middle East. The Turks were uneasy about the over-all situation, particularly along their borders. There was some doubt as to the attitude of Iraq. The new government, under General Kassim, a dictator of uncertain temperament, had quickly professed a desire to be friendly with the Western powers and had been cooperative in protecting United States and British lives and property when we evacuated some of our nationals. However, the purposes of that government were unknown, and we realized that it had the capability of sudden military action against Jordan or Kuwait. In Saudi Arabia there was always the danger of a coup.

As some insurance against these possibilities and to reassure our friends in the region, I approved a Joint Chiefs' recommendation for a seaborne movement of a Marine Corps regimental combat team, located on Okinawa, to take station in the Persian Gulf. There it could guard against a possible Iraqi move into Kuwait or be available in case of threats to the security of friendly governments. I approved the movement of a Composite Air Strike Group[11] from Western Europe to our base at Adana, Turkey.

Finally, I instructed General Twining to be prepared to employ, subject to my personal approval, *whatever* means might become necessary to prevent any unfriendly forces from moving into Kuwait. In the state of tension then existing, these measures would probably bring us no closer to general war than we were already.

* * *

On the informational and propaganda side I was disappointed to learn that Free World capabilities and efforts were far from satisfactory. The British, in fact, had been required, because of lack of funds, to shut down a radio station in the Middle East that would have been valuable at the time. In Washington I had been told that a representative of the Voice of America (our governmental radio overseas) had tried to obtain

[11] A Composite Air Strike Group is a balanced tactical air task force. This one was composed of RF-101s, F-100Ds, and RB-66s, among others.

from a senator a statement opposing our landing of troops in Lebanon. In a state of some pique I informed Secretary Dulles that this was carrying the policy of "free broadcasting" too far. The Voice of America should, I said, employ truth as a weapon in support of Free World objectives, but it had no mandate or license to seek evidence of lack of domestic support of America's foreign policies and actions.[12]

Upon Foster's recommendation I approved the dispatch to Lebanon of a qualified and authoritative representative. Ambassador Robert Murphy was sent at once to achieve the best possible coordination between United States officials on the spot and Lebanese authorities.

During all this time we were in finger-tip communication with Prime Minister Macmillan. In the two days following the landings, the British Cabinet discussed the possibilities of further action in the Middle East. On July 17 that government decided, in compliance with King Hussein's plea, to send twenty-two hundred British paratroopers from Cyprus to bolster his shaky regime. The British were undoubtedly influenced by reports of a dangerous plot against the King's life.

Selwyn Lloyd, sent to Washington by Harold Macmillan to confer with Foster and me, repeated the Prime Minister's arguments in favor of making the Jordan expedition a joint U.S.-British operation. I explained that, as of that moment, I had committed myself to the Congress to go only as far as Lebanon. Aside from combat troops, however, we could and we would support the British in every feasible way, including the provision of logistical support. Furthermore, I pledged, if the British got into trouble I would take all necessary measures to make their operation a success.

One problem facing the British was that of access into Amman, the Jordanian capital. The quickest and best air route into Amman was over Israel, and permission to overfly Israel was accordingly requested. Prime Minister Ben-Gurion agreed to grant the overflight rights, but only after he had called Foster Dulles, at 2:30 in the morning Washington time, to insure the United States' backing of the British request. The authority having been given, British troops landed in Amman on July 17 without difficulty. They were enthusiastically welcomed by the populace.

Problems of access, however, were not completely solved. Ben-Gurion's action was not popular in his own country and Soviet pressure on him to withdraw the authorization was heavy. There were other routes of resupply into Jordan that we hoped could soon be used. One of these

[12] During World War II the Office of War Information had, on two occasions in foreign broadcasts, opposed actions of President Roosevelt; it ridiculed the temporary arrangement with Admiral Darlan in North Africa and that with Marshal Badoglio in Italy. President Roosevelt took prompt action to stop such insubordination.

would be from the U. S. Air Force Base at Dhahran, Saudi Arabia. Plans had been made for resupply from this area, but at the last minute the Saudi Arabian government (without a doubt Prince Faisal, King Saud's younger brother, acting in this instance) withdrew permission for U.S. planes to sortie to Jordan from this base. In extreme emergency it might have become necessary to ignore the Saudi Arabian decision.

There remained, however, the port of Aqaba, Jordan's surface outlet to the sea. In the course of time supply through this port could be made practicable, but the fifty-mile road between Aqaba and Amman was practically nonexistent, and the route ran through difficult country. Thus it was, much to King Hussein's chagrin, that for the time being the main supply line for the British and the Jordanians had to be through the air space of Jordan's professed mortal enemy, Israel.

When Ambassador Murphy reached Beirut on July 19 he immediately called on President Chamoun and found him nervous and depressed.[13] Chamoun was so weary that his mind seemed almost at times to black out; he had difficulty in recalling what he had said only moments before. He had suffered two heart attacks and had been sixty-seven days without leaving the presidential residence. He indicated at one time that he was contemplating resigning before July 24 in order to force Parliament to meet. The arrival of American troops, however, seemed to increase his confidence, and he talked of issuing a peremptory order to General Chehab to attack the rebels. Our ambassador, Mr. McClintock, remarked that he had heard similar talk over the past two months, but the President now said the situation was different.

One unexpected diplomatic difficulty had to be straightened out at once. On the day preceding Mr. Murphy's arrival, Adil Osseiran, the President of the Chamber of Deputies of Lebanon, sent a message to me and to the Security Council of the United Nations, protesting the U.S. landing. This gave some fuel to those who were feeding the flames of Arab nationalist resentment. When the international impact of Osseiran's message was pointed out by Bob Murphy, however, President Chamoun agreed to write me an official letter of explanation. On July 21 it arrived. After expressing the gratitude of the Lebanese people and of himself to the United States, he wrote:

> It has been brought to my attention that Mr. Adil Osseiran has in his capacity as President of the Chamber of Deputies objected to this landing in a message he sent to you and to the Security Council of the United

[13] "There," Murphy wrote later, "I found a tired and worried man, who for sixty-seven days had been a self-made prisoner. Apparently he had not so much as looked out of a window during that time, and this undoubtedly was wise as his chances of assassination were excellent." (*Diplomat Among Warriors,* p. 400.)

Nations. This message does not express but Mr. Osseiran's personal opinion. For the President of the Chamber of Deputies has no constitutional status, as is clearly proven by the fact that there is no mention whatsoever of him in the provisions of the Constitution of Lebanon. He is a Deputy like and among other Deputies; he is elected only to preside over the meetings of the Chamber of Deputies; to administer the Secretariat, and to represent it on formal occasions.

I want to assure you, Mr. President, that we are both happy and honored to find ourselves side by side with the Great American nation defending not only our independence and integrity against direct aggression, but the high principles in which the free world believes and by which it lives.

Faithfully yours,

/s/ Camille Chamoun

Ambassador Murphy remained on the spot and kept in close communication with the State Department. He went later to Iraq to give our assurances to Premier Kassim and finally to Cairo to confer with Nasser.

Though the military and diplomatic situation in Lebanon seemed now to simmer down, anxiety continued over the precarious supply situation of the British in Jordan. Because petroleum supplies from Iraq had been cut off, we were now obliged to supply Jordan with oil and gasoline. Requirements in these items alone came to 105,000 barrels per month. In spite of this additional strain on supply arrangements, both King Hussein and Prime Minister Macmillan again requested that United States troops be placed on the ground in Jordan along with British. For the moment, however, I thought such a move would be unwise and unnecessary.

A week after our Lebanon landings, Harold Macmillan reported that British troops in Jordan had only twelve days' supply of food and oil, with ammunition for only a few days' local operations. Moreover, he was still experiencing difficulty with Ben-Gurion regarding overflights of Israeli territory, the Israelis already having cut down the length of time during the day in which the supply operation was permitted. Consequently Harold requested some United States support and asked that the United States take over the airlift from the British to fly in essential supplies. To this I answered:

Dear Harold:

I received yesterday your message about Jordan. Taking up first the matter of supply, we are quite ready in principle to help out further in this respect. I understand that we are flying POL[14] from Lebanon to Jordan,

[14] A British term, adopted during World War II by the United States Army, meaning Petrol, Oil, Lubricants.

overflying Israel close to the Syrian border. The Israelis acquiesce in this but do not like it. We have told them that we think this need will be over by this week and that an adequate substitute can be found in Aqaba where, I believe, intensive work is being done to improve the facilities and communication route with Amman.

We would be willing to use our Globemasters to assist you in flying from Cyprus supplies to your forces in Jordan. As you say, a smaller number of these larger planes could do the job you are doing. However, we would have to seek and find some accommodation with Israel. Foster has already talked with their Embassy here about the matter, and we hope to get a reply by tomorrow. I am convinced that whatever be the immediate outcome, we cannot look upon these overflights of Israel as a permanent solution. We must concentrate upon getting what is needed into Aqaba. . . .

The introduction of our ground forces [into Jordan] raises much more difficult problems. Our public opinion and Congress would, I know, be extremely averse to seeing us take this further step. We believe, as you indicate, that your forces there already stabilize the position and we hope that it will continue thus, until through the UN or otherwise you are able, logically, to lay down this burden.

This United States aid in aerial delivery of supplies I felt would be adequate, particularly since General Twining advised me that the communications line between Amman and Aqaba should be open by about July 28 both by rail and by road.

All these detailed concerns were dwarfed by the fears that gripped the rest of the world over what the Soviet reaction might be to the United States and British interventions. Personally I had always discounted the probability of the Soviets doing anything as "reaction." Communists do little on impulse; rather their aggressive moves are invariably the result of deliberate decision. Nevertheless, we were watchful. Soviet actions, despite polemics and some damage to the United States Embassy in Moscow, remained cautious and negative. They staged extensive military maneuvers in the south of Russia, but confined their external moves to the diplomatic.

Our announcement to the United Nations of our landings on July 15 had carried with it a proposal that the Secretary-General arrange for an emergency force to be dispatched to Lebanon to replace United States troops. This proposal immediately encountered a Soviet veto in the Security Council and inspired a Soviet counterproposal calling upon the United States and Britain immediately to cease armed intervention in the domestic affairs of Arab states. This barren proposal received only one aye vote.

A Swedish proposal to suspend the United Nations observation team was likewise overwhelmingly defeated. A few days later a proposal by the Japanese—completely sensible, I thought—for the United Nations to "make possible the withdrawal of the United States forces from Lebanon" was also vetoed by the Soviet delegation. Now the spotlight turned to a voluminous and largely fruitless exchange of correspondence between Mr. Khrushchev and the West, particularly with the United States.

On July 10, while the series of proposals in the United Nations were being considered, Khrushchev returned to his favorite formula for solving world problems—a summit meeting. This he proposed in a letter to me that he simultaneously made public. The letter contained the usual professions of desire for peace and a rather surprising polemic against the commander of the Sixth Fleet, throwing in for good measure a boast of Soviet military capabilities. After contesting the validity of the requests on the part of the local governments that formed the justification for the United States and British forces to go into Lebanon and Jordan, and after again warning of the danger thus brought on, Chairman Khrushchev proposed the immediate convocation of a conference of the heads of government of the U.S.S.R., the United States, Britain, France, and India "in order to, without delay, adopt measures for the cessation of the military conflict which has begun." Khrushchev proposed further that the meeting also consider the question of a cessation of delivery of arms to the countries of the Middle East. He suggested that Secretary-General Hammarskjold participate in the meetings and that the recommendation resulting from the conference be then submitted to the UN Security Council for review. In this review he suggested participation by representatives of the Arab countries.

This proposal was attractive on the surface and, I understand, made a strong impression in the United Nations. Nevertheless we could not accept it. First of all, the resources of the United Nations for maintaining order and stability in the Middle East were far from exhausted, provided the organization was given time to mobilize its assets. Furthermore, the spectacle of five "great powers" sitting down to decide the fate of the nations of the Middle East without the participation of Israel was contrary to the whole idea of the United Nations. After studying the letter, I authorized a public statement emphasizing our desire to continue with efforts within the United Nations.

I then addressed myself to a reply to the Chairman. I began by refuting his arguments on the legality of the United States' action in going into

Lebanon, and called attention to the constant Soviet abuse of its veto power in the Security Council. I pointed out that implementation of his proposal would not conform with the Charter of the United Nations, and ventured the view that the "recommendations" regarding the Near and Middle East would in reality be decisions that would make the United Nations nothing more than a rubber stamp for a few large powers. Then I came to the real substance of my reply:

> The Security Council is already dealing with certain phases of the problem alluded to by your note. If you or we believe that other aspects of this problem or other problems should be urgently dealt with in the interest of peace, then it lies open to any of us to enlarge the scope of the Security Council consideration. Furthermore, under the Charter, members of government, including Heads of Government and Foreign Ministers, may represent a member nation at the Security Council. If such a meeting were generally desired, the United States would join in following that orderly procedure.
>
> I do not, of course, exclude the discussion, outside the United Nations, of world or regional problems, not posing alleged imminent threats to the peace. I cannot but deplore the persistent refusal of your Government for so many months to agree to the adequate preparation of a "summit" meeting, at which we could exchange considered views on the great problems which confront the world. . . .

Harold Macmillan answered in similar fashion, giving but a little leeway for the possibility of informal meetings outside the Security Council framework, an idea that I considered dangerous.

Khrushchev was not long in answering. In a letter the next day, July 23, he implied that the Western powers, and Britain in particular, had accepted his proposal almost in toto. He emphasized the opportunity for discussion outside the Security Council meeting and repeated his proposal that India be a party to Security Council discussions. He went on: "It goes without saying that representatives of the interested Arab states must be brought into a discussion of the questions in the Security Council with the participation of the chiefs of government of the above mentioned five powers." He proposed July 28 as the date for the meeting.

I lost no time in answering. The Chairman, I felt, was arrogating to himself the privilege of determining who should sit on a Security Council discussion. Furthermore, we desired to put him on notice that any discussion of the Middle East would not be confined to Jordan and Lebanon alone, but would also include such items as Soviet attempts at subversion [see Appendix N].

My letter insisted that the matter belonged to the United Nations and that the precedent established by that organization should be followed; I rejected the idea that Khrushchev either alone or in conjunction with a few other heads of government could alter the composition of the Security Council.

Then I pointedly reminded him:

> You will also recall the 1950 "Peace through Deeds" Resolution of the General Assembly which condemns the "fomenting of civil strife in the interest of foreign power" as among the "gravest of all crimes."
>
> It is my earnest hope that through the United Nations Security Council steps can be taken in regard to the Middle East which, by making peace more secure there, will help promote it elsewhere.

Then I again told him that if he should still want a "summit" meeting, all that was necessary was to secure general agreement among the affected "heads of government" to represent their respective countries in the United Nations Security Council.

Again Harold Macmillan took a position almost identical with ours. Unfortunately President de Gaulle of France did not, insisting that a summit meeting could not be held within the Security Council framework and suggesting that a meeting of heads of government be held in Europe. As a result, Khrushchev seized on De Gaulle's statement to repeat his desire that a summit meeting of the five powers be held as soon as possible somewhere in Europe. His letter was obviously calculated to throw the onus of any refusal to negotiate on the United States.

Our correspondence was becoming fruitless. Accordingly I briefly answered the Chairman on August 1, repeating once more my points regarding the responsibilities of the United Nations organization and my determination to call a special meeting for August 12. I said I would be there and hoped that he would be.

The whole debate by correspondence came to an end a few days later. While on a visit to Red China, Khrushchev issued a joint communiqué with Chairman Mao Tse-tung, calling upon Britain and the United States to withdraw their troops. Upon his return to Moscow, Khrushchev sent me a message asserting that we were responsible for the fact that a summit meeting would not be held. He was, he said, calling for a special session of the United Nations General Assembly.

Immediately on receipt of Khrushchev's message we contacted the British, who were much disturbed over this development for fear of being embarrassed in the General Assembly should their rights in Jordan be attacked. It was, of course, clear that we could not prevent a meeting of the General Assembly.[15] Under the UN Charter it would take place inevitably, if only on Soviet request. However, in the light of the British treaties with Jordan, we could see no real reason for embarrassment for them. We prepared for a meeting of the General Assembly.

Things were now beginning to stabilize in the Middle East. On the 31st of July the situation in Lebanon was sufficiently calm to justify the special presidential election there that Mr. Murphy had done much to bring about. General Chehab, a Christian, was elected the new President. He was an almost ideal candidate, acceptable to both the rebels and to the government.

Immediately upon his election I sent a message of congratulations to General Chehab, to which he responded warmly. I was a little amused at his expression of regret over having to leave the military life after so many years. His statement struck a responsive chord.

By the end of July conditions in Iraq improved. Premier Kassim was showing traces of friendliness to the West and seemed to be in complete control of the government. Although he had signed a non-aggression pact with the United Arab Republic, there was no overriding reason for the United States to withhold recognition any longer. This was accorded on July 30.

On August 8, our total strength in Lebanon reached its highest peak —114,357 men, of which 8515 were Army and 5842 Marine Corps.[16] That strength had been built up because of uncertainty during the early stages of the operation. Now we had more troops there than were needed, and decided to begin some withdrawals. To avoid the appearance of doing so on the demands of the Soviets when the General Assembly opened, we arranged for sufficient troops to depart to attract some public notice before the convening of the Assembly. This would also reassure Premier Kassim, who had expressed doubts about our sincerity in using our troops only for the security of Lebanon. At the same time, the Joint Chiefs of Staff set about making plans for a mass withdrawal of our forces when the need for them was clearly gone.

[15] On July 29 Secretary Dulles had come back from a Baghdad Pact meeting and reported that Macmillan had been anxious to move rapidly on a summit conference because he was feeling the awkward position of the British in Jordan and believed he had to accede to a view in the Parliament that in all these matters one should sit down and "talk it over." Foster had still felt that the Soviets wanted a meeting very much and would take it on our terms.

[16] This force included a tank battalion and an Honest John rocket battery with atomic capability. The bulk of the Army troops arrived in very early August. The peak strength of the Marine Corps contingent was over 6300 in late July.

* * *

When the General Assembly convened, it seemed wise for me to request the opportunity to address it. I hoped it might be possible to establish a constructive atmosphere conducive to real results.

We made up a list of six items important to peace in the Middle East. The first two, as might be expected, involved the preservation of peace in Lebanon and in Jordan. Also vital, I felt, was an end to the fomenting of civil strife from sources outside the region. To guard against this kind of indirect aggression, we hoped the United Nations would establish a standby United Nations peace force to constitute permanent "ready" machinery for immediate action. Furthermore, to alleviate the tensions between Israel and the Arab states—still a basic cause of Middle East conflict—our government proposed that the nations concerned in the 1948 conflict (Israel on the one hand, Jordan, Syria, and Egypt on the other) call for a United Nations study and possibly a permanent United Nations body to control the flow of heavy armaments to the region.

Last, we favored an economic development plan to accelerate improvement in the living standards of the Arab peoples, and suggested consultations between the Secretary-General and the Arab nations of the Near East to devise a regional development organization. Its task would be to accelerate progress in such fields as industry, agriculture, water supply, health, and education. Other nations and private organizations which might be prepared to support it should be consulted at appropriate times. We were convinced that only improvement of living standards could bring stability to the Middle East.

Promising United States support for such an organization, I said:

> The institution would be set up to provide loans to the Arab States as well as the technical assistance required.
>
> The institution should be governed by the Arab States themselves. . . .
>
> . . . the best and quickest way to achieve the most desirable result would be for the Secretary-General to make two parallel approaches. First, to consult with the Arab States of the Near East to determine an area of agreement. Then to invite the International Bank for Reconstruction and Development, which has vast experience in this field, to make available its facilities for the planning of the organizations and operating techniques needed to establish the institution on a progressive course.

During the following week the diplomatic logjam in the United Nations finally broke. Appropriately enough, the resolution the United Nations General Assembly passed on August 21 was instituted by the Arabs themselves. It pledged non-interference among the Arab states in each others' affairs and instructed Secretary-General Hammarskjold to make practical arrangements leading to the withdrawal of the West's troops from Lebanon and Jordan.

Fundamentally, this action in the United Nations terminated the Lebanon crisis, although American troops were to stay there for another two months. President Chamoun retained his office until September 23, its legal date of termination. Troubles, of course, did not suddenly end. The general strike which had long before been called by the Arabs against President Chamoun did not cease until early September, when its leaders concluded it was impossible to force that capable but harassed statesman into early retirement. Then, upon the assumption of his presidential office, General Chehab had some difficulty in forming a Cabinet satisfactory to all factions, but with a duly constituted government, elected by legal means, the independence and integrity of Lebanon were preserved.

On October 25, 1958, the final withdrawal of United States troops took place, almost without public notice. This lack of attention contrasted vividly with attitudes in the early days of our intervention when some international critics were crying that America's purpose was to establish a permanent and imperialistic foothold in the Middle East.

But even with this highly satisfactory development, the situation in Iraq was still far from satisfactory. General Kassim—something of a mystery figure whose basic purposes were never made plain—retained dictatorial powers. In December 1958 the State Department sent Assistant Secretary William Rountree on a visit to Iraq, where he was greeted with rioting and threats. However, he managed to visit extensively with the Prime Minister, explaining to him the peaceful character of United States' objectives in the area. Rountree came home to report in the latter part of the month, somewhat encouraged by his visit with Kassim and by his visit with President Nasser of the United Arab Republic.

During the next year, uncertainty continued. Periodic reports came in of the growing power of the Communists in Iraq—groups that were certainly not completely preoccupied with pan-Arabism and Nasserism but were, apparently, responsive to directions from the Kremlin. For a while these groups were permitted to form paramilitary organizations and carry arms. Eventually even Kassim seemed to recognize the danger to him and his regime and, possibly under pressure from the army or from Colonel Nasser, began to curtail the status of these Communist organizations.

During 1959 the attitude of President Nasser seemed to become progressively less aggressive. From October 1958 to the end of 1963, stability in the Middle East and northern Africa improved remarkably. Although two governments were overthrown by *coup d'états,* the Menderes regime in Turkey in 1960 and the Kassim regime in 1963, such leaders as King Hussein, President Nasser, General Chehab, the Shah of Iran, President Habib Bourguiba of Tunisia, and the ruling house of Morocco have retained their positions and influence. Algeria, after painful travail, has become free. President Nasser has continued to run the Suez Canal in a way satisfactory to all users. An acceptable relationship seems to have blossomed between the region and its former colonial masters, particularly the British and French. The peoples of the Middle East, inscrutable as always to the West, have nevertheless remained outside the Communist orbit.

* * *

A year after the Lebanon landings, the Premier of Lebanon, Rashid Karami, formerly a leader of rebel forces, came to visit me. At the time of his visit he was only thirty-eight years old, but Mr. Karami, a confirmed Arab nationalist and admirer of Nasser had, in the term of his office, developed a reputation for moderation. He was strictly an orthodox Arab, and was far from convinced, even at the time of his visit, that the Communists constituted a worse threat to the Arabs than did Israel. He passionately supported the Algerians against the French, despite President de Gaulle's proclamation in September 1959 offering Algeria the right to choose its own future by referendum. He claimed that President Nasser was now fighting the Communists as hard as he had formerly fought the imperialists.

I enjoyed that conversation. In the course of it I happened to mention the landings in Lebanon the year before; Mr. Karami said with a laugh that it would have been better had the United States held off sending troops but had merely sent Mr. Murphy to straighten out the situation. I was highly pleased with the implicit compliment to Bob Murphy, who had long been my good friend and who was participating in our talk. But on the other hand, neither Murphy nor I could agree with the substance of the Prime Minister's statement. No one man could possibly have composed the differences that were then tearing Lebanon to pieces and which brought about that government's cry for American help. However, as our conversation ended, I could not completely smother the thought that if our visitor's statement had been true, every one in my administration could have been saved a lot of anxious hours.

Apart from the successful outcome of the intervention to save Lebanon, I believe that one additional benefit to the West, intangible and unpublicized but nevertheless important, came out of that affair. This was a definite change in Nasser's attitude toward the United States.

The Suez incident, and our long negotiations to reach a satisfactory solution to all the problems arising out of it—a period during which we almost invariably found ourselves at odds with President Nasser—had led him into the egregious error of doubting America's firmness in carrying out her pledges. He seemed to believe that the United States government was scarcely able, by reason of the nation's democratic system, to use our recognized strength to protect our vital interests. America's traditional devotion to negotiation in preference to military action for the settlement of international disputes reinforced his notion that under no conditions would the United States ever resort to force to support its friends and its principles.

Nasser was in Yugoslavia when the Lebanon landings took place and, reportedly in a state of near-panic, took off speedily for Moscow for conferences with the Soviets. Undoubtedly expecting Khrushchev to move violently and noisily in Egypt's favor, President Nasser was disappointed.

In our action and the Kremlin's cautious reaction he found much food for thought, it would appear. Presumably he concluded that he could not depend completely on Russia to help him in any Middle East struggle, and he certainly had his complacency as to America's helplessness completely shattered.

* * *

On the military side the Lebanon operation demonstrated the ability of the United States to react swiftly with conventional armed forces to meet small-scale, or "brush fire" situations. Our rapid buildup to over fourteen thousand men during a three-week period could have been even faster had there been a necessity. At the time this buildup was in progress we were also providing airlift for the British in Jordan.

Besides those forces deployed in Europe and Asia (five divisions in Europe and two in Korea), the United States kept six more in mobile reserve. These consisted of three Marine divisions and three Army divisions organized in a "Strategic Army Command" (STRAC). These divisions were available for rapid deployment anywhere in the world. True, the major problem was transport. It was far easier to deploy forces across a beach such as at Beirut than it might have been into a landlocked area such as Afghanistan. Incidentally, the complications, including costs, of major instantaneous deployment are gigantic.

In Korea the maximum number of United States divisions in combat at any one time was seven—one Marine and six Army. The Lebanon operation was not to be compared with the serious fighting of the Korean War. But such operations had convinced me that if, "small wars" were to break out in several places in the world simultaneously, then we would not fight on the enemy's terms and be limited to his choice of weapons. We would hold the Kremlin—or Peking—responsible for their actions and would act accordingly.

These facts were not secret; they were well-advertised. The Communists had come to be aware of our attitude and there was reason to think that they respected it.

CHAPTER XII

The Troubled Islands Again—Quemoy and Matsu, 1958

We are in for a long, hard struggle to protect what is left of the free world from further encroachment. But we can win it and we will win it unless we are stupid enough to listen to the counsel of supercaution from those who say we can't afford to arm ourselves for modern war or to help arm our allies.

—*George E. Allen*

Concessions to despotism lead inevitably to a "point of no return. . . ."

—*John Foster Dulles*

IN early August 1958, while the Lebanon issue was being debated in the United Nations, the Communists made their next provocative move. This time they stepped up their belligerencies against islands off the Chinese mainland, the Quemoy and Matsu groups.[1] The Red Chinese had not seriously challenged these Chinese Nationalist-held islands since the crisis four years before that had brought on our Far East Resolution of January 1955.

The first definite word that the Chinese Communists might again try to seize the offshore islands came to me through intelligence sources on the 6th of August. Their broadcasts had become increasingly shrill. They had been building up military strength locally. Over the Formosa Strait, Sabre jets of the Chinese Nationalist Air Force began encountering Soviet-built MIGs with more frequency.

This information was given to me one day after Mr. Khrushchev had

[1] Map "The Quemoy and Matsu Island Groups," appears following page 360.

announced his refusal to attend a projected summit meeting within the framework of the United Nations Security Council. The Soviet Premier had just returned from a visit to Communist China. What relationship if any there was between the news from the Far East and his conferences with Mao Tse-tung was an intriguing subject for conjecture.

Why, we wondered, were they choosing this moment to stir up trouble in the Far East? Was Khrushchev still trying to hold Mao back, as some believed, or was he urging him on? For my part, I was quite sure that, to disturb and divide the Free World, Khrushchev would never fail to suggest dark and dangerous possibilities whenever he had an excuse.

One possibility we considered was that he may have been rankled because we had ignored his threats on Lebanon, and had concluded that a reopening of the offshore island issue might divert the attention of the world from Lebanon to the Far East and show that the Communists were still on the offensive. Perhaps he thought that the Far East would be a good place once again to test Western unity and resolve—a place where, in the light of divergent viewpoints among Western allies, the Communists might exploit apprehensions regarding Soviet advances in weaponry.

In the stridency of Mao's public boasts and threats to seize Formosa by force, this new challenge resembled the earlier one of 1955. But the current situation included new dangers that seemed to make our position more difficult, and in the days following we assessed the current circumstances.

For one thing, the Soviets had used the intervening years to build up their nuclear striking force, which now included a more formidable arsenal of hydrogen weapons. I did not doubt our total superiority, but any large-scale conflict stimulated here was now less likely to remain limited to a conventional use of power. At the same time the Communists had built a complex of military airfields in the Fukien area near the coast that would enable them to launch air attacks not only against the tiny offshore islands but against the main Chinese Nationalist base on Formosa as well. Extensive artillery emplacements now almost ringed Quemoy.

Chiang Kai-shek had helped complicate the problem. Ignoring our military advice, he had for many months been adding personnel to the Quemoy and Matsu garrisons, moving them forward, nearer the mainland. By the summer of 1958, a hundred thousand men, a third of his total ground forces, were stationed on those two island groups. From a sensible military viewpoint, those little islands should have been organized and defended only as strong outposts, with the permissible minimum in personnel strength. However, Chiang had always insisted that the loss of the offshore islands would inevitably mean the loss of Formosa itself.

It seemed likely that his heavy deployment to these forward positions was designed to convince us that he was as committed to the defense of the offshore islands as he was to that of Formosa.

But with the gauntlet thrown down, we prepared to react—and the nature of our reaction would be determined by the nature of the Reds' next move.

We had to consider that the Chinese Communists might attempt to starve out the offshore islands by blockade. There was also the possibility of an amphibious assault against the offshore islands, against Formosa, or against both. There was the likelihood that they might employ air forces to strike the Nationalists' airfields on Formosa. The Joint Chiefs of Staff thought they would.

We assumed that under the circumstances of the moment, we would probably have to come to the aid of our ally, Chiang, no matter where an assault occurred. If the assault were directed toward Formosa, our assistance would be full-out. To save the offshore islands against a first phase attack limited initially to those islands alone, a lesser response would be required and would conform to the terms of the Formosa Resolution.

While the Formosa Resolution proclaimed an American determination to defend that island and the neighboring Pescadores, an attack on the offshore islands would justify our military participation only if, I, as President, should judge the attack to be a preliminary to an assault on Formosa.

It was quite possible, of course, that the current threat to Formosa had long been planned by the Chinese Communists with the support of the Soviet Union, constituting only a part of an intermittent but continuing campaign to drive the United States out of the Far East. If the capture of the offshore islands should, in fact, lead to the loss of Formosa, the future security of Japan, the Philippines, Thailand, Vietnam, and even Okinawa would be placed in jeopardy and United States vital interests would suffer severely. Such a chain of disaster would not be wrought instantaneously, perhaps, but assuming success in the initial blow, disintegration would follow, we thought, within the course of several years. This modern possibility that "for want of a nail, a shoe was lost" had led to reaffirmation of the conclusion that Quemoy and Matsu were essential to America's security. Moreover, the Communist threats and propaganda were never directed primarily to these two small island groups; rather, the announced objective was Formosa.

We concluded that if the Reds became convinced that the United States would avoid intervention they would in all likelihood launch an amphibious assault against Quemoy and possibly Matsu. On the other hand if the Communists were convinced that we would come to the aid of Quemoy, they would probably refrain from outright attack, confining their actions, at least initially, to blockade and interdiction tactics.

For our part, once we had intervened with major military force to save Quemoy, we would accept nothing less than victory; only in this way could we maintain the confidence of the Free World. We recognized, however, that to be successful we might face the necessity of using small-yield atomic weapons against hostile airfields, for from vastly dispersed locations, enemy bombers could concentrate their lethality on the target area of Formosa, the Pescadores, and the offshore islands. This immense geographical advantage, extremely difficult if not impossible to eliminate with conventional weapons, would have to be offset by our sheer power. The use of even small atomic bombs could scarcely fail to result, for a while, in a worldwide feeling of revulsion against the United States, a feeling which might be lessened if these relatively small weapons were used solely against military installations, minimizing fallout and civilian casualties. However, having recognized the possible necessity of such future use, there was no compulsion upon me to make an immediate decision. We felt also, if the issue could be decided quickly, the consequences on world opinion of decisive, successful action by the United States would certainly be less damaging than the political disasters caused by failure. This line of reasoning was spelled out in detail in a memorandum that Secretary Dulles and I studied, edited, and agreed on, to insure that there was no discrepancy in our thinking [see Appendix O].

However, I was determined that by every possible means we should avoid expanding hostilities more than absolutely necessary. I was by no means convinced that the Chinese Communists would be willing to risk war with us; I doubted that they would bomb the airfields on Formosa as part of a limited attack on Quemoy.

After considering all the possibilities and probable consequences, my directive was this: If we were forced to intervene to save the offshore islands—and even if I had concluded that the true objective of the attack was Formosa—we initially would restrict our air strikes to shipping and to the nearby Communist airfields. We would not launch an immediate attack on the interior of China as a "punishing" operation. The intensity, scope, and effectiveness of the Communist attack as it developed would, of course, influence my later decisions.

When these possibilities were first discussed, disagreement arose among my associates about putting out an immediate, strong statement of United States intentions. I knew that Foster Dulles, who was absent at the time, was much in favor of it. But in this instance I thought that the Joint Chiefs of Staff, who felt it wiser to "keep the Communists guessing" for the moment, were correct. A reason for so doing was the difficulty of defining in advance—and thus limiting—what we might do. We could not say that we would defend with the power of the United States every protruding rock that was claimed by the Nationalists as an "offshore island." On the other hand, if we specified exactly what islands we would defend, we simply invited the Reds to occupy all the others of those groups.

Also, the effect on Chiang Kai-shek of a definitive statement might be undesirable. He was a proud, sometimes stubborn, sovereign ruler, and our ally. Though he derived the bulk of his war-making capabilities from us, he had a right to expect our ready assistance under appropriate conditions. But to restrain him from his cherished ambition of aggressive action against the mainland was not always easy. One way of inducing some caution on his part was to keep some doubt in his mind as to the conditions under which the United States would support him. Normally he was cooperative; now he was reportedly restless and uneasy. Under these circumstances a statement of unqualified support could encourage him to attack. A statement expressing less would be harmful to him and helpful to the enemy.

Therefore, at the moment nothing was put out. Chiang became increasingly uneasy. To try to reassure him, indirectly, Foster and I on August 23 made use of a letter from the Chairman of the House Foreign Affairs Committee to Secretary Dulles as an excuse for Foster to issue the following, which we made certain was well-publicized:

> Dear Mr. Chairman:
>
> I have received your letter of August 22.
>
> We are, indeed, disturbed by the evidence of Chinese Communist buildup, to which you refer. It suggests that they might be tempted to try to seize forcibly the Quemoy or Matsu Islands.
>
> As you know, these islands have been continuously in the hands of the Republic of China, and over the last four years the ties between these islands and Formosa have become closer and their interdependence has increased.

Then, the letter came to the key statement:

> It would be highly hazardous for anyone to assume that if the Chinese Communists were to attempt to change this situation by attacking and seeking to conquer these islands that this act could be considered or held to a "limited operation."
>
> It would, I fear, constitute a threat to the peace of the area. Therefore, I hope and believe that it will not happen.

That same day, the Chinese Communists initiated a massive artillery bombardment of the offshore islands, firing twenty thousand rounds.

From then on the Communists continued to fire about eight thousand rounds a day, causing no extensive physical damage to the fortifications, but inflicting casualties among both the military and the civilian populations. Quemoy was strafed and the Reds sent out fighter planes in strength. In addition the Communists set up a blockade which for two weeks prevented the Nationalists from convoying supplies to the islands.

Nevertheless, Chinese Nationalist morale, for the moment, was said to be high. I now ordered certain limited supporting measures. The United States Seventh Fleet was directed to take a position where it could quickly intervene in the defense of Formosa. We reinforced the fleet's carrier strength from two to four.[2] All United States forces in the area were to be placed on a "readiness alert," prepared for immediate war operations. The number of destroyers patrolling the Formosa Strait was to be augmented, as were the United States Air Defense forces on Formosa. United States forces were directed to be ready to escort Nationalist Chinese resupply vessels to the offshore islands.

These movements were not secret; in fact, to insure that they were noticed, I instructed the Department of Defense to permit a few revealing words to reach the press. These would not escape the notice of the Communists.

Under ideal circumstances, I would have preferred that the Seventh Fleet merely patrol the Formosa Strait rather than provide escorts for convoys. However, on Admiral Burke's information that the Chinese Nationalist naval forces were not sufficiently strong and experienced to give assurance that they could resupply the islands without our help, I assented to this, with the proviso that United States vessels should halt three miles off the unloading beaches, remaining in international waters. In this way we hoped to provide protection for most of the journey from Formosa, while avoiding clashes with the Communists within their territorial waters. On Sunday, September 7, the first daylight convoy from Taiwan to Quemoy went through, escorted by American ships headed

[2] The carriers *Hancock* and *Lexington* were already on hand. One of the carriers brought in to reinforce (the *Essex*) came from the Mediterranean. (As an example of the intricacy of our diplomatic problems, we found it necessary to notify President Nasser, through our Ambassador, of the movement of this carrier, assuring him that it was not being transferred to the Persian Gulf area which he would interpret as a hostile gesture.)

by the heavy cruiser *Helena* (on which I had returned from Korea in 1952).

More than a week earlier Allen Dulles had reported that the Communist radio had begun new and violent broadcasts calling for the surrender of Quemoy, and announcing that they would "liberate" Formosa. This announcement worked to our advantage. If the Reds were to attack the offshore island as a declared preliminary to moving against Formosa, their intentions would be on record, and under the Formosa Doctrine we could instantaneously come to the tactical aid of the Nationalists. Accordingly, I asked Allen Dulles to contact the Secretary of State and arrange for the State Department to make public these Communist broadcasts [see Appendix P].

A few days after the heavy shelling began I received a frantic letter from President Chiang. Much of the information on which he based his apprehensions differed markedly from that provided by our intelligence services. His version of the effectiveness of the Communist artillery bombardments on the Quemoy garrison surpassed anything that had been reported to me. He mentioned the recent loss of three Nationalist general officers and described in anguished terms the effects of Communist Chinese air and naval attacks.[3] He feared that communication between Formosa and the offshore islands would be cut any time and, surprisingly, questioned the capability of the Seventh Fleet to control the Formosa Strait. The fact that Quemoy was hemmed in by hostile artillery batteries on the east, west, and north, meant to him that unless the Nationalists were permitted to take aggressive actions on an extensive scale, Quemoy and Matsu would fall to the enemy because of starvation.

The Generalissimo asked for a categorical statement of an intention to employ our full military power to defend Quemoy and Matsu, to provide convoys for Nationalist shipping all the way from Formosa to the beaches, and to delegate to Vice Admiral Roland N. Smoot, the Commander of the Taiwan Defense Command, authority to employ United States forces to defeat any Red attack without reference to Washington.

Sympathetic as I was with the Generalissimo's general intentions, I was puzzled by much of what he wrote. His present concern over Quemoy's vulnerability to blockade seemed totally inconsistent with his earlier insistence on loading down the offshore islands with far more troops than

[3] A week later it was reported that the Generalissimo was shown detailed analyses of the Nationalist-Communist artillery duel on Quemoy. It turned out that the damage on Quemoy had been remarkably light and troop morale was high. The Commander of the Taiwan Defense Command believed that this was the first time the Generalissimo had been given a clear picture of the situation.

were necessary for defensive purposes. Naturally, I disagreed with his lack of confidence in the capabilities of the Seventh Fleet and suggested that if the Nationalists were more active in firing counterbattery on Red artillery positions the situation would look better.

I thought our military arrangements were satisfactory. The blockade of Quemoy had not yet been broken, but we were optimistic. Furthermore, in view of the efficient communications available between Taipei and Washington, I saw no need to delegate to any subordinates my authority as Commander-in-Chief to commit United States forces to action.[4]

To allay the Generalissimo's concern, however, as well as to make our position clear before the world, I approved a statement by John Foster Dulles on September 4, 1958. It presented our arguments in support of Chiang Kai-shek's legal position on Quemoy and Matsu and repeated our determination that these territories not be seized by force. The statement repeated the portion of the Formosa Doctrine that authorized the President to employ the armed forces of the United States for the protection of Taiwan and related positions and announced that

> . . . the President has not yet made any finding under that Resolution that the employment of the Armed Forces of the United States is required or appropriate in insuring the defense of Formosa. The President would not, however, hesitate to make such a finding if he judged that the circumstances made this necessary to accomplish the purposes of the Joint Resolution. In this connection, we have recognized that the securing and protecting of Quemoy and Matsu have increasingly become related to the defense of Taiwan (Formosa). . . . Military dispositions have been made by the United States so that a Presidential determination if made, would be followed by action both timely and effective.

In order to keep the door for negotiations open, however, we included the following paragraph:

> The United States has not, however, abandoned hope that Peiping will stop short of defying the will of mankind for peace. This would not require

[4] Throughout this whole period it seems that I was continually pressured—almost hounded—by Chiang on one side and by our own military on the other requesting delegation of authority for immediate action to United States commanders on the spot in the case of attack on Formosa or the offshore islands. On September 6, a request came from the Joint Chiefs of Staff asking authority for the United States Air Force to support the Chinese National Air Force in the event of a major landing attack on the offshore islands. In potentially explosive situations and with attendant communications only vaguely understood, such delegations were at times necessary. But for this case I insisted that I would assess developments as they occurred. Therefore, I kept to myself the decision to employ U.S. forces.

it to abandon its claims, however ill-founded we may deem them to be . . . . at Geneva between 1955 and 1958, a sustained effort was made by the United States to secure, with particular reference to the Taiwan area, a declaration [from Red China] of mutual and reciprocal renunciation of force, except in self-defense, which, however, would be without prejudice to the pursuit of policies by peaceful means. The Chinese Communists rejected any such declaration. We believe, however, that such a course of conduct constitutes the only civilized and acceptable procedure. The United States intends to follow that course, so far as it is concerned, unless and until the Chinese Communists, by their acts, leave us no choice but to react in defense of the principles to which all peace-loving governments are dedicated.

Two days later, September 6, I learned that Chou En-lai, the Red Chinese Premier, had just said over the radio that the Chinese were accepting our proposal, made on July 28, to resume ambassadorial talks in Warsaw, Poland, between the Communist Chinese ambassador and our own, Jacob D. Beam. These talks, after having gone on for three long years, had been suspended on June 30.

I made public the gist of the Communist broadcast and said that if the Chinese Communists were now prepared to respond constructively to our policy announcement of September 4, we would welcome such action. We assured our Nationalist ally, however, that we would not, in these talks, be a party to any arrangement that would prejudice the rights of the Republic of China. This was the first sign of a lessening of the crisis.

Our method was hardly blessed with unanimity of opinion. Harold Macmillan, for example (replying to a letter Foster had written on September 4 at my behest), quoted Winston Churchill's statement during the 1954–55 crisis: "A war to keep the coastal islands for Chiang would not be defensible" in Britain.[5]

Even more remarkable, the Defense Department now seemed willing to shift its position. On the afternoon of September 11, only a few hours before I was to deliver a televised report to the nation, the Secretary of Defense, Neil McElroy, informed me that the Joint Chiefs of Staff now felt the Quemoy and Matsu islands should be vacated (or lightly manned as outposts only). From a military standpoint alone, the latter solution had

[5] Harold Macmillan summarized the rather negative attitudes that he anticipated from the various Commonwealth countries, including Britain. Harold suggested a demilitarization of the offshore islands (a thought that he attributed to Foster Dulles). The idea he felt might be advanced by the British government either in the UN or in a separate approach to the Soviets. He did not hold out hope that our September 4 statement would induce the Communist Chinese to confine their actions to bombardment of the islands.

long been desirable, but Mr. McElroy now felt that Chiang's refusal to do so was a reflection of his hope of promoting a fight between the United States and the Chinese Communists as a prelude to a Chinese Nationalist invasion of the mainland.

To add to the afternoon's events, Foster delivered to me a report from our ambassador on Formosa that the Chinese Nationalists, fearful of our talks in Warsaw, and apprehensive over difficulties the convoys were getting into, were experiencing a severe case of jitters.

In my televised report that evening I spoke of the bombardment, of the Chinese Communist naval craft which were trying to break up the supply of Quemoy, of the fact that over one thousand people had been killed or wounded, in large part civilians. In 1955, I recalled, the Reds had broken off their attack on the offshore islands when we moved to support Free China. We had hoped they would act peacefully but now that they were not, we were bound by our treaties, and our principles, and authorized to act by the Formosa Resolution. There would be no retreat.[6] The security of the western Pacific was essential but we were there not just to save the islands but also to demonstrate that force should not be used for aggressive purposes in the modern world. "There is not going to be any appeasement," I said, and "I believe there is not going to be any war."

I had repeatedly sought to make our position clear so that there would be no danger of Communist miscalculation—but I also interpreted the congressional Joint Resolution backing up the Formosa Doctrine as requiring me not to make absolute advance commitments, covering every contingency, but to use my judgment according to the circumstances of the time. I expressed hope that the reopened Warsaw talks could find measures to resolve the problem.

Reaction to these statements was mixed. The press reported that Republicans stood behind me. Many Democrats applauded my expressed preference for peaceful negotiations over war but argued that the defense of Quemoy was not necessary to the defense of Formosa.

[6] A letter just received from Mr. Khrushchev was mentioned in this report and two days later I answered it, saying in part:

"I agree with you that a dangerous situation exists in the Taiwan area. I do not agree with you as to the source of danger. . . .

". . . United States military forces operate in the Taiwan area in fulfillment of treaty commitments to the Republic of China. . . . They are there to help resist aggression—not to commit aggression. No upside down presentation such as contained in your letter can change this fact."

I concluded with regret that I could not find in his letter any effort to find that common language which would remove the danger or that he had not written a similar letter to the Chinese Communists urging moderation. But I suggested that he encourage them toward negotiation as a civilized method of advancing one's views.

One senator declared, "The United States is being dragged into war through the back door by a dictator, a Chinese war lord who was driven off the mainland of China."

Abroad, our allies, not unexpectedly, emphasized the part of the talk that called for negotiation, rather than the sections that proclaimed the firmness of our stand. On Formosa, the country most affected, the talk, reportedly, was well received. However, a few days later the Chinese National Assembly issued an extraordinary statement saying ". . . we wish solemnly [to] advise our American ally that [the] government of the Republic of China, as [the] duly constituted government of [the] Chinese people in accordance with [the] constitution, will not tolerate any commitments reached which are detrimental to legal interests and status of [the] Chinese Republic. . . . Furthermore, we also wish [to] sound [a] solemn warning to any countries which attempt to trade our vested interests to appease Reds. . . ."

* * *

But while speeches were made, statements issued, and resolutions passed, the crisis was really eased by the success of the Nationalist Navy, with the help of United States advisers, in defeating the Red interdiction of Quemoy. For many days, almost throughout September, we had watched with keen interest this rather tiny military action.

That first convoy movement in which United States vessels participated was on September 7 and it had consisted of escort ships and two medium landing ships (LSM) carrying three hundred tons of ordnance. The convoy arrived at Quemoy and discharged its cargo without interference or incident. This good news was short-lived. A second convoy was caught in heavy fire; one cargo ship was abandoned aflame and the other withdrew. There was no shelling of the United States escort vessels, which were standing three miles offshore, as ordered. More convoys were planned, but the failure of the second one instantly created doubt in many quarters that the Communist "blockade by land gunfire" could be defeated. Failure followed failure for days, during which the feeling grew among both the Chinese and Americans on Formosa that the resupply situation was one that could scarcely be retrieved. Stores of food, medicines, and ammunition steadily dwindled.[7]

But the Chinese Nationalist sailors began to benefit from instruction in

[7] All accounts of supply levels varied. At one point they were said to consist of roughly fifty days' supply across the board, not a desperate situation but one which could easily become so if no more convoys could get through.

techniques known to the United States Navy, and they were becoming adept at handling specialized equipment that our forces had used so expertly in World War II. A particularly helpful item was the LVT, a tracked-landing, low-propelled vehicle designed to operate both in water and on land. The Nationalist Navy started to use these "swimming" trucks on September 14. Three days later, thirty-two LVTs transferred seventy-five hundred tons of cargo from the ships anchored three or four miles off the mainland and drove them right up onto the beaches of Quemoy. The next day Nationalist landing craft transported three 8-inch howitzers, particularly effective in counterbattery fire. Even junks were used in landing supplies as were, also, transport planes.[8] Sizes of daily deliveries grew. By the end of the month it appeared that air drop alone could maintain supply levels in essentials.

On October 5 the Communist Chinese, apparently admitting the failure of their efforts to subdue Quemoy by artillery fire, turned back to psychological warfare to try to split us from our ally. Their Defense Minister announced that Communist guns would cease firing for a week on Quemoy supply convoys if United States destroyers would cease to escort. The fire stopped, and United States vessels went back to normal patrolling of the Strait, ready to resume convoying if necessary.

The Nationalists took full advantage of the respite and on a single day unloaded nearly a twenty-day supply. On October 12 the Communist Defense Minister announced another suspension of firing for a period of two additional weeks.

With the temporary cease-fire, public support for our stand on the offshore islands issue rapidly developed. It was apparent that the Chinese Reds did not choose to precipitate a major war. So I made another attempt to convince the Generalissimo of the wisdom of reducing his garrisons on the islands. He finally did reduce them somewhat.

With this breathing space I thought it would be well for Secretary Dulles to have a serious talk with the Generalissimo. So Foster, after completing a visit in Rome, took the polar route to Formosa, though fearing that the Communists might make of his presence there an excuse to resume shelling the offshore islands. This they did, on October 16, but this could have been mere coincidence.

Foster's talks with the Generalissimo, held intermittently over a period

[8] In the aerial battles the Chinese Nationalists' fighter planes, some equipped with Sidewinder air-to-air missiles, took a heavy, one-sided toll against the Communist Air Force.

of three days, were most satisfactory. The Secretary, in order to dissipate the fears and anxieties created by Communist propaganda, emphasized the need for renouncing force as an acceptable means of regaining the mainland. The Communist propaganda theme, previously mentioned—namely, that Chiang was simply trying to involve the United States in a war with Communist China in order to gain the China mainland—had convinced many peoples and nations. Chiang's renunciation of aggressive force was therefore in his interest and ours.

The Generalissimo also accepted, in principle, the need for gradually developing better military arrangements for the offshore islands. Chiang did not say that he would start removing troops immediately, but indicated that discussions between his military people and ours would probably result in some redeployment, to Taiwan, of perhaps approximately fifteen thousand to twenty thousand men.

The Chinese Communists now suddenly announced that they would fire on Nationalist convoys only on odd days of the month, and would permit the Chinese Nationalists to resupply the offshore island garrisons on even-numbered days. I wondered if we were in a Gilbert and Sullivan war. In any event the Nationalists could easily build up any level of supply desired by simply shipping in all they desired every other day.

While saying nothing to Chiang, I expressed to our own military authorities the hope that he would continue to resupply on any day of his own choosing, to test the true intentions of the Communists. The shelling was costing them much more in expensive ammunition than it was accomplishing in material damage to the Nationalists. However, as a concession to the "terms" of this weird little war, the United States would not engage in any convoying operations unless the Chinese Communists attempted to interfere with the supply program on the even-numbered days in international waters.

Thus the crisis passed. The supply situation on the offshore islands was solved. The Chinese Communists, after issuing an astronomical number of "serious warnings" to the United States, gradually seemed to lose interest in Quemoy and Matsu and, except upon unusual or ceremonial occasions, ceased firing. The Nationalists reduced the size of their forces on the offshore islands, but not to the extent I thought desirable. The Chinese Communists have, as of this writing, refrained from reopening the issue by the use of force.

CHAPTER XIII

The Departure of Sherman Adams

When sorrows come, they come not
single spies,
But in battalions.

—*Shakespeare,* Hamlet

THE year 1958 brought economic recession which, for the most part, repeated the story of the 1954 recession: a dip in the economy, frenzied Democratic calls for action, the administration's determination not to panic, and the economy's gradual emergence from difficulty.

Recovering from the recession of 1954, the American economy had climbed to new heights.[1] But while the growth in businesses' physical plant—such things as factories, laboratories, and machinery—angled acutely upward sales and output did not keep pace. The result was an excess of productive capacity.

This excess, plus such other things as high costs of equipment and wages, high interest rates, a tightening of bank credit, and what businessmen describe with a wince as a "cost-profit squeeze," brought on a decline in business investment after June of 1957, and the economy started on a downward course.

Between August 1957 and April 1958, industrial production fell off 14 per cent. During the winter unemployment increased by more than a million, reaching about 7 per cent of the labor force in April; corporate profits declined more than 25 per cent.

In January 1958, the former Chairman of the Council of Economic

[1] Between the third quarter of 1955 and the third quarter of 1957, business investment in new plant and equipment went up 27 per cent; manufacturing investment went up 37 per cent.

Advisers and one of my most highly valued consultants, Dr. Arthur F. Burns, wrote to me about a meeting of the American Economic Association, which he had recently attended: He reported on the "gloom of the academic fraternity about our economic prospects. If there was an optimist in the crowd, he kept his counsel to himself."

Of course, political opponents rushed in with all the stereotyped criticisms and with dozens of patent remedies.

Early in January of 1958, just as in 1954, the head of the United Steel Workers, David McDonald—a man whom I liked personally—once again sketched out a free-wheeling program of federal outlays to end the downturn with little apparent regard for their likely long-term economic consequences. In a later meeting with members of the executive committee of the AFL-CIO, we went over one sobering statistic after another. Their single suggestion was posed as a question: "Why don't you act now?"

In reply I reminisced a bit: "You know, the same thing happened in the war. Whenever a crisis occurred, some interested but excitable people began screaming for action. And when they did, I had only one answer, 'I guess I'm just too stubborn to act fast until all the facts are in.'"

The story broke the ice at that particular meeting. But it did not stop the calls for crash federal action to bail the country out of its troubles.

For example, early in the 1958 session, the Congress passed a stupid bill—I choose the adjective carefully—authorizing appropriations for rivers, harbors, and flood control projects. It authorized fourteen projects with an estimated cost of $168 million, in which local participation did not measure up to the possible local benefits. In another group were four projects with an estimated cost of more than $27 million, on which adequate project reports (advance surveys and plans) did not even exist. Worse, it authorized three projects, with an estimated cost of $115 million, on which Corps of Engineers reports did exist, but they were all negative because the projects made no economic sense whatever.

"I cannot overstate my opposition to this kind of waste of public funds," I said, and on April 15 I vetoed the bill. I did so despite the specious argument that it would stimulate the economy. This, I said, bordered on the ridiculous for the reason that we then had on hand a backlog of technically valuable public works projects estimated to cost nearly $5 billion. Moreover, with a few minor exceptions, I pointed out, the projects in the objectionable rivers and harbors bill could not possibly have been started for many months or, in some cases, for years.

In another attempt to appear to be taking "vigorous action" against the recession, many members of the Congress voted for Joint Resolution

162, which would freeze farm price supports for one year. This piece of legislation appealed not only to its Democratic sponsors, but equally to quite a few "conservative" Midwestern Republicans. At a White House meeting one of these men passionately declared: "It's high time the Republicans gave better evidence they're in the farmer's corner." The "evidence" he meant was clearly a heavier dose of federal largesse, demonstrating that neither party's adherents are simon pure on issues of political philosophy.

But another Republican, Senator Knowland, with more than a few farmers as voters in his home state of California, flatly disagreed. He telephoned me on March 25. "Thirty-seven Republicans," he said, "hope you will sign that farm freeze bill. Fourteen hope you will veto it. I'm one of the fourteen."

I vetoed the bill, saying that it was one which would pile up more farm products in government warehouses, restrict the growth of markets, and postpone the day when agriculture could be released from the straitjacket of controls.

Despite my determination to do all I could to prevent this bill becoming law, I suspected that its political appeal, particularly in time of recession, might prove irresistible to many members of Congress. One member of the staff came to me after a strenuous meeting on the subject and said, "Mr. President, I'll bet you a dollar that the Senate will sustain your veto."

I jumped at the chance. "I'll take that bet," I told him, "because I've never heard of any other I would so enjoy losing."

Happily, my veto was sustained.

From the outset of the recession, my associates and I took the view as we had in 1954 that we should prepare strong programs to prevent a serious lengthy decline but should never be swayed from reason by the purveyors of gloom. We watched with concern the increase in unemployment, but we refused to take action that would fail to cure unemployment and cause more acute trouble later on.

"From the best advice I can get, and on my own study of the facts regularly placed before me," I had said on February 12, "I believe that we have had most of our bad news on the unemployment front. I am convinced that we are not facing a prolonged downswing in activity. Every indication is that March will commence to see the start of a pickup in job opportunities. That should mark the beginning of the end of the downturn in our economy, provided we apply ourselves with confidence to the job ahead."

As evidence of specific government action which could effect good results quickly, I announced that I had directed the Postmaster General to submit to the Congress a $2 billion program to modernize Post Office buildings and equipment—a program which could put men to work quickly in big cities where many of the unemployed lived.

By the end of February we felt certain the economic decline was "bottoming out." We watched and waited. At my direction, the White House Special Assistant for Public Works Planning, Major General John S. Bragdon, worked on a continuous survey of public works projects which, ready to go, could be started soon and finished up within two years. The Bureau of the Budget instructed the Executive Departments and Agencies to speed up work on those projects which were already under way and on those for which appropriations had been made. But I deplored the sudden upsurge of pump-priming schemes such as the setting up of huge federal bureaucracies of the PWA or WPA type.[2]

Fortuitously, there was warm encouragement several weeks later from an unusual corner. I had an interesting talk at the White House with Ludwig Erhard, the West German Vice Chancellor and Minister of Economics, who was then visiting the United States. In 1951, the United States government had sent to West Germany a team of economic experts—including several who became prominent in the administration succeeding mine—to advise the German government on measures to stimulate Germany's advancement. They came up with a number of shopworn recommendations, including more easy money, more government spending and management, less fear of inflation. But Erhard refused to listen. He rejected that course. Above all, he was the man who set the German economy free, swept away its economic shackles, gave industrial enterprise a chance, and thereby produced one of the most extraordinary economic booms in European history.

As I talked with Dr. Erhard in my office on March 24, his words came as welcome relief to alarm bells I had been hearing. He said, "I would not really worry about the American economy. Because of Sputniks and fear of other developments in the uneasy world, your recession may have psychological causes which will disappear as public apprehensions lessen. I believe with you that the federal government should not start too early to intervene directly in economic affairs but should continue to reassure the public as to its own security as well as to the basic soundness of the economy."[3]

[2] Public Works Administration and Works Progress Administration devices of the 1930s for the creation of "make-work" jobs during the depression.

[3] My Special Assistant for Economic Affairs, Dr. Gabriel Hauge, sent me a quotation from another, as it happened, distinguished West German, Franz Etzel: "The state is not a cow, fed in heaven and milked on earth."

The weeks rolled by and several of my leading economic advisers came to the conclusion that, as in 1954, the administration should urge the Congress to cut taxes. This question prompted an exchange of letters with Dr. Burns.

His attitude had been set out in mid-February in a talk he made at Columbia University. It was widely reported in the press. He saw no compelling evidence, he said, of an upturn by the middle of the year, though he did not rule one out. But the press, misreading his words, reported that he had urged massive federal intervention at once, in opposition to the administration. Dr. Burns quickly wrote to me to correct the record.

He consistently opposed the suggestion of public works as a cure-all —a proposal, he believed, that would do little to counter the recession and would increase federal spending in later years, when the country would face the danger not of recession but of inflation.

"The fellows on Capitol Hill," he wrote, "want to criticize but don't want effective results." Nonetheless, because he still could see no convincing signs of early recovery, he had come to the belief that a tax cut was desirable. A delay in cutting taxes, he believed, would only lead to the enactment of ineffective and dangerous public works schemes now, plus a big tax cut later. Senator Knowland also urged a Republican tax cut as a device to head off radical proposals from political opponents.

In reply to Dr. Burns I wrote:

Dear Arthur:

I trust that I am not getting stubborn in my attitude about logical federal action in this business slump, but I am bound to say that I cannot help but feel that precipitate, and therefore largely unwise, action would be the worst thing that we could now do. I realize that to be conservative in this situation—and flatly to say so—can well get me tagged as an unsympathetic, reactionary fossil. But my honest conviction is that the greatest service we can now do for our country is to oppose wild-eyed schemes of every kind. I am against vast and unwise public works programs (they would need some years to get truly under way) as well as the slash-bang kinds of tax-cutting from which the proponents want nothing so much as immediate political advantage. . . .

We shall continue to push on with the things that we believe are useful. One of these, of course, is the acceleration of public works already under way. These have to be paid for in any event; acceleration of the work will cost nothing in the long run, and the additional work will be helpful now.

Administrative actions have already been taken to support home building and we have asked for legislation to push harder on this particular matter. However, some of the bills on this subject are bad.

> Tax cuts *may* have to be made, and with the general proposition made in your last two letters I completely agree. But how I pray that when and if such action is necessary, we may have some statesmen and economists in controlling [congressional] positions.

On a tax cut, there was little difference between the judgment of Dr. Burns and the consensus of the administration (he was advocating, among other measures, a tax cut of about $5 billion a year). But, as I wrote to him, I had to weigh against the advantages of an immediate tax cut now, the mounting costs of the already authorized programs of the federal government. According to our estimates, the entire budget, including programs already scheduled or almost certain to be adopted, would probably amount to about $80 billion in fiscal year 1961. Vast and continued deficits could become inflationary and, like recessions, endanger the economy also.

Nonetheless, by the end of April, other economic advisers of mine were becoming more concerned. Dr. Raymond J. Saulnier, Dr. Burns' successor—a distinguished economist and man of integrity with whom I consulted constantly on economic trends throughout my second term—pointed out at a Cabinet meeting on May 2, 1958, that while the downward trend had abated, it had not yet flattened. Most economists, he said, did not predict an upturn before the end of the year.

However, I still refused to advocate a tax cut without more evidence that it would help rather than hurt. In this judgment I had the solid support of Secretary of the Treasury Robert B. Anderson, who reminded his fellow Cabinet members that built-in stabilizers were helping the economy and warned of the dangers of premature federal action. Moreover, beyond the economic argument lay a political one. As I wrote to Dr. Burns on May 15, any bill for a tax cut would face an "overwhelming assault by amendments" proposed by pressure groups.[4]

As in 1954, the clouds of pessimism gradually began to roll back. Between the middle of April and the middle of May unemployment had dropped by thirty thousand, in the first reversal in the upward movement since November. By June or July the experts' charts were showing rises in industrial production, personal income, non-agricultural employment, and new home construction. The Gross National Product, in the second quarter of 1958, was on its way upward again.

The storm was over.

[4] Before all else we wanted Congress to act to keep at their current levels excise and corporate income tax rates which were scheduled to be dropped on July 1, 1958. Until this was done, I refused to propose any tax reductions in other categories.

* * *

The recession was only the beginning of my troubles. This stormy year also saw a sad end of my official affiliation with Governor Sherman Adams.

On June 10, 1958, staff investigators of the Subcommittee on Legislative Oversight of the House Committee on Interstate and Foreign Commerce made public a number of hotel bills (at the Sheraton-Plaza Hotel in Boston) incurred by Governor and Mrs. Adams and dated from 1955 to May of 1958. Totaling approximately $2000, they had been paid by New England industrialist Bernard Goldfine, whose relations with the Federal Trade Commission and the Securities and Exchange Commission the subcommittee was investigating. Along with the bills, the House investigators reported allegations that, because of his friendship with Adams, the two regulatory commissions had given Goldfine preferred treatment.

* * *

From our first meeting in 1952 Sherman Adams seemed to me best described as laconic, abrupt, businesslike, and puritanically honest. Never did he attempt to introduce humor into an official meeting. On the many occasions during our White House years when I called him on the telephone to ask a question, he never added a word to his "yes" or "no" if such an answer sufficed. It never occurred to him to say "Hello" when advised by his secretary that I wanted him on the phone or to add a "Good-bye" at the end of the call. For Sherman Adams this was neither bad manners nor pretense; he was busy. Absorbed in his work, he had no time to waste.

Members of the Congress and the press often misinterpreted him; many wanted to see in him something of a Rasputin. Actually he was a tireless, able, and devoted assistant. I never saw him by a single word or action try to act as a "power-behind-the-throne" or to assert an authority beyond that expected of him as my principal White House Assistant.

He spent far less time with me than had my principal subordinates in other times and places. We never built up between us the easy informality I had enjoyed with such men as Bedell Smith and Alfred Gruenther, who served with me in the Army in somewhat similar positions. Nevertheless, I liked, trusted, and highly respected Sherman Adams and admired his powers of concentration and his judgment.

In social gatherings he was a pleasant, often an entertaining member of the party. He loved to sing and his voice was good. Beyond this he had a knowledgeable and talented wife—Rachel was one of the most charming persons in Washington, a lady whose company I always enjoyed.

As would be suspected, Adams' mannerisms were not to endear him to the average politician. Many congressmen like to have their importance recognized by the people with whom they come in contact; Adams had little skill for solidifying his relations with politicians except with those who could see beneath his craggy exterior to the true worth of the man.

Early in 1958, the governor had made a speech in Minneapolis flaying the Democratic party. The text was so tough that even some members of the White House staff who normally delighted in vigorous partisan polemics had urged him to tone it down. But the governor merely asked: "Are the charges in this speech supportable?" Upon being assured that they were, he said, "Well, then, I'm going to make them. I will not give a namby-pamby speech." His decision had delighted some Republicans but left resentment among Democrats.

From the beginning of my first administration, Adams had insisted that the conduct of White House personnel should be impeccable whether dealing with people in government or out of it. He refused to take any perquisite that did not pertain to his office. Although he held Cabinet rank he always declined to use any kind of governmental transportation for other than strictly official purposes. To and from the office, he drove his own car. Never once in the years of our association did he ask me for himself, for any member of his family, or for a friend, any special consideration or favor. He was frugal in his habits and simple in his tastes.

As a consequence, when the stories appeared alleging that he had used his position improperly in behalf of his friend Goldfine in return for prior favors, I was not only astounded but unbelieving, to say the least. I could understand his having cordial friendships, but I was confident he would never have allowed friendship to influence his official acts. I was supremely confident that Adams' explanation would quickly settle the matter.

In a letter of June 12 to the subcommittee and in a personal appearance[5] before it a few days later—and in 1961 in a book—Governor Adams answered the charges against him with characteristic directness.

His association with Goldfine dated back to the early 1940s when Adams was Speaker of the House of Representatives of New Hampshire. At a time when other textile manufacturers were closing their New England mills and moving out, Goldfine had had the courage to stay on. Adams—

[5] Presidential staff members are not required to appear before congressional committees, but Adams did so voluntarily, to clear up the matter.

like other public officials—admired this courage and deeply appreciated the stimulus it provided to the economy of the state of New Hampshire. Thus begun, the friendship between the Adams and Goldfine families had flourished. They had often exchanged gifts: the governor had given Goldfine a gold watch, for example, and Rachel Adams had given the Goldfines a painting. As old friends, the Adamses accepted hotel accommodations, which the governor mistakenly thought Goldfine maintained "on a continuing basis" for the use of his visiting friends and business associates; to this hospitality no strings were attached. The governor had accepted a vicuña coat which he said had cost the Goldfine mills $69. He further testified that the Adamses had accepted, for the living room of their Washington home, the loan of an oriental rug; on their departure from Washington Goldfine was to get it back. Adams' testimony (and Goldfine's later) made clear the governor was only one of a number of prominent men in public life, Republican and Democratic, who were similarly favored.

In return for these gifts, Governor Adams stated that he had neither promised nor performed any act to influence any regulatory agency. In late 1953 Goldfine had asked Governor Adams for additional information on a complaint of the Federal Trade Commission that one of Goldfine's companies was violating a wool-labeling regulation. Governor Adams handled the request as routine and asked the chairman of the commission, Edward F. Howrey, for a memorandum setting forth the facts, which he sent on to Goldfine. The company subsequently agreed to comply with the regulations. In 1955 Goldfine asked the governor to arrange an appointment between him and Chairman Howrey to discuss a problem, which he did not further describe, under the commission's wool-labeling regulations. Adams made the appointment. If his "influence" was felt, the results were oddly expressed: The end of this sequence of events was a cease and desist order issued by the commission against Goldfine's company.

The next year Goldfine complained to Governor Adams that the SEC was probing into his affairs because his East Boston Company, a realty firm, had failed to file reports with the commission on its financing practices. Governor Adams asked Jerry Morgan, then my Special Counsel, to look into the question. Without using Governor Adams' name, Morgan did so, getting from the SEC the same facts on the dispute as Goldfine had given the governor. Because the inquiry turned up no new information, Adams made no report to Goldfine.

Adams was particularly sensitive to this type of inquiry coming into the White House. In 1955 he had laid down a strict order to the members of the White House staff that any White House call made to any regulatory agency should come from only one of three responsible officials: the governor himself, his deputy, Fred A. Seaton, or Jerry Morgan. To the Legislative Oversight Subcommittee, the governor asserted that the FTC and SEC had given Goldfine exactly the same response as they would have if he and Adams had been total strangers.

Despite this disclaimer, the clamor would not die down. The gifts themselves could not have caused concern. Neither could the phone calls, of themselves. But the gifts plus the phone calls—despite the absence of a connection between them—and the eagerness of his enemies to attack, were in the end to destroy his usefulness in public life.

Adams himself recognized that "implications can be drawn" from any telephone call, however innocent, to a regulatory agency when the man on the other end of the line is the Assistant to the President.

"If I had those decisions before me now," Adams concluded, "I believe I would have acted a little more prudently."

Despite Governor Adams' forthright and courageous defense, I could see that he was deeply hurt and depressed over the accusations. The day after he made his appearance on Capitol Hill, I had a news conference scheduled. I was determined to begin that conference with a strong affirmation of my own confidence in the governor's integrity and honesty. I dictated a statement and redrafted it several times before going to the conference. It began by suggesting that every gift is not a bribe, and went on:

> The circumstances surrounding the innocent receipt by a public official of any gift are therefore important, so that the public may clearly distinguish between innocent and guilty action.
>
> Among these circumstances are the character and reputation of the individual, the record of his subsequent actions, and evidence of intent or lack of intent to exert undue influence.
>
> Anyone who knows Sherman Adams has never had any doubt of his personal integrity and honesty. No one has believed that he could be bought; but there is a feeling or belief that he was not sufficiently alert in making certain that the gifts, of which he was a recipient, could be so misinterpreted as to be considered as attempts to influence his political actions. To that extent he has been, as he stated yesterday, "imprudent."
>
> . . . My own conclusions of this entire episode are as follows:
>
> I believe that the presentation made by Governor Adams to the congressional committee yesterday truthfully represents the pertinent facts.
>
> I personally like Governor Adams. I admire his abilities. I respect him because of his personal and official integrity. I need him.
>
> Admitting the lack of that careful prudence in this incident that Governor Adams yesterday referred to, I believe with my whole heart that he is

an invaluable public servant doing a difficult job efficiently, honestly, and tirelessly.

Now ladies and gentlemen, so far as I am concerned, this is all that I can, all that I shall, say.

But it was not the end. Two weeks later the subcommittee staff revealed that on his federal tax returns Goldfine had charged off as business expenses the cost of the rug and the hotel bills; ten days later the subcommittee came out with more figures on more hotel bills, which brought the total for Adams and his family to more than $3000. As the subcommittee brought out additional evidence and Goldfine himself testified, things did not improve. Goldfine had paid hotel bills, it turned out, not only for Governor Adams, but also for several senators; he had given presents to twenty-three governors. He testified that he had contributed about $100,000 to both political parties, that he had sent Christmas gift baskets, costing as much as $800, to as many as three hundred persons a year; one of the recipients was a predecessor of Governor Adams in the White House.

On August 13, the House, by a vote of 369 to 8, cited Goldfine for contempt of Congress for refusing to answer twenty-two questions which he claimed were not pertinent to the investigation. Meanwhile, with the headlines on Goldfine going from bad to worse, Republicans as well as Democrats, in that election year, wanted Adams' scalp. Republican supporters in the Congress—who included Senators Everett Dirksen, Ralph Flanders, George Aiken, and Jacob Javits—were outnumbered by his Republican critics, who included Congressman Richard Simpson, Chairman of the Republican Congressional Campaign Committee, and Senators Arthur Watkins, William Knowland, Roman Hruska, Frank Barrett, and Charles Potter. His supporters thereafter had my undying gratitude.

During the summer months the Adams affair continued to occupy much space in the press. However, my confidence in his integrity was unshaken. Of course he had made a mistake; against this, however, was my conviction that his own story was not only accurate but persuasive on the two points that I regarded as central to the entire controversy. These were that the governor had, in fact, accepted the items from Goldfine as nothing more than personal or family presents given from one friend to another; the second was that the governor had not undertaken to obtain for his friend any official assistance that would not have been accorded, as a matter of routine, to any other citizen. Completely convinced, therefore, of his innocence as far as intent of wrongdoing was concerned, I refused to ask for his resignation.

The governor and I had several serious talks. Then, thinking that my association with him might make it difficult for me to be completely objective, I asked the Vice President to keep in touch with developments, advising me from time to time of their nature. In mid-July Mr. Nixon had a long discussion with the governor and reported to me the gist of the conversation. The Vice President's principal points were that the vast majority of Republicans in both Houses of Congress thought Adams should resign and that if the governor declined to do so the matter would become a major political issue in the November election.

In the meantime, in addition to the evidence in the press I had been getting reports from individuals who knew of Mr. Goldfine and his business dealings in New England, that his reputation was not of the kind that should have encouraged Governor Adams to seek his friendship. (My own first impression had been—as I am certain Governor Adams' initial impression had been—that Mr. Goldfine was a high-minded and enterprising businessman. Now I was told that this first impression was far from accurate. This was serious because of the implication that the governor had been less than alert or wise in forming his friendships.)

On September 4, I telephoned Meade Alcorn, Chairman of the Republican National Committee. His reports confirmed those I had been receiving: that the Goldfine case was a cause of "hopelessness" in the Republican Party all over the country.

I had to conclude that, in spite of my deep conviction of Adams' honesty, his retention of his office would be a mistake both for him and the office.

A few days later the results of the Maine election became known. The Republican candidate's overwhelming defeat was ascribed, by many, to the governor's relations with Goldfine. At the time of that election, I was at the summer White House in Newport; Sherman Adams was on a brief fishing expedition in New Brunswick with General Persons and their wives. Jerry Morgan telephoned the governor, asking him to return to Washington where, by appointment, he immediately met with the Vice President and Meade Alcorn. The latter told the governor what he had already told me: that unless Adams resigned, the party would be badly handicapped in the forthcoming election.

By this time I was convinced that there was nothing more that could be done to restore the governor's former usefulness in the White House, and decided it would be best for him to resign, feeling sure that he would voluntarily conclude to do so.

The next morning, September 17, Governor Adams telephoned me from Washington telling me his decision to resign; he wanted some time, he said, to consider his resignation statement. This was satisfactory to me.

Within a few days the governor came to see me at Newport with a draft of his resignation statement. That evening, from Broadcast House in Washington, he read it to the country on nationwide radio and television: "A campaign of vilification," he said, "by those who seek personal advantage by my removal from public life has continued up to this very moment. . . . An easy and obvious way to bring such an attack to an end is to remove the target. . . . Against my distaste for giving any grounds whatever to the charge of retreating under fire . . . I must give full consideration to the effect of my continuing presence on the public scene. . . .

"Within the past few days," he concluded, "I have reached a decision . . ."

In my letter accepting his resignation I said, "I deeply deplore the circumstances that have decided you to resign. . . .

"Your performance has been brilliant; the public has been the beneficiary of your unselfish work . . .

"I accept your resignation with sadness. . . ."

Before he left the White House I gave Governor Adams as a personal gift a silver bowl inscribed:

To Sherman Adams
The Assistant to the President
1953–1958
For Tireless Service to the Public
Brilliant Performance of Every Duty
and
Unsurpassed Dedication to his Country
From his devoted friend
Dwight D. Eisenhower

Those words still summarize my judgment and feeling today. In his going I lost a man as dedicated to duty and as selfless in his motives and actions as any other person I have known. The White House was, for some time, a sad place, for there was scarcely an individual on the staff who was not Adams' partisan.

My own deep regret about the entire episode caused me to reflect on, among other aspects, the hazards always besetting the path of any man accepting an appointive office in the federal government. The careless acceptance of casual gifts can bring trouble; good intentions, long-standing personal integrity and competence are no defense when a storm of criticism and vilification whips up around his head. Certainly we must never be complacent about slack or careless conduct in official life. What does seem somewhat unfair is that members of Congress are practically immune from the microscopic examinations and investigations that are so often the portion of appointed public figures.

Adams' trust in his friend was strong but obviously misplaced. Therefore his failure to check up on the nature of the favors and gifts he received is at least understandable. But no one who really knew him ever questioned the nature of the man who received them or questioned his integrity for a moment. The fate of Governor Adams was determined by several unrelated sets of facts which, when brought together in an atmosphere of hostile suspicion, made any other outcome impossible. Even today, if I were called upon to suggest the names of men for a position of trust—men in whose character I had confidence—I would never hesitate to list Sherman Adams among them.

* * *

The departure of Governor Adams created the need for some reorganization in my personal staff, and I quickly began conferring with some of my associates about a replacement. Among the names suggested were those of military men, known for their capacity for handling staff duties expeditiously.

General Alfred Gruenther, then President of the American National Red Cross, General Lauris Norstad, the Supreme Allied Commander of SHAPE, and Vice Admiral George W. Anderson, Jr., of the Navy were of this group; so was Brigadier General Andrew Goodpaster. In my opinion each was fully capable, by reason of his knowledge, personality, and character, of handling the responsibilities of the position. Other names brought forward were those of Secretary Seaton of the Interior Department and Ambassador Lodge, still serving in the United Nations. Scarcely any of these men could have been spared from his present post, however.

I became convinced that the man who could most easily be fitted into the position was Governor Adams' outstanding deputy, Major General Wilton B. Persons, long since retired from the Army.

While Jerry Persons' military record was a distinguished one, he had been taken off field duty as early as 1930 and assigned to official duties of a civilian character that had given him extensive background information about the members of Congress and the legislative process. His final five years in this kind of work had been performed in the White House. I had come to respect his abilities, particularly as a coordinator among individuals holding vigorous and differing views. I decided to promote him to the vacant post, and so he became the general supervisor of the entire staff. Though his over-all responsibilities were thus heavier than before, I was able to free him of one particular function. Because of my own intimate participation in the conduct of international affairs, I thought it would needlessly burden the chief of the White House staff to be involved deeply in national security affairs. So I arranged for all Defense and State Department problems coming to the White House to be brought to me directly either by Gordon Gray, the Special Assistant for National Security Affairs, by the White House Staff Secretary, General Goodpaster[6] or by my son, John, who served as Goodpaster's assistant. Of course Persons could voluntarily attend conferences on these subjects.

Having decided to fill the top post by promotion within the staff, with one or two exceptions I followed the same policy throughout. I promoted Gerald Morgan from the post of Special Counsel to that of Deputy to General Persons. Through six years of service in the White House he had established himself as one of my truly valuable staff officers and one capable, in the absence of his superior, of handling all the responsibilities of the Assistant to the President.

Bryce Harlow was given a new title, "Deputy Assistant to the President for Congressional Affairs," replacing Jerry Persons in that position.

Under Harlow were some very capable and hard-working men. One was Jack Z. Anderson, a former congressman who was very successful in furthering among congressional members a clear understanding of legislation we recommended. Other members were Edward A. McCabe, Earle D. Chesney, and Homer H. Gruenther, all of whom had been with me from

[6] Gordon Gray had succeeded General Cutler in 1958 when the latter, for personal reasons, had to resign. Mr. Gray had previously served as Secretary of the Army during President Truman's administration and, for some months, had been the Director of the Office of Defense Mobilization in mine. I was delighted to have him close to me: he served with real distinction.

General Goodpaster continued to carry the title of Secretary of the White House staff, but so far as I was concerned, his most important duty was to handle all correspondence reaching the White House that dealt with national security affairs. As such, his duties overlapped those of Gordon Gray, with Gray's responsibilities covering the long-range planning of the NSC, and Goodpaster's involving day-to-day operations. Immediately under him were several assistants. The first of these, as I have mentioned, was my son, John, who came from the Pentagon to become Goodpaster's assistant specifically assigned to the international field—particularly subjects that came to us directly from the State and Defense Departments, the AEC, and the Central Intelligence Agency. Arthur Minnich was the assistant responsible for general correspondence and activities pertaining to domestic issues. E. Frederic Morrow, a capable man, and a negro, who had campaigned for the ticket in 1952, served as Administrative Officer for special projects, giving attention also to the field of civil rights.

my first term. Early in 1959 this group was joined by Clyde A. Wheeler, Jr., who later left us to run for a congressional seat from Oklahoma.

Robert E. Merriam, formerly Deputy Director of the Bureau of the Budget, had joined the White House staff early in the fall of 1958. After Adams' resignation he became responsible for interdepartmental affairs; like Morgan and Harlow he had the title of Deputy Assistant to the President.

David W. Kendall, an experienced lawyer, succeeded Jerry Morgan as Special Counsel, assisted by H. Roemer McPhee and Phillip E. Areeda.

Two months before Governor Adams' resignation, Gabriel Hauge, my Special Assistant for Economic Affairs, had accepted a position with Manufacturers Trust Company in New York City. He was an outstanding man and I tried to dissuade him from leaving the government. Indeed, I told him that I had already decided to offer him a post in the Cabinet to fill a prospective vacancy, but this did nothing to change his mind. I felt his loss keenly but I secured a former Assistant Secretary of Agriculture, Don Paarlberg, as his successor. It proved to be a fortunate choice.[7]

[7] Several other staff members retained positions they had held under Governor Adams:

Thomas E. Stephens, who had returned to the post of Appointments Secretary several months after the resignation of Bernard Shanley in late 1957; Lieutenant General Elwood R. Quesada, a comrade of World War II days, but now retired, who had joined me in mid-1957 as a Special Assistant for Aviation Planning, and who some months later was confirmed as the Administrator of the Federal Aviation Agency; Rocco C. Siciliano, a former Assistant Secretary of Labor, who in 1957 came to the White House as Special Assistant for Personnel Management; Robert Gray, who in the spring of 1958 became Cabinet Secretary, succeeding Maxwell Rabb, who resigned to go into private law practice; and Karl G. Harr, Jr., who with previous experience in the State Department and as a Deputy Assistant Secretary of of Defense, had become the Vice Chairman of the Operations Coordinating Board, serving that body much as Gordon Gray did the National Security Council; Dr. Malcolm Moos, who in September of 1958 came into my office to assist me in the drafting of speeches and statements, replacing Arthur Larson, who went to Duke University.

Early in 1957 the Assistant Press Secretary, Murray Snyder, had gone to the Pentagon as an Assistant Secretary of Defense. To fill his position, with the title of Associate Press Secretary, I appointed Mrs. Anne W. Wheaton; she had formerly served with the Republican National Committee, and her presence had the effect of improving our communication with that office. She became the first woman to hold a position of this importance in my White House staff.

W. Allen Wallis, an economist from the University of Chicago and, at the time of this writing, President of the University of Rochester, joined the White House staff in 1959 with an unusual type of assignment. I had organized a board at Cabinet level to advise me on problems of inflation; he served as Executive Vice Chairman of this Cabinet Committee on Price Stability for Economic Growth. The Vice President was the official chairman of this committee, and it included such

* * *

Though the year 1958 was characterized by controversy it was, happily, not exclusively so. There were significant achievements, some in quiet corners of government.

For one thing, it was an outstanding year in the annals of natural resources conservation in the United States—and it was a year in which, after previous attempts had failed, we approved the admission of a new state to the Union, setting the stage for admission of a second new state the following year.

Fifty years earlier, in 1908, President Theodore Roosevelt had convened a historic Governors Conference at the White House to "consider the question of the conservation and use of the great fundamental sources of wealth of this nation."

Those of us who venerated Theodore Roosevelt's example were determined that, with our rapidly increasing population and proliferating industrialization, our extraordinary natural resources and national beauty would not be "civilized off the face of the earth."

The year 1958 saw, for example, the passage of legislation to provide more funds for acquiring wildlife refuges and to make the improvement of fish and wildlife resources a specific purpose in federal water resource construction; legislation long urged by conservationists was enacted to make applicable on military lands the fishing, hunting, and trapping laws of the states and territories in which such lands are located. New restrictions were applied to oil and gas leasing on federal wildlife refuges and game ranges, and a commission was established to survey the future needs of our expanding population for recreational areas.[8]

---

persons as Secretary Robert B. Anderson and Raymond Saulnier, Chairman of the Council of Economic Advisers. On specialized economic questions I continued, as in my first term, to have the valuable counsel of two distinguished corporation executives, Clarence Randall and Clarence Francis.

[8] This sequence of laws and administrative actions were part of a pattern of fish and wildlife conservation which were not confined to 1958. On August 8, 1956, for example, I had signed the Fish and Wildlife Act of 1956, a bill which for the first time established the office of an Assistant Secretary of the Interior for Fish and Wildlife. And between January of 1953 and January of 1961, the administration added to our system of wildlife areas—which had previously included only about seventeen million acres—thirty-four new ones of more than 11 million acres. The unprecedented total figure of nearly twenty-nine million acres includes the Arctic Wildlife Range in Alaska—a nine-million-acre area in northeast Alaska above the Arctic Circle, nearly twice the size of Massachusetts, which, abounding in animals and migratory birds, will long stand as the largest single addition to federal wildlife lands in our history.

The conservation achievements of 1958 included another signal piece of legislation, one to assure the abundance of one of the most important natural resources on this planet. On September 2, 1958, I signed a bill authorizing the expenditure of $10 million for five plants for the conversion of salt water into fresh [see Appendix Q].

When I took office in 1953, the saline water conversion program in the Department of Interior had been under way for a bare six months. From the evidence of laboratory and pilot plant work through the succeeding years, scientists by 1958 estimated the cost of converting sea water at about $1.75 per thousand gallons. Through the new demonstration plants, we hoped to reduce that cost to $1 and then to fifty cents. This last figure would fall within about ten cents of what many Americans pay for fresh water today. Our expectation was that in city after city the curves of costs—of converted water and of water from rivers and wells—would come together.[9] When they do, Americans will have a new source of supply, economically justified. I am confident we can look forward to the day, however distant, when, because of the success of this undertaking, new industries will rise on the Gulf Coast, and arid portions of our Southwest will bloom and become a home for many thousands of American families. And beyond our borders one can foresee the habitation of now vast, vacant spaces in Mexico, Brazil, Africa, Saudi Arabia, West Pakistan, Israel, and Australia—an island continent as large as the United States with no more fresh water than that flowing through our Columbia River Basin.

One other achievement, spurred by the Department of the Interior, merits mention here: the advancement of the American Indian, particularly their progress in education.

In 1953, when I entered office, only about half of all the school-age children on the Navajo reservation were attending school. By 1958 the number in school had increased from fourteen thousand to twenty-seven thousand—nearly 90 per cent of the school-age population. On all our Indian reservations together, in 1953, only 79 per cent of the children were in school; by 1961 that figure had risen to 91 per cent. In this

[9] To be sure, people were already using converted water, produced at high prices. Kuwait, for example, used five million gallons of converted water a day, out of the Persian Gulf; every thousand gallons cost nearly $3. At Morro Bay in California, the Pacific Gas and Electric Company was converting about 144 thousand gallons a day for use in generating electricity; every thousand gallons cost about $2.60. The city of Coalinga, California, had become the first community in the history of the United States to produce its water supply by converting brackish well water—less salty than sea water—at a cost of $1.45 per thousand gallons. In these places and elsewhere people were using converted water because they had no less expensive alternative.

advance the government was helping, and so were the Indians themselves. Between 1950 and 1958 the number of Navajo students attending college increased from 37 to 294. To assist such students, the Navajo tribe was putting into scholarships the entire income from $5 million in tribal funds. In 1947 the Navajo tribe had been one of our poorest; after 1956 and the discovery of oil on their reservation they became probably the wealthiest, their resources scrupulously protected by honest administration in Washington.

* * *

That year, 1958, was the first year since 1912 when the United States admitted a former territory into the Union. Statehood for Alaska and Hawaii, like the St. Lawrence Seaway, had for years been among those perennial causes which few people believed could become a reality [see Appendix R].

Objections to Alaskan and Hawaiian statehood came from both parties. Southerners opposed the addition of new congressional members who might support the cause of racial integration. Republicans feared Alaska might go Democratic; Democrats feared Hawaii might vote Republican. Others argued that no territory should become a state that, geographically, was noncontiguous with the mainland of the United States. Hawaii had to contend with two additional arguments: (1) that Communists dominated its twenty-five-thousand-member branch of the International Longshoremen's and Warehousemen's Union headed by Harry Bridges—a union which, opponents of statehood claimed, could tie up the islands' economy; and (2) that only a third of the Hawaiian population was Caucasian.

The Democratic platforms of 1948 and 1952 had pledged immediate statehood for both territories. The Republican platform in 1952 had urged immediate statehood for Hawaii and statehood for Alaska "under an equitable enabling act." Though I shared some of the uneasiness of many others about the prospect of taking non-contiguous territories into the Union as states, I accepted my party's platform pledges as binding on me, and took action accordingly. A long and difficult struggle ensued, but once we had set statehood for the two territories as an administration goal, we were determined to keep up the fight until victory was attained.

In my opinion, Hawaii had the stronger case of the two, having a greater population and industrial and tax base than its sister territory. In my first State of the Union message in 1953, I had declared that statehood for Hawaii "should be granted promptly with the first election scheduled for 1954." I repeated this request each succeeding year of my first term.

The Congress, however, did nothing on either territory.[10]

Because of its location across the Bering Strait from the Soviet Union, Alaska had a particular strategic significance: within the northern and western parts of Alaska, it was essential that our military forces continue to have maximum freedom of movement.

With this national need in mind, I recommended to the Congress in January of 1957 for the first time—along with statehood for Hawaii—"that, subject to area limitations and other safeguards for the conduct of defense activities so vitally necessary to our national security, statehood also be conferred upon Alaska." To satisfy the security requirement, the administration worked out a new legislative formula: that the entire territory of Alaska should become the state of Alaska, and that in conferring statehood the Congress should grant the President special powers to set aside large sections in the north and west of the new state for the purposes of national defense—sections totaling 276,000 square miles inhabited by twenty-four thousand people, including five thousand in the military service.

The final drive began, energetically led for the administration by the new Secretary of the Interior, Fred Seaton, long an ardent advocate of statehood for both Alaska and Hawaii.

Proponents of Alaskan statehood pointed to its giant size—more than 586,000 square miles, an area more than twice the size of Texas—and to its resources—its 136 million acres of forests, its hydroelectric potential nearly twice the existing capacity of the power-rich state of Washington, and its hundred billion tons of coal.

Beyond this, an intensified search for oil by American companies, operating under enabling legislation and governmental leases, began in the mid-1950s. Small-scale explorations had been going on for a number of years; the Navy had conducted some searches in the far northern Point Barrow region.

By July of 1957 a considerable success had been achieved; oil was discovered on the Kenai Peninsula. By April of 1958 the Interior Department, with my approval, had under lease or subject to application here

[10] The House passed an Hawaiian Statehood Bill in March of 1953. But the following year the Senate amended that bill to include Alaska, and then passed the combined bill. This maneuver, which invited the House opponents of Alaskan statehood to team up with the House opponents of Hawaiian statehood, killed statehood for either territory that year. The next year the House committee came up with another joint bill; the House sent it back to the committee and thus defeated it.

and elsewhere in Alaska nearly forty million acres of land, a figure equivalent to more than half the total acreage under lease in the entire continental United States, including the continental shelf. By May of 1958, private oil companies had spent more than $30 million on exploration in the territory. Alaskans began to argue that Alaska's emergence from territory to state would spur the development of these enormous natural resources.[11]

(Incidentally, as a result of the cruises later in 1958, of the atomic submarines *Nautilus* and *Skate* under the Arctic ice cap, an arresting long-term possibility came up—the commercial transportation of Alaskan oil by undersea nuclear-powered submarines to European ports, which lie closer to Alaska by such a route than they do to the Middle East.)

The supporters of statehood, this time avoiding the trap of a combined Alaskan-Hawaiian bill, began to win over the unconverted, asserting that with Alaska admitted statehood for Hawaii would become inevitable. In the summer of 1957 both Senate and House committees put up Alaska statehood bills. In May of the following year, a bill passed the House. A month later statehood for Alaska passed the Senate, and on July 7 I signed the bill into law.

As predicted, the case for Hawaii now became irresistible. To counter the argument that Communist subversion would threaten the young state, advocates of Hawaiian statehood cited the war records of Hawaiians in the Korean War where the enemy was not only Asiatic but Communist. With a population of approximately 635,000, Hawaii had a far better claim to statehood, based solely on numbers, than Alaska. Beyond this, Hawaii was a self-sustaining area with flourishing industries, producing each year nearly $150 million worth of sugar and $115 million worth of pineapple, and earning $80 million a year through tourism. In 1958 the Hawaiian economy was producing federal revenues amounting to more than $166 million—a figure higher than that in ten of our states.

On March 11, 1959, the Senate passed the Hawaiian Statehood Bill, and the House passed it the next day.

[11] Opponents of statehood cited the fact that the territory had a population of no more than 220,000, including 50,000 military personnel. Advocates of statehood countered this with several arguments. First, they said, the territory's civilian population, between 1950 and 1956, had increased nearly 50 per cent. Second, in the past hundred years, eleven states had come into the Union with populations smaller than Alaska's; only six had more. Alaska in 1958 had approximately one-tenth of 1 per cent of the nation's total population—a figure equivalent to the percentage Idaho and Wyoming had when they were admitted and a percentage far larger than had been the case for Nevada.

On March 18 I signed it.[12] By an ironic coincidence, that week the Dalai Lama began his long and tragic flight from Tibet to India. Thus, while the people of Tibet were losing even the small measure of self-government which the Chinese Communists had previously allowed them, American citizens of Asian extraction in Hawaii were gaining new political rights through a peaceful process.

[12] Fears of both Democrats and Republicans over fixed voting tendencies in Alaska and Hawaii proved to be exaggerated. In 1958 Alaska went Democratic, in 1960 Republican. In 1959 Hawaiians elected a Republican governor and one Republican senator; in 1960 the state went for Senator Kennedy.

BOOK FOUR

We cannot build peace through desire alone. Moreover, we have learned the bitter lesson that international agreements, historically considered by us as sacred, are regarded in Communist doctrine and in practice to be mere scraps of paper. The most recent proof of their disdain of international obligations, solemnly undertaken, is their announced intention to abandon their responsibilities respecting Berlin.

As a consequence, we can have no confidence in any treaty to which Communists are a party except where such a treaty provides within itself for self-enforcing mechanisms. Indeed, the demonstrated disregard of the Communists of their own pledges is one of the greatest obstacles to success in substituting the Rule of Law for rule by force.

Yet step by step we must strengthen the institutions of peace—a peace that rests upon justice—a peace that depends upon a deep knowledge and clear understanding by all peoples of the cause and consequences of possible failure in this great purpose.

—State of the Union message,
January 9, 1959

CHAPTER XIV

Berlin

When Berlin falls, western Germany must be next. If we mean . . . to hold Europe against Communism, we must not budge.

—*General Lucius Clay*

ON Monday, November 10, 1958, Soviet Premier Khrushchev declared his intention of signing at an early date a "peace treaty" with East Germany, thus—he contended—terminating Allied rights in West Berlin. With this pronouncement he transformed the city of Berlin, which had remained relatively quiet for more than nine years, into a tinderbox.

At the end of World War II, Germany's capital was divided into four sectors; the larger and more populous area comprised the sectors occupied by British, French, and American forces, the smaller area by Soviet troops. Since Berlin lay within the Soviet Zone in East Germany, the Western sector of that city was dependent for access on narrow corridors some 110 miles long through East German territory, completely controlled by the Soviets.[1]

This access was maintained by political agreements, the most specific of which were the Potsdam protocol signed in 1945 between the United States, Britain, France, and the Soviet Union, and the agreement reached by the four powers at Paris in 1949. The Western nations were committed to the eventual reunification of the entire German nation and did not recognize the "German Democratic Republic," a puppet government set up by the Soviets; the Soviet Sector in East Berlin was made the "capital" of this regime.

[1] Map, "The Berlin Corridors," appears following page 360.

Under these awkward conditions it was always easy for the Soviets to create varying annoyances involving Berlin and Allied right therein. In this latest instance Mr. Khrushchev bluntly declared that the four-power occupation of Berlin was out of date and must be ended. He asserted that East Germany should have its capital free of the "state within the state" (his term for West Berlin), and that the situation in that region should be "normalized."

Khrushchev did not at first threaten drastic action, such as the blockade of 1948. Instead he called on the Western nations to begin negotiations with the East German government toward a complete withdrawal of Allied forces from the city. The Soviet Union said it intended to transfer all its administrative functions in the city to the East Germans; but politically we would not, under any circumstances, do business with the East German mock government.[2]

I of course at once recognized the dangerous potential of the Russian declaration, though it was no surprise that the Communists should continue to make trouble wherever they saw a promising possibility. But there was little room in the Berlin situation for negotiation or compromise. Militarily, our forces in the city were token garrisons only. Berlin's actual defense lay only in the West's publicly expressed intention that to defend it we would, if necessary, resort to war.

The physical and psychological condition of West Berlin had changed dramatically in the decade since the blockade, when the Allied airlift saved the city from starvation. No longer were West Berliners barely scraping along on subsistence amounts of food and fuel; they now had a fully-geared industrial economy. Its new prosperity required supplies and raw materials multiplied many times over those needed a decade before.

This thriving industrial metropolis was showing to the world, and to the East Germans in particular, the contrast between the Communist and free ways of life. West Berlin had long provided a haven for thousands upon thousands of unhappy, escaping East Germans of whom, to make matters even worse from Khrushchev's viewpoint, a considerable proportion were professionals and intellectuals. Small wonder he was to call the city a bone in his throat. An Allied retreat would remove it.

Moreover, any concession that Khrushchev could wring from a crisis-weary West could be pictured in Communist propaganda as a magnificent victory. Tacit recognition of the Grotewohl regime in East Germany could

[2] Later on Khrushchev apparently changed his mind. His puppet Prime Minister, Otto Grotewohl, said that Soviet withdrawal would be contingent on simultaneous Western withdrawal.

be politically disastrous to Chancellor Konrad Adenauer, the man who, more than any other, had been responsible for the rapid rehabilitation of West Germany and for her solid, courageous alignment with Western philosophy. Khrushchev now hoped to exploit differences among the four Western governments—differences, for example, over the kind of Communist provocation that could compel the West to go to war.

When the news of Khrushchev's statement first broke, there was no reason for an immediate public reply by the United States government; too much eagerness to counter Khrushchev's statement would give the impression that our government was edgy. Our rights, which had been observed for years, were evident. The people of Berlin were unshaken by the news; indeed no overt action had been taken, and thus there was really nothing to react to as long as Western rights had not been infringed. So, for the moment, we said nothing. But I kept in close touch with developments. The next one was not long in coming.

On Friday, November 14, four days after the initial announcement, the Soviets detained three United States Army trucks for 8½ hours at a checkpoint on the Autobahn just outside Berlin. General Norstad, the Supreme Allied Commander in Europe, sent a message that, in the absence of other instructions, he was planning to dispatch a test Berlin–Helmstedt convoy. If the Soviets were to detain it and if protest did not effect "early release"—within two or three hours—he planned to extricate the convoy "by minimum force necessary."

Clearly, however, if such action were to be taken, it should first be made known to our allies. Therefore, even though the administration was generally sympathetic to Norstad's approach (the Chiefs of Staff thought we should move at once), his plan could not be put into effect immediately. To give time for consultation an order was sent temporarily suspending all convoys to Berlin.

Soon thereafter Foster Dulles informed me that the initial combativeness of the military had eased and the Chiefs of Staff and General Norstad now recognized the necessity for bringing our allies in line prior to taking drastic action. At a meeting a few days later—on the twentieth—Secretary Dulles observed that if Khrushchev should carry out his intention of transferring Soviet responsibilities to the East German government, he would create the most complicated situation in Berlin since the end of the 1949 blockade. Foster believed that Khrushchev would probably move soon to carry out his threat.

By November 21 I felt the time had come to make some sort of low-key announcement that the United States would stand on its commitments. I directed Jim Hagerty to make the announcement for me to the assembled press representatives in his routine briefing. The transcript gives an idea of the atmosphere of one of these informal, speak-but-say-little Hagerty press conferences, at which he was a master when he chose to be:

Mr. Hagerty: "There isn't much I can tell you, but I can say this: that the President and our government are keeping in close touch with the situation in Berlin and are also keeping, as a government, in close touch with the government of the United Kingdom and the government of the Republic of France.

"This [Berlin], as you realize, is not a unilateral problem. . . . It is a problem that concerns our two allies as well. And I can say, speaking for the U.S. government, . . . that our firm intentions in West Berlin remain unchanged."

Q. "Speaking there for the U.S. government or for the three allies?"

Mr. Hagerty: "Well, I can't speak for the governments of the UK and France, but as I say, we are keeping in close touch with the Allies and I would think that would also be true, but I can't speak for them."

Q. "Jim could spell out those intentions?"

Mr. Hagerty: "No, and I do not intend to."

Q. "Well, [it] certainly involves permanent intention to stay in West Berlin, doesn't it, Jim?"

Mr. Hagerty: "If you ask me what our 'firm intentions' mean, I can say that those firm intentions remain to maintain the integrity of West Berlin. That is all I have to say this morning—(laughter)—unless you have some questions."

I soon learned from Prime Minister Macmillan that he had sent a message to Khrushchev, warning of the worry which Khrushchev's recent statements on Berlin had caused. Harold, possibly with tongue in cheek, had said that he found Khrushchev's statements difficult to reconcile with the many previous expressions he had made expressing a desire to reduce tension in the world. He reminded Khrushchev that the position of the allies was well known. For us the crux of his message was "the British government have every intention of upholding their rights in Berlin, which are soundly based."

Meanwhile the allies began, through their embassies in Bonn, an effort to compose a four power note (including West Germany) to the Soviets. At the same time we lifted our ban on truck convoys from West Germany to Berlin, and soon one was reported to have passed unhindered.

There matters stood until the 27th of November, when my son John arrived in Augusta with an extensive summary of current State Department, CIA, and military reports. Together, the reports stated that none of the Western governments or any member thereof advocated pulling out of Berlin. However, there had been Allied discussion on various subjects including (1) the degree with which the Western powers could deal with the East German government without loss of prestige or undue damage to Adenauer, (2) the procedures to be followed (including the degree of force to be used) in the event of serious harassment by East German police, and (3) the timing of Western moves, such as the proposed note to the Soviets or any proposed message to Adenauer. The report concluded that, of the nations involved, West Germany had taken the firmest and most unequivocal position; that France was uncommitted (apparently President de Gaulle preferred to wait a little longer before moving), and at the "working level" (the men below the Prime Minister) the British appeared to be the most conciliatory.

The only startling aspect of the report was found in the British paper. It had been received informally from the British government, apparently representing only the views of the lower echelons of the Foreign Office, and not pretending to commit the government. The paper suggested a Western readiness not only to deal with the East German puppet government but, eventually, to recognize it, rather than expose Berlin to the danger of a blockade. These views reportedly had been communicated to our ambassador, John Hay Whitney, by the British foreign secretary, Selwyn Lloyd, who implied that there was no reason why dealing with East Germany should lead to our ejection from Berlin. He claimed, furthermore, that the French Foreign Minister, Maurice Couve de Murville, agreed with him that "low-level" recognition of that regime was better than a risk of war.

On reading the report I telephoned the Secretary of State, saying "Until this morning I didn't know of the existence of this British paper and I'm astounded by its arguments." I said that I was amazed also at the alleged sentiments of Couve de Murville, whom I had always considered a stout-hearted individual.

Foster's reply was that the working level British paper had been repudiated by Harold Macmillan himself!

Foster had more to report. The State Department had just received a note from Moscow that seemed to defer any move on Khrushchev's part for six months, during which time negotiations over Berlin should take place. Khrushchev had also proposed that West Berlin become a "free city" under the United Nations, and that all occupying powers' military forces withdraw from Berlin.

If an agreement to this effect could not be reached at the end of six months, Khrushchev concluded, the Soviets would go ahead with their program.

We discussed the free city concept for a few moments. I would be willing to study the possibility of creating a free city, I said, if it included *all of Berlin,* East and West; if the avenues to the city from the West were placed also under the jurisdiction of the United Nations, and if the West German government approved. If the proposal applied to West Berlin only, I would have nothing to do with it. At the end of the conversation I asked Foster to urge a four-power conference of Western foreign ministers with a view of concerting the stand which the West would take.

At the conclusion of this conversation, I turned to John and we speculated for a few moments. The immediate crisis was averted. But Khrushchev's latest pronouncement had, nevertheless, the tone of an ultimatum. At the end of six months, on May 27, 1959, to be exact, we presumably would be faced with a far more serious crisis—unless Khrushchev backed down or a solution satisfactory to all interested parties, not yet in sight, could be found. During the interim we could be sure that the Russians would use every weapon in their arsenal to divide the West and to play on the already taut nerves of some of its leaders. There seemed to be no avoiding a showdown because Khrushchev had apparently laid his prestige on the line.

* * *

During the next few days I had ample occasion to reflect at length on Berlin. I had lived with this problem intermittently for the past thirteen years. Inevitably, despite intimate acquaintance with it, the question kept coming back to me: "How, or rather why did the Free World get into this mess? How did we ever accept a situation in which our only feasible response to an attack on a thirteen-thousand-man garrison[3] surrounded by numerous Communist divisions would likely mean the initiation of World War III?"

From a conventional military viewpoint alone, the situation was so lopsided as to be ridiculous. But far more was at stake than the fate of military men surrounded by a sea of potential enemies.

The Western position in Berlin was the result of political agreements made by United States, British, and Soviet governmental leaders during World War II, agreements which the Soviets never carried out.

The arrangements they established for occupation of Germany were intended to be temporary only. Allied governments never visualized that the

[3] The United States and Great Britain had four thousand to five thousand each and France about three thousand. There was probably a like number of civilians from all three nations. Informed estimates set the number of Soviet divisions at 180, of which twenty-two were deployed in East Germany.

occupation zones for Germany would one day become enduring political boundaries, dividing the population and condemning millions of unfortunate peoples to live under dictatorship for decades, possibly generations.

Moreover, the decisions made regarding the division of Germany and the status of Berlin were not reached impulsively or without long study. When the allies were preparing for Operation OVERLORD,[4] they set up in London the European Advisory Commission, composed of political representatives of the United States, Great Britain, and the Soviet Union, and charged them with responsibility for recommending plans to govern a defeated Germany. They were to suggest boundaries for occupation zones.

During the 1944–45 campaign in Europe, my headquarters came to the conclusion that the boundaries recommended by the Advisory Commission would give more territory to the Soviets than they could take by force of arms. We reported this. But because the Western governments undoubtedly looked upon the division of Germany as a temporary arrangement, the exact lines may have seemed, at that time, as of little importance.

My headquarters also proposed as an alternative to the use of Berlin as the temporary capital of Germany the building of a cantonment capital to be located at the junction of the American, British, and Soviet Zones.[5] But the Commission's recommendations for Germany's division were adopted, with the retention of Berlin, over one hundred miles within the Soviet Zone, as the site from which all Germany should be governed.

For months following V-E Day I, as the United States representative on the Four-Power Allied Control Council, visited Berlin periodically. The Council attempted to run the country from this traditional seat of au-

[4] Code name for the Normandy invasion.

[5] Although the scheme brought no positive response, President Roosevelt might have had something similar in mind when in February of '44 he reportedly sketched out a plan for Germany's division. In his rough diagram the national occupation zones were triangular in shape with the points joining at Berlin.

My pie-shaped plan was similar except that the center of the pie was located elsewhere—at the junction of the U.S., British, and Soviet Zones. The President seemed little concerned about Berlin in contrast to Winston Churchill, who thought it would be greatly to our advantage to capture it even though by the prior decision to which he was a party, the area in which it was situated would be surrendered to the Soviets.

Mr. Roosevelt's only interest, as I recall, was in our control of the northwest sector; there was nothing in the southwest, he remarked, "except tourists and scenery." I did not believe we should have sectors, and said as much to the President when I was ordered back to consult with the Joint Chiefs at Staff in 1944.

thority in accordance with the joint directions of our respective superiors. As it turned out, Soviet cooperation was so lacking that Germany was soon, in effect, governed by two authorities, the Soviets in the East and the Western allies in the West. Both parts of the nation were later accorded recognition by their respective occupiers. The West, however, retained their rights in and access to Berlin.

Trouble was always afoot. Possessed, geographically, of the power to control access to the city, the Soviets never lost an opportunity to harass the West as much as they dared. The Free World was kept acutely aware of this during the following years, a period that witnessed the initiation of the Reds' Berlin blockade in 1948 and its later defeat. When in 1951 I was recalled to duty as Supreme Allied Commander in Europe, Berlin became once more a matter of my immediate direct responsibility but little difficulty was encountered.

Soon after my inauguration as President, the East German revolt of 1953 broke out. It was quickly quelled. The Western part of Berlin was subjected to periodic harassment, and the city always held my attention. At innumerable meetings, we examined, against the possibility of future emergency, methods of support, including financial support, of the city, increased air transport, stockpiles of materials for emergencies, and limited retaliatory measures to discourage Soviet proddings. As the city grew from a heap of rubble to a brilliant showplace, we were determined to leave no doubt in the mind of Stalin and his successors that challenging our rights in the city could have painful consequences.

* * *

Now at the end of 1958, with the threat suspended for the moment, we began to plan the United States' response.[6]

Foster Dulles and I put less credibility in Khrushchev's threat to move

[6] Many people seemed to assume that, because Mr. Khrushchev had made an announcement, I should abandon my determination to enforce strict economy on defense expenditures. This showed a total lack of understanding of our military problem. If resort to arms should become necessary, our troops in Berlin would be quickly overrun, and the conflict would almost inevitably be global war. For this type of war our nuclear forces were more than adequate. Why so much of our populace has always seemed to feel that our defense would be immediately improved by an increase of a billion dollars or so, or by the quick call-up of a hundred thousand ground troops, has always been beyond my ken. I determined that this crisis should not affect our long-range plans for assuring the defense of America without waste. Indeed, it was always my conviction that one purpose of Khrushchev's manufactured crisis was to frighten free populations and governments into unnecessary and debilitating spending sprees.

in the following May than he possibly expected. But every tick of the clock brought us nearer to the moment when we had to be ready to meet him head on, if necessary. Though six months can sometimes seem like an age, there was little enough time to perfect contingency planning with our allies.

The problem was delicate: We could leave no doubt in the Soviets' minds of our intentions, yet we could not be provocative. First of all, the work we had done over the previous six years, and the concepts behind it, had to be coldly examined in the light of existing circumstances.

On December 11, immediately following the regularly scheduled meeting of the National Security Council, I asked the Vice President and a dozen others to come into my office. Before the meeting I had been informed by Foster Dulles that certain assumptions or attitudes about Berlin on which our previous planning had been based had turned out to be obsolete or invalid. For example, the State Department had thought it possible that when Khrushchev announced his intention of turning over controls of access routes to the East Germans the West should simply announce its intention to treat the East Germans as the "agents" of the Soviets. There were precedents for dealing with unrecognized Communist governments on specific problems. In Korea we had negotiated with the North Koreans and the Chinese Communists; in Indochina we had sat at the table with the North Vietnamese; indeed, in Germany, East Germans had administered transportation, utility, and other systems with our tacit approval on the assumption that they were responsible to the Soviets. Now, however, Khrushchev's belligerent message of November 27 left no doubt in anyone's mind that the East Germans would act in their own right, officially at least, once control of facilities should be turned over to them.

This position surprised me. Until that meeting, I said, I had not been aware that our petty dealings with the East Germans had become, by any distorted interpretation, a basis for virtual recognition of East Germany. I had no difficulty in rejecting the State Department's proposed "agent" expedient. An individual could be treated as an agent; a nation could not. However, I was troubled that up to this time we had always justified our position in Berlin solely on our rights as "conquerors." After all, we had recognized the Federal Republic of Germany (West Germany) as a sovereign nation four years before, and she had joined the North Atlantic Treaty Organization. The soundest basis for our remaining in Berlin, I felt, was our solemn obligation expressed to the two million Germans of West Berlin and to the entire world to stand by a city that had freely chosen to stay with the West and the cause of freedom. If our word to them would be broken, then no one in the world could have confidence in any pledge we made.

However, my feeling that the conqueror theory was obsolescent did not, in my mind, absolve the Soviets from respecting their obligations. I could listen to and perhaps participate in a proposal regarding Berlin that might appeal to reasonable people, but I would not do so on the basis of Soviet repudiation of agreements made earlier among responsible governments; nor would I do so under the shadow of a threat.

We would now have to be adamant in our attitude toward the East Germans in matters so small as to seem almost totally inconsequential. Once we tacitly agreed that the East Germans were in control, then, with a foot in the door, they would later find ways of gradually opening it, with each move so seemingly insignificant as to preclude decisive action on the part of the West.

The line had to be held where it stood. I directed that talks with the French, British, and West Germans begin immediately. We knew that getting agreements acceptable to all would be difficult. The British seemed to stress practical access and tended to downgrade the implications of tacitly recognizing the East German regime. Such an attitude infuriated Chancellor Adenauer, whose political standing rested on the hope of eventual reunification of Germany through free elections. Moreover, among the Germans themselves there were splits. West Berlin's mayor, Willy Brandt, while strong in his support of a stand against the Communists, seemed for a time to be somewhat amenable to Khrushchev's idea of a "free city." To this Adenauer could not agree. In France, President de Gaulle adhered to his position that we should do nothing in a hurry, that immediate response would only show nervousness to the Soviets.

Near the close of this meeting, Vice President Nixon expressed the opinion that Khrushchev was angling for another summit conference. He pointed out the parallel between Berlin and the Quemoy-Matsu situation of 1955, stressing that the Soviets had stirred up trouble in both places as devices to lure us into a meeting. Under Secretary of State Christian A. Herter, while not disagreeing, felt that the difficulties the Communists were having bolstering their regime in East Germany could be a major factor. I myself had no objection to talks, provided they were not under duress, and had been properly prepared.

While giving Khrushchev every opportunity to be sensible, we were determined that he should have no reason to question our readiness and capacity to defend our rights. "In this gamble," I said, "we are not going to be betting white chips, building up the pot gradually and fearfully.

Khrushchev should know that when we decide to act, our whole stack will be in the pot."

The next day Foster Dulles, just out of the hospital, came to see me on his way to Paris for a meeting of the four Western foreign ministers and, subsequently, of the North Atlantic Council. Our most immediate problem at the NATO meeting would be a grimly related subject: to prod our allies to live up to the NATO force levels they had earlier agree upon.

On December 14 the foreign ministers reaffirmed our resolve never to negotiate under threat. A few days later, the North Atlantic Council issued a declaration on Berlin that associated all the NATO countries with the earlier statement of the foreign ministers. Then coordinated replies from the United States, Britain, France, and West Germany went out to Khrushchev. The messages were carefully worded. The East German regime, for example, was repeatedly referred to in our message by the laborious phrase, "the regime which the Soviet government refers to as the German Democratic Republic." Most significant was the sentence which read, *"Since the agreements can only be terminated by mutual consent, the government of the United States will continue to hold the Soviet government directly responsible for the discharge of its obligations undertaken with respect to Berlin under existing agreements."*

A note arrived on January 9, 1959, from Harold Macmillan, who was optimistic, but both his note and his optimism were soon overtaken by events. First, a message which in fact contained nothing new came from the Soviets, dated January 10—a long, tedious argument for a German peace treaty and for reunification of Germany through negotiations, not through free, all-German elections. In addition, its insistence that a "free city" would mean *only* West Berlin, not all of Berlin, dispelled any illusions. The message ended in a characteristically somber tone:

> No one can prevent the Soviet Union from renouncing its functions regarding Berlin and its communications with West Germany, and from settling the questions arising in connection with this through an agreement with the German Democratic Republic.

A week after receiving this letter, I held a forty-five-minute conversation with Mr. Anastas I. Mikoyan, one of Khrushchev's deputies and an expert on trade affairs. His request for a visa was, ostensibly, to permit him to visit Soviet Ambassador Menshikov, but many believed that his journey must have more serious purpose. I hoped that he was prepared to talk constructively. It was not so: I found Mr. Mikoyan a relatively affable personality, but he "mouthed" only the current Communist line.

I was disappointed to find no evidence whatsoever of a softening of the Soviet attitude.

On Mikoyan's trip home, one of his plane's engines caught fire. Fortunately, an emergency landing at our Argentia base in Newfoundland averted disaster for those aboard.

Informed of this news at a dinner, Foster Dulles commented dryly, "Maybe Mikoyan won't yell so loud about our overseas bases from now on."

* * *

In late January I called a meeting of Defense and State Department officials to discuss Berlin developments. On the question of the Soviet desire to turn control of Berlin access over to the East Germans, we reaffirmed our demand that the U.S.S.R. observe its obligations. But how to find an effective method for enforcing this demand? It would not be easy to explain to the public why a nation would risk war over an issue so seemingly slight as the nationality of the man who stamps the papers as a convoy proceeds through a checkpoint. The central point was that all rights the allies had in Berlin were brought about by agreement with the Soviet government, not with the puppets they had installed in a fragmented part of Germany. There would be no way in which we could hold the East Germans responsible for carrying out Soviet promises made years before. Chris Herter supplied what I thought was an apt phrase: Acquiescence in the substitution of East German officials for Soviets at a checkpoint would "simply start us down a slippery slope toward East German control of everything."

To show the Soviets that we meant business, the Chiefs of Staff were instructed to send sufficient replacements to Europe to fill out the rosters of all our military units, both combat and support. This routine movement of replacements would be done quietly but quickly; it was certain that the Soviets would detect the movements and probably interpret them correctly as evidence of our determination.

One disagreement at this meeting was between Foster Dulles and the Joint Chiefs of Staff. The Joint Chiefs believed that the United States should be prepared to go into action with a fairly substantial force—one division—on the day the first truck convoy should be stopped. Foster objected: world opinion, he argued, would not be sufficiently mobilized on May 27 to permit the immediate use of a force this size.

I tended to side with Foster, but for different reasons. One division was far too weak to fight its way through to Berlin and far more than necessary to be a mere "show of force" or evidence of determination. The deployment of an entire division would be played up in the press and would put the pressure on the Soviets to "put up or shut up." Such a move could be regarded, elsewhere, as aggression. Its use would raise other questions. For example, having used military force to open the way, would we not then have to keep open the 110-mile-long road by force? Such a task would require far more than a division. If a mere probe became necessary a much smaller unit should be employed and I so decided.

Once action was called for, the move would obviously have to be swift; delay could only confirm to the Soviets and to the world that we had accepted the new status quo.[7]

The plan, as I approved it at the meeting, included these steps: (a) A refusal to acquiesce in any substitution of East Germans for Soviet officials in checking the Western occupying powers movement to and from Berlin. (While it would be permissible to show an East German official a pass for identification purposes, such official would not be permitted to stamp a pass); (b) A decision to begin quiet military preparations in West Germany and Berlin prior to May 27, sufficient to be detected by Soviet intelligence but not sufficient to create public alarm; (c) Should there by any substitution of East German officials for Soviets, a small convoy with armed protection would attempt to go through, and if this convoy were stopped, the effect would be discontinued and the probe would fire only if fired upon; (d) Transit would then be suspended and pressure would be brought to bear on the Soviets by publicizing the blockade and taking the matter to the United Nations Security Council and, if necessary, to the General Assembly. In these circumstances our further military preparations would be intensified by observable means such as the evacuation of dependents from West Berlin and possibly from all Germany; (e) In the event that this moral and other pressure was not sufficient, use of additional force would be subject to governmental decision; (f) We would at once attempt to bring about a foreign ministers' meeting with the Soviet Union to be held about the middle of April.

One purpose of the meeting would be to provide a means by which Khrushchev could, without losing face, modify his position regarding

[7] Fortunately the supply situation in Berlin was good. When I checked, I was informed that we had military supplies in the city to last about ninety days; the civilian supply situation was even more favorable. In no category did the stocks fall below a two-month level. Assuming an initial repulse, this supply situation would give us time to maneuver before we found ourselves in a major emergency. On the debit side, General Twining warned that Tempelhof Airport, used in the earlier, propellor-age Berlin airlift, probably could not take our largest jet air freighters.

Berlin.[8] Should he not do so, the West would be on notice that a showdown was imminent.

The meeting at which this program was developed was informal, yet the drama of the hour was not missed by participants. We all knew the potentials of the decisions which had been made. Possibly we were risking the very fate of civilization on the premise that the Soviets would back down from the deadline when confronted by force. Yet this, to my mind, was not really gambling, for if we were not willing to take this risk, we would be certain to lose. Our approach was cautious, controlled, and I was confident it was correct. We were trying to give the Soviets every opportunity to be reasonable without humiliation but we were keeping our powder dry.

* * *

During the following sixteen weeks, Premier Khrushchev executed a remarkable diplomatic retreat. So skillful and subtle was each step backward that its significance was hardly noticed and for this reason the retreat, although absolute, caused scarcely any loss in Khrushchev's public standing. The Western governments deliberately encouraged this evolution.

On the afternoon of February 3, 1959, for example, Foster Dulles, Livingston T. Merchant, Assistant Secretary of State for European Affairs, and I discussed our expectations for Foster's forthcoming trip to Britain, France, and Germany (a journey we thought desirable, but which none of us dreamed would be his last). We had just learned of Prime Minister Macmillan's decision to make a personal exploratory pilgrimage to Moscow, and it was obviously desirable to reach the best possible meeting of minds among the interested Western governments before his departure on the 28th of February.

Arriving in London February 4, Foster met that evening with Macmillan. Though the Prime Minister had no objection to our plans for meeting an immediate emergency, he still seemed less concerned than we about accepting the East Germans as "agents" for the Soviets; he felt

[8] One further small evidence of changing times: As the meeting broke up, I was informed that West Berlin Mayor Willy Brandt would soon be in the United States. I thought that his flight from New York to Washington might be the occasion to provide him with an escort of the new B-58s, which should prove an impressive show.

On reflection, I realized that B-58s are scarcely designed for such short-run escort duty. If their speed were held down to only Mach 2, their flight time between New York and Washington would be about eight minutes. This flashing "escort" would leave Mayor Brandt's plane behind before he would have time to see them.

that the status quo in Berlin could not endure indefinitely, certainly not after Adenauer passed from the political scene. He was particularly intrigued by an idea originally advanced by Foreign Minister Rapacki of Poland—a proposed "thinning-out" of military forces in Germany, leading eventually to some sort of neutralization, like that of Austria. Harold believed the Russians would have more to lose than to gain by a mutual withdrawal of troops from Germany.

In Paris, Foster found that President de Gaulle shared our misgivings about East German control of Berlin's access routes. Indeed, remembering the failure in 1936 to resist Hitler's occupation of the Rhineland, De Gaulle seemed to be prepared to use force a little more suddenly than we felt advisable.

In Bonn, Foster obtained confirmation of earlier indications that Chancellor Adenauer had become uneasy about British policy toward Germany and particularly about Macmillan's proposed trip to Moscow. The British ambassador in Bonn had reportedly said that sooner or later it would become necessary to recognize the East German government, an idea hardly designed to make the Chancellor sleep better. However, Adenauer and his aides seemed to be satisfied with the United States contingency plans.

When the Secretary arrived home and after we had met for extended consultations, he sent me a note that held disturbing implications. It requested permission to turn over temporarily his duties as Secretary of State to Under Secretary Herter because of the need for an operation for a recently developed hernia. He had also, he indicated, not wholly thrown off the effects of an abdominal inflammation which had appeared the previous December. I could not but feel apprehensive.

As a result of Foster's European talks, we had concluded that a meeting of some type with the Soviets probably would be inevitable; even Adenauer had agreed to this idea in principle. Khrushchev himself seemed to be showing signs of amenability. True, the Communists had held up a Western convoy for over two days, after it had proceeded from Berlin to the very door of Western Germany, and Khrushchev was still boasting of his missile strength. However, at the meeting of the 21st Congress of the Communist Party, he had expressed the desire for an early end to the cold war and, surprisingly, had invited me to make a visit to the Soviet Union, claiming that I would be received with "heartfelt hospitality."[9] In addition we were getting high-level Soviet hints of a possible postponement of the May 27 Berlin deadline.

[9] This invitation was highly diluted. It was included in a lengthy speech which also included hostile references to U.S. leaders. On February 6 I put out a statement through Mr. Hagerty observing that it seemed strange that Khrushchev would, if

With the situation easing ever so slightly it seemed an appropriate time to make a formal proposal for a meeting. Therefore, in replying to the Soviet note of January 10, we proposed a meeting of the foreign ministers of the U.S.S.R., France, the United Kingdom, and the United States with the time and place to be settled through diplomatic channels. Our note stated that the conference should cover the problem of Germany in all its aspects. It was our plan, without giving in to pressure, to reduce tensions by extending the area of discussions beyond the narrow issue of Berlin itself.

In the meantime other, more pleasant, matters engaged my attention. One was a visit to Mexico. On the 18th of February I took advantage of an invitation extended by the new President of Mexico, Adolfo Lopez Mateos, to join him at Acapulco, a beautiful spot on Mexico's Pacific Coast. For two days, in a balmy atmosphere, I was privileged to become acquainted with this dynamic new leader of our nearest southern neighbor. To be sure we had problems too, involving such things as cotton, fishing rights, territorial waters, and border disputes, but it was a relief to be able to discuss such questions in a spirit of amity.[10] My brother Milton, who had often served as my personal representative on visits to many Latin American nations, sat in on our conversations. I was pleased when President Lopez Mateos suggested that he and I keep in close touch with one another by having my brother serve as a traveling intermediary. This arrangement proved to be helpful. When Project Mercury required for its success a control station at Guaymas, Mexico, my brother carried on the sensitive negotiations with President Lopez Mateos and ultimately obtained full Mexican cooperation.

---

he really welcomed a visit, extend an invitation in such a manner. I had no plans for such a visit under these circumstances. The statement left the door open in event future developments would suggest a visit to the U.S.S.R. in the cause of peace.

In a press conference on February 10, I said, "I would think I would have to wait for some more official type of, and more, let us say, persuasive kind of, invitation than that."

[10] While at Acapulco I learned that agreement was said to have been reached between the governments of Britain, Turkey, and Greece on the future status of the island of Cyprus. The solution had been long in coming but finally, by dint of statesmanship on the part of all three nations concerned, Cyprus was to become an independent nation. There were difficulties yet to be overcome in the implementation, but the accord was of sufficient importance that I sent Harold Macmillan a congratulatory cable from this rather remote location.

Another pleasant aspect of the visit to Acapulco was a chance to meet and talk briefly with Anthony Eden, now retired and vacationing there, attempting to regain his health while writing his memoirs.

* * *

Returning to Washington, I learned that Harold Macmillan was leaving on his planned trip to Moscow.

As he had promised, Harold kept me well informed. He was impressed, he reported, by the apparent feeling of insecurity which still persisted among the Soviets in spite of their power, but with respect to Germany and Berlin he detected no signs of weakening in the long-term Soviet purpose. Khrushchev flatly said there was no room for maneuver, or for retreat from his intention to sign a peace treaty with East Germany in the following May. Furthermore, the Soviets would not, at this point, admit any relationship between Berlin, reunification of Germany, a peace treaty, and European security. Discussions on all these, Khrushchev said, would result in a labyrinth of negotiations which might last ten years. To Harold's message I replied on February 24, in part:

> This morning, February twenty-fourth, we received cabled extracts from the statement that he [Khrushchev] made today in Moscow that are seemingly even more belligerent and unyielding than those he has made in the past. . . .
>
> . . . it seems that he is intensifying his efforts to create division within the Western group and thus to weaken our resolution. In effect he is saying, "We are destroying the Western rights in Germany and in Berlin, and if you make any attempt to defend those rights you are guilty of aggression and warlike acts."
>
> Tomorrow morning I shall probably have some searching questions put to me by the press respecting the latest statement of Khrushchev, and the rigidity of the line he is taking. I shall say as little as possible, particularly during the duration of your visit. However, I believe I should reiterate that the West is a unit in its determination to defend its rights and to carry out its responsibilities respecting Berlin, and that, while we are completely ready to negotiate where there is any possible negotiable ground, we are not going to be divided or defeated by threats.
>
> With warm regard,
>
> *As ever,*
>
> Ike

Harold answered on February 26 to the effect that he not only agreed with my assessment of what Khrushchev was saying to us, but had told the Premier that it was he who was threatening war.

While Harold was still in Moscow, Khrushchev took time out from their talks to deliver a hard, even insulting public speech, an act of incredibly bad manners. Harold, however, seemed to take the insult rather philosophically. In describing the incident to me he admitted that the welcome in Moscow had cooled ever since he had shown his support of Adenauer, who was Khrushchev's chief personal target. Harold emphasized to Khrushchev that the very danger of the situation required him to understand that the British government would line up with its allies.

About the only agreement that Harold could report from Moscow was that both sides realized the seriousness of the situation. He did not feel that he had shaken Khrushchev's resolve any more than ours had been shaken, but at least Khrushchev could no longer harbor any mistaken notions regarding the strength of British determination. He concluded:

> It is on this rather dark note that I am now leaving for a four-day journey around Russia. I thought that you would like to have my latest news before I set off.

When Harold returned to Moscow the clouds seemed a little less black. He reported that Khrushchev had recovered from his toothache, which had been the Chairman's last-minute reason for failing to accompany Harold on his trip, and Mikoyan had unexpectedly turned up to greet him in Leningrad. This gave Harold encouragement. He hoped that this improvement in Soviet deportment was the result of his own attitude, which I would describe as solid but patient and polite determination.

In a note of March 2, I congratulated him

> . . . on the firmness of your presentation respecting Western rights in the Berlin situation. At the very least you demonstrated to the world that strength does not depend upon discourtesy, a great contrast to the provocative attitude and statements of Khrushchev during your visit there. Thank you very much for the care you took to inform us on a day-by-day basis of your Russian experience.
>
> . . . I am quite sure that nothing is so important as to have our ideas and plans concerted among the four of us and, so far as possible, with the complete NATO group. Certain elements of the situation constantly change. . . .

Harold was a solid ally—I admired him the more for the frankness in which he always presented his views.

Now, in a long note to the Western leaders, the Soviets reversed their field. After eight pages devoted to speeches, drivel, specious reasoning, and threats, the document called for a new summit meeting. But the men in the Kremlin were well aware of our long-standing insistence that, while we would always go the extra mile to negotiate where there was any logical hope of progress, we would not, in its absence, go to a summit. They therefore added that, if the Western powers insisted, they would agree to a meeting of the foreign ministers of the U.S.S.R., the United States, Britain, France, Poland, and Czechoslovakia—a meeting limited to a German peace treaty and Berlin.

This was a step forward, because only a few days before Khrushchev had scornfully denounced the idea of a foreign ministers' meeting. Despite this concession, world tension did not abate; questions in press conferences clearly evidenced how seriously the Berlin question was on the minds of all. Trivialities were largely avoided and queries dwelled on such matters as the health of the Secretary of State, the necessity for instituting an air alert for the Strategic Air Command, the possibility of negotiation with the Soviets in light of the latest note, the need for improving the defenses of Europe, and the desirability of making use of the experience of Bedell Smith who had been ambassador to Moscow. With the country so concerned, I thought it was advisable to hold a conference with the legislative leaders of both parties. On the morning of March 6, 1959, I met with a few of them, along with some of my closest advisers. The value of this meeting was so obvious to all of us that I held another later that evening with broader congressional representation.[11] These meetings, held in ordinary times as well as when the nation approached an emergency, often brought out the best in men. Their concerns reflected the concerns of our people; their sense of national interest could transcend party. This did not mean that such sessions were easy-going, rubber-stamp get-togethers. On the contrary, the quality of brisk give and take was among their finest features.

These encounters also revealed something about the character and interests of the legislators. Sam Rayburn, for example, was always anxious to make certain that the United States would do everything possible to negotiate. Senator Lyndon Johnson, on the other hand, appeared to be anxious to be able to take some action, visible to the world, to indicate we had—or the Senate had—strengthened our Armed Forces.

I assured Speaker Rayburn that we would not go to war because of rigidity in attitude and emphasized the recent exchange of notes in which we kept the chances for negotiation open. To Lyndon Johnson, I reiterated my confidence in the nation's military power. In fact, I said, "If we were to release our nuclear stockpile on the Soviet Union, the

[11] Present were Vice President Nixon, Acting Secretary of State Herter, Defense Secretary McElroy, CIA Director Allen Dulles, Speaker Sam Rayburn, Senators Everett Dirksen, J. W. Fulbright, Lyndon Johnson, Richard Russell, Leverett Saltonstall, Alexander Wiley; Representatives Leslie Arends, A. S. J. Carnahan, Robert Chiperfield, Charles Halleck, Carl Vinson; General Persons, Mr. Bryce Harlow, and Major Eisenhower.

main danger would arise not from retaliation but from fallout in the earth's atmosphere."

The purpose was to talk over the abnormal situation facing us, to ask for the ideas of the Legislative branch, and to make certain that we were all thinking along the same lines. Allen Dulles briefed the groups on the status of our, the Soviets', and the East Germans' forces.

"How reliable are the East German troops?" "Can our Germans beat their Germans?" were questions posed to Mr. Dulles. He said that in his opinion, the Soviets would not depend on theirs in any serious action.

"Then," said Mr. Halleck, "if there is action, this would of necessity involve Russian participation?"

The answer was "yes."

Neil McElroy stressed the need in all our planning to bring our allies into accord, saying, "This is what necessitates that we be quiet and refrain from committing ourselves to the public, at the risk of giving the false impression we are doing nothing. Though nothing has come to a head," he said, "we are approaching these problems as if a decision were required tomorrow."

Commenting on this point, the legislators agreed that excessive warnings could cause undue alarm not only to our own people but to the Russians as well.

The recurring question was the seeming contradiction between our plans, made much earlier, for reductions in the size of our Armed Forces and our need to be prepared to defend West Berlin. "The Soviets are engaged in confronting the United States with a series of crises," I said. "The United States has the need for an efficient military system. But it has to be realized that if we program for the sum total of all recommendations for increasing military strength, the mounting burden would call for full mobilization," putting our country on a wartime footing. I said that we could not have ground forces to match those that the Soviets could mobilize in middle Europe.

However, a number of the conferees continued to express anxiety about the adequacy of our Armed Forces. I inisted that if we were to respond with frantic haste to every annoying threat of the Soviets we would merely be dancing to the tune they called, with the result that they could destroy effective planning on our part and push us toward bankruptcy. "We are going to live with this type of crisis for years," I warned, "and our great problem will be to prevent the Communists from throwing us off balance." I expressed the conviction that all-out war would not come, but even if we could be miscalculating and it did come, we still had the courage and the means to follow through successfully. I went on to say that we had no intention of opposing, with ground troops only, a full-out attack by a couple of hundred Soviet divisions, but that we would take care of the situation.

This disposed, at least for the meeting, of the argument that we were making a mistake, in the midst of a critical period," to reduce the army by thirty thousand men.

As was normal in all meetings between legislators and the Executive branch on security matters, the question of mutual security came up. I was told, as often before, that this was "a most wasteful expenditure of money." I replied that if we wanted to abolish mutual security and provide instead for eighty or ninety divisions deployed around the periphery of the Soviet Union, this would solve any unemployment problem but it would also make certain that we became a garrison state.

Several times I said that I would consult with the Congress insofar as possible if the Berlin situation seemed to intensify. And several times Senator Russell assured me that consultation was appreciated but not necessary—the initiative was mine and the Congress would support me. There was an almost amusing quality of "Don't call us" about it, but I did remark appreciatively on their backing and on the statesmanlike restraint shown by the Congress. As Vice President Nixon said, this was especially helpful while we were trying to draw into an exact alignment with our allies.

Needless to say, the foregoing are only excerpts from the two meetings, but perhaps the quoted exchanges give an insight into the Executive and the Legislative branches working together, a phenomenon that frequently gets less space and attention than it deserves.

* * *

One crucial point remained in my mind, namely, the relationship, in public thinking, between the Berlin crisis and the numerical strength of our Armed Forces. The question came up again at the next press conference and again I tried to explain the fundamentals. But it seemed advisable to expand the answer into a short television talk, which I delivered on the evening of March 16.

Once more I covered much of the ground the leaders and I had gone over. I stressed that history had taught us the grim lesson that no nation had ever been successful in avoiding the terrors of war by refusing to defend its rights, and that we would never negotiate under a dictated time limit, with an agenda imposed on us, or on other unreasonable bases. I expressed the hope that we could reach an agreement on respectable terms and went on to describe the nation's defense structure.

The next morning in reading the newspapers I was amazed to learn that my remarks of the evening before had been interpreted to mean that I agreed to a summit meeting as long as a foreign ministers' conference was held first. The words referred to were these:

> It is my hope that thereby all of us can reach agreement with the Soviets on an early meeting at the level of foreign ministers.
>
> Assuming developments that [would] justify a summer meeting at the summit, the United States would be ready to participate in that further effort.

I saw immediately what the difficulty was. Those who were anxious for a summit meeting took my words to mean that no matter what happened at the foreign ministers' meeting I would interpret it in such a way as to justify going ahead at the summit. This was exactly the opposite of what I sought to convey. I was determined to make the Soviets show ahead of time that there would be promise in a summit, before I would attend such a meeting.

We were now preparing for a planned conference with Prime Minister Macmillan, the summit issue seemed to occupy the center of the stage in all the Western capitals. Reports from overseas indicated considerable variance on this question among the British, the French, and the West Germans. Recent statements by Chancellor Adenauer had apparently implied that summit talks might well become routine affairs. This seemed an unlikely eventuality to me. But what did cause concern was a late report that Harold Macmillan was ready to participate in a summit meeting without any sort of promising preliminary sessions with the Soviets. I was disturbed to hear a highly respected British friend of mine quoted as saying "Britain will not be atomized over the stamping of papers," indicating to me a lack of appreciation of the implications of seeming trivialities. Harold, I knew, was soon to be faced with an election, and sentiment in Britain for a summit meeting was strong. Nevertheless I was quite certain that in any showdown he would see to it that Britain could not be belittled. For my part I was in no mind to change our basic position.

We had many other questions to discuss with the British. As always, I wanted them on our side and everything understood between us. Any conference with the British requires the most detailed discussion. They do not like to sign any generalizations in a hurry, no matter how plausible or attractive they may be, but once their signature is affixed to a document complete confidence can be placed in their performance. French negotiators sometimes seem to prefer to sign first and then to begin discussion.

The most thorny question was the unification of Germany. Our government believed that the problem of Berlin could be solved only in the context of German unification and that, until success in this matter had been achieved, the rights of the Western allies in Berlin must not be violated.

On this matter Chancellor Adenauer's problem was particularly difficult. He had staked his political career on West Germany's individual sovereignty, association with the West, and eventual reunification of Germany. For this reason any negotiation with the Soviets that involved even the slightest kind of indirect recognition of the East German government was anathema to him. He feared that minor operational dealings with the East Germans would spell political disaster to his Christian Democratic Union. Thus, in advance, he refused to accede to any arrangements whatsoever that might be made with the East Germans, despite the fact that some of these could appear to the other Western allies to be logical. Herein lay one source of rift between Adenauer and the British.[12]

But regardless of difficulties, it was at least essential that we do what we could to bring the British and West Germans closer together. We also had to insure that the West German viewpoint would be represented in either a foreign ministers' or a summit meeting. At the Geneva Conference of 1955 Adenauer had taken residence in the vicinity and we had kept in close touch with him; it was obvious that some arrangement of like nature would have to be made if a later summit conference should ever take place.

Other matters that we expected to discuss with the British would be European security and nuclear test negotiations. Regarding the first issue, support for the Rapacki "thinning-out" of forces plan was reported to be widespread in Britain. However, this sympathy could hardly be

[12] Adenauer, however, had recently been talking of a "federation" between West and East Germany. He would not, by any means, accord to the East Germans a status equal to that of the Federal Republic, and, according to the East Germans, was adamant against any veto power over his own actions. However, Germans on both sides of the fence were apparently working at lower levels to find a solution whereby a federation of German states might be initiated, beginning with some unification at lower staff levels, without involving the two governments.

Other obstacles to coordinating a "Western position" existed in Germany itself. It was possible that Adenauer's party could be defeated if elections were one day held throughout East and West Germany, a possibility that did nothing to bring the two major political parties in Germany together in developing a solid German position on unification. Khrushchev once told me categorically that Adenauer's support of unification was nothing but a show; in Khrushchev's opinion it was merely a ruse on Adenauer's part to stay in power. However, Khrushchev made no reply when I asked him why he did not put his theory to the test by holding free elections throughout Germany.

shared by the West Germans and French, particularly in view of their never-ending concern that United States military forces might be withdrawn from Europe.

On nuclear testing, my goal was modest. I hoped it would be possible to reach at least a small, enforceable agreement between West and East which might generate confidence for more ambitious plans in this or related fields. I was convinced that the Soviets would not sign a comprehensive self-enforcing agreement respecting armaments, even one on nuclear testing, unless they gained confidence through experience and minor successes in first operating under treaties that were limited initially, practically to trivialities.

Concerned by a reported increase of Free World anxiety about nuclear fallout, I was beginning to feel that we should for the time being strive for a treaty involving only tests within the earth's atmosphere, ignoring those tests of small weapons below ground or sufficiently far into space to preclude fallout. Our concern, however, was that Prime Minister Macmillan might be willing to enter into a treaty with the Soviets which was not realistically enforceable.[13]

On March 20, 1959, the day of the Prime Minister's arrival, he and I, after a short word of greeting, set out for Walter Reed Army Hospital to visit Foster Dulles, who was undergoing treatment for a malignancy.

On the way I thought again of how good it was to have as the leader of our closest and strongest ally a man with whom my acquaintance had been cordial and intimate since the days when we were together in North Africa in 1942. True, we had a troubling difference of opinion on Berlin policy, but he was a statesman upon whose integrity and friendship I could depend.

At Walter Reed we went up the back elevator to Ward 8, a trip which was becoming all too familiar to me. There we met the Secretary of State and the four of us (Selwyn Lloyd joined us) engaged in an hour's conversation that turned out to be anything but casual. The meeting gave Foster full opportunity to express the views we had developed in our

[13] There were other less earth-shaking matters which we might discuss with our friends. One, strangely enough, concerned a wool tariff quota which was currently under study in the State Department. Since wool was a large industry in Britain, the tariff which the United States put on this commodity while subsidizing our own sheep herders with portions of the proceeds, was a matter of concern to the British. (I would not ordinarily have expected to be discussing a subject such as this in such a meeting, were it not for the fact that when unhappiness develops among friends on one monumental subject it's always good to make sure that some other smoldering minor resentment does not complicate communications.)

many conversations together. Whatever treatment he had been given in the hospital had done nothing to dull his mind.

The British attitude toward the Berlin situation was the main topic. Foster made a forceful plea that we avoid giving the people of the world the impression that we were frightened of the Soviets or that the Soviets were in the "driver's seat." Foster asked wryly why we spent $40 billion a year or more to create deterrent and defensive power if, whenever the Soviets threatened us, our only answer would be to buy peace by compromise. "If appeasement and partial surrender are to be our attitude," Foster said, "we had better save our money." In some parts of the world —notably Asia, Africa, and Latin America—people were watching closely to see whether they thought the Soviet Union or the Western allies would be the more powerful. He admitted that we could not prevent Khrushchev from strutting across the stage and making grandiloquent speeches; but we could avoid the impression that whenever he sounded conciliatory we would rejoice, and whenever he sounded threatening we would become "fearful as though he were the Lord of Creation."

Finally, after an incomplete discussion of the nuclear test issue, we found that time had run out and it was necessary to depart via helicopter for the retreat in the Catoctin Mountains known as Camp David.

At Camp David Prime Minister Macmillan, Foreign Minister Selwyn Lloyd, Acting Secretary Herter, Ambassador Whitney, and our respective advisers met for a lengthy joint discussion. The Prime Minister gave us a complete account of his trip to Moscow. It had, he said, three phases: "the honeymoon, the cold spell, and the final resurrection of courtesy by the Russians." No business could be done with the Russians, he observed, except with Khrushchev. The trip had been extremely useful and he hoped it had served to change the Soviet tactic from one of unilateral action to one of negotiation. The Prime Minister reported that there seemed to be renewed Soviet interest in test ban ideas, particularly in a spot-check system of inspection.

Somewhat flabbergasting, in view of his earlier bombast, was Khrushchev's statement to Macmillan that the May 27 deadline on Berlin was in no sense an ultimatum.

Selwyn Lloyd believed that the Soviet bosses would like to ease the burdens which their military establishment made on their own economy and that the Soviet government had no intention of going to war. This statement did not seem to me to square well with Harold's previously expressed anxiety about a nuclear attack on Britain.

The Prime Minister referred sketchily to the views of President de Gaulle, whom he had visited. But his news about Adenauer was of interest. The German Chancellor was beginning to favor a five-year "standoff," an agreement between East and West that the status quo between the two Germanys would not be disturbed. He was also willing to discuss—although he made stipulations which practically negated the offer—the possibility of limitation on armaments in specific areas within Germany. It further appeared that Adenauer was relaxing somewhat in the rigidity of his refusal to deal with the East Germans, a change which, he hastened to add, was not to be confused with de facto recognition.

The Prime Minister's report was not nearly so pessimistic as I had anticipated. However, our discussion exposed an important disagreement between the British and ourselves on a summit conference. Selwyn Lloyd, in particular, seemed to feel that a foreign ministers' meeting would be meaningless if it were not designed to point toward a prearranged summit meeting. My stand was that the basic purpose of the ministers' meeting was to determine the desirability of a later one at the summit, and I could not agree to participate personally unless there was evidence of good faith and some progress that promised results from a summit.

Before our conversation ended, we talked about such details as the best place for a possible summit meeting. Harold made a tongue-in-cheek proposal that Newport, Rhode Island, would be splendid because the luxurious surroundings might appeal to the Soviet taste. The site was a matter of indifference to me. A good place might be San Francisco, where the United Nations Charter was signed in 1945, I suggested. At this point, with the conversation moving into minutia, Harold and I left the meeting to drive over to Gettysburg to look around the farm.

When we returned to Camp David, we again met with our associates and on this occasion our differences and convictions were expressed emphatically—and at times emotionally. It now became abundantly clear that the gravest question before us was that of a summit meeting. Harold said that we were dealing here with a matter which affected the whole future of mankind. "World War I—the war which nobody wanted—came because of the failure of the leaders at that time to meet at the summit. Grey [Sir Harold Grey, British Foreign Minister at the time] went fishing and the war came in which the United Kingdom lost two million young men."

I reminded Harold that World War II had been preceded by a summit meeting attended by Neville Chamberlain, and I intended to be associated with nothing of the kind.

The Prime Minister said that he could not take his people into war without "trying the summit first." Eight bombs, he said, would mean twenty or thirty million Englishmen dead and would destroy their country.

We were not without sympathy for our friends' position but I said that in the event of war, the United States would probably have losses many times those of Britain, and the American people had strong convictions, too. I had put the matter to the British on the premise that I would go to a summit only if developments justified the trip. "We do not escape war by surrendering on the installment plan; one way to prevent war is to be willing to stand on solid ground." I would "not be dragooned into a summit meeting."

"I owe a duty to my people," Harold said. "This question of agreement now to a summit meeting is probably the most fateful decision I will ever have to make." We could only speculate on Harold's insistence upon a promise to attend such a meeting regardless of preparatory measures, but we had no question of his sincerity or the visible depth of his feelings. Without personal animosity, we agreed to think things over during dinner and overnight.

The next morning, when we met at 9:30, Harold told me that his assistants had been working with our advisers and that he thought they were close to an agreement on a formula for a note to the Soviets. Momentarily, I suspected that somebody had come up with clever or ambiguous phrasing which would result in our using the same words but with different meanings in our minds. However, when Mr. Macmillan read the text, I was pleasantly surprised. The formula was to propose a foreign ministers' meeting on a specific date and then to state the purpose of the foreign ministers' meeting, following which these words would be used: *"On this understanding and as soon as developments justify the holding of a summit meeting."* We promptly agreed on the language of a note to be dispatched to the Soviets [see Appendix S].

Throughout that day advisers from the Department of Defense, Atomic Energy Commission, and other agencies came and went hourly by helicopter. Harold and I, and our closest aides, never left the premises—indeed hardly left the spacious living room of Aspen cottage, whose picture window overlooks a beautiful valley to the east.

Our work on the foreign ministers' conference, the summit, and other questions completed, Harold and I attended church at Trinity United Church of Christ in Thurmont, Maryland, on Sunday morning, March 22, and then returned to Camp David. That afternoon, on the way back to Washington, we made another call on Foster Dulles, who happily had been moved temporarily from the hospital to his own home.

* * *

On March 30 Khrushchev accepted the Western proposal for foreign ministers' talks to begin on May 11.[14] But this did not mean that everything was calm and serene. Petty harassments and difficulties were continually cropping up. For example, a Soviet trawler was detected off Newfoundland cutting transatlantic telephone cables which connected the United States and Europe. This act, while conceivably an accident in the process of deep-sea fishing, was suspicious. The trawler was boarded by the United States Navy and taken to port for questioning of the personnel before being released.

At the end of March a more serious annoyance occurred. As a matter of habit, United States aircraft flying from Western Germany to Templehof Airport in West Berlin had observed a 10,000-foot ceiling because there had never been reason to go higher. However, with the advent of new equipment, which performed better at higher altitudes, it had become apparent that, in the remote possibility that an airlift became necessary, higher altitudes might well be used. Therefore, despite Soviet objections, we sent a flight to Templehof at a high altitude on March 27. The Soviets officially protested, and on April 11 I sent the following message:

> The United States Government rejects the Soviet contention that flights above 10,000 feet are precluded by regulations covering flights in the corridors, and that the flight of the C-130 aircraft in question, duly notified to the Soviet Element in accordance with established practice, constituted a violation of presently existing rules. . . . Flights by aircraft of the United States do not require any prior agreement from the Soviet Element [of Berlin Command], and the United States never has recognized and does not recognize any limitation to the right to fly at any altitude in the corridors. As has been previously pointed out, the altitude at which aircraft fly is determined in accordance with the meteorological conditions prevailing at the time and the operational characteristics of the aircraft. . . .
>
> The flight by Soviet aircraft in dangerous proximity to the United States C-130 on March 27, as witnessed by thousands of persons in the Berlin area, constituted not only a serious violation of the flight regula-

[14] At the same time a press report came in to the effect that in mid-March Khrushchev had told West Germany's Socialist Democratic leader, Karlo Schmidt, that nothing would happen regarding Berlin before a summit meeting. While ordinarily we would place little confidence in a story on such a subject this conversation did seem consistent with the estimates we held of Khrushchev's real intentions.

tions that obtain in the air corridors and the Berlin Control Zone but intentionally created the very hazard to flight safety about which the Soviet representatives have professed concern. . . .

The United States expects the Soviet Government promptly to issue instructions to its personnel in Germany to ensure fullfillment of their responsibility for flight safety in the air corridors to Berlin.

* * *

That same day, Allen Dulles and Jerry Green, personal assistant to the Secretary of State, came in, their faces sober. They told me that Foster (then recuperating in Florida) was experiencing considerable pain in his neck and shoulders and was becoming weaker. He had made up his mind that it would no longer be possible for him to continue as Secretary of State. In the meantime he intended to go back to Walter Reed for further checkups. I insisted that Allen tell the Secretary that there was no need to make a change hurriedly. While I would comply with Foster's desires I did not want to rush. I sent the *Columbine* to Florida to return him to the hospital.

Two days later I asked Acting Secretary of State Herter and General Goodpaster to visit me. I told Mr. Herter that at a reasonably early date I would like him to take the post of Secretary of State. No announcement would be made immediately; in the meantime I requested Mr. Herter to submit to a thorough physical examination, so that a group of doctors could determine his physical capacity for performing the arduous tasks of the position. Secretary Herter suffered from arthritis, but his experience and character were such that if he were physically able, his would be, in my judgment, a splendid appointment. We made arrangements with my brother Milton, President of the Johns Hopkins University, for Secretary Herter to undergo a complete physical examination at the Hopkins Medical Center.

On April 15, I talked with Foster on the telephone. In view of the new findings of his doctors, he had made up his mind to submit his resignation immediately. I conveyed the unhappy news at a press conference that morning and announced my intention to appoint Foster as a consultant so that he might continue his service to both the State Department and to me. I said that while his physical incapacity would prevent his carrying out the arduous duties of Secretary of State, I was determined to keep him close where he could be useful in considering everything that might affect our foreign relations.

His letter arrived, dated April 15:

Dear Mr. President:

It is apparent to me that I shall not be well enough soon enough to continue to serve as Secretary of State. Accordingly, I tender my resignation to be effective at your convenience.

I am deeply grateful for the opportunities and responsibilities you have given me.

I was brought up in the belief that this nation of ours was not merely a self-serving society but was founded with a mission to help build a world where liberty and justice would prevail. Today that concept faces a formidable and ruthless challenge from International Communism. This has made it manifestly difficult to adhere steadfastly to our national idealism and national mission and at the same time avoid the awful catastrophe of war. You have given inspiring leadership in this essential task and it has been a deep satisfaction to me to have been intimately associated with you in these matters.

If I can, in a more limited capacity, continue to serve, I shall be happy to do so.

Faithfully yours,

Foster

So now on April 16, 1959, I answered:

Dear Foster:

I accept, with deepest personal regret and only because I have no alternative, your resignation as Secretary of State, effective upon the qualification of your successor.

In so doing, I can but repeat what the vast outpouring of affection and admiration from the entire free world has told you. You have, with the talents you so abundantly possess and with your exemplary integrity of character, employed your rich heritage as well as your unique experience in handling our relations with other countries. You have been a staunch bulwark of our nation against the machinations of Imperialistic Communism. You have won to the side of the free world countless peoples, and inspired in them renewed courage and determination to fight for freedom and principle. As a statesman of world stature you have set a record in the stewardship of our foreign relations that stands clear and strong for all to see.

By this letter I request you to serve in the future, to whatever extent your health will permit, as a consultant to me and the State Department in international affairs. I know that all Americans join me in the fervent hope that you will thus be able to continue the important contribution that only you can make toward a just peace in the world.

With affectionate regard,

As ever,

D.E.

The announcement of Christian A. Herter's appointment as Secretary of State was made on April 18, 1959. Because of the delay brought about by his physical examination, it was not possible for me to announce his appointment at the same time as Foster's resignation; we had not then received the verdict of the Johns Hopkins physicians. A suspicion arose that I had someone else in mind. I regretted this; I had considered others, of course. We thought of giving the post to Robert Anderson and offering the job of Secretary of the Treasury to Douglas Dillon. But Mr. Herter was my choice, as well as Foster's, and it was only the question of his physical ability that took the extra time. Mr. Herter was sworn in on the 20th of April at Augusta, Georgia, and at Walter Reed Army Hospital, Foster soon took the oath in his new capacity as consultant.

Four days after Chris Herter assumed the post of Secretary of State, the scheduled meeting of the four foreign ministers was to begin. The issues outstanding were many. Apart from those mentioned earlier, they included restrictions on the deployment of IRBMs in Germany, assurances against surprise attack and, far from least, the principles for a peace treaty. Secretary Herter was intimately aware of my views on these complicated problems; as he departed for the conference, we had some hope but no huge expectations of constructive results.[15]

Unfortunately, soon after the conference began, it became obvious that little or no progress was to be expected. Gromyko, in the formal meetings, maintained his tiresome attitude of intransigence. This news reminded me of a cable we had received in early March from Llewellyn Thompson, our ambassador in Moscow. The cable predicted that if Gromyko were to represent the Soviet Union in these meetings, we could expect little progress. Apparently Gromyko did not enjoy the confidence of Khrushchev to the extent that he was empowered by the Kremlin to negotiate seriously on important issues; he was little more than a messenger and one, I often thought, whose every word and action, including his bad manners, were dictated by his Soviet master.

[15] The first big difficulty that Secretary Herter encountered was not with the Russians but with the French. He had an unpleasant talk with Premier Michel Debre, who informed him that President de Gaulle was withholding permission for the basing of nuclear warheads on French territory pending our favorable action on three items: (1) full, public acceptance of a "Big Three" organization he had proposed, (2) our acceptance of proposals supporting the position of the French government regarding Algeria, and (3) the accomplishment of nuclear equality among the French, British, Americans, and Soviets.

These proposals were a little more than unrealistic, and they implied that France was far more concerned with obtaining endorsement of her own ambitions than in acting as a partner in seeking an East-West settlement.

For two weeks the talks remained in a practical deadlock and so produced no surprises. The one potentially striking news story occasioned almost no comment. As the pages of the calendar turned and the clock ticked the seconds away, May 27 approached and finally arrived. This was the date which Soviet Premier Khrushchev some six months earlier had declared he would turn over to East Germany control of access to Berlin. It was the ultimatum that, only a few months before, many had feared would bring up the curtain of World War III. The day came and went—a day lost in history.

But for the Free World the day brought no cause for elation. The Berlin situation would continue to be a challenge. And on May 27 the four foreign ministers, including Gromyko, entered an airplane for a transatlantic journey to Washington, D.C. The occasion for their coming was, for me and one American family in particular, an event of almost unspeakable sadness: the funeral of John Foster Dulles.

WAGING PEACE: MAP PORTFOLIO

Maps by Rafael Palacios

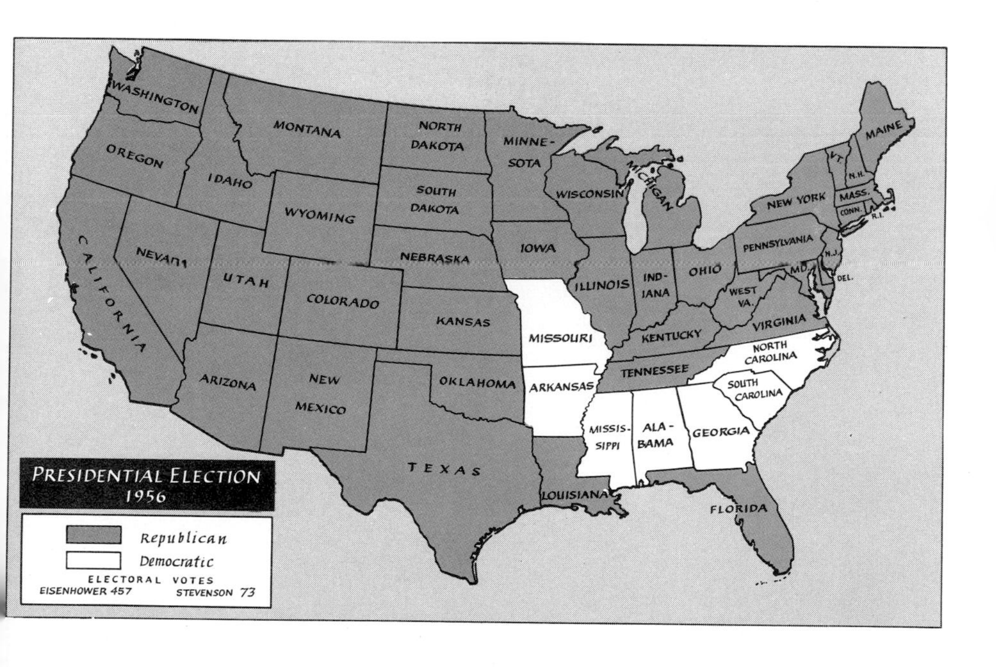

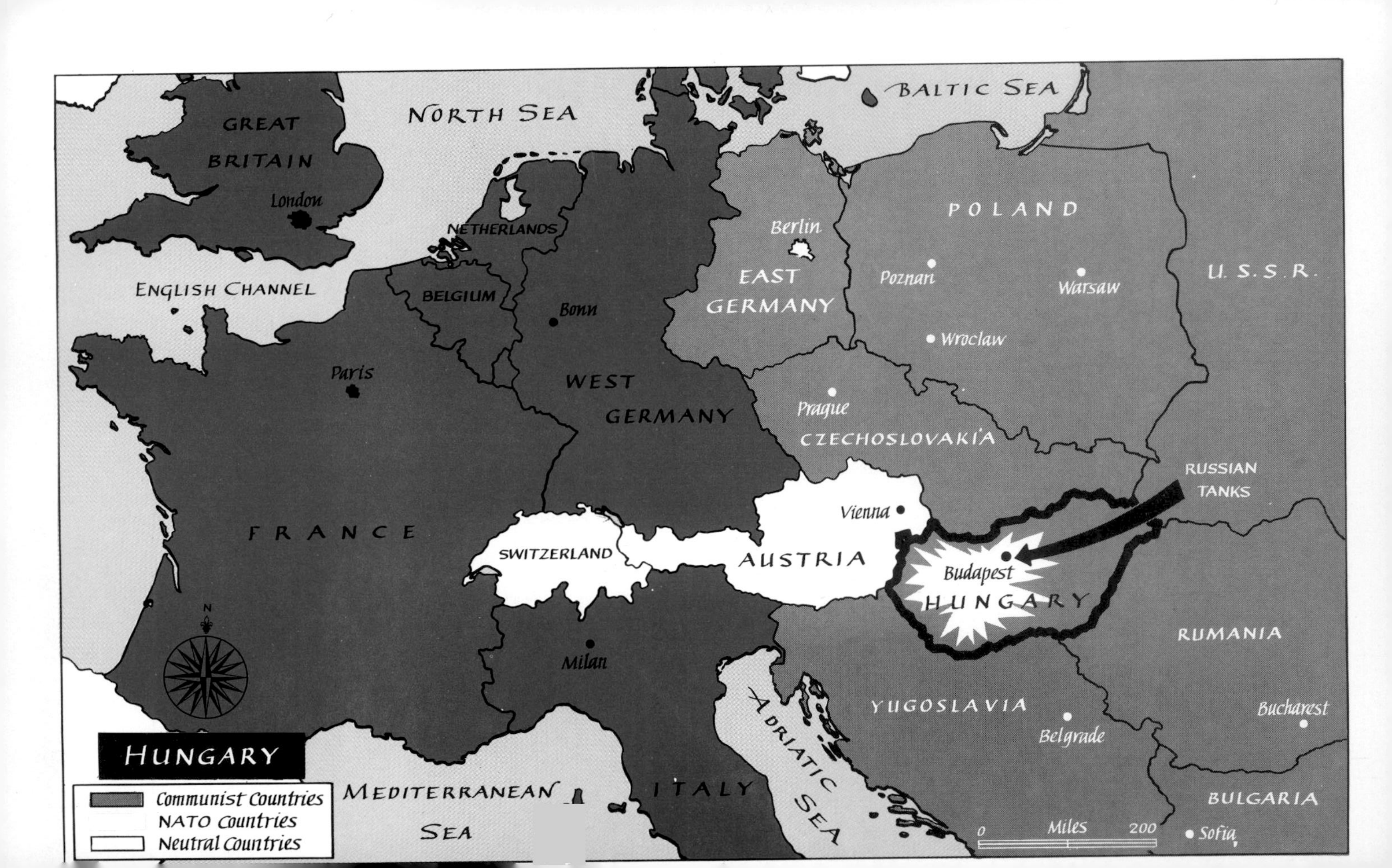
HUNGARY
Communist Countries
NATO Countries
Neutral Countries
GREAT BRITAIN
London
NORTH SEA
BALTIC SEA
ENGLISH CHANNEL
NETHERLANDS
BELGIUM
Bonn
Paris
FRANCE
WEST GERMANY
EAST GERMANY
Berlin
POLAND
Poznań
Warsaw
Wroclaw
U. S. S. R.
Prague
CZECHOSLOVAKIA
RUSSIAN TANKS
Vienna
SWITZERLAND
AUSTRIA
Budapest
HUNGARY
RUMANIA
Milan
YUGOSLAVIA
Belgrade
Bucharest
BULGARIA
Sofia
ADRIATIC SEA
MEDITERRANEAN SEA
ITALY
N
0 Miles 200

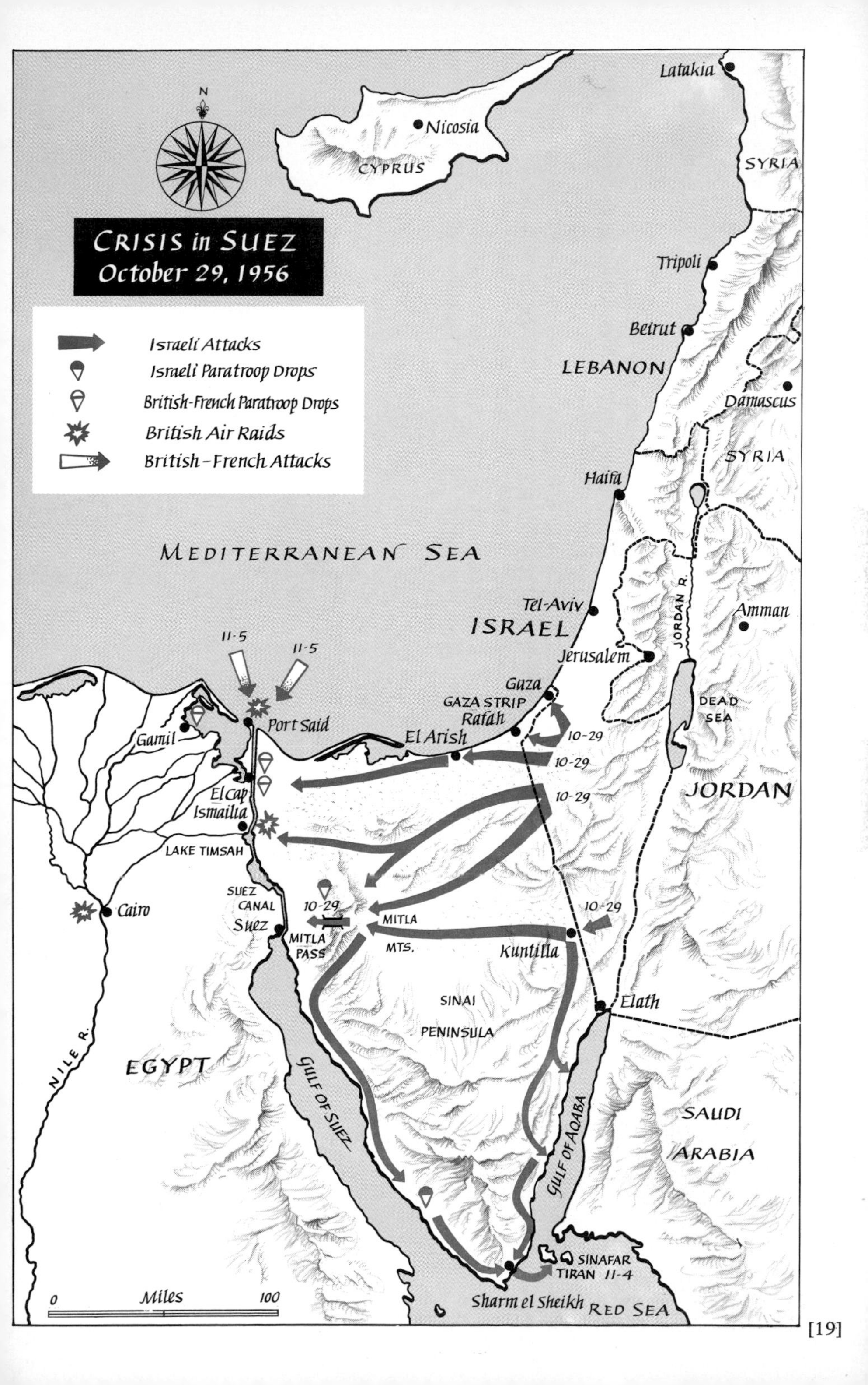

CRISIS in SUEZ
October 29, 1956
Israeli Attacks
Israeli Paratroop Drops
British-French Paratroop Drops
British Air Raids
British-French Attacks
Latakia
Nicosia
CYPRUS
SYRIA
Tripoli
Beirut
LEBANON
Damascus
SYRIA
Haifa
MEDITERRANEAN SEA
Tel-Aviv
ISRAEL
Amman
JORDAN R.
Jerusalem
DEAD SEA
JORDAN
Gaza
GAZA STRIP
Rafah
11-5
11-5
Port Said
Gamil
El Arish
10-29
10-29
10-29
El Cap
Ismailia
LAKE TIMSAH
SUEZ CANAL
Suez
Cairo
10-29
MITLA
MITLA PASS
MTS.
10-29
Kuntilla
SINAI
PENINSULA
Elath
NILE R.
EGYPT
GULF OF SUEZ
GULF OF AQABA
SAUDI
ARABIA
SINAFAR
TIRAN 11-4
Sharm el Sheikh
RED SEA
0
Miles
100

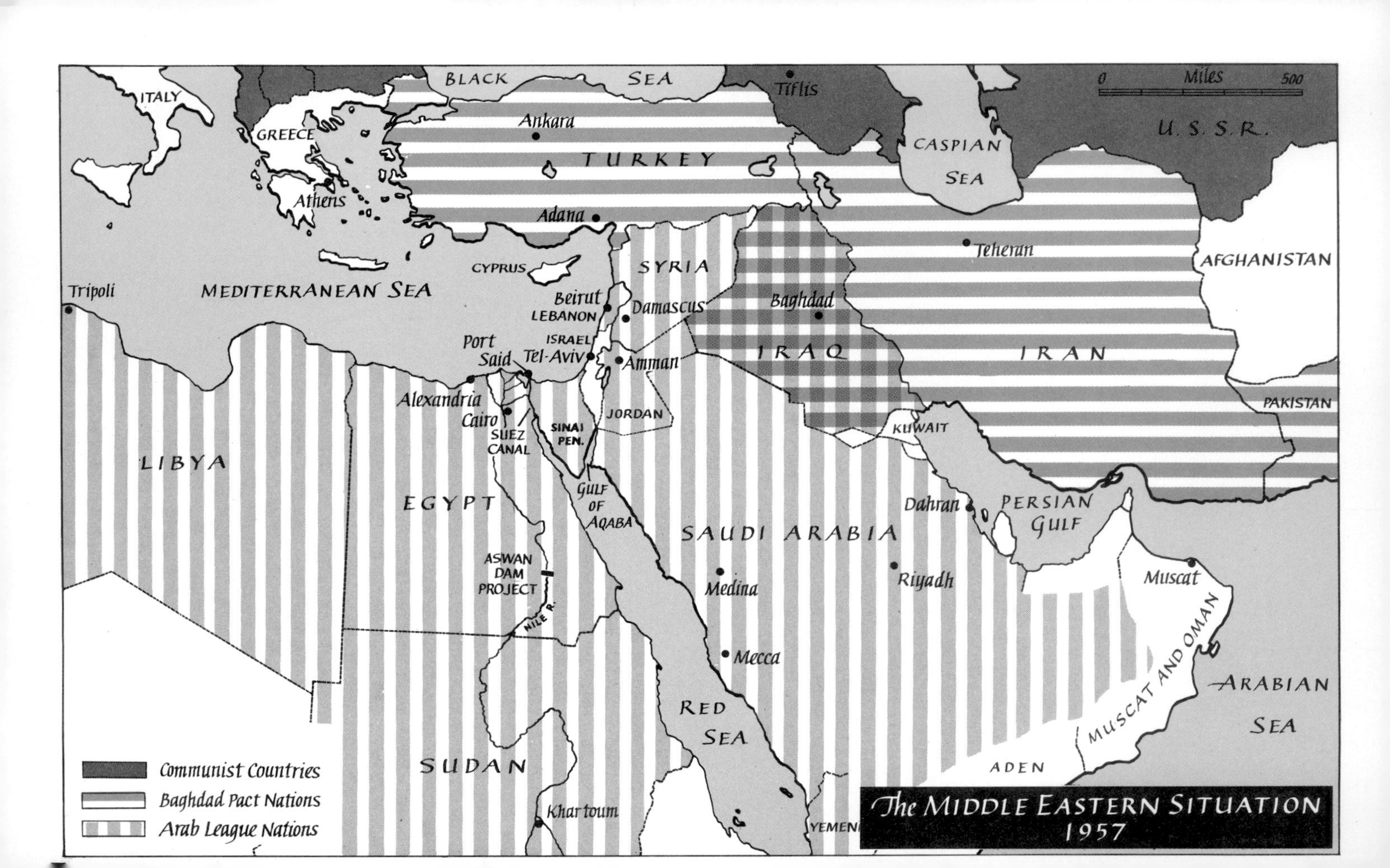
The MIDDLE EASTERN SITUATION 1957
0 Miles 500
Communist Countries
Baghdad Pact Nations
Arab League Nations
BLACK SEA
Tiflis
U.S.S.R.
ITALY
GREECE
Athens
Ankara
TURKEY
Adana
CASPIAN SEA
Teheran
AFGHANISTAN
CYPRUS
MEDITERRANEAN SEA
Tripoli
SYRIA
Beirut
LEBANON
Damascus
Baghdad
IRAQ
IRAN
ISRAEL
Tel-Aviv
Amman
Port Said
Alexandria
Cairo
SUEZ CANAL
SINAI PEN.
JORDAN
PAKISTAN
KUWAIT
LIBYA
EGYPT
GULF OF AQABA
Dahran
PERSIAN GULF
SAUDI ARABIA
ASWAN DAM PROJECT
NILE R.
Medina
Riyadh
Muscat
MUSCAT AND OMAN
Mecca
ARABIAN SEA
RED SEA
SUDAN
ADEN
Khartoum
YEMEN

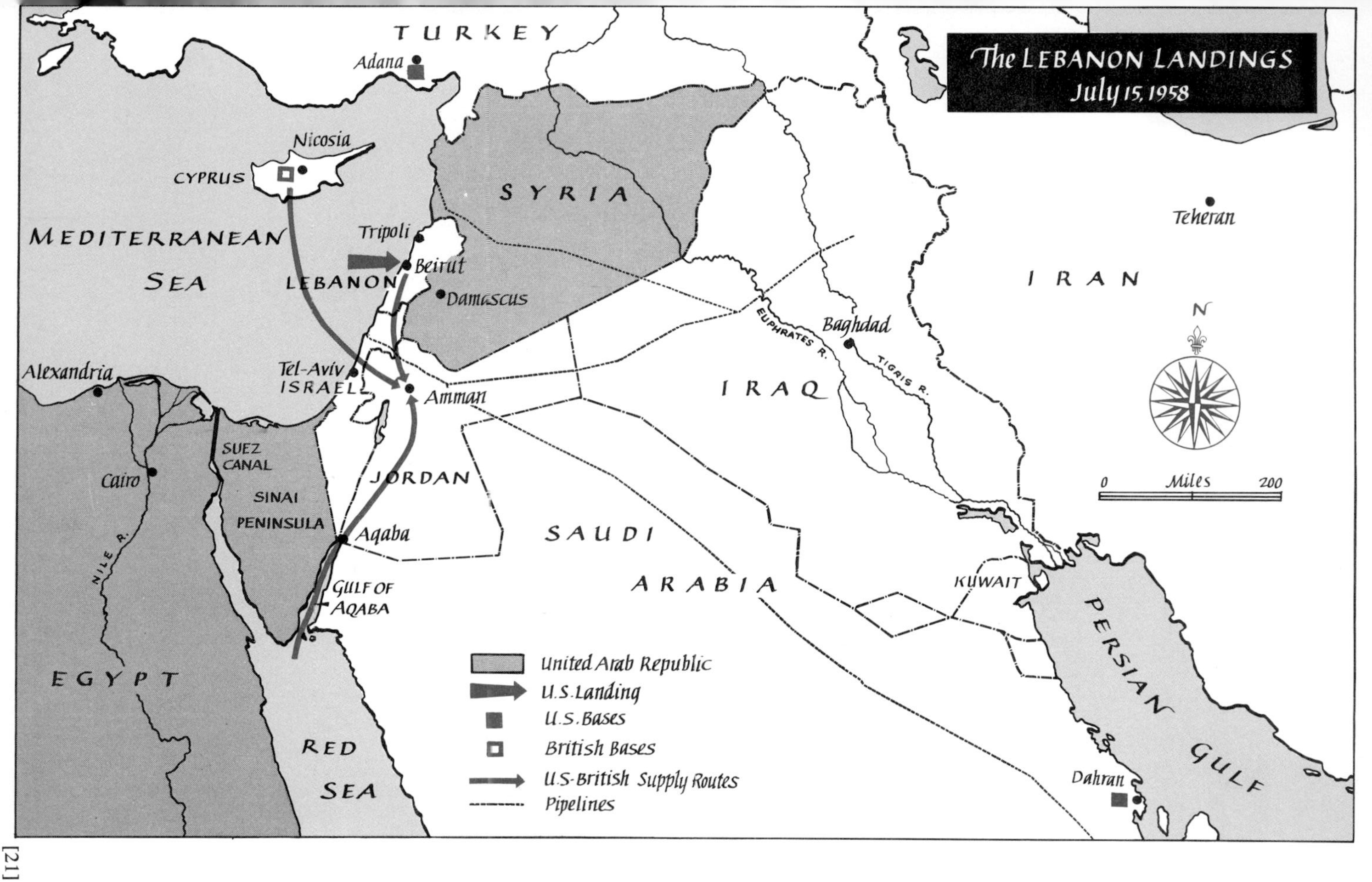
The LEBANON LANDINGS
July 15, 1958
TURKEY
Adana
Nicosia
CYPRUS
SYRIA
MEDITERRANEAN
SEA
Tripoli
Beirut
LEBANON
Damascus
Teheran
IRAN
N
Baghdad
EUPHRATES R.
TIGRIS R.
Alexandria
Tel-Aviv
ISRAEL
Amman
IRAQ
SUEZ
CANAL
Cairo
JORDAN
0
Miles
200
SINAI
PENINSULA
Aqaba
SAUDI
ARABIA
NILE R.
GULF OF
AQABA
KUWAIT
PERSIAN
GULF
United Arab Republic
U.S. Landing
U.S. Bases
British Bases
U.S.-British Supply Routes
Pipelines
EGYPT
RED
SEA
Dahran

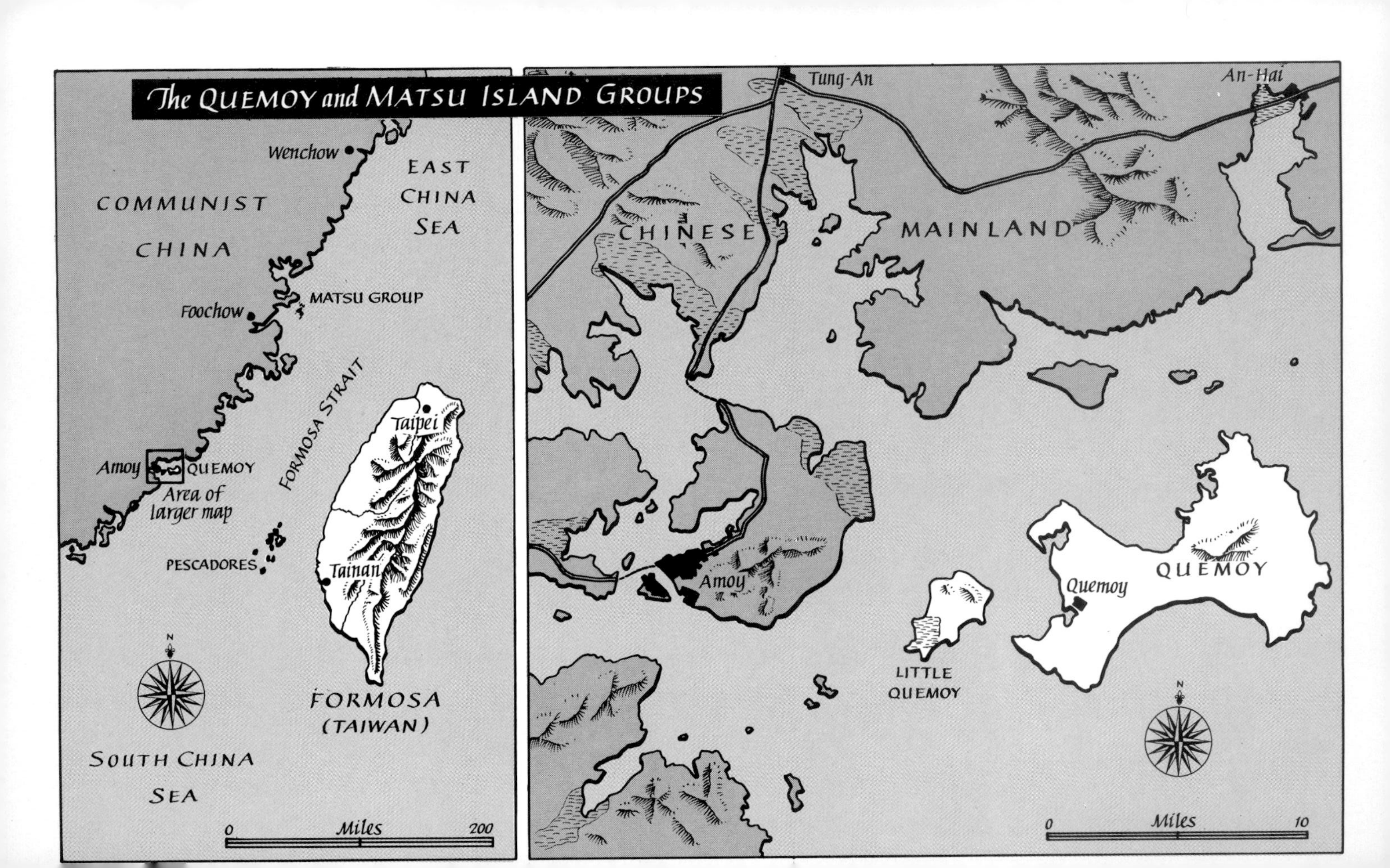
The QUEMOY and MATSU ISLAND GROUPS
Wenchow
EAST CHINA SEA
COMMUNIST CHINA
MATSU GROUP
Foochow
FORMOSA STRAIT
Taipei
Amoy
QUEMOY
Area of larger map
PESCADORES
Tainan
N
FORMOSA (TAIWAN)
SOUTH CHINA SEA
0
Miles
200
Tung-An
An-Hai
CHINESE
MAINLAND
Amoy
Quemoy
QUEMOY
LITTLE QUEMOY
N
0
Miles
10

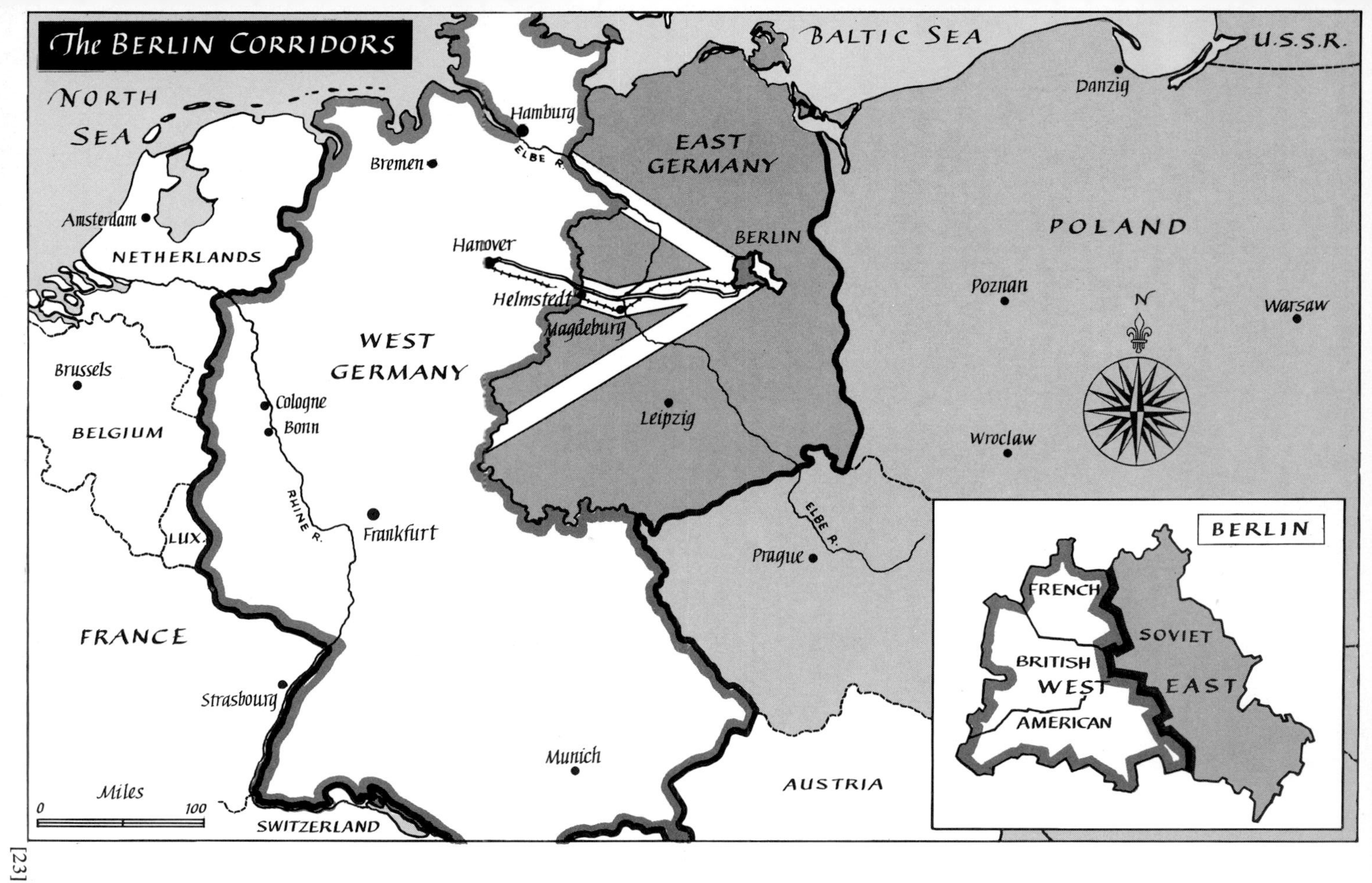
The Berlin Corridors
North Sea
Baltic Sea
U.S.S.R.
Danzig
Hamburg
Elbe R.
Bremen
East Germany
Amsterdam
Netherlands
Berlin
Poland
Hanover
Helmstedt
Magdeburg
Poznan
Warsaw
N
West Germany
Brussels
Cologne
Bonn
Belgium
Leipzig
Wroclaw
Rhine R.
Lux.
Frankfurt
Elbe R.
Prague
Berlin
French
Soviet
British
West
East
American
France
Strasbourg
Munich
Austria
Miles
0
100
Switzerland

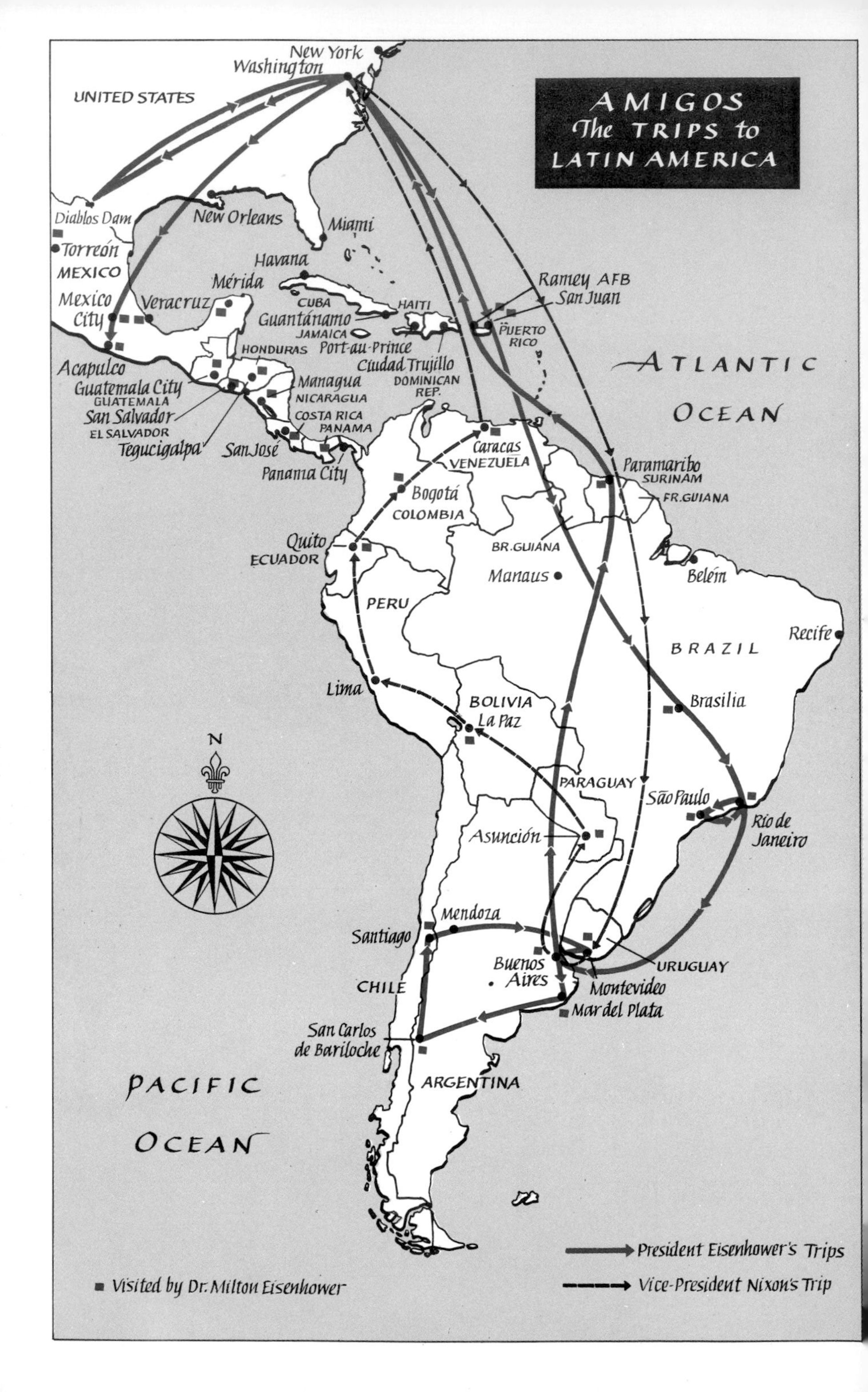

AMIGOS
The TRIPS to
LATIN AMERICA
New York
Washington
UNITED STATES
Diablos Dam
New Orleans
Miami
Torreón
MEXICO
Havana
Mérida
Mexico City
Veracruz
CUBA
Guantánamo
JAMAICA
HAITI
Port-au-Prince
Ciudad Trujillo
DOMINICAN REP.
Ramey AFB
San Juan
PUERTO RICO
Acapulco
HONDURAS
Guatemala City
GUATEMALA
San Salvador
EL SALVADOR
Tegucigalpa
Managua
NICARAGUA
COSTA RICA
PANAMA
San José
Panama City
ATLANTIC
OCEAN
Caracas
VENEZUELA
Paramaribo
SURINAM
FR.GUIANA
Bogotá
COLOMBIA
BR.GUIANA
Quito
ECUADOR
Manaus
Belém
PERU
Recife
BRAZIL
Lima
BOLIVIA
La Paz
Brasilia
PARAGUAY
São Paulo
Rio de Janeiro
Asunción
N
Mendoza
Santiago
Buenos Aires
URUGUAY
Montevideo
Mar del Plata
CHILE
San Carlos de Bariloche
ARGENTINA
PACIFIC
OCEAN
President Eisenhower's Trips
Vice-President Nixon's Trip
Visited by Dr. Milton Eisenhower

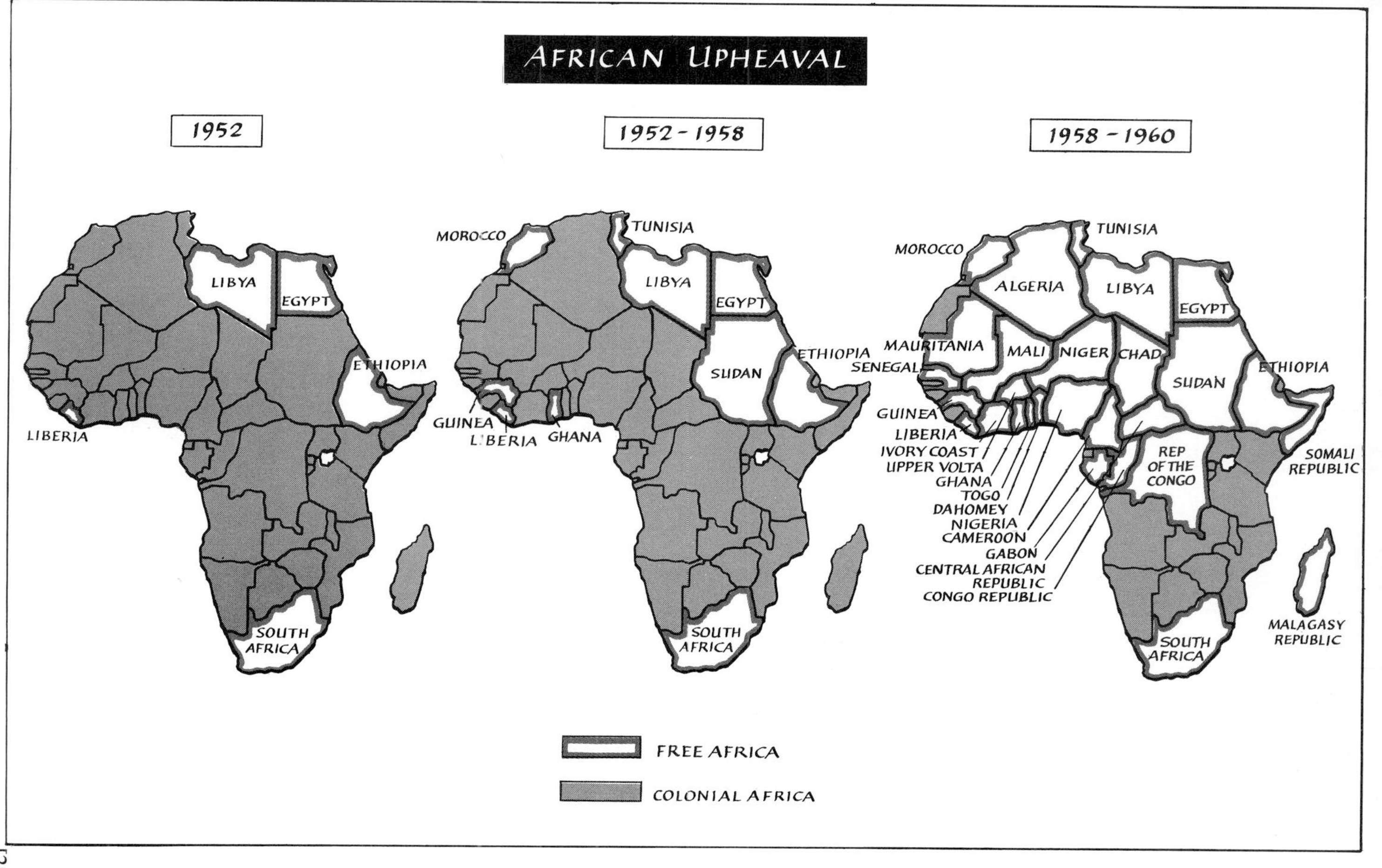
AFRICAN UPHEAVAL
1952
LIBYA
EGYPT
ETHIOPIA
LIBERIA
SOUTH AFRICA
1952 - 1958
MOROCCO
TUNISIA
LIBYA
EGYPT
SUDAN
ETHIOPIA
GUINEA
LIBERIA
GHANA
SOUTH AFRICA
1958 - 1960
MOROCCO
TUNISIA
ALGERIA
LIBYA
EGYPT
MAURITANIA
MALI
NIGER
CHAD
SUDAN
ETHIOPIA
SENEGAL
GUINEA
LIBERIA
IVORY COAST
UPPER VOLTA
GHANA
TOGO
DAHOMEY
NIGERIA
CAMEROON
GABON
CENTRAL AFRICAN REPUBLIC
CONGO REPUBLIC
REP OF THE CONGO
SOMALI REPUBLIC
MALAGASY REPUBLIC
SOUTH AFRICA
FREE AFRICA
COLONIAL AFRICA

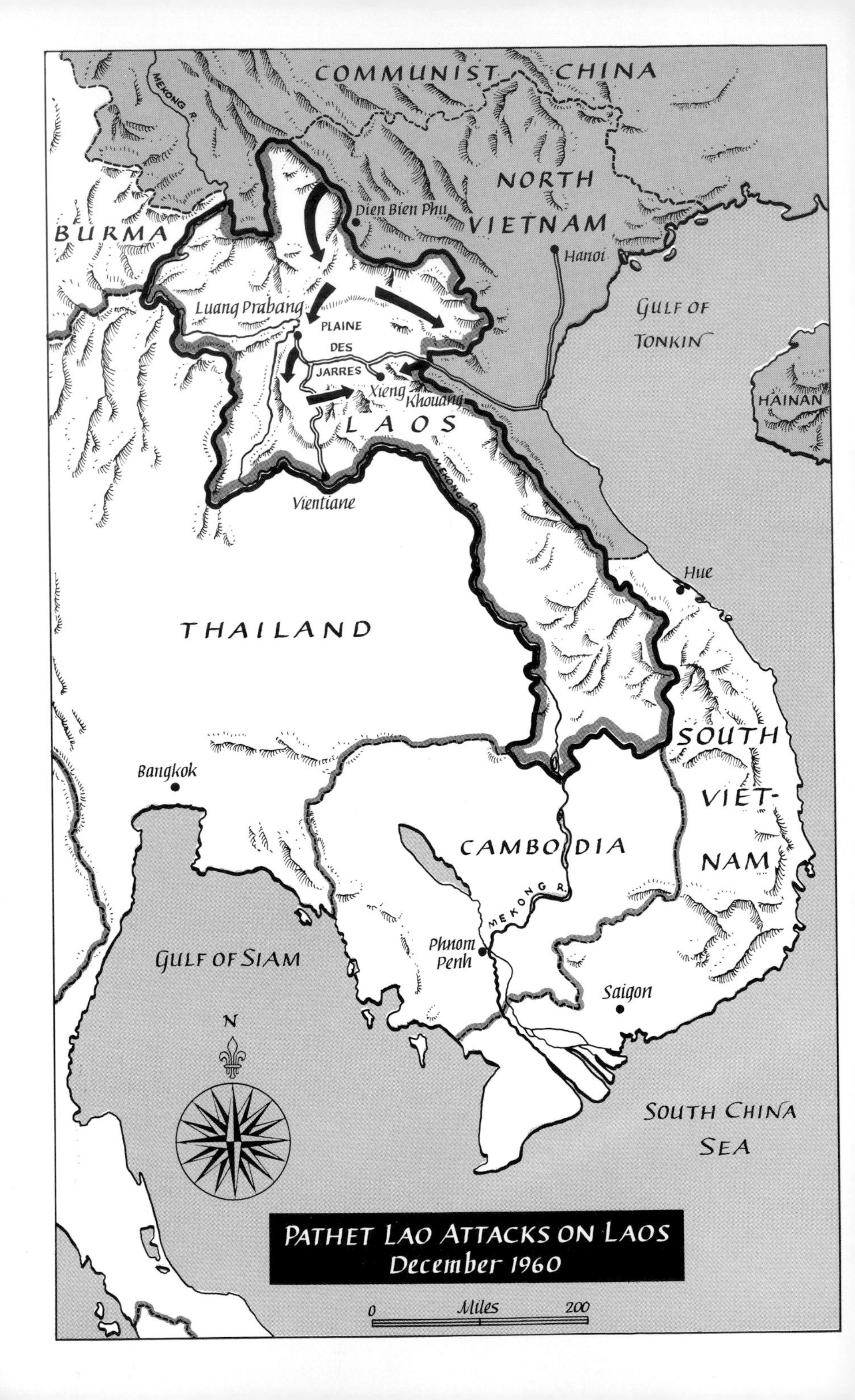
COMMUNIST CHINA
MEKONG R.
NORTH
VIETNAM
Dien Bien Phu
BURMA
Hanoi
Luang Prabang
PLAINE
DES
JARRES
Xieng
Khouang
GULF OF
TONKIN
HAINAN
LAOS
MEKONG R.
Vientiane
Hue
THAILAND
SOUTH
VIET-
NAM
Bangkok
CAMBODIA
MEKONG R.
Phnom
Penh
Saigon
GULF OF SIAM
N
SOUTH CHINA
SEA
PATHET LAO ATTACKS ON LAOS
December 1960
0
Miles
200

The Brandenburg Gate, with Communist East Berlin beyond

"I would be willing to study the possibility of creating a free city, I said, if it included *all of Berlin,* East and West."

"The physical and psychological condition of West Berlin had changed dramatically in the decade since the blockade....This thriving industrial metropolis was showing to the world, and to the East Germans in particular, the contrast between the Communist and free ways of life."

"His calm approach, his comprehension of the important factors in every problem, his firm conclusions, and his moral courage were majestic."

Secretary of State
John Foster Dulles

"Adams had little skill for solidifying his relations with politicians except with those who could see beneath his craggy exterior to the true worth of the man."

Sherman Adams,
Assistant to
the President

epresentative Joseph Martin and
nator William Knowland

Representative Charles Halleck
and Senator Everett Dirksen

"During 1958 and 1959 and with the election of 1960 rumbling beyond the horizon, Republicans and Democrats fought with more than normal intensity. Four main engagements were the congressional elections of 1958, the battle of the budget of 1959, the short and confused skirmish over the nomination of Clare Boothe Luce, and the disgraceful fight against confirming Lewis Strauss as Secretary of Commerce."

are Boothe Luce,
nbassador to Italy

Admiral Lewis L. Strauss, Chairman, AEC;
Secretary of Commerce

"With the assurance of the veteran that he was, [Secretary Christian A. Herter] stepped into the experiences ahead that were to be enough to frustrate and exasperate any man, even one with his wisdom and patience."

Premier Nikita Khrushchev and Vice President Richard Nixon continue their debate in front of a model kitchen. Anastas I. Mikoyan, First Deputy Premier, is shown between them; Leonid Brezhnev, Party Secretary, far right

"At Sokolniki Park, where the Vice President opened the U. S. Exhibition, Khrushchev deliberately took advantage of what was supposed to be a purely ceremonial occasion to attack both Dick and the United States. But the Vice President met him point by point."

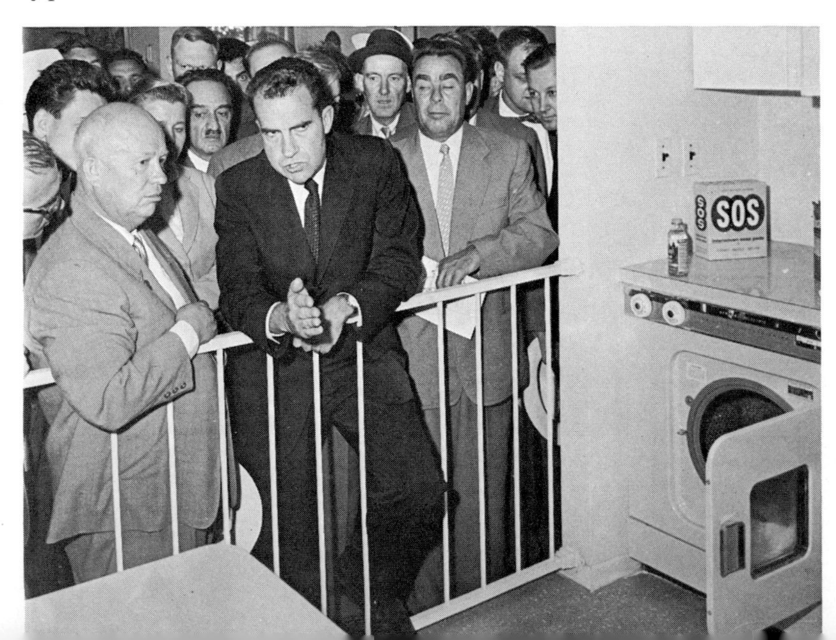

PERSONAL DIPLOMACY

"...The search for some break, some avenue of approach, as yet unexplored."

"We arrived at 6:30 P.M., just at dusk and the ceremonies at the airport were impressive... the exchange of greetings with Chancellor Adenauer was short, and soon the two of us were in an open car en route to the American Embassy."

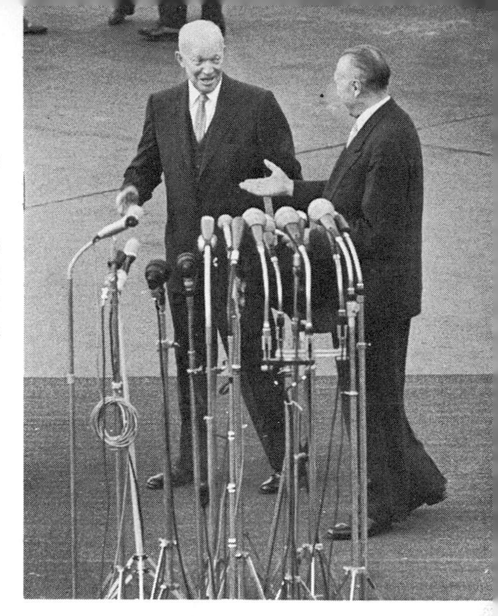

Prince Philip, Princess Anne, President Eisenhower, Queen Elizabeth at Balmoral Castle, Scotland

"One quality of the Royal Family that has always intrigued me is the informality which prevails when its members are at home among themselves, particularly at Balmoral."

President Charles de Gaulle elcomes President Eisenhower to Rambouillet Castle

"I at once sensed important changes that had occurred since I had last seen him.... All in all, he now appeared a more benign, less forbidding individual than the fiery division commander who had made himself the symbol of French resistance in World War II."

PERSONAL DIPLOMACY

"As I once told the legislative leaders, I wanted to make 'one great personal effort, before leaving office, to soften up the Soviet leader even a little bit. Except for the Austrian peace treaty,' I said, 'we haven't made a chip in the granite in seven years,' even though we had blocked all their forays against the Free World."

Meeting at Andrews Air Force Base, September 15, 1959, before the Camp David talks

"Cabot Lodge, who had undergone an ordeal in keeping up with our energetic and unpredictable visitor, told me in detail of Khrushchev's activities. They would, he remarked, fill a book. This much could be said: Khrushchev responded vigorously to every incident."

CHAPTER XV

John Foster Dulles

It is by presence of mind in untried emergencies that the native metal of a man is tested.

—*James Russell Lowell*

Now he belongs to the ages.

—*Edwin M. Stanton* (*of Lincoln*)

ON Sunday, May 24, 1959, it was my sad duty to write an announcement which began:

John Foster Dulles is dead.

A lifetime of labor for world peace has ended. His countrymen and all who believe in justice and the rule of law grieve at the passing from the earthly scene of one of the truly great men of our time.

Throughout his life, and particularly during his eventful six years as Secretary of State, his courage, his wisdom, and his friendly understanding were devoted to bettering relations among nations. He was a foe only to tyranny.

Because he believed in the dignity of men and in their brotherhood under God, he was an ardent supporter of their deepest hopes and aspirations. From his life and work, humanity will, in the years to come, gain renewed inspiration to work ever harder for the attainment of the goal of peace with justice. In the pursuit of that goal, he ignored every personal cost and sacrifice, however great.

We, who were privileged to work with him, have lost a dear and close friend as all Americans have lost a champion of freedom. United, we extend to Mrs. Dulles, to her children and to all members of the Dulles family our prayers and deepest sympathy, and the assurance that in our memories will live affection, respect, and admiration for John Foster Dulles.

He was born in Washington, D.C., on February 25, 1888. The year 1907, when he was only nineteen, saw his first diplomatic service in the peace conference at The Hague. He chose law as his profession, specializing in its international phases. His reputation as an authority was soon established, and as a very young man he served as an adviser to President Wilson at the 1919 Paris Peace Conference, as well as a member of the Reparations Commission and the Supreme Economic Council. From the start, he never lost his consuming interest in diplomacy and, as a highly regarded international lawyer in his more mature years, he was from time to time drafted for specific State Department tasks. For him these were both agreeable and exciting opportunities for, as a grandson of one Secretary of State and the nephew of another, he had developed from boyhood a high regard and abiding respect for the office and the department in which he was one day to serve so brilliantly.

In 1945 he was a member of the United States delegation at the initial United Nations meeting in San Francisco; it was his task to participate in drawing up the documents for the UN organization. Thereafter, he was rarely absent from international conferences convened to further human betterment and universal peace.

From 1949 to 1950 he served as an interim United States senator from New York, having been appointed by Governor Thomas E. Dewey to fill the unexpired term of Robert F. Wagner, Sr.

In 1950–51, as an ambassador-at-large, he was given the mission of devising a peace treaty with Japan. In this work he visited many nations in Asia and Europe. In the course of this assignment the high officials of the U.S.S.R. missed no opportunity to denounce and vilify his efforts. Nevertheless, his work was climaxed in September of that year by the signing of the treaty at San Francisco by forty-eight non-Communist nations. He resigned from the State Department in the spring of 1952, and as the time of the Republican nominating convention approached was chosen to write the foreign policy plank in its platform.

When I was elected to the Presidency that November, I promptly named him as Secretary of State-designate. Foster and I had met four years earlier, but I had known him before my election to the Presidency through reading his articles and speeches, particularly those of the postwar years, and through the reports of friends such as Governor Dewey, General Marshall, and others. From 1952 onward our relationship ripened into one of deep personal friendship and close collaboration in the work of conducting the foreign relations of the United States.

* * *

Soon after my first inauguration, Foster sought my approval of what he called "a few guideposts for formulating and implementing a sound foreign policy." Some of these were by no means new, but it was characteristic of Foster, who took nothing for granted, that he should want to make certain of our common understanding of basic considerations as we attacked the many problems we would certainly encounter in the years ahead.

Quite naturally we agreed that a determined pursuit of peace with justice should be, as indeed it always had been, the foremost objective of the American government. Such an objective in the world situation of the early 1950s could be reasonably pursued, we knew, only if the United States spoke from a position of power. The first guidepost was, then, to make certain always that our strength was equal to the most strenuous demand that could be made upon it. Without a fully satisfactory military position—one that would compel the respect of every nation in the world, including the Communists—we thought that the pursuit of peace would be merely an exercise in futility.

But the needed power would have to comprehend not only military strength, the age-old single criterion of civilizations long since reduced to rubble, but moral and economic strength as well. Moral strength in a free nation could be sustained only with a public understanding of America's mission in the world. The Secretary believed that every kind of educational program should be pursued to assure clear comprehension of the importance of the "American mission" and its problems. To assist in this educational process, he felt, was one of the duties of every governmental official carrying responsibilities in foreign affairs.

We emphasized economic strength, not merely because an adequate military force could be developed, improved, and indefinitely supported only with a vigorous and highly developed economy, but also because there was clearly laid upon us, if we were to maintain the peace, the responsibility of assisting, often at much expense to ourselves, impoverished peoples to attain gradually rising standards of living. Squalor and starvation worked to the advantage of Communist ambitions. Only as human standards rose could there be real hope for the further development of a peaceful and prosperous Free World.

To promote a just peace and the rule of law, Foster believed that we should strengthen the United Nations. Here, an obstacle, practically insurmountable, would be encountered in the veto power exercised by the Soviets in the Security Council of the United Nations. Nevertheless, in his six years as Secretary of State, Foster never ceased trying to bring about some kind of worthwhile improvement in the world organization that would lessen the possibility of war and make feasible a degree of disarmament.

If we were to be helpful in transforming the cold war into something better than a temporary truce, Foster believed that the firmness of our purpose to assist any free nation seeking our cooperation in defending itself against Communist penetration should be understood throughout the world. Whenever a crisis of this kind impended, our own intentions should be announced at the earliest possible moment. He was convinced that the Korean War would never have started if the Communists had known in advance that the United States would defend that country with our troops and with those of our allies that could be mobilized.

Still another purpose of our global policy was the development of a ring of strong and binding alliances with other nations dedicated to freedom.[1] He believed that forging these links was necessary, especially to protect those weaker nations around the Eurasian land mass that were directly exposed to the Communists. As far back as 1947, President Truman had announced the American determination to support Turkey and Greece in opposing Communist violation of their borders, and had obtained from the Congress resources to implement this policy. These arrangements, while necessary and suited to the particular problem, were not a part of a permanent network of defensive alliances such as Foster visualized. In 1949, the North Atlantic Treaty Organization had been authorized by the Brussels Treaty, and the outbreak of the Korean War in 1950 had stimulated the members of NATO to mobilize strength for their collective security. The key to NATO was the agreement that an attack upon any one of the member nations would be considered an attack upon the others. Foster believed that this kind of alliance could be and should be extended into other areas.

One of the ensuing advantages that would develop, he thought, was better morale in the exposed areas, and a readiness on the part of each to take a more definite stand against an invasion of its rights or territory. In the event of emergency, such treaties would permit without further negotiation a rapid shift of American military strength to assist in the defense of the threatened area. As a result, during my administration, NATO was extended to include West Germany; the Southeast Asia Treaty Organization was established; and the Central Treaty Organization—CENTO, previously the Baghdad Pact—(which the United States supported but was not a member of—was created. Bilateral arrangements for mutual security were made with Japan, Korea, and Formosa. The net result was that in the aggregate, these treaties committed the United States to support the defense of almost every free area that was directly facing the Sino-Soviet complex.

These accomplishments did not guarantee the universal peace settle-

[1] Map, "The Ring of United States Alliances," appears on the front endpapers of this volume.

ment which Foster dreamed of, but they stood as a monument to a linking of trust and strength that would prevent the step-by-step deterioration of the world during his years in office—and beyond.

Though Foster was a man of great intellect and stature, he was a perfect advocate not of the perfect or the theoretical best but of the possible. He was called legalistic, arrogant, sanctimonious, and arbitrary—but such descriptions never occurred to those who knew Foster Dulles as I did. It was said also that he sought not only to be influential in the conduct of foreign affairs, but to be responsible only to his own convictions and inclinations. What his critics did not know was that he was more emphatic than they in his insistence that ultimate and personal responsibility for all major decisions in the field of foreign relations belonged exclusively to the President, an attitude he meticulously maintained throughout our service together. He would not deliver an important speech or statement until after I had read, edited, and approved it; he guarded constantly against the possibility that any misunderstanding could arise between us. It was the mutual trust and understanding, thus engendered, that enabled me, with complete confidence, to delegate to him an unusual degree of flexibility as my representative in international conferences, well knowing that he would not in the slightest degree operate outside the limits previously agreed between us. The association was particularly gratifying to me because of the easy partnership we developed in searching for the answer to any complex problem. But although behind closed doors we worked as partners, he in all our conversations lived his conviction that he was the adviser, recognizing that the final decision had to be mine.

Foster had a fine sense of humor, but he was nevertheless all business when there was business to be discussed. For this reason he was sometimes considered by strangers as abrupt, even brusque. This often made him a target for the venom of smaller men, especially anyone who felt slighted by his serious, almost sharp form of address. This circumstance partially distorted the average citizen's picture of Foster, who, in truth, was filled with human kindness and understanding.

Foster was far from being the only strong personality habitually at my conference table, and when his opinions brushed against another's there were always sparks to brighten the moment. As an example, at a meeting dealing with a volatile situation in the Middle East, an exchange between Secretary Dulles and Admiral Radford brought out the following remarks in rapid order:

The Secretary remarked that certain items in the preparations just announced with certain plans which its Joint Chiefs of Staff had recently made with our ally, Britain, "were news to me. The State Department would like to know more about such plans."

Admiral Radford replied: "Military plans for the area could be more specific if the Department of State would tell the Joint Chiefs what was likely to happen in the Middle East."

"I have no idea what the military plans for the Middle East are," Foster retorted. "If I knew in advance what our capabilities were, it would help a great deal."

"I wonder whether details could help the State Department," Radford countered.

"Your comments at this meeting have helped me," the Secretary said, his tone not exactly all gratitude.

When I suggested that the Joint Chiefs prepare a memorandum for the State Department, the Admiral offered to brief the Secretary instead.

To which I facetiously added: "*I* have a little curiosity in this matter too."

But we all knew (and this applied to every principal member of the administration) that the government could not only tolerate disagreement, but needed it. These differences always involved issues and courses of action and, of course, never became personal.

One trait I can recall which was not among his most winning was that Foster, having explained something once, was apt to forget that he had and, within a day or so, tell it over again. At least it showed consistency and it is, in any event, a not uncommon fault.

Foster was the first Secretary of State to adopt on a major scale the practice of flying personally to the trouble spots of the world instead of depending almost exclusively on letters, cables, and messages. In the earliest days of my administration he undertook an extended visit to the Middle East and it has always been my impression that he then found the distinct advantage, from his standpoint at least, of seeing situations for himself, reporting his findings to me daily. During our six years together there were only a handful of days when, either abroad or at home, he did not communicate to me the essentials of his activities and the results of his work.

In nearly all his trips, he was accompanied by his devoted wife, Janet. Without her, I do not believe he could have undertaken and maintained the schedule of travel and work that amazed his associates and often led me to ask him to "Slow down, take it easy."

One trip was particularly difficult. In late 1958 (less than a year before he died), he went to Rome, heading a delegation to represent me at the funeral of Pope Pius XII. While there he heard that the critical situation in Formosa was seemingly growing worse. The only suitable aircraft available in Rome for an immediate journey was an Air Force jet tanker, a wonderful plane for speed and range but not for passenger comfort. The bleak prospect of riding halfway around the world in an outsize plane, devoid of beds, or even chairs, save for a couple of cots and small seats fastened to a vast, dim, and drafty deck, did not deter Foster in the least.[2]

His favorite retreat was Duck Island, a tiny islet he owned in Lake Erie. He and Janet, whenever opportunity arose, took off to the island, where they lived in complete isolation, without household staff and normally without visitors. He gloried in chopping firewood and performing all the manual chores required for living in what was hardly more than a small wilderness.

I have no reason to believe that his arduous and continuous efforts to achieve better understanding among nations contributed to his untimely death. But in the last days of his illness he constantly gave to us all a final shining example of courage, fortitude, and dedication. From the time of his first operation, in 1956, he insisted upon knowing the exact character of his disease and his chances of survival. Even with this knowledge, he continued his work without thought of self; he had to be pointedly reminded whenever the time came for another checkup at the hospital.

* * *

The dialogues between John Foster Dulles and me were by no means limited to official meetings, memoranda, and phone calls. We developed between ourselves a habit that, for me at least, proved stimulating and satisfying.

Foster's favorite time for coming to my office, of all the many sessions, was toward evening, around six o'clock. Then, after completing the day's business, we would engage in more general conversation. We would lean back in our chairs, he in his accustomed place to the left of the desk, and the two of us would, in a somewhat philosophical vein, talk about and try to analyze the broader aspects of the world drama we saw unfolding. We turned away for the moment from day-by-day problems, concrete or abstruse and absorbing as they were. Where was the Free World going? Will the trend toward incentive payments in Russia lead it

[2] Having myself made a short trip in an identical plane I can admire all the more the sense of duty and Spartan acceptance of prolonged inconvenience and discomfort that made such a trip routine for Foster and Janet Dulles.

eventually away from Communism to something akin to competitive enterprise? Was the termination of the cold war a slow matter of generations or might the Soviet Union one day, seeing the futility of its dreams of conquest, suddenly reverse its policy? Where will the world be in fifty years if the population explosion is not checked? There was no limit to the subjects that entered our conversations.

One of the speculations that Foster returned to over and over was the motivation behind the decisions of the men in the Kremlin. As the world knows, the West—and particularly the United States—has presented a number of sincere proposals which, if accepted by the Soviets, would do much to reduce the amounts and costs of armaments, relieve anxieties in the world, and provide unprecedented opportunities for improving the quality of life in less developed nations. Starting with the Baruch Plan of 1947, which would have, at a time when our nation possessed a monopoly in atomic bombs, placed the entire development of the nuclear science in the hands of an international agency, and going on through the long list of peaceful and eminently fair proposals for peaceful progress the United States had made, our best efforts had been flatly rejected by the Soviets. "Why?" Foster would ask, "Why?"

No answer was to be found merely in the personal ambitions of dictators; neither could conflicting ideologies be solely blamed, because they would not have prevented reasonable men from reaching agreements where results would be to the advantage of both. Slavic temperament provided no answer: there were many instances in the past to prove the conciliatory capacities of educated Russians. To be sure, one element was the ideological gulf between a government which is atheistic and one which is religiously based. All our laws are rooted in values very different from the Soviets'. For example, we speak of "good faith"; they believe, as part of their creed, in any form of deceit and treachery which advances the cause of Communist domination. Foster was intensely aware of this ideological difference. In all our dealings with the Kremlin, we concluded that only a pragmatic approach was useful.

Nevertheless we came early to the conclusion that the Soviets would not, save under the most extreme provocation, risk a global nuclear war. They might undertake, as in the past, probes that would alarm populations and some governments, but would never carry such activities to the point where all-out retaliation would be the only response a self-respecting nation could take.

In the reasoning behind this conviction, Foster frequently referred to two vulnerable points that we deemed particularly important. The first was that dictatorships, by their nature, always have a narrow base of popular support; in a political sense their vulnerability to modern destructive attack is greater than in the case of people occupying a large geographical area and practicing self-government. In the U.S.S.R. the entire Communist Party numbers only a few million out of over two hundred million, and the Party's solidly authoritative heads are few. These leaders could not fail to fear that even a partial political paralysis under attack could easily cause not only mammoth casualties but general bewilderment among the survivors, possibly open revolution.

The other factor in the Soviet situation that seemed to us a deterrent to reckless action on their part was their feverish effort to attain maximum industrialization. Soviet leaders must have realized that the industrial complexes they were striving to develop, including their large hydroelectric developments, would be highly vulnerable to attack, and their destruction could have incalculable effects on their economy. Therefore we believed that in spite of Soviet bluster, boasts, and often repeated threats, their definite progress in building an organized and productive society provided still one more well-founded reason for their reluctance to provoke global nuclear war.

No matter what differences in culture and tradition, values or language, the Russian leaders were human beings, and they wanted to remain alive. In the early weeks of my administration, when we decided, through indirect channels, to warn the Communists that either a reasonable armistice would be promptly achieved in Korea or we would no longer be bound by formerly understood limits regarding types of weapons and geographical boundaries of the battle zone, we did so on these basic conclusions as to the Soviet situation and Soviet intentions.

It was in such convictions, also, that we took our firm position in the Formosa Strait, warned the Soviets when they threatened to intervene with force to support Egypt in the 1956 Suez crisis, later sent troops at the request of President Chamoun and against Communist opposition, to Lebanon, and stood visibly ready to defend Western rights in Berlin. We knew that the Soviets would strive to keep the Free World off balance and stretch tensions to the breaking point—but Soviet bombast was not the same as Soviet bombs.

We kept a sharp eye on the Red Chinese for many reasons. For one thing, the Chinese are smart people. For another, they are tremendous in number, and their leaders seem absolutely indifferent to the prospect of losing millions of people. Among Western statesmen, human life is weighed carefully—to understate our attitude. Not only in political life, but in the military, our thought processes are enormously at variance with Communist values. Marshal Zhukov and I once discussed methods of getting through a mine field, of clearing a path. "Why," he said, "you just march them through!" In a situation like Red China's, where industry is needed more than people, a truck or a tractor can seem more important than a man.

We did not see any new African countries looming large in our time—that is, large to the point of attaining full, mature power. But we could see all of them developing. There were promising leaders in some nations and a number of large cities throughout the continent, but there was not the experience or the underlying fabric of productivity to make nations great and prosperous and there probably would not be for decades.

Foster was hopeful about the possibilities of really helping the Latin Americans even though we recognized the likelihood that in solving their immense difficulties they would more than likely have to face a struggle over birth control. He cared deeply about Latin America, but our most pressing problems arose initially in areas which were geographically closer to Russia and China—for example Iran, Korea, and Formosa—and quite possibly his and our concern did not register sufficiently.

We thought that in the long run, Communism, because it was not attuned to the best in human nature, was doomed to destruction or, at the very least, major modification. For decades, perhaps a century or two, freedom and Communism might live in the same world in some form of co-existence. But we felt that empires and ill-conceived governmental systems would probably not endure so long as in the past; the pace of almost everything had accelerated, and civilizations would rise and fall in a comparable tempo. The eventual free flow of information, bringing in its wake a dawning awareness within the Communist world that there were other, better ways of life, would one day in a worldwide open society bring about the mutual understanding and the acceptance of global cooperation essential to the establishment of peace with justice for mankind.

At home, Foster displayed an abiding interest in our political system. He often observed that the basic theory of government for, of, and by the people is easy to understand. It was less easy to see why a supposedly literate and informed citizenry and their elected representatives would abuse their own rights and fail in their own responsibilities in the practice of self-government.

One evening Foster mentioned that a Republican senator had flatly told him that if he, Foster, failed to recommend for appointment to an ambassadorial post an individual the senator favored, the senator himself would not thereafter support the foreign policies of the United States. This was a shocking sort of thing and one that disturbed Foster mightily. In it he saw definite evidence that even some of our highest officials of government were motivated by such narrow and sometimes selfish purposes that the successful functioning of self-government, as established by our forebears, was getting more and more unlikely.

Why would pressure groups, each organized to seek special and often obviously unjustified favors from government, fail to acknowledge that spreading and intensification of this practice could eventually wreck the free institutions of our nation?

Above all "Why," he would ask—"why would any man elected to high office sell his soul to the selfish purpose of pecuniary gain or to the mere hope of re-election when already he had achieved the honor of selection by his fellow citizens to represent them?"

"Of course," Foster would say, "anyone can answer, 'human nature' to excuse shortsighted actions of the selfish and the vain. But many Americans have given us shining examples of selflessness, men living and dead, who have commanded our respect and admiration. Does not democracy presuppose that anyone would prefer to be remembered in history because of loyalty and devotion to the nation rather than because he became rich, or because he was elected by a well-controlled political machinery for twenty congressional terms?" He would recall many Americans who had placed national service first: for example, George Washington, John Quincy Adams, Abraham Lincoln, John Marshall, George Marshall, Daniel Webster, Woodrow Wilson, Benjamin Franklin, John Adams, Henry Clay, Thomas Jefferson, Robert Taft, Arthur Vandenberg. He now belongs to that list.

Foster had read and pondered deeply. He was fully aware of the warnings found in the words of De Tocqueville and Macaulay respecting the pitfalls inherent in a system of popular government. Time and again he repeated, "Representative government is still on trial."

One circumstance constantly irritated him, at times causing him to speak explosively. "I spend at least a fourth of my time testifying before the congressional committees," he would say, "and the galling thing is that much of my time there is wasted at the very moment I have so many other things I must do." Among the time-consuming appearances before congressional committees were those dealing with State Department appropriations. One year Foster determined to change the routine: Instead of sitting through weeks of detailed hearings, he would make a broad opening statement on the work and needs of the Department and then turn over to the Under Secretary the task of following and coordinating the testimony of Assistant Secretaries and Bureau Chiefs. When the Secretary failed to put in an appearance at the Appropriations subcommittee the day following his opening testimony, the chairman of the subcommittee phoned him and snapped, "Mr. Secretary, my subcommittee has just reduced the budget for your immediate office by 50 per cent; if you wish to restore the original figure I'd suggest you come back here and stay throughout our hearings." Angry but realistic, Foster went back.

* * *

But these interludes never interrupted the workings of his remarkable mind; rather they were a part of his whole life. Without stop his mind met, absorbed, and digested facts and concepts in the vast fields of interest to which his life was devoted. He talked about *The Federalist Papers* as though he had begun their study in kindergarten. His dissertation to me, one day, on the unwisdom of the Bricker amendment was almost overpowering in its conviction that the adoption of that proposal could do nothing less than eventually wreck the Constitution and our nation.

And when engrossed in any problem of foreign affairs, and particularly when we were going through anxious periods, he was a figure to inspire confidence in his associates. His calm approach, his comprehension of the important factors in every problem, his firm conclusions, and his moral courage were majestic.

In dealings with subordinates he was always anxious for them to understand the broad reasoning behind specific policies. Here are excerpts from a cable he sent to Douglas Dillon, our ambassador to France, on October 4, 1956:

> The Western European nations have been preserving their political divisions which keep them weak, partly because they have felt that they could afford this luxury so long as they had more or less a blank check on the U.S. for economic, military, and political support everywhere in the world. This Suez matter is bringing into the open the fact that they cannot count upon us outside the North Atlantic Treaty area automatically and without the exercise of our independent judgment. Under those circumstances they feel weak and frustrated.
>
> I believe that their answer is to be found in increased European unity so that they will have together the strength which they need to be a powerful force in the world comparable to that of the Soviet Union and the United States, and more able to carry out their own policies. This unity movement is taking on new strength and is, I think, doing so largely because the European countries are increasingly aware that they cannot count unreservedly upon U.S. support everywhere.
>
> Obviously we do not want anti-Americanism, but I do not think that we can, or indeed that we should, try to buy pro-American sentiment by leading the Western European countries to feel that we will blindly support them in any course which they may wish to pursue.

> . . . the historical and cultural ties which bind the British, French and ourselves so deeply together shall of course always lead us to seek to work together and to regard any sharp difference as a grave misfortune. . . .

Foster feared the effects of making national riches our major goal. He felt we were too eager for soft living, for living without rising to our responsibilities. Occasionally he would hint that perhaps the Communist challenge offered the West an unintended benefit by counteracting the potentially damaging effects of affluence among our citizenry. Not only change but struggle is the rule and the joy of life. Possibly human beings would not be as happy without something to fight for—peacefully.

Essentially he was an optimist. At the end of a talk about our form of government and its future, he would often get up, go to the door, and just before leaving turn and chuckle: "Well, it's served us pretty well for two centuries, I guess it will keep on doing so."

In countless ways there were revealed his terse candor, his knowledge, the largeness of his spirit. It is no wonder that when he was called from among us his closest associates and friends felt an overpowering loss, a gap that could never completely be filled.

CHAPTER XVI

Principally Politics

Liberty exists in proportion to wholesome restraint.

—*Daniel Webster*

DURING 1958 and 1959 and with the election of 1960 rumbling beyond the horizon, Republicans and Democrats fought with more than normal intensity. Four main engagements were the congressional elections of 1958, the battle of the budget of 1959, the short and confused skirmish over the nomination of Clare Boothe Luce, and the disgraceful fight against confirming Lewis Strauss as Secretary of Commerce.

In the first of these, the Republicans suffered a resounding defeat. When the votees were counted in November 1958, Democrats outnumbered Republicans in both Senate and House by nearly two to one. In gubernatorial races, 26 Democrats won, bringing their national total to 35 and leaving the Republicans with 14. With these results came a dubious distinction: I became the first President in American history to face three successive Congresses in which the opposition had majorities in both houses.

Scattered but impressive good news did come in on election night. The Republican Mark Hatfield, a young professor of political science, swamped his Democratic gubernatorial opponent in Oregon. Christopher Del Sesto became Republican Governor of Rhode Island, a state normally controlled by the Democrats. Representative Hugh Scott defeated Governor George Leader for a Senate seat in Pennsylvania. In Arizona Senator Barry Goldwater overwhelmed his Democratic opponent, while Republican Paul Fannin won the governorship. And in New York state Nelson Rockefeller bested the incumbent Governor, Averell Harriman, by more than a half million votes, while Republican Congressman Kenneth B. Keating won his way into the Senate.

Nevertheless, the over-all results were discouraging and, to me, all the more disappointing in view of the overwhelming majority our national ticket had attained only two years earlier.

One of our Senate losses particularly saddened me, that of Senator John W. Bricker of Ohio. Despite our long wrangle over the Bricker amendment in 1953–54, (an attempt to limit the treaty-making powers of the President), I respected the senator. He and I agreed on many issues, and the administration had often benefited from his counsel and support.

Senator Knowland's loss in the California gubernatorial race, even though freely predicted by pollsters, was another unhappy piece of news. Because I wanted to strengthen common sense government at both state and national levels, I wanted Knowland to succeed in his fight for the governorship. While pre-election Republican internal struggles in that state accounted partially for the defeat, the basic causes for the state's turn away from its traditional Republicanism were obscure and difficult to define.

During the campaign I had been annoyed by the efforts of some political writers to prove that Republicans were a deeply divided party. Often cited were differences between Senator Knowland and me. There had been a number. But, in writing to Republican National Chairman Meade Alcorn as early as August 30, 1957, I had observed, "Senator Knowland stands among the first four or five of the Republican senators in his record of voting for measures which I have proposed. With one or two exceptions over the five-year period, his differing vote has been based upon some detail or technical feature. We have, at times, differed on applicable policy in foreign affairs—but in important administrative projects he has led the fights for approval."

The charge that he and I were at opposite ends of the political spectrum was gross exaggeration.

In a television talk on election night in 1956 I happened to use the expression "modern Republicanism"—meaning only the application of Republican principles to the problems of today. Some seized upon the casual remark as an indication of the existence of a schism in the political thinking of the party. To me a modern Republican was one who supported the 1956 platform—a definition which should certainly have been acceptable to all except a number of malcontents. But, as I told Chairman Alcorn, I would be happy to abandon the phrase if necessary and substitute another which meant the same thing because all that I wanted was to emphasize that the mainstream of Republican thinking was guided by hard common sense. Phrases, prophecies, and punditry interested me less than a man's voting performance.

Nevertheless, despite the substantial areas of basic agreement within our party—certainly disrupted by no more than a fissure as compared to the deep chasm separating the wings of the Democratic party—we had lost. Why?

No single reason explained the defeat.

One, no doubt, was the recession of that year. Though unemployment had dropped off from a peak of 5.2 million since July, it still stood at 4.7 million by the middle of October, and at 4.3 million by the middle of November. In the forty-nine congressional districts in which incumbent Republicans lost seats, thirty-eight districts suffered from substantial unemployment.

Another contributory cause in the Middle West was an increasing unhappiness over the laws on agriculture. For six years the administration had tried urgently to change these, but both parties were so badly split on the issues involved that our efforts had little effect. In the twenty congressional districts which led all the rest in the value of their farm products, the Democrats in 1952 had elected only three congressmen, in 1954 only four, and in 1956 eight; but in 1958 they elected thirteen.

Still another reason was a set of "right to work" proposals in some states—laws designed to eliminate compulsory union membership provisions in labor contracts. Section 14 (b) of the Taft-Hartley Act authorized each state to settle this matter as it saw fit, and the retention of this provision in the federal law was, I thought, wise and proper. Through the campaign I held to this view, refusing either to modify it, as the AFL-CIO urged, or to call for federal legislation banning compulsory union membership, as Senator Knowland and others advocated. In 1958 the citizens of Kansas, California, Colorado, Idaho, Ohio, and Washington had the opportunity to vote for or against the enactment of such state laws. Leaders of organized labor fought them tooth and claw. In one state only, Kansas, the voters gave their approval. In the other five, the "right to work" referendums went under in a landslide. And so did three leading Republicans who had favored them—Senator Knowland in California, and Senator Bricker and Governor C. William O'Neill in Ohio.

Another factor in our defeat was "COPE," the Committee on Political Education of the AFL-CIO, whose main line of education seemed to be propagandizing for the election of Democrats. Of the nearly $2 million which organized labor reported it had spent on the 1958 election, 42 per cent went to state and local labor committees, 55 per cent directly to Democratic candidates, and less than 1 per cent to Republicans. The Republican party had no associated organization to counterbalance this lopsided labor support.

During the campaign Vice President Nixon traveled from coast to coast just as he had in 1954, trying to spur Republicans into action. As a fighting campaigner he let no opposition charge go unanswered.

In early October, for example, the Democratic Advisory Council announced its considered conclusion that "six years of leaderless vacillation have led us to the brink of isolation from our Allies and to the brink of having to fight a nuclear war inadequately prepared and alone."

"In a nutshell," the Vice President shot back in rebuttal, "the Acheson foreign policy resulted in war and the Eisenhower-Dulles foreign policy resulted in peace."

I had long disliked and discouraged the use of foreign policy as a political football. But the other side had started this one. Our action had, in my conviction, kept us out of war and halted the sweeping, population-gulping Communist advances that had lost China in 1949. In 1953, when our administration took over, they were threatening Indochina, Iran, Guatemala, and Korea, threats that we effectively countered. I urged that the record be set straight, and I wrote to Dick that the truth was the most effective weapon we could use.

Though such clashes were featured in the press, a mysterious apathy among the Republicans persisted. Part of it seemed to come from the Adams controversy. As I wrote to Clifford Roberts on September 4:

> The thing that disturbs me most about your report is that a spirit of "hopelessness" seems to you to be a Republican attitude discernible throughout the country. This defeats me. The six-year record of the Administration has been remarkable in view of the political complexion of the Congress. One man admittedly made a mistake, but no one has ever accused him of crookedness. Yet this circumstance, almost alone, seems to account for the alleged "hopelessness."

For various offenses, officials of considerable rank in the prior Democratic administration were indicted and convicted. In view of these circumstances, why was it, I asked, that the Democrats were not plagued, equally, by a spirit of hopelessness?

But none of the reasons advanced for the alleged Republican listlessness was truly convincing. Neither then, nor since, have I been able to develop a logical explanation or even an excuse that sounded plausible to me.

Before the campaign started, I had decided to hammer away on one overriding theme: my conviction that the deficit-producing, inflation-inviting, irresponsible-spending proposals of self-described liberal Democrats in the Congress had to be combatted at every turn.

In fiscal year 1960 the government would be forced to spend *one dollar in every ten of its revenues just to pay the interest on its debt*. This was five times as much as we were investing in natural resources. In the twentieth century there had been thirty-four unbalanced federal budgets, a number of them, in my opinion, wholly unnecessary; these had contributed to the dramatic decline in the value of the dollar during our lifetime. So I was opposed to every federal expenditure over and above the demonstrable needs of the nation.

The congressional hoppers were filled with bills that I thought both extravagant and useless. Just three introduced by Democratic congressmen in the 1958 session would, over a five-year span, have taken $150 billion out of the federal treasury.[1] To raise that much money, the government would either have had to sink out of sight into debt or levy a tax increase of nearly $1000 on every man, woman, and child then living in the United States.

I was getting alarmed by the spirit of recklessness that sought constant increases in spending, and by the apparent inability of our side to stem it.

Denied the power to veto specific items within a bill, I wrote to George Humphrey in the summer of 1958 with a sense of frustration that for the larger good contained in them, I had been compelled by circumstances to sign bills "which I personally considered as imposing unwarranted drains on the federal treasury." I cited in particular a bill for Civil Service pay raises, and the postal bill, incorporating a rate reform but including also a pay increase for the service. I told George I wished I could "be somewhat more persuasive" in my efforts to make the Congress understand the "danger of unwarranted expenditures." Some members of Congress gave clear indication of socialistic objectives, I thought, while some others were trying to be politically clever, pushing preposterous money bills that would unquestionably bring on a presidential veto, but would give them a voting record to appease pressure groups in the next election.

For increasing the likelihood of their own re-election, not a few legislators of both parties seemed ready to mortgage not only the coming decade but the next century. Yet some had the effrontery to campaign not only on their own spending plans but, oddly, on an alleged "support of the President."

Happily, there was still enough common sense in controlling places in

[1] Congressman George McGovern's agricultural bill would have cost the government $36.5 billion; Congressman Thomas Abernethy's proposal to increase income tax exemptions to a thousand dollars would have cost $50 billion, and Congressman Wright Patman's proposal for pensions to everybody over sixty-five would have cost $66 billion.

the Congress to prevent the most outrageous bills from reaching my desk. In any case, I determined to wage the most intensive campaign within my physical powers to hold the line against the prodigals. I argued that unless a Congress was returned to Washington prepared to fight this trend, the federal government would remain powerless to preserve the purchasing power of the taxpayer's dollar.

In the fall of 1957 Dr. Arthur Burns had delivered a series of lectures at Fordham University which he later published as a book: *Prosperity Without Inflation.* He sent me a copy; the lectures focused not on the danger of "galloping" inflation—the sort which had in the past, for example, caused German employers to pay their employees three times a day, because of the almost hourly decline in the value of the German currency —but rather on the insidious danger of "creeping" inflation. Since 1933, he pointed out in this book and in later correspondence, prices in the United States had risen appreciably during business expansions but had not fallen at all, or only a trifle, during business contractions. In 1929–33, between the peak and the trough of the business cycle, consumer prices had fallen off 26.6 per cent. In contrast to this, in the recession of 1953–54 they had risen 0.3 per cent, and in 1957–58 had risen 2.6 per cent. Obviously we were experiencing some inflation even in "deflationary" periods.

This slow-moving increase in the aggregate cost of such things as food, clothing, industrial products, and services, Dr. Burns explained, could have several causes, not all of which were necessarily bad: the government's policy of striving always to cut short economic declines and prolong economic expansions; increases in private debt (in 1955–56, for example, individuals and corporations added $91 billion to their debt, while states and localities added $9 billion); and increases in wages, even in times of recession.

If prices and wages were to stay high or go higher in economic contractions, the outlook for stability at other times was bleak.

Why worry, some asked? Why not let prices creep upward forever? To such questions Dr. Burns had some plain and, I thought, accurate answers:

(1) Inflation can get out of hand; beginning with a creep, it can end with a gallop.

(2) Inflation hurts people. Price increases averaging merely 1 per cent a year will in twenty-five years cheapen the dollar by more than one-fifth. Inflation, Dr. Burns concluded, "is bound to deal harshly with the plans and hopes of millions of people in the course of a generation."

To check insidious advances in prices, Arthur Burns mentioned a variety of measures, but in his major recommendation he insisted that *"government must lead the economic community in the practice of restraint."* By this he meant more than balanced budgets. He noted that huge federal spending, even when covered completely by tax revenues, can in itself provoke inflation. He cited as causative factors: government officials tend to be less efficient shoppers than private buyers; government prices are often computed by the "cost plus" method; government contracts are subject to special labor provisions; government spending, especially for defense, is unlikely to contribute to the improvement of industrial capacity and productivity as much as the same amount of private spending would; when federal spending and federal taxes increase, private spending does not necessarily decline by an equal amount. The result is an increase in total spending, which is inflationary.

So he argued that when the economy was performing at capacity and the federal budget was in balance, the government should try to increase its surplus by cutting spending, by postponing projects which, however desirable, are not immediately necessary. For, at a time of full employment, an increase in either federal or private spending will tend to bring on an increase in prices.

But, Dr. Burns observed, "The Government is not yet prepared to act as decisively to check inflation as it is to check recession. . . . Such weighting of the scales of economic policy, however slight, is probably unavoidable in the existing state of public opinion."

Whether or not these things were widely understood, I believed in them, and launched a drive, in the 1958 campaign, attempting to change public opinion. All Republicans, I thought, should join in such an effort, one that in its way might be remembered as a historic accomplishment. I would strive toward this objective, even if I had to do it alone. To my dismay, I had to write to Arthur Burns on September 29, not too many Republicans seemed to agree.

On October 20 in Los Angeles, I delivered what some writers called the most unvarnished political speech of my career: The Democratic party, I said, "is not one—but two—political parties with the same name. They unite only once every two years—to wage political campaigns.

"But at one extreme is a wing where the campaigns of this year were largely settled in southern primaries held weeks ago. At the other extreme is the stronger wing, dominated by political radicals. . . ." These were the ones who really challenged sane, forward-looking governmental fiscal policy in the United States.

"Most Americans are against reckless public spending. As to this, the record of congressional radicals is too clear and too recent to need explanation. . . .

"This year in Congress . . . One after another administration bills were mangled or mushroomed. . . .

". . . And only sturdy Republican resistance in Congress and my vetoes blocked over $5 billion of this spending. And I remind you—these federal billions are your money—your own money. Either they come out of your paycheck through higher taxes, or your pocket is picked by inflation."

This campaign, I argued, gave us the crucial choice between irresponsible government and forward-looking, common sense government; overpowering federal government or government kept close to home; frustrated, stymied government or efficient government able to keep its promises to America.

"If you are for trustworthy, progressive government," I concluded, "then it is clear you should talk Republican, work Republican—and, on November 4, vote Republican."

It was a futile effort.

On the night of November 4 the bad news came in. At my press conference the next morning reporters asked me about those passages in the Los Angeles speech that described the choices open to the electorate.

To start with, one friendly reporter, in adroit paraphrases, summed up my campaigning by saying that I had told the public that Democrats were left-wing apostles of phony doctrines, committed to demagogics.

I had to point out emphatically that I never levied such charges against the Democratic party as a whole, but against its "spender-wing," and that apparently I had not made any impression with the message.

As for the rest of the questioning, I did not attempt to sidestep. The voters, I said, had obviously cast their ballots for people whom ". . . I would class among the spenders. . . . And I promise this: for the next two years, the Lord sparing me, I am going to fight this as hard as I know how."

The electorate, I told White House staff members privately that day, seemed to want to throw all responsibility to the federal government. They had returned a Congress with scarcely enough Republican votes to sustain a veto. But we had lost a battle, not the war.[2]

For my part I sought no scapegoat. Possibly I was as much at fault as anyone. At least there were just too many, including some Republicans,

[2] Among many letters of condolence I received a thoughtful personal note from Prime Minister Macmillan on November 7 [see Appendix T].

who, though loudly proclaiming their adherence to political concepts featuring fiscal sanity and common sense, were so beguiled by prospects of federal spending in their respective districts that they pitifully failed to participate wholeheartedly in the campaign.

When Larry Burd of the *Chicago Tribune* had asked what factors I thought had caused the Republican defeat, I said that I did not know but that I would say, in agreement with what Vice President Nixon and Republican Chairman Meade Alcorn had observed earlier, "If the Republicans don't start fighting this morning, this very day, for the next election, they're going to be in a bad way."

* * *

Obviously there was much to do within the Republican party. As Meade Alcorn said, many people saw our party "as a kind of hibernating elephant who wakes with a mighty trumpet blast at election time and then rests calmly until the next campaign comes." That was nicely put. I asked Alcorn to come to see me at intervals of no longer than two weeks to discuss his efforts to get unified and effective support for administration programs.

Seeking a villain for the 1958 defeat, several persons urged me to fire Alcorn himself. I refused. To my mind, he had been an excellent chairman. His intelligence, energy, imagination, and dedication had been exemplary. Indeed, he had worked so hard during the campaign that at times I feared he might be risking his health. I continued to support him vigorously and when he finally did resign on April 1, 1959, he carried with him my sincere regrets.

On December 6, 1958, I wrote a long memorandum for the record describing measures to put life back into the Republican party. It was based upon conversations with Dick Nixon, who would be, I believed, the Republican standard bearer in the national election of 1960.

We agreed on a number of things, including methods for studying and revising organization, for raising and utilizing money, for discovering mistakes in our recent campaigning and in correcting them. In the end our ideas were not implemented in the form we visualized, but some progress began.

We established a Republican Committee on Program and Progress under the chairmanship of Charles Percy of Chicago, to set forth the long range political goals of the Republican party in every area of foreign and domestic policy. This organization worked hard through the spring and summer of 1959 and came up with a constructive report in the fall.

We likewise sought to encourage members of the 1952 and 1956 Citizens for Eisenhower-Nixon organization to work for the improvement and strengthening of the regular Republican party. One day I dictated a draft of a letter outlining some of the results we could hope for in this particular effort.

> Starting from the premise, in which I firmly believe, that a two-party system is essential to the preservation of the democratic processes of our country, and that the vast majority of the people of our country want to see that system maintained, I suggest the following lines of activity . . .
>
> First, I would hope that your present organization might not only be kept alive, but strengthened, during the two-year period before the next campaign. I realize the "glamor" . . . that a national election carries, but there is solid and interesting work to be done every day of the year in every local political front.

I urged "Citizens" to continue to support the principles upon which I had waged both the 1952 and the 1956 campaigns and while doing so, seek out possible candidates who not only shared their faith in these principles but who were energetic, dedicated, and persuasive leaders:

> I would suggest that Citizens work among themselves and with the regular Republican organization in an effort to interest and build up into local prominence attractive, young candidates with sensible and progressive political philosophies. Such men should be approached and, if possible, interested in service to the public in political office, even though they may have taken no prior part in political activity. When feasible, the television camera should be used to introduce such men to the public and to make certain they become well known. . . . the American people are relying more and more—and rightly so—upon their own estimates of the kind of people they want to elect to office. . . .
>
> While interest is undoubtedly easy to focus on personalities," I added, "I think we would all do far better, for the time being, to concentrate [mainly] on *issues*. . . .
>
> . . . all of us know that a solid—and broad—grass roots base is the only permanent way of building the type of progressive organization that we must have. There is no room, as we have learned, for such a luxury as party disunity in a local or a national campaign. . . .

Next I called in General Persons and asked him to telephone every presidential appointee in the government (except those in non-political fields) to ask each what he could do, within his particular geographic or professional area, to help the Republican party during the next two years. I wanted individual appointees to take on specific responsibilities among labor groups, for example, and among conservationists, educators, and men of business and the professions.

The administration's principal and immediate battleground was Capitol Hill. On the morning of November 19 the House Minority Leader, Joseph W. Martin, Jr., of Massachusetts, came to breakfast. We discussed the need for revitalizing the organization and operations of the Republican party, and for getting candidates of natural leadership to run on our ticket. But when I suggested that we ought to have several younger Republican members of Congress come regularly to the White House to attend the leadership meetings, I encountered reluctance.

Both in 1954 and in 1956, when the Republicans failed to achieve control of the House, Congressman Charles Halleck had come to the White House to inform me that he intended to oppose Congressman Martin for the post of Minority Leader. He wanted my blessing on the attempt but both times I had refused, and he had gone along with my decision. But after the rout of 1958, Halleck came once again.

"The time has come," he said, "when I can no longer work under Martin's nominal leadership. Twice before I have held off, but now I'm determined to unseat him. And I have the votes to do it."

"Charlie," I replied, "as you know, I've done my best to unify the Republican members in the House and try to get them to pull together. But now, with the poor showing the Republicans have made throughout the country, I simply say to you that, while I shall make no attempt to influence any congressman's vote, I shall no longer stand in your way."

On January 6, 1959, in a secret ballot vote of a Republican caucus, Halleck defeated Martin 74 to 70. Martin charged that "Nixon's people actively opposed" him, and he alleged that several members of the White House staff had intervened to help Halleck. In the latter belief he was mistaken. Following my instructions, my assistants had kept "hands off."

I invited Mr. Martin to remain as one of the members of the weekly leadership meetings, but he declined. On the Senate side, Republicans also had to choose a new leader, following the departure of Senator Knowland.

Senator Knowland had been a zealous champion of congressional prerogatives. "Certainly you do not want the Senate of the United States to become merely a rubber stamp," he would say again and again in leadership meetings. He always reacted impulsively to any fancied slight by the liaison officers upon whom we so much depended in maintaining coordination between the White House and Republican congressional leaders. Naturally, when everyone in an entire organization is working at top speed and sometimes under high tension to further a common purpose, it is not always easy to keep sand from fouling the gears of cooperation. Though Senator Knowland was hypersensitive in such matters, he was an effective party leader in the Senate.

After the 1958 elections, rumors circulated around the Capitol that the recently victorious Senator Goldwater might seek the post of Minority Leader. Among those who mentioned the possibility to me was the Majority Leader of the Senate, Lyndon Johnson, who was, naturally, interested in the identity of the leading Republican with whom he would be working. I could give him no information, but when the Republican Senate caucus met on January 7, the two principal candidates who emerged were Senator Everett McKinley Dirksen of Illinois and Senator John Sherman Cooper of Kentucky. Dirksen defeated Cooper by a vote of 20 to 14. One of Cooper's supporters, Senator Thomas Kuchel of California, was selected as Minority Whip. Dirksen was well-informed, friendly, and a loyal lieutenant. He might have been able to work wonders with majority support.

The problem for him, and for Charlie Halleck on the House side, was to get the small Republican numbers to stick together as a fighting phalanx, to rally backing for administration bills rather than individual legislators' pet projects, and above all, to hold the line against the central danger in the 1959 legislative session—soaring spending proposals from the overwhelming Democratic majority.

* * *

"Every sort of foolish proposal will be advanced in the name of national security and the 'poor' fellow," I told the legislative leaders at our first meeting on January 13. "We've got to convince Americans that thrift is not a bad word."

The fight revolved around the fiscal year 1960 budget which I submitted to the Congress in January of 1959—a budget balanced at $77 billion. Advisers had warned me against moving, in a single year, from a recession budget in the red by an estimated $12.9 billion to one in balance. Some had thought we could not cut spending much below $80 billion. But in the end, deciding on still other advice, I sent up a balanced budget.[3] I planned to let the Congress know that if it materially added to the budget, I would respond with a veto, and that if the veto were overridden I would propose a tax increase to cover the increase in spending, and if necessary call a special session for the purpose.

[3] Secretary of the Treasury Anderson in particular argued for a balanced budget as a means of strengthening foreign bankers' confidence in the dollar; he was already concerned about the outflow of gold, a problem which came to a head in late 1960.

Though under the circumstances a good deal of give and take would be necessary, I was determined to use the power of the federal government to prevent the cheapening of our currency. "This is going to be one of the bloodiest fights we have ever had," I told a group one morning in my office. I knew we could not expect to win it completely but neither could the spenders.

In preparing the budget, the giant military demands gave us, as usual, the gigantic headaches. No major item budgeted in each of the Armed Services was approved for inclusion unless the question "why?" was answered to my satisfaction. After a series of tough meetings, we got the appropriations estimates for the military functions of the Department of Defense down to $40.8 billion.

In health, education, and welfare, I insisted that spending more money did not necessarily hasten progress. Preventing deterioration of our currency was not only an economic necessity but a *humanitarian goal as well,* because failure to preserve the purchasing power of the dollar spells hardship for those who will one day live on pensions, insurance policies, and savings in government bonds. Moreover, prosperity depends in large part upon avoiding an inflation that could destroy incentives.

In an effort to cut spending on agriculture, I wrote Secretary Benson suggesting that he consider putting money ceilings on the amounts that any one farm could receive. "Isn't there something we can do," I asked him, "to avoid using federal subsidies to create millionaires [which in some cases the long established farm subsidies had done] under programs ostensibly devised to protect the little farmer?" This idea, though attracting spotty support, was watered down and thus made ineffective by the legislators.

Having hammered out the budget, we turned to legislative tactics. On December 15, Dr. Arthur Burns wrote to me proposing an excellent plan:

> I would suggest that you request the Bureau of the Budget to provide you with an estimate of the total cost of the high-sounding programs put forward by the Democratic [Advisory] Council. This job of estimation will, of course, prove very difficult since most of the Democratic proposals are vague. Nevertheless, I believe that an estimate of costs should be made, and that at an appropriate time the figure should be put before the country, either by you or someone else whom you would designate.
>
> The kind of thing I am talking about might well become a continuous project of the Budget Bureau, so that you or others can use it aggressively. The Democrats, let us grant, will keep busy this year and next in proposing one spending program after another. The Budget Bureau should keep just as busy translating vague talk into figures and adding the different figures, no matter how they emerge, together. This budgetary arithmetic should

> be brought before the country unremittingly. If work of this sort is done well . . . there will be less uncertainty in the minds of the American people as to which political party is the principal architect of inflation.

Under Maurice Stans, the Budget Bureau went to work. With a determination and dedication that amazed as much as it delighted me, he deluged the Cabinet and—when possible—the public with statistics that made truly fearsome ogres of the gaudily garbed promises of the spenders [see Appendix U].

As in the struggle over defense reorganization the year before, I wrote to hundreds of friends asking them to do what they could to persuade the Congress to hold the lid on federal spending. Administration speakers spotlighted the problem of rising prices, giving plain answers to the question: "What's wrong with inflation?" They pointed out that inflation hurts the government; clearly if today's dollar sinks to tomorrow's dime, fewer and fewer people will buy government bonds or patronize savings banks. Rising prices hurt defense, because as the dollar deteriorates, the costs of munitions go higher. Inflation hurts our foreign trade: the higher American prices go, the easier it becomes for foreign competitors to undersell us. The loss of markets through inflation means loss of jobs. In short, inflation hurts people, the worker and the family on a fixed income most of all. I concluded that the Democrats' idea of cutting the budget —which would admittedly be helpful in avoiding inflation—was to slice primarily into foreign aid, never a politically popular cause, and then to keep on seeking larger appropriations for domestic purposes with scant thought of priority.

There was, in the end, only one way to win: to alert the country to the dangers of cheap money, to turn a bright spotlight on the Congress and, in view of the scarcity of Republican members, to get enough Democratic votes to defeat the outlandish proposals brought forward by those who believe that bigger appropriations mean always a better America.

We did not have to wait long for a test. At the legislative leaders' meeting on February 3, I warned we were facing our first crucial vote—on a Democratic proposal to expand the administration's program for federally financed housing.

The Republicans, united, soon showed what they could do; together with conservative Democrats, they voted down a proposal by Senator Joseph Clark of Pennsylvania to provide an exorbitant $450 million a year for the next four fiscal years for urban renewal; 32 Democrats and one Republican voted for this proposal, 26 Democrats and 30 Republicans voted against it. Later in the year, when both chambers of the Congress had enacted a housing bill, its cost was still out of bounds, and

I vetoed it. On August 12 the Senate supported my veto: 53 Democrats and 2[4] Republicans voted to override, 10 Democrats and 30 Republicans stood by me. Three weeks later, the Congress sent me another housing bill, one that was still too big. I vetoed it. And once again the Senate failed to override.

In voting patterns like these throughout the session, again and again the thin line held. Only once that year did the Congress override my veto, when 20 shortsighted Republicans in the House voted with the Democrats against my disapproval of an over-fat pork barrel measure.

When the session was ended, Congressional Quarterly reported the average Democrat in the Senate and House had opposed measures to limit federal spending on 72 per cent of 97 roll call votes. As a result of our Spartan-like economy we actually completed fiscal year '60 with a surplus of more than a billion dollars.

Even more significant than this fiscal victory, however, was the victory in public education evidenced by the grass roots support that turned the tide. Out of the jaws of a political defeat we had snatched at least a partial victory for common sense.

* * *

Next, we were anxious to obtain legislation to combat the abuses and racketeering uncovered by the McClellan Senate Investigating Committee.

In a television talk on the evening of August 6, 1958 I said:

> For many months, newspapers have carried extensive accounts of racketeering and corruption in labor-management matters. Many of you have actually witnessed disclosures of this corruption on television in your own homes. It is a national disgrace.

I wanted a reform law—a law to protect the American people from the gangsters, racketeers, and other corrupt elements who had invaded the labor-management field. I insisted, moreover, that we must be careful to protect the rights of the individual worker:

> . . . any reform bill worthy of the name must also protect the individual rights of union members—within their unions. It must assure them of fair elections. It must assure them of honest handling of their money—money made up by dues often collected under auspices of federal law. It must also give to the govenment effective authority to investigate and enforce these provisions. Unless it does these things . . . it is not a reform bill at all.

[4] Jacob Javits of New York and William Langer of North Dakota.

Now let us examine what Congress has done so far this year. Has its action measured up to the minimum requirements I have outlined to protect the American people? I regret to say that, as yet, the answer is no. . . .

I pointed out that a bill proposed by Senator Kennedy and supported by the Democratic leadership, which passed the Senate in April, would not give the individual worker and the public the protection they deserved.

"It does not," I said, "deal with or curb the picketing or boycotting practices I have described."[5] Against the "no man's land," it gave no real relief. ("No man's land" is the legal area into which a labor dispute falls when neither the state nor the federal government has any authority to help settle it; the result is usually a damaging test of naked strength between the disputants.)

Secretary of Labor Mitchell was active and effective in carrying on the administration's fight for the enactment of a better bill.

At a legislative leaders' meeting, some members pointed out that it was going to be difficult to get that bill enacted; it was neither pro-management nor pro-labor. I replied that I would not approve any labor bill unless it provided for correcting the conditions that were so glaringly unjust. I wanted a reform bill, not a surrender bill, I said. On September 14, I signed into law S 1555, the bipartisan Landrum-Griffin Labor-Management Reporting and Disclosure Act of 1959, a definite improvement on the legislation previously existing.

* * *

In 1959 we had to contend with Senator Stuart Symington's repeated charges of a "missile gap"—the allegation of an alarming inferiority in the numbers and power of the missiles of the United States as compared to those of the Soviet Union. (He had earlier made headlines with similar allegations of a "bomber gap.")

On August 29, 1958, he sent me a long letter charging that we were lagging unjustifiably behind the Soviets in missiles, giving as his authority his own intelligence sources. The full extent of the danger, he said, the Central Intelligence Agency had not accurately estimated.

[5] As an example of coercive—or "blackmail"—picketing, I cited union officials' use of picketing to force a company's employees to join a union against their will. As an example of the secondary boycott—the boycott against an "innocent bystander" in a labor dispute—I cited picketing of a furniture store to force indirectly the employees of the furniture factory to join a union against their will.

It is no exaggeration to say that, during all the months while our scientists were struggling to perfect the reliability and effectiveness of our missiles, there was rarely a day when I failed to give earnest study to reports of our progress and to estimates of Soviet capabilities. But in analysis of comparative military power there is never complete certainty; seasoned judgments are needed if the nation is to be neither defenseless nor bankrupt. Moreover, it was perfectly clear, as I told the legislative leaders, that we could not provide security merely with a checkbook. "The people who are advocating more spending think . . . it is money rather than brains and courage which we need now."

It is of course true that on entering office in 1953 we *had* inherited a missile gap—from an administration of Senator Symington's own party and we had been laboring to close it. Though by early 1959 we knew the Soviet Union still led us in certain areas of missile research and production (especially high-powered boosters), we also knew that our total defense capabilities—including manned bombers, emerging long-range ballistic missiles, and nuclear weapons of all kinds—had a superiority overwhelming enough to deter the Soviet leaders from aggression. By January of 1960 new intelligence reports narrowed almost to negligibility the extent of the Soviet lead in long-range and sea-launched missiles; this lead would soon disappear.

Nonetheless, in the 1960 campaign, the charge of a missile gap remained a useful piece of demagoguery. But within a month after my successor took office, word conveniently leaked out of the Pentagon that the "missile gap" had been closed. Indeed, several months later, in November of 1961, news out of the Pentagon indicated that the latest intelligence estimates gave the United States nearly a two to one lead over the Soviet Union in combat-ready ICBMs. The non-existent missile gap had been suddenly closed by unabashed partisan politics.

* * *

Two controversies of 1959 swirled around two presidential appointments, those of Clare Boothe Luce and Lewis Strauss.

On February 26, 1959, I nominated Mrs. Luce as United States ambassador to Brazil. From 1943 to 1947 she had served as a Republican congresswoman from Connecticut. Between 1953 and 1956 she had represented the United States skillfully as ambassador to Italy during trying and sensitive years. With her qualifications for a new ambassadorship, I looked forward to her service in Latin America, where first-class representation was always important.

Unhappily, Clare Luce ran headlong into the headstrong opposition of Senator Wayne Morse of Oregon. Alone among the members of the Senate Foreign Relations Committee, he voted against her. In the Senate debate which followed he again berated her for having asserted on October 11, 1944, during the political campaign of that year, that President Roosevelt was "the only American President who ever lied us into a war because he did not have the political courage to lead us into it." This remark, some fourteen years before, was hardly diplomatic, but Mrs. Luce had admitted the intemperance of her wording (though in her own defense she cited former Secretary of War Stimson on Roosevelt's repeated assertion during the 1940 campaign that the United States would not have to go to war). This did not satisfy Senator Morse. Moreover, he took violent exception to a passage in another speech which Mrs. Luce had made, this one in April of 1952: "If a general loses a division he is shot. When Acheson, as Under Secretary of State, lost 100 million people a year to Communism, including the friendly 500 million Chinese, he was promoted to Secretary of State."

"I call that subversion," Morse said, adding his suspicion that "Mrs. Luce is one more example of the Eisenhower administration's practice of paying off political 'hacks' with ambassadorial appointments."

Despite the noise, the Senate confirmed her on April 28, 79 to 11. But then a new spurt of trouble began. Mrs. Luce had a press conference and in the course of it got off a remark which many senators "deplored," behind scarcely hidden smiles.

"My difficulties," she said, "of course go back some years when Senator Wayne Morse was kicked in the head by a horse."

Several senators voiced their "shock." If they had known she felt this way about a fellow member of the Senate, they said, they wouldn't have voted for her.

"This is part of an old pattern of mental instability on her part," Senator Morse responded gallantly.

Senator Lyndon Johnson telephoned me, asking that I induce Mrs. Luce to temper her "kicked in the head" remark.

"Well, I have not felt exactly complimented by some things that Wayne Morse said about me," I told the Senate Majority Leader. He observed that he sometimes found himself in the same boat.

At six o'clock that evening Henry Luce announced that he had asked Mrs. Luce to resign because the controversy had become a political vendetta. Although I told a news conference the next day that I believed that Mrs. Luce's remarks represented a very human reaction to attack, and did not impair her usefulness, she submitted her resignation. With Wayne

Morse as Chairman of the Latin American Subcommittee, she knew that she would be subjected to "continuing harassment" and that her effectiveness as United States ambassador to Brazil would unquestionably suffer.

* * *

While this disagreeable but faintly comic scene was being played out on the Senate floor, another and far more bitter quarrel was being argued in the committee room of the Senate Committee on Interstate and Foreign Commerce.

On October 24, 1958, I had announced the recess appointment of Lewis L. Strauss as Secretary of Commerce. Admiral Strauss had declined reappointment as Chairman of the Atomic Energy Commission in 1958, at the expiration of his statutory term. His reason was the evident hostility of Senator Clinton Anderson, the junior senator from New Mexico, who would become, in 1959–60, Chairman of the Congressional Joint Committee on Atomic Energy. The Admiral felt that in the circumstances it would be difficult for him as commission chairman to maintain good relations with the congressional committee.

On November 13 Lewis Strauss took the oath as Secretary of Commerce. Upon the reconvening of the Senate, the nomination went to that body for confirmation. Three times before, Admiral Strauss had been confirmed by the Senate: when appointed rear admiral in 1945, when appointed to the Atomic Energy Commission by President Truman, and when appointed chairman of the commission by me in 1953. Further, Admiral Strauss had served four Presidents of the United States with distinction; as a member of the AEC he had been the first to insist upon the monitoring program which detected the first tests of atomic bombs by the Russians, and he had stood alone in advocacy of the development of the hydrogen bomb. He had been one of the stanchest supporters of the 1953 Atoms-for-Peace proposal, and was among the first to insist upon dedication of a portion of atomic production to the development of nuclear science for peaceful purposes. It should not have taken the Senate more than minutes to confirm his appointment as Secretary of Commerce, a post for which, by virtue of his extraordinary experience in government and in business, Lewis Strauss was supremely qualified; he would have been one of the most outstanding Secretaries of Commerce in the history of the office.

Despite a wealth of *prima facie* evidence of the Admiral's fitness, the Senate committee did not begin hearings until March 17; it did not conclude them until nearly two months later, on May 14. Newspaper after newspaper deplored the curious deviousness and delay and detail of this proceeding. Even the *Washington Post*, normally against my administration, declared in an editorial: "It ill becomes the Senate to use its power of confirmation as an instrument of harassment."

The Senate, however, was using its power of confirmation for exactly that. The junior senator from New Mexico, appearing at the hearings by reason of senatorial courtesy, declared that Admiral Strauss in 1949, in opposing a shipment of certain radioisotopes to Norway, had given as his reason that "this isotope was to be used for research in the development of more heat resistant alloys for jet engines."

"I say to you," the senator declared, "that that is an unqualified falsehood."

Admiral Strauss thereupon produced a cable from the United States Embassy in Oslo to the State Department confirming that the Norwegians wanted the isotope "to develop alloy for jet or gas turbine use" at temperatures above 700° Centigrade if possible.

The senator from New Mexico charged Admiral Strauss further with failure to cooperate with the Joint Committee on Atomic Energy. That charge was refuted by three who had served as chairman of the committee—Senator Bourke Hickenlooper and former Congressman W. Sterling Cole, both Republicans, and Congressman Carl Durham, a Democrat; all gave testimony in favor of Admiral Strauss. A fourth chairman, the late Senator Brien McMahon, had in 1950 written a letter on behalf of the Joint Committee praising the service of Admiral Strauss.[6]

The senator also charged that Admiral Strauss had refused to transmit information to the Congress. He cited a statement of Chairman Cole in 1954 that the commission had declined to submit information until the Congress had adopted a formal resolution forcing it to do so. In refutation, Admiral Strauss pointed out that the decision against submitting information was not his decision; it was the decision of the majority of the members of the Atomic Energy Commission. Further, he himself had voted with the minority, that is for sending the information to Congress. But during the Senate debate this charge was repeated, as if he had never shown it to be baseless.

The next complaint was that the Atomic Energy Commission had made a key decision on uranium procurement and announced it, on October 28, 1957, without giving prior notification to the Joint Committee on Atomic Energy. This was proved false when Admiral Strauss produced a copy of an AEC document on that very point which had been

[6] When the full Senate finally voted, only two of the nine members of the current Joint Committee opposed Strauss.

delivered by hand to the joint committee three days before the announcement.

Another leader against Senate confirmation was Senator Estes Kefauver of Tennessee. Testifying in the hearings, Kefauver alleged that the Joint Committee on Atomic Energy and the Senate Anti-Trust and Monopoly Subcommittee had been unable to get a copy of the Dixon-Yates contract until it was published in the *St. Louis Post-Dispatch* in August of 1955. Rebutting this, Admiral Strauss pointed out that immediately upon the signing of the contract, on November 11, 1954, the commission had forwarded a copy to the Joint Committee on Atomic Energy. This meant nothing to Senator Anderson: "The one great point," he declared during the debate, "is that the contract was not available to the committee until it was printed in the *St. Louis Post-Dispatch*. That is the essential charge. It is true." It was not true.

Senator Kefauver's entry into the conflict intensified the acrimony on both sides. The *Richmond News Leader,* an outstanding newspaper in a state whose two senators, Harry F. Byrd and A. Willis Robertson, were full out in backing Admiral Strauss, editorialized, ". . . it is a pity that so big a man [Strauss] will have to suffer public abuse from so small a politician."

As the hearings ground on, Admiral Strauss offered to do anything I asked, even submit his resignation. As I told the legislative leaders, however, I had assured Strauss I would carry the fight through to the very end, and if that end were not reached in this administration, I would make sure the next Republican candidate pursued it. The shocking performance in the Senate was not only hurting the Admiral; it was increasing the danger of mediocrity at the top of government by discouraging men of real stature from submitting themselves to such a pounding.

Though a man of sensitivity and deep personal feeling, Lewis did not weaken. He addressed a moving reply to all those who had testified against him before the joint committee:

> Certain witnesses demand that your committee drive me from my present position as Secretary of Commerce, to which new duty the President appointed me last November. Their criticism, as I have listened to it, is twofold. First, they differ with me on public policy, mostly in connections other than in the field of the Department of Commerce; and second, they attack my integrity.
>
> It would be a human impulse to strike back in anger when a man's record of a lifetime is distorted and defiled. Instead, when you permit me to do so, I shall answer in detail from the record with truth, but without rancor. I shall present facts to refute the false charges.
>
> So far in the several weeks since the hearing started, except for the

> opening day, and my own testimony, only witnesses known in advance to be hostile to me have been called for statements and questioning.
>
> I greatly appreciate the fact that members of the committee of both parties . . . questioned the testimony. And I trust that, eventually, witnesses in my favor may be permitted to add their evidence.
>
> Hearing both sides is the fair American method of inquiry. . . . With deep sincerity, Mr. Chairman and Gentlemen, I declare that if the cruel accusations as to my character made in these hearings, and thereafter reported in the press, were accurate, I would never have accepted President Eisenhower's appointment last November. I would not have betrayed his trust, nor would I come before this committee knowingly with unclean hands. . . .
>
> I believe the American people in these critical days of national security, threats from the Communist bloc, Soviet trade war, and grave economic problems, want something better from Washington than what appears to be the pattern of persecution through long-drawn-out attempts at defamation of a plain man who has done his best as he sees it for his country over many years.

And he added, painfully, that he had never thought when he was a young man, that he would ever be called upon for such a statement.

Finally, on June 4, a majority of the committee reported favorably on the nomination: six Republicans and three (of eleven) Democrats, Senators John Pastore, Strom Thurmond, and Frank Lausche. A minority report, however, catalogued once again the charges against Admiral Strauss and concluded, "mostly on the basis of his conduct and demeanor before us" that he was "lacking in the degree of integrity and competence essential to proper performance of the duties of the office [to] which he had been nominated."

A sharp debate on the Senate floor followed. While largely partisan, a dedicated and fair-minded group of Democrats, led by Senator Harry Byrd, rallied to the Admiral's support. Then, on the night of June 19, 1959, came the vote. The Senate refused to confirm the nomination, 49–46.

So close was the vote that two senators were generally held to be responsible for the disaster. They were Margaret Chase Smith of Maine and William Langer of North Dakota, two short-sighted Republicans who alone among the members of their party voted with the Democrats against Admiral Strauss. Shortly before the final vote Senator Lyndon Johnson made known his intention of voting against the Admiral; Democratic senators Richard Neuberger and John Kennedy, who had reportedly promised Admiral Strauss they would vote for him, reversed their positions before the roll call was taken. Admiral Strauss and I were grateful that fourteen Democrats had the courage to vote for confirmation.

This was the first occasion in which the Senate refused to confirm a presidential nomination since 1925, when it had rejected Charles B. Warren, President Coolidge's nominee as Attorney General. After the vote against the Admiral, *Pravda* rejoiced: "The United States Senate has torn the down and feathers from Strauss, and he has appeared before the public stark naked as a dyed-in-the-wool reactionary and an inveterate enemy of peace."

I have little doubt that there was a similar rejoicing elsewhere. My own feelings were expressed by this statement:

> Last night the Senate refused to confirm the nomination as Secretary of Commerce of Lewis Strauss—a man who in war and in peace has served his Nation loyally, honorably, and effectively, under four different Presidents.
>
> I am losing a truly valuable associate in the business of government. More than this—if the Nation is to be denied the right to have as public servants in responsible positions men of his proven character, ability, and integrity, then indeed it is the American people who are the losers through this sad episode.

Both then and in retrospect I have considered the Senate rejection of Admiral Strauss as one of the most depressing official disappointments I experienced during eight years in the White House. This sprang not so much because of my personal feelings of sympathy and affection for the man—nothing his persecutors could do would ever diminish the respect and admiration in which he is held by all who truly know him—but because the incident shook, for the moment, my faith that democracy could be expected to detect and successfully defend integrity, ability, and bigness against the maneuverings of jealous, vindictive and little men.

But whenever I am tempted, even silently, to express violent criticism of such people or rail at the lack of courage in some holding positions of responsibility in our democratic institutions, I think again of George Washington and the scandalous attacks hurled at him again and again during his second administration. He never lost faith in self-government; though cursed and reviled he kept his temper, his dignity, and the admiration and respect of history. So has and will Lewis Strauss.

CHAPTER XVII

Collapse at Geneva

I do desire we may be better strangers.

—*Shakespeare,* As You Like It

CHRISTIAN A. Herter stepped into the office of Secretary of State under trying circumstances. Only a few days after being sworn in, he had to go to Geneva where the foreign ministers of the United States, Britain, France, and the Soviet Union began exploring the feasibility of a later summit conference. The chances for genuine achievement seemed remote.

Secretary Herter was well prepared for his difficult role. He had been Under Secretary of State since the retirement from the post of Herbert Hoover, Jr., in 1957, and, during Foster Dulles' final illness, had served as Acting Secretary of State. With the assurance of the veteran that he was, he stepped into experiences that were to be enough to frustrate and exasperate any man, even one with his wisdom and patience.

When Secretary Herter returned to Washington for the funeral of Foster Dulles on May 27 I told him of my appreciation of his success in sustaining during the first weeks of the foreign ministers' meeting the kind of posture we always hoped to maintain—that of firmness without belligerence, of conciliation without appeasement.

That same morning I had the opportunity to talk with Chancellor Adenauer who, admiring Foster Dulles deeply, had come to the funeral. He outlined once more the attitude which he believed the West should sustain in all dealings with the Communists. He proposed nothing new. Indeed, had he advocated any change I would have been disappointed, for I approved of the Chancellor's steadfastness and his conviction that the Communists respected nothing but strength.

Regarding the tactics to be followed in the light of the Russian pressures on Berlin, we acknowledged that some differences remained among the Western powers. The Chancellor was disturbed by the course he feared the British government might follow, especially by the possibility that Prime Minister Macmillan might be inclined to make significant concessions to the Soviets. I stated my conviction that on questions of principle, the British government—and Mr. Macmillan in particular—stood squarely with us. Regarding tactics and public statements we should keep in mind that Macmillan faced difficult economic and political problems. Thus, British public opinion on the subject of Berlin was sharply divided, a fact which caused Macmillan to walk softly; but in a final showdown on any major issue he would be firm.

On the day after the funeral, four foreign ministers—Herter, Gromyko, Lloyd, and Couve de Murville—came to my office. I emphasized that I attached importance to the success of the Geneva conference, and dwelled on the conditions under which constructive results might be achieved. Much depended, I insisted, upon the degree of flexibility possessed by each of the participants in the negotiations. Our Secretary of State was empowered to negotiate on all matters falling within the broad outlines of previously approved policy. I hoped that each of the others might enjoy the similar confidence of his own government.[1]

Later, at a luncheon, I urged the four to take advantage of the informal atmosphere to get together and clear away some of the debris of detail in negotiation. Somewhat facetiously I suggested a radical approach. "I think I will instruct the pilot of your plane," I said, "not to land at Geneva until you four have reached the basis of some agreement. To do this I will provide the services of an American tanker airplane to extend your flight time indefinitely."

Secretary Herter later said that the trip back to Geneva took place in a better atmosphere. The four principals removed their coats, sat around a table in shirt-sleeves, and discussed their common problems. But no agreement of even the smallest kind was reached.

A few days after his return to Geneva, Herter sent me a message saying that the time had come when I might try personally to give an assist in breaking the impasse. Gromyko had made no concessions that in our view would remotely justify a summit, while Khrushchev, then on tour in

[1] This point I brought up deliberately because of the well-known practice of the Soviet rulers to treat their representatives, in international conferences below the summit, as little more than couriers—requiring that even minute details be checked and no concessions, even of a procedural nature, be made until approved in the Kremlin itself. Such a degree of centralization not only immeasurably slowed up the entire process of negotiations, but in itself almost completely defeated the legitimate purposes of diplomatic meetings.

Albania, had been making threatening statements. The Secretary, with Selwyn Lloyd concurring, hoped I would make clear in my next press conference that nothing had happened at Geneva to justify a summit conference.

Before meeting the press, I thought it best to inform Prime Minister Macmillan of my intentions; therefore, on June 3, 1959, I sent him the following:

> As you know, I adhere to my position that a summit meeting based on nothing more than wishful thinking would be a disaster. The world would interpret such a move as being virtual surrender, while Soviet prestige would be enhanced. . . .
>
> While I shall not try to give at my press conference a full list of the things that would spell additional . . . progress at the foreign ministers' meeting, we might hope for a widening of contacts between the two sides of the Iron Curtain, particularly in the fields of press exchanges, books, and travel by private citizens. Other ways in which progress might be achieved would be by some firm agreement for initial steps in banning of particular tests and control thereof.
>
> I repeat that the production by the foreign ministers of a reasonable paper for us to work on at a summit conference, together with the assurance that there will be no further attempts to restrict our rights and privileges with respect to Berlin, constitute the very minimum that would jusify a summit meeting.
>
> These are not new ideas; so far as I know, all of us are agreed on them.

As expected, the question came up in in the press conference, and I answered in nearly the same language I had used in the message to Macmillan.

My statement had no effect. Soon I began to receive more messages from Secretary Herter, all indicating that the Geneva meeting was nearing a crossroads; if it continued as an acrimonious and futile debating society, it would soon look ridiculous in the eyes of the world. The alternative was to adjourn—or possibly to take a long recess. The Soviets now produced a new proposition that in some respects seemed to be the worst up to that time. It set a new deadline, a year from the date of issuance, at which time all Western rights in Berlin would terminate. Never before had the Soviets in a conference stated their intentions so baldly. Public knowledge of this proposal would almost automatically end the Geneva conference.

Prospects for the future of the conference were made no brighter by the failure, in the opening sessions of the nuclear test talks, to reveal anything more in the Soviet attitude than the old, tiresome spirit of intransigence and *Nyet.* Then came a new message from Chris Herter.

He was beginning to suspect that the Soviets were stalling for time; they seemed to assume that Prime Minister Macmillan would press for a summit regardless of the outcome of the foreign ministers' conference.

At once I telephoned Under Secretary Dillon. If Herter's impression had any validity whatsoever, Harold, to avoid a complete collapse of negotiations, might conceivably take it upon himself to issue personal invitations to Khrushchev, De Gaulle, and me to come to London for "conversations without an agenda." Whatever name might be attached to such a meeting, the world obviously would regard it as a "summit."

With such a possibility in mind I decided to communicate directly with Khrushchev, and on June 15 sent the following:

> Dear Mr. Chairman:
>
> The point seems to have been reached in the discussions among the four Foreign Ministers in Geneva at which I feel impelled to address to you this personal and private note. . . .
>
> The Soviet Delegation, while unwilling to discuss in a serious way the broad peace plan which we put forward, has now, after some weeks of both private and plenary sessions, put forward proposals with respect to Berlin which are from our viewpoint a clearly unacceptable challenge to our position in that city. At the same time, Mr. Gromyko has stated that "in the opinion of the Soviet Government there is no foundation for any link between the results of this conference and the convening of a summit meeting." . . .
>
> It seems to me, unfortunately, that the latest Soviet position at Geneva as presented by Mr. Gromyko creates an impossible situation for the United States in that it implies the convocation of a summit meeting without prior progress of any kind. . . .
>
> I add only that if such a meeting were to offer hope of success it would certainly have to take place in an atmosphere in which neither side was posing a threat to the other and on the basis of such preparatory work by our Foreign Ministers as could give us reason to believe that the Heads of Government would be able to reach agreement on significant subjects. Anything less, it seems to me, would be a betrayal of the hopes of men everywhere.

On the day the message was sent, I received word through Under Secretary Dillon that Gromyko had now extended the time when, according to Soviet views, Western rights in Berlin would terminate; instead of one year from the date of issuance the new proposal would allow two and one-half years. Further, reduction of Western forces in Berlin might be progressive rather than immediate. We were amused at Gromyko's claim that his original demand for a one-year termination had been made on his *own initiative;* moreover, the two and one-half years termination date seemed, transparently, an effort to tempt an American President to leave the problem to his successor. The entire proposal was manifestly unacceptable.

But the real shock for me that day was confirmation from Chris Herter that his earlier impression had been correct: he reported that Harold Macmillan, while in Moscow, *had definitely agreed to press for a summit, regardless of conditions.* During our Camp David talks Harold had dropped several such hints, but my own contrary purpose had been so strong that it had not occurred to me at the time to question him more closely on the matter. While I conceded that he had a right to his view, I still held to my own—that a summit without more than blind hope to justify it could not be regarded as less than an egregious mistake. In any event, this news seemed to explain, partially at least, why Gromyko had been so stubborn in refusing to make any concessions that deserved the name of progress.

The divergence in thinking between ourselves and the British was emphasized when on June 16, I received a new communication from the Prime Minister: he predicted the breakdown of the Geneva foreign ministers' meeting in the near future. What disturbed him was the next possible step. Khrushchev, after the breakdown of negotiations, might invite the other three powers to a summit conference and this invitation, he thought, would be equally difficult to accept or reject. To forestall it, he proposed holding, on a Western invitation, an "informal" meeting of the four heads of government—not a "summit," of course, but rather a small gathering with no more than two advisers accompanying each head of government. If I should be the one to propose such a meeting, the idea would be widely acclaimed.

When the British ambassador, Sir Harold Caccia, arrived at the White House that evening, I came to point quickly. What was behind the Prime Minister's latest note? What was on his mind? I reminded the ambassador that our foreign ministers were not schoolboys who lacked authority to negotiate seriously and confidently within the limits of approved policy. They were engaged in an earnest effort to learn where we stood with the Russians and to try to develop solid reasons for a summit meeting. Now, in the Prime Minister's current message, I was presented with a suggestion of going hat-in-hand to see the Russians at a summit, almost in an attitude of supplication. This did not appeal to the American people, I suspected, and certainly not to me; moreover, I suspected that British people would not like it either.

The ambassador, aware of our attitude, was far from comfortable in carrying out his errand. However, he explained his own government's theory that the purpose of such an informal heads-of-government meeting would be to consider how to get the foreign ministers' meeting started up again.

The only reason I could see for the Prime Minister's proposal was that, in his judgment, Khrushchev was exercising such complete personal control in the Soviet Union that there was no prospect of success in negotiating with anyone else. To operate on this basis, however, would negate the entire diplomatic process. I informed the ambassador that I disagreed completely with the theory, set forth in the Macmillan letter, that if no agreement were reached at the foreign ministers' meeting it would be all the more necessary to hold a summit conference. While I understood and sympathized with Harold's domestic problems, I emphasized that I would not participate under such circumstances.

As an alternative to a summit of any description, we discussed briefly the possibility of a personal meeting between Khrushchev and me. But I emphasized that I would not suggest such a meeting to Khrushchev save in response to the expressed desire of our allies and, if held, it would be exploratory only and would not imply a promise on my part to suggest a summit.

On one point we were agreed: the foreign ministers should not actually adjourn the Geneva meeting. It would be better for them to recess than to break off negotiations. As a result of this meeting, I wrote to Harold Macmillan:

> I shall probably want to write you further as soon as we know Khrushchev's reaction to my letter of June 15. As you probably know, it was a most urgent suggestion to him to reconsider the Soviet position at Geneva, which has in fact retrogressed in recent days, and to live up to his own pledge to us last March that the Soviet Government would do everything possible to make a positive contribution to the work of the Foreign Ministers' Conference. As to his reaction to my message I am not particularly sanguine but I also do not believe that we have yet necessarily reached an impasse.

The message went on to remind Harold that I adhered to our Camp David agreement concerning our insistence upon substantive accomplishment at the foreign ministers' conference, and added that if I surrendered on this point I would no longer have any influence with Khrushchev who would, thereafter, consider me a "pushover." Indeed, I said, I would myself interpret such an agreement as an exhibition of weakness.

I next took up the suggestion that we have an informal meeting of the four governmental heads. My conclusion was that no matter how informal the meeting, the world would view it as a full-fledged and official summit conference. Each head of government would want his own foreign minister with him, who in turn would insist upon a number of his selected advisers. To all of this would be added clerical helpers, interpreters, security, and other personnel. "The presence of 1000 representatives of the press," I said, "would be the frosting on the cake."

Referring to the Prime Minister's belief that if an invitation should come from Khrushchev it would be difficult for us either to accept or decline, I replied that I would feel no embarrassment whatsoever in saying "no." However, I referred to the possibility that if Khrushchev were to head the Soviet delegation that would soon visit their exhibition in New York, I could take advantage of that fortuitous circumstance, if our allies so desired, to meet him and indulge in exploratory discussions on future plans for negotiations. I promised to communicate with him upon receipt of a reply to my letter to Khrushchev.

For that reply we did not have long to wait—it arrived on the same day that my message went to Harold. Although the tone was conciliatory, there was in it little basis for optimism. Khrushchev argued that the foreign ministers had achieved results by defining the differences between us and by making attempts to narrow divergences. He asserted that the earlier Soviet proposals (in which Western rights were to terminate in one year and two and one-half years, respectively) were not to be considered ultimatums, and concluded, in unconscious irony, I would think, by expressing approval of these letter exchanges as a profitable means of communication between the two of us.

I informed Harold that I saw little encouragement in the Soviet note but could be just as patient and persistent as Khrushchev.

It was now clear that the foreign ministers' meeting in Geneva should come to a close, at least temporarily.[2] They had been able to agree on one thing only—the wisdom of a recess for three weeks, starting on June 20. The first session had wound up in deadlock after forty-one days.

* * *

Another subject that now required attention was that of an American Exhibition, to be opened in Moscow in late July as a counterpart to the Russian Exhibition, just opening in New York. The exchange had been agreed upon months earlier, but now I wanted to explore the possibility that through these two exhibitions we might widen our contacts with the Soviets. The hope—faint though it might be—was that we could en-

[2] Before doing so, however, the three Western foreign ministers made one final effort, submitting to Gromyko a memo [see Appendix V].

courage the Soviet rulers to relax the rigidity with which they kept their society closed. Obviously if such a process could be progressively expanded, it would increase our knowledge and understanding of the U.S.S.R., its people, and its economy—and their knowledge of the United States.

The experiences of Harold C. McClellan, who was in charge of the American Exhibition in Moscow, were little less than maddening as he desperately worked to open our exhibit at the time scheduled. One day the Soviets would be cooperative, apparently anxious for the exhibit to take place; the next they would seem fearful of its effect on the populace and would find every kind of specious excuse to delay preparations. Finally, however, we made our deadline.

In other ways the Soviets continued their wearisome policy of alternating sweet words with saber-rattling. Three days after the foreign ministers recessed, Mr. Averell Harriman, a former ambassador to the Soviet Union, was granted an interview with Chairman Khrushchev which Harriman later described as "terrifying." Khrushchev announced his intention to terminate Western rights in Berlin and boasted of rockets poised in China that could immediately liquidate Formosa. He claimed that Soviet fighters could shoot down our air-breathing long-range missiles and made lavish claims regarding the quantity and capabilities of the Soviet ICBMs. He alleged that for an expenditure of 30 billion rubles on ballistic missiles the Soviets could destroy every industrial center in the United States and Europe, but that he, of course, *preferred* not to do so!

Concurrently with this harangue, the Soviet commander in Berlin was attempting to transfer jurisdiction over Allied Autobahn traffic to the East Germans. Three attempts were made by the East German police to control the movement of American convoys. They were not successful, but when we protested at the annoyances the Soviets replied that these were matters we should settle with the East Germans.

When I returned to Washington on June 26, after a pleasant visit with Queen Elizabeth and Prince Philip at the opening of the St. Lawrence Seaway, I accepted an invitation from the Soviets to visit their exhibition in New York. Three days later I flew to New York with a sizable party. Struggling through the crowds, I had the opportunity to view the display which was in some ways quite remarkable, and to form a preliminary personal impression of First Deputy Premier Frol R. Kozlov.

He was a personable, yet obviously tough and capable man. He spared no effort to be ingratiating and treated our party with the utmost cordiality. This was demonstrated, for example, at the art exhibit in which I was especially interested. The paintings were all representational. Mr. Kozlov asked me to select one to keep. Feeling it would be impolitic to decline,

I chose a colorful landscape depicting a rapid-flowing stream through snow-covered fields, entitled "Spring Comes to the Farm." (When the picture reached the White House I had it hung in a conference room; later it went to a museum.)

Two days later in Washington I had a further opportunity to become acquainted with Mr. Kozlov. Again he was pleasant, but our talk was unproductive. The First Deputy Premier then left for a ten-day tour around the United States.

At my Wednesday news conference, a week later, Merriman Smith asked:

> Mr. President, there is a story from Moscow this morning that Premier Khrushchev told the American governors who visited him yesterday two things: That he is available for travel—(laughter) and that he would like very much to visit the United States.
>
> But, a new and somewhat significant point is that he thinks, he told them, that he thinks a visit by you to Russia would be very beneficial to relations between both countries.
>
> I wonder what your feelings on this subject are?

This was the first I had heard of Khrushchev's statement. I so admitted, and went on to point out a few of the difficulties, including the need to maintain cooperative relations with our allies in all dealings with the Soviets. I differentiated between purely ceremonial state visits and serious substantive discussions between heads of government.

As soon as the press conference was over, however, I called Secretary Herter to say that the Khrushchev suggestion might possibly provide a device to break the stalemate. If such an exchange were to come about, a meeting in a fairly secluded spot would be desirable.

The State Department studied the idea. Talking alone with Khrushchev offered some real possibilities. Mr. Herter and his advisers suggested to me that we send word promptly to Khrushchev through Kozlov, who was scheduled to return to Moscow on July 12.

After pondering the question I decided to extend a qualified invitation to Mr. Khrushchev.

The mechanics of the invitation were fairly simple. Under Secretary of State Robert Murphy was to meet Kozlov at the airplane as he was departing from New York. Murphy was to give him a letter for Khrushchev. It would be general in nature, and would refer to a more specific oral message that Bob Murphy would deliver at the steps of the airplane.

The next day I signed the letter to Khrushchev and gave it to Bob Murphy for presentation. We then discussed the "talking paper," that is, the notes from which Murphy would speak to Kozlov. Murphy was to refer to Khrushchev's reported interest in visiting the United States, to point out the possibility that a personal meeting between the two of us on an informal basis might lead to a better understanding, to specify that we were thinking not of negotiation but of mere discussion and especially to express my hope that the foreign ministers, resuming their meeting on July 13 at Geneva, would make such progress as would justify a meeting of the four heads of government. If they did so, I would support plans for a four-power summit meeting in a place such as Quebec. If all this should be agreeable, a meeting between Khrushchev and me at Camp David, near Washington, at a mutually suitable moment should be arranged.

Furthermore, if Khrushchev were interested in visiting points of interest in the United States, I would be pleased to make the necessary arrangements. Timing, of course, would be a matter on which Khrushchev's views would be necessary. Finally, Murphy was to mention to Kozlov the possibility of my making a trip to Moscow later in the year.

Our government now viewed the reconvening of the foreign ministers at Geneva with faintly revived hope. Both Khrushchev and Kozlov had told our ambassador in Moscow, Llewellyn Thompson, how delighted they were at the treatment Kozlov had received on his tour in this country. With this turn of events we felt we had reason to expect at least some sort of a change of attitude when the Geneva meetings got under way.

However, when the foreign ministers returned to Geneva the Soviets, far from smiling, had grown more difficult. Gromyko had become not only obstructive but on occasion even indulged rudely in personalities. Meanwhile, the East German customs police attempted to interfere with an American military train, the first time that an incident of this type had happened. This was one in a new rash of incidents involving Western access rights to Berlin.

On July 21 I discussed with Under Secretary Dillon and General Goodpaster a message from Chris Herter at Geneva. In it the Secretary expressed the opinion that the conference seemed to have reached a stalemate. He had in mind calling for its early termination, an action designed to make Gromyko either produce or show his hand.

This move would have been satisfactory to me, except for the fact that Vice President Nixon was due to board a plane soon for a trip to Moscow. If the foreign ministers' meeting were to break down, the Vice President would then find his task, already certain to be difficult, even more so. Consequently, I advised Chris not to terminate the foreign ministers' discussion at once, but rather to seek a recess for a few days to allow the Vice President time to complete his trip.

The explanation for the Soviet attitude came to my attention forcefully the next day. Having received a message from Khrushchev accepting the invitation to visit the United States, I was struck by the apparent lack of connection in Khrushchev's mind between this exchange of visits and the need for progress at the foreign ministers' meeting. Accordingly, I sent for Under Secretaries Dillon and Murphy and for General Goodpaster to go over the draft of a reply that I had begun to compose.

To my surprise, Mr. Dillon voiced objection to the fact that my draft implied the same conditions for a meeting with Khrushchev as for a four-power summit meeting. I retorted that this was so because I wanted it so; the link was automatic and was in conformity with Bob Murphy's conversation with Kozlov.

At that point Bob Murphy spoke up with admirable candor. He said he had never understood any link to exist in my mind between an invitation to Khrushchev and progress at a foreign ministers' meeting; the invitation which he had conveyed to Kozlov had been unqualified.

To say that this news disturbed me is an understatement. My invitation was to a meeting that I had described as a prelude to a summit; since my readiness to attend a summit was conditioned on assurance of progress at Geneva, it was difficult for me to understand how the misinterpretation occurred.

An informal conversation between Khrushchev and me at Camp David, while some progress at the Geneva conference might still occur, was one thing; an extended trip by Khrushchev around the United States and a personal conference between the two of us, after the foreign ministers had produced nothing, was quite another. For the only time that I can remember I lectured the assembled group regarding the need for proper measures, such as Foster Dulles had consistently employed, to insure that State Department action and my own thinking were exactly in step. After all the important meetings we held, I reminded them, Foster would go back and dictate a memorandum of the conference. He would then call me on the phone and read it to me to assure that it was in accord with my understanding. I was chagrined at the way this whole matter had developed; I remarked that I would now personally have to pay the penalty of going through with a meeting which, under the circumstances, would be a most unpleasant experience, and would be subject to serious misinterpretation.

After a bit of cool reflection, I realized that the cause of the difficulty lay more in my own failure to make myself unmistakably clear than in the failure of others to understand me. After all, here were some of the most capable men I knew in their field, and apparently all had failed to comprehend the idea in my mind. It was now up to me to make the best I could of the situation.

But having momentarily fallen prey to a sense of frustration, I soon began to believe that there was still a glimmer of hope. I could not cancel the invitation to Khrushchev, but I could at least point out to him the difference in the reception he would receive in the United States if progress at Geneva were actually apparent. I could emphasize strongly how hopefully, then, the American people would view a meeting between us. On the other hand, I could not *order* a warm reception for Khrushchev, and I could not guarantee one if he came to the United States as the person responsible for the breakdown of fruitful negotiations. On July 29 I wrote to the Chairman to explain these circumstances.

* * *

An effort related at least distantly to East-West summits was that of encouraging exchanges of visits between United States and Soviet officials at all levels in the hope that such exchanges might lift the Iron Curtain somewhat. It was to help gain acceptance for this idea in the U.S.S.R. that Vice President Nixon flew to Moscow that summer. Accompanied by my brother, Milton, he went to officiate at the opening of the United States Exhibition there, as First Deputy Premier Kozlov had earlier done at the opening of the Soviet Exhibition in New York. We hoped that his going would represent more than a mere courtesy call. It seemed possible that some encouraging results might well flow from it.

A week before his departure, however, I had issued in response to a Congressional Joint Resolution, Proclamation 303 entitled, "Captive Nations Week, 1959," the third week in July. Quite naturally I was in sympathy with the Resolution which set aside a week of prayer dedicated to the peoples held captive under Communist domination, but given a choice as to timing, I would have delayed its passage for some days. Despite the fact that the peaceful means of expressing our concern were stressed, Khrushchev had taken a less peaceful view of it (or at least he so pretended). Although the captive nations themselves could have received little word of the Resolution had he willed it otherwise, he took occasion in Warsaw to criticize me for signing such a proclamation and to express doubts as to the desirability of Mr. Nixon's coming to the Soviet Union at all.

When Dick Nixon came to see me just before his departure, however, he was not discouraged. He recognized the difficulties inherent in the journey, but he was optimistic and even eager. While the Vice President was not being sent as a negotiator, I advised him not to have any hesitation in talking plainly with the Soviets and particularly to be positive in his conversations with Khrushchev.

One pertinent question in Dick's mind was my personal definition of the word "progress" in relation to the foreign ministers' meeting. I said that this meant at the very least an assurance that Western rights would be maintained in Berlin until changed by four-power agreement and the setting up of effective machinery to study the over-all German problem of which Berlin was only a part.

Dick agreed. He intended, he said, to meet Khrushchev head-on in debate if forced to do so. By countering Khrushchev's points, one by one, Dick felt he would have an excellent chance to probe Khrushchev's mind and possibly to gain some real knowledge of the Chairman's convictions. Furthermore, he hoped to change some of Khrushchev's misconceptions about America.

* * *

Whenever the foreign ministers' meeting seemed on the verge of recess or termination, our exchanges of views with our British friends became more frequent.

The Prime Minister was now placing considerable emphasis on the possible advantage of a moratorium—simply a period of specified length during which the subject of Berlin would not be brought up as an issue by either the Soviets or the Western allies. While I could not see this as much of an advance, I agreed that, as long as Western rights at the end of the moratorium would be in no way reduced, such an arrangement might be beneficial in removing the crisis mood then prevailing in some quarters. Harold's idea was that the period should be at least two and a half years, a terminating date that would follow the next German election.

But Harold had something more drastic in mind than a mere moratorium. He suggested that I should, without further ado, couple the idea of Khrushchev's visit to the United States with a proposal for a formal summit meeting in Washington or Quebec toward the end of August, a month later. He also proposed that I should suggest a preliminary pre-summit meeting in Paris of the heads of government of France, West Germany, Britain, and the United States.

Of course I simply could not agree. But despite my feeling of frustration I had no intention of bickering with one of my best friends. So I decided to state my views in detail once more, reviewing the entire history of the problem but making no new proposals.

As this message was going out, I learned that Harold's idea of a "pre-summit" by the four Western heads of government was dead before it was ever formally proposed; De Gaulle would have none of it.

Harold replied to my message the next day: He would be willing to hold a Western summit in London, with Premier Debré of France representing De Gaulle. But I had to remain firm; the requirements for a formal four-power summit were still, despite my friend's conclusions and assumptions, not met.

Part of the problem was solved by Chairman Khrushchev. Having been warned of the hot summer weather in the United States, he expressed a preference to postpone his visit to this country until some time after the first week of September. This would put a summit meeting much later than Harold Macmillan had suggested.

While all this was going on, the Vice President had been keeping me intimately informed of his trip. Khrushchev had expressed considerable anger over the Captive Nations Resolution and had made it a point to jeer at the Vice President about it on every occasion, particularly during the early stages of the tour. This he did both in public and private.

At Sokolniki Park, where the Vice President opened the United States Exhibition, Khrushchev deliberately took advantage of what was supposed to be a purely ceremonial occasion to attack both Dick and the United States. But the Vice President met him point by point and in my opinion came out considerably better than even. The debate continued even at social events, such as on a boat trip on the Volga River. The Vice President's popular reception throughout the Soviet Union, however—and even more so in Poland, on his return trip—had been amazingly good. In one instance, at least, the police apparently had orders to suppress the enthusiasm of the crowd. I was delighted with the way things went.

Our Moscow exhibition served a constructive purpose by bringing thousands upon thousands of Soviet men, women, and children face to face with the products of American industry and above all with American citizens. I was particularly impressed with reports of the group of outstanding United States college students who served as guides and who day after day stood up and in fluent Russian fielded questions of the greatest diversity about life in the United States. In fact, these bright young men and women so impressed their hearers that when some trained Communist agitators began infiltrating the crowd and throwing loaded questions, friendly Russians in the audience would help out by supplying answers in loud whispers.

I had long advocated—and still advocate today—this kind of direct people-to-people exchange as one fine, progressive step toward peace in the world. In September of 1956 I initiated a broad-scale People-to-People program—an effort to stimulate private citizens in many fields (the arts, education, athletics, law, medicine, business) to organize themselves to reach across the seas and national boundaries to their counterparts in other lands.

> If we are going to take advantage of the assumption that all people want peace, then the problem is for people to get together and to leap governments—if necessary to evade governments—to work out not one method but thousands of methods by which people can gradually learn a little bit more of each other.

In 1958 I studied and worked on a proposal (which I never got to make) for a massive exchange of undergraduates by the United States and the Soviet Union—an exchange which, far outstripping the handful we normally send and receive each year, could come to a total of as high as ten thousand. (I even drafted a message to Chairman Bulganin offering to invite "several thousand" Soviet students here, with their expenses paid, leaving to Soviet leaders the decision as to whether it would invite an equal number of American students to their country.) In checking out the security aspects of this idea, I telephoned J. Edgar Hoover, who said, "Though bringing ten thousand Soviet students into the United States would undoubtedly cause some additional problems, I'm all for the idea. It's an affirmative, dynamic proposal."

I was getting tired of dealing with a Communist generation set in their prejudices. One day a new crop would wield the power in the Soviet Union, and it was this generation I was trying to reach. My proposal for a massive exchange was never made public, for at that time the State Department was negotiating with the Soviet Union for cultural exchanges in the magnitude of a hundred or so; these were not having much success, and so I was persuaded that I would only disrupt current negotiations if I made a more daring proposal. However, as a nation we must never stop trying.

* * *

With the Nixon trip now drawing to a close, there was no reason to extend the futility at Geneva [see Appendix W].

Every attempt to achieve agreement on even inconsequential points had been in vain. On August 5 the end came. It was with anything but enthusiasm that I went to a press conference that morning to announce the planned exchange of visits with Mr. Khrushchev. I described how I had suggested to the State Department some time before that an unusual type of effort to melt the ice might be useful; explained that this visit had no direct connection with a possible later summit meeting, and recognized that there was no hope that this announcement could favorably affect the dying foreign ministers' meeting which again had been characterized by the enduring negative attitude of the Soviets.

* * *

The residual effects of all this caused me some chagrin: I now had to meet Khrushchev and allow him to tour our country in spite of the fact that he had deliberately engineered the breakdown of the foreign ministers' meeting. But I did have the satisfaction of knowing that our diplomats at Geneva had done a good job. Under the strong tutelage of the new Secretary of State our delegation had tried to work constructively and patiently, and had given away no Western rights.

The world knew how earnestly we were striving for peace. The original Soviet ultimatum on Berlin had been so firmly met that it was now taken less seriously in Western governmental circles, and people were losing much of their apprehension that we might, without warning, be plunged into the holocaust of World War III, possibly over some small incident.

Ahead lay months, I knew, of strenuous work with our Western allies as well as with Khrushchev—and some time later possibly a summit meeting. In many ways, especially from the viewpoint of precedent, I regretted that normal diplomatic channels, even including formal meetings among foreign ministers, were being so markedly ignored. Prospects for even the slightest progress in easing world tensions now seemed to lay, for the time being at least, in direct contacts between the heads of governments.

CHAPTER XVIII

Personal Diplomacy

So likewise ye, except ye utter by the
tongue words easy to be understood,
how shall it be known what is spoken?
For ye shall speak in the air.

—*I Corinthians 14:9*

It is generally better to deal by speech than by letter.

—*Francis Bacon*

THE news of Chairman Khrushchev's impending visit to the United States was received with consternation by Chancellor Adenauer and President de Gaulle. They were reportedly concerned over any possible appearance that I would be representing the views of all the West when the Chairman and I should sit down to confer. Prime Minister Macmillan, on the other hand, applauded the idea of this personal visit but still seemed somewhat at odds with the rest of us on conditions for a summit meeting.

These facts indicated a necessity to confer with the heads of government of these three allies before Khrushchev arrived on September 15, 1959.

For some time I had been searching for an opportunity to renew personal contact with General Charles de Gaulle, who had returned to power in France only the previous year. His unfavorable stance toward certain Western problems was caused by an unwavering and understandable purpose: restoring the prestige of France. I hoped that by renewing old associations and revealing my sympathetic understanding of his purpose, I possibly could encourage him to become more flexible in his views respecting NATO's command arrangement.

A friend, C. D. Jackson, knowing of my desire soon to meet with

President de Gaulle, suggested August 27, 1959, as a possibility. This would be the fifteenth anniversary of the day when, as Supreme Allied Commander in Europe during World War II, I had paid my first official call on General de Gaulle, then in his office in the newly liberated city of Paris. It was a date that might have some sentimental significance, for that call had given public notice that the forces under my command recognized him as Provisional President of France. Should such a visit be agreeable to him, I thought that while I was in Europe I could also confer briefly with Adenauer and Macmillan. With all three leaders I would discuss NATO, realistic plans for disarmament negotiations with the Soviets, the Berlin situation, and possible ways to reduce world tensions.

The State Department sought to find out whether De Gaulle might find such a visit acceptable; if the 27th of August was not convenient for him, I could come to Paris some time in early September.

De Gaulle replied that he welcomed the idea but because he had previously scheduled a trip to Algiers for the end of August he preferred a September date. He would be quite willing to make adjustments in his plans, if necessary. I appreciated his offer, but, having no overriding reason to prefer the earlier date, chose a later one.

In the meantime we learned that Chancellor Adenauer desired that I come also to Bonn, even if for only a matter of hours. I told the planners to include Bonn in the schedule—a brief stop before going from the Continent to London. Finally, plans were set to everyone's satisfaction.

I was scheduled to leave from Washington early in the morning of Wednesday, August 26. I came down from Gettysburg the previous Sunday and spent Monday and Tuesday in conferences. Congress was still in session and it was necessary of course to leave our affairs with Congress in order.[1]

I then held a press conference and summarized the purposes of the trip. But the interest of the group was focused not on this trip to Europe, but on the forthcoming visit of Premier Khrushchev, nearly a month away, and my possible return trip to Russia.

Peter Lisagor of the *Chicago Daily News* asked:

[1] At a meeting with the Republican leaders that Tuesday we discussed possibilities for obtaining action on labor legislation, civil rights, interest rates, public works, PL 480 (use of U.S. agricultural surplus for export to underdeveloped countries), mutual security, highway legislation, federal health insurance, veterans pension, and counterpart funds. One piece of disturbing information from the legislators was that a public works bill would probably be passed, authorizing expenditures far greater than I could approve.

> Mr. President, . . . part of the criticism is that your visit to Russia somehow or other will erode the presidential prestige to a ceremonial visit of that kind.
>
> Would you care to comment on that?

In a rather long answer I discounted the contention that a foreigner's visit to me or a visit of mine to another nation could hurt the prestige of the Presidency itself, even though I might personally be widely criticized. Observing that my own "prestige" was not particularly important, I emphasized that the search for some break, some avenue of approach, as yet unexplored, through which we might move to a better relationship between East and West, was truly vital. The costs Americans bore every year for armaments were staggering. If this went on indefinitely, we could reach a breaking point. Consequently, any President who recoiled from using the last atom of his own prestige or energy in the attempt to find an acceptable approach to the dilemma should be condemned by the American people.

"I get a little bit weary," I observed, "about people who say, 'Well, this would be a terrible blow to presidential prestige,' or any other prestige. We are talking about the human race and what's going to happen to it."

I did concede that particular circumstances could arise which would make a visit to Russia unrealistic.

My final day in Washington was a bit full—twenty-five meetings in all, with Cabinet officers, staff, congressional leaders, and the press—all business, none ceremonial.

The next morning I left the White House at 3:20 A.M. accompanied by Mamie, who came to the airport to see us off. The brief ceremonies at Andrews Air Force Base were eerie, with flashing photographic bulbs punctuating the blackness beyond the floodlighted area around the nose of the strange jet airplane. Before departure I took Mamie aboard to show her around the mammoth machine which was almost completely new to me. Both in size and speed the new airplane completely dwarfed the *Columbine,* the Super Constellation that we had long considered the last word in luxurious transportation. However, no airplane ever looked attractive to Mamie.

Afterward I settled back in my compartment with the Secretary of State and underwent an exhilarating experience, that of my first jet flight, with its silent, effortless acceleration and its rapid rate of climb. The deep coloring of the sunrise, seen from a height of thirty-five thousand feet, was an unforgettable sight. We stopped to refuel at Harmon Air Force Base in Newfoundland, where the officers and ladies of that station—at what must have been considerable inconvenience to themselves—brought us refreshments and a warm welcome at 7:30 A.M. Then we continued to our destination, Bonn, Germany.

We arrived at 6:30 P.M., just at dusk, and the ceremonies at the airport were impressive. While this German army bore little resemblance to the old, there was still no question about Teutonic efficiency in things military. The exchange of greetings with Chancellor Adenauer was short, and soon the two of us were in an open car en route to the American Embassy.

The welcome given to the American party along the twenty-mile route to the Embassy was astonishing to me—a feeling the Chancellor said he shared. The exuberant crowds exceeded severalfold the aggregate of the populations of the towns we went through; the road became so jammed that it took our convoy an hour and a half to cover a distance that had been estimated as requiring only a third of that time.

Even in the excitement of such a journey I could not fail to see overwhelming evidence of the remarkable transformation that Germany had undergone in the course of the seven years since I had left my post at NATO. The extent to which American styles and American products had influenced the country in dress, manners, and even billboards was remarkable.

To return the greetings of the crowd, the Chancellor and I were compelled to stand in the tonneau throughout the journey, even after night had fallen, and we were weary by the time the American Embassy came into sight. The Secret Service still had the chore of making a passageway through the crowds so that we could penetrate the few yards between our car and the residence, but the feat was finally managed. After a quiet evening with Ambassador and Mrs. David K. Bruce—both old friends of mine—I put an end to an eventful twenty-seven-hour day.

The first scheduled item the next morning, following a ride through the American community, was a ceremonial visit to Theodor Heuss, President of the Federal Republic of Germany. I met him at the Villa Hammerschmidt, where within a few minutes we were joined by President-elect Heinrich Luebke. Proceeding then to the Palais Schaumburg, Chancellor Adenauer and I began our private conferences.

Our first topic was the France-Algeria situation. During the months just past President de Gaulle and Chancellor Adenauer had kept in close contact, and the State Department had predicted that Adenauer might urge American support for President de Gaulle's position respecting Algeria. I explained that I was in sympathy with the constructive efforts President de Gaulle was making to reach a satisfactory composition of the French-Arab difficulties in that revolt-torn region.

The Chancellor and I discussed a proposal on Algeria that the Arab nations planned to bring before the United Nations. I reminded the Chancellor that an Arab proposal concerning French-Algerian relations had been made recently in the General Assembly and that France had refused to defend herself on the ground that the French-Algerian struggle was an internal affair. The sequence of the voting had been arranged by lot; fortunately it had so happened that the United States had voted last. Our government had been able to abstain, in the knowledge that the resolution had already failed to obtain the necessary two-thirds majority. However, I stressed that we could not expect such a fortuitous voting order to occur again. In the light of our anti-colonial tradition, the United States would find itself on the horns of a dilemma in the next session if asked to support France wholeheartedly *in the absence of sturdy French participation in the debate.* I thought it advisable for the French not only to take a positive stand but to submit to the General Assembly an appropriate resolution of its own and to support it vigorously. Then, if the proposal were reasonable, we would be glad to support it. I recommended that the Chancellor urge President de Gaulle to consider seriously the advantages of such a move.

The Chancellor seemed almost obsessed with the Algerian problem. He believed that the Algerian rebellion could never have become a serious affair except with heavy Communist support; were it to be totally successful, we could expect to lose Algeria to the Communists, followed in order by Morocco, Tunisia, and the Middle East. In such a procession of tragic events, he said, the position of Western Europe would be precarious.

While I could not foresee such a chain of disaster, I did agree that the situation was serious enough. The Chancellor knew, of course, that I was expecting to discuss Algeria with President de Gaulle who, according to my information, was developing an over-all Algerian plan, soon to be submitted, that might be deemed satisfactory to both sides.

The meeting with the Chancellor lasted longer than planned, and I was late for a press conference scheduled for eleven o'clock. I was pleased to find that the press representatives were in a serious mood, and important subjects were undiluted by the trivial questions that too often beset such affairs.

Lunch that day was held at the Palais Schaumburg, with the Chancellor and some of our German and American associates. The atmosphere was convivial. The Chancellor, a known connoisseur of Rhine wines, had personally selected those to be served, and had ordered the dessert pudding flavored with one of his favorites. When the pudding arrived, he found it to be lacking the desired ingredient, whereupon he spoke sharply and at length (in German, of course) to his chief of protocol, Sigismund von Braun, the brother of our noted missile scientist, Wernher von Braun. He also took occasion in the course of his after-luncheon toast to apologize to his guests for the lack of flavor in the pudding. "I'll be thankful if this disappointment is the most serious one I encounter during my European visit," I remarked, and he replied, with a laugh, that he not only agreed but that he would regard such an outcome as a miracle of the highest order.

After lunch we immediately turned again to business. This time the Chancellor and I met alone with only our interpreters. Such an arrangement, I often found, does much to encourage an easy exchange of views and confidence on both sides.

I was gratified to find that on the Berlin situation the Chancellor, while firm, was not so rigid as had been suggested. We agreed that the Soviets, no matter how belligerent or objectionable their deportment, would be careful to avoid any move that might set off a major war. The German buildup of armed forces for NATO then came under discussion, with the Chancellor promising to meet commitments. I told him that I, for one, hoped that the German contingent would later be materially increased in size so that eventually the strength of the American ground forces in Europe could be drastically reduced; he quickly replied that the possibility should not be even mentioned at the time.

I was disappointed that the Chancellor saw substantial difficulties in developing better East-West German contacts. He feared that the United States government misunderstood the extent of the repressive measures used by the East German Communists in punishing their own people who illegally benefited from these contacts. On the whole, the Chancellor was quite pessimistic on this important subject.

This informal exchange was so absorbing that I felt we should continue without calling in our advisers, who had been directed to join us about half an hour after the start of our private talks. As a result, many eminent professionals of both nationalities cooled their heels in the anteroom until word came at 4:30 that it was time to depart. The Chancellor and I virtually flew out the door; three minutes later we were on our way to the airfield and were at Wahn Airport in eight minutes.

The brief departure ceremony ended on an unusual and, to me, highly pleasing feature. A splendid German band, providing the music for the occasion, played as its final selection the *Official West Point March.* I was deeply touched by the gesture, the more so when I learned they had practiced the strange piece for weeks.

* * *

An hour and a half after takeoff we reached London International Airport, landing, as on the day before, at dusk. Harold Macmillan and members of his Cabinet were out to meet us, and after a brief welcome by the Royal Air Force Honor Guard, we left the airport for the United States ambassador's residence.

On the way Harold told me that he had given a minimum of publicity to our route. Hence, he had been surprised to find, as he had driven to the airport, crowds lining the streets, in spite of approaching darkness. He and I had designed the trip for business only, to be conducted with a minimum of ceremony, because of a tentative plan, to which I had agreed, for my wife and me to make a formal official visit in December to the British Isles. Although no public announcement of the plan could then be made, Harold was anxious that the later trip would, in the public mind, overshadow the informal one I was now making. I had not visited Britain since the unhappy Suez incident, and because some British papers at that time had said I had let their government down, some people had warned me to expect a cool reception. For my part, having spent many of the most trying and dramatic moments of my life in Britain, I knew I had friends there and, in a sense, felt as if I were coming home. Even though I was sure we would encounter no general hostility, I must confess that I was happily overwhelmed by the reception accorded our party.

As we made our slow way toward the city, the crowds grew ever denser and Harold kept repeating, "I never would have believed it, I never would have believed it." As we reached the region of Grosvenor Square, where my wartime headquarters had been located for a time, he turned to me and said, "The state visit in December is off. Anything after this would be anticlimax; I would not think of broaching the subject with Her Majesty after such a demonstration!"

Finally we reached the Embassy residence and settled down for a short but pleasant evening with Ambassador Whitney and his charming wife, Betsey.

* * *

The next morning, we prepared to depart for Balmoral[2] to call on the Royal Family. The Prime Minister came to the Embassy residence at ten minutes of eight—a wretched hour by European standards—and

[2] Balmoral Castle in Scotland, the vacation residence of the Royal Family.

accompanied me to the airport. In half an hour I was airborne for Dice, Scotland, accompanied only by General Snyder, Sergeant Moaney, and my son John, who acted as my aide.

We were met by Prince Philip, an interesting personality and a man for whom I had formed a genuine liking. After a motor trip of some fifty miles, we reached Balmoral Castle. I had seen this beautiful spot thirteen years before when my family and I had visited Their Majesties, the then reigning King George VI and Queen Elizabeth.

As the Prince and I entered the Palace grounds we were met at the gate by the Queen. Together we inspected the Guard of Honor. We then spent a delightful few hours with the Royal Family and their household guests, and had a tour of the Balmoral estate, with the Queen herself taking the wheel of a station wagon to drive us to the many points of interest.

We went over rugged, heather-covered hills, where the Royal Family was fond of stalking stag, and stopped at a small house built for Queen Victoria, where the party enjoyed an afternoon picnic. From there we went to pay a visit to the Queen Mother, that gracious lady who lived in a modest dwelling not far from the castle.

One intriguing feature of the afternoon was my temporary illusion that I had escaped from the anxious eyes of the ever-faithful Secret Service detail. Mile after mile we had rolled over isolated roads with not a person to be seen; certainly no car full of security agents was following us, much to my relief. But, not long after we left the picnic area, I noticed a man standing by the side of the road. He was Secret Service Agent John Campion, looking not the least bit concerned. I knew then that a system of "sentry" surveillance had been worked out in advance; the Service was not relaxing its constant and protective care.

One quality of the Royal Family that has always intrigued me is the informality which prevails when its members are at home among themselves, particularly at Balmoral. At the afternoon picnic by the lake, the Queen acted as hostess and simple housewife, gracefully cooking the "dropped scones" over a charcoal burner for her eight or ten guests. I tried to help as a waiter; I am quite sure that I was adjudged by Her Majesty as somewhat less than competent in this department. In any event, after tasting dropped scones for the first time I asked the Queen for the recipe and she later sent it to me.

While we had tea the Prince raced a sailboat up and down the lake in a stiff breeze. It was cold for that time of the year by our standards. Their two children, dressed in windbreakers and sailing togs, were the Prince's shore helpers.

The next morning, Saturday, August 29, I had to depart—all too soon—from Balmoral. Retracing our route to Dice, we were airborne once more in the special jet aircraft of the "Queen's Flight."

* * *

Harold Macmillan met me at twelve noon, and without delay we proceeded to Chequers, which has been the country home of the Prime Minister ever since, years ago, a wealthy American presented the property to the British government for that purpose.

This attractive estate had become quite familiar to me during the days of World War II, when I visited there often as a guest of Mr. Churchill. Sufficiently isolated from London and surrounded with pleasant fields and forests, it was an ideal place for an informal gathering.[3]

We wasted little time in getting down to business. With lunch at 2 P.M., Harold and I, with our advisers, met immediately afterward in a spacious room on the second floor. As always the discussion was wide-ranging. The first subject was that of bases in Trinidad which had been leased to the United States during World War II in exchange for fifty destroyers.[4]

From there the discussion turned to the current Communist aggression in Laos. We decided to ask the United Nations to send observers to Laos, at least to determine the accuracy of our suspicion that the aggressors—the Pathet Lao units—were Communists.[5]

I brought Harold up to date on the discussions with Chancellor Adenauer. He seemed satisfied with what I had learned of Adenauer's

[3] The house had a notable history long before it became a residence for the Prime Minister. Some portions are four hundred years old, and the dwelling—I do not know how much was then in existence—was owned by Oliver Cromwell's son-in-law in the seventeenth century. Paintings of Cromwell and his daughters and other bits of Cromwell memorabilia provide additional interest for a visitor. The room in which my secretary, Ann Whitman, stayed on the third floor was the one in which Lady Mary Grey had been imprisoned for a couple of years. More fortunate than her sister, Lady Jane Grey (beheaded by Queen Mary in 1554), Mary Grey was apparently treated quite well by her keeper, and survived the ordeal.

[4] The lease was supposed to run for one hundred years, but now that Trinidad was becoming independent, it was difficult for the United Kingdom to continue to guarantee the agreement. Nothing could be decided until the new West Indies Federation had a chance to take a look at the proposals respecting the matter made recently to the new nation by the British government. However, it was good to know that the British understood our position and were in accord.

[5] Other subjects discussed included contingency planning for Berlin, a World Bank loan for development of the Suez Canal, currency reform in Indonesia, and the inevitable communiqué. See Chapter XXV.

attitude, although we were disappointed that East-West contacts within Germany could not be rapidly expanded.

The first meeting over, we took our golf clubs to the surrounding green gardens and set about devising a makeshift golf game. Surrounding the house at Chequers is a stone wall several feet high, and beyond this, on one side, is a sizable field. We placed a golf bag at the foot of the wall as a target and, by going to the far end of the field, were able to set up a shot of something over 150 yards. This provided a competitive setting and we played the British against the Americans—Harold Macmillan and Selwyn Lloyd against Jock Whitney and me. With each side given an equal number of shots, we tried to hit the bag more often than they did, but at the end of two rounds all was well for national pride on both sides. The British won the first round, five to four, and the Americans the second, four to three. This was a good point at which to quit, and so we went back to get ready for the evening.

At 7 P.M. Harold and I met with only our two foreign ministers present. We discussed the forthcoming Khrushchev visit. I told Harold that I felt sure Khrushchev would attempt to make a good impression in the United States, despite the tough language he had been employing to impress visiting Americans. This surmise, I felt, was strengthened by the fact that he was bringing his family.

As to the reasons for inviting Khrushchev to visit America, little explanation was needed, for Harold had been heartily in favor of it from the beginning. We agreed that the most important objective was to urge Khrushchev to accept a moratorium on threats and counterthreats respecting West Berlin. Beyond that I thought we should discuss with our visitor nuclear tests, the wider aspects of disarmament, and the broadening of contacts between the United States and the U.S.S.R.[6]

The next morning, Sunday, the four of us again conferred. This time the major subject was nuclear testing. The British seemed less concerned at this point than were we with the growth of Soviet military might, including nuclear weapons. They appeared more concerned with world opinion, particularly among the "uncommitted" nations, some of which seemed to believe it possible to solve our problems with the Communists through the mere exchange of unsecured promises. To the making of such "agreements" I was opposed. This discussion, therefore, was left in

[6] Broadening of contacts among our two peoples under appropriate agreements should be, I think, a continuing American objective if for no other reason than the ease with which the Russian government can obtain information of our life, culture, and industry as compared to the difficulties in obtaining similar information on the Soviet Union.

an inconclusive state. I would not make any unilateral declaration on our part to suspend tests beyond a previously announced moratorium on atmospheric tests, which was to terminate at the end of 1959. Harold said that he might find it necessary eventually to announce that no further British tests of any kind were to take place.

Following this conversation we attended church. The Elesborough Church near Chequers is a quaint structure; on this occasion its quaintness was strained by overcrowding. I was offered the privilege of reading the daily lesson, but felt it proper to decline in favor of my host. Accordingly, Harold did so himself, as apparently was his habit whenever he went to Chequers.

In our final meeting, which took place that afternoon, we took up the technical aspects of "decoupling"—a method of reducing shock waves in the earth so as to conceal underground nuclear explosions.[7] Then we talked about preparations for the television discussion that Harold and I planned for the following evening. Though we agreed on the general subjects to be discussed, the program was to be unrehearsed. On this I insisted because of my distaste for predigested conversation.

Monday morning we returned to London. On the way I had the privilege of stopping at St. Paul's Cathedral for a very brief ceremony in which I dedicated the American chapel in memory of the Americans based in England who lost their lives in World War II. From there we continued to the Embassy residence, where I received a call from the Spanish minister. On behalf of Generalissimo Franco he extended me an invitation to visit Spain at any time convenient to me; I said I would try to do so and thanked him.

That evening we went to the Prime Minister's residence at No. 10 Downing Street to appear before the television cameras and report to the British public on our Chequers talks. The report went well, I felt, although some differences in our viewpoints must have been obvious.[8] At least the performance gave us a chance to express our confidence in the future, a not inconsiderable message in an age of worry.

[7] Possibilities such as these vastly increased the difficulty of reaching any test ban agreement with inspectional features at this time.

[8] With respect to a possible summit, Harold Macmillan said, "I have always wanted a summit meeting and I believe your initiative will put us into position to get it under the best conditions." Later I said, "I will not be a party of a [summit] meeting that is going to depress and discourage people. Therefore we must have some promise of fruitful results."

No. 10 Downing Street is rather ancient. The British were planning to rebuild it on the inside. Because of the number of people and the amount of equipment necessarily present in the television room, some feared that the second floor, on which the program was to be held, might not be able to sustain the weight concentrated in the room. One British aide later commented wryly on the embarrassment that would have resulted if the floor had given way. It might have been curious, with both principals falling out of sight of the viewing public while expressing confidence in the future.

The televised talk over, we went to the dining room. Present that evening in addition to Harold were three men, who at various times had been British Prime Ministers: Winston Churchill, Clement Attlee, and Anthony Eden. Each made a short talk, which, together with the general after-dinner conversation, made it a most enjoyable and memorable occasion.

The next day I rested at the American Embassy residence, known as Winfield House, thought over my forthcoming talks with President de Gaulle, and caught up on correspondence. The only event planned for the day was purely personal. Ambassador Whitney had invited about thirty of my British wartime friends for supper. I had looked forward to this reunion. It fulfilled a deep ambition I had long cherished.

* * *

The following morning we left by helicopter from the lawn of Winfield House for the London airport. I said good-bye to Harold Macmillan and to Sir Frederick Handley Page, representing the Queen, and by nine o'clock the doors of the Boeing 707 were closed and we were bound for Paris.

On meeting President de Gaulle at the airport, I at once sensed important changes that had occurred since I had last seen him. The most notable of these was scarcely definable—it included a relaxed confidence that contrasted with his more aggressive attitude in the years when he was fighting for recognition as France's leader. All in all, he now appeared a more benign, less forbidding individual than the fiery division commander who had made himself the symbol of French resistance in World War II.

It was quickly apparent that President de Gaulle had left no stone unturned to make this visit a spectacular one. Upon meeting us, he took us into the *Salon d'Honneur* to meet dignitaries of his government. Then, passing through cordons of handsomely uniformed *Gardes Républicaines,* the party departed for Paris. The *Garde Républicaine,* incidentally, is a spectacular ceremonial warrior with a shiny brass helmet, dark blue coat, white trousers (for certain occasions), knee-length boots, and a curved saber. He is a figure out of the past, standing guard in the present.

As the motorcade approached Paris, the crowds progressively grew larger. Because our convertible top was in place, it was practically impossible to acknowledge the salutes of the crowd, even though both President de Gaulle and I sat hunched up in an attempt to peer through the small windows. I asked if we might have the top taken down, the President immediately told the driver to do so. The driver indicated that he would comply within a matter of moments. I supposed he was looking for a convenient place to stop. With nothing happening, the President spoke again to the driver, who muttered something, unintelligible to me, and kept on going. Again the performance was repeated and I came to the conclusion that we had a single-minded chauffeur who had received prior orders to keep his proper place in the motorcade and would do nothing else. But at long last the driver stopped the car, apparently without instructions, and nonchalantly lowered the top. We proceeded from there in relative comfort. I was later informed that because our route had taken us through a district known to be a hotbed of Communism, the driver had been told by his commander to keep the top up as a protection from any thrown missile, regardless of any contrary instructions from the car's occupants. Since every uniformed individual is far more sensitive to the wishes of his immediate superior than those of any other person, I could now understand better the driver's seeming inability to comprehend the simplest instructions from the President of the French Republic.

Although I had at first planned to stay at the United States Embassy, my party and I stopped, at President de Gaulle's hospitable insistence, at the Quai d'Orsay guest house, a courtesy, I was informed, that was reserved for V.I.P.I.s.[9] Having reached our living quarters, we looked over the schedule of events planned for us by the French government and learned that the visit was to be more formal and ceremonial than any other of the tour.

That night we attended a state dinner at the Elysée Palace in a beautiful setting and, the following noon, an equally splendid luncheon at the same place. We spent one night at the Quai d'Orsay and one night at the Palace of Rambouillet, some miles from Paris. These compliments were difficult to repay in the short time we were to be in Paris, but I did, on the second day, have President de Gaulle as my luncheon guest at the United States Embassy. During our two-day stay we participated in several other ceremonies, among them a placing of a wreath at the

[9] "Very Important Personage, Indeed," a popular expression in the governmental services.

Arc de Triomphe, in tribute to France's Unknown Soldier, and a reception at the Hotel de Ville. I also found time to visit at the Embassy with several diplomats whom I had been anxious to see[10] and to make a short address to the NATO Council, then meeting in Paris.

But the most important aspect of the visit was the chance for serious conversations with President de Gaulle. As usual, such talks were not expected to produce specific decisions; their real purpose was to facilitate an exchange of viewpoints and possibly to sweep away some of the underbrush of misunderstandings that grow up when positive personalities communicate only through the written word and diplomatic channels. I found the meetings more than rewarding.

There were many thorny issues to take up. While General de Gaulle's call back to public life had been triggered by the Army, he had received overwhelming popular support, its virtual unanimity unmatched in modern democratic societies. Thus his position in France was at that time unassailable. With his almost mystical self-confidence and his unswerving dedication to the restoration of French prestige and leadership, I concluded it would be naïve to expect much in the way of flexibility in any position he would take.

As a preliminary move, I went to some length to assure President de Gaulle that, in my forthcoming meeting with Khrushchev, I had no intention of putting forth new proposals or of beginning negotiations on any substantive matter that concerned any nation other than my own. I would never presume, in a bilateral meeting with the Soviets, to represent the views of all the West.

While President de Gaulle obviously regarded the invitation to Khrushchev as a futile gesture, he remarked that it was a decision for the United States alone and that little harm could come from it.

On the subject of a summit, our views were identical; we agreed that such a meeting, without tangible signs of progress in advance, would be unacceptable to both of us. Likewise we stood together on Berlin contingency planning; we must avoid letting the Soviets believe that we were weak, vacillating, or divided.

The President's views on the North Atlantic Treaty Organization were much as had been reported to me earlier. While he vigorously supported the general idea of the North Atlantic Alliance, he was obviously against integration of national military forces in a supranational command structure such as then existed. The NATO organization, he said, had now

[10] Paul Henri Spaak, Secretary-General of NATO, J. M. A. H. Luns, the Dutch foreign minister in his capacity of President of the North Atlantic Council, and Premier Antonio Segni and Foreign Minister Guiseppe Pella of Italy.

been established for some years, and the situation in 1959 was entirely different from that which had faced Europe at the time of the organization's founding. He pointed out that the 1949 threat to Western Europe had been urgent, compelling the Western European nations to submit to the principle of integration under a Supreme Commander on the basis of immediate military need. This situation no longer applied. Moreover, when NATO was founded in 1949 the Communist threat had not developed on a global scale; Algeria had not become a serious scene of uproar; tropical Africa had not begun to erupt; the Indochina War was still a local affair, and the Korean War had not begun. President de Gaulle's point was that NATO as now organized no longer provided a satisfactory mechanism to meet the worldwide problems.

What he suggested to rectify the situation likewise held little surprise for me. Indeed, his proposal had been the subject of letters exchanged between us ever since he had taken office more than a year before. He proposed an organization comprising France, Britain, and the United States—the only free nations, he said, with global responsibilities—the purpose of which would be to coordinate the political policies of the three nations in every area of the world.

Appealing as the idea sounded, in part, I thought it one to work on in confidence rather than to proclaim publicly. I tried to point out the impact that publicizing such an arrangement might have on many of our allies and on newly emerged nations and neutral nations, each of which commanded a full vote in the United Nations General Assembly. I believed that any attempt to organize a coalition of the "Big Three" NATO nations would be resented by all the others to the point that NATO itself might disintegrate. He discounted this possibility but did not seem too disturbed even at the prospect of its coming about. I tried to convince him of my desire to coordinate our respective policies and actions around the globe, particularly when any two of us had important interests. What we should be seeking, I said, was the substance and benefits of coordinations, not the façade of self-assumed authority among three great nations. I was quite willing, for example, to organize a permanent staff, representing the heads of all three governments, to look into such problems as alleged arms shipments from Tunisia to the Algerian rebels. Although this was not what De Gaulle had in mind, he accepted my views in good grace and did not push further the matter of a formal tripartite organization.

Returning to problems of NATO, De Gaulle believed that each nation in the last analysis must be responsible for its own security. To tell a Frenchman that the defense of France is the responsibility of an organization such as NATO is automatically to make him less zealous in his performance of duty. General de Gaulle was convinced that the influence of national rather than multinational organization on morale was overriding. In that spirit he had set the development of a French nuclear capability as a matter of first priority, and he seemed determined to develop all three of Frances' armed services to an extent that the nation might be considered "in business for itself" from a military point of view. This to me would be needlessly expensive; if all nations of NATO took a similar attitude, the result would be a hodgepodge of fragmented military power that could not be used effectively as a unit, while each national force, by itself, would be helpless against the Soviet juggernaut.

But I knew we had not merely a broad question to debate, but a specific problem to face. Earlier in the year De Gaulle had removed the French fleet from its previous commitment to the Supreme Allied Commander, Europe (SACEUR) in time of war. The French naval force, De Gaulle announced, would cooperate fully with NATO in the event war occurred, but would not operate under orders from SACEUR. His excuse for this action was concern for Algeria, requiring the French fleet to keep open a lifeline across the Mediterranean in time of war.[11]

Another De Gaulle decision forbade stationing Allied nuclear weapons on French soil without giving him a veto power on their use. This power, in justice to our other allies, we could not give. Therefore, we had been compelled to move several fighter squadrons armed with nuclear weapons from France to bases in Germany.

Because of geography and international politics, France was, and is, vital to the successful functioning of NATO. Fully aware of this, De Gaulle was able to force other members of the alliance to accommodate many of their own arrangements to his actions. Fortunately, the others appreciated the need for a collective defense; they patiently accepted the difficulties caused by De Gaulle's unilateral decisions, and made the best of them.

When we took up the subject of Africa, the President first expressed his grave concern over the events transpiring on that continent, both in tropical Africa, particularly on the west coast, and in the Arab regions to the north. This former group of nations, he pointed out, is distant from Europe, separated by a vast sea of sand. In tropical Africa, France formerly had held substantial possessions, broken down into numerous and artificially separated political divisions.[12] One of De Gaulle's first

[11] Actually the French fleet, as a result of losses incurred during World War II, was not strong enough to make much difference. But the attitude seemed a departure from reality.

[12] At that time the nations of the French Community included, besides France itself, Mauritania, Senegal, Sudan, Upper Volta, Niger, Ivory Coast, Dahomey, the Congo Republic, Central African Republic, Chad, the Malagasy Republic, and Gabon.

acts after taking office was to go to Africa to offer to each nation the choice between complete independence and autonomy within a French "community." All but Guinea had accepted membership in the French Community. De Gaulle attributed Guinea's choice completely to its young leader Sékou Touré, of whose motives and far leftist leanings he was, at that time, particularly suspicious. He regretted the impatience for immediate independence that uncontrolled nationalist ideas had engendered in all these peoples. The Community was, of course, a good compromise between complete independence—with its attendant responsibilities and heavy costs—and a colonial status with France. It maintained economic and social ties, meanwhile providing to each nation one of the gains they most coveted: a vote in the United Nations. De Gaulle suspected that considerable pro-Communist subversion was going on within the borders of many nations in the French Community, with its local sources probably found in Guinea and to some extent in Ghana, formerly a British colony.

Algeria brought forth his intense official and personal concern. De Gaulle started out on the premise that eventually the status of Algeria should be decided by the Algerians themselves, in a free vote. The problems were complex, however. France had been in Algeria for 130 years, and more than a million Frenchmen, in a total population of over ten million, had long considered Algeria their home. These people were as determined to maintain close connections with the mother country as were the Moslems to attain a separate status. In addition there was no homogeneity among the peoples of Algeria or any recognized spokesman for them. An Algerian nation as such had never existed in contrast to either Morocco or Tunisia.

General de Gaulle's main point of contention was that a rebellion was going on, headed by a small band of self-proclaimed leaders, who did not really represent the views of the bulk of the Moslems of the region. He refused to deal with these individuals, remarking that he would never recognize a group that existed only through the terror of machine guns. He pointed out, reasonably, that it was impossible to hold a referendum or a vote of any kind in an atmosphere of active rebellion. A vote would be held, to be sure, but only when there was a stop to the shooting. De Gaulle's concern over suspected Communist influence in Algeria was strong. If a totalitarian group took over control of Algeria, he feared that this would soon result in a fully communized state.

Then we got down to the hard problem of what to do in the United Nations if a resolution should come up again in the near future similar to the one barely voted down the year before. De Gaulle, as expected, hoped that the United States would avoid abstaining, as we had done the year before, and instead would support the French. "We would like to stand by our traditional ally in this matter," I replied, "but I hope that France will make it possible for us to vote with you by taking some prior constructive action respecting Algeria that would prove acceptable to world opinion—or at least present a full explanation of their point of view—should a United Nations debate ensue."

In spite of my urging, the President declared flatly that if a debate should arise in the United Nations as a result of an unfriendly Afro-Asian resolution, then, France would make no defense whatsoever.

For a moment it seemed we had reached an impasse, but De Gaulle immediately came up with a reassuring program of action. He said that France would, within a matter of days, promise the Algerians the opportunity to determine their own future by free vote, to be taken as promptly as possible after rebellion ended. He assured me that once I had read his forthcoming speech carefully, I would be able to support his position in the United Nations. I replied that if his public speech was as clear, reasonable, and positive as the plan he had just described, I would, immediately after its delivery, say so.

Our talks were cordial. Despite our admitted disagreements, I left Paris with a renewed admiration for what President de Gaulle was trying to do in Algeria and the French Community,[13] and for him as an administrator and political leader of a great nation. Popular morale was far improved over what I had encountered two years earlier.

For at least two years before he became his country's President, I had often remarked to Secretary Dulles and others interested in the future of that nation that only General de Gaulle's accession to power could save France.

Shortly before leaving Paris a White House aide arrived, Associate

[13] On September 16, 1959, President de Gaulle made a speech recognizing the right of Algerians to self-determination. While it made no mention of dealing with the provisional Algerian government, it promised that within four years after the end of a cease-fire, the Algerians, observed by the rest of the world, could elect whether to (1) form a completely independent Algerian state free of ties with France, (2) remain as part of an integrated intro-metropolitan France, or (3) retain an association with France similar to the status of the members of the French Community.

While the timing of such an election, four years after a cease-fire, seemed long in view of the realities, the fact that the general conceded to use the word "independence" at all was considered a great step forward. His speech was overshadowed in the American press by the antics of Mr. Khrushchev, who had just arrived in the United States, but its impact was worldwide. For one thing it delayed a crisis in the United Nations, by postponing the submission of an Afro-Asian resolution on Algeria. At the same time it created a feeling of disillusionment and abandonment on the part of both the French army in Algeria and the French colonials. While an act of statesmanship, to which I could refer in my later dealings with Arab leaders, the speech represented the beginning of De Gaulle's difficulties with the right-wing elements of France, with whom he had supposedly been formerly aligned.

Special Counsel Roemer McPhee, with an armful of bills that had just passed the Congress. One of these was a reckless and wasteful "pork barrel" public works bill which I refused to sign even though Roemer warned (correctly, it turned out) I was probably setting the stage for the first overriding of one of my vetoes in nearly seven years.

As we spent our last evening at Rambouillet, someone, knowing that I was planning to spend a few days of recreation at Culzean Castle in Ayrshire, Scotland, suggested that my visit there might prove a little lonely and suggested that I ask a couple of friends to fly overseas to meet me in Scotland for some golf and possibly a bit of bridge. The idea struck me as intriguing, in certain respects the brightest I had heard during the entire trip. Forgetting the time differential, I picked up the telephone and within minutes was talking to Bill Robinson in New York. My call got him out of bed; in New York it was two o'clock in the morning. Without a moment's hesitation he accepted my invitation and a few hours later he and "Pete" Jones were on their way. I was indeed fortunate to have friends who were such light sleepers.

The next morning, September 3, we flew by United States Army helicopter from the magnificent grounds at Rambouillet to the airfield. Shortly thereafter we were airborne for Scotland. Once in the air, I sent short messages to all of my former hosts. The trip had been memorable, not only for the unquestioned benefits of the discussions but also for the renewal of warm friendships in three countries.

Our short stay at Culzean Castle was a delight. Pete Jones and Bill Robinson arrived, slightly worse for wear, but repaired immediately to the golf course without rest except for catnaps the night before in the airplane. With Jock Whitney we formed a congenial bridge and golf foursome and thoroughly enjoyed the interlude. One evening I invited in the Pipe Major from the Ayrshire (Bag) Pipe Band, of which I am a proud honorary member, to play for my guests in a colorful traditional dinner ceremony. With the lights dimmed, the band, resplendent in uniforms and with kilts and medals, marched several times around the dining table—pipes blaring out "Scotland the Brave" and other stirring Scottish battle tunes.

Such a pleasant interlude could not long endure. Our stolen holiday was interrupted the following morning by bad news from Laos, and we started back for Washington.[14]

[14] In Laos, reports were becoming more urgent regarding the activities of the Pathet Lao units. The Pathet Lao, under the leadership of Prince Souvannavong, were known to be pro-Communist, but the amount of direct aid which they received from the North Vietnam government was unknown. My action on return to the United States was to approve increased aid to the pro-United States government. Soon a degree of calm returned to the area.

* * *

Hence on September 7, I was quickly plunged into the endless routine of the President's office, beginning with the regular Tuesday meeting with legislative leaders and going on to conferences on State Department matters, particularly Laos.

For the next few days, I was intermittently engaged in planning for the visit of Nikita Khrushchev. While I still felt some annoyance because of the circumstances that brought about the visit,[15] I was determined to be courteous and correct in public but never silent in the face of any flamboyant claims and assertions that I felt certain he would scatter about the country.

In meeting the Chairman, I planned to concentrate on three main points: The first was our firmness on Berlin and on our rights elsewhere in the world. The second was my willingness to go anywhere to discuss matters of mutual interest (such as disarmament) if by so doing I could genuinely advance the cause of peace—even to a summit if it offered a reasonable promise of success and took place under no Soviet threat or ultimatum of any kind. The third was Mr. Khrushchev's priceless opportunity to go down in history as one of the truly great statesman of all time, my thesis being that if he would use the power of his position in the furtherance of disarmament, relaxation of tensions, and support of peace, he could capture the respect and admiration of the world for years to come. My proposal was by no means merely a sop to the man's ego. It was a chance which I sincerely believed he had before him. This effort I would reserve for private conversations, not for conferences.

In any event, as I once told the legislative leaders, I wanted to make "one great personal effort, before leaving office, to soften up the Soviet leader even a little bit. Except for the Austrian peace treaty," I said, "we haven't made a chip in the granite in seven years," even though we had blocked all their forays against the Free World.

In order to have an advance agreement on subjects for discussion, the Secretary of State and the Soviet foreign minister got together on Sep-

[15] Many Americans nursed serious misgivings about the forthcoming Khrushchev visit. Some of the more vociferous were those who opposed any kind of contact with the Soviets, but others were persons of standing, not only in political life, but also in business, labor, and the clergy. One outstanding leader who expressed some misgiving was Francis Cardinal Spellman. I telephoned to assure him we would stand firm on Berlin; the exchange of visits implied no hint of a surrender. The cardinal, always my great friend, promised he would continue to pray for the successful outcome of my endeavors.

tember 16 and prepared an agenda that included such items as Germany and Berlin, disarmament, nuclear test negotiations, mutual exchanges and contacts, Laos, Iran, and even nuclear reactor information. It seemed to me that this was an ambitious list for such a short meeting; if I could get my three main points seriously considered, I would be satisfied.

There were other problems to occupy the staffs, particularly Mr. Khrushchev's itinerary, and the security measures for his safety. In order to facilitate the Chairman's tour about the United States I had, several weeks earlier, selected Cabot Lodge to act as my personal representative and host. Cabot had unusual qualifications. As head of the United States delegation to the United Nations, he was familiar with Soviet thinking and methods and could easily answer any question or debate any claim Khrushchev might bring up during the trip.

But as we developed plans and made suggestions to the Soviets, their attitude was anything but cooperative. Even before I had left for Europe, we had noticed evidence that their customary rigidity and suspicion would carry over to our arrangements for the visit.

One of the items of petty contention concerned the itinerary. Perhaps the original ideas advanced by our staffs regarding places that Khrushchev should visit had little appeal—but every suggestion we made was accompanied by assurance that the Chairman's wishes in every instance would govern.[16]

Regardless of the ideas we had, the Soviets had their own and were insistent to the point of ignoring good manners. At times I was tempted to cancel the trip, at least to cancel the invitation to confer quietly at Camp David. For some reason, an invitation to Camp David had come to confer a special distinction upon a guest.

And of course there were minor but endless matters involving protocol. One of no importance which took time and much discussion was that of dress for formal occasions. Khrushchev had announced that he would not wear customary formal dress or even tuxedo to the White House

[16] In one early meeting with some of the planners, I had to chuckle to myself about the local pride that inspired many recommendations. The Governor of South Dakota, for example, thought that the town of Yankton would be a typical American town for the Chairman to see. Mr. Nixon thought Los Angeles would be a place that he should not miss. Secretary Anderson, from Texas, thought that Mr. Khrushchev ought to visit there, to see the ranches of that state. My amusement was increased when I realized that I had been guilty of the same thing; I had been thinking that the very place for Khrushchev to see would be Abilene, Kansas, and the refrigerating plant where, before entering West Point in 1911, I had worked my way up to the exalted position of night engineer, with a schedule of eighty-four hours a week. One purpose, of course, was to impress upon him that, even though a "capitalist" in his eyes, I knew what hard work was.

dinner given in his honor. These, in Communist eyes, were symbols of capitalism. Without further discussion I announced that Khrushchev would be free to wear anything he desired, but that we Americans would follow our own customs. More vexing to the State Department was the problem of determining the protocol status of the Chairman. Strictly speaking, Khrushchev was not a chief of state; he was a head of government. The position of chief of state is invested in someone who, even if only a figurehead, nevertheless typifies the sovereignty of the state he represents. When the State Department, at my direction, asked the Soviets about the order of precedence for Khrushchev, they were obviously discomfited. They pointed out that Khrushchev was the "boss" of Russia. To that we merely asked whether he was the head of state or the head of government. Finally they compromised with some such wording as coming "in the capacity of the head of state," and asked that procedures for the position be observed.

Minor irritations continued up to the moment that Khrushchev's TU-114 landed at Andrews Air Force Base. Three days before his arrival, the Soviets shot a large rocket to the moon. This was a noteworthy feat, but the propaganda purpose of the timing was blatant.

A bit of comic relief among these last annoyances was provided by the Soviet ambassador, the genial-appearing Mikhail Menshikov. In a final burst of poor taste he attempted to dictate the greeting procedure at the airport when Khrushchev landed. Menshikov insisted that he personally, as Soviet ambassador, should board the airplane when the door opened; from there he should escort the Premier to meet those assembled below. The question, minor as it appeared, raised diplomatic temperatures so much that I was finally called upon for a decision. This was easy. I gave him a flat no. He would do it our way or Menshikov would not be present at the ceremony.[17]

* * *

The day of arrival was September 15. Shortly after noon I met the Chairman at Andrews Air Force Base. There were only minor exceptions to our normal reception procedures. One was the presence in the welcoming party of several children from the Soviet Embassy, heavily bedecked with flowers, who added a pleasant touch of color. Then, instead of speaking extemporaneously, I read my message of greeting from a prepared

[17] Our practice is for the host to wait at the bottom of the airplane's ramp to greet the visiting dignitary as he alights, with no intermediary allowed to enter the plane.

text to emphasize its official nature. The crowds, of good but not notable size, greeted Mr. Khrushchev good-naturedly but in restrained fashion along the route. I escorted him to the Presidential Guest House and returned to my office to complete plans for the afternoon.

At 3:30 Mr. Khrushchev and members of his party appeared for our first formal business meeting. We were joined by advisers—among others, Gromyko and Menshikov for the Chairman, and the Vice President, Secretary of State, and Cabot Lodge for me.

Khrushchev at once presented me with a gift, a model of the spherical projectile called Lunik II, which had been used in the recent Soviet moon shot. This seemed, at first, a strange gift, but it then occurred to me that quite possibly the man was completely sincere. I accepted it, of course, with all the grace I could command.

Because the amount of time allotted to this meeting was limited, I advised Khrushchev that we would probably be able to cover only the outlines of what we would want to talk about later at Camp David. I emphasized that I had no desire to curtail the agenda; my purpose was only to achieve greater understanding between the two of us. I recognized that unpleasant subjects such as Laos would probably come up and would have to be dealt with, but said that I was especially interested in Berlin, in a summit if it could be held under circumstances offering real progress toward easing world tensions, and in Mr. Khrushchev's special opportunity to make a dramatic move in progress toward peace. Of course, I recognized that we might probably talk about other matters such as disarmament, broadening contacts, trade, and reduction of exacerbating propaganda. I described Camp David to Khrushchev and told him of its simple surroundings. He seemed happy to learn that the climate was a little cooler at Camp David than it was in Washington.

The Chairman said that he had come to the United States empowered to talk in the broadest terms, his purpose to find agreement on many things. The Soviet Union, he said, did not want war and furthermore he believed that we realized this fact. I agreed that there was no future in mutual suicide, but remarked that the attitudes shown at the latest meeting of the foreign ministers gave a contrary impression. Mr. Khrushchev stressed that his purpose was to try to establish trust between us, a trust based on acceptance of each other's existence; as to the differences between us, which we both recognized, he said, "let history decide."

There was nothing in our guest's stated intentions to quarrel with. However, in saying so, I felt it necessary to word things a little differently. We should, I said, attempt to find ways to clear away the underbrush of confusion and mutual distrust, so that we could begin to solve our important outstanding problems. I assured the Chairman that the big obstacle, on the American side at least, was not a matter of personalities at all. It was a matter of national psychology. We had read Marx and were fully aware of what Marx and Lenin claimed was going to happen to our society. I remarked also that because the Communist Party in the United States was a militant group, supported by Moscow, it was only natural that we should be alert and watchful against subversion. I admitted that our anti-Communist feeling sometimes degenerated into witch-hunts.

The Chairman claimed that the United States was basically afraid of Marxism and pointed to the contents of a recent speech by the Vice President. Mr. Nixon, who was present, broke in to say that he was complimented because the Chairman had read it. Khrushchev argued that the speech was mere propaganda, deliberately calculated to arouse feelings of animosity against himself and his party on their arrival. As an aside he warned that it was impossible for anyone to influence foreign people over the heads of their government, and he proudly claimed that such an effort would be futile in the Soviet Union because he himself represented the feelings of the Soviet people.

Returning to the speech of the Vice President, however, Khrushchev's attitude indicated that he thought he had scored a bull's-eye. He said, "After having read that speech, I am surprised to find on arriving here that people in the United States welcome us with such tolerance and obvious friendliness." Then he added, "In the Soviet Union there would have been no welcome whatsoever if I had, in advance, publicly spoken against the visitor."

"That is the basic difference," I said, "between our two systems."

This exchange tried the patience of the Vice President. He reminded Mr. Khrushchev of the speeches the Chairman had made upon Mr. Nixon's own arrival in the Soviet Union two months earlier. Khrushchev retorted that he would be glad for me to read them all, and compare his own with Mr. Nixon's speeches. To add to the snowballing comedy of the situation, Mr. Khrushchev suggested that I be the referee as to which speeches were more provocative.

Khrushchev was obviously much concerned about the extent of the newspaper and television coverage that would be given to his speeches while he was in the United States. He alleged that our publicity media had not covered his side of things adequately in the Moscow debates. To this I replied that our press, radio, and television companies were free to report what they regarded as news, or to decline to disseminate any story that had, in their opinion, little news value. I said that his utterances would be reported according to this kind of editorial judgment, not mine. Despite my insistence, he refused to believe that we have in this country a free press, without governmental censorship. He said, "Of course, the American government gets printed what it wants printed and is able to suppress what it does not want printed."

At about this point I steered the conversation into another channel. There was no point in propagandizing ourselves on propaganda, I said, and an argument about Mr. Khrushchev's speeches versus Mr. Nixon's was not much to the point. I offered to provide facilities so that Khrushchev could invite editors, journalists, and reporters to meet him alone. He could, by observing the results, see whether he was reported fully. Khrushchev shrugged it off and finally said he believed me. However, because of a natural concern about the possibilities that could arise in a press conference scheduled for the next day, I told him I could not predict or guarantee the kind of questions he would receive; some might seem to him unnecessarily provocative. He seemed completely confident and said that he thought he knew our press quite well.

There was no question in my mind of Khrushchev's skill as a debater. He was a master at picking up another's proposals and using them—with his own interpretations—to advance his own point of view. In this instance he seized on my idea that we should encourage exchanges of television programs and increase the numbers of visitors to one nation from the other. His reply was "My speeches will probably not be reported in the television and radio system of the United States; then the same thing would happen in the Soviet Union." His last word on this subject was "such an effort would soon become a dialogue between deaf persons." Obviously we were getting nowhere rapidly.

After a short exchange on Berlin in which each side reaffirmed its previously established position, the conversation went to more personal matters.

The Chairman expressed some concern over the number of speaking and visiting engagements on his trip around the United States.

I could not resist replying that every engagement on his calendar had been put there on the insistence of Soviet officials. Then, in an effort to avoid any hint of wrangling, I said, "Perhaps I can take on some of the speeches in your stead." This finally caused him to laugh.

I asked casually whether he would have any interest in visiting any of our big atomic plants, knowing that there would be little a layman could learn from such a visit. If he should accept, I knew also he would be impressed by the size of the plants which were then producing nuclear material and weapons at a rapid rate. He replied that he saw no value to such a visit and would prefer not to see anything of this sort. I assumed that such a visit might have created an undesirable precedent for my visit to his country.

The whole conversation, except for the one fleeting argument between Khrushchev and the Vice President, produced no sparks of visible animosity. At the end, the Chairman expressed confidence that we could find a way out of our difficulties and alluded to the high regard in which I was personally held in the Soviet Union. While he did not, perhaps, expect it to be flattering, he made quite a point of saying that Stalin had had a great repect for some of my actions during World War II operations, but failed to specify what these actions were. We ended the conversation by directing our respective foreign ministers to spend the next couple of days together working out an agenda for Camp David.

At this point the photographers came in and soon thereafter the Chairman and I were left alone with only interpreters. It was at this point that I was able to express my conviction regarding Mr. Khrushchev's opportunity to go down in history as a towering statesman if he would use his power constructively. The Western alliance was not so solidified as the Soviet Bloc. I had only sixteen months left in office, I reminded him; his own opportunity was more far reaching than mine.

Mr. Khrushchev took this idea graciously but said that such things could not be accomplished by actions on one side only. "There should be good will and tolerance on both sides," he said solemnly, "to do everything possible to solve our differences."

At that moment the two of us went to the White House lawn to begin a helicopter ride around the city. One of the suggestions I had made, long before the Chairman's arrival, was an offer to arrange such a tour. To this he had sent a courteous but firm refusal on the ground that he disliked that sort of machine. But while riding with him from the airport that morning I deliberately expressed my regret that he could not join me on this kind of sightseeing, for I had found them convenient and always interesting.

"Oh," he replied, "if you are to be in the same helicopter, of course I will go!"[18]

[18] This brought back to my memory a small incident, almost fifteen years in the past. Shortly after the close of hostilities in 1945, Marshal Zhukov was invited by the President to visit our country and his government had, on his behalf, accepted. When next I saw the marshal he began to express in a roundabout way some doubt about the wisdom of his coming. He first wanted to know whether I would travel with him as his host. I replied that I could not do so because of a number of duties keeping me then in Europe. This seemed to disappoint him, and he next remarked that because his government had no long-range passenger planes he would be compelled to use short-range types and go "island hopping" to America. This, he said, would be both inconvenient and time-consuming. I quickly suggested that he use the plane assigned to me by my government, and when this was interpreted to him

Our craft hovered over the city and its suburbs for more than half an hour. Fortunately, it was a beautiful afternoon and I was confident that Mr. Khrushchev was interested, but I saw no expression revealing his reaction to what must have been, for him, unusual sights. I would have given a good deal to know what he thought of the spectacular flow of thousands of automobiles so dramatically displayed below us. In Moscow, Khrushchev had simply refused to believe Vice President Nixon's statement that most American families owned cars. Our helicopter trip occurred as the government offices were closing; so cars formed literally continuous ribbons of movement, on highways and bridges, for as far as we could see. He must have been persuaded of the truth of Nixon's statement, but stoically refrained from saying so or even changing expression.

However, he openly expressed his admiration for the helicopter itself, and later gave an order for the purchase of three of them for his own use, specifying that each should be identical with the one in which we were then riding. On return to the White House lawn he and his party proceeded back to the guest house.

That evening the Chairman and members of his family joined us on the second floor of the White House, prior to our state dinner.[19] The mixed garb of the guests did, I must admit, present an odd spectacle—black, double-breasted business suits for the Soviets, white tie dress for the Americans. The Soviet men seemed to be fully at ease—except for Ambassador Menshikov, who appeared self-conscious, probably because at Washington social events he normally wore white tie and tails. The women, being feminine even though Communist, were obviously uncomfortable.

The state dinner itself followed the routine of all others, and would not have been remarkable were it not for the unusual toast which the Chairman offered.

Admittedly my toast concentrated more on the long and peaceful history between our countries than on personal compliments to the Chairman. That of Mr. Khrushchev was a splendid example of combined propaganda and political argument, prepared for delivery at the banquet table:

---

he came out with another question: "May your son go as my aide?" and I replied, "Of course!" "Well," he beamed, "with your plane and your son going with me I know I shall be quite safe. I shall go." He later, however, refused again, perhaps because he was losing favor in Moscow.

[19] Mr. Khrushchev brought with him his wife, his daughter, Mrs. Julia Nikitichna, his other daughter, Mrs. Rada Adzhubei, his son, Mr. Sergei N. Khrushchev, and his son-in-law, Mr. Alexi Adzhubei, editor of *Izvestia.*

Mr. President, Mrs. Eisenhower, Ladies and Gentlemen:

I wish to thank you, Mr. President, for the good wishes that you voiced, and to state on my part that we have come here on the invitation of the President with our intentions based on the need to come to an agreement on the improvement of our relations, because our countries are much too strong and we cannot quarrel with each other. If we were weak countries, then it would be another matter, because when the weak quarrel, they are just scratching each other's faces and it takes just a couple of days for a cosmetician and everything comes out right again. But if we quarrel then not only our countries can suffer colossal damage but the other countries of the world will also be involved in a world shambles.

But I am sure that we can live in peace and progress together for peace. . . .

Our countries have different social systems. We believe our system to be better—and you believe yours to be better. But surely we should not bring quarrels out onto the arena of open struggle. Let history judge which of us is right. If we agree to accept this principle, then we can build our relations on the basis of peace and friendship.

You are a very rich and strong country. I read very many speeches made by many of the senators and representatives present here today, and so although I have made their acquaintance here for the first time today, in actual fact they are my old acquaintances by their speeches.

What we should now do is to strive together to improve our relations. We need nothing from the United States, and you require nothing that we have. It is true that you are richer than we are at present. But then tomorrow we will be as rich as you are, and the day after tomorrow we will be even richer.

But is there anything bad in this? After all, we are going to do this by our own forces—by our own strength. I must say that the meeting I had today heartened me. When some of our journalists approached me after the meeting and asked me my impressions, I said that there was an agreed communiqué that was to be published and they should abide by what was said in that communiqué. But I could not help mentioning that I would inform my government that a good beginning had been made, and one could only hope that the final outcome would be even better.

And so I would like to raise my glass and propose a Toast to the President, to his wife, to all of you esteemed ladies and gentlemen.

Dinner was, as usual, followed by a short musicale. This evening's program consisted of some robust music by Fred Waring and his Pennsylvanians that our guest seemed to enjoy thoroughly.

I did not see Khrushchev again until the next evening, when my wife, son, daughter-in-law, and I arrived at the Soviet Embassy to attend the customary return dinner. This was a pleasant affair; typically the Soviets had spared no effort to make it a sumptuous one. They even imported raw fish and caviar directly from Russia for the purpose. The elaborate table was not altogether show, of course; Russians love a feast, and they are hospitable people. This dinner reminded me of similar occasions fourteen years before when our four-power meetings in Berlin shortly after World War II had been characterized more by good food than by good progress.

* * *

The next morning Chairman Khrushchev and his family left Washington for a ten-day tour around our country. His itinerary took him first to New York City, where he made speeches at the Economic Club and the United Nations; later in the day he visited Hyde Park. Thence he proceeded to Los Angeles, where in a film studio he professed himself offended by an exhibition of *Can Can* dancing. Then he went on to San Francisco for a meeting with labor leaders and a visit to an IBM plant. In Iowa, on his only visit to an agricultural region, he stopped at a farm featuring a hybrid corn and then went on to the Unviersity of Iowa. From there he went to factories in Pittsburgh. He returned to Washington on September 25.

On his return Cabot Lodge, who had undergone an ordeal in keeping up with our energetic and unpredictable visitor, told me in detail of Khrushchev's activities. They would, he remarked, fill a book. This much could be said: Khrushchev responded vigorously to every incident. When things went right, he showed pleasure; when he was displeased or heckled, he displayed a scowling, enraged countenance. A crisis had occurred in Los Angeles, where he publicly condemned in intemperate language the refusal of the mayor of the city to take responsibility for his safety were he to go to Disneyland. I later learned that Soviet security officers had vetoed the suggestion for a visit to Disneyland and, of course, the mayor could not make necessary arrangements when Khrushchev at the last minute expressed his own desire to see that fabulous place. He merely said that "suitable arrangements could not be made."[20]

[20] This Disneyland incident came up in a conversation between Mr. Khrushchev and my brother, Milton, after the former had returned to Washington. Milton opened by saying, "I was interested in your reaction to the Disneyland affair, because when I was in Siberia with Vice President Nixon I grew weary of industrial plants and one day asked (twenty-four hours in advance) that I be permitted to visit state farms and collective farms rather than a copper mine. At the expiration of the twenty-four hours I was told that 'suitable arrangements could not be made.' "

Mr. Khrushchev, with a look of honest astonishment, exclaimed, "I have no idea why that happened."

One significant development, according to Cabot, was a progressive lessening of Khrushchev's preconceived notions regarding control of American publicity media. He now seemed to have developed some comprehension of a free press, and even of the American division of responsibilities between federal and local governments. He had come to realize that whenever he was heckled by local people in a small town in the West, this was not the deliberate design of the government in Washington—it was simply the way people felt and reacted.

* * *

On the afternoon of his return to Washington, Chairman Khrushchev came again to my White House office. Without delay we boarded a helicopter on the lawn for the trip to Camp David. We arrived at 6 P.M. and went to the cottage named "Aspen," where the Chairman and I, with a couple of others, were housed. Our guests having been made comfortable in the several cottages of the Camp, we had supper and a short entertainment. The entire Soviet party had experienced an exhausting day, and we all retired after nothing more than small talk.

As the group gathered around the breakfast table the next morning, it was obvious that the atmosphere was becoming more informal. Mr. Khrushchev was in a relaxed mood. Dressed in a rather decorative embroidered white shirt, he was the picture of ease. He had much to tell, addressing himself directly to me, without appreciable humor and without emotion.

He spoke about World War II. Perhaps he wanted to show me that he was a practical man who had seen battlefields at first hand, as indeed he had. Punctuating his points with his index finger, Khrushchev leaned across the table and told me of the days during the war when he had been a commissar with the Red Army on the various battlefronts. He mentioned the difficulties that the Soviets encountered in preventing looting, even by high-ranking Army officers, once the Soviets began to drive into German territory. For this crime the Red Army had a simple remedy. They would not bother to court-martial and dismiss an officer for looting, he said; they would merely shoot him on the spot, regardless of rank. I understood the interpreter to say that a couple of major generals were so punished.

Khrushchev mentioned my former counterpart in Berlin, Marshal Zhukov, who was reportedly involved in an attempted coup in 1957 to supplant the Chairman. Here, for the only time in the conversation, Khrushchev developed a twinkle in his eye. He merely remarked, rather parenthetically, "Your old friend Zhukov is all right. Don't worry about him. He's down in the Ukraine fishing—and like all generals he is probably writing his memoirs."

Khrushchev's most interesting talk, however, involved his relationship with the Red Army commanders in the field and with the Kremlin in Moscow. The commissar's job, basically, was to act as political adviser to the local military commander and to insure that the commander stayed politically reliable; the commissar reported to Moscow on the commander's non-tactical activities. I am sure that Khrushchev performed this function well, but judging from this account, given me fifteen years after the event, he seemed to have sided more often with the field commanders than with Stalin. For example, at Stalingrad where Khrushchev was commissar during that historic defense, he said that the Army group commander recommended that the city be evacuated so as to conduct the defense on the high ground to the east. This, Stalin overruled because of the significance of the name of the city. As a result of occupying the city and fighting for every street, Khrushchev said, the Russian losses were far higher than were necessary.

A similar situation occurred the next year during the Soviet offensive of 1943. In this instance the military commander recommended against a certain large-scale attack in the Kharkov area. Khrushchev agreed and, as in the previous year, he called the Kremlin by phone direct. This time, according to his tale (as he waggled that index finger), he talked to Marshal Zhukov, Stalin's military chief at that time, and presented his arguments. Zhukov alleged that Stalin was unavailable to talk, although Khrushchev was certain, from his intimate knowledge of the room in which the call was being handled, that Stalin's desk was only some twenty feet away. Zhukov heard Khrushchev's story, but insisted that the attack go on as planned. Khrushchev expressed some grudging admiration for Zhukov. He said Zhukov was blunt, bold, direct, and non-diplomatic—as a soldier should be. The attack jumped off, and as Khrushchev had predicted the Soviets lost some three hundred thousand men.

This particular story had a sequel. Five years after the battle, Khrushchev went on, a group of the Politbureau was sitting at a meal. Mikoyan, having become a little "tipsy," began to twit Stalin on the wisdom of this Kharkov decision. "You see, Comrade Stalin," he was quoted as saying, "Comrade Khrushchev was right! The Kharkov attack should never have been made." In his exuberance, Mikoyan had failed to see Stalin rising in anger from his chair.

Hard put to save the situation, Khrushchev barely placated Stalin with a hurried assurance: "Don't worry, Comrade Stalin, we would have lost those three hundred thousand men had we defended or attacked."

In these interesting stories I was not sure whether Khrushchev was trying to make me understand Stalin's weaknesses or, possibly, his own skill in handling his master. The Chairman's recounting of tales of World War II did, however, fascinate us all.

In all sessions we practically ignored the agenda which our foreign ministers had put together. Numerous problems were brought up somewhat haphazardly, but again and again we seemed to come back to Berlin and the latest Soviet ultimatum.

During the sessions the Chairman and I seized several opportunities for strictly private conversations, some at Camp David, others while sightseeing around the countryside. Because my purpose in these man-to-man talks was to learn more about his intentions, objectives, and personal characteristics, we used a single interpreter only—his own. On one of our rides we stopped at my farm near Gettysburg, where we visited with my grandchildren. In such surroundings and circumstances Mr. Khrushchev was a benign and entertaining guest. He told our grandchildren about his own. He asked each child, ranging from eleven years of age to four, for his or her name, and gave to each the counterpart in Russian—each, that is, except for Susan, whose name apparently had nothing to correspond. He issued to them and their parents, who were also present, urgent invitations to accompany me to Russia when I returned his visit the next year. The parents appeared more than hesitant but the children were enthusiastic.

He was interested in the cattle I was raising—the Black Angus breed—and said he was working to improve the cattle breeding industry in his own country. I told him that I would like to send him one as a present. This seemed to please him, and I was happy when Lewis Strauss, who has a large and fine herd of the same breed, later offered to augment the gift by sending him a young bull and another heifer. This we subsequently did.

In our more serious private conversations the Chairman told me that he had decided to abandon all development of naval equipment except submarines and possibly some destroyers. His government, he admitted, had already begun the building of five new cruisers—one of which had been more than half completed—but he had stopped all work on them. He was interested, he said, only in the subsurface part of naval power. In reply I said that we were, as he well knew, developing a fleet of atomic submarines including the Polaris type. Indeed, my naval aide, Captain E. P. Aurand, brought a model of the Polaris submarine (it was procurable in toy stores everywhere) to give to the Chairman as a memento of his visit. In addition I told him that while we were busy developing an atomic submarine fleet, we were alive to the dangers to us posed by any powerful hostile submarine force. We were giving close attention to the problems of contacting and destroying such vessels in the event of an emergency. To this he simply said, "Of course—I understand."

Aside from these private talks, our plenary sessions naturally dealt with subjects of interest to one or both of our nations. Frequently he interspersed his expositions with comments on his two-week tour around America. Obviously he had, as Cabot Lodge had reported, gained some comprehension of the privileges of a free press, and of the workings of our federated system of government. When he learned, for example, that the President of the United States has no control over the Mayor of Los Angeles, he said, "Now I begin to understand some of the problems of President Eisenhower." Again he implied that our vast numbers of automobiles represented only a waste of money, effort, and time.

We discussed the relative strengths of our military forces, the characteristics of our two economies, and specific international problems, including Germany, Berlin, and the Far East.

Referring to Red China, Khrushchev said he had some personal viewpoints about our attitude toward that nation. He asked if I would like to discuss the subject. I answered that I thought there was little use to do so, for the simple reason that Red China had put herself beyond the pale so far as the United States was concerned. I cited in particular Communist China's refusal to return to us certain of our citizens who had been unjustly imprisoned, and her failure to purge herself of the United Nations resolution branding her as an aggressor. The Red Chinese had never, I said, repudiated their often repeated intention of capturing Formosa by force. Instead they were constantly stirring up trouble in Southeast Asia by economic and military interventions in that region.

He took my refusal in good part and implied that he had been specifically asked to bring up the subject with me; by whom, he did not say. He did add, however, that allegations of differences between the Soviets and Red China, while not necessarily deliberate, were ridiculous by their very nature. He and Mao Tse-tung were good friends; the two nations, he said, would always stand together in any international dispute.

He said the Soviet economy must produce more consumer goods; he had personally been striving for a long time to improve the quality and quantity of food, clothing, and housing for the Russian people. He claimed that they were making remarkable progress in multiple family housing. He belittled the usefulness or desirability of the individual home so much in evidence in the United States. He said this type of dwelling entailed increased work and expense for the householder because of high heating costs, expensive transportation, repairs and upkeep, and care for surrounding grounds. When I again called his attention to our magnificent highways and the automobiles that crowded them—as I had done on our helicopter trip around Washington ten days earlier—he now had a ready answer. He said that in his country there was little need for this type of road because the Soviet people lived close together, did not care for automobiles, had slight interest in driving around the countryside on a Sunday afternoon, and rarely changed their residences from one city to another. To this he added to my amusement: "Your people do not seem to like the place where they live and always want to be on the move going someplace else."

Mr. Khrushchev thought that my projected visit to Russia should come soon, saying that the tour could be of whatever duration I might desire and that I alone would decide on the itinerary to be followed. He emphasized that I would be welcome "to see every kind of thing he had seen in this country."

The only question that produced a real argument was his conviction that we should quickly have a four-power "summit." I replied that, like mountain summits, political summits are normally barren, but that, under proper circumstances, I would have no particular objections to such a meeting. I would never go to it as long as there existed the faintest semblance of an ultimatum by his government respecting its purpose to make a peace treaty with East Germany and, according to him, to terminate the rights and privileges of the allies in Berlin. I told him that he should understand without any possibility of error that our nation would never agree to the surrender of West Berlin either to the Soviets or to East Germany, and that so long as the Russian ultimatum went unrepudiated I would not even talk about attending a summit conference.

He continued to rationalize his attitude but I told him that my simple statement of refusal would have to stand. This brought on a long explanation of his prior announcement that he would conclude a separate German peace treaty: the gist of it was that the existence of West Berlin as an unwelcome irritant in the body of "peace-loving" East Germany was growing intolerable. The situation was not only abnormal, he said, but was based upon wartime decisions, then fourteen years in the past.

He knew, of course, that I was familiar with all his prior announcements on the subject; so, rather than go over old ground again and again, I simply said, "You're correct in saying that the situation grew out of an agreement among the forces that destroyed Hitler—but in one of those agreements you got much territory that the Western allies had captured in Germany as well as the Kuriles in Japan; without those wartime agreements the Soviets would not be in any of these areas. Are you going to give them back?" He made no reply.

This part of the conversation came to a head late Sunday morning, our last day at Camp David. As we were obviously at an impasse, he and I, by common consent, moved away from the remaining members of the conference, taking with us again only his interpreter, Oleg Troyanovski. He talked about Germany and Berlin without rancor, but obviously felt he had committed himself so firmly that he saw no way to retreat immediately from his position. However, the Chairman finally said he recognized my determination in this matter and said he would take steps publicly to remove any suggestion of a time limit within which he would sign a Soviet-East German peace treaty, thus making the future of Berlin a proper subject for negotiation, not one for unilateral action.

I replied that by this concession he was putting the matter back into the status quo ante, with the result that all of us could honestly seek for a decent solution to the problem of a city divided. His reversal on this vital matter came shortly before luncheon time, so we arose, each to go to his own quarters for a few minutes. As he left the room he said something to his ambassador and foreign minister, both of whom jumped up to accompany him outside for a walk.

At luncheon, to which we had invited other officials from Washington, including Dick Nixon, there was no serious discussion, but the Chairman seemed to take particular delight in hurling barbs at the Vice President. Dick replied briskly and pointedly to each of the Chairman's sallies. I was a little astonished that Khrushchev should take advantage of a social occasion to try to make another guest feel uncomfortable, but all of us came to suspect that he might have become annoyed with his advisers, who had probably been less than enthusiastic over the Berlin decision he had communicated to me privately. We speculated that his manner at luncheon was merely his way of showing irritation.

Immediately after luncheon we met again. Khrushchev said he would not want his concession to appear in a joint communiqué at the end of our meeting.

"This ends the whole affair," I said, "and I will go neither to a summit nor to Russia."

But he quickly interposed to say that before he could publicize such a statement he needed an opportunity to explain to the members of his own government the reasons that led him to his decision. Consequently he asked me to wait until Tuesday morning to make a public statement describing the agreement and he would, in his own capital, attest to its accuracy. This I accepted. (Forty-eight hours later I made a public announcement of the agreement and he responded immediately in the same vein.)

On the practical side, I pointed out to the Chairman that my schedule for the fall was relatively full, as I understood his was. Therefore I proposed that my return trip to the Soviet Union be delayed until the following spring. He agreed and suggested that the summit meeting be held shortly before my return visit. On this I could not speak for America's allies, of course, and we agreed that timing on a summit meeting could be worked out later.

Throughout the two days Khrushchev stressed the difference in the Soviet Union between his own policies and those of his predecessor. He pointed out what he considered to be some of Stalin's mistakes, such as refusing to be a party to the Japanese peace treaty. Here Khrushchev seemed to have an idea that we had denied to the Soviets their right to participate in the Japanese occupation, as they would like to deny ours in Berlin. I lost no time in pointing out to him that the Soviets had never captured any portion of Japan, and their occupation of the Kuriles was a concession from the Western powers.

With the conferences finally coming to a close, the Chairman and I took an automobile, shortly after two o'clock, and drove from Camp David to Washington. He was much interested in the countryside and continued to talk about his visit throughout the nation. When I dropped him off at the Presidential Guest House in midafternoon of Sunday, September 27, he again repeated his hope that my family and I would visit his country during the coming year.

* * *

As Khrushchev left the United States, we thought he had come to realize that he had a bear by the tail on the Berlin issue, and was relieved at having found a way out with reasonable dignity. I am sure he was pleasantly surprised with the degree of consideration with which he was treated in the United States. Beyond this he implied that the personal acquaintanceship between us should prove helpful in approaching some of our common problems, such as disarmament. The trip through the United States had seemingly given him a new feeling of confidence. Coming to us with an apparent suspicion that he would be treated as an unwelcome guest, he now seemed to enjoy thoroughly every exposure to the public. I felt that he had thrown off a bit of that peculiar defensive complex so noticeable in some Russian officials. At any rate he had gone in good spirits and with many warm messages for my grandchildren. (Mr. Khrushchev later sent them Russian dolls and Christmas tree ornaments for Christmas.)

It seemed that at the end of the Khrushchev visit there was less public pessimism than when he came to our shores. He himself later talked much about "the Spirit of Camp David," but it was a term that I never used or deemed valid.

Nevertheless, a crisis over Berlin had been averted without the surrender of any Western rights. True, the crisis had been an artificial one of Khrushchev's own making, but on the other hand it carried with it the danger that by overstepping himself, he might have gotten into a position where a far worse situation could have developed for all nations. At least it now seemed that we should have a better atmosphere in which to approach such questions as expanding exchanges of visitors and information between East and West, finding an acceptable solution to the problem of a divided Germany, and developing mutual trust through satisfactorily enforced disarmament treaties, even though limited at first in scope.

But, as always, we would have to wait for deeds to determine the sincerity of Soviet words.

BOOK FIVE

But armaments must also be controlled here on earth, if civilization is to be assured of survival. These efforts must extend both to conventional and non-conventional armaments.

. . . Today, I solemnly declare, on behalf of the United States, that we are prepared to submit to any international inspection, provided only that it is effective and truly reciprocal. This step we will take willingly as an earnest of our determination to uphold the preamble of the United Nations Charter which says its purpose is "to save succeeding generations from the scourge of war, which twice in our lifetime has brought untold sorrow to mankind . . ."

—Address before the 15th
General Assembly of the
United Nations, New York
City, September 22, 1960

CHAPTER XIX

The Steel Strike and the Economic Record

The principle of spending money to be paid by posterity, under the name of funding, is but swindling futurity on a large scale.
—*Thomas Jefferson*

AT one minute past midnight on Wednesday, July 15, 1959, the United Steel Workers of America, a half million of them, walked off their jobs, and the fires were banked in the giant blast furnaces of Gary, Youngstown, Birmingham, and Pittsburgh, where more than 85 per cent of this country's steel is produced. The union members wanted a wage increase. Industry, though offering to improve the workers' pension and insurance benefits, opposed a pay increase at least until the following year. Even more sensitive was the issue of factory work rules. The steel companies demanded the right to change these rules in order to increase workers' efficiency and end "featherbedding." A prior ten weeks of hard and often acrimonious bargaining had failed to yield an agreement, and the strike was begun.

A strike of this magnitude inevitably involves the entire country and becomes of deep concern to the federal government. The first thing, therefore, was to define the government's proper role and fix its limits. The objective was to get the steel workers back to their jobs voluntarily and the industry producing again for consumers, for defense, and for tax revenue—without stimulating inflation.

The nation's welfare demanded an agreement be reached that did not involve a necessary increase in unit production costs, which would obviously be inflationary, and could make us less competitive in world markets. This, in turn, could further intensify our "balance-of-payments" problem (roughly, the difference between our annual payments abroad and our receipts from abroad), which had become serious starting in 1957. The difficulty was to determine how to do this without using the full weight of the federal government to impose a settlement, which might irretrievably damage the process of free collective bargaining.

To settle such controversies, some politicians of course have a quick and easy remedy: "In the public interest, let the federal government take charge." They contend that in basic industries—such as steel and other metals, machinery, automobiles, paper, and chemicals, which have an inescapable influence on the entire price structure—the federal government should intervene directly in wage and price decisions. Some propose compulsory arbitration by the federal government; others urge the creation of special courts or review boards to hear and judge industrial disputes, in each case with decisions that would be binding upon labor and management.

I opposed such answers. Let the federal government fix wages, I argued, and it will next have to fix hours and work rules, moderate grievances, and finally set prices. Once it regulates wages and prices in major industries, it can run the entire economy—and will soon run it for political, not economic, advantage.

Moreover, government compulsion not only threatens economic liberty; it is also ineffective. In foreign countries that have tried it, it has brought on hit-and-run strikes, and work slowdowns and stoppages. Here in the United States we had learned, before 1953, that federal intervention in labor-management disputes had often produced neither a satisfactory settlement nor prevented wage and price increases.[1]

Shortly after my inauguration I had designated the Secretary of Labor as my primary adviser on labor-management problems. This seems elementary, but in the previous administration the use of a presidential staff officer as a labor authority had tended to reduce the Department of Labor to a compiler of statistics and had injected the White House into all manner of labor-management quarrels. Following a general policy of White House "hands off" in this type of negotiation, I had, for example,

[1] In 1946 a fact-finding board, convened at the direction of the President, had not ended that year's steel dispute which came to a settlement only after the federal government adjusted its wage and price formulas to let the companies raise their prices. Another federal board failed to produce a settlement in 1949, which saw fringe benefits and prices rise again. In 1952 the steel companies rejected the recommendations of the Federal Wage Stabilization Board; that year's strike ended only after the board approved both a wage and a price increase—and after the U. S. Supreme Court had declared unconstitutional President Truman's seizure of the steel mills. In a speech in Pittsburgh during the 1952 campaign, I charged that that particular fifty-four-day steel strike—which cut total non-farm employment by 670,000—would have been shorter if Washington had kept out of it.

refused to use presidential authority in the Louisville-Nashville railroad strike of 1954, the Southern Bell Telephone strike of 1954, and the United Auto Workers' campaign for a guaranteed annual wage in 1955. Left to their own devices, the disputants had composed their quarrels among themselves.[2] So, in 1959 I rejected the perennial suggestion that the government "settle" the steel conflict.

It *was* the duty of the government, nevertheless, to keep fully abreast of every development, and steps to this end were taken at an early date. If at any time the disagreement should mushroom into a real danger to the nation's security and economy, it would be the further duty of the administration to ask the Congress for special powers until the emergency could be surmounted.

The strike continued. On September 8, in its fifty-sixth day, it became the longest since World War II. Two weeks later the Department of Commerce reported to me that its effects were becoming more apparent throughout the economy: work weeks were shortening, plants were shutting down, and a shortage of alloy steel plates and beams threatened to delay the construction of missile bases.

On September 30 I held two separate sessions on the problem, one with a number of executives in the steel industry, the other with labor leaders.

I told both sides that it would be exceedingly unwise for them to force the government to intervene directly in the struggle and urged each to show a conciliatory spirit. Both claimed that they wanted a non-inflationary agreement, and both agreed that negotiations, which had been suspended for days, would resume at once. Three days later industry made its first money proposal and, not unexpectedly, labor called it "completely unacceptable."

In the meantime, industrial consumers were beginning to buy up the backlog of warehoused steel at increased prices, to use uneconomical sizes, and to cut the work week further. Mass layoffs were becoming imminent. Shortages threatened to delay the construction of new units of the Polaris. Imports of steel were increasing.

Because of this clear threat to the country's security, the time had come to use the resources of existing law. On October 9, I invoked the

[2] By the time I left office, the record showed the results of these policies. In a computation of the number of workers involved in work stoppages, the four best years since World War II fell within my years in the White House. In a computation of the number of days lost because of work stoppages, six of the seven best years since World War II fell within my administration; six of the seven worst years fell within the previous administration.

Taft-Hartley Act, and ordered a three-man presidential fact-finding board to investigate and report upon the facts of the strike. Ten days later, after the board reported that the disputants were unlikely to reach a voluntary settlement, I ordered the Justice Department to go to court to seek an eighty-day "back to work" injunction. On October 21, a federal district court issued the injunction; and on November 7 the Supreme Court of the United States upheld the Taft-Hartley injunction. For the next eighty days—until January 26—the steel workers would be back on their jobs, after 116 days on strike.

Meantime, the national interest did demand a settlement.

On the afternoon of November 5, I met for a long discussion with David McDonald, President of the United Steel Workers, and Secretary of Labor James P. Mitchell, who had been following the course of the strike night and day during the past months. After the meeting, Secretary Mitchell returned to his office in the Department of Labor where I telephoned him.

"McDonald was, of course, presenting only his side," I told the Secretary, "but I believe he wants to settle. He wants to compromise. Maybe management could give some pledge that the steel workers wouldn't lose their jobs to automation." I was referring, of course, to the industry's demand for an increase in efficiency.

It appeared that McDonald was more concerned with "work rules" than with wages. He argued that the changes in the work rules demanded by management were unfair and might wreck the union; this fear, he said, had encouraged the workers, despite their hardships, to rally behind him and stay out on strike. (Management, on its side, argued that the work rules were antiquated and that they compelled inefficiency and helped price American products out of foreign markets.)

Through the month of November steel production moved toward 90 per cent of capacity. But the dispute continued, and on November 15, the union rejected a company offer of 30 cents an hour in increased wages and fringe benefits over the next three years.

Quite naturally, during all this time, I reviewed the legal resources available to the President in such crises and pondered the wisdom of asking for more legislation. Through the injunctive process the Taft-Hartley law provided a breathing spell. But I was beginning to believe that the law might be amended advantageously to give the President a choice of several different courses of action, instead of just an eighty-day injunction. Giving the President a choice would put the contending parties in doubt as to the course he might elect, and might induce them to resolve their differences sooner. On November 12, I dictated a draft of a letter to Secretary Mitchell outlining an idea for preventing strikes which involved the national security. Its purpose was to induce serious study and discussion by interested parties on possible actions, including that of temporary reduction or elimination of tariffs on the products of an essential industry tied up by a prolonged strike.[3]

By the end of November, time was running out. The administration had no choice but to try a further means of persuasion.

On the eve of an overseas trip on December 3, I spoke to the nation by television. A key section of the talk focused on the steel strike:

> Responsible citizenship in a free country means what it says—the nation's welfare demanded responsible action on both sides. Unless they decided to so act, the country would see to it that they did. The exact methods the parties agreed upon to advance the negotiations were unimportant. What was important was a fair settlement.
>
> Indeed, it is so important that I am instructing the Director of the Mediation . . . Service to do all that he can to keep the parties negotiating around the clock.
>
> America needs a settlement now.

Earlier, on July 7 at the All-Star baseball game in Pittsburgh, before the strike began, Mr. McDonald had talked with Vice President Nixon and asked him to use his good offices to induce the steel manufacturers to come to an agreement with the union. Through the fall, the Vice President had talked frequently with Jim Mitchell, watching the course of the strike. Finally, at my request, he and the Secretary began a series of secret meetings with officials on both sides of the dispute, meeting among other places at the Nixon home in Washington and at the Waldorf-Astoria in New York. The efforts of my two emissaries were conciliatory only; they were not to promise or threaten any governmental action to bring about a settlement.

These closed meetings went on intermittently throughout the month of December, while in public the disputants held a round of talks with federal mediators. Manufacturers of cans and makers of aluminum products signed new agreements with the union (which includes workers in aluminum as well as steel), but the eleven major steel companies did not. By the end of the month the presidential fact-finding board reported that the two sides were growing even farther apart. The steel companies filed with the board their "final" offer, providing for the increase in benefits estimated at 30 cents an hour and for binding arbitration on

[3] This letter was not sent, though its ideas were passed along by phone and in person during this rapidly worsening period. The draft is included in Appendix X to show the trend of my thinking at the time.

the issue of work practices. By the 13th of January—less than two weeks before the Taft-Hartley injunction would expire—union members would, under the law, vote on this offer. Every indication was that they would vote negatively and walk off the job once more.

Both sides now knew that, should this negative vote come about, the union negotiators' bargaining position would be stronger than ever. But they also knew that the Congress was returning to Washington, and that, if the steel workers walked off the job again, the result could be new legislation, probably requiring compulsory arbitration; neither side looked forward to such a law.

At this moment of impasse, neither management nor labor wanted to make the first move. Secretary Mitchell called David McDonald.

"Dave," he said, "the time has come when you have to break the line and come down."

This time McDonald did reduce his demands, not as much as the steel companies wanted, but at least the Vice President and Mitchell had a measurable concession.

At once, on Wednesday, December 30, 1959, they flew to New York City to meet with officials of the steel industry. In a brief conference with the executives the Vice President "laid the issue on the line," reminding them that if the strike resumed, "the country will have no place to go for a remedy but to the Congress, which as you know, the Democrats control. In an election year, management won't like the labor-management legislation such a Congress will produce."

That meeting broke the deadlock. The company negotiators agreed that they would voluntarily accept the settlement recommended by Nixon and Mitchell. Feverish negotiations followed.

At ten o'clock on the morning of January 2, from Augusta, Georgia, I had a three-way telephone conversation with the Vice President in California, and Secretary Mitchell and General Persons in Washington. Nixon and Mitchell described the recent negotiations. I agreed to their announcing that, with my approval, they had served as an unofficial committee of the government and that both had recommended the settlement.

"This is the best settlement we can work out on a voluntary basis," I concluded.

But this whole episode had strengthened my conviction that in the long run the country would need better and stronger laws to protect the public interest in labor-management disputes that could seriously hurt the economy and national security. This would inevitably give the government more power over the economy, which would be deplorable, but the lack of wisdom on both sides in voluntary negotiations seemed to me to leave no alternative.[4]

On the morning of January 4, after Jim Mitchell had gone sleepless for two nights, the two sides announced their agreement. Industry would pay approximately 41 cents an hour in increased wages and fringe benefits over thirty months, from January 1, 1960, to July 1, 1962, and management abandoned its attempt to change the work rules. Dave McDonald signed the settlement with much enthusiasm; the steel executives with less. While relieved that the immediate crisis was ended, I had misgivings: The money settlement, higher than the 30 cents previously offered, probably would not be inflationary, but the effort to modernize work rules should not have been dropped.

The government economists conclusion that the settlement would not be necessarily inflationary[5] was vindicated in the succeeding months.

In the State of the Union message a few days later, I expressed my gratification that despite the increase in wages and fringe benefits the steel companies did not plan to increase prices at present; I called on management and labor to do their utmost to increase efficiency and thus to hold prices down. Because experience showed that similar difficulties would certainly recur in the future, I said, . . ."It is my intention to encourage regular discussions between management and labor outside the bargaining table, to consider the interest of the public as well as their mutual interest in the maintenance of industrial peace, price stability, and economic growth."

* * *

As the economy moved out of recession in 1958 and began to overcome the effects of the steel strike of 1959, the government's fiscal position rapidly improved. From a $12.4 billion deficit in fiscal year 1959, we were moving toward a $1 billion surplus in fiscal year 1960, a result of success in the battle of the budget and of the economy's recovery, which lifted federal tax revenues by nearly $10 billion and, by obviating the need for certain anti-recessionary expenditure programs, made it possible to reduce federal spending by $3.8 billion.

[4] This was my belief at the time. However, a study made at the request of Secretary Mitchell by a group headed by Professor E. R. Livernash of Harvard University resulted in a report released in January 1961, that did not agree with me. Its conclusions are found in Appendix Y.

[5] Lower than the average 1959 wage settlement, it was only about half the size of other steel wage settlements since World War II, all of which were accompanied by price increases, as this one was not.

Further improvement would, of course, depend in part on economic conditions but also, among other things, on the continuation of certain tax rates which, without specific congressional action, would have been reduced. Accordingly, in January of 1960, I asked the Congress to extend corporate income tax rates at their prevailing rates for another year, beginning June 30, 1960, and to postpone for the same period the reduction of excise taxes on such things as alcohol, tobacco, and automobiles. On the correct assumption that these tax proposals would be adopted, I presented to the Congress with considerable satisfaction in January 1960, a fiscal 1961 budget with a projected surplus of $4.2 billion.[6]

Later some economists challenged these policies.[7] In swinging too rapidly from deficit to surplus, they argued, the administration had demonstrated a wholly needless concern about inflation; by refusing to reduce taxes, we had failed, they averred, to assure the continuance of the economy's upswing out of the trough of the 1958 recession and, instead, had induced a slowing down in the economy which had contributed to the $4 billion deficit in 1961. A slowdown actually did begin in the spring of 1960 and intensified during the fall and winter; unemployment increased.

Though the deficit-to-planned-surplus swing may have been abrupt, I felt then and do now that the criticisms overlooked some of the causative factors for the actual disappointing results.

First, so far as the $4 billion deficit of 1961 was concerned, the criticism ignored the fact that, under the Kennedy administration, between fiscal year 1960 and fiscal year 1961, federal spending went up $5 billion—an increase far greater than the $2.4 billion one we planned.

[6] In this effort three influential advisers and co-workers were Secretary of the Treasury Robert Anderson, Chairman of the Council of Economic Advisers Dr. Raymond Saulnier, and Director of the Bureau of the Budget Maurice Stans. Another whose counsel I valued highly was the Chairman of the Federal Reserve Board William McChesney Martin. Though not a member of the Executive branch, he worked tirelessly to further fiscal responsibility and sustain the value of our currency.

[7] A number of respected business analysts, one of whom was Gabriel Hauge, cautioned me against the damaging effects that might result from trying to return too quickly to a balanced budget in fiscal year 1960 after the $12 billion deficit of the previous year. I was impressed by Dr. Hauge's arguments but an overriding consideration, in my mind, was the worsening situation in our balance of payments. I felt that a rapid return to a balanced budget would help reassure other nations as to America's ability to pay her debts and lessen their desire to convert their dollars into gold.

Second, the criticism ignored the impact of the long 1959 steel strike[8] on federal revenues in both fiscal year 1960 and 1961, a shutdown producing an economic downturn equivalent to recession.

Third, the complaint that fiscal policy was overly restrictive during this period overlooks the fact that between September 1958 and September 1959 the Federal Reserve Banks raised discount rates from 2½ to 4 per cent and that by December 1959 average rates on short-term business loans made by commercial banking institutions had risen to a peak of 5.4 per cent. For people borrowing to start or expand businesses, money was therefore more expensive, harder to get. Not until June 1960 did the Federal Reserve Banks begin to reduce discount rates, and not until September 1960 did all rates get down to 3 per cent. It is not my purpose to quarrel with the credit policy of the independent Federal Reserve System in this period, for I believe that we were engaged then in a battle against an inflationary psychology—a battle that had to be won. Monetary policy had an essential part to play in that struggle. But advocates of the theory that fiscal policy should have been strongly expansionary, appear to imply that expenditure and tax policy in this period should have been launched into a kind of tug-of-war with monetary policy. Obviously, policy cannot be evaluated except as a whole.

Fourth, critics overlooked the inflationary psychology which prevailed during the mid-fifties and which I thought it necessary to defeat. In 1957, for example, consumer prices were rising at an unacceptably high annual rate of 3.2 per cent. Ten years of this could devalue the current dollar more than 30 per cent while if the rate accelerated, we would have had an entirely intolerable situation on our hands. Even during the 1957–58 recession, prices rose more than 2 per cent; wages and salaries were simultaneously continuing upward nearly as rapidly as during periods of economic expansion.[9] Most important of all, these cost increases were

[8] In the first quarter of 1960, for example, inventories were building up at an annual rate of more than $9 billion; in the fourth quarter they were declining at an annual rate of $3 billion; between the beginning and the end of 1960, production and employment fell off and unemployment rose. But this inventory swing largely resulted from the steel strike. In the inventory buildup of the first quarter of 1960, durable goods manufacturers and automobile retailers accounted for 85 per cent of the total accumulation. It is not surprising, therefore, that between January and December of 1960, while total industrial production was dropping 7 per cent, iron and steel production was falling off 47 per cent. Final demand, however—demand excluding that which results in changes in inventory—continued to rise throughout the year.

[9] Whereas the Gross National Product fell about 4.5 per cent during the recession, personal disposable income fell less than 1 per cent. If consumer purchases had fallen as much, proportionally, as they did in the corresponding part of the 1929–30 depression, they would have fallen $28 billion; as it was, they fell only $1.3 billion.

far outstripping the historical rate at which American industry achieved improvements in productivity, and for this reason were tending to raise prices or squeeze profit margins.

The administration believed that if wages and prices could *increase* during a recession, we could get into real inflationary trouble in time of prosperity. Monetary and fiscal policy had to be so fashioned as to forestall such a result and to re-establish confidence in the dollar. Above all, we had to strengthen public faith in the willingness as well as in the ability of government to take the steps necessary to curb cost and price inflation. This was our purpose, and it is my conviction that we were successful.

At the end of January the Joint Economic Committee of the Congress, while differing on some administration policies, agreed, Republicans and Democrats alike, that a time of prosperity was pending and that we should strive to produce a budget surplus. By a bipartisan vote the committee rejected a permanent policy of "easy money," and went on record against a broad-gauged expansion of federal spending.

As we looked backward from the spring of 1960, we enjoyed a moment of satisfaction. A year earlier, with a $12.4 billion deficit superimposed on rising wages, rising stock prices, and an uneasiness caused by an increased foreign payments deficit, we might well have despaired of preventing a powerful upward thrust in prices. Now evidence was appearing that that inflationary thrust, powerful as it was, had been blunted.

The anti-inflation battle is never-ending, though I fear that in 1959 the public was apathetic, at least uninformed, regarding this issue. This attitude caused me to recall a laconic comment of Winston Churchill when someone asked him during World War II what the allies were fighting for: "If we stop," he replied, "you will find out."

Economists who now look back to the 1959–60 period and wish we had discontinued the struggle because the enemy had seemingly vanished, shrug off the good results of that struggle. After the campaign of 1958, the battle of the budget, the steel strike of 1959, and the refusal to continue deficit spending in 1960, prices rose much more slowly. This fact was not only a boon to men and women living on fixed payments from insurance, pensions, and social security, but it has been helpful in preserving markets abroad. For whereas our wholesale prices, for example, remained roughly on a plateau between 1958 and 1963, prices in West Germany rose 4 per cent, in Sweden 11 per cent, and in France 17 per cent.

The policies and struggles of those years made a significant contribution, I think, in puncturing public apathy toward the dangers of inflation and the political manipulations which invite it. For evidence, consider the reluctance of vast numbers of Americans in 1963 and 1964 to accept a tax reduction unless the government at the same time should assure them it would hold down federal spending and deficits. The people took this lesson to heart, and the results are in the record.

Nevertheless, the fight is never over. I believe that today there is a dangerous looseness in federal fiscal affairs and a too-ready popular assumption that "we are so prosperous we can afford anything."

Recently I was visited by a young Doctor of Philosophy, engaged in writing a paper on the appropriate role and responsibilities of the minority party in the American political system. I suggested that one task, especially in times of prosperity, was that of opposing deficit financing. He disagreed, supporting the practice even in times of record prosperity, and saying that this was one of the major reasons he was a member of the Democratic party. To my query as to the desirability of paying off some of our huge debt when circumstances permitted, he replied that, in his opinion, there was no virtue in doing so. While he disclaimed expertise as an economist, he was confident in the soundness of his convictions, citing several well-known economists of the "new school" as his authority. In brief, he expressed his beliefs in this fashion:

"The federal government should pump into the economy more than it collects so as constantly to spur expansion and vigor.

"The size of the debt is immaterial because it largely reflects the costs of war and, after all, while it steadily grows in absolute terms, in its ratio to the Gross National Product, it is constantly decreasing. So long as this condition obtains, deficit spending would not be a factor in inflation.

"As a consequence, piling up the debt with its growing interest costs poses no threat to the future; the view that we were passing on to our grandchildren a growing financial burden is obsolete and erroneous; the debt should be looked upon merely as a bookkeeping record to be passed on from generation to generation like the Constitution and the fertility of the continent."

My counterarguments reflected the convictions on this matter that guided my administration for eight years. My view is unshakable: When the economy is booming and the federal government concurrently is spending so heavily as to create sizable deficits, inflationary pressures are bound to build up and the cost of living can be expected to increase. This is economic irresponsibility, practiced only by those who believe that next month's profit and loss statement is more important than the long-term and steady growth of a free economy. Playing with inflation is the height of reckless folly. Plentiful examples past and present, demonstrate the validity of these convictions.

My visitor was not impressed, even when I invited his attention to huge but unpublicized federal obligations—far in excess of the funded debt—that must some day be paid for by all our citizens.

Unable to disturb my visitor's complacency, I had to content myself with suggesting that he talk with an economist of the kind I respect—such as Arthur Burns, Gabriel Hauge, or Raymond Saulnier—my faint hope being for his conversion in thinking, if not in party allegiance.

* * *

The foregoing account may leave the impression that we were interested only in reducing federal costs—that we wanted the country to step backward into puritan austerity. That would be a completely erroneous view. Our overriding purpose was to promote economic growth while keeping prices reasonably stable. The record, including that of antitrust action, matches that purpose.

In the years 1952–60 the Gross National Product rose about $100 billion (in constant prices), or nearly 25 per cent.[10] Average weekly earnings in manufacturing increased 34 per cent, national income 42 per cent, and private domestic investment nearly 45 per cent. Incidentally, in these years the average salary of public school teachers went up nearly 50 per cent, while private gifts to colleges and universities rose nearly 200 per cent.

In those eight years Americans broke all previous records, and established a new one, by building more than eight million new homes. And into those homes science and technology brought time-saving and work-saving appliances on an unprecedented scale. While refrigerator-freezers and automatic washing machines certainly did not guarantee happiness, they provided more leisure time in which to pursue it.

But science was not only remaking the American home; it was also, more and more, helping to make Americans a cosmopolitan people. Between 1952 and 1960 the number of airline passengers more than doubled; by the end of 1960 our airlines were annually carrying passengers nearly a billion miles. In 1950 American overseas travelers totaled 676,000; by 1960 that number had multiplied neary 2½ times, going to 1.6 million—most of them traveling by air and all of them, together with travelers to Canada and Mexico, spending more than two billion dollars.

[10] And whereas the 1939 dollar was worth only 52 cents by January of 1953, the 1953 dollar had lost only about 5½ cents of its value by 1961.

At home 60 million automobiles were now being driven on a vast new network of superhighways; travel, once the pleasure of the rich, had become the privilege of the majority.

Gratifyingly, more than a score of American-made satellites were orbiting in space and many atomic-powered submarines were at sea. In our defense establishment and throughout our economy, sophisticated instruments were remaking the world of work—electronic computers capable of adding a column of figures as high as the Empire State Building in a second or solving in hours complicated problems that formerly would literally have required generations of time; machines capable of lifting from hands and minds routine tasks of men on production lines and at office desks; capable perhaps one day of forwarding at an unimagined speed the dazzling (although sometimes troublesome) process by which fewer and fewer people turn out a greater and greater abundance of food, apparel, shelter, and tools.[11]

Few of us, riding on the whistle-stopping campaign train of 1952, and promising to do a better job in government, would have dared to predict all of these developments. Not every achievement was governmentally inspired by any means. But looking back from 1960, we could see that in those intervening years the achievement of a widespread prosperity, and the repulse of an insidious inflation, had helped to bring a chance for the good life to more Americans than ever before.

[11] In 1953, 13.5 million production workers added to manufactured products a value of $121.6 billion. In 1960, 12.2 million workers added $164 billion.

Nonetheless, through these years some politicians professed to believe Khrushchev's prediction that in economic competition, as in the space race, the Soviet Union would "bury" us, and that our grandchildren would live under "Socialism." As late as the 1960 campaign they protested that the Soviet Union's economic growth rate was three times ours, conveniently forgetting (a) that the Soviet GNP (if we could believe their figures) equaled only 40 per cent of ours, and (b) that even the Soviets' claimed rate of annual economic growth had long been *declining,* from 26 per cent in 1948 to 16 per cent in 1951 to 10 per cent in 1957.

Once the opposition took over the government, however, this "growth gap" evaporated with the same ballistic speed as the "missile gap." By September of 1961, administration officials were comforting us with their conclusion that—despite Khrushchev's continuing boasts—the Soviet Union's economy would, by 1971, still trail the United States by 25–40 per cent, and that Russia would probably not overtake us economically within the twentieth century.

CHAPTER XX

Disarmament

We must take as our working hypothesis that what is necessary is possible.

—*John Foster Dulles*

WAR, with its suffering and destructiveness, has produced notable victories and notable men, but in temporarily settling international quarrels it has not guaranteed peace with right and justice. War is stupid, cruel, and costly. Yet wars have persisted. In the name of self-defense, nations have paid the human price and, spurred on by fear and competition, have continued to accept the burdens of armaments, the size and cost of which grow ever more fantastic.

In the past, when military machines grew to such a size or awesomeness as to create arrogance in the powers possessing them, these powers by domineering acts sometimes drove other nations, in despair or utter hopelessness, to resort to force. Ancient Rome and Napoleon's France provide but two examples. In other instances—Japan in 1941—the ambitions for military power became so expensive that the nation's economy could no longer bear the cost; whereupon political leaders resorted to war in the hope of recouping national losses.

It is no wonder, then, that vast majorities among all peoples of the civilized world have long since become weary of wars, and of the bloody and taxing penalties incurred to wage or prevent them.

With the desire for peace so universally and deeply felt, the obvious question is "Why do wars occur?" The answer is not to be found in peoples themselves (save where they have been deliberately misled), but in the blind arrogance and conflicting ambitions of governments, especially those whose philosophy is essentially hostile to others and whose objective is nakedly imperialistic.

The Soviets' shocking postwar seizure of and political domination over the Eastern tier of European nations, the curt refusal of the Soviets to accept the Baruch proposal in 1947 to turn over to the United Nations exclusive responsibility for nuclear development, the blockade of Berlin in 1948, and the outbreak of the Korean War in 1950 are a few of the dramatic warnings to all nations that the promise implied in the founding of the United Nations in 1945 would not soon be translated into worldwide peace.

But hope is more difficult to kill than men, and humanity is not ready spinelessly to accept the cynical conclusion that war is certain to recur, that the law of the jungle must forever be the rule of life.

Men have begun to realize that the best interest of all, no matter how mutually hostile their ideologies, might be served by agreeing upon *controlled* reductions of armaments. If nations, large and small, feel compelled to produce costly weapons of war because of alleged or genuine fear of attack, these fears would be lessened and costs markedly reduced if trustworthy agreements on levels of military power could be achieved. Such measures, while not fully assuring peaceful settlement of all international issues, should lessen the diversion from useful purposes of the materials, money, and manpower that go daily into the production of weapons. Psychologically, the effect would be to diminish the influence of military might in international issues.

The problem has compounded with the increase in the destructive power of weapons and in the improved means of delivering them. Atomic and hydrogen bombs and long-range ballistic missiles, preposterously destructive, have so enormously increased mutual apprehensions that effective measures toward universal disarmament are essential in achieving a world of security—at least of reducing the fear of global cataclysm and the practical extinction of civilization.

Of the various presidential tasks to which I early determined to devote my energies, none transcended in importance that of trying to devise practical and acceptable means to lighten the burdens of armaments and to lessen the likelihood of war. Any progress would be an important step toward the ultimate goal of establishing a universal peace with justice and freedom.

* * *

From the very beginning of my administration, we sought creative proposals that might, if accepted by others, lead to progress. For eight years the effort was unremitting. No matter how deeply preoccupied my associates and I became with other urgent situations, never for a day was there absent from our minds and organized work the search for some kind of agreement that would mark a first, even if only a small, step toward a satisfactory disarmament plan.

In the end our accomplishments were meager, almost negligible. Except for the considerable accomplishment of the founding of the IAEA, following my Atoms-for-Peace speech before the United Nations in December of 1953, the most significant, possibly the only, achievement of the entire effort was the wider education of all civilized peoples in the growing need for disarmament and the reasons for our failure to achieve tangible results.

That failure can be explained in one sentence: It was the adamant insistence of the Communists on maintaining a closed society. Their obdurate attitude was based on fear—fear that once they lifted the Iron Curtain their own people, discovering the goodness and richness of life in freedom, might repudiate Communism itself, and, learning of the sincerely peaceful intentions of free peoples who had been proclaimed to them as deadly enemies, would soon reject the Communist goal of world domination.

Every realistic plan for mutual disarmament automatically creates a need for impartial inspection. This is essential no matter what nations are involved; it is imperative in any arrangement made with the Soviets, for they have flagrantly violated nearly every agreement they ever made. But so consuming is the Soviet fear of opening Russia to others that every system so far proposed by the imagination and good will of the Western nations has been flatly rejected by the Communists, even where these would provide opportunity for only a modicum of inspection.

My first major disarmament proposal following the general pronouncements in my 1953 Inaugural Address came three months later in a talk before the American Society of Newspaper Editors. I called upon all nations to set limits on the sizes of their military and security forces and on the proportion of their total production of certain strategic materials to be devoted to military purposes; I proposed international control of atomic energy and the promotion of its use for peaceful purposes only; and called for the enforcement of all agreed limitations and prohibitions by adequate safeguards, including a practical system of inspection under the United Nations.

Eight months later in a speech before the United Nations, I outlined an Atoms-for-Peace proposal, whereby governments would,

> . . . to the extent permitted by elementary prudence, . . . begin now and continue to make joint contributions from their stockpiles of normal uranium and fissionable materials to an International Atomic Energy Agency.

Though the Soviet delegates seemed pleased with this widely applauded suggestion, I was to learn that at every opportunity their government would throw obstacles, in the form of legalistic and technical objections, across the path of progress. Two years after my talk before the United Nations, the agency I had proposed had not yet come into being. As an interim measure, therefore, I announced on Washington's Birthday, 1956, that the United States would make available to United States licencees and to friendly governments abroad, 40,000 kilograms of U-235 for peaceful purposes (in addition to smaller amounts previously made available for research). A year and a half later, on July 29, 1957, the International Atomic Energy Agency became a fact and reinforced my hope that time and patience might bring forth more significant achievements.

* * *

During the many months following my original proposal, disarmament was a subject of varying, and often sharply opposing, views among departments and agencies of the United States government and outside them.

I determined to find a method to help compose them. One step was to call on former Minnesota Governor Harold E. Stassen, an energetic and imaginative man, to serve as my Special Assistant for Disarmament. Mr. Stassen was then head of the Foreign Operations Administration, charged with executing the Mutual Security Program. That organization was about to be incorporated into the State Department,[1] a move that freed him for the new assignment.

Governor Stassen would report directly to me (but was to cooperate closely with the State Department). He was to evaluate the many departmental views on disarmament and to identify the areas of disagreement. At the same time it seemed logical that he should also represent the United States on the five-nation disarmament subcommittee, which had been established in 1954 as a working group of the United Nations Disarmament Commission. In his capacity as a negotiator for the United States he was, therefore, reporting to our ambassador to the United Nations, Cabot Lodge, to Foster Dulles, as well as to me. This need for an individual to "wear several hats" is not uncommon in government, but almost invariably it causes some misunderstandings among the respective staffs, even when the principals themselves cooperate smoothly. This case was no exception.

Before taking over his duties on the United Nations subcommittee, Governor Stassen studied our over-all disarmament position. A chief result

[1] As the International Cooperation Administration.

of his many meetings was a conclusion that the security of the United States would be well served if initially we could secure agreement for an exchange of blueprints of military forces with the Soviets, opening our military bases reciprocally with the Soviets to inspection. Others, notably Nelson Rockefeller, at that time my Special Assistant for Psychological Warfare, enthusiastically advocated this idea.

The Open Skies proposal that I offered at the summit conference at Geneva was akin to this concept, but the idea had its limitations. Obviously aerial inspection would be of little value in itself as a means of discovering where any nation stored its stockpile of nuclear weapons. But it assumed that even in the day of "push-button warfare" a modern nation would find it impossible to prepare a massive surprise attack without a stepping-up of military activity sufficient to be noticeable from the air. As always there was our hope that the success of such a first step might develop mutual confidence for future progress.

There is no question that following the Geneva conference in the summer of 1955 the United States held the initiative in winning the good opinion of the world.[2] Most governments were highly favorable to our Open Skies proposal, as evidenced by a December 16, 1955, General Assembly resolution which, adopted by a vote of 56–7, urged early implementation of:

> Such confidence-building measures as the plan of Mr. Eisenhower, President of the United States of America, for exchanging military blueprints and mutual aerial inspection, and the plan of Mr. Bulganin, Prime Minister of the Union of Soviet Socialist Republics, for establishing control posts at strategic centres.

But our objective in this endeavor was not approbation or propaganda. We wanted a real beginning of mutual disarmament.

As always, the result was nothing but disappointment. The Open Skies proposal was criticized by the Soviets because, they said, it covered only the territories of our two homelands and would fail to cover territory where United States forces were stationed overseas (ignoring, of course, the forces that the Soviets were maintaining in the European satellite nations). Bulganin decried the proposal because it was limited—

[2] Also, there had been a phenomenally successful conference (also in Geneva) on the peaceful uses of atomic energy which had brought scientists of the Free World and from behind the Iron Curtain together for the first time in a generation. Our initiative in having proposed this conference was widely recognized and our participation in it by means of full-scale exhibits, including a complete nuclear reactor built at Oak Ridge and flown to Geneva, was spectacular and inspiring.

it did not cover the entire world in the first step.[3] He promised to keep it under consideration, but preferred instead his own scheme for a series of static control posts to be located at communications centers, railroad marshaling yards, and the like. To this idea we had no objection, realizing, however, that it was so inadequate as to be virtually useless. This we knew from our experiences with "fixed posts" of inspection in Korea, which were consistently bypassed by the North Koreans and Red Chinese after the signing of the Armistice. We argued, therefore, that fixed posts and an inspection system should be simultaneously established.

Through all our correspondence in the following year, Bulganin objected to the priority I accorded to inspection to prevent surprise attack. Glibly he extolled the alleged value of friendship treaties and joint announcements pledging reduction of manpower levels and "prohibition" of atomic weapons.

He must have known that such relatively meaningless, unenforceable treaties between the United States and the U.S.S.R. built on these sweeping generalities would have dismayed our allies and would have practically shattered NATO.

Then on May 14, 1956, the Soviets announced their intention to reduce their armed forces by 1.2 million men. Naturally they pointed to this statement of intentions (the Soviets would permit no verification of the announced manpower reductions) as an example we should emulate.[4] Furthermore, our intelligence services estimated that the aggregate strength of Soviet forces after their announced reductions[5] would be four million men, something more than a million in excess of our own.

During the second half of 1956 the disarmament issue was all but obscured by the thundering events in the Middle East, Hungary, and

[3] In a later letter he was to come up with a still more curious argument: if the military in both the United States and the Soviet Union were to learn all about each others' armed forces, they would automatically begin agitation for increases in their own; therefore the Open Skies would increase rather than decrease armaments.

[4] I had predicted in a message to the House Foreign Affairs Committee the week before the announcement that the Soviets would probably soon shift a considerable body of manpower from the armed forces to the farms and factories.

[5] There was no conflict in principle regarding conventional force reductions. Shortly after the Soviet announcement of May 14 they agreed to a Western proposal in the UN disarmament subcommittee that forces be reduced among the "big five" to levels of 2.5 million men each for the United States, the Soviet Union, and Red China—and to 750,000 each for Britain and France. However, Soviet refusal to permit verification of its enforcement prohibited the signing of any formal treaty. The next year the United States voluntarily reduced its own forces to the 2.5 million-man level, although we did so without appreciably reducing our fighting strength.

Suez, but in January 1957, Cabot Lodge was instructed to submit to the United Nations a new set of disarmament proposals. These involved certain ideas we had proposed before: reduction of nuclear stockpiles and transfer of fissionable material to peaceful uses; force reductions under adequate inspection to fixed levels for ourselves and principal allies (previously coordinated with them); and progressive installation of aerial and ground inspection teams as guards against surprise attacks. But some of our suggestions were new. We expressed willingness to work out methods of limiting and finally eliminating nuclear test explosions and proposed (even though the first orbited manmade satellite was still months in the future) that satellites, intercontinental missiles, and space platforms should all be brought within the purview of reliable arms control systems.

This proposal, along with those of other nations, was referred as usual to the Disarmament Commission subcommittee, scheduled to meet again in London late in March 1957.

During the spring of that year Governor Stassen became convinced that the Soviets were sufficiently disturbed over Britain's development of atomic weapons that they would go to new lengths to reach agreements to prevent a further spread. He sensed, he said, the sincerity of Soviet fears and the necessity for immediate action. He also thought that the Soviets now believed that progress would be furthered through informal Soviet-American negotiations rather than within the United Nations.

Impelled by these conclusions, Stassen prepared a paper outlining what he called a new approach to disarmament negotiations. He sought authority to use it as a "talking paper" in conversations at the London Conference. The paper, as presented to me and others at the White House by the governor, dealt primarily with the United Kingdom, Russia, and the United States and only secondarily with those nations that were not so far advanced in nuclear research. It proposed that all nations except these three would be prohibited in the future from the manufacture or use of nuclear weapons. The three "nuclear powers" would be prohibited from the use of nuclear weapons except for defense under the United Nations Charter, for retaliation in case of atomic attack upon themselves, or in accordance with a United Nations decision. After July 1959 (the date on which Stassen estimated an effective inspection system could be installed), all future production of fissionable material would be devoted to non-weapons purposes. Each of the three nuclear powers was to maintain substantial nuclear weapons capability.[6]

[6] The paper went into other aspects of disarmament: a limited aerial inspection system together with fixed control posts, the exchange between the United States and the Soviets of blueprints of significant conventional armaments, and the placing of 15 per cent of the major significant armaments shown in the blueprints in "moth-

It was to be made clear in the London talks that the paper was not an official United States proposal; it could be used simply as a basis for starting confidential conversations.

Shortly after Stassen's return to London on May 31, 1957, he showed the gist of this paper to the Russians, but without prior coordination with our allies, which was, of course, a mistake, particularly in view of the warnings given him by a number of officials of the administration. When word of this reached Harold Macmillan, he immediately wrote me a letter that, while restrained, did not mask the genuine distress this new gambit had caused him. After remarking that disarmament was the paramount issue facing the civilized world, he added, "As we correspond on so many questions very freely, I would have hoped that we could have examined together the possible consequences of these proposals before they were put forward." He went on to describe the reactions he anticipated from our partners in NATO:

> . . . A cynical critic might say that, at the end of the process which they [our NATO partners] envisage, two great nuclear powers would remain: the United Kingdom would be prevented from developing the nuclear strength which she is just beginning to acquire: and all the other countries of Europe would have signed away their right to defend themselves with these weapons for the rest of time, whatever changes may take place in the political conditions of the world. . . .

He was particularly concerned over French and German opinion, and was anxious to discuss the matter as soon as possible.

This development caused me acute embarrassment. The Prime Minister and I had met that very spring in Bermuda for the express purpose of restoring the close teamwork and confidence that had existed between Britain and the United States before the Suez crisis. Now the United States was in the position of being the first violator.

I hastened to assure the Prime Minister that the memorandum given by Governor Stassen to the Russians was meant to be an "exploratory" or "talking" paper only, and to inform him fully of its nature. I did this even though I realized that my implied reprimand might be injurious to Stassen's status as our representative. The Prime Minister cheerfully accepted this explanation, and the diplomatic squall blew over.

In any event, the Soviet answer to Stassen's memorandum largely negated the suggestions it contained. The Soviets haggled over the pro-

---

balls." It proposed that the two nations would reduce their armed forces to 2.5 million each and cut their military expenditures by 15 per cent, at the same time reducing their armed forces located in the Russian and European inspection zones by 20 per cent.

posed levels of armed forces, asserting for the first time that with a smaller population the United States did not need to maintain armed forces as large as those of the Soviet Union. As for the gradual prohibition of nuclear weapons and their fissionable materials, the Soviets harked back to their proposal of April 30 calling, as usual, for all nations to prohibit the manufacture and use of atomic weapons. The Soviet response made it clear that the premises on which the Stassen memorandum had been submitted, i.e., that the Soviets would be genuinely interested in progressive disarmament and protection against "fourth country" nuclear capabilities, were not valid.

Still, we did not give up. In late August 1957, we presented a position in the UN disarmament subcommittee which had the approval of all member nations of NATO. These proposals made major concessions, one of which was the inclusion of a two-year moratorium agreement on nuclear testing.

The Soviets rejected the entire paper.

In the fall of the year the disarmament subcommittee of the United Nations was expanded to include representatives from all countries signatory to the United Nations. This enlargement reduced the disarmament subcommittee to a futile debating society and ended its usefulness.

* * *

With these negotiations coming to naught we now concentrated on securing an agreement on the regulated cessation of nuclear testing. This effort was not an integral part of disarmament, but if successful would do much to allay the fears of mankind about atomic fallout.

The widespread and growing fear of radioactive fallout from nuclear tests was, according to the best authorities, unreasoning; but it was real. Blast and heat were properties of conventional weapons; mankind had come to regard flamethrowers and fire bombs, terrifying as they are, as acceptable tools of war. But the dangers of radioactivity were little understood and therefore deeply feared by populations.

Concern over testing in the atmosphere was given a sharp impetus when, in 1954, a large thermonuclear shot in a test series turned out to have yield about double that previously calculated. A Japanese fishing vessel, apparently oblivious to warnings to avoid the area, strayed into the danger zone and was caught in radioactive fallout. The reaction on the part of many responsible persons was, "What next?" The neutralist nations and the Japanese were particularly vehement in voicing their apprehensions.

Domestic misgivings were stirred up further when, in the 1956 political contest, our nuclear test policy became a campaign issue. As I have said, I did not believe that such a question could be debated intelligently in public on a partisan basis. Moreover, I was opposed to a unilateral suspension of tests, which seemed to be the intent of my opponent's initial suggestion, later to be modified. To cease testing without a satisfactory system of mutual inspection was no solution at all, and I so stated.

Nevertheless, the campaign brought the problem forcefully to the forefront. Many of the misleading statements presented by partisans, on the advice of their "experts," nearly drowned the sober and largely contrary testimony about the dangers of testing given by the Atomic Energy Commission and the National Academy of Sciences, the nation's foremost scientific body.[7]

The furor died down somewhat at home, but abroad nuclear testing was also a matter of intense emotional interest and argument. Justified or not, the fears of such nations as Japan had to be taken into account. In October of 1957, for example, a year after my re-election, I received a letter from the Prime Minister of Japan, Nobusuke Kishi, a Japanese statesman of unquestioned pro-Western sympathies and a brave opponent of Communism:

> Japan as a peace-loving nation ardently desires prompt realization of a general disarmament, particularly prohibition of the manufacture, use and test of nuclear weapons as is clearly stated in the several resolutions of the Diet, which have been duly transmitted to Your Excellency's government. My government, recognizing the urgent necessity of ending all nuclear test explosions, has repeatedly requested your government to suspend such tests. But to our profound disappointment, none of the countries concerned has so far taken the initiative to suspend nuclear test explosions. But they all go on repeating their tests, creating a vicious

[7] The report by the National Academy of Sciences received little publicity by comparison with the scare headlines which were generally to be found in the press over statements denouncing all tests of weapons. The National Academy had engaged in an independent study of the biological effects of atomic radiation with 150 of the most distinguished authorities in the several fields participating. The report stated that except for accidents, biological damage from peacetime test activities had been "essentially negligible." A White House statement of October 24, 1956, said the following regarding effects of strontium 90:

"As regards fallout of strontium 90 from weapons testing, Dr. Willard F. Libby of the Atomic Energy Commission has stated that the present rate of testing, if continued indefinitely, would not produce a dangerous level of concentration of strontium 90 in the human body. Dr. Shields Warren, eminent radiologist, has stated that bone deposition of strontium 90 is well below the natural background level of radiation, and that to cause harmful effects the dose would have to be increased many times."

> circle of the most regrettable kind, which does nothing to lessen distrust among nations.
>
> . . . I, therefore, earnestly request Your Excellency to make a thorough study of the proposal of the Japanese Delegation. Acceptance will, my government believes, pave the way for the solution of the question of disarmament and nuclear test explosions, which is eagerly wished by the Japanese people and all peoples of the world.

Two months before receipt of Prime Minister Kishi's letter I had come to the conclusion that, in view of worldwide apprehensions, we should propose a ban, strictly limited as to time, on the testing of nuclear weapons. Accordingly, on the 21st of August 1957, Governor Stassen was instructed to propose an agreement for the suspension of nuclear testing for a period of up to two years.

Canada, France, and Britain joined us in the proposal. To implement it, the Soviets would have to agree to certain conditions and safeguards: ". . . within that period, there will be initiated a permanent cessation of production of fissionable materials for weapons purposes, and installation of inspection systems to insure performance."

My proposal for a suspension of testing was apparently regarded by the Soviets as only one part of the broader proposals on disarmaments which we submitted almost simultaneously. Both were rejected.

* * *

It was now becoming apparent that both East and West needed a common understanding of the scientific technicalities involved before the possibilities of a comprehensive, regulated test ban could be intelligently discussed. Such an understanding could be established only by experts. So on April 28, 1958, I formally proposed to Chairman Khrushchev a measure we had been considering—a meeting of experts whose technical studies would precede any political conference.

The Chairman, eleven days later, sent an acceptance. Details of the meeting to be held during the summer were soon worked out. To represent the United States I appointed Dr. James Brown Fisk head of the delegation, and Drs. Ernest O. Lawrence and Robert F. Bacher.

The committee, which met in Geneva on July 1, 1958, was made up of representatives of the United States, Great Britain, France, the Soviet Union, Poland, Czechoslovakia, and Rumania. Their work was conducted in an atmosphere of singular cooperation and objectivity. The committee's report covered such vital subjects as the basic methods of detection and identification of nuclear explosions, through the recording of acoustic waves, the collection of radioactive debris, and the recording of seismic waves and radio signals. It discussed methods of detection of nuclear explosions carried on at altitudes of 30 to 50 kilometers above the earth. The technical equipment needs of a control system were evaluated, and the over-all outline for the control system itself was drawn up in remarkable detail.

The most important part of the committee's report defined the control system necessary to guard against infraction:

> 3. The network of control posts would include from 160 to 170 land-based control posts (equipped in accordance with Section III of this report) and about 10 ships. . . . the exact number of control posts within the limits indicated above, can be determined only in the process of actually disposing them around the globe . . . [see Appendix Z].

The committee, Eastern and Western experts alike, definitely recommended the adoption of the measures suggested in the report. This was surprising. We had expected the Soviet technicians to be more politically oriented and negative than they turned out to be.

On receiving this news, our government on August 22, 1958, proposed to the Soviets a follow-up series of diplomatic negotiations, to begin October 31; we pointed out that "If there were an agreement to eliminate such tests, its effective supervision and enforcement would be technically possible."

To encourage the new meeting, the statement went on, the United States would be prepared, unless testing should be resumed by the Soviet Union, to withhold further testing of atomic and hydrogen weapons for a period of one year from the beginning of the negotiations. Moreover, we said that if an agreed inspection system were installed and working, and if satisfactory progress were being made in reaching an agreement on implementing major and substantial arms control measures, we would be prepared to continue the suspension of tests on a year-to-year basis. It was emphasized that the suspension of testing was not in itself a measure of disarmament or a limitation of armament but that its significance would be felt if it led to other, more substantial agreements. "It is in this hope," the statement ended, "that the United States makes this proposal."

Our willingness to suspend testing for one year had its risks, which we clearly recognized. Indeed, some of my most trusted advisers in government were against suspension. Reducing the risks, to an extent, was the fact that the moratorium would not go into effect until after the completion of our Hardtack series of tests in the Pacific. Furthermore, the moratorium was to be contingent on Soviet abstinence from testing during a like period. On balance, I felt that this was a risk that must be taken if there was to be any hope whatsoever of achieving a workable and properly supervised nuclear test ban.

The United States proposal for talks was accepted by Chairman Khrushchev, and they began on October 31. As announced, the United States' test ban—and that of Britain as well—went into effect.

To represent the United States in the talks I chose Ambassador James J. Wadsworth, who had served throughout my administration as Deputy United Nations Delegate under Cabot Lodge. Ambassador Wadsworth was an experienced negotiator, a man of patience and with a sense of humor, two qualities essential in what promised to be a tedious task.

When the discussions began, it soon became apparent that the technical conclusions reached by the experts two months earlier posed problems for the Soviet system which their political leaders could not abide. Particularly unacceptable was the over-all scheme for control posts stationed around the world. The Soviet political negotiators began immediately to propose modifications which they asserted would not destroy the effectiveness of the system. The control commission, for example, would be composed of members from each nation signatory to the treaty. However, before the commission could rule that a given seismic event required investigation by an inspection team, *the finding would have to be concurred in by representatives of all nations present,* thus giving the Soviets a veto within the control commission. Further, the Soviets said each projected control post would have to be staffed by *nationals of the government on whose territory the post was located,* with the representatives from other nations limited *to one or two observers.*

These points, on which the Soviets insisted, made it obvious they had no intention of agreeing to a practicable control system. The reason was not altogether clear. One conjecture was that the Soviets intended to cheat on any treaty they signed. More likely, however, was the probability that the Soviets feared free movement within their territory by international teams far more than they feared or wanted a ban on testing. Regardless of the Soviet motivation, discussions went slowly.

Moreover, optimism diminished when the AEC discovered that on November 1 and November 3 the Soviet Union had done some further testing of nuclear weapons despite the fact that the United States had hinged its own suspension on a similar halt in testing by the Russians. On November 7 I announced that this Soviet action relieved the United States of its obligation to cease testing. But I added that our suspension would remain in effect, as would that of the British, "for the time being." In the months following we detected no further Soviet tests, and our suspension continued.

At the end of 1958 I was confronted by another unpleasant fact. Careful analysis of the results of the United States operation Hardtack during the previous summer indicated, strangely, that some of the data the United States scientists had used in agreeing to the technical report at the Geneva meeting of experts had been incorrect. A system known as "decoupling," by which a nuclear device could be shielded and set off in a large underground cavern could, it was found, reduce the strength of a seismic reaction (and thus reduce detection) by a ratio of 300 to 1. It would be possible, using this method, to test large weapons without producing a signal clearly identifiable as a test explosion.

Confronted with this word, I had no choice but to pass the new information on to both Britain and the Soviet Union. This threw a pall on the conference at Geneva. Not only could it represent to a suspicious negotiator evidence of bad faith, but even among our own negotiating group there was a loss of confidence in the accuracy of the data with which they worked. If such discoveries could bring about drastic changes in the structure of fact upon which we made our calculations, what new discoveries were in the offing?[8]

The disarmament talks recessed on December 18, 1958, to resume about four months later. On April 20, 1959, I made a new proposal to Premier Khrushchev, one I had discussed with Prime Minister Macmillan during his visit to the United States the previous March. I suggested a limited nuclear test ban, prohibiting only atmospheric shots (up to 50 kilometers in height). This conformed to the experts' findings that detection systems could reveal shots of any size up to that altitude. Agreements for banning underground shots and those conducted in outer space would have to be delayed for a later time.

True to form, Premier Khrushchev turned down my proposal. It would not solve the problem, he contended, since shots underground and in outer space and under water would still be possible, thus deluding the world that a test ban treaty of significance had been made, whereas actually such would not be true. He ignored the feared effects of fallout in the atmosphere, about which he had evinced so much concern on previous occasions.

* * *

Toward the end of 1959 arrangements were finally reached for another meeting of scientists to study the Hardtack data. The United States delegation, again headed by Dr. James Brown Fisk, met at Geneva be-

[8] Out of this discovery came an emphasis on a problem called that of describing a "threshold." It now seemed, in view of these figures, no longer possible to detect all nuclear shots underground. Therefore, later phases of negotiations included the magnitude of seismic disturbance with which a treaty would concern itself. Having set a minimum standard, a treaty might confine its concern to tests giving more than one kiloton, five kiloton, or other specified size of detonation.

ginning November 25. Unfortunately, the harmony of a year and a half earlier was no longer evident. The "Technical Working Group No. 2" completed its studies on December 19, in disagreement. The Soviet experts' statement in the group's report was immediately refuted by Dr. Fisk [see Appendix AA].

The failure of the experts to come to an agreement after fourteen months of work left little basis on which to seek a political treaty. In announcing the result, I called attention to the unwillingness of the Soviet technical people to take advantage of the Hardtack data. And while promising to resume negotiations, I repeated that our voluntary moratorium, which had been extended to permit more time for negotiations, would expire on December 31, 1959.

The United States therefore considered itself free to resume nuclear weapons testing, but we pledged not to resume without announcing our intention in advance. During this period of voluntary suspension, however, the United States would continue an active program of weapons research, development, and laboratory experimentation.

By this time, an effective ban on nuclear testing had become an essential preliminary to—even though not a definite part of—attaining any worthwhile disarmament agreement. Consequently, I ordered that we continue our efforts to achieve this first step. I was still unwilling to give up. In February 1960, I announced that the United States was presenting another limited test ban proposal designed to end, under assured controls "(1) all nuclear weapons tests in the atmosphere; (2) all nuclear weapons tests in the oceans; (3) all nuclear weapons tests in those regions in space where effective controls can now be agreed to; and (4) all nuclear weapons tests beneath the surface of the earth which can be monitored." The plan would permit, through a coordinated research and development program, a systematic extension of the ban in remaining areas.

On March 19 the Soviet Union expressed its willingness to:

> Conclude a treaty halting all nuclear weapons tests in the atmosphere, the oceans, and cosmic space, and all underground tests of seismic magnitude 4.75 or more;
>
> Agree to the U.S. proposal for the carrying out of a program of research and experimentation among the U.S., U.K., and U.S.S.R. with all parties to the treaty undertaking at the same time an obligation not to conduct any nuclear weapons tests during this period below the threshold of seismic magnitude 4.75 [4.75 kilotons TNT equivalent].

This reply was so general in nature—it did not deal with important matters of operation—that Ambassador Wadsworth requested clarification.

The British and the United States were willing to confine negotiations to detonations above 4.75 kilotons (as the Soviets proposed), in which connection the points now at issue were adequate quotas of on-site inspections, the composition of a control commission, control post staffing and voting matters, as well as arrangements for detonations for peaceful purposes. To reach agreement on a practical plan for barring tests above the threshold, which were easily detectable, we would first be willing to declare a voluntary and temporary moratorium for tests below that seismic level if the Soviets would join us.

When, on May 3, 1960, the Soviets indicated a willingness to engage at once in a seismic research program, we moved immediately to go ahead with our share of this scientific effort. This expansion of our scientific research program, known as Project Vela, evolved from recommendations of the Berkner Panel. While only $10 million had been provided for this research during 1960, we planned to spend about $66 million in fiscal year 1961.

Four days after the announcement of this research program, scientists from the three "nuclear" nations met in Geneva to continue exchange of information on seismic research. Difficulties were soon encountered. Following the abortive summit in Paris,[9] the Soviet political representative at Geneva directly contradicted the Soviet technical experts' previous presentation. Early seismic research was unnecessary, he said, and the U.S.S.R. would carry out no research program. In a display of arrogance astounding even in a Communist negotiator, he further announced that the Soviets would insist on participating in any measures taken by the United States in their own program, would assert the right to inspect "internally" any devices which we might employ, and would exercise a veto power over our seismic research.

This completely ridiculous gesture terminated, so far as I was concerned, the dreary exercise. In our years of effort there had been accomplishment—unfortunately too much of it theoretical—but it was obvious that for the moment we had reached a blind alley.

It was now clear that further voluntary suspension of testing was useless and would, if continued, place us in a disadvantageous position. Prudence demanded a resumption of testing, and except for the fact that my administration was reaching its end, I would have immediately announced such a decision. However, I felt that if the incoming President had a different judgment, it would be unwise to tie his hands by my action at this late date. Accordingly, we did no more testing during the remaining few months of my administration, but I emphasized to President-elect Kennedy my conviction that our nation should resume needed tests without delay.

[9] See Chapter XXIII, "The Summit That Never Was."

* * *

In retrospect: I may have acted unwisely in suspending nuclear testing for a fixed length of time, but as yet I have found no compelling reason to regret that the United States thus provided proof to the world of our readiness to relieve anxiety and fear and to negotiate in good faith. We did everything possible to encourage the Soviets to act with us and to remove this cloud that so darkened the skies at mid-century.[10]

* * *

While the highly publicized negotiations on test bans were in progress, other disarmament conferences were held intermittently. Among these, one highly important event was a gathering of scientists to study the practical aspects of minimizing the possibility of surprise attack.

I had proposed such a study to Premier Khrushchev in the same note (of April 28, 1958) which advanced the idea of a study on enforcement of a nuclear test ban. Two months later, the Premier accepted my proposal, but it was not until November 10, 1960, that representatives of the United States, the United Kingdom, France, Italy, and the Soviet Union convened to begin discussions.[11] The talks achieved nothing. No sooner were they under way than the Soviet political delegate, Vasily Kuznetsov, supported by his technical experts, asserted that the only way to prevent surprise attack would be through a "complete ban of nuclear weapons, elimination of foreign bases, and reduction of conventional armed forces."

[10] The aftermath of the nuclear test problem is already history. Within a few months of the inauguration of President Kennedy, the Soviets conducted a series of thermonuclear tests in the atmosphere, dumping radioactive fallout into the atmosphere in unprecedented amounts. These tests, begun in early September 1961, may have been carried out primarily for political purposes; however, it is clear that their preparation required a considerable period of time, persuasive evidence that the Soviets, even while negotiating across the table, had no intention of ever agreeing to a self-enforcing agreement.

In 1963, a partial test ban between the United States, Great Britain, the Soviet Union, and other countries was signed, prohibiting nuclear tests in the atmosphere, under water, and in outer space, and all underground explosions that would permit the escape of nuclear debris beyond the boundaries of the responsible nation. In some of its features this treaty was similar to the proposal we had made in the spring of 1959.

[11] The chief delegates from the United States were Mr. William C. Foster, Vice President of Olin Mathieson Chemical Corporation; Professor George B. Kistiakowsky; and General Otto P. Weyland, former Commander of the Air Force Tactical Air Command.

These political matters lay outside the competence of the scientists present, and the meetings, when recessed on December 18 as scheduled, were never resumed.

The final effort for a political agreement was the convening in March 1960, at Geneva, of a ten-nation disarmament conference under United Nations auspices.[12]

It too failed when, on June 27, 1960, the Soviet representatives walked out.

* * *

Since an acceptable treaty for controlled disarmament was not realized, we continued to build an overpowering military establishment as the only feasible defense against the menace and probings of international Communism and as the indispensable platform from which to continue negotiations for a peaceful world.

When the Soviets rejected my Open Skies proposal in 1955 I decided that more intelligence about their war-making capabilities was a necessity. So I directed that we would begin aerial reconnaissance, making use of the then relatively invulnerable, high-flying U-2 aircraft. It had been making some weather flights, but from 1956 onward its basic mission was to provide us with current information on the status of the Soviet missile and armaments programs.

During the same period a new weapons system, the Polaris, a solid-fuel, submarine-launched missile instituted in 1955, came into the United States arsenal. With its almost complete invulnerability to surprise attack it became a critically important factor in deterring any rash adventure by the Communists.

It seems a wry and sad commentary on human intelligence that the development of a unique weapons system did more to restore a feeling of Western confidence in a stable future than had all the disarmament talks conducted over a period of years.

* * *

We must not give up our efforts to achieve arms limitations agreements. Some day a real breakthrough may come about, possibly from an unlikely direction. Near the close of my second term, a treaty on Antarctica was signed by twelve interested countries including the United States,

[12] Representatives from the United States, Great Britain, France, Canada, and Italy for the West, and Poland, Czechoslovakia, Rumania, Bulgaria, and the Soviet Union for the Communist bloc.

the Soviet Union, and the United Kingdom. It provided for an unlimited right of inspection among the various nations sending expeditions to that region, specifically including the right of overflight at any time.

In an address made by Under Secretary of State Robert Murphy at Louisville, Kentucky, he said: "The record shows that, in the few instances where there has been a mutual desire for agreement, meaningful agreements are reached. Where those agreements provide for means of enforcement, they have been enforced."

The Antarctica Treaty is one small example of what might be accomplished in more populous and significant areas.

* * *

Disarmament, or at least controlled and coordinated reduction of armaments, is as important now as it was when I took office in 1953. Though I believe that during those years the Soviet Union gradually learned caution about provoking us and our allies to the point of war, the arms burden upon the respective populations has not lessened.

The world today is faced with an immense expansion of population; Latin America, for example, is expected to triple its population by the turn of the century. This multiplication of people will mean also a vast multiplication of needs. The newly awakened, underprivileged populations are certain to grow less and less tolerant of wastefulness on the part of those productive and more fortunate peoples who could, relieved of paying for the weapons of destruction, be of greater help in providing the tools for life. They will learn that eighty thousand people could be adequately housed out of the money spent on a single armed Polaris submarine; that more than four hundred modern American-style elementary schools could be constructed at the cost of one squadron of Minuteman I missiles—and their patience will wear thin. Their discontent could flame into further world disorder. An acceptable disarmament agreement between the Western and Eastern power blocs might not save sufficient resources to meet all the basic requirements of the world's needy, but so long as such proportions of the world's assets are wasted on excessive armaments, our ability to help poorer people to help themselves will be sorely and uselessly impaired.

Though disarmament, alone, cannot guarantee a just peace it would, today, be the one practical accomplishment that could pave the way toward this greatest of all goals.

CHAPTER XXI

Friends

We are not a nation, so much as a world.

—*Herman Melville*

IN September 1959, I began seriously to consider the feasibility of a personal visit to the Mediterranean area and the Middle East. The general idea of such a trip had been in my mind for some time. As my second term of office was more than half over, I reflected on a fact in American history: a President's influence on domestic affairs normally wanes in the last days of his administration. The thought of marking time waiting for January 20, 1961, did not appeal to me, particularly since my health was good and even seemed to be improving. How, I wondered, could I make the best use of this remaining time for the benefit of the United States?

I realized that internationally I enjoyed a measure of good will, or at least a wide acquaintanceship, garnered during my many years abroad, performing duties assigned by our government. This might be put to some use. Possibly a trip or a series of trips to visit representative regions of the Free World might be a means of doing so.

This prospect was appealing. Experiences both before and after becoming President had confirmed my instinctive feeling that at all levels of government, face-to-face, friendly discussions offer advantages that can scarcely be realized through written communications and secondary representations. In the White House I had welcomed many heads of government and heads of state who had come to the United States either for ceremonial visits or for pertinent political conversations. Without exception I had found them informative and rewarding. Moreover, every such visit carried the implication that the gentleman or lady making it wanted to demonstrate the friendliness of his people toward ours.

Presidents did not ordinarily travel far and wide. My own hope, in the event I undertook such as ambitious and somewhat dramatic venture, unprecedented in peacetime, would be to assure all the people I could reach of the sincerity of our search for peace and our desire to be helpful. I wanted to try to raise the morale of struggling and underprivileged peoples, to enhance confidence in the value of friendship with the United States, and to give them assurance of their own security and chances for progress.[1]

I had often talked with the Vice President about these ideas, and he had helped me to put them into practice. Not only had he acted as my personal representative in visiting important sectors of the world, but as the next in succession to the Presidency, he helped to make my trips possible by always staying close to the seat of government during any prolonged absence of mine.

On one occasion a group of us, including John and Barbara, our friends George and Mary Allen, and Mamie, went to the Vice President's home for dinner. It was the night of Friday, December 19, 1958, a date made memorable for all of us by the successful orbiting of our communications satellite, Score. While we were there my notion of a Middle East tour came into the conversation. I was surprised to find that every person in the party was highly favorable to such an expedition. (Unanimity in Washington, even among people this close to each other, was uncommon.) The Vice President assured me that if I took a trip, no matter what its duration, he would remain in Washington. He felt that such a journey would have incalculable benefits for the United States and the Free World, and thought I should also plan as many other trips as possible before my term of office was completed.

So I took the matter up with the Secretary of State. Mr. Herter, though warning that careful diplomatic scheduling would be necessary, responded enthusiastically, adding his thought that a visit to the Indian subcontinent would be especially useful.

No idea could have pleased me more. In fact, my desire to visit that region went back to the days of my youth. Upon graduating from West

[1] To Americans it may seem passing strange that any special effort would be needed to convince other peoples of these motives. We like to think that our record of the last one hundred years has been almost exemplary in its concern for justice, fairness, and decency in its relations with others. Nonetheless, while the United States, with no designs on the lands and treasures of others, has traditionally been faithful to a policy of anti-colonialism, the fact remains that some of our closest allies have been among those popularly associated with colonial systems; Communist propaganda has long classified us, with some success, as an imperialist nation, bent on "economic domination." Such allegations, though deliberate falsehoods, cannot be discounted when endlessly repeated to the illiterate and the starving of the world.

Point, I was asked, as was then customary, to express my preference for a duty station. "The Philippines," I replied. My notion was that I could then use my graduation leave on a lengthy eastward tour, finishing up at the islands, and with a lengthy stay in India along the way. The Army sent me to Texas.

My present-day purpose was not tourism. It was an obvious fact that the Free World should do everything possible to make certain that India —an announced neutral in the polarized power struggle—should never be allowed, with its 400 million people, to fall within the Communist orbit. Moreover, during Prime Minister Nehru's visit to the United States in 1956, I had become so intrigued by the picture he painted of the region, its people, and their aspirations that my desire to see that country for myself became the stronger.

Impressed by the time-saving capability and the convenience of the jet airplane I used during my most recent European trip, I came to believe that it might be reasonable for me to accept an Indian invitation to come to that country to dedicate, in December 1959, the United States Exhibition at the World Agricultural Fair in New Delhi. The exhibition had been arranged to help improve farming methods in that part of the world, and to increase markedly the food supplies of an immense number of needy people.

Here, the diplomatic wire-walking foreseen by Secretary Herter began. It would be almost unthinkable for an American President to make a courtesy call on India without including Pakistan in his itinerary. Both nations were our friends; each looked to the United States for private and public investment, and each, because of their mutual distrust heightened by differences over Kashmir, was watchful of every acquisition by the other of military supplies—or any other relative advantage. Further, Pakistan was our ally through common membership in the Southeast Asia Treaty Organization, and indirectly through her membership in the Central Treaty Organization.

Then, in falling domino fashion, a visit to Pakistan would almost compel a visit to Afghanistan; there were rival territorial claims causing some antagonism between these two. Any trip to this region automatically raised the desirability of stopping in Iran. The Shah of Iran had always been in sympathy with the United States and had paid us both informal and official visits; Iran was also a member of the CENTO Alliance. Clearly it was wise to include all four of these nations in an itinerary that would touch any one of them.

If these stops could be arranged, there were yet other countries to consider.

An airplane going to the Middle East would necessarily overfly Turkey and Greece, providing me an opportunity, with little inconvenience, to stop in both. They were members of NATO, the former a member of CENTO. Moreover, such a route would cross Italy, the only one of the four most populous Western European nations that I thus far had failed to visit as President. I quickly resolved to include these three in my schedule.

The possibility of visiting Saudi Arabia was examined closely. King Saud had earlier come to Washington and had warmly invited me to make a return call whenever it was convenient. If on such a journey, however, we should touch down in Saudi Arabia, we ought to go also to Egypt, the principal nation of the Arab League—and a visit to either of these would be unwise indeed, unless Israel was then included. The diplomats argued that even such a schedule would fail to satisfy the rampant prejudices in the region; certain rulers believe that "If you are my friend, my enemies are your enemies." Any slight action, even normal mannerism, on my part that could be interpreted as favoring either the Arabs or the Israelis would add fuel to the fires of mutual suspicion among these nations.

As a substitute for a stop in the eastern Mediterranean, it seemed quite logical to include one or more of the Moslem nations farther westward. I selected Tunisia. Two reasons made the prospect attractive.

The first was that President Habib Bourguiba of Tunisia was a true friend of the West and we respected him as an enlightened leader of his people. The second was purely personal. The final events of the North African campaign of World War II had taken place in Tunisia, and I wanted another glimpse of the country.

Then, we thought it not only polite but beneficial to stop briefly in Morocco, whose King had made a ceremonial visit to the United States in 1957.

In between these two visits, I was to go to Paris for a long-planned "family" summit, a conference among four Western powers. Because the flight from Paris to Morocco would go directly over Spain, it seemed desirable to stop briefly in that country, where our air bases were among the most important of our military installations abroad.

Eleven nations—a typical governmental expansion of a youngster's wish to see India and a more mature citizen's wish to visit a place or two in the Middle East.[2]

[2] Map, "In Search of Peace, 1959–1960," appears on the back endpapers of this volume.

FRIENDS

The visit with Pope John XXIII, December 6. Center, official interpreter Lieutenant Colonel Vernon Walters; in the background, Mrs. John Eisenhower

"'You were a general and became President,' he said jokingly, 'and I was a sergeant and became Pope.'
"...Time fled, and at the Pope's invitation other members of our party were invited in to be presented briefly."

Karachi, Pakistan, December 7. At the presidential palace with President Mohammed Ayub Khan

"There seems to be something in the chemistry of humans that often determines at first contact whether or not any two easily become friends or are mutually repelled. From the very beginning I conceived for President Ayub a warm affection which still endures."

New Delhi, India,
December 9

"The human sea closed upon us and compelled a halt. . . . When tra
remained at a standstill, [Prime Minister Jawaharlal Nehru] dismoun
and forced his way to the front of the car. Using the stick he alw
carried, the Prime Minister began laying about him."

Civic Reception, Ramila Grounds, New Delhi

"The crowd—estimated by my hosts as well over a half million—was seated on the ground in a great grassy field. Both Prime Minister Nehru and I spoke through a most efficient public address system to a throng that astonished me by its close attention."

Madrid, Spain, December 20. Evening motorcade with Generalissimo Francisco Franco

"I was impressed by the fact that there was no discernible mannerism or characteristic that would lead an unknowing visitor to conclude that he was in the presence of a dictator."

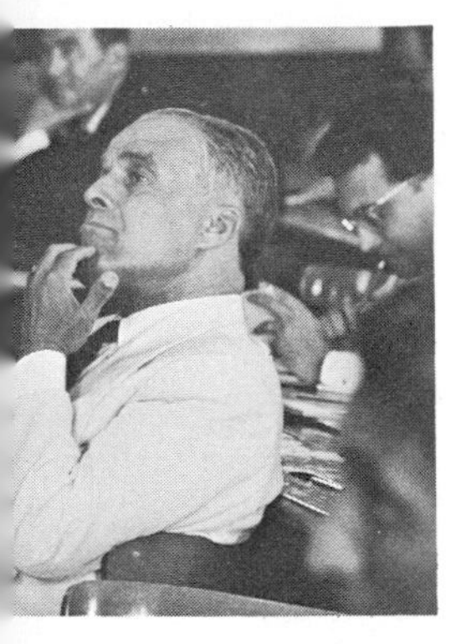

:sident Habib Bourguiba Tunisia

esident Bourguiba reminded me, in tain respects, of . . . Ayub. . . . Each, ong his associates, seemed to enjoy espect and loyalty gained far more personality, ability, and character n by the official position he held."

Iorocco, December 22. King Mohammed V accompanies President Eisenhower into Casablanca

"Among the crowds along the road to Casablanca were Berber tribesmen, who had received word unofficially that some kind of a celebration was in the offing. Without the knowledge of the Moroccan government, these hardy warriors, with their antique muzzle-loading rifles and their flowing robes, lined the route of the motorcade to fire salutes, one-handed, straight into the air."

"To attempt an estimate, even a rough one, of the number of people we saw during those eighteen December days would be a futile gesture, but obviously it ran into the millions.

"Their faces are interestingly different and their lands exotic, but their fate and ours are one."

Rome

India

Greece

Pakistan

Washington, D.C., December 22

"As Mamie and I drove down Pennsylvania Avenue, approaching the White House, we found hundreds of sparkler-carrying well-wishers filling Lafayette Square with a dazzling midnight illumination."

AMIGOS

"On May 12 [1958, Vice President Nixon] was in Bogota, Colombia..."

"...and from that city went to Caracas, Venezuela. There, the next day, a howling and ugly mob smashed the car in which he was riding, and threatened to overturn it and drag its occupants into the street."

"After a flight of nearly six hours from Puerto Rico we arrived at the first stop in South America, the new inland capital of Brazil, named Brasilia.... The exterior lines of the buildings seemed to me graceful and the basic construction unique, featuring use of cantilevers—great overhangs without visible support."

Motorcade through Rio with President Juscelino Kubitschek, February 24, 1960

"Entering Rio de Janeiro the next day we met crowds of spectacular size, estimated by the police at a million. Along a five-mile motorcade route, which took an hour to travel, people jammed the roadways and streets and filled office windows."

"President [Arturo] Frondizi expressed his enthusiasm for the beautiful Presidential aircraft. I knew, of course, about the Latin American tradition that whenever a guest admires an object, the host must give it to him...."

San Gregorio Housing Project, Santiago, Chile. President Jorge Allesandri is to President Eisenhower's right

"The pride of the builders in their new homes was indescribable. Every face was shining."

Dr. Milton S. Eisenhower meets some Costa Rican citizens

"Some significant advances were a direct result of the appointment in 1953 of my brother Milton as my personal representative and special ambassador on matters affecting Latin America."

* * *

Not for a moment during the earlier years of my administration could such an ambitious trip have been deemed practical. But at the beginning of winter in 1959, with travel by jet becoming commonplace, with the Congress not in session, with the Soviet Premier having just completed a visit to America, and with the world relatively calm, such a journey was clearly feasible.

With a list prepared of the states I proposed to visit, Colonel William Draper, my chief pilot and air aide, was called in to advise on the itinerary from the viewpoint of flight times, airports, and so on. After considerable study in Washington and consultation with the appropriate embassies, the route was laid out. First stop, Rome, Italy. From there we were to go to Ankara, Turkey; Karachi, Pakistan; Kabul, Afghanistan; New Delhi, India; Teheran, Iran; Athens, Greece; Tunis, Tunisia; Paris, France; Madrid, Spain; Casablanca, Morocco; and back home. Our longest stay would be for five days in India; the shortest, several hours each in Iran, Tunisia, and Morocco.

The route established, the necessary staff work began. Schedules to the hour and minute had to be worked out with the representatives of each nation, to insure that every necessary visit within the nation be made but to allow time also for rest and recuperation. Quite often the estimates of American diplomatic officials on the ground, eager to make maximum use of every moment of a visitor's time, so crowd a schedule as to drive the victim into near exhaustion.

Planning included supply considerations. Proper fuel at the proper points is one need requiring close attention. In Turkey, for example, fuel for a Boeing 707 jet transport had to be flown across the mountain ranges from our United States base in Adana to the south.

Another special item was drinking water. My doctors had insisted, ever since my operation for ileitis in 1956, that I drink only bottled water—always from the same source—to minimize risk of internal upset. Consequently Sergeant Moaney packed and carried along on this trip twelve large cases of Mountain Valley water.

Security is of grave concern to the Secret Service, especially when a President becomes involved in crowds, and this problem takes on delicate diplomatic aspects when it appears that the feelings of a host government might be hurt by the implication that its protective arrangements are less than satisfactory. Facilities have to be provided for proper press coverage, particularly in countries where transportation, and above all electrical communications, is meager, again without offense to the local officials.

Even billets for the many newsmen who accompanied me on this trip were, in some locations, difficult to provide. For all these reasons we sent over the approved route an advance party of staff officers.

As we reached the final stages of planning, a personal disappointment was Mamie's conclusion that she was not physically strong enough to make the trip. It would have been an even more rewarding experience for me—and better for my mission—had she been able to do so. In her place, because John was to accompany me in his routine capacity as a staff officer, I asked my daughter-in-law, Barbara, to be one of the party. She agreed enthusiastically, setting out promptly to buy suitable clothes and see to the several thousand arrangements that a mother of four must make before leaving home for almost three weeks.

I was fortunate for this trip to have the company of Under Secretary of State Robert Murphy, a dedicated public servant. We had first worked together in the days of the 1942 North African invasion. This was his final assignment before retirement. Bob had decided, much to my regret but with my complete understanding, that as of the date of his retirement from the career foreign service, he would also leave the appointive position of Under Secretary. At my request he stayed on to give me invaluable assistance on the intricacies of this journey.

* * *

We took off from Andrews Air Force Base, landing about ten hours later at the Ciampino Airport, Rome, at twelve noon on Friday, the 4th of December. President Giovanni Gronchi was on hand to greet our party, and before long we were driving through a persistent gray drizzle along the old Appian Way with its tombs, monuments, and the glorious debris of ruins left by the ancient Romans, finally reaching the party's quarters in the Quirinale Palace. (The Quirinale had, until 1870, long been the summer residence of the Popes.)

The President was a highly intelligent and aggressive type of executive. He was determined to make the Presidency of his country something more than a ceremonial office; he was well informed, and any talk with him turned out to be enlightening.

His country needed increased American assistance, said Gronchi. He argued that Italy had a particularly heavy defense burden because, in addition to providing its quota of troops to NATO, its geography presented a long flank exposed to Communist attack across the narrow Adriatic. The defense problem had become even more difficult, he said, with Italy's present agreement to station our Jupiter missiles in its territory; their security would require, he thought, additional Italian troops, which meant more American aid.

I promised to give urgent consideration to the President's requests, but was insistent, apparently to U. S. Ambassador J. D. Zellerbach's astonishment, that under no circumstances would the United States ever press our allies to "take" intermediate-range or any other kind of missile as a supposed obligation to us; missiles must be accepted voluntarily and without any thought on the part of our allies that the arrangement placed any additional obligation on the United States.

The next morning, we met at the Viminale Palace with Prime Minister Antonio Segni. Mr. Segni, thoughtful, studious, was soft-spoken, even shy, but his conversation left no doubt that he was courageous in upholding his own convictions. Possibly it was because of these characteristics that he reminded me of Mr. Nehru. I liked Segni and thoroughly enjoyed my meetings with him. It was encouraging to know that both he and President Gronchi were for a firm stand on Berlin.

These Italian leaders, more especially the President, felt that their government should have a more important position in Western councils than it now enjoyed. Plaintively, President Gronchi said, "We hope it will not be forgotten that after the Italian nation succeeded in getting rid of the Mussolini dictatorship it also placed its resources at the disposition of the Allies so as to bring about a victorious end of World War II. We are not asking any voice in helping to solve the Berlin question," he said, "but whatever happens to Germany as a whole is, of course, of much interest to the future of Italy."

I replied that, "I had not realized that Italy had felt neglected, but the right of Italy to be present at international conferences involving her interests is axiomatic."[3]

Another subject important to the Italians was a diplomatic quarrel with Austria over a disputed area situated in the upper Adige Valley between Austria and Italy. Only recently, said Mr. Segni, the Austrian foreign minister had made a chauvinistic statement about the area; where a series of violent incidents had taken place. These were instigated, the Italians had concluded, by the Austrian government; and the Austrians now wanted a change of the border in their favor. Mr. Segni assured me earnestly that no Italian government accepting such a change could stand. I told him I would see what the United States might properly do to compose the difficulty.

[3] The following summer, Italy became one of the five Western nations represented at the ten-nation disarmament talks.

* * *

Sunday was the final day of our stay in "sunny Italy" but our first of sunshine. I attended services at St. Paul's Episcopal Church and from there went to make a scheduled call on the Pope.

In the apartment of His Holiness Pope John XXIII on the second floor of the Vatican, I visited for approximately an hour with this remarkable person. Bright and active at the age of seventy-eight, he had the vivacity and zest of a far younger man. The conversation included reminiscences, observations on the cold war, some of our hopes for the future, and cheerful banter about our respective careers and present positions. Before Pope John's elevation to the Papacy we had met in Paris where he was in the diplomatic service. We talked of those days. "You were a general and became President," he said, jokingly, "and I was a sergeant and became Pope." He said that he almost had not made sergeant and if he hadn't, he might never have become Pope. But time fled and at the Pope's invitation other members of our party were invited in to be presented briefly.

On the way out of the Pope's apartment I noted, with some amazement, that the United States Army had penetrated even the Vatican. Nonchalantly sitting on a table in the anteroom was a member of the Signal Corps, equipped with a telephone, ready to connect me instantly with any spot that could be reached by American communications. The efficiency of this dedicated group of signalmen brought forth expressions of admiration as well as smiles from members of the Pope's circle.

* * *

Once in the air it seemed a short jump to Esenboga Field, Ankara. We were greeted by President Celal Bayar, and members of his government, and we proceeded along the two-lane blacktop highway across the lonely Anatolian Plain to the city. I recall that during the progress of the motorcade, the thought occurred to me that more Americans should visit Turkey. Here was a nation of nearly twenty-seven million people with a per capita income of a little over $100 a year, inured to hardships and, whatever their internal politics, traditionally strong in their defiance of the Russians, whether Czarist or Communist. They were fast friends of the United States.

Once settled at the guest house, our party soon departed for the residence of President Bayar, where a brief business meeting took place. The President opened the meeting with the remark that we really had nothing to talk about, since we all knew that our views were identical in every respect.

However, both Prime Minister Adnan Menderes and Foreign Minister Fatin Zorlu were concerned over risks they felt that the government of Afghanistan was incurring. They suggested that I was in an ideal position to carry a warning to the King of Afghanistan who, they feared, was accepting so much Soviet help and so many Soviet "technicians" in the country as to make Afghanistan an easy target for an eventual Communist takeover.

"I think another Asian might better take up such questions with the Afghans," I replied, but agreed to find out whether or not the Afghans would welcome any word of mine on such a sensitive subject. I later learned that neither Pakistan nor Iran was free of similar anxieties concerning Afghanistan.

I thought Mr. Menderes a shrewd, knowing man, clear in his mind as to the military and economic needs of his nation and reasonable in his presentations of his government's desires for American aid.[4] Turkey was one Moslem country where, since the time of the national hero, Ataturk, women were not required to be veiled in public. While some clung to old customs, those that did not showed, I thought, a high level of pulchritude—not a few, in fact, were beautiful.

* * *

Departure on Monday, Pearl Harbor Day, found us bound for Karachi, flying along a narrow Turkish-Iranian corridor between the southernmost portion of the Soviet Union and Iraq, the government of which was then far from pro-West. The corridor is not wide. Members of our group had expressed doubts about flying this route, recalling that not too long before one of our C-130s had been shot down by the Soviets in the same area. These trepidations were baseless, in my opinion. I laid no claim to a charmed life nor was I careless of risk, but I could think of nothing more disastrous, from the Communist viewpoint, than to shoot down the President of another nation when it was universally known he was engaged in a trip to promote peace and good will. There was no hint of any danger or attempted interference throughout the trip.

[4] It was difficult for me to reconcile, months later, my impressions of the government's stability with the violence that developed and which swept the Bayar government out of power and into disgrace, resulting finally in the execution of several members, including Menderes and Zorlu. Of course, when the upheaval did come, it would have been highly improper for me to comment, and fortunately the new government has proved strongly anti-Communist. But I could not, when the revolt occurred, refrain from a deep regret that such a violent upheaval had taken place.

* * *

In Pakistan President Mohammed Ayub Khan met us at the airfield and we headed a motorcade to Karachi in perfect weather. The route, running largely along the shoreline, was flat. Balmy breezes—though sometimes a bit odorous—came in from the sea. Crowds, in numbers to which we were gradually becoming accustomed, lined the streets, cheering and shouting. Races and types of dress were mixed.

Entering town, President Ayub and I left his open Cadillac and, to complete the journey, mounted to a horsedrawn royal carriage traditionally used in Karachi in greeting a head of state. President Ayub showed me to a room in a large, comfortable palace, and took his leave.

All activities that evening took place out of doors. Dinner was served under a large, flat-topped, multicolored canopy suspended over nearly an acre. Luxurious oriental rugs completely covered the ground. Guests were seated in small groups, with the head table in the center, the whole creating a feeling of space and splendor.

"How can you plan such a wonderful party to be held outdoors," one of us asked, "with no alternative for moving inside if the weather is poor?"

President Ayub replied, with confidence that would have done credit to a man from the Miami or Palm Springs Chamber of Commerce, "Here you *know* that the weather will be good."

President Ayub presented a variety of entertainers whose athletic and martial skills revealed why Indian and Pakistani units are famous for this kind of exercise. There was a brilliantly executed sword dance, with men in white costumes swirling flashing steel swords perilously close to the figures of their companions racing past. (The next day we saw a dashing exhibition in which Ayub's horsemen rode at full tilt, bearing down upon small tent pegs in the sand, and then bringing them up on the point of their lances.) It was an interesting evening, and our hospitable host postponed all serious talk until the following morning.

The most difficult problem between Pakistan and India involved Kashmir.[5] The immediate quarrel was about the division of the waters of the Indus River, of which both nations desired a considerable share for irrigation and power. Ayub (and Nehru, as it developed) believed that a

[5] Kashmir is a province, the bulk of whose population is Moslem, like Pakistan's. It is controlled by India, a Hindu nation, and heated feelings remain from the bloody skirmishes between Indians and Pakistanis for control.

reasonable solution would soon be forthcoming so long as the negotiations did not get involved directly in the Kashmir question.

Since, however, some of the sources of the Indus waters were found in Kashmir, the negotiations could not be freed completely from emotionalism. I told the President, and later Prime Minister Nehru, that the United States was willing to help in the huge conservation projects that would permit efficient use of the Indus waters, but only if the two nations quickly agreed upon a compromise program. I expressed conviction that if both would accept the leadership of the World Bank, trusting to its impartiality and its technical competence, there should be no insuperable difficulty in reaching a reasonable answer. I was glad to find that both showed a degree of flexibility and conciliation in the matter.[6]

Friction between Pakistan and Afghanistan was created by conflicting claims to territories with ill-defined boundaries and a population of nomadic tribes.

Using a map, President Ayub pointed out regions in Afghanistan through which he said the Soviets were building important roads solely for their own strategic purposes. He spoke earnestly and emphatically on the subject and I agreed to attempt to explore it while in Afghanistan and later have it studied in Washington.

Inevitably, the level of United States aid came up for discussion. Indeed, in one guise or other, this question was part of every business conference I held in every nation throughout the entire tour. In general my answer was always the same: We wanted to help those nations who wanted to help themselves in raising their own living standards and combatting Communism. I said that all should understand, however, that our resources were limited, that other industrialized nations should help shoulder a portion of the costs, and that all of us should cooperate closely to maximize security and progress and to minimize expense. Only in this way could real results be achieved in the long run.

President Ayub candidly admitted that when he first came into power it had been necessary to establish a virtual dictatorship; but he said that his basic ambition was to lead his people to democratic institutions at a speed dictated by their capacity to absorb them. He asserted it was useless to try to implant democracy suddenly and on a nationwide basis; any such experiment would be doomed to the same disaster as had overtaken the earlier one in his country, initiated immediately after the founding of the nation in 1947. He planned to begin training towns and villages

[6] Later it was to become a source of satisfaction that before the end of my administration, India and Pakistan signed an amicable agreement on the division of these waters.

to govern themselves locally and he had a schedule of elections for installing these islands of self-government. He then proposed to go ahead with the same process, step by step, into even larger geographic areas, so that within a reasonable number of years the nation would gradually control itself under democratic processes. The final step would be the election of a national legislature and chief executive.

In our conversations I found President Ayub an agreeable, intelligent, and persuasive gentleman. He spoke English as if it were his native tongue; he was forthright in speech, athletic in physique, outgoing in manner, and possessed a fine sense of humor. He was a good companion. Ayub is pleasant and modest, but incisive—characteristics that gave an aura of credibility to his avowed purpose of steadily developing healthy democratic institutions in his country.

There seems to be something in the chemistry of humans that often determines at first contact whether or not any two easily become friends or are mutually repelled. From the very beginning I conceived for President Ayub a warm affection which still endures. As would be expected, I have more than once disagreed with his views and some of his actions but I had no reason to doubt the sincerity of his motives. I count him a friend.

It was typical of his plainspokenness and candor that Ayub said, speaking in public at a reception while we were in Karachi, that a major part of the world "takes it for granted that the maintenance of [global] peace and promotion of universal prosperity is the bounden duty of the U.S.A." But certain countries, he added, while quite willing to receive what the United States gives, are not willing to acknowledge it and cooperate in return. Countries other than those of the Free World do not deny the unique role the United States plays in the cause of keeping the peace—at least not in private, he added—but "they reserve to themselves the right to do otherwise. So . . . the U.S.A. is today placed in the most unenviable position of returning hostility with consideration, coldness with warmth, indifference with attention, and friendship, of course, with friendship."

We could not have asked from any leader in the world a more understanding expression of America's international purposes and problems.

* * *

About this time I came to realize that our delegation had an effective diplomat in the person of Barbara. She had been ill on departure from Ankara and had arrived in Pakistan with a stomach upset, hungry and weak. The understanding Pakistanis insisted on canceling all of the events scheduled for her that afternoon. But she would have none of it; instead, she visited hospitals and clinics and despite her affliction appeared to enjoy her tour thoroughly. From then on, throughout the trip, I asked for a daily report on Barbara's activities. In many instances her schedule was as heavy as my own, I learned, while the warm appraisal of her efforts shown by the press and our hosts must have been as gratifying to her as they were appreciated by all of us in the party.

* * *

We began the next day's journey to Afghanistan, lifted by helicopter from Ayub's residence to the airfield in pre-dawn darkness. The hours I keep on trips sometimes wear a little thin with the staff. One comment made by Tom Stephens, Appointments Secretary, was overheard as he was standing, in the early dawn, irritably awaiting transportation. "When this administration is over," he muttered, "I'll never work for a farmer or an Army officer again."

The flight from Karachi to Kabul took less than two hours. During the latter part of the journey we were accompanied by Russian-built MIGs—part of the Afghan Air Force. We flew over rugged mountains through which, a century before, the British had so often fought, with mixed success, against primitive tribes.

At Bagrum Airport we were met by His Majesty Mohammed Zahir Shah, Premier Sardar Mohammed Daud Khan, Foreign Minister Sardar Mohammed Naim, and other dignitaries. The day was cold, the skies were heavy, and our pleasure in our reception was dampened by the presence of MIG aircraft on the field.

From Bagrum Airport to Kabul is about fifty miles through mountainous country. The landscape is bleak and forbidding with little discernible evidence of industrial improvement or activity. The road, I understood, had been paved primarily for this occasion, ironically, with major Soviet assistance. The area, while fairly densely populated, was primitive and desolate; many houses were constructed of unbaked mud. Grapes are the principal agricultural product of this region, but at that time of the year the extensive vineyards were nothing but fields of brown and black stems.[7]

As the motorcade sped southward, crowds of people came out from

[7] I was told that the Moslem religion prevents the manufacture of wine from grapes. I suppose that if it were permitted, the income of Afghanistan would be considerably higher. Fortunately, there was an export market for those grapes, principally in India, a circumstance that produced modest income.

small villages—often hidden behind the foothills—to line the roadside. Faces were weatherbeaten, often hidden by full beards and turbans, more than faintly similar to Biblical pictures of the time of Abraham. Few if any women were present. The obvious poverty of the countryside and the grimy yet friendly people contrasted with the majesty of the Hindu Kush Mountains in the background. Together they presented a picture of colors and contrasts I shall long remember.

The conversations with King Zahir and Foreign Minister Naim at Chilstoon Palace were informative. I was able to express our concern over the amount of aid the Afghanistan government was accepting from the Soviet Union, and I added that some of their neighbors felt a similar uneasiness.

The King said, "I appreciate your concern but I can assure you of the fierce, independent spirit of the entire Afghan nation." He referred to historic attempts by others to keep his people in subjugation. "I doubt that accepting aid will result in our enslavement," he said.

The King then emphasized the needs of Afghanistan for economic assistance and recited statistics to prove his case. Per capita income, he said, was $48 per year. Life expectancy was twenty years, the same as in the days of Julius Caesar. There was in his country an understandable desire for rapid improvement—a desire for change that had created a willingness to accept aid from any source. "Afghanistan," he said, "is the one country where the Soviets have rendered more concrete aid than has the United States."

Again I repeated my exposition of America's record and capacities in the field, but I told him I would have the matter examined once more.[8]

After luncheon at Chilstoon Palace, our party started for a helicopter pad from which to fly to the airfield, and experienced for the first time in the tour the excitement of a mob bursting out of control. Suddenly, and without warning, we found our vehicles unable to move, almost sinking in a sea of strange faces. But the faces were friendly and in spite of the inconvenience and the unavoidable delay, I was heartened to see such a spirit in people of whose sympathies we had been doubtful.

On the journey back to Bagrum, Pete Aurand notified me, in a mock serious tone, that we were setting "a new altitude record for presidential

[8] The King, supported by his Premier, Prince Daud, and foreign minister, Prince Naim—both are blood relatives of his—gave me the clear impression that they exercised absolute authority over the nation. However, a prominent Pakistani, expressing his own opinion to me, doubted that this was the case. He thought the Royal Family was weak, was not in close touch with the people, and felt little security in its position. If this conclusion was valid, it was not apparent to me.

trips by helicoptering" at more than seven thousand feet. This was a trifle less than notable information inasmuch as I was the first President to make much use of "choppers" and because the territory below us was itself around seven thousand feet above sea level.

* * *

After a two-hour flight from Kabul, we arrived in India a half hour late. I was relieved to learn, however, that our tardiness had been fortunate, since a severe traffic jam on the roads from New Delhi to the airport delayed Mr. Nehru's arrival beyond the time scheduled for our landing.

The airport ceremonies that evening took place in an almost eerie setting. Darkness was approaching and, save for the spaces cleared for the ceremonies, every square foot of the broad field was jammed with people. I reviewed the long line of Indian troops completely unaccompanied, a local custom unique in my experience. Then I returned to the spot where President Rajendra Prasad and Prime Minister Nehru awaited me on an elevated platform about fifteen feet high, illuminated by glaring floodlights. President Prasad and I exchanged the customary public greetings, while Mr. Nehru sat sideways on the top rung of the ladder on the rear of the platform. When offered the chance to speak he waved it off impatiently, to the amusement of the crowd.

The motorcade had not even left the airfield before it became obvious that anything resembling a timetable had to be discarded. Crowds began swarming around the vehicles, immediately forcing us to slow down to a maximum of five miles per hour. Along the road, among fantastically dense crowds of pedestrians, were automobiles, bullock carts, donkeys, and even camels. The whole teeming, boisterous, confused, happy crowd outdid in size anything I had ever seen, including those of the victory celebrations in the great cities of America and Europe. The pace of the motorcade necessarily became so slow that enthusiastic well-wishers could approach the car from the rear and fill it with garlands of flowers, especially marigolds, heaping them upon us.

Despite my fatigue I was deeply touched. It was an overwhelming experience. Along the way were hundreds of thousands who, I was told, had been standing in place for four hours or more. Mr. Nehru told me that people had come from miles away, spending days in travel on foot or by cart, to participate in a welcome to the representative of the United States.

As the motorcade finally approached Connaught Circle in New Delhi, the human sea closed in upon us and compelled a halt. For more than twenty-five minutes we could not move.

Members of the Secret Service were almost helpless. Fortunately, the people jamming the area wanted only to touch me, the car, or any member of the party, or to shout greetings that could not possibly be heard above the general din. Though the Secret Service did manage to protect me from the loss of buttons and clothing (eagerly snatched at by the exuberant crowds), Dick Flohr, my personal bodyguard, bore bruises and sore muscles for days afterwards.

The Prime Minister finally took a hand himself. When travel remained at a standstill, he dismounted and forced his way to the front of the car. Using the stick he always carried, the Prime Minister began laying about him. He tried to whip the blocking crowd toward one side or the other. This was lively non-violence but the Prime Minister could no more get the attention of even those he was striking than I could get his. His presence in the crowd was almost unnoticed. It did not take him long to recognize the futility of trying to control the almost hysterical fervor, however, and he crawled resignedly on an escorting jeep, stalled only three feet ahead of my car. At long last, with the help of police reserves, the jam loosened. We were allowed, slowly, to proceed.

Arriving at the President's house, known as the Rashtrapati Bhavan, the party, including President Prasad, Prime Minister Nehru, Mrs. Indira Gandhi, Mr. Nehru's daughter and hostess, Ambassador and Mrs. Ellsworth Bunker and our personal staffs, gathered in the apartment which had been assigned to us. Everyone talked at once about the magnitude, spontaneity, and enthusiasm of the reception. Mr. Nehru said this was the largest demonstration he had seen since Independence Day eleven years before. He was obviously delighted.

* * *

The next morning, December 10, I had the opportunity, before my first scheduled event, to become acquainted with my surroundings. Although I have, through many years, become largely insensitive to the appointments of the quarters where I lay my head, I must confess I experienced a feeling of amazement in the Rashtrapati Bhavan. The palace is gigantic, occupying four blocks, larger in square footage than the Palace of Versailles. Outside each door of every room in our part of the palace stood a rigidly immobile lancer,[9] insuring the safety and pri-

[9] These lancers were from the same unit as the palace guard at Karachi, who had put on the tent-pegging demonstration. When the countries split in 1948, one part of the unit went with Pakistan, the other with India.

vacy of the occupant. My apartment, which included several large rooms, adjoined the one in which Barbara and John were housed. A spacious balcony was shared by the two suites, and beyond the balcony lay the beautiful Moghul Gardens, which gave the palace much of its dignity and grandeur.[10]

At 8:30 A.M. I was escorted formally from my apartment and went by auto to pay a visit to the Tomb of Mahatma Gandhi. There, with shoes removed, I rendered my respects to the memory of the architect of Indian independence.

Later in the morning, for a conference, the Prime Minister and I drove to his residence, where we were joined by Ambassador Bunker, Under Secretary Murphy, and Ambassador Mahomed Ali Currim Chagla, the Indian ambassador to the United States. Discussion consisted largely of Mr. Nehru's explanation of the origins of some Indian-Pakistani problems, together with his suggested solutions. He also described the nature and potentialities of the current Chinese invasion into India,[11] but was unable to ascribe a logical reason for the move. I did not comment except to remark that Communists needed no logical reason for causing trouble because the creation of trouble was, for them, an end in itself.

In the afternoon I addressed a joint session of the Indian Parliament, where I became aware of the oratorical prowess of Vice President Sarvepalli Radhakrishnan. He spoke simply but eloquently of the significance of this visit to India, giving the entire speech in fluent English without a note and without a pause. My own speech was received with an unusual response: the members simply tapped for a time on the desks with their open palms. By American standards this could have meant almost anything—possibly something unpleasant—but veterans of Indian politics later told me that it was an ovation, that in their terms I had brought down the house.

In the evening a dinner was given by President Prasad in the state dining room, formerly used by the British viceroys of India. I was pleased to see that the pictures of the viceroys still hung on the walls alongside that of their successor, President Prasad. I took this fact as evidence that, though the nation had been ready to make any sacrifice to achieve independence, neither the connection or the separation had left a concerted hatred. When I noted an impressive statue of King George V standing in a prominent place near the Palace I could not help wondering whether

[10] The Moghul Gardens are apparently so named because of the style of formal landscaping introduced by the Moghuls, Moslems originally from Central Asia, in their occupation of India some three hundred years previously.

[11] An incursion into the district of Ladakh, high in the Himalayas.

we in our early days of independence would have tolerated among us a statue of King George III.

* * *

On December 11, I visited Delhi University. I met the members of the Vice Chancellor's charming family. His two daughters, both university students, and I compared features of college life in our respective countries.

Late that afternoon came the event around which the entire trip had been planned, the formal opening of the World Agricultural Fair. The ceremonies were elaborate and some of the speeches were the same, running to considerable length. Much attention was given to a message of congratulations from the Soviet government, to maintain, I assumed, the official neutrality on which India insists.

This was the first occasion on which I was privileged to hear Prime Minister Nehru make a public address. His speaking style was conversational. He used no gestures, his tone was almost professorial, and he held the audience, despite its vast size, completely spellbound.

Following the dedication, the party was taken to the United States Pavilion of the fair, stopping along the way to view one of the few white tigers in captivity. The United States Exhibition was extensive, with items ranging from "Atoms for Peace" to instructions in ballroom dancing. I was there as a guest, principally; my only ceremonial function was to press a button starting a nuclear reactor. For half an hour we walked through the various wings of the pavilion but, as the hour grew late and the crowds dense, we saw less of it than we would have liked.

* * *

Following church attendance on Sunday (President Prasad, to my delight, insisted on accompanying us) came an event which I had looked forward to from my days in Abilene, Kansas. Conducted by Mr. Nehru, my entire official party and I took off from Palam Airport to visit Agra, the site of the Taj Mahal.

It would be idle for me, after ages of picture postcards and gifted travel writers, to attempt a description of this magnificent building. Perhaps it would be best to say simply that anyone visiting that site will never be disappointed. Soaring imagination, ingenious craftsmanship, and meticulous effort had obviously gone into a monument to one man's love for his wife. I was told that in one of the mosaics which adorn its walls, the petal of each life-size flower contains sixty separate stones. The Taj stands in an extensive and completely walled enclosure which includes two mosques, with its rear elevation facing the Jumna River. Contrary to the impression I had carried from childhood, it is located in a fairly populous area. I should have known; nearly all India is populous.

From the Taj Mahal we traveled by helicopter to a small Indian village named Laraonda. Here I saw at first hand the poverty in which so many people of India live. Dwellings were constructed of mud. Modern sewage, lighting, and running water were, of course, nonexistent. Houses were virtually unfurnished. In the city hall, the only plastered building in the village, I noted posters from the government and a few news bulletins placed for the benefit of those who could read. These, except for one small and dilapidated radio, provided the only source of news for the entire community.

As we left by helicopter for the airport, the Prime Minister suggested that we fly over the deserted city of Fatehpur Sikri. It was built by an ambitious Moghul emperor four centuries ago as a new capital of India. It had taken ten years to build. Many buildings, with more than half of the city wall, still stand. This emperor had made one small error: along with the splendor in which he planned to live he had failed to provide an adequate source of water. As a result the city soon became only a magnificent monument to absent-mindedness.

We returned to New Delhi in the early forenoon, and shortly thereafter the Prime Minister conducted me to a civic reception. The crowd—estimated by my hosts as well over a half million—was seated on the ground in a great grassy field. Both Prime Minister Nehru and I spoke through a most efficient public address system to a throng that astonished me by its close attention.[12]

That evening I dined with the Prime Minister privately. We sat alone, and during the time we spent there I felt closer to Mr. Nehru than on any of the other occasions we had been together. He talked of India, her history, her needs, her principal problems, both domestic and foreign and of his hopes for her. His views were palpably honest and sincere. While I sensed that he felt almost bewildered by the unjustified and

[12] Obviously Mr. Nehru had a tremendous hold on the Indian people. I was told that on one occasion when he was speaking to a vast assemblage numbering in the hundreds of thousands, the public address system suddenly ceased functioning. In spite of this, the Prime Minister, who continued talking, held the rapt attention of his audience, which, according to my informant, seemed to understand every thought he was expressing even though they could not hear his spoken words. Indians openly recognize this spiritual or intellectual communion between a revered leader and a crowd; it is a sort of mystique into which Westerners are not initiated. Its name, as I understood it, is *darshan*.

brutal Red Chinese attacks against India's frontiers, he still showed little rancor or anger, even though he made clear his determination to resist.

He emphatically denied that his aim was the socialization of India. Referring to the public and private sectors of the Indian economy, he thought that the two sectors should be about equal. He expressed the hope that other nations would recognize this dual programing and would find it possible to help in either direction, each according to its own decisions. His government, he said, would welcome both kinds of assistance.

Throughout his conversation, there was discernible his preoccupation with India's primary problem: it was people, people, and more people everywhere—people in such numbers, always increasing, that every plan and program for their betterment invariably set up goals too modest to assure progress as rapid as population growth.

While we did not mention the matter specifically I came to understand, not only from his conversation but out of my own observation, that all plans for India's progress were going to fail unless some effective and practicable system of population control were adopted. At one time I had publicly stated that the problem of population growth in other countries was not a proper responsibility of the United States government. My trip to India convinced me that we could not stand aloof if requested to help. In spite of a high rate of infant mortality and inadequate health facilities, India was adding each year more than five million souls to her population. This could not go on. Until this Indian problem is solved all others will grow worse rather than better.

This was my last evening in New Delhi. Understanding between our two governments had been deepened, I felt, and our ease of communication improved. During my stay there I constantly asked myself, "Who could possibly be qualified to take Mr. Nehru's position if he should be forced to give up?"

* * *

From New Delhi onward to the end of our tour, we were flying in a direction opposite to the rotation of the earth. The result was that our working days were lengthened. On this journey, after almost four hours in the air, Bill Draper set his Boeing down at Teheran at 8:40 A.M. local time.

In Teheran, the Shah of Iran and I went through welcoming ceremonies in bitterly cold weather. The trip from the airfield to the Marble Palace was neither long nor strenuous, but it brought another new experience. As in Ankara, arches had been constructed at intervals, to span the highway along which we traveled. As we approached the first of these arches, I found that the entire road for something like a hundred yards on each side of the arch was carpeted by beautiful Persian rugs. Somewhat taken aback, I exclaimed to the Shah, "I assure Your Majesty that in America we show far more respect for Persian rugs than you do."

"In the 'old days,'" he replied casually, "the entire road from the airport to the Palace would have been covered, rather than merely at each of the arches."

Upon arrival at the Marble Palace the Shah and I immediately retired to a sitting room for a private conversation of about an hour.

The Shah had always impressed me as a man of good intent, concerned for the welfare of his people. Though far from being a dictator he possessed much more authority than any constitutional monarch of Europe. He did not hesitate to plunge directly into serious discussion, and impressed me as a man who was acquainted with each major problem of his nation and its relationship with others. The Shah was not the product of a long line of royalty; his father rose from the ranks of the army to become Shah of Iran. This fact may account for my impression that he was working hard to be accepted intellectually and sentimentally as the respected leader of his nation. Possibly it accounted, too, for his anxiety to have a son and heir to succeed him.

He told me of some of his internal problems, one of which was the serious maldistribution of wealth and land. He had already devised a bill by which he hoped to bring about a redistribution of land holdings. He expressed confidence he could do so.

The Shah presented me with a desk of a mosaic pattern, rivaling any example of fine craftsmanship that I have ever seen. He said that each square centimeter of the desk's surface contained over one hundred separate pieces of material. It had taken master craftsmen two years of unremitting work to construct the desk. (It is now in the Smithsonian Institution as a gift from him to the American people.) In addition, each of the provinces of Iran had representatives on hand with mementos of more modest nature. A gift in itself was the freshness and beauty of the young people who made the presentations. I could not but remark upon this to the Shah. I have always since wished that our stay in that fascinating region could have been much longer. But, like tourists everywhere, the time came when we had to hurry to begin the next leg of our journey, to Greece.

* * *

On hand to greet us as we reached Athens were King Paul and Crown Prince Constantine. The crowds on the way into the city were in a holiday mood and seemed almost as large as those in Karachi. To extend their greetings many had sought vantage points in trees or on rooftops or telephone poles; some chose such precarious locations that I feared for their lives.[13]

At the Palace we were greeted by the charming Queen Frederika and her two lovely daughters.

The next morning, accompanied by Premier Constantin Karamanlis, I went to Parliament to address that body. The political opposition in Greece includes some 12 to 15 per cent Communists. In the Parliament their leader, sitting immediately in front of the group, determines when they are to applaud a speaker and when they are to refrain.

At one point this scheme broke down. I mentioned "peace": the Communists obeyed their leader and broke into vigorous applause. And then, as I frequently do, I added, "with justice": the leader turned back and frantically tried to get the group's attention, but it was too late. The flurry was so noticeable that all others present, including me, had a momentary chuckle.

Later in the morning I met with the Prime Minister and his advisers. Mr. Karamanlis raised a wholly unexpected question—the future employment of the United States Sixth Fleet. He brought this up, he said, because of a rumor that the United States government was planning to remove the fleet from the Mediterranean. Such an action, he exclaimed, would insure the loss of the entire region to Communism.

I did not ask the source of the rumor. "As long as I hold my present office," I said, "you may be assured of the fleet's continued service in those waters and of America's concern for the safety of the region." From his reaction to my answer I felt that the most important point he wanted to make during my visit had been settled.

Mr. Karamanlis, I soon decided, was one of the most able men I had met on my tour.

Next on the schedule was a formal luncheon. During the meal, the Royal Family made lighthearted efforts to convince us we should stay over another day rather than departing as planned on the cruiser U.S.S. *Des Moines*. Most elaborate of these hospitable plots was a false weather report circulated on an official-looking slip of paper by the Crown Prince, predicting "severe storms and rough seas" on the Mediterranean. One

[13] We learned the next day that one young boy had broken away from his parents, and while sitting on top of a roof had been injured when the building collapsed. While he lay in serious condition at the hospital, Barbara found an opportunity to drop by for a quick visit. The doctors said the boy was doing well, and we were relieved to learn later that he recovered.

of my companions remarked that our entire party was so sleepy that a hurricane would never be noticed, whereupon the Crown Prince laughed and said, "In that case I may as well change the prediction."

In a drizzling rain, appropriate to the way we felt at leaving this land and their splendid people, we took off by helicopter and, tracing the route of the ancient walls from Athens to the port of Piraeus, landed by helicopter aboard the *Des Moines*.

* * *

The *Des Moines* was then the flagship of the U. S. Sixth Fleet. An old friend, Vice Admiral George Anderson, formerly one of my assistants at SHAPE and now commander of this force, courteously vacated his suite for my use.

After some thirty hours of comfortable sailing we reached Tunis, a city of special significance to me since the days of World War II. Early on the morning of December 17 my party and I departed by helicopter for the Dar es Saada Palace at La Marsa, just outside Tunis. Here we had a sumptuous breakfast, and I was privileged, in addition to ceremonial responsibilities, to confer once again at length with the President of Tunisia, Habib Bourguiba.

President Bourguiba thought that President de Gaulle's recent offer of self-government to Algeria had been a constructive step, but he added that there were powerful forces in the French government and army which did not want De Gaulle to be successful. Those people, he said, opposed any solution to the problem other than complete Algerian integration with France and would accept nothing short of victory in crushing the rebellion. The French commander in Algeria, General Maurice Challe, had made a speech shortly after De Gaulle's offer and had indicated that, come what may, the French armed forces would remain in Algeria.

President Bourguiba said: "I am certain that if the French are successful in putting down the rebellion in Algeria, they will move to recover their position in Tunisia and Morocco."

I tried to assure Bourguiba that his fears were groundless, and in doing so learned that he had never met General de Gaulle. "Would you have any objection to my telling General de Gaulle of your feelings and maybe suggesting to the French President that he arrange a meeting between you?" I asked. President Bourguiba said that he would have no objection whatsoever.

He said that Tunisia could be made an example for all nations of Africa of the benefits arising from friendship with the West. It was not a large country and would not, therefore, require large sums of money. He outlined his problems, mentioned Tunisia's material resources—largely underdeveloped—and said he hoped to have help in meeting his needs.

President Bourguiba reminded me, in certain respects, of President Ayub of Pakistan. While he did not have Ayub's commanding physical presence, he was direct and pleasant in manner, and definitely Western in orientation. Like Ayub's, his statements were modest, clear, and concise and he lived for the welfare of his nation and his people.

Both men struck me as natural leaders. Each, among his associates, seemed to enjoy a respect and loyalty gained far more by personality, ability, and character than by the official position he held.

* * *

On Friday, December 18, at 1:30 P.M., we debarked at Toulon, France, and after a swift and bumpy railway trip pulled into the Gare de Lyon in Paris at 10:30 P.M.

The ensuing period was a busy one. On Saturday the four Western heads of government met twice at the Elysée Palace. The next day we spent at Rambouillet in nearly continuous session until midafternoon, at the end of which I drove back to Paris with Chancellor Adenauer.

The liveliest conversations were those I had with President de Gaulle. He raised again the subject of an organization of governments—French, British, and American—establishing themselves as a kind of triumvirate to promote their common interests throughout the world. He believed that only in this fashion could we handle the emerging problems of Africa and Asia. He thought that this could be done without inciting the jealousy and antagonism of other nations.

On this last point I found it necessary to disagree, and both of us held to our respective positions. The talks were, as always, friendly and there was no personal unhappiness or recrimination.

In our formal meetings the heads of government reaffirmed the principles set forth in the four-power communiqué of December 14, 1958, and in the Declaration of the North Atlantic Council of December 16, 1958, on Berlin.[14] We agreed, in principle, on a summit meeting with the Soviets and agreed to communicate with that government, proposing April 27, 1960, as a date to meet in Paris. Chairman Khrushchev had withdrawn his ultimatum on Berlin while both the U.S. and the U.S.S.R. were ob-

[14] These were the meetings, it will be recalled, that Foster Dulles attended on his last trip abroad. The powers agreed to stand unified on Berlin; they denied the Soviet right to abrogate unilaterally any wartime obligations.

serving an unofficial suspension of nuclear testing. The atmosphere seemed better and both President de Gaulle and I believed it best to go along with the idea that a summit might be helpful.

* * *

When we reached Spain, I was able to meet and talk with Generalissimo Francisco Franco, something I had wanted to do ever since we had established bases in that country.

It had not seemed appropriate during the months I spent in Europe immediately after conclusion of hostilities in World War II for me to seek an opportunity to meet him. I was then thought of as a quasi-belligerent and it was scarcely fitting to make a visit to a government which had remained neutral throughout the conflict. Years later, when I went back to Europe to command NATO forces, I again thought it impolitic to visit a non-member nation against which certain members were deeply prejudiced. However, since I had been President our nation had drawn a step closer to Spain, at least to the extent of making arrangements for establishing air bases there. Now in 1959, I considered it proper to stop briefly at the capital of that country to discuss, among other things, the practical matter of cooperation concerning these installations that were highly valuable to each of us.

Landing at Madrid's Torrejon Airport, we proceeded to the historic Moncloa Palace and then to a formal dinner with Generalissimo Franco. To us, accustomed to the American custom of formal dinners beginning around eight in the evening, it seemed almost incredible that normal Spanish practice was to begin no earlier than ten, and often later. When our advance party had visited Madrid in November, Tom Stephens found it difficult to persuade the Spanish government to adopt a compromise that would set the dinner hour at 9:30. Such matters, of course, seem to be trifling to the average citizen; to the protocol officer they are highly important, as indeed they were to a President nearly seventy years old, then on his seventeenth day of almost incessant travel.

When Generalissimo Franco delivered the traditional dinner toast, he mentioned that the day was also the birthday of my youngest granddaughter, Mary Jean. This personal mention caused Barbara, who was sitting next to the Generalissimo, to glow.

I was impressed by the fact that there was no discernible mannerism or characteristic that would lead an unknowing visitor to conclude that he was in the presence of a dictator. Generalissimo Franco is a rather small man of regular features and modest manner. Whatever the reasons for the Spanish Revolution, it was clear that Franco had proved himself a strong and enduring leader.

We had one sporting interest in common, though his proficiency put him in quite another class; he is reputed to be one of the finest bird shots in Spain and possibly in the world. My first brief visit with him certainly provided no basis on which to form anything more than a hasty impression, but I found him personable and agreeable—indeed, sufficiently so that I wonder what the consequence would be if he became willing to hold free elections?

* * *

Early the following morning I went to the Pardo Palace, Generalissimo Franco's private residence, for breakfast and serious talk. The atmosphere of the conference was cordial and Franco gave the impression of being secure in his position and pleased with the presence in Spain of important American air bases. He made no specific requests of me for additional aid, but did outline some of the economic problems of his country, especially those arising out of its lack of industries.

On my part I seized the opportunity to convey to him the request of Protestant churchmen in America to eliminate what these churchmen called intolerance toward Protestant people and activities in that country. A Protestant church built in Madrid a few years earlier had never been allowed to open. He promised to look into the matter, and I later heard that the restrictions were somewhat relaxed.

* * *

Our last stop was in Morocco. There we were met by King Mohammed V, who had visited Washington two years earlier. Among the crowds along the road to Casablanca were Berber tribesmen, who had received word unofficially that some kind of a celebration was in the offing. Without the knowledge of the Moroccan government, these hardy warriors, with their antique muzzle-loading rifles and their flowing robes, lined the route of the motorcade to fire salutes, one-handed, straight into the air. I think the Secret Service agents were not so fearful that a tribesman might deliberately take aim and shoot, but the possibility did occur to them that one of the old weapons might explode alongside our car. Having been accustomed, as a boy, to muzzle-loaders and black powder—the same kind used by the Berbers—I knew that the agents needed to have no fear of an explosion from the size of the charges they were using. These tribesmen were just as conscious of the cost of powder as I had had to be sixty years earlier.

After luncheon at the Palais Royal, I gathered with King Mohammed, El Mehdi Ben Aboud, ambassador to the United States, the two princes, my son, and an interpreter. The King, like King Zahir of Afghanistan, was quiet and reserved in manner; both seemed to prefer to keep their basic political and economic aims enshrouded in mystery.

The Moroccan King was emphatic in his declaration that his nation would remain a kingdom, loyal to the ruling house, and that the people, having thrown off the overlordship of France, would remain independent of all other types of domination. While he seemed to defer markedly to the expressed opinions of his son, the crown prince, I could not determine whether he did so out of respect for the young man's abilities or because he did not want, in front of strangers, to differ openly with his heir apparent. At times both the King and the prince hinted that Soviet help would be welcome in their country, but they belittled any thought that the Communists could convert Morocco to Communism. In both Afghanistan and Morocco I noted that, though these two kings were reputed to be despotic rulers, both tried to avoid giving the impression of living extravagantly—even while dwelling in palaces. One the surface, at least, they were genuinely interested in improving the lot of their people, and in maintaining their nation's independence of outside powers.

One subject on King Mohammed's mind was the fate of the new nations of Africa. He was anxious that the independence of all colonial Africans be bolstered with all the influence we had at our disposal. He brushed off the idea that any colony could benefit by a period of preparation for freedom. "Only immediate action," he insisted, "can satisfy African ambitions." Furthermore, the West must support these newly independent nations financially after setting them free.

I argued that precipitate action would create many difficulties; in particular I said that President de Gaulle had been constructive in his pronouncement of September 16 and I thought his proposals were reasonable. Independence was a worthy ambition, I told him, and certainly dear to American hearts, but it also had its costs. Those seeking a separate political status should be concerned first, I said, with the economic capacity to meet at least the minimum costs incurred. He was not convinced.

* * *

Flying home, we crossed the Atlantic and landed at Washington on December 22, at 11:30 P.M. local time after a 21½-hour day. Mamie was there to greet us, along with the Nixons and members of the Cabinet. We were truly happy to see them.

As Mamie and I drove down Pennsylvania Avenue, approaching the White House, we found hundreds of sparkler-carrying well-wishers filling Lafayette Square with a dazzling midnight illumination. It was a unique reception and, because of the cold and the lateness of the hour, one that we deeply appreciated.

When we reached the second floor of the White House I saw a startling formation.

Seated around a table in the West Hall were General Gruenther, Bill Robinson, George Allen, and Slats Slater, all engaged in what appeared to be a routine bridge game. As we came in, Al Gruenther turned around slightly, said "Hi," turned back to his bridge hand, and said, "I double."

George looked up long enough to ask, "What's new?"

Another asked, "Just in?"

But despite their best efforts at nonchalance and indifference, they had succeeded in displaying a welcome sight to a tired and glad-to-be-home traveler.

* * *

Looking back over our long journey, we could point to no concrete or specific achievements, nothing to loom large in official records. We brought back no new treaty or agreement to enhance the security of the United States or to strengthen its economy. We had solved no problems nor revolutionized, in our favor, any trends threatening our vital interests.

But the purpose of the trip was not to solve specific problems. We wanted to create a better understanding of our nation and, hopefully, to develop a strengthened confidence in our country and its global purposes. And of course we wanted to learn more about others and their aspirations.

To attempt an estimate, even a rough one, of the number of people we saw during those eighteen December days would be a futile gesture, but obviously it ran into the millions. Yet never once did I see a patently hostile face; the welcoming placards along the roadsides and the glad shouts of "America!"—recognizable in spite of language differences—left no doubt of the friendly sentiments the teeming populations felt for our nation.

I believe that our talks, formal and informal, helped to persuade national leaders and millions of people that the United States had no selfish purpose in cooperating with them; that we sought no territory; did not wish to dominate; and believed in freely chosen governments for peoples and nations everywhere. Charges of colonialism against us, I repeated over and over again, were not only blatantly false but were a tactic to divert world attention from the real imperialism and new harsh colonialism of the Communist conspiracy.

For myself, I had no doubt that the trip was worth the effort it required. By no means does such a conclusion imply that an American President should spend a large portion of his time traveling the earth. But when any future Executive may find the circumstances favorable for undertaking a similar journey, then whatever trouble and inconvenience he might be subjected to in visiting the less well-known parts of the world will be repaid many times over. He will be showered with kindnesses and courtesies to the point of exhaustion, but he will be rewarded richly by the eagerness of whole populations to learn about America, and by his better understanding of the peoples he, directly or indirectly, as head of the strongest nation on earth, is destined to serve.

Their faces are interestingly different and their lands exotic, but their fate and ours are one.

CHAPTER XXII

Amigos

We cannot afford the luxury of ignorance;
it costs too much.

—*Milton S. Eisenhower,* The Wine Is Bitter

AT seven-thirty on the morning of Washington's Birthday, 1960, I took off, with a considerable party, from snow-covered Washington, D.C., for Ramey Air Force Base in Puerto Rico. When we landed there, in its sunshine with the temperature in the eighties, we were embarked on a fifteen-thousand-mile trip which would take us to the four southernmost countries of Latin America.[1]

* * *

For nearly half a century I had been interested in Latin American life. While waiting in 1915 to hear whether a serious knee injury would preclude a career for me in the United States Army, I had earnestly considered, should I be rejected, the possibility of trying to carve out a career in Argentina—a place which, I understood, resembled our own West in the 1870s. A favorable decision on my physical fitness by the West Point authorities removed this temptation.

I had often visited Mexico. During the early 1920s I had lived for three years in Panama and there met visitors from other Latin American nations. After the close of World War II I had done considerable traveling, and in South America had managed to go to the vast republic of Brazil.

Any American should understand that as we are bound to our neighbors to the south geographically (indeed, with our nearest southern

[1] Map, "Amigos–The Trips to Latin America," appears following page 360.

neighbor we have an undefended border more than 2000 miles long), it behooves us to join with them in developing a stronger Western Hemisphere economy, higher standards of living, and faith in freedom's future. But blocking the way to Latin American development are a host of acute problems, including a lack of development capital, ruinous up-and-down swings in the prices of their exports, a need for common markets, lack of housing, education, transportation, and health facilities, and an archaic social system. Compounding these difficulties is the incredible population explosion—one of the largest on the face of the globe. A half century earlier Latin America had only one-third its population of 1960. In the next forty years we could expect its population to triple again, reaching six hundred million, a number approximately double the population predicted for the United States and Canada at the same time.

Between 1953 and 1960, to help in finding solutions, we had done many things, starting with that popular export, money.

We had broken all records in increasing the new flow of United States public and private capital to Latin America. Whereas in 1953, for example, that flow totaled $232 million, in 1957 it reached a peak of $1.6 billion, of which most was private funds. Aggregate American assets and investments in Latin America totaled about $7 billion in 1952; by 1960 they had nearly doubled, with only $2 billion coming from public funds.

In 1938 the Export-Import Bank[2] had begun its loans to Latin American governments with a commitment of $200 million spread over two years. In 1958, at the request of the administration, the Congress increased the lending authority of the bank, which does about half its business in Latin America, from $5 billion to $7 billion.

Largely through efforts of the United States, the World Bank set up two new agencies: the International Finance Corporation, established July 20, 1956, to lend money to private companies; and the International Development Association, set up in 1959 to make loans repayable on unconventional terms—"soft" loans.

We substantially increased our technical assistance to Latin America, sending agricultural, mining, and financial experts to help our neighbors to the south; tripled cultural exchanges; settled with Mexico a longstanding dispute over migrant workers; intensified our program to eradicate malaria throughout the region; shipped nearly half a billion dollars' worth of surplus foods and feeds to Latin American countries, getting in return local currencies which we then used to finance development projects in those same countries.

[2] Set up in 1934 to help finance exports and imports between the United States and foreign countries.

Since 1953 our assistance to Latin America, however, had been not only more extensive than ever before, it had also incorporated precedent-shattering innovations.

The first of these involved United States backing for a new Inter-American Development Bank, which we announced at a meeting of the Inter-American Economic and Social Council in July of 1958. On April 8, 1959, an agreement among twenty-one American nations established this bank with a total capitalization of $1 billion, of which the United States would supply as much as $450 million. For more than a half century Latin American nations had wanted such a bank, but the United States had repeatedly rejected it. Now, we reversed that long-standing policy. This reversal was highly significant. Traditional unilateral aid was sustaining a prevailing social order which was unjust to the masses of the people, but we could do nothing directly about this without violating the policy of non-intervention in the internal affairs of other nations. The creation of the new bank changed this, for now the Americas had a multinational instrument, secure against control by any one country, for bettering the life of people throughout the Americas; if this instrument insisted upon social reform as a condition of extending development credit, it could scarcely be charged with "intervention."

The second reversal was United States support for establishment of Latin American common markets. Previous administrations had either opposed such regional economic associations or had refused to discuss them. Beginning in 1957, however, high administration officials, including Dr. Milton S. Eisenhower, Secretary Dulles, Under Secretary Dillon, and Assistant Secretary Roy R. Rubottom, Jr., emphasized on numerous occasions that the United States favored such regional agreements so as to improve prosperity, trade opportunities, and credit worthiness. Two began to develop, one in Central America[3] and another primarily in the southern part of Latin America.[4] If each of the participating nations were ready to negotiate and cooperate with its neighbors, the beneficial effects would be incalculable. As in Europe, these common markets could be the first move toward turning a system of barbed barriers into one of open gates, permitting free exchanges of products to mutual advantage.

Only history, however, will have the full answer.

A third reversal in policy was a United States decision to support "international commodity study groups" and, under the right conditions,

[3] Original signatories: Guatemala, Honduras, El Salvador, Nicaragua, and Costa Rica.

[4] Comprising Argentina, Brazil, Chile, Mexico, Paraguay, Peru, and Uruguay.

"commodity stabilization agreements." What would they accomplish? They were aimed at these situations:

Nicaragua obtains 55 per cent of its total export earnings from bananas; Guatemala and El Salvador, roughly 60 per cent from coffee; Chile, 66 per cent from copper; Bolivia, 69 per cent from tin ore; Colombia, 71 per cent from coffee; and Venezuela, 92 per cent from oil. The prices of some of these commodities swing up and down as much as 50 per cent from one year to the next. When the prices for such commodities plummet—and prices of manufactured goods stay steady—the effects on the economies of these nations (and therefore the welfare of the peoples) is drastic. For years Latin American governments have wanted to discuss with us methods by which these steep ups and downs in the price graph could be smoothed out; previous administrations steadily refused. But on June 23, 1958, a twenty-three-nation international coffee study group met in Washington to begin an examination of remedies for the damage done to income by a surplus in coffee. In September of the same year fifteen Latin American coffee-producing countries agreed to limit their exports of the next crop year. Concurrently, other commodity study groups were created. In the fall of 1959 the United States sanctioned an international coffee agreement.

Some of these significant advances were a direct result of the appointment in 1953 of my brother Milton as my personal representative and special ambassador on matters affecting Latin America. He gave most of his governmental interest to this region.

But despite this record, trouble persisted. Our aid was considerable, the problems gigantic. Repeatedly Milton warned of Latin Americans' resentment over what seemed to them to be our preoccupation with other areas of the world, especially those closer to Communist military forces. In a report to me in late 1958, following an extensive study tour in Central America (his studies of South America having occurred earlier), Milton wrote: "I must add a note of urgency to my general recommendation that the nations of Latin America and the United States re-examine their attitudes and policies toward one another and constantly seek to strengthen their economic, political and cultural relations, to their mutual benefit." Behind the lines of his note, one could see that he meant that time was running out in Latin America.

I shared his continuing concern.[5] My trip to Panama in 1956, to meet

[5] On June 14, 1955, for example, I wrote Foster Dulles: "I probably have written you more often on the subject of Mexico than any other single matter. This is yet another communication, just for your personal contemplation. . . .

"I have the uneasy feeling that somewhere along the line we are not really appreciative of Mexico's economic and political and social problems. I believe that

with heads of state of Latin American nations, was symptomatic of my awareness.

Sometimes our Latin American problems arose out of the damage done to their economies by such things as our subsidized sale of cotton on the world market, or again, by restrictions we placed on our imports of their lead and zinc. A variety of other complaints, most of them untrue, were constantly launched against us, and at times resentment flared into violence. In March of 1959, an American newsmagazine quoted an unidentified United States official in La Paz, Bolivia, to the effect that the only way to solve Bolivia's problems was to abolish the country and divide it among its neighbors. This observation, carried only in the magazine's special Latin American edition, prompted an angry Bolivian mob to take to the streets of La Paz, burn the American flag, and stone the American Embassy and USIA office. In the rioting a fifteen-year-old Bolivian boy was shot and killed.

With Panama our relations were necessarily closer than with any other of these nations because of the existence there of the Panama Canal, built by the United States, owned by the United States, and covered by a treaty written in 1903 that gives the United States the authority to operate within the Canal Zone "as if it were sovereign." Through all the years since 1903 there have been irritations and difficulties, springing mainly from Panamanian dissatisfaction with what they deem to be the small advantage accruing to them because of the presence of the Canal.

In November of 1959 trouble blazed in Panama: a mob of Panamanians, stirred up over the sovereignty issue, as well as the old issue of allegedly unfair rates of pay for native workers in the Canal Zone (and mistakenly believing that the United States made huge profits from the Canal), attempted to "invade" the Zone. There were elements of justice in the Panamanian complaints,[6] and we had been working on a nine-point program for the Zone, including a low-cost housing project and re-

---

there is a holdover in our country today of the thought that Mexico is inherently an enemy of ours—I rather sense this feeling often when I hear people talking of the country.

". . . I am so earnestly of the opinion that the soundness and friendliness of our relationships with Mexico must be a first and continuing concern of ours, that if we could arrange for an early visit of President Ruiz Cortines I would be perfectly willing to go through with it. I think that possibly you and I could profit a lot to hear his personal thoughts about his own country and its needs, especially capital—public and private."

[6] As early as 1934, when I had been studying the problems of the Canal Zone in the War Department, I had believed that we should make some reasonable changes in response to the requests of the Panamanians.

vised wage rates. But before the program could be started, the mob marched. After calm returned, parts of the program gradually went into effect.

Prior to this incident, in May 1958, a worse explosion had occurred, during the Latin American trip of Vice President and Mrs. Nixon (described by him in dramatic detail in his book, *Six Crises*). On May 8, a mob at San Marcos University in Lima, Peru, shoved, stoned, and booed the Vice President and his party. As soon as I received word of this shocking incident, and was assured of the Nixons' composure and safety, I dictated a cable: "Your courage, patience, and calmness in the demonstrations directed against you by radical agitators have brought you new respect and admiration in our country."

He replied in good humor. ". . . The only casualties we have suffered to date are a couple of Ben Freeman's[7] suits which I will be unable to wear again."

On May 12 he was in Bogota, Colombia, and from that city went to Caracas, Venezuela. There, the next day, a howling and ugly mob smashed the car in which he was riding, and threatened to overturn it and drag its occupants into the street.

The moment this news reached me I ordered a thousand United States troops flown to Guantanamo Bay and Puerto Rico, ready to move in and rescue the Vice President and Mrs. Nixon if necessary.

This day seemed marked by fate for localized crises around the globe. The Vice President was under attack in Venezuela. The United States was somehow getting blamed for trouble in Algeria. Burmese mobs were conducting anti-U.S. demonstrations. Rioting groups in Lebanon (before the Lebanon landings) burned two American libraries, to which area I ordered units of the Sixth Fleet.

"Maybe I should be digging out my uniforms," I told Mamie that evening, "to see whether they still fit."

When I telephoned Dick Nixon in the American Embassy at Caracas, he reported that he had been able to carry out most of his planned program and would start back that evening.

A hundred thousand Washingtonians turned out the next morning to welcome the Nixons when they arrived at Washington National Airport. The Vice President's tour, Radio Moscow was declaring, was a "disgraceful fiasco." It was not that; in fact, as one good friend of mine, William Ewing, who had gone with him, wrote about the Vice President's earlier stopover in Argentina: "Everybody was talking about the way he faced

[7] A Philadelphia tailor.

unfriendly demonstrators, but we thought the friendly crowds would tear him to pieces. It was a moving sight to see."

Nonetheless, the events of that week in May 1958 brought home to all of us the clear truth that, as the Vice President reported at the end of his trip, "the threat of Communism in Latin America is greater than ever before."

* * *

This threat, though none of us knew it at the time, was to be thrust into the open first, not on the Latin American mainland, but on the island of Cuba. There a bearded young man named Fidel Castro had succeeded in gathering together a band of about a thousand guerrillas in the Escambray Mountains, a force promising to throw out the self-enriching and corrupt dictator Fulgencio Batista and end the suppressions and brutalities of his police state.[8]

Throughout 1958, in accordance with the charter of the OAS, the United States carefully followed a policy of non-intervention in Cuba, although sentimental support for Castro was widespread. We repeatedly seized cargoes of arms headed for Castro and in March suspended the delivery of arms to Batista. We would not take sides or intervene, I told a news conference on November 5, 1958, except to protect American citizens in Cuba.[9] A month later Castro launched a major attack against Santa Clara, the capital of Las Villas province in central Cuba. Batista's local forces, unable to defeat Castro, decided to join him. Obviously

[8] Castro's struggle had been going on for years. On the 26th of July 1953, a date which gave his movement its name, he and a little band of followers had unsuccessfully attacked the Moncado Barracks in Santiago de Cuba. After a tempestuous 3½ years of fighting, imprisonment, and exile in Mexico, Castro returned to Cuba, where he hid out in the Sierra Maestra jungles, conducting intermittent guerrilla forays. Herbert L. Matthews of the *New York Times,* having held exclusive talks with Castro in his mountain hideout, proclaimed him "the most remarkable and romantic figure to arise in Cuban history since José Martí, the hero of the Wars of Independence." And in the absence of reports to the contrary, and the universal revulsion against the Batista government, it is not surprising that large numbers of his readers should have echoed Matthews' views.

Castro promised free elections, social reform, schools, housing, and an end to corruption. Though some individuals, in and out of government, voiced suspicions that the Castro movement was Communist-inspired and -supported, these rumblings were drowned out by the chorus of plaudits encouraging the "liberator."

[9] In late July of 1958 Castro's rebel forces in Oriente province threatened the water supply for the United States naval base at Guantanamo Bay, which comes from the Yateras River, across the boundary in Cuba. The United States at once, by agreement with the Cuban government, sent a contingent of Marines into Cuba to protect the Yateras pumping station until government soldiers, temporarily withdrawn, could return to guard it.

Castro had won the emotional, and now the significant material support from the Cuban people.

During the rush of these last events in the final days of 1958, the Central Intelligence Agency suggested for the first time that a Castro victory might not be in the best interests of the United States. (Earlier reports which I had received of Castro's possible Communism were suspect because they originated with people who favored Batista.)

"Communists and other extreme radicals appear to have penetrated the Castro movement," Allen Dulles said. "If Castro takes over, they will probably participate in the government." When I heard this estimate, I was provoked that such a conclusion had not been given earlier.

One of my advisers recommended that the United States should now back Batista as the lesser of two evils. I rejected that course. If Castro turned out to be as bad as our intelligence now suggested, our only hope, if any, lay with some kind of non-dictatorial "third force," neither Castroite nor Batistiano.

On New Year's Day 1959, Batista sought refuge in the Dominican Republic, and Fidel Castro prepared to enter Havana in triumph.

Despite our apprehensions, Castro's first moves in the new year gave some observers cause to hope for the best. On January 2, for example, he proclaimed the appointment of an acceptable Provisional President, Carlos Manuel Urrutia Lleo, who in turn a few days later appointed as Premier the respected Dr. José Miro Cardona.[10] A group of Latin American governments had extended recognition to Castro by January 6.

From the intelligence digest prepared in my office during the early weeks of 1959:

> January 2, 1959: The Fidel Castro rebels are consolidating their control in the country. Santiago has fallen to them. An interesting facet which the State Department considers partly cheerful is the turning over of the armed forces by Cantillo to a Colonel Ramon Barquin, who has aided the rebels in their consolidation. Favorable aspects of the turnover are (1) that Barquin is an apparently well-thought-of officer, and (2) his opportunity to take a hand may strengthen the military's position, vis-à-vis Castro, and add a certain amount of stability to the situation. Castro is short on experienced and responsible personnel. The Communists can be expected to exploit a fast-moving situation, perhaps by supporting a general strike.

> January 6, 1959: Provisional President Urrutia established himself in the Presidential Palace in the early evening on January 5 after a delay of several hours caused by a non-Castro rebel group known as the Directorate. The Cabinet announced on January 3, however, contains

[10] Two years later Dr. Miro Cardona headed the Cuban exiles during the weeks of preparation for the invasion at the Bay of Pigs.

three or four members of this Revolutionary Directorate, a fact which our Embassy believes will add to the prospects for stability. The foreign minister is a man named Agramonte, who is a leading figure and is considered friendly to the U.S. Urrutia has agreed to give protection to the Embassy in Havana, in accordance with requests of a committee of ambassadors. Meanwhile, we have received requests for recognition from the Urrutia government and are assessing the situation. Costa Rica, Ecuador, Peru, Honduras, and Mexico have extended recognition.

January 7, 1959: President Urrutia has announced additional appointments to his Cabinet, including Prime Minister José Cardona, who is a highly respected former dean of the Havana Bar Association. He has announced that he will dissolve Congress and criminal courts and rule by decree for eighteen to twenty-four months. American businessmen meeting in Havana are urging rapid recognition on the basis that this government appears far better than anything they had dared hope for.

January 9, 1959: The Cuban Communist Party has obtained a minority voice in the organized labor movement. The party is attempting openly to create an impression of legality, although Urrutia has not recognized the party. Meanwhile, speculation on the orientation of the Urrutia government remains doubtful.

January 12, 1959: Castro and other leaders of the July 26 movement have declared the Communist Party will now be permitted to operate legally.

January 21, 1959: CIA reports several responsible men in the new Cuban government are being disillusioned over the delays and inefficiency occasioned by the constant deferral of decisions to Fidel Castro, whose time has been spent largely in public appearances. Prime Minister Miro Cardona, for these reasons as well as his anger over Castro's inflammatory attacks on the U.S., has submitted a letter of resignation.

Mass executions of Castro's enemies were under way.

Toward the end of January the press carried reports that Communists, long underground, were now supporting Castro. A Cuban delegate to the 21st Congress of the Soviet Communist Party in Moscow announced that the Cuban Communists had occupied the forefront of the struggle against Batista. And at that Congress, we later learned from sensitive clandestine sources, all foreign Communist Parties, and especially those in Latin America, were directed not to advertise their association with Moscow but rather to display themselves as "national" Communist movements. On February 13 word arrived that Castro himself was to become Premier.[11] In the ensuing weeks the number of executions mounted. Castro declared that he would not side with the United States in the cold war. He de-

[11] During these weeks our intelligence people continued to worry less about Castro's own leanings than about the danger of a breakdown of the machinery of government, labor unrest, and widespread unemployment, which the Communists could exploit.

nounced us for fifty years of "interference" in his country, interference which he would now end.

On the last day of February Castro announced a two-year postponement of the election he previously had promised, and on March 26 Allen Dulles reported that "the Castro regime is moving toward a complete dictatorship. Communists are now operating openly and legally in Cuba. And though Castro's government is *not* Communist-dominated, Communists have worked their way into the labor unions, the armed forces, and other organizations."

We learned that the American Society of Newspaper Editors had invited Castro to come to Washington to give a speech at the National Press Club on April 17. I was more than irritated by the news of the invitation and of Castro's acceptance.

Having personally become highly suspicious that Castro was a Communist and deeply disgusted at his murderous persecution of his former opponents, I inquired whether we could not refuse him a visa. Advised that under the circumstances this would be unwise, I nevertheless refused to see him.[12]

In Washington, Castro held a three-hour conference with the Vice President. At the end of this the Vice President wrote a long memorandum for the State Department and the CIA which had one clear conclusion: that Castro was "either incredibly naïve about Communism or under Communist discipline." Such a statement, about a government we had recognized, could not, without corroboration, be made public at that time.

Subsequent events more and more confirmed the Vice President's opinion. Major Ernesto ("Che") Guevara, an Argentine physician and soldier of fortune known to have been associated with the leftist Arbenz in Guatemala, welcomed the support of the Communists for the Castro government. Mao Tse-tung and other Communist leaders began speaking in praise of Castro. Che Guevara made a trip to Asia, where he told Indian Communists that as soon as Cuba could get rid of the United States naval base at Guantanamo Bay, Castro could show his true colors in foreign policy.[13]

[12] In his speech to the editors, Castro denied any Communist influence in his government. In a later television interview he denied that Cuba had gone neutralist. Meanwhile in Cuba, Castro's brother Raul delivered another anti-American speech. "Raul Castro must certainly be a Communist," I told Allen Dulles when I read what he had said.

"If he's not," Allen answered, "he's awfully close to being one."

[13] In Cairo, Nasser reportedly told Guevara that if Cuba did business with the West, it might lose 5 per cent of its resources, but that if Cuba did business with the Communists, it would lose 100 per cent.

Though our intelligence experts backed and filled for a number of months, events were gradually driving them to the conclusion that with the coming of Castro, Communism had penetrated this hemisphere.[14]

Communist newspapers, including one in Chinese, began to sprout up in Cuba. Cuban delegations visited Peking and talked over their achievements with Chairman Mao. The Deputy Director of the CIA revealed that the Soviet Union had sent an expert to Cuba to help guide the course of its revolution. Castro denounced the United States on October 26, and soon the government contained only one top official without some sort of Communists affiliation. A few weeks later all private businesses came under government control.

In the meantime, within a matter of weeks after Castro entered Havana, we in the administration informally began to examine measures that might be effective in restraining Castro if he should develop into a menace. By the end of 1959[15] we were seriously discussing a change in the law that, reflecting the protective attitude the United States had maintained toward Cuba for six decades, required the United States to buy about half of Cuba's sugar crop annually at premium prices. Another suggestion was to begin efforts to induce all Latin American governments to watch Castro carefully and to counter any move of his to promote revolution in the Western Hemisphere.

Even though, at times, Castro's public performances appeared to be the acts of a man mentally unbalanced, it was clear we would have trouble getting unanimous agreement that Castro posed in fact any threat to an American nation.

[14] In spite of the contrary evidence of his actions, Castro, up to the end of my administration, still posed as a democratic reformer. He did not confess his true color until December 1961.

[15] In the United States, admiration for Castro died slowly through the year 1959. In January Congressman Adam Clayton Powell (Democrat of New York) urged the government to recognize Castro at once and give him $200 million in aid. Both Powell and Congressman Charles O. Porter (Democrat of Oregon), accepted Castro's invitation to visit Havana. Herbert Matthews described the Castro government's "conservative tinge." By July former President Truman was repeating in a syndicated column what he had earlier told a Columbia University audience: "I think that Fidel Castro is a good young man, who has made mistakes but who seems to want to do the right thing for the Cuban people, and we ought to extend our sympathy and help him to do what is right for them. During Franklin D. Roosevelt's administration and my own, we sought to do what we thought was in the interest of the natives of South America." By January of 1960, Senator John F. Kennedy was writing, in a book called *The Strategy of Peace,* "Fidel Castro is part of the legacy of Bolivar." He implied that we might have given "the fiery young rebel a warmer welcome in his hour of triumph."

One suggestion was that we begin to build up an anti-Castro force within Cuba itself. Some thought we should quarantine the island, arguing that if the Cuban economy declined sharply, Cubans themselves might overthrow Castro.

In any event, by early 1960 there was no longer any doubt in the administration that "something would have to be done"—the questions were what, when, and under what circumstances? We knew that precipitate, unilateral action could easily be fatal to our hopes of strengthening the Western Hemisphere's Organization of American States for dealing with international problems of common interest. For one thing we did know: Fidel Castro was a hero to the masses in many Latin American nations. They saw him as a champion of the downtrodden and the enemy of the privileged who, in most of their countries, controlled both wealth and governments. His crimes and wrongdoings that so repelled the more informed peoples of the continent had little effect on the young, the peons, the underprivileged, and all others who wanted to see the example of revolution followed in their own nations.

* * *

Given these problems and the need for collective action to solve them, I decided by early 1960 that the time had arrived for a presidential journey to South America.

Recognizing the need for the trip was easy. Planning for it was no simple matter. To the south of us are many proud and sensitive peoples and governments. While it was manifestly impossible for me to visit each of these countries, I did hope, by following a well-laid-out itinerary, to make the entire continent feel that our interest extended to all of the Latin American republics. So I directed the State Department to make representations to Latin American ambassadors in Washington to the effect that I would hope that a restricted visit would not be interpreted merely as a desire to see and study sympathetically particular areas, but as an effort to pay my respects to all peoples of that vast region.

It was important to include Argentina and Chile in my itinerary because a visit to these two, lying at the southern limits of the continent, would reveal that I was not interested in a gesture or token journey but rather in a serious effort to learn. Naturally, I could not go to the two southernmost nations without stopping also in Brazil, the largest and most populous of all of the countries below the Rio Grande. It seemed, too, that if we were to stop at Rio de Janeiro and Buenos Aires, it would appear discourteous simply to overfly Uruguay, a friendly nation often praised for its democratic institutions. Finally, it seemed appropriate to visit our own Commonwealth of Puerto Rico, an island that since 1898 had been closely associated with our country and that since 1950 had nearly doubled its gross product, demonstrating the kind of economic progress I hoped to see begun in American nations farther south.

The travelogue aspects of the journey are soon told.[16] After a flight of nearly six hours from Puerto Rico, we arrived at the first stop in South America, the new inland capital of Brazil, named Brasilia. This handsome city, located six hundred miles from Rio, was the brainchild of President Juscelino Kubitschek, who was on hand to meet us at the airport.

With a horde of automobiles, jeeps, buses, and pickup and construction trucks in procession behind us, we drove the ten miles from the airport to the main intersection of the city for ceremonies on an improvised platform. The new buildings, many of them still empty, the enthusiasm of the parade, and the red mud reminded me of the historic fact that the United States' own young government, originally located in the established city of Philadelphia, had decided to build a new capital in a largely unoccupied area called the District of Columbia. Brasilia also called to mind the "boom town" spirit that had been so much part of the winning of the West in our own nation.

President Kubitschek, acting as guide, described the fundamental purpose of the new city. It was an ambitious project, he said, to induce the population of his nation to desert the feverishly crowded areas along the ocean and migrate into the central Brazilian plateau. This region, according to the President, had not only a much more salubrious and equitable climate than the damp coastal regions, but was blessed with such rich and fertile soil that the economy of the country, if this region were exploited, would leap forward, bringing about early and marked increase in living standards of the whole population.

The architecture of Brasilia is ultramodern. The exterior lines of the buildings seemed to me graceful and the basic construction unique, featuring use of cantilevers—great overhangs without visible support. Streets, roadways, and overpasses are constructed with the single purpose of promoting the flow of traffic and preventing congestion at any point.

Although later some of President Kubitschek's associates expressed to

[16] In addition to members of my own staff, I was accompanied by Secretary of State Herter, Assistant Secretary for Latin American Affairs Rubottom, and the citizen members of the Advisory Committee on Inter-American Affairs. These included my brother, Milton, former ambassador to Venezuela Walter J. Donnelly, Dr. G. Kenneth Holland, President of the Institute of International Education, O. A. Knight, a labor leader and authority on Latin American labor, Charles A. Meyer, a Vice President of Sears, Roebuck, and Dr. Dana G. Munro, Professor of International Studies at Princeton.

me much skepticism about the project and its chances of success, I agreed with his conviction that if a large part of Brazil's population could not be induced to settle and work in the huge central plateau, there was little to be done to make the Brazilian nation the powerful and prosperous country it could otherwise become.

Entering Rio de Janeiro the next day, we met crowds of spectacular size, estimated by the police at a million. Along a five-mile motorcade route, which took an hour to travel, people jammed the roadways and streets and filled office windows. Along the way I heard one band after another play "God Bless America," but it was less comforting to see a sign proclaiming: *We like Ike; We like Fidel too.*

The next morning we were up at dawn for a flight to the industrial center of São Paulo, and an eleven-mile open-car motorcade in pouring rain. From under their umbrellas hundreds of thousands of Paulistas threw sodden confetti and shrieked "Viva EEKE!" I was struck by the variety of the faces in the crowd—many Japanese, Germans, East Europeans, Negroes—the faces of immigrants who had poured into São Paulo from all over the globe to work in its booming industries. Soon I was addressing a luncheon of two thousand business and civic leaders.

On the way back to Rio, at the São Paulo airport, I had word of a shocking disaster: a United States Navy transport plane carrying members of the Navy Band who were then touring South America and were to play at a presidential reception in Rio that night, had collided with a Brazilian airliner. Sixty-one had died in the crash. Sadly, and as soon as possible, I went to the Miguel Conto Hospital to visit the three Navy men who had miraculously survived.

* * *

At 10:45 the next morning, February 26, my party touched down at the International Airport in Buenos Aires. At the foot of the ramp I shook hands with Arturo Frondizi, the President of Argentina.

In yet another motorcade later that day we headed for the Argentine National Congress, escorted by the Grenadier Guards, cantering along in crimson and blue uniforms trimmed with gold, giving a dashing aspect to the parade. This time the crowds stood not in drenching rain but in a broiling ninety-degree summer sun. Here for the first time we heard of some difficulty: it was reported that before my arrival supporters of the exiled Peron had exploded five bombs at different places around the city.

The next day I flew south for a brief visit to the seaside resort of Mar del Plata, where a million Argentinians warmly greeted the combined Argentine-U.S. party. As we prepared to leave from the Mar del Plata airport, President Frondizi expressed his enthusiasm for the beautiful presidential aircraft. I knew, of course, about the Latin American tradition that whenever a guest admires an object, the host must give it to him. Unhappily, however, the plane was not mine to give away. So I did the only thing possible: I invited President Frondizi to ride along to our next stop—the Andean resort city of San Carlos de Bariloche. He readily agreed. To make room for him, the crew had to throw off the suitcases of several staff members—baggage that turned out to contain their dinner clothes, without which they were unable to attend a formal dinner that evening.

The next morning, with Milton, Jim Hagerty, and Dr. Walter Tkach,[17] I went in search of land-locked salmon in a nearby mountain stream. They were water-locked, too—we had no success. We caught only a few small trout, which we threw back; and Milton provided the morning's entertainment by losing his balance and falling into the icy water.

The next morning, after a farewell to President Frondizi, we vaulted the Andes and came down in the third country of our visit, Chile, to be greeted by its intelligent and impressive President, Jorge Alessandri.

* * *

The next day, Tuesday, March 1, 1960, was crowded with interest.

Early that morning I received a long letter from the President of the Federation of Students of Chile, an organization claiming a membership of twenty-five thousand drawn from the country's seven major universities. The letter came right to the point: "Has the United States become a satisfied nation, one which fights for the maintenance of the prevailing order in the world and in Latin America? This dangerous image is becoming accepted more every day. If this is true, we must respectfully say to you that the United States will have little or nothing to offer the younger generation and the immense multitude of the poor, who compose 90 per cent of the Latin American population. And we will have little or nothing to expect from the guidance and genius of North America. . . .

". . . The United States apparently finds its best friends . . . to be those . . . to whom the prevailing order in this starved and illiterate America means the right to enjoy a standard of living which would be envied by the multimillionaires of the United States.

"But they are not the friends of the United States. They are the friends of their own privileges, which they aspire to identify with North American interests in order that they themselves may be supported by the United States."

[17] The assistant presidential physician.

This letter made its impression on me. I could not answer it immediately, for I was due within a few minutes at a nearby theater to address members of the American Embassy staff and of Santiago's Chilean-American societies. When I greeted the audience and began to talk, I could not put the students' letter out of my mind. So in the middle of my address I looked up from the typed script:

"This morning, I received a letter signed by some individuals who are officials in student bodies. They say they represent twenty-five thousand . . . university students.

"This was a letter speaking to me, or of me, in the most respectful and even affectionate terms, but telling about the tremendous errors they think [that I, as President of] the United States [am] making with respect to South America. It says that every bit of the work in the Organization of American States and similar organizations is all in favor of the rich nation, all in favor of the rich individual, is against the weak, whether it be a nation or an individual.

"Now I am not going to detail all of the things where they believe the United States is in error. I want to point this out: before individuals who do not carry great responsibilities in the world make decisions and spread information, or what they call information, we should be sure of our facts, we should read history carefully.

". . . these students happen to be the people that I am interested in more than any others in the world. The young people of today, with all of their opportunities for learning, the certainty that they are going to take over the responsibilities of government, of business, of the social order, and of education—these are the people in whom we must be interested.

"If the United States is to help, we must have some understanding between us. The United States had never, at the end of two World Wars and Korea, added an acre to its territory. We have sought no advantage anywhere, either as result of war or peaceful help, that would give us an advantage at the expense of others.

"We are not saints—we know we make mistakes, but our heart is in the right place, and we believe that aid given by the United States to the people who want to work, who welcome some help, who are energetically working for themselves to raise their standards of living, not merely for themselves as individuals but for every single individual in the nation, those are the people from which we get great satisfaction in helping."

That afternoon a second thing happened which I shall long remember. By helicopter we flew to San Gregorio, on the outskirts of Santiago, to see a new low-cost housing project under construction with American aid.

Here in this suburb the government had provided land, concrete foundations, and minimum utilities for about four thousand homes. But the people themselves were building the houses out of large varnished wooden blocks. On each concrete foundation, with washroom facilities in the center, two families would build. I took a close look at the blocks of wood, each of which was about a foot long and about four inches square in cross section. Each block was nailed to the others with long spikes. In response to my questions, I learned that this was an economical, new method of construction, one that produced a strong product. The people had finished about six hundred of their houses, and were working hard to complete the others before winter set in, in the month of June.

Under the blazing sun the children of the village crowded around, cheering and applauding. One man came up and pushed a big block in my direction: it was to go into his house and he wanted me to sign it. Almost immediately a dozen others came up with their unique "autograph books." The pride of the builders in their new homes was indescribable. Every face was shining.

That night I saw a huge crowd fill the Plaza de la Moneda, in front of the Presidential Palace. Bands and orchestras played, and hissing fireworks lit up the warm evening sky. It was good to see this festive demonstration. But my mind kept returning to both the evidences of ominous unrest I had seen and to the hope and promise in the faces of the men, women, and children building their own homes.

I could not at that time reveal what was shaping up in my mind—that the private and public capital which had flowed bounteously into Latin America had failed to benefit the masses, that the demand for social justice was still rising. But upon my return home I determined to begin planning, and the plans would culminate eventually in historic measures designed to bring about social reforms for the benefit of all the people of Latin America.

* * *

In Montevideo, Uruguay, where we touched down at two o'clock the next afternoon, I rode through the remaining traces of tear gas the police had used on a small crowd of demonstrators at one of the city's universities. The incident, involving perhaps a hundred agitators—some of whom threw tin cans off the roof of the school—was a slight thing amid the enthusiasm of hundreds of thousands of well-wishers who jammed the three-mile route of our motorcade. Indeed, all the Montevideo newspapers except the Communist press emphatically condemned the demonstration. But it was another reminder of a seething unrest not far beneath the surface.

The next day we flew back toward Puerto Rico, again a long trip, enlivened by the loss of an engine over the Amazon jungle that forced us to transfer to our follow-up plane when we landed at Paramaribo, Surinam.

I was fatigued. As I wrote Prime Minister Macmillan later that month: ". . . Frankly, no prior tour of mine in the past fifteen years has been so [physically] tiring as the one I [have just] completed in South America. The combination of dust, crowded days, and summer heat persuaded me that I'm not as young as I was when we were together in Algiers."

On the trip I had made thirty-seven addresses and toasts, including two nationwide telecasts. The effort had not been unproductive, at least as seen by our journalists. At the end of the trip, Tad Szulc, a *New York Times* reporter who had gone along, wrote that: "relations between the United States and South American lands appeared today to stand on the highest plateau since the end of World War II. . . ." The expedition, at least in the eyes of the press, was a real success.

* * *

In the messages I delivered I reminded Latin Americans of the fact that United States policy and actions in their region had no ulterior or narrowly selfish purposes. I hammered away on several themes:

One was the need for widely shared economic advance. "We wish, for every American nation," I said on my departure from the United States, "a rapid economic progress, with its blessings reaching *all the people.*"

The second was the need for a continuation of American aid, public and private, to Latin America. "I assure you that my government," I told the Brazilian Congress, "while honoring its commitments outside this hemisphere, is in no mood to allow its special responsibilities among the American states to go by default." In private conversations with the four Presidents I visited, I reminded them of the fact that if Latin America is to progress, it must attract increased private investment from overseas, a flow that is certain to dry up unless foreign investors believe that Castroism is to be repudiated by the nations of the Latin American continent. ("Give private capital the right conditions," I said in a toast to the President of Argentina, "and you can't keep it away.") Unhappily, not one of the four felt able, for local political reasons, to assert an all-out opposition to the Castro movement. None would admit that the happenings in Cuba were helping to block his country's economic advance, because of the reluctance of investors to come into any nation where they fear expropriation. The Presidents' comments were so similar as to appear coordinated in advance: "Castro, the revolutionary, has been a hero to our people; Castro, the political leader, has lost some of his prestige," apparently meaning that he was losing a measure of influence in their respective countries.

My third major topic was the need for peace. In addressing the Joint Session of the National Congress of Chile, I praised President Alessandri's imaginative plan for a reduction of armaments in Latin America. I observed that even partial success would release money for more useful purposes, help prevent inflation, and prevent competitive buildups of national armies and navies.

Another recurring subject in all my talks was a refutation of the charge that the United States favors imperialism and dictatorship.[18] (In fact, though the United States is not the cause, between 1953 and 1961 the number of Latin American dictators declined by two-thirds.) "We repudiate dictatorship in any form," I told an audience in Santiago, "right or left." I assured all I met that the United States believes in the right of all peoples to follow their destiny in their own way, and repeatedly I turned both the charges of colonialism and dictatorship against Castro and Communism.

I assured every audience that my country would not intervene in their local affairs. My Latin American hosts, like their neighbors and fellow citizens throughout the hemisphere, had by no means forgotten the earlier years of this century when the United States had intervened in Colombia, Panama, Nicaragua, Honduras, Haiti, the Dominican Republic, and Mexico; this was the period of United States gunboat diplomacy and, in their view, of American corporations' exploiting the "Banana Republics." Since the early 1930s intervention as an American policy had gone into the discard, replaced by the policy of the Good Neighbor.

I had upheld this traditional policy of non-intervention. At the same

[18] The charge, I declared, was a "blatant falsehood."

"In all history no nation has had a more honorable record in its dealings with other countries than has the United States.

"The Philippines are independent today—by their own choice.

"Alaska and Hawaii are now proud partners in our federated, democratic enterprise—by their own choice.

"Puerto Rico is a Commonwealth within the United States system—by its own choice."

And I said once more—it can hardly be repeated too often—that the United States, counter to almost all of recorded history, did not, following the last three wars, seek to permanently annex a single acre.

time, however, I urged upon all leaders the need for internal social reforms if United States assistance was to be truly useful. Moreover, I realized that the time seemed to be rapidly approaching when the United States would probably have to modify its historic reluctance to push officially for political and social changes within the countries to which it was supplying economic help. We would not only have to bring the American nations together in a collective effort to protect the hemisphere from Communist imperialism; we would also have to organize the same kind of collective action to end, within individual countries, traditions of economic injustice by which the rich continued to get richer and the poor poorer.[19]

* * *

In the months of 1960 following my trip to South America we pursued both these purposes.

On March 17, 1960, less than two weeks after my return from Puerto Rico, I ordered the Central Intelligence Agency to begin to organize the training of Cuban exiles, mainly in Guatemala, against a possible future day when they might return to their homeland. More specific planning was not possible because the Cubans living in exile had made no move to select from among their numbers a leader whom we could recognize as the head of a government-in-exile.

In trying to get other countries to work with us against Castro, we

[19] These two tasks were related. It is wrong, however, to see the drive toward a kind of new "collective intervention" for social progress as a reflex response to Castro and Communism. As far back as July 22, 1956, at the meeting of Presidents in Panama City, while Fidel Castro was still in training in Mexico, I had successfully proposed that each American President name a special representative to a group which would recommend ways to make the Organization of American States more effective "in those fields of cooperative effort that affect the welfare of the individual." This group, I said, should make "practical suggestions in the economic, financial, social, and technical fields." In 1958 Milton returned from his trip to Central America convinced of the urgent need for low-cost private housing, health facilities, better education, and land reform on a grand scale throughout Latin America. In February of 1959, the month after Castro seized power, the United States presented to the Committee of Twenty-One of the OAS suggestions for increasing credit, improving development planning, expanding foreign trade, and financing low-cost housing. We made plain our dislike of all dictators—Richard Nixon and my brother both suggested that our distinction between dictatorships and democratic governments should mean "a formal handshake for one, an *abrazo* [embrace] for the other."

At Caracas in 1954 the American states declared their solidarity and their opposition to international Communist intervention. In 1959 in Santiago the American foreign ministers reaffirmed their joint determination to protect democratic institutions in this hemisphere.

confronted still a further problem—the fact that most of his Latin American neighbors considered him less of a threat than the Dominican Republic's Generalissimo Rafael Leonidas Trujillo Molina, who at sixty-eight, after a thirty-year rule, could claim the undisputed title of "oldest surviving one-man dictatorship." *"El Jefe,"* as his three million subjects knew him, boasted efficient secret police with an extensive record of mysterious deaths and disappearances. Both Castro and Romulo Betancourt, the influential reformed ex-Communist President of Venezuela, had unsuccessfully tried to unseat Trujillo through invasions in 1959. In January of 1960 Trujillo smashed another plot against him, imprisoning more than a thousand people. By May, intelligence reports told me, the life expectancy of the Trujillo regime once again appeared uncertain. Trujillo had begun to attack Dominicans associated with the Catholic Church.

"This kind of attack," I remarked on hearing the report, "is usually the last desperate resort of a dictator." But we knew that until the American nations made some effective move together against Trujillo, they would do nothing against Castro—a far more menacing presence in the hemisphere.

On June 8 after a four-month investigation, an Inter-American Peace Commission—an arm of the OAS—declared Trujillo's regime guilty of "flagrant and widespread violations" of human rights. Two days later Secretary Herter reported the possibility of a coup in the Dominican Republic, which could lead to the establishment of a provisional government.

"If such a government takes over," I answered, "we should recognize it quickly. Then, if necessary, we could move in troops at its request."

Meanwhile, Castro himself was becoming more and more of a problem. Che Guevara, now the economic power in Cuba, announced the State would own and operate all industry. José Miro Cardona broke with Castro and sought asylum in the Argentine Embassy in Havana. The possibility that Cuba's government might definitely become a Communist satellite, though still discounted by most of my advisers, was disturbing. I remarked in one meeting that if the Soviet Union had the temerity to make a mutual security treaty with Cuba, we would have a sitation that the United States could not tolerate.

The CIA now started to build a fifty-kilowatt radio station on Swan Island, 110 miles off the coast of Honduras and four hundred miles southwest of Cuba, a station which, when completed, could cover the whole Caribbean area at night. "This new station," Allen Dulles said, "will first attack Trujillo and then Castro."

It continued to be difficult, however, to get a consensus among the

American governments as to the true significance of Castro's various actions. President Betancourt, of Venezuela, for example, opposed a number of Castro's policies but, as he told Cuba Foreign Minister Raul Roa, he would be the first to help defend Cuba against foreign intervention.[20] This meant that if we brought charges against Cuba in the OAS before that organization declared itself against Trujillo, Venezuela would line up in defense of Castro.

But in the meantime, there were moves we could make. It was silly, for example, to continue to give Cuba favored treatment regarding its sugar exports. Therefore, on July 6, 1960, I signed legislation authorizing presidential action to fix the quota on Cuban sugar imported in the United States until March 31, 1961. A proclamation was issued cutting the 1960 quota by 700,000 short tons. (Later I set the quota for the first three months of 1961 at zero.) "This action," I remarked on the day I signed, "amounts to economic sanctions against Cuba. Now we must look ahead to other moves—economic, diplomatic, strategic."[21]

But before we could intervene, we would first have to prove to the Organization of American States, beyond any shadow of doubt, that Cuba had become a Communist base; otherwise, resentment at "arrogant intervention" could lead to serious difficulties for us in Latin America. It was certain that public opinion in the Americas would not condemn Castro until we had moved against Trujillo who, in July, was accused of attempting the assassination of President Betancourt. The attempt took place on a Caracas street when an automobile full of explosives was detonated as the President's car was passing. Only a closed rear window saved Betancourt's life; the riders in the front seat, with open windows, were killed.

Manifestly our hands were tied until we knew for certain that a Castro-type would not succeed Trujillo, and this was difficult to determine in a nation that had for so many years lived under absolute, ruthless dictatorship. We continued, however, to keep emergency plans for Cuba ready. These included such possibilities as blockade, military action, and joint action with Latin American countries.

[20] Interestingly, as time passed, Betancourt became Castro's bitterest critic and foe. Indeed, Betancourt helped persuade other Latin American countries to withdraw recognition from Cuba and to eliminate trade and travel to the island.

[21] The law, incidentally, required that, to replace the sugar from Cuba, the United States purchase additional sugar from Trujillo's Dominican Republic. I was concerned about reports I had heard of bribes coming into the United States to influence the government to buy Dominican Republic sugar, and I did everything in my power to counter this unwise provision.

* * *

On the day I signed the proclamation reducing imports of Cuban sugar, I met with foreign policy advisers to discuss a new aid policy for Latin America. Because of the unrest and the situations in both Cuba and the Dominican Republic, the flow of private investment to Latin America had slowed considerably. One remedy, Douglas Dillon said, was to ask the Congress to authorize an increase in the capital of the Inter-American Development Bank, primarily to support "economic and social projects." Among other things, he said, we should include in our recommendation to the Congress a provision for land reform.[22]

This appealed to me, and I approved immediately. We had to find all possible means to show Latin America that the United States wanted to raise the standard of living of *all* her peoples. The letter I had received in Santiago from the Chilean students had left its impact on me.

Four days later, on July 11, in Newport, Rhode Island, I began a press conference by announcing our future course of action—a course which included both cooperation against dictatorships and cooperation for economic and social progress.

* * *

During the next two months, we continued to get significant reports out of the Caribbean. On July 9, Khrushchev had threatened to use rockets to protect Cuba against a military attack by the United States, a threat that we dismissed. But in the middle of July, Allen Dulles said to me: "As you know, Khrushchev has publicly ridiculed the idea that the Soviet Union would ever put missiles in Cuba when he can launch them from the Soviet Union. But recently a number of large unidentified packages have been brought into Cuba, and one military base has been put off bounds. It may be that the Soviets are putting up a short-range missile base somewhere on the island. We're watching carefully to see what they are doing."

All through the summer the CIA kept watching, but no solid evidence was obtained that the Russians were transporting any major military items to Cuba. However, our Army attaché in Havana had gotten hold of photographs of Czech semi-automatic rifles in the hands of Cuban

[22] On April 20, 1960, Secretary Herter, in an address at the Pan American Union, had foreshadowed this sharp change in American policy we had been formulating when he pointed out that the problem of land distribution now demanded the attention of all the American nations.

soldiers. These photographs, for the first time, confirmed reports of the entry of Communist arms into Cuba.

We had reports that Castro was not well, that he was increasingly nervous and susceptible to lapses of memory. We continued to hear of Dominican agents lurking in Venezuela with a determination to assassinate Betancourt. And my reaction to Trujillo's "resignation"—when he installed Vice President Joaquin Balaguer in the Presidency but retained power in his own hands—was "Whom does he think he is fooling?"

* * *

Constantly before us was the question of what could be done about the revolutionary ferment in the world. We knew, for example, that we could not indefinitely support governments that refused to carry out land and social reforms. We needed new policies that would reach the seat of the trouble, the seething unrest of the people, but without causing bloodshed and more suppression. One suggestion was that perhaps we should try to raise the pay of teachers and start hundreds of vocational schools in underdeveloped countries. The productive nations, I said, "had to disabuse ourselves of some old ideas if we are to keep the Free World from going up in flames"—specifically the idea that we could remain aloof from the blaze and retain, at the same time, both prosperity and security for ourselves.

By August 8 Under Secretary Dillon's group had finished working out the details of the new program. I asked the Congress to authorize the expenditure of $600 million in Latin America in addition to the amount then estimated for mutual security. Of this, $100 million would go for earthquake rehabilitation in Chile.[23] The remaining half billion would go for "projects designed to contribute to opportunities for a better way of life for the individual citizens of the countries of Latin America." We wanted in particular to help our Latin American neighbors to accelerate their projects to improve land settlement and use; housing; vocational, technical, and scientific training; and such public facilities as water and sewer systems.

Testifying before the Senate Foreign Relations Committee a week later, Dillon gave the reasons for this new program: the density of the populations, the low base from which Latin American economic growth was beginning to rise, the "far from equitable" distribution of incomes, and the "outdated economic, legal, and social institutions" which had

[23] A series of earthquakes in late May had left more than 2000 dead and 2 million homeless and caused property damage of more than $300 million.

impeded the area's progress. He asked the Congress to make the authorization so that at a forthcoming meeting of an OAS group at Bogota, Colombia, the United States could say that we were ready to cooperate, with not less than half a billion dollars. Acting in record time, the Congress passed the authorization (Public Law 86-735) on September 8.

Meanwhile, on August 20—in response to United States leadership—the American foreign ministers, meeting in San José, Costa Rica, passed a resolution condemning the Dominican government's actions against Venezuela—including the attempt to assassinate Betancourt—and calling on all members of the OAS to break diplomatic relations with the Dominican Republic and to impose a partial economic blockade, beginning with a blockade on the shipment of arms. The vote was 19–0, with the Dominican Republic and Venezuela abstaining. (In accordance with this resolution, I asked the Congress to cut most of the Dominican Republic's sugar quota. Three days later we broke diplomatic ties with Trujillo. These moves contributed to the downfall of his dictatorship.)

At the same conference, after reports that Castro had been trying to bribe delegates to the meeting and that several of them were taking a weak-kneed stand against Castroism, the foreign ministers agreed on a Declaration of San José. This farsighted indictment condemned "emphatically the intervention or the threat of intervention . . . from an extra continental power in the affairs of the American republics. . . . Rejects, also, the attempt of the Sino-Soviet powers to make use of the political, economic, or social situation of any American state. . . . [and] Reaffirms that the inter-American system is incompatible with any form of totalitarianism." Though this declaration did not mention Cuba by name, and though the Mexican delegate claimed that no one intended in these words to offend Fidel Castro, anyone who could read could see in it a clear indictment of the Cuban regime,[24] an indictment that echoed the earlier condemnation of Trujillo.

On September 5, 1960, the Special Committee for Economic Cooperation met in Bogota, Colombia. Douglas Dillon announced the change which we hoped it would bring about: "To our steadily increasing programs of economic development we must add the new and broad dimension of social development in a conscious and determined effort to further social justice in our hemisphere. . . . We must bring fresh hope to the less privileged people who make up such a large proportion of the population in many of the countries of Latin America. . . . We must

[24] As soon as the Declaration was approved, the Cuban delegation walked out of the meeting and left for Havana.

help them to acquire ownership of the land and the means for its productive use. . . .

". . . The task is nothing less than to lift whole segments of the population into the twentieth century."

On September 13 the OAS Special Committee (Cuba dissenting) adopted the historic Act of Bogota. This specified cooperative measures for the improvement of land, of housing and community facilities, educational systems, tax reform, and public health facilities. For the first time the delegates declared their recognition "that the preservation and strengthening of free and democratic institutions in the American republics" required the speeding up of social and economic progress in Latin America. "Non-intervention" had given way to a new idea—the idea that *all* American nations had an interest in ending feudalism, the vast hereditary gulf between rich and poor, the system that assured to a handful of families opulence without labor and condemned millions to near-starvation without opportunity.

Thus was launched a new program for inter-American cooperation which the succeeding administration enthusiastically carried on, giving it a bright and dramatic new label. On March 13, 1961, at a White House reception, President Kennedy called "on all the people of the hemisphere to join in a new Alliance for Progress . . . to satisfy the basic needs of American people for homes, work and land, health and schools." Later that year, in a meeting at Punta del Este, Uruguay, the countries of the Americas committed themselves to such an alliance, setting specific goals. The delegates saw this as a ten-year, $100 billion undertaking; and the United States committed itself to "provide a major part of the minimum of $20 billion, principally in public funds, which Latin America will require for the next ten years from all external sources in order to supplement its own efforts." This meant that our country essentially guaranteed on an average a total annual flow to Latin America of $2 billion, in private and public funds.

The Alliance for Progress carries forward the progressive departure from the traditional American doctrine which we began as early as 1957 and carried on intensively upon my return from Latin America. In my judgment the basic concepts and the agreements in the Act of Bogota are right. Whether the noble purposes proclaimed there will be realized, only the Latin American nations themselves can determine, for only they can change their tax, land, and other laws, and only they can foster widespread educational opportunities, health facilities, and an expanding economy.

If Latin American nations do abide by their commitments, our assistance, as promised at Punta del Este, should be generous.

BOOK SIX

The generating force behind a successful United Nations must be the noble idea that a true international community can build a peace with justice if only people will work together patiently in an atmosphere of open trust.

In urging progress toward a world community, I cite the American concept of the destiny of a progressive society. Here in this land, in what was once a wilderness we have generated a society and a civilization drawn from many sources. Yet out of the mixture of many peoples and faiths we have developed unity in freedom—a unity designed to protect the rights of each individual while enhancing the freedom and well-being of all.

This concept of unity in freedom, drawn from the diversity of many racial strains and cultures, we would like to see made a reality for all mankind. This concept should apply within every nation as it does among nations. We believe that the right of every man to participate through his or her vote in self-government is as precious as the right of each nation here represented to vote its own convictions in this Assembly. I should like to see a universal plebiscite in which every individual in the world would be given the opportunity freely and secretly to answer this question: Do you want this right? Opposed to the idea of two hostile, embittered worlds in perpetual conflict, we envisage a single world community, as yet unrealized but advancing steadily toward fulfillment through our plans, our efforts, and our collective ideas.

Thus we see as our goal, not a super-state above nations, but a world community embracing them all, rooted in law and justice and enhancing the potentialities and common purposes of all peoples.

—Address before the 15th
General Assembly of the
United Nations, September 22, 1960

BOOK SIX

CHAPTER XXIII

The Summit That Never Was

For a man by nothing is so well bewrayed,
As by his manners.

—*Edmund Spenser*

FROM the autumn of 1959 to the spring of 1960 most people of the Western world felt that a slight but discernible thaw was developing in the icy tensions which had become normal between the West and the Soviet Union. This impression resulted partially from Mr. Khrushchev's agreement at Camp David to remove his threat to end the presence of Allied forces in West Berlin. His action made it possible for the Western nations in December to agree to attend a summit meeting without sacrifice of self-respect and under no hint of blackmail. Plans for a spring conference began with a place and date: Paris, in mid-May of 1960.

That meeting at the summit was never to be held.

* * *

On the afternoon of May 1, 1960, General Goodpaster telephoned me: "One of our reconnaissance planes," he said, "on a scheduled flight from its base in Adana, Turkey, is overdue and possibly lost." I knew instantly that this was one of our U-2 planes, probably over Russia. Early the next morning he came into my office, his face an etching of bad news. He plunged to the point at once. "Mr. President, I have received word from the CIA that the U-2 reconnaissance plane I mentioned yesterday is still missing. The pilot reported an engine flameout at a position about thirteen hundred miles inside Russia and has not been heard from since. With the amount of fuel he had on board, there is not a chance of his still being aloft."

* * *

The U-2 reconnaissance program had been born of necessity. In the middle fifties the United States found itself, an open society, faced by a closed Communist empire which had lost none of its ambitions for world conquest, but which now possessed, in airplanes and guided missiles armed with nuclear weapons, an ever-growing capacity for launching surprise attacks against the United States. As long as the Communist empire remained closed, this capability would become ever more dangerous. It could grow without our knowledge; it could mobilize for instantaneous attack; at the very least its hierarchy could continue to attempt blackmail campaigns, boasting of a nuclear strength and delivery capability out of all proportion to that which actually existed.

To anyone bearing responsibility for the security of the United States, the situation was highly unsatisfactory. When I had submitted the "Open Skies" proposal at Geneva in 1955 we knew that, if taken seriously and agreed to by the Soviets, it would have done much to reduce this danger to the United States and the chances of a global war. The Soviets were unwilling to present to the world this valid evidence of a desire for the peace they professed to want. The proposal was never even seriously considered.

Obviously we had to have accurate intelligence. In the circumstances Allen Dulles believed that the answer was a new type of aircraft being built specifically for high-altitude reconnaissance missions.

Back in November of 1954, Foster Dulles, Charlie Wilson, Allen Dulles, and other advisers had come to see me to get authorization to go ahead on a program to produce thirty special high-performance aircraft at a total cost of about $35 million. A good deal of design and development work had already been done. I approved this action.

"Go ahead and get the equipment," I said, "but before initiating operations come in to let me have one last look at the plans."

Foster agreed with the decision.

"Of course difficulties might arise out of these operations," he said, "but we can live through them."

Secrecy was of the essence. Any leak of information either at home or abroad could compel abandonment of the entire idea. Consequently, all conferences affecting it were held only at the highest level; even the manufacture and assembly of the plane were so conducted as to minimize the chances that its intended purpose might be exposed to public gaze. Within the White House itself, according to my recollection, the only persons aware of the existence of these planes were General Goodpaster, Gordon Gray, and, somewhat later, Goodpaster's principal assistant, my son. The small consultative group I assembled had as its members the Secretary of State, the Secretary of Defense, the Chairman of the Joint Chiefs of Staff, the Director of the Central Intelligence Agency and one of his special and trusted assistants, Mr. Richard Bissell.

The importance of the effort at that time cannot be overemphasized. Our relative position in intelligence, compared to that of the Soviets, could scarcely have been worse. The Soviets enjoyed practically unimpeded access to information of a kind in which we were almost wholly lacking. For example, some years earlier a book had been published by a member of the Atomic Energy Commission giving detailed descriptions and locations of several of our most important nuclear establishments. At almost every book store in important cities accurate maps of important bridges, industrial establishments, highways, and railroad centers in the locality were available to any traveler in the country. No so in the Soviet Union, a region in which information of this kind was known only to a selected few, and to no foreigners. On top of this we knew that the Soviets maintained in America an active and comprehensive spy system from which there was constantly pouring into the Kremlin information of the kind that in the event of war might be decisive. Considering all these things, I approved the recommendation of the intelligence chief that he employ the U-2 reconnaissance planes over Soviet territory.

The U-2 was more of a flying glider than a conventional airplane. So large were the wings and so light the construction that wheels were provided for the wingtips to prevent them from dragging on the ground on landing and taxiing. Several characteristics made the U-2 an almost ideal craft for its purpose: It was constructed in such a unique configuration that there was little chance of its being mistaken for a bomber; it was capable of carrying heavy camera equipment to altitudes well in excess of sixty thousand feet, high enough to be safe from any known Soviet fighter interceptors. Proof of the plane's capacity to produce photography of excellent definition was striking. I was shown photographs, taken from an altitude of seventy thousand feet, of some of our important cities. On these we could easily count the automobiles on the streets and even the lines marking the parking areas for individual cars. There was no doubt about the quality of the information to be obtained.

We then tested the probability of the U-2s being discovered by the Soviets as it flew over the territory of that nation. So, a number of test flights were made over our own country. Even though our radar systems had been warned of strange airplanes flying over our national territory, the U-2 flights were either unseen or were tracked imperfectly. This gave us confidence that, in the then-existing state of radar efficiency and the inability of fighter planes to operate at altitudes above some fifty thousand feet, U-2 reconnaissance could be undertaken with reasonable safety.

A final important characteristic of the plane was its fragile construction. This led to the assumption (insisted upon by the CIA and the Joint Chiefs) that in the event of mishap the plane would virtually disintegrate. It would be impossible, if things should go wrong, they said, for the Soviets to come in possession of the equipment intact—or, unfortunately, of a live pilot. This was a cruel assumption, but I was assured that the young pilots undertaking these missions were doing so with their eyes wide open and motivated by a high degree of patriotism, a swashbuckling bravado, and certain material inducements.

The U-2 reconnaissance flights began in 1956. They were flown intermittently and infrequently because of the exacting requirements for nearly perfect weather, which thus afforded only a few operational days a month, and then only in favorable seasons. Each series of intrusions was planned and executed with my knowledge and permission, in the full awareness of the stern diplomatic consequences we would face if a combination of events should go wrong.

During the years since World War II, the electronics industries of all nations were (and are) making tremendous progress in perfecting radar equipment and techniques. Almost from the very beginning, we learned that the Soviets knew of the flights and had from time to time made partial radar tracks of the courses flown. Moreover, in both the Soviet nation and ours, intensive work was going ahead on improving defensive rockets—types designed to knock down planes flying beyond the range of antiaircraft guns and interceptors. Knowing of these developments, each time a new series of flights was proposed, we held a closed meeting to determine whether or not new information on developing technology might indicate the unwisdom of proceeding as before.

Of those concerned, I was the only principal who consistently expressed a conviction that if ever one of the planes fell in Soviet territory a wave of excitement mounting almost to panic would sweep the world, inspired by the standard Soviet claim of injustice, unfairness, aggression, and ruthlessness. The others, except for my own immediate staff and Mr. Bissell, disagreed. Secretary Dulles, for instance, would say laughingly, "If the Soviets ever capture one of these planes, I'm sure they will never admit it. To do so would make it necessary for them to admit also that for years we had been carrying on flights over their territory while they, the Soviets, had been helpless to do anything about the matter." We knew that on a number of occasions Soviet fighters scrambled from nearby air bases to attempt an interception, but they could never come close enough to damage a U-2; probably the pilots never even saw one of these attempts. However, I said that while I wholeheartedly approved continuation of the program, I was convinced that in the event of accident we must be prepared for a storm of protest, not only from the Soviets but from many people, especially from some politicians in our own country. There would never be a good time for a failure.

But, with a record of many successful flights behind us, the intelligence people became more and more confident that the outcome of each future venture was almost a certainty. Furthermore, the information obtained was important.[1] So when a spring program for 1960 was proposed, I again approved. All of these things were clear in my memory as Goodpaster finished his climactic report to me the morning of May 2.

* * *

There was, to be sure, reason for deep concern and sadness over the probable loss of the pilot, but not for immediate alarm about the equipment. I had been assured that if a plane were to go down it would be destroyed either in the air or on impact, so that proof of espionage would be lacking. Self-destroying mechanisms were built in.

Beyond this there was the possibility that Foster Dulles' judgment might prove right: Khrushchev, unwilling to admit that United States planes had been for years penetrating deep into his territory, might suppress the facts. We knew, for example, that he was aware of a similar flight that had traversed Soviet territory on the 9th of April; for his own reasons, he had said nothing of it.

There being nothing further to do about it that May morning, I asked General Goodpaster to keep me informed and continued with my daily schedule. I addressed the United States Chamber of Commerce, dedicated windows in the Washington National Cathedral commemorating pioneers of the labor movement, and, in the evening, attended a dinner sponsored by the Committee for National Economic Growth and the Committee to Strengthen the Frontiers of Freedom. The day ended with a brief stop by Mamie and me in the East Room of the White House,

[1] During the four years of its operations, the U-2 program produced intelligence of critical importance to the United States. Perhaps as important as the positive information—what the Soviets *did* have—was the negative information it produced—what the Soviets *did not* have. Intelligence gained from this source provided proof that the horrors of the alleged "bomber gap" and the later "missile gap" were nothing more than imaginative creations of irresponsibility. U-2 information deprived Khrushchev of the most powerful weapon of the Communist conspiracy—international blackmail—usable only as long as the Soviets could exploit the ignorance and resulting fears of the Free World.

where we were giving a party for a group of friends of John and Barbara. The next morning I departed for Fort Benning to witness a firing exhibition of the Army's newest weapons.

Nearly two days after Goodpaster's first report went by without a word reaching me from any source as to the fate of the missing pilot. While I was on the way to Fort Benning, the National Aeronautics and Space Administration, acting in good faith, put out a statement that one of its weather reconnaissance planes was missing.[2]

Then, on May 5, while I was attending a meeting of the National Security Council, we learned of the Soviet reaction. Early in the meeting, Allen Dulles reported on the first portion of a current speech by Khrushchev before the Supreme Soviet, in which he made lavish promises to the Russian people—less work and lower taxes, for example. The remainder of the speech text had been coming in on the wires when Mr. Dulles had left for the Council meeting, but he thought a tough statement of some kind regarding the United States and the summit was the next item. At this point, General Goodpaster, with the missing U-2 very much on his mind, got up and left the meeting to arrange for the complete text to be sent to us by secret teletype.

The text arrived just as the meeting ended. Khrushchev had announced the shooting down of a United States reconnaissance plane that had penetrated deep into Soviet territory. The theory that Khrushchev would never admit such an occurrence was demolished.

[2] "A NASA U-2 research airplane, being flown in Turkey on a joint NASA-USAF Air Weather Service mission, apparently went down in the Lake Van, Turkey, area at about 9:00 A.M. (3:00 A.M. E.D.T.), Sunday, May 1.

"During the flight in southeast Turkey, the pilot reported over the emergency frequency that he was experiencing oxygen difficulties. The flight originated in Adana with a mission to obtain data on clear air turbulence.

"A search is now under way in the Lake Van area.

"The pilot is an employee of Lockheed Aircraft under contract to NASA.

"The U-2 program was initiated by NASA in 1956 as a method of making high-altitude weather studies."

A major problem in pursuing a program such as the U-2 was that of maintaining secrecy in the field. Although the existence of the plane itself could not be fully concealed, its major mission could be. The Reconnaissance Detachment performing these reconnaissance missions was assigned to NASA and flew weather missions for that organization, but NASA was purposely kept in the dark as to the unit's intelligence activities. The NASA information officer who gave out this statement was telling the truth as he knew it.

* * *

I asked the senior officials of the State Department, the Department of Defense, and the CIA—only those concerned with U-2 operations—to remain behind to consider the situation that now faced us. To avoid confusion it was advisable that any public information on the subject should be given out by one agency of the government only, in this case the State Department. For the moment the White House was to stay aloof from the incident.

When an immediate statement was suggested I voiced serious doubts. My belief was that enough had been said in the NASA release and we should now remain silent until we knew what Khrushchev's follow-up was to be. However, it was the unanimous advice of the others present that a statement should be made without delay; otherwise it was felt the "explanation" would lose credibility. I accepted the recommendations of my associates and instructed Acting Secretary Dillon to have the State Department prepare immediately an appropriate statement harmonious with the previously designed "cover story."[3] As for the White House position, I instructed Jim Hagerty to tell the press that I had directed a complete inquiry, the results of which would be made public by the Department of State and NASA. Meanwhile, I directed General Twining to suspend temporarily peripheral electromagnetic reconnaissance by our RB-47s and other military craft, routinely conducted by the Air Force and the Navy.[4] The next day the U.S. ambassador in Moscow gave the Soviet government a note requesting full facts of the Soviet investigation into the U-2 incident, to include information on the fate of the pilot.

On that afternoon, Friday, May 6, Mr. Khrushchev, appearing before the Supreme Soviet once more, announced what to me was unbelievable.

[3] "The Department has been informed by NASA that, as announced May 3, an unarmed plane, a U-2 weather research plane based at Adana, Turkey, piloted by a civilian has been missing since May 1. During the flight of this plane, the pilot reported difficulty with his oxygen equipment. Mr. Khrushchev has announced that a U.S. plane has been shot down over the U.S.S.R. on that date. It may be that this was the missing plane. It is entirely possible that having failure in the oxygen equipment, which could result in the pilot losing consciousness, the plane continued on automatic pilot for a considerable distance and accidentally violated Soviet airspace. The United States is taking this matter up with the Soviet Government, with particular reference to the fate of the pilot."

[4] This instruction, which later leaked to the press, was confused in many minds first as constituting a cessation of U-2 flights, and further an admission that the U-2 flights had been conducted by the military. This was totally untrue; General Twining had nothing to do with the operation of the U-2. There was no need to suspend U-2 flights because further series was scheduled or approved.

The uninjured pilot of our reconnaissance plane, along with much of his equipment intact, was in Soviet hands. Francis Gary Powers, the pilot, had confessed to those aspects of the flight that were obvious from the evidence and thus the world was aware that his mission had been to penetrate deeply into the Soviet Union. Pictures of Powers were made public and parts of the reconnaissance airplane were put on display. (As a mildly ridiculous sidelight, Mr. Khrushchev had, even though the authentic evidence was available, presumably on its way to Moscow, initially displayed wreckage of what was obviously another airplane.)

At home, and abroad, reaction was mixed. Some Americans seemed to receive the revelation with a sense of relief. One columnist, a habitual pessimist, entitled his column for the day, "The Wonderful News," in elation over the fact that the United States had been able to conduct such reconnaissance missions with impunity over Soviet territory for so long. Others greeted Khrushchev's belligerent manner with heavy resentment. A few were fearful that his rage could touch off general war. Still others began debating the wisdom of going ahead with the scheduled summit.

The State Department put out a statement pointing out the necessity for intelligence-collecting activities, but still lamely adhering to the cover story. This I thought might prove to be a mistake, but Mr. Herter felt it important to proceed in such fashion as to afford Khrushchev an "out" in the event that he desired to minimize the whole affair.

The next morning Secretary Herter called me again, this time to recommend a statement admitting the essential truth of the Soviet allegations. It would, on the part of the administration, disclose the fact that I had directed information-gathering by every possible means to protect the United States and the Free World against surprise attack. Several of my colleagues emphasized—and I fully agreed—that any statement should be utterly and meticulously accurate. I approved a draft after changing some of the wording to eliminate any phrase that seemed to me to be defensive in tone.[5] I felt anything but apologetic.

My acknowledgment of responsibility for espionage activities was practically unprecedented in history, but so were the circumstances. Francis Gary Powers was no individual traveler sneaking across borders between

[5] "Under these directives, programs have been developed and put into operation which have included extensive aerial surveillance by unarmed civilian aircraft, normally of a peripheral character but on occasion by penetration."

The State Department statement added that specific missions had not been subject to presidential authorization, which meant that I had not ordered the single flight in question. I had approved the reconnaissance of broad areas of the Soviet Union within a time period of certain weeks.

guards and living in concealed garrets in the land of a potential enemy; Powers had been apprehended thirteen hundred miles within Soviet territory, flying a piece of expensive machinery, equipped with the most intricate sets of cameras and data-gathering material available. In the diplomatic field it was routine practice to deny responsibility for an embarrassing occurrence when there is even a 1 per cent chance of being believed, but when the world can entertain not the slightest doubt of the facts there is no point in trying to evade the issue.

Furthermore, it seemed to me that Mr. Khrushchev's outbursts were hypnotizing the world with a passionate but highly distorted presentation of one particular phase of international espionage. His government had been so notoriously involved in spying, especially in the United States, as to dwarf our activities, but by separating this particular type of espionage from all others he hoped to make convincing his charge of "warmongering." To claim that because the equipment employed was an airplane with a camera, and therefore provocative of war, was plain silly, and I felt it necessary that the matter be put in perspective.[6]

The real issue at stake was not the fact that both sides conducted intelligence activities, but rather that the conduct and announced intentions of the Communists created the necessity for such clandestine maneuvers. As a consequence, the West—more specifically the United States as the major military power of the West—had to maintain constantly the capacity to detect any possible prelude to an infinitely more destructive Pearl Harbor.

At a White House meeting later that day, May 9, I brought up the U-2 incident as the first order of business. There was nothing for the moment requiring new instructions—all of the actions had been taken. However, I thought it well to review the events surrounding the U-2 incident and the nature of the storm it had created. This I did, and advised the group that Allen Dulles was meeting that afternoon with congressional leaders to explain our reconnaissance work "fully but without apology." I reviewed the long and successful history of the flights, and a few reasons for my unequivocal acceptance of personal responsibility for the over-all conduct of the U-2 program. Also, to set their minds at ease, I assured them that all the "principals" involved were unanimous in their conviction that the program "has provided us a volume of indispensable information."

[6] Espionage was distasteful but vital. And, as I remarked later to the group of bipartisan congressional leaders, the decision was mine. One had to weigh the risks, keep the knowledge in as few hands as possible, and accept the consequences if something went wrong. There is no glory in this business, if it *is* successful, it cannot be told.

Turning to the future, I specified that there should be one department only within the government authorized to speak on the U-2 incident: the State Department. No one else was to comment.[7] I anticipated, correctly I believe, that any statements by others would inevitably contain minor discrepancies, which the press would dissect. "We will now just have to endure the storm," I said, with everyone fully realizing that it was I personally—and rightly so—who would do the enduring.

* * *

In the midst of all this turbulence, it was necessary to avoid losing sight of the next immediate issue: the effect of the U-2 on prospects for success at the forthcoming summit meeting in Paris. On the question of the advisability of my attending a meeting where Mr. Khrushchev would be present, I told the Secretary of State that I had no intention of changing my plans. The only developments that could prevent my attending would be information that the meeting was to be canceled or that Mr. Khrushchev would not be present.

We knew that at such a summit there would be no sign, even on the surface, of geniality. In a sense this was advantageous; there would be no necessity to try to conceal, under a false cloak of camaraderie, the sharply conflicting views both sides held about the major problems of the cold war. For me, the attendance had become a duty. It might prove unpleasant, but I had no intention of evading it. Indeed, I welcomed the opportunity to uncover more Soviet hypocrisy.

On May 14, 1960, I started for Paris.

Before my departure, I informed the appropriate agencies that U-2 flights over Soviet territory would not be resumed. For this there were two reasons, one fairly obvious, the other less so: the first being that in view of the rapid advances in ground-to-air rocketry and radar efficiency the U-2 was probably no longer a reliable plane to use for this purpose. The second was that considerable progress was now being made in photography of the earth from satellites. At the same time, a few of my associates (and certain members of Congress) were recommending that I punish, either by reprimand or dismissal, selected officials who had been closely engaged in the U-2 operations. The thought was that such action would provide at least an implication that the flights had taken place

[7] It was reported to me that there soon broke out a rash of Washington cocktail party conversationalists who had been on the "inside" and had "known" about the U-2 before it fell. This had its funny side—but the talk, at times, was misleading.

without my authorization or possibly even without my knowledge—that I had been a victim of overzealous subordinates.

This argument I could not see. To deny my own part in the entire affair would have been a declaration that portions of the government of the United States were operating irresponsibly, in complete disregard of proper presidential control. And it would have been untrue. Moreover, to enter a conference with Khrushchev when he could refer in pity to my "inability" to control important matters in our government and scornfully dismiss any argument of mine on the ground that obviously I could not speak authoritatively for my government was out of the question. Finally, to pretend, by taking punitive action against subordinates—when all involved in the operation well knew of my personal approval—would have been to do a glaring and permanent injustice to whatever person or persons could have been designated as guilty. I rejected the whole notion out of hand.

* * *

We landed at Orly Airport near Paris on the morning of the 15th.

Not long after arrival, I learned from Prime Minister Macmillan, who had reached Paris ahead of us, that he was in receipt of a message from Khrushchev which was apparently a copy of one sent to President de Gaulle, the chairman of the planned conference.

The message, after reciting in extended fashion the feelings of outrage and resentment experienced by the Soviet government and its entire people at the effrontery of the United States government in authorizing flights over Soviet territory, laid down conditions that would have to be complied with by me before Chairman Khrushchev would attend the summit meeting. The first of these conditions was that I should denounce the U-2 flights as acts of inadmissible provocation committed by the Air Force of the United States in regard to the Soviet Union; secondly, that I should renounce the continuance of comparable acts for the future and, finally, that I should have to "pass severe judgment" on those immediately responsible "for the premeditated violation of the frontiers of the U.S.S.R. by American planes." Khrushchev's message went on to say that unless all of this were done, "I cannot be among the participants in negotiations when one of them has made perfidy the basis of its policy toward the Soviet Union." It concluded by saying that if all of these things were done, Mr. Khrushchev would, as the head of the Soviet government, be ready to participate in the conference and do everything possible to contribute to its success.

I promptly told the Prime Minister that there was no possibility that

I would apologize for acts that I thought necessary to the security of the United States, particularly in view of the proof in our hands of persistent and flagrant espionage activities in our nation by numbers of Soviet agents.

That same evening President de Gaulle invited Prime Minister Macmillan and me to join him at the Elysée Palace for preliminary discussions, especially of Khrushchev's note. I remarked that the Khrushchev complaint was about me and I saw no reason it should not have been made directly to me. Khrushchev had communicated with both President de Gaulle and Prime Minister Macmillan to register his protest and set forth his conditions but had made no move to inform me.

I frankly admitted to the Western members of the conference that the U-2 work we had carried on was both distasteful and disagreeable, but our relative intelligence position was so dangerous that I had decided there was no recourse. Both understood my reasons and appeared to be sympathetic. By no means did I intend, at the forthcoming conference, I told them, to raise my hand and swear that we would never again do anything in the field of espionage. I would not permanently tie the hands of the United States government for the single purpose of saving a conference.

Our conversation turned to the kind of reply that I should make to Khrushchev if he opened the meeting the following morning with a violent blast. President de Gaulle thought the best reply would be, "Everyone does this, you Soviets do it too."

At first the Prime Minister believed it possible that Khrushchev was being adamant because he had gotten into something of a spot at the Kremlin. Everyone agreed that the Soviet message, delivered to De Gaulle and Macmillan, had all the earmarks of one carefully prepared in Moscow. We wondered why Khrushchev bothered to come to Paris at all. Exchanges of communications between his government and ours had already put him on notice that I would never apologize.

President de Gaulle remarked that this particular incident should not be construed as the real cause of tension in the world. To this Prime Minister Macmillan replied that the incident merely provided evidence of the necessity for doing something to relieve tensions.

We then turned to a number of other subjects that could be expected to come up if there were a conference. In all these matters—the principal one was Berlin—there were no major disagreements.

We agreed that because Khrushchev's letter of complaint about me was sent to both De Gaulle and Macmillan, it would be appropriate, upon the convening of the conference on Monday morning, that the Chairman

(President de Gaulle) first recognize me so that I might promptly reply to the accusations already put before my two Western associates.

However, when the principals met the following morning, Khrushchev quickly broke up this arrangement. President de Gaulle, presiding, had not even finished calling the meeting to order before Khrushchev was on his feet, red-faced, loudly demanding the right to speak. General de Gaulle looked rather quizzically at me and upon my nod to him, turned to Khrushchev and said this would be quite satisfactory.

The chairman of the Soviet delegation then launched on a long diatribe, speaking from a prepared text. He not only repeated the allegations and demands made in the message previously sent to President de Gaulle and Prime Minister Macmillan, but went on into a much longer dissertation on the reasons it had now become necessary for him to revoke the invitation that he had previously extended to me to visit the Soviet Union later in the spring.

The length of his explanation and the emphasis he gave to this subject clearly indicated that he was determined to keep me out of Russia. His document was repetitious, and at one point he became so vehement that I could not help grinning. He happened to notice this, and thereafter kept his eyes glued to the text of his speech.

I then asked for the floor and made a brief reply, restating the reason why my government had felt it necessary to conduct intelligence activities, pointing out that these activities had no aggressive intent but were to assure the safety of the United States and the Free World against surprise attack. I informed them that the overflights themselves, conducted by unarmed planes, were suspended and not to be resumed. I remarked also that if Mr. Khrushchev's basic purpose was to keep me out of his country he did not need to go into such a long and dreary explanation of why he chose to do so; a simple statement that I was no longer welcome would have served his purpose more quickly and just as conclusively.

I went on:

> I have come to Paris to seek agreements with the Soviet Union which would eliminate the necessity for all forms of espionage, including overflights. I see no reason to use this incident to disrupt the conference.
>
> Should it prove impossible, because of the Soviet attitude, to come to grips here in Paris with this problem and the other vital issues threatening world peace, I am planning in the near future to submit to the United Nations a proposal for the creation of a United Nations aerial surveillance to detect preparations for attack. This plan I had intended to place before this conference. This surveillance system would operate in the territories of all nations prepared to accept such inspection. For its part, the United States is prepared not only to accept United Nations

> aerial surveillance, but to do everything in its power to contribute to the rapid organization and successful operation of such international surveillance.
>
> We of the United States are here to consider in good faith the important problems before this conference. We are prepared either to carry this point no further, or to undertake bilateral conversations between the United States and the U.S.S.R. while the main conference proceeds.

When I finished, General de Gaulle made the interesting observation that within the last few days a Soviet satellite had been passing over France and for all that the French had been told about the nature of the orbiting vehicle, reconnaissance photographs could have been made of all French territory.

Khrushchev broke in to say he was talking about airplanes, not about satellites. He said any nation in the world who wanted to photograph the Soviet areas by satellites was completely free to do so.

In any event, deadlock was apparent, and Khrushchev, with his delegation, stalked out, saying that he was going to give his written statement to the press, at the moment of his own choosing. After his departure the three of us remained in informal conversations for a little time, discussing the whole performance. Both President de Gaulle and Prime Minister Macmillan suggested that Khrushchev was acting more like a student reciting a difficult lesson than as a person who was speaking his own convictions and beliefs.

As we walked out of the meeting, General de Gaulle touched me on the elbow and said, "Whatever happens, *we are with you.*" The loyalty of my two colleagues, De Gaulle and Macmillan, was the brightest spot in the whole affair.

The following morning the Western allies met again at the Elysée Palace. At that meeting it was decided that President de Gaulle should send, in writing, an invitation to Khrushchev to meet with the group at three o'clock that afternoon, and request an answer, in writing, of his intentions. While we had been informed by telephone that he intended to be present, he deliberately boycotted the meeting without notice. However, we took the opportunity to decide on the West's future course of action. We decided to draft a perfectly truthful statement of the entire incident and to issue it as soon as we saw that any effort to get together was completely hopeless. We met again late in the evening at the Elysée Palace to agree among ourselves on the exact wording of the announcement.

Because I had already made an engagement to stop in Lisbon on the 19th, I spent the day of the 18th visiting Notre Dame Cathedral and having lunch at the Elysée Palace; that evening, at the American Embassy, we enjoyed, in a family atmosphere, dinner with Amory and Laura Houghton. While there I received a curious telegram from Senator Lyndon Johnson, who with Adlai Stevenson, Sam Rayburn, and Senator Fulbright, asked that it be delivered to Khrushchev. It was a request to the Soviet Chairman that he not torpedo the conference. This was a somewhat awkward attempt, I thought, to interfere in the day-to-day conduct of foreign relations. In any event, I told my staff to reply that the conference had already broken up, so whether or not the cable was transmitted to Chairman Khrushchev, I was leaving Paris early the following morning. Secretary Herter telephoned Senator Johnson to tell him of my decision and to ask whether the authors desired to withdraw the cable. Senator Johnson hoped it would still be delivered. Why, I've never known but the message, as I recall, was delivered by a staff officer to the Soviet Embassy in Paris.

* * *

Departing Paris on the 19th, I stopped at Lisbon for a day's visit with that Allied government. I had interesting talks with the Portuguese Prime Minister, Mr. Salazar. In the evening, our party attended a state dinner and the following morning I left for Washington.

For a few days after the breakup of the Paris meeting, the American public and, I suspect, those elsewhere, were uneasy and apprehensive. The atmosphere was strained by a doubly unfortunate coincidence: an American C-47 transport was forced down over East Germany. At the moment we did not know the facts. If it were to become standard Soviet practice to shoot down all American planes approaching the border, then we could be close to war. Soon we learned that this was not the case; our plane had lost its way and the incident was of no larger or lesser diplomatic significance than many others.

Even after the immediate tension abated, Khrushchev continued to bluster. But significantly he made no additional threat against Berlin; indeed, he scarcely made mention of the city. He said, in fact, that he would wait to discuss it with my successor after January 1961. At last ended his futile ultimatum of November 1958.

* * *

The Paris meeting was the last time I saw Khrushchev in person. In a way I was sorry this was so. There was no denying that he was an interesting man. Of course he stood for everything in government that, to me, was unacceptable, even abominable. He was shrewd, tough, and coldly deliberate, even when he was pretending to be consumed with anger. Certainly he was ruthless. In personal conversations he was blunt but witty; he laughed often and seemed devoted to his family. The Khrushchev of the tea table was scarcely recognizable to one who knew him at the conference table.[8]

True, I think the Paris summit, had it been held, would have proved to be a failure and thus would have brought the Free World only further disillusionment. Khrushchev could have used the failure as an excuse for revoking the invitation for me to visit Moscow; the U-2 incident made this easier.

The big error we made was, of course, in the issuance of a premature and erroneous cover story. Allowing myself to be persuaded on this score is my principal personal regret—except for the U-2 failure itself—regarding the whole affair. But our position was not helped by those who chose to carp and view with alarm when the moment called for national calm and perspective.

Regarding the U-2 program itself, I know of no decision that I would make differently, given the same set of facts as they confronted us at the time.

I deeply regret that one of our young pilots had to pay with imprisonment for the failure of his plane in its final flight over Russia. Francis Gary Powers was freed after my retirement from the Presidency. Through an exchange on a bridge in Europe, Powers was delivered safely back into American hands as we turned over one Colonel Rudolf Abel, a master Soviet spy caught in Brooklyn, U.S.A. This, as others have observed, was a tacit admission by Khrushchev that our "outrageous" U-2 pilots have their opposite numbers operating within the borders of this country.

Technically, the entire program was a success. The information acquired did much in influencing the size and character of our security structure, in revealing the pattern of Soviet industrialization, and in locating military establishments of greatest threat to us in the Soviet Union. Armed with U-2 knowledge, which supplemented the strength of our Armed Forces, we were better able to plan our own political-military course.

One aspect of Khrushchev's scuttling of the Paris conference was the

[8] The indication that his anger in Paris was largely spurious was more than a little strengthened when, shortly after I left official life, in 1961, a roundabout invitation reached me to visit the Soviet nation. And I would have gone except that I felt such a journey could have been interpreted at home as an effort of a private citizen to project himself into American foreign affairs. I sent word back that should the invitation be renewed through my government I would accept. (In relating this incident I am barred from mentioning names because I gave my word to respect the request for secrecy concerning the intermediary.)

conclusion reached by my two colleagues as to the reason for Khrushchev's actions. It was, they thought, to prevent me from visiting the Soviet Union. President de Gaulle and Prime Minister Macmillan outlined their reasons for such a conclusion.

It was necessary, they said, to keep in mind that Khrushchev had known of the U-2 flights for quite some time, but had not revealed that knowledge. When Powers was brought down, obviously Khrushchev could have kept the matter secret, at home and abroad, if he had wished. So clearly he deemed it wise to publicize the matter.

At this point, they went on, we must recall Nixon's visit to Russia and Khrushchev's to the United States. In Russia, Nixon had talked to hundreds of thousands of men and women who had never before heard what life was like in the United States. On one occasion Nixon spoke by national television to all parts of the Soviet Union. Most did not believe the fantastic (but truthful) things he told them about our production, our schools, our culture, our transportation, and—most fascinating of all—what a laborer's family could buy on his income. Khrushchev pretended he did not believe Nixon,[9] but he was, according to Nixon and my brother Milton, disturbed by this exposure of his people to Western ideas and facts.

When Khrushchev visited the United States he of course had no further excuse to pretend ignorance about life in our nation. And if a visit by the United States Vice President had raised misgivings and questions in the minds of his people, what would be the consequence of a visit by the United States President who, offered reciprocal courtesy, would be free to speak to the masses throughout Russia, as Khrushchev had done in the United States?

When I have been questioned about the wisdom of the U-2 flights, I have replied with a question of my own: "Would you be ready to give back all of the information we secured from our U-2 flights over Russia if there had been no disaster to one of our planes in Russia?"

I have never received an affirmative response.

[9] Khrushchev had such full opportunities to learn about American life that it was not possible to give any credibility to his expressions of disbelief.

CHAPTER XXIV

Turbulent Summer

> But today the winds of change are blowing over our society, and if we are indifferent to them, we may find too late that the wind has become a destructive hurricane. . . .
> —*Grayson Kirk,* Responsibilities of the Educated Man

FROM the breakup of the Paris meeting in May 1960, to the end of my administration, the Soviets indulged in an intensified campaign of vituperation and false charges. The peaceful line was gone; in its place was a Kremlin attitude reminiscent of the days of Stalin.

Their professed explanation, the one Mr. Khrushchev would have liked us to believe, of course, was that the Chairman had become indignant at the "impudence" of the United States in conducting air reconnaissance over his land in mid-1960. This was ridiculous: As I have said, Khrushchev had known of many earlier U-2 flights. He had long been well aware, also, that we had volumes of evidence on Soviet espionage in our nation and had apprehended their spies in our territory regularly. This knowledge had not deterred him, in apparent good will, from coming to the United States, visiting at Camp David, and arguing for a summit conference.

For whatever reason, it was obvious the Chairman had concluded that his policy of conciliation had not paid off. It may have been costing him support in the Soviet hierarchy.

The cancellation of Khrushchev's invitation to visit the Soviet Union caused a revision in my plans for going to Japan. Originally I had expected, after traveling in the Soviet Union for several days, to fly eastward across Siberia and arrive in Tokyo on June 19. I saw no reason to change this arrival date in Tokyo, but the extra time now available made it possible to accept a long-standing invitation to revisit the Philippines, Korea, and Formosa. Immediately upon my return from Europe on May 20, intensive planning was started for what quickly became a tour of several bastions of the Free World in the Far East.

But the Communists, having canceled the trip to the Soviet Union, set about to disrupt this one also. In Japan, with its stray Communist elements and its far left Socialist party, the Communists wielded a strong influence with a consequent ability to stage public disturbances.

Japan was not properly equipped to handle this kind of difficulty. The reason largely stemmed from her extreme pacifism. The only nation to have suffered atomic attacks on civilian populations and determined to prevent a resurgence of Samurai dictatorship, she had disarmed to an extent that not even billy clubs were provided her police forces. The police were thus completely unable to control large and unruly mobs. Moreover, while Communist elements began urging violence to prevent my entry into their country, the U-2 incident was intensively advertised as warlike aggression against the Soviets and increased the apprehensions of the populace.

The Communist tactic in Japan was fundamental: their propaganda set out to create in the public mind a direct link between my visit and the forthcoming ratification of the New Japanese-American Security Treaty. This treaty, a revision of the agreement of 1952, obligated the United States more definitely to participate in the defense of Japan and increased Japanese rights as partners in this effort. Socialist opposition to the treaty had been felt as early as November of the previous year, with persisting demonstrations staged by both labor federations and student organizations.

As my advance party, including Jim Hagerty and Tom Stephens, flew toward Haneda Airport to review our detailed travel arrangements, the Communists and extreme left-wing Socialists were able to organize a massive demonstration, announcing it to be a sample of what would transpire on my visit to Japan.

On their arrival at Haneda Airport on June 10, Stephens and Hagerty were greeted by surly, noisy mobs, consisting partly, as we later learned, of paid demonstrators,[1] along with thousands of the merely curious. It was an unpleasant situation. Stephens, Hagerty, and our ambassador, Douglas MacArthur II, traveling by car and trying to go to the American Embassy, became immobilized by the demonstrators for fifteen minutes. They had to be rescued, amidst flying stones, by a United States

[1] A peculiarity of this demonstration was the lack of real ill will on the part of some of the wildest demonstrators. One individual, beating on the hood of an automobile with a large stick, inadvertently nudged a Secret Service man. He very politely excused himself and then continued beating on the hood of the car.

helicopter. My emissaries conducted themselves magnificently; one of the news pictures of the episode showed Jim Hagerty coolly taking photographs with a miniature camera of the howling crowd while they rocked his car.

Only later was I to learn, to my amusement, that there had been no film in the camera.

The incident caused real concern to our representatives who were planning for my arrival some days later. However, Ambassador MacArthur retained his confidence that the unrest would soon fade away and Prime Minister Kishi, with his own prestige deeply committed to the security treaty and to this visit, continued to hope that my visit could take place as arranged. But a United States Secret Service representative in Tokyo, Mr. Floyd Boring, took a pessimistic view of the ability of the police to control the mobs and reported to his superiors, Chief U. E. Baughman and James Rowley, that the situation was explosive. Allen Dulles shared this concern. "A kamikaze-type operation," he said, "is the thing most to be feared."

On a daily basis I had been kept aware of these developments. Though none of the reports was encouraging, I refused to be deterred. The responsibility for any cancellation of the invitation rested squarely upon the Japanese government officials, I said. If I had to change my plan, it would only be on their request. They had to be the ultimate judges of whether or not they could provide the security that would be due a visiting head of state.[2] While I knew that the invitation might be canceled, I thought also that a Far Eastern tour, even with Japan removed from the itinerary, was still worthwhile; so I was not unduly disturbed.

On June 12 I left Washington. The dean of the diplomatic corps in Washington, Dr. Guillermo Sevilla-Sacasa of Nicaragua, apparently unable to hide his concern for our safety, bade farewell to my son and daughter-in-law as they were mounting the plane with the remark, "We shall always remember you." Barbara laughed but later admitted that the ambassador's remark gave her a quiet chill.[3] We started our tour with the invitation to Japan still standing. After a stop in Alaska, which I was visiting for the first time since it had become a state, we went on to the Philippines.

In that land, where sentimental ties with America existed, I spent a nostalgic three days briefly revisiting such familiar scenes as Fort McKinley, Malacanang Palace (where President Manuel Quezon twenty-five

[2] The Communists and extreme left-wing Socialists had served notice that the presence of the Emperor himself would not deter them from demonstrations and violence.

[3] Two of my grandchildren, David and Anne, were down at Andrews Air Force Base to see me off; on this trip, as on the Middle East trip, Barbara was accompanying John once more to serve as my unofficial hostess.

years earlier had provided me with an office), the Manila Hotel, and many other places I remembered well from my tour of duty there as a major and lieutenant colonel in the late 1930s. I met with former and current officials of the Philippine government, and even had a short reunion with Maximo, my chauffeur of former years. As we went about the city, happy throngs crowded the streets. The greetings and hospitality of the Philippine people were, I thought, a monument to the success of American policy toward this former possession, whose people had at the end of the nineteenth century fought to the point of exhaustion against annexation to the United States.

During our stay in Manila, reports came in that the situation in Tokyo was continuing to degenerate. Student demonstrations outside the Japanese Diet building reached a fever pitch. On the evening of June 16, while attending ceremonies on the Luneta,[4] I was notified that the Japanese government had finally "postponed" its invitation for my visit. I could not help being disappointed. Viewed from any angle, this was a Communist victory.

Even Mutual Defense treaty ratification a few days later, the defeat of which had been the primary goal of the Communist riots, did not seem to anyone who chose to feel otherwise to have much significance. Neither did the fact that the Communists lost ground in all Japanese provinces where local elections were held shortly thereafter. These elections included Tokyo, where the demonstrations had occurred.

From the Philippines, I went on with the trip to Formosa, Okinawa, and Korea. I resolved that upon my return I would try to use the Japanese incident as one device to help explain to the American people once more what we were up against in dealing with international Communism.

* * *

In my private conversation with President Carlos Garcia, as well as in my speech to the Philippine Congress, I stressed America's admiration for the truly magnificent job the Philippines had done in cleaning up the debris of the war. I lost no opportunity to assure them that we viewed them as equals and with no feelings of condescension. I emphasized also that in their turn the Philippines should not use the United States as a whipping boy for their troubles.[5] This admonition was accepted in good humor and, I believe, with good results.

[4] A grassy city park along Manila Bay.

[5] Ever since our control of the Philippines began near the turn of the century, the favorite target for the Philippine demagogue had been the United States. Regardless of our efforts to improve health and education, social reform, to install representative government, and of our pledges to accord full independence as soon as Philip-

* * *

Conferences with Generalissimo Chiang Kai-shek in Free China were, of course, rather different in nature. Free China lived under the threat of the Chinese Communists to take Formosa by force. Indeed, to emphasize this, the Reds welcomed my arrival on Formosa with an intensive bombardment of Matsu and Quemoy.

Obviously disturbed by the recent student demonstrations in Korea and Turkey, as well as Japan, the Generalissimo was determined that such occurrences would not happen in his own domain.[6] He was convinced these upheavals were Communist-inspired, staged at much expense by the Communist leaders of both Red China and the Soviet Union. The Generalissimo was particularly concerned over the future of Japan and feared it might be lost to the Communists. Such an outcome would be, he remarked and I agreed, an irretrievable disaster for the remainder of the Far East.

The Generalissimo emphasized the high priority that Soviet planners gave to the Far East. He disputed categorically the growing assumption elsewhere that evidences of disagreement between the Soviets and Communist Chinese would result eventually in a split advantageous to the Free World. This, he asserted, was impossible. Mao Tse-tung might argue heatedly with the Soviets, but, the Generalissimo thought, Mao could never afford to split off from the Soviet Union, for he owed his own power to Kremlin support.

Significance should be attached, he felt, to a recent Soviet-Chinese agreement recognizing the link between Red China and the state of (Outer) Mongolia, previously considered a neutral buffer state. The Soviets had always been oriented toward Asia, and these recent happenings indicated a continuing trend toward heightened Soviet interest in the Far East and increased danger for Formosa.

Again and again he repeated that Asia was the prime target of the Communist world and the weakest link in Free World defenses. How-

---

pine economy and organization could sustain it, the Filipino still liked to picture himself as a patriot dedicated to throwing off the yoke of Yankee oppression.

President Manuel Quezon used to quote to me with considerable pride: "A government run like hell by the Filipino is better than one run like heaven by the American." At this time, fourteen years after independence, some Filipino politicians, having won the race, felt this was still a good horse to ride.

[6] The demonstrations in Korea had resulted in the overthrow of President Rhee the previous April. In Turkey student rioting was successful in overthrowing the Menderes regime in late May 1960, only about three weeks before my visit to Taiwan.

ever, he was optimistic in one regard; unrest was growing steadily among the people and even in the Army on the Chinese mainland. He mentioned uprisings in recent years in Sinkiang province, and in the Sikang region of China and Tibet. The Generalissimo thought it might be possible to exploit this unrest, if he were to conduct small guerrilla operations, particularly in the outlying districts. This idea had appeal, but could be dangerous to local citizens suspected of collaborating. While always ready to support such ventures where conditions gave reasonable promise of success and without too much danger of involving innocent people, I thought that in this instance great caution would be required. An aggressive program could result in disaster for many mainland Chinese loyal to Chiang. He assured me that he had pondered deeply the stern lessons of the Hungarian revolt of 1956.

The operations then discussed by Chiang have since been intermittently carried out, to the benefit of Nationalist morale. Some recruits have been obtained from the mainland on those expeditions.

During these conversations the Generalissimo was accompanied and aided by his charming wife, Madame Chiang, who served at times as both an assistant and translator. The talks were satisfying and reassuring.

* * *

I next landed at Okinawa, the most important island of the Ryukyu chain, seized at fearful cost by the Americans in World War II. In the uneasy postwar situation, the United States had maintained Okinawa as a military base while recognizing Japan's titular sovereignty. For the moment the island was administered by an American high commissioner, Lieutenant General Donald P. Booth. The chief representative of the Ryukyuan people was Mr. Seisaku Ota. Here, during our short conference, we witnessed a small "snake dance" demonstration among the crowds outside.

The conversations brought out one illustration of the consequences many thousands of miles away of ill-advised governmental actions in Washington. Mr. Ota earnestly protested a cut of about a million and a half dollars in the United States appropriations for economic support of the Ryukyus. On checking with General Booth I ascertained that this support was critically necessary and that the appropriation had been supported by the Bureau of the Budget and the administration. The matter was still under consideration in the Congress, but the harmful reduction had been recommended by a subcommitte under the chairmanship of the uncomprehending Mr. Passman. I informed Mr. Ota that there had been a restoration by the Congress of at least $200 million in the over-all military assistance fund, but I did not know whether the restoration included that particular $1.5 million. So I asked General Goodpaster to make a transpacific call to General Persons in Washington with instructions to mobilize all possible effort for the restoration of the money, or failing that, to find another way of dealing with the problem. The effects of uninformed action in Washington on distant peoples, whose good will is vital to the United States, can often be out of all proportion to any savings which may have been achieved.

* * *

My conversations in Korea with Prime Minister Huh Chung, a most personable gentleman, were interesting but limited in possibilities because his was a "caretaker" government, scheduled to endure only from the April revolution that had ousted President Rhee until the free elections, which were to be held soon.

One topic we did discuss was Japanese-Korean relations. The Prime Minister alleged that his nation had suffered many injustices under Japan's half-century domination over Korea and that some of these effects were still apparent. Expressing a fear that the Japanese were heading toward neutralism or even Communism, he gave me a long list of grievances against Japan; the most important was his complaint that the Japanese were currently repatriating certain Koreans located in Japan to North Korea without even consulting South Korean authorities.

In the hope of furthering political stability in the country, I suggested, at a breakfast with a number of Koreans, that a *coup d'état* was not the best way to change governmental regimes. Present were two or three students who had been ringleaders in the demonstrations to overthrow President Rhee in Seoul the previous April. Their pride in their accomplishment was so enthusiastic that it was seemingly impossible for them to comprehend the calmer thought I wished to convey. Actually, assuming that the accusations regarding the Rhee regime were accurate—that it was tyrannical and in complete control of the ballot box—it might have been impossible to vote him out of power. Under such assumptions, I recognized that the demonstrations were justified. However, I expressed satisfaction that the coup had not resulted in personal violence to Rhee or in reprisals and blood baths, such as had occurred so often, as in Cuba eighteen months before. I urged them to seek stability and foster democratic processes.

* * *

On our departure from Korea, my party spent a few delightful days of rest in our fiftieth state of Hawaii before proceeding back to Washington.

Upon my return, I discovered that some sections of the American press, once so laudatory on the subject of all kinds of "summits," were now, in the light of the cancellation of the visit to Japan, suggesting that presidential visits to Allied nations had been a poorly conceived idea in the first place. For my part, I saw little to regret and little to change in supplementing normal diplomatic exchanges with personal contacts between national leaders whether in Washington or abroad, now that jet aircraft had made such visits to distant lands practicable. In a nationwide broadcast I said:

> . . . it seems apparent that the Communists, some time ago, reached the conclusion that these visits were of such positive value to the Free World as to obstruct Communist imperialism. Thus they have sought every possible method to stop them. Through their propaganda they bitterly opposed my entry into the Philippines, . . . Taiwan, . . . Okinawa, . . . Korea, and, of course, Japan.
>
> . . . These disorders were not occasioned by America. We in the United States must not fall into the error of blaming ourselves for what the Communists do; after all, Communists will act like Communists. . . .
>
> So far as any future visits of my own are involved, I have no plans, no other particular trip in mind. Considering the shortness of the time before next January, and the unavoidable preoccupations of the few months remaining, it would be difficult to accept any invitation for me, again, to go abroad.
>
> But so long as the threat of Communist domination may hang over the Free World, I believe that any future President will conclude that reciprocal visits by heads of friendly governments have great value in promoting Free World solidarity.
>
> And this I assure you. If any unforeseen situation or circumstances arising in the near future should convince me that another journey of mine would still further strengthen the bonds of friendship between us and others, I would not hesitate a second in deciding to make still an additional effort of this kind.
>
> No consideration of personal fatigue or inconvenience, no threat or argument would deter me from once again setting out on a course that has meant much for our country, for her friends, and for the cause of freedom—and peace with justice in the world.

One of the most indelible memories I have of the many journeys into other countries is that of the people I saw—masses of glowing faces, friendly shouts, songs, gaily printed placards, and homemade signs of welcome. Their message, I felt, was one of kinship with the United States. No matter what the color of the skin, the shape of the eyes, the character of the costume, all were met for one purpose: to show, in this rather vicarious way, their favorable conception of American freedom, American purpose, and American aspirations for all men.

* * *

On the evening of July 1, 1960, as my wife and I were celebrating our forty-fourth wedding anniversary with our family at Gettysburg, I received word that a United States patrol plane, an RB-47, had disappeared over the Barents Sea, north of Russia. The plane had been on a routine mission, collecting electromagnetic, radio, and radar information, and was operating under orders to remain clear of Soviet territory by a distance of at least fifty miles. Our own radar tracking of the aircraft had indicated that the plane at one point had gone a little closer, but never to a distance less than thirty miles. It was headed away from Soviet territory at the time it disappeared.[7]

For the moment we did not have all the facts. We did not know, for example, why the aircraft had gone down. Large complicated pieces of machinery such as these aircraft carry do, occasionally, malfunction and even explode mysteriously (witness the inexplicable losses occasionally of domestic airliners). The mystery was deepened during the next couple of days when the Soviets began taking part in searching the Barents Sea for debris from the disaster.

The truth was to come out ten days later in the form of a note delivered to the United States *chargé d'affaires* in Moscow: the aircraft had been shot down by Soviet armed forces. The note itself was full of allegations we knew to be false. The body of the chief pilot of the airplane had been recovered, the Soviets revealed, as well as two survivors, 1st Lt. John Richard McKone and 1st Lt. Freeman Bruce Olmstead. The other three members of the crew were still missing. The note identified the base in Britain from which the flight had originated, and contained language almost unprecedented, even for Soviet communications:

> If the fate of American pilots . . . may be regarded as an internal affair of the United States, then this can by no means be said of the enormous threat to the general peace which arises from the provocatory actions of the Government of the United States. This is a question to which neither the Soviet Union nor any other state showing genuine concern for the preservation of peace can be indifferent.
>
> Considering that a violation of the border was in the present case cut off in its initial stage, the Soviet Government considered it possible

[7] Other incidents of this type which come immediately to mind are the loss of the Navy patrol plane in the Bering Strait on June 22, 1955, just as we were preparing for the Geneva conference; the loss of the Navy patrol plane off the China coast on August 22, 1956, during the Republican National Convention; and the loss of a C-130 along the southern borders of the U.S.S.R. on September 2, 1958.

to limit itself to destruction of the violating plane and calling to account of the surviving members of its crew, who will be judged according to the full severity of Soviet law.

At the same time the Soviet Government in all seriousness warns the Government of the United States of those dangerous consequences to which continuation of provocative actions by American aircraft will lead and the responsibility for which will rest on the Government of the United States.

It concluded with a threat to our allies:

> The Soviet Government with deep regret has to state that the governments of some states who are allies of the United States in military blocs have not yet drawn the necessary conclusions from known facts connected with the aggressive actions of the U. S. Air Force. Permitting the use of American military bases situated on their territory, they continue to pursue a policy of participation in the aforementioned aggressive actions, and through this bring great danger upon the peoples of their countries.

Such drivel could not be ignored. Accordingly, the next day we released the following statement:

> The American RB-47 plane was over international waters and at no time flew over Soviet territory, Soviet territorial waters, or Soviet airspace. The shooting down of this plane, as the Soviet Government alleges, can only have been a deliberate and reckless attempt to create an international incident.
>
> For 11 days the plane has been reported as missing. Indeed, it has also been reported that at least one Soviet ship was assisting, in good faith, in the search for the missing aircraft.
>
> Any attempt to connect the flight of this aircraft with the U-2 flight of May is completely without foundation, and the Soviet authorities, including Mr. Khrushchev, know this.

In plain words, they were deliberately lying.

The official reply to the Soviets went into more detail, exposing falsehoods in the Soviet note. We expressed our willingness to undertake, with the Soviet government, a joint examination of the entire incident and, reserving our right to demand full compensation, we concluded with a warning of our own:

> It should be clear to the Soviet Government that a repetition of acts of this nature cannot fail to have the most serious consequences, responsibility for which would rest upon the Soviet Government alone.

Again it was difficult to discover any logical motive for the barbaric Soviet actions. The bluster about the incident, we suspected, would continue for a while, most likely as an effort to frighten our allies and possibly to pressure them into denying us the use of bases.[8] To substantiate this view, Allen Dulles quoted Tass, the Soviet news agency, as saying that the Soviets planned to "scare the daylights" out of all United States allies until I left office, apparently on the theory that our election period would neutralize the administration into inaction.

If this general hypothesis were correct, the Soviets were certainly disappointed in the attitude of the British government. Harold Macmillan, speaking in Parliament, strongly defended our right to fly our planes in this geographical area.[9]

Whatever his ojectives, Mr. Khrushchev got another disappointment when the issue came up before the Security Council of the United Nations. On Monday, July 25, Cabot Lodge gave the Security Council the facts of the entire flight. Using a detailed chart he gave the exact route followed by the aircraft and described the precautions taken to insure that Soviet territory would not be violated. He demolished the Soviet assertion that the plane had been twelve miles north of Cape Svyatoy Nos and had been shot down over Soviet territorial waters east of Svyatoy Nos. He described the Soviet moves (which the American intelligence services had accurately pieced together), including the efforts of a Soviet fighter to force the American aircraft toward Soviet territory. Possibly Khrushchev had been lied to by his own people, Cabot conjectured, something that, he pointed out, occasionally happens in a dictatorship. As a final blow, Cabot requested the Security Council to make an impartial investigation or to give the matter to the International Court of Justice for adjudication.

The results were electric. The Soviet draft resolution condemning the "provocative action" of our Air Force and insisting that our government take immediate steps to put an end to such acts was rejected 7 to 2. Our own draft resolution calling on the governments of the United States and the U.S.S.R. to resolve their differences either "through investigation of the facts by a commission . . . or authority acceptable to both parties . . . or through referral of the matter to the International Court of Justice . . ." was blocked in the Security Council by the eighty-ninth veto cast by the U.S.S.R. Khrushchev's effort to make the RB-47 a little brother to the U-2 had turned out a miserable failure. Charles E. Bohlen,

[8] Speculating on the reasons for the long Soviet delay before announcing that they had been responsible for the loss of the airplane, Allen Dulles noted that the announcement coincided with the long-scheduled debate in the British House of Commons on the subject of foreign bases.

[9] A few days later Harold was to be even more firm. He wrote a long letter to Mr. Khrushchev, taking him to task for his actions.

who had listened to the reply of the Soviet representative, said that the Soviet argument at the end was the weakest effort he had ever heard from them.

In subsequent speeches Cabot Lodge continued with an exposé of Soviet activities. For example, he told of the appearance of the Soviet trawler *Vega* off the Atlantic coast of the United States in April of 1960. This vessel had gone so far as to attempt to retrieve one of the loaded test vehicles shot by our nuclear submarine *George Washington.* Cabot, tracing the path of this Soviet vessel to points thirteen miles off Cape Henry, Virginia, produced detailed photographs of this unusual "fishing" vessel with its numerous antennae capable of picking up long-range ultra-high-frequency radio and radar emissions. Twisting the knife, he pointed out that there had been no fishing gear at all on this so-called fishing boat; nevertheless we had photographed the *Vega, not sunk it.* He then continued with a series of other intelligence activities of the Soviets to include four aircraft flights in 1959 and two in 1960 that had come within twenty-five miles of United States territory, three of which had approached within five miles. Again he produced fairly close-range photographs, emphasizing again that we had photographed these planes but had not shot them down.

For a period the RB-47 incident appeared to presage new danger. Every day aircraft of NATO nations flew on legitimate missions around the periphery of the Sino-Soviet bloc. Most of these aircraft were not capable of living in the air against modern fighter planes. If the Communists should choose, they could shoot our planes down practically at will. It would, of course, be equally intolerable as a matter of principle for the United States abjectly to cease all peripheral flights over international waters and friendly territory. Consequently, if the Soviets had persisted in shooting down such aircraft, I could in the end only have gone to Congress for authority to systematically retaliate and punish.

Fortunately, the RB-47 episode took its place as but another expression of the ugly Soviet pattern of the day. The United States grieved for the four young airmen lost and for their families, and patience was growing thin, both in the administration and in the public. Apparently the Soviets sensed this for from then on, until the end of my administration, there was no further incident of this kind.

* * *

During the exchange over the RB-47, and, incidentally, at the beginning of the political campaign, world attention was attracted to the violence and chaos that had broken out in the newly independent Republic of the Congo.

This former Belgian colony, with a population approaching fourteen million, was only one of seventeen African nations achieving their independence that year.[10] In flood force, the spirit of nationalism had grown in all Africa.[11] The determination of the peoples for self-rule, their own flag, and their own vote in the United Nations resembled a torrent overrunning everything in its path, including, frequently, the best interests of those concerned.

Most of the former colonies, did, to be sure, have strong economic and cultural ties with their former rulers. Furthermore, key positions in communications, armed services, government, and such industry as existed were, in many instances, necessarily held by European technicians.

The United States was not directly involved, for we had no territorial claims in Africa. But, with a position of leadership in the Free World, we did not want to see chaos run wild among hopeful, expectant peoples and could not afford to see turmoil in an area where the Communists would be only too delighted to take an advantage. In spite of the relatively high regard in which the United States was held in most of the newly emerging nations because of our anti-colonial tradition, our close alliances with some of the former colonial powers caused vexing complications in Africa.

The picture was not all pessimistic. The evolution of the so-called Central African "French Community"—eight independent nations, formerly French colonies—seemed to be going well.

On my 1959 visit to Paris, the Prime Ministers of these various French Community nations, not yet independent, had been present one evening at the Elysée Palace. I had been privileged to talk to several and their outlook appeared remarkably well disposed toward the French.[12] Thus it was that those nations that elected to take the route to independence via the French Community did so with relative smoothness.[13]

[10] Map, "African Upheaval," appears following page 360.

[11] Cameroun, Togo, Senegal, Sudanese Republic (later Mali), Malagasy Republic, Republic of the Congo (formerly Belgian), Somali Republic, Dahomey, Niger, Upper Volta, Ivory Coast, Chad, Central African Republic, Congo Republic (formerly French), Gabon, Nigeria, and Mauritania.

[12] One of the Prime Ministers, Fulbert Youlou, President of the Congo Republic, sent me a gift, which caused much interest and some consternation at the State Department when it arrived. It was a small elephant.

[13] In early 1960, when the independence movement really began to snowball, it became obvious that our traditional policy of refraining from involvement in areas considered to be under the hegemony of other nations had to be re-examined. Accordingly, in early April I approved a policy, which came as the result of much study, that the United States would be prepared on the basis of a case-by-case appraisal of a country or project to extend economic development assistance where needed to

But the Belgian Congo was something else. As late as the middle of 1959, I had heard many European officials say that the Belgian Congo was one area that would remain tied to the mother country simply because, they contended, the Belgians had deliberately avoided training anyone to take over control of government. Consequently the world was surprised when, in January of 1960, riots broke out in the capital, Leopoldville—riots of such violence that Belgium granted independence to the Congo as of the following June 30. The Belgians began feverish preparations, training Congolese for the positions they would have to assume, but unfortunately time was insufficient. Without administrative capacity, political stability was almost impossible, and the situation was made worse by the existence of numerous fragmented political parties and by the conflicts between the tribes in the Congo. Nevertheless, with a restless and militant population in a state of gross ignorance—even by African standards—the Congo was almost overnight hurled into the family of independent nations.

Things went badly from the start. Even the ceremonies marking independence in the Congo portended ill. With Belgian King Baudouin present, the radical and unstable Congolese Prime Minister, Patrice Lumumba, took the occasion to excoriate Belgium for afflicting "atrocious sufferings" on the Congolese, although he promised that the Congo would remain on friendly terms with Belgium. The President, Mr. Joseph Kasavubu, a man of considerably more moderation, was obviously discomfited and embarrassed.

Rarely has a government proved in so short a time its lack of ability to govern. Within two days of the independence ceremonies, tribal disturbances began. These reached alarming proportions four days later when the troops of the *Force Publique,* a Belgian-led constabulary of twenty-five thousand, revolted against their white officers. To pacify the troops the Lumumba government promoted all native personnel one grade and summarily dismissed the Belgians. The respite was of hours only. On July 7, as the UN prepared to welcome the Congo into the fold, mobs of soldiers from the *Force Publique,* now joined by civilians, looted

---

the nations of Africa. Furthermore, we felt it necessary to go further and to extend special assistance for the improvement of education and training in the region, particularly emphasizing the needs which would be common to all the countries of the area.

In such instances as the French Community, of course, where newly independent nations would retain close ties with the former mother country, we would coordinate closely with the latter in the planning of such aid. Several members of the administration were particularly concerned over developments in Africa, Under Secretary of State Dillon, for one, and above all the Vice President.

and pillaged Leopoldville, causing Belgian residents to flee in terror across the Congo River to Brazzaville, the capital of the formerly French Congo Republic.[14] Four days later another long-feared move occurred: the rich province of Katanga, which included the majority of the Congo's wealth and resources (and incidentally most of the Belgian investments) announced under the leadership of Moise Tshombe its secession from the central government.

Now began a long series of riots, alarms, and rebellious outbreaks that should not have surprised the world, but did, to say the least, cause both dismay and disgust. The first reaction to the Katanga secession was by Belgium. That government moved in with troops to protect her interests. Lumumba, who we were now convinced was a Soviet tool, screamed in protest against this "aggression"—in spite of his own helplessness to maintain order—and the matter came to the attention of the United Nations. This is not the place to describe, even in capsule form, all the political, economic, and military actions and counteractions that make up the turbulent story of the first six months of Congolese independence; but inevitably the United States became involved when, within a few weeks of the initial rioting, the whole sorry mess fell to the United Nations.

The Security Council, working around the clock, adopted on July 14 a Tunisian resolution calling on the Belgians to withdraw their troops and authorizing the Secretary-General to provide the Republic of the Congo with military assistance until the Congolese government could fully meet its needs with its own national security forces. The United States supported this resolution.[15]

Speed was essential, and response was immediate; the United States Air Force flew in logistic support of this United Nations movement. With hundreds of tons of United States supplies, the first of a contingent of one thousand Tunisian and twelve hundred Moroccan troops arrived in Leopoldville July 15. In addition, the United States provided helicopters and light airplanes and, as a gift, four hundred tons of flour for the

[14] Both the Belgian and the French Congos chose to retain their names. Therefore the only distinction lay in the terms "Republic of the Congo" (Belgian) and "Congo Republic" (French).

[15] The vote was 8–0. Britain, France, and China abstained, objecting to the first paragraph, calling on Belgian withdrawal. Although, in view of the urgency of the problem the United States supported this resolution, Cabot Lodge pointed out that our interpretation of the first paragraph should be taken to mean that Belgian troops should withdraw only as soon as the United Nations forces were in sufficient strength to replace them. (Belgium had promised to withdraw to previously agreed bases as the troops arrived. Lumumba, who had broken relations with Belgium, would not accept this offer. As it turned out, the Belgians had pulled back to two bases everywhere except in Katanga by July 25.)

United Nations' use. Dr. Ralph Bunche was the representative on the spot of the Secretary-General of the United Nations. From the beginning he had been vilified and unjustly attacked by the Soviets.

The United States sent in no combat troops; we confined our contribution largely to supplies and air transport. However, we did station an attack carrier near the mouth of the Congo River. To support all these operations, I found it necessary to request an additional $100 million for the Mutual Security Contingency Fund.

With the foregoing actions the stage was set, but the situation was by no means stabilized. On the contrary, confusion continued, which the Soviets, as could be expected, did all they could to exploit. On July 15, Mr. Khrushchev issued his now familiar and routine denunciation of the United States in a message to Congo leaders and threatened to enter the Congo with force. This we squashed effectively by saying in the Security Council that no troops should be introduced into the Congo other than those requested by the Secretary-General and that we would do whatever was necessary to prevent the intrusion of any other military forces.

In early September the situation reached another phase of crisis. A Soviet ship with trucks and technicians had arrived in the Congo in the latter part of August, and it was estimated that two hundred Soviet technicians, in addition to some air crews, were in the Congo without United Nations authority. Secretary-General Hammarskjold suspected that the Soviet fliers might be military personnel prepared to engage in military activities in support of Lumumba. The Secretary-General lodged a protest to the Soviets, bringing on his own head a violent denunciation in the United Nations that seemed, temporarily at least, nearly to break his gallant spirit.

The Soviet invasion received a setback the first week of September when President Kasavubu dismissed Prime Minister Lumumba, a Communist sympathizer if not a member of the Party. The move was engineered awkwardly, according to reports reaching me; for example, after announcing the Prime Minister's removal over the radio, the President left the radio station unguarded and Lumumba seized it to issue an impassioned plea to the Congolese population. Soon thereafter a former sergeant in the *Force Publique,* Joseph Mobutu, proclaimed himself dictator. He announced that he was removing from their respective offices Kasavubu, Lumumba, and Joseph Ileo, the newly appointed Prime Minister. Mobutu, who set up a government of students and technicians, immediately closed the Soviet Embassy and ordered all Soviet diplomats out of the Congo. Many left. The Congo was able to boast, at this point, of being a nation with three full-fledged "governments"—Kasavubu's, Lumumba's, and Mobutu's. For a while Lumumba stumped the country, trying to achieve support for himself, and for a period took refuge in the protection of certain sympathetic United Nations troops while the Congolese searched for him. Eventually he was arrested and in February of 1961 was shot while trying, reportedly, to escape.

In the meantime, the Governor of Kantanga province, Moise Tshombe, succeeded for a period in maintaining the independence of his area. Allegations that the Belgians were planning to support a permanent split caused us much concern, but even if the charges were originally correct, the Belgians quickly abandoned the effort. They were largely gone by August 18, and the move was completed by the end of the month.

The troubles in the Congo remain even as of this writing, in late 1964. The United Nations force has now left, and disorder is rising again.

Reviewed as a whole, the Congo crisis represented a forward step in the influence of the United Nations.[16] Taking action in an area where direct participation on the part of European powers would cause only an exacerbation of resentments, the United Nations succeeded in achieving some stability in the area and a feeling of participation on the part of the African nations involved, even though the situation there is still far from settled. Most important, dictatorial ambitions of certain of the heads of new states were thwarted by the resolution of the United Nations officials. Khrushchev's attempts at subversion with an eye to Communist takeover were checked by the common sense and good will among free nations—American, European, Asian, and African alike.

* * *

As the Congo situation was approaching its climax in the United Nations, we received word, on September 1, 1960, that Premier Khrushchev was about to launch another propaganda offensive. On that date, Moscow announced that he would come to New York to head the Soviet delegation to the United Nations General Assembly, scheduled to open on September 20. This, of course, he had a right to do, as authorized by the charter.

Although the announced purpose of Mr. Khrushchev's visit was to give added weight to discussions on disarmament, I did not, for a moment, believe it. There had been too many discussions and conferences on this

[16] At the same time, United Nations activity here, as well as peace-keeping activities elsewhere, threatened the future of the organization, for the U.S.S.R. has stubbornly refused to pay its share of the United Nations costs thus incurred. This question of costs is, at this writing, an unresolved and exceedingly serious one, for it seems to me that the United States must continue to insist that the U.S.S.R. lose its voting rights in the United Nations if it fails to meet its financial obligations to the organization.

subject in which the Soviets' purely negative contributions were already too well known to warrant belief in such a story. We had only to recall the Soviet walkout from the ten-nation disarmament talks at Geneva on June 27, 1960, to discount the claim. Perhaps he merely wanted a wider stage for a tough-talking performance, but for whose benefit it would be difficult to say. Perhaps he hoped in some way to influence our presidential election. Perhaps he was taking this platform as a means of reaffirming before the world his position as the spokesman for Communism. Some suggested that he was merely taking an easy way of meeting Castro, thereby increasing our suspicion of Castro's ultimate purpose.

Others thought he was seeking a genuine rapprochement with the West. There was talk, particularly among neutrals, of another meeting between Mr. Khrushchev and me, but in the absence of assurance that any benefits could be expected from such a meeting, I could not have had less interest.

Mr. Khrushchev's announcement did, however, affect my scheduled plans for participation in the General Assembly activities. It was known that the Soviets were pressuring other leaders of the Communist and neutralist nations to come to New York. If any considerable number should agree to do so, the General Assembly meeting could evolve into something of a "summit" meeting under United Nations auspices.[17] When asked at a September news conference whether I planned to address the United Nations again (and also possibly to see Khrushchev), I could answer only in tentative fashion. I admitted that I had been giving serious thought to making another visit to the United Nations but emphasized that I was not going to the General Assembly to debase that body by being a party to a "battle of invective and propaganda." At that time my thought was to address the Assembly sometime after our national election.

An immediate problem confronting the government, if we suddenly found ourselves the hosts to a number of heads of government, would be to provide security for the visitors. True, our State Department security people and the New York police were accustomed to handling foreign dignitaries, but never on such a massive scale as this. Even though Mr. Khrushchev had visited the United States the year before without incident, the atmosphere since then had changed drastically; public opinion was such that he might be subjected to annoyance and even physical harm if not heavily guarded. Worse, there were indications that

[17] It will be recalled that we had proposed this device two years earlier during the Lebanon crisis, except that on that occasion the meeting was to take place in the Security Council rather than the General Assembly.

Prime Minister Janos Kadar of Hungary and Premier Fidel Castro of Cuba would be among those attending the meeting, and feeling among certain segments of our population was even stronger against these two than against Mr. Khrushchev himself.

We finally decided we should have to insist that four persons—Mr. Khrushchev, Mr. Kadar, Mr. Castro, and General Mehmet Shehu (whose government of Albania we did not recognize) confine their movements to the island of Manhattan. By so doing, the New York police force could provide adequate security for them to travel at will and with no interference in the performance of their functions as chiefs of delegations. More than this I felt the United States was not required to do. Accordingly, on September 10, each of the four governments concerned was issued an *aide-mémoire* setting forth the travel restrictions. As might be expected, these notes evoked anguished protests from those concerned, particularly the Soviet Union. Mr. Khrushchev lost no time in lodging a formal protest with the State Department. By the same token, I lost no sleep over the protests of these four, but my decision to take such restrictive action would have been far more difficult had the security problem not been genuine. The whole matter, did, however, cause me to remark that the only benefit accruing to us from having the United Nations in New York at this point was that it decreased the outflow of gold.

Not until September 12 did I definitely decide to address the United Nations at this session, by which time Mr. Khrushchev was already en route to New York. But, now my original hope to address the General Assembly later in the fall had to be abandoned. However, the possibility now arose that Mr. Khrushchev might well stay in New York until Christmas, by which time the debate could have become so intense that I could not avoid entering the melee if I should delay speaking until that time. Therefore, the best thing to do, I believed, was to address the Assembly on its first day. By this timing, I could try to set a reasonable and restrained tone at the start. In addition I could give strong affirmation of United States support for the United Nations, a gesture made essential by the unjustified attacks the Communists had been making on that body and on Secretary-General Hammarskjold personally.

Accordingly we announced that I would address the Assembly on the morning of Thursday, September 22. Secretary Herter suggested that I might take an opportunity during the several days I planned to be in New York to meet some of the visiting heads of government, particularly those from the Afro-Asian lands.[18]

[18] One group that supported my seeing Nasser were representatives of the Conference of Major National Jewish Organizations (B'nai B'rith, American Zionist Council,

In planning my talk before the General Assembly I was determined it would not be limited to platitudes and generalities. It was necessary, I thought, to make specific proposals on the main topics then holding the attention of the world.

When I began speaking to the General Assembly, I lost no time in reaffirming our government's full support of the Secretary-General:

> In response to the call of the Republic of the Congo, the United Nations, under its outstanding Secretary-General, has recently mounted a large-scale effort to provide that new Republic with help. That effort has been flagrantly attacked by a few nations which wish to prolong strife in the Congo for their own purposes. The criticism directed by these nations against the Secretary-General, who has honorably and effectively fulfilled the mandate which he received from the United Nations, is nothing less than a direct attack upon the United Nations itself. In my opinion, he, the Secretary-General, has earned the support and gratitude of every peace-loving nation.

Emphasizing that small nations and particularly the new African states were the ones having the greatest stake in the United Nations organization because of their relative weakness in material resources and production, I stressed the importance of United Nations protection for them. I therefore proposed a program of five major elements:

> (1) A pledge by all countries represented at this Assembly to respect the African peoples' right to choose their own way of life and to determine for themselves the course they choose to follow. . . .

I urged others to avoid any intervention, emphasizing that the United States had refrained from so doing.

> (2) The United Nations should be prepared to help the African countries maintain their security without wasteful and dangerous competition in armaments.

I expressed the hope that African states would strive to establish regional groupings (such as I had earlier urged in Latin America), thus eliminating political frictions among themselves and improving their economies.

> (3) We should all support the United Nations response to emergency needs in the Republic of the Congo, which the Secretary-General has shown such skill in organizing. . . .
>
> (4) The United Nations should help newly developing African countries shape their long-term modernization programs. . . .

American-Jewish Congress, Union of Orthodox Congregations of America) who came to visit me on September 20. These representatives were hopeful that I could persuade Nasser to moderate his attitude toward Israel.

Saying that there were already in existence a United Nations special fund and a technical assistance program, I recommended these should be considerably expanded. In addition I suggested other ways and wider avenues through which the new nations could receive valuable assistance.

> (5) As a final element to this program, I propose an all-out United Nations effort to help African countries to launch such educational activities as they may wish to undertake.

The United States would, I said, be ready to contribute to an expanded program of educational assistance to Africa by the family of the United Nations—in accordance with the wishes of the African nations, of course.

In addition to this five-point program for Africa, I noted that other areas likewise needed assistance. I mentioned the Food for Peace program and expressed the hope that the Assembly would consider a specific proposal[19] for carrying it forward.

I again argued the need for standby United Nations forces and recommended that the members of the organization take action on the Secretary-General's suggestion that a qualified staff be set up in the Secretariat to assist in meeting the future needs for United Nations forces. The United States, I said, endorsed Mr. Hammarskjold's suggestion that member nations maintain specific national contingents earmarked for prompt United Nations service. Besides maintaining combat forces, our government was ready, also, to earmark substantial air and sea transport facilities for United Nations use.

I discussed outer space and offered to the Soviets and to the rest of the world the opportunity to cooperate with us in demilitarization of all space efforts—to agree, among other things, that "subject to appropriate verification . . . no nation will put into orbit or station in outer space weapons of mass destruction"; and that "all launchings of spacecraft should be verified in advance by the United Nations."[20]

[19] A proposal by which the Food and Agriculture Organization of the UN would help channel surplus food from the wealthy to the poorer nations. This plan to feed the hungry would carry forward our continuing work, under Public Law 480 of 1954, to sell surplus food to friendly countries for foreign currencies, which we then used for such purposes as defense, economic development, and international educational exchange.

[20] The Joint Chiefs of Staff were concerned over this last point. The fear of the Joint Chiefs was, of course, that this paragraph would be interpreted to mean that we would allow the Soviets detailed inspection of all aspects of our spacecraft whether they were weapons or not. The wording used in the speech simply indicates that United Nations verification would need only establish that the spacecraft was not a weapon of mass destruction.

I ended with a final plea for support of the United Nations:

> Thus we see as our goal, not a superstate above nations, but a world community embracing them all, rooted in law and justice and enhancing the potentialities and common purposes of all peoples.

On the morning of this address, September 22, fourteen new nations were represented in the United Nations for the first time. My proposals, particularly those for Africa, were well received, as I was later to learn in my informal talks with the heads of the African delegations.

Because of increased United States-Soviet acrimony, the attitude of Mr. Khrushchev in the audience was of course a subject of much conjecture. He was present and attentive but quiet; while he did nothing to lead a chorus of approval, he conducted himself properly.

But the atmosphere of conciliation that I attempted to set was to be short-lived. The next day, Mr. Khrushchev took the stand and launched into an intemperate, vituperative attack on the West in general, on the United Nations, and on the Secretary-General in particular.

> The colonialists tried to bring this [their own reinstatement] about by crude methods and direct interference, as they always do in such cases. Unfortunately, in the case of the Congo they have been doing this unseemly work through the United Nations Secretary-General, Mr. Hammarskjold, and his staff.
>
> This is shameful. . . .
>
> The Soviet Government has placed the Congo question on the agenda of the Fifteenth Session of the General Assembly. The Assembly should give a rebuff to the colonialists and their stooges and call Mr. Hammarskjold to order so that he should not abuse his position as Secretary-General and should discharge his duties in strict conformity with the provisions of the United Nations Charter and the decisions of the Security Council.

This attack shocked and disillusioned the representatives of neutralist countries. Khrushchev's performance, together with the subsequent 4½-hour harangue by Fidel Castro did much to reinforce the bad impression created by their boorish antics in public a couple of days earlier. These two had met and while we knew nothing of their conclusions, their visit strengthened our suspicions that Castro was a Communist, even though it was not until December 1961 that Castro announced that he was a Communist and "always had been one."

* * *

At the end of my address I gave a luncheon at the Waldorf for the delegation heads of the Latin American states. During the next few days

I had the valuable opportunity of talking with many leaders of the Afro-Asian world, some of whom I had not met before.

One fact heightened my interest in these talks; except for their universal support of the United Nations, no two viewpoints were similar. Each took the opportunity to refer to some preoccupation of his own nation.

Premier Saeb Salaam of Lebanon and Crown Prince Moulay Hassan of Morocco, for example, while Arab in their outlook, had immensely different problems and preoccupations. Prime Minister Salaam seemed obsessed with Arab problems everywhere, particularly, I thought, with Algeria. Prince Moulay Hassan, on the other hand, was concerned primarily with the position of Morocco as a leader of the Moslem world, and with the American aid he wanted in order to keep it so. Prince Norodom Sihanouk of Cambodia, an energetic, suave, unpredictable man, was pleasant in manner and appearance. Professing awareness of the threat of Communist China to the north of his country, he felt that Cambodia was receiving less than its share of United States support. I gave no promise other than to say I would review the matter.

Deputy Premier Aklilou Abde Wold of Ethiopia I found to be a most enthusiastic person, particularly about the United Nations, and I asked him to convey my warm greetings to Emperor Haile Selassie, whom I had met some years earlier. Prime Minister B. P. Koirala of Nepal, calmly, and in a matter-of-fact manner, told me of Nepal's problems in building a five-hundred-mile road from east to west. He pointed out that, strangely, the Communist Chinese were far more reasonable in negotiating their border disputes with Nepal than with India.

My schedule in New York included talks with only two leaders of tropical Africa, Kwame Nkrumah of Ghana and Sylvanus Olympio of Togo. In talking with them, my main objective was to advance the recommendation I had made in my United Nations address for the formation of regional groupings of nations. This idea seemed to be of little interest to Nkrumah, a leftist who was reputed to harbor an ambition to expand the borders of Ghana by means other than voluntary federation.

On the other hand, Mr. Olympio, whose tiny nation of Togo had originally been part of the German colony of Togoland, had already effected a partial economic union with neighboring Dahomey. Mr. Olympio pointed out that one problem militating against progress in Africa was the almost continuous bloody tribal warfare. In view of this condition, he stressed that the United Nations should not have any inhibitions about "meddling" in the internal affairs of these countries, since these tribal wars were regional, not national, in scope. He had a wonderful sense of humor—an unusual trait in the leaders of some of the newer nations. I found Mr. Olympio the most impressive of the African leaders I met in New York.[21] (His assassination in January of 1963 was a loss to his nation and all Africa.)

Mr. Nkrumah professed, to my surprise, considerable optimism regarding the situation in the Congo. He said the situation was not insoluble, and stressed that the solution had to be worked out through the United Nations. Indicating his respect for the United States, he said he had taken special steps to arrange a visit to me before going to see Mr. Khrushchev, upon whom he had been invited to call. Later that day I learned that Mr. Nkrumah went directly from my room to the United Nations General Assembly and within forty-five minutes cut loose with a speech following the Khrushchev line in strong criticism of Secretary-General Hammarskjold.

Three other world figures I wanted to see were Tito, Nasser, and Nehru. I met President Josef Broz Tito for the first time on the afternoon of my United Nations address. He was shorter than I had expected, and reserved; in contrast to Khrushchev, he was a good listener. I felt he could have profited much from a trip around our country. I told him I was glad of the opportunity to meet him, since I had commanded Allied forces in the theater of war adjacent to Yugoslavia until 1943 (and dropped materiel in to him), but had never been in his country myself. The conversation, by and large, was innocuous. He seemed anxious to convince me that Yugoslavia was not on the best terms with all members of the Communist bloc.

"The Red Chinese," he said, "hate the Yugoslavs more vehemently than they hate the Americans. Despite this I have supported admission of the Chinese Communists to the United Nations. It seems only logical to admit a government that controls a nation of six hundred million people."

"Our people feel a special animosity toward the Red Chinese government," I answered, "for such good reasons as their invasion of South Korea and their holding and torturing some of our soldiers. Furthermore, they won't cease their persistent threats against Formosa, and their con-

[21] Two weeks later, Prime Minister Sir Alhaji Abubakar Tafawa Balewa of Nigeria came to visit me in the White House. This arrangement had been arrived at because Sir Alhaji had not been in New York during my visit. This official I found as impressive as Mr. Olympio but in a different fashion. Stately and solemn in his native garb, he spoke in a clipped and precise British accent of the problems of the divisions of his country and his hope for the future. In particular I appreciate the fact that he seemed to harbor no strong resentment against the British. Rather, he backhandedly praised them for the conscientious job they had done in training their public servants in preparation for independence. "After all," he said, "I have been in a position of responsibility for thirty years."

tinual pressure on Southeast Asia. When I met with Khrushchev last year at Camp David I told him that on that issue, the issue of Red China, we simply had to disagree."

President Tito seemed to understand this viewpoint and made quite a point of the affection that the Yugoslavs feel for the United States because of our help to them during World War II. This feeling, he said, would constitute a good basis for the improvement of relations.

* * *

Another leader I was meeting for the first time was President Nasser of Egypt. Ever since his assumption of power in Egypt, quarrels had characterized relations between his government and most others throughout the Middle East (to say nothing of Britain and France), and I was eager to learn more of his character and ambitions.

In presence he was impressive, tall, straight, strong, positive. His features, dark eyes and dark hair with graying temples, gave him a vivid appearance.

He quickly got to specifics. The United Nations actions in closing the Congo airfields to outside traffic was not to his liking, he said, and had shaken the confidence of the "entire world." I told him I thought this assertion more than a little overstated. He did not explain why he was anxious for those airfields to be open to aircraft of the United Arab Republic.

He complained also about the United Nations' inability to enforce the United Nations boundary line between Egypt and Israel as laid down in 1948. Until the United Nations enforced that arrangement, he said, he could not accede to United Nations resolutions calling on him to permit Israeli shipping to go through the Suez Canal. He did not say that the "quid" would certainly be rewarded with the "quo."

Nasser hoped that Africa would not become a battleground for the East-West cold war; criticized both presidential candidates in the American political campaign then current for what he called pro-Jewish and anti-Arab statements; referred rather pointedly to some of the "unfair" speeches made on the floor of the United States Senate, and argued that the nine hundred thousand Arab refugees concentrated mainly in the Gaza Strip and on the border of the Jordan should be repatriated with United Nations assistance. He denied that he had ever advocated destruction of Israel, and assured me that he wanted to cut back as soon as possible on his military budget, but said that so long as Israel was supported by Jewish contributions from all around the world he had no recourse but to look to his own security.

He insisted there was no danger that Egypt would surrender to Communist domination. He was willing to accept Soviet aid but only as long as it could not place his nation in jeopardy.

I repeated that the policy of the United States advocated friendship with all nations of the Middle East and would not deliberately take sides in the Jewish-Arab quarrels unless we became convinced that one was guilty of aggression. I assured him that the United States had no political or territorial ambitions in Africa and wanted to be helpful to those nations that were prepared to work peacefully and energetically toward raising their own standards of living. Whatever the validity of all the points Nasser made during the conversation, the meeting was for me a highly interesting experience.

I was glad, as always, to have another chance to talk with Prime Minister Nehru. Remarking on Mr. Khrushchev's diatribe three days earlier, the Prime Minister said rather wistfully that everyone, including himself, had been astonished at the attack. He was much concerned over the situation in the Congo, but stated emphatically that the Belgians had "left the country in ruins" and with few qualified administrators. The Prime Minister said that he had not yet decided what position he could assume in the current discussions in the United Nations that might be useful in calming tempers and ruffled feelings.

We talked about successful negotiation for the division of the Indus River waters and about the Red Chinese penetration of India's borders. He was remarkably calm in discussing this last subject, but did say that all India was determined to protect its territory no matter what the cost. Needless to say, perhaps, I heartily approved of this expression of strength by one whose philosophy had been passive resistance.

My final meetings, on September 27, were with Prime Minister John G. Diefenbaker of Canada and Prime Minister Macmillan. As an interesting example of the widely different interpretations that can be made of another man's motives, Mr. Diefenbaker told me that Indian Defense Minister V. K. Krishna Menon had concluded that the purpose of my talk to the Assembly was to "stir up the cold war."

I found Harold Macmillan fairly optimistic. "The mood in the General Assembly," he said, "seems to be changing, and a feeling is growing that Khrushchev has badly overplayed his hand." As to this, Chris Herter quoted Dag Hammarskjold: "It begins to look as though the United Nations has imported some of the political chaos of the Congo." We compared views on the latest moves in Katanga, the troublesome activities of Patrice Lumumba, and the problems of the Nigerians in New York City, where the delegations were experiencing difficulties in securing lodging because of their color. I made certain that the matter was taken up with Mayor Robert F. Wagner and the police commissioner, Stephen P. Kennedy, at once.

* * *

The days following these conferences were full ones, too. I returned to Washington on the night of September 27 to greet Their Royal Highnesses Crown Prince Akihito and Crown Princess Michiko of Japan. The day following was given entirely to catching up on the work that accumulates when a President is absent from Washington even for a few days.

Then, on the 29th, I received word that Mrs. Eisenhower's mother, Mrs. John S. Doud, had died in Denver after a long illness. I went to our private quarters to talk to Mamie, and found her bearing up well. I had commitments in Chicago that evening and determined that I would carry through with them; Mamie would travel on ahead and I would go on after that to Denver to join her.

"Min's" funeral was a particularly sad event. She and I had always been close friends. Surviving her husband by more than nine years, she had been with Mamie and me almost constantly in the White House until in 1958 she decided to return to her home in Denver, which she was destined never to leave again. She had been failing badly for two years and in her final months could scarcely recognize anyone; nevertheless, with her passing at the age of eighty-one, I felt a deep sense of personal loss, while Mamie was inconsolable.

* * *

On our return to Washington on Saturday, October 1, I learned that a group of five "neutral" nations had jointly submitted to the United Nations General Assembly a resolution calling for a meeting between Mr. Khrushchev and me.

It was apparently assumed that such a meeting would solve many of the problems plaguing East-West relations. Four of the five leaders —Nkrumah, Nehru, Tito, and Nasser—had met with me the previous week and not one had even hinted at an intention of participating in such a proposal. The fifth, President Sukarno of Indonesia, I had not seen for some years. Their purpose was far from clear. At best it seemed totally illogical; at worst it seemed an act of effrontery. The participation of Prime Minister Nehru was particularly puzzling. The others had no reputation as students of the world scene, but I could interpret Nehru's action only as a sign of confusion as to what his own role ought to be at a meeting where much might be expected of him.

Obviously, if a majority in the United Nations voted for the resolution, I would be in a most embarrassing position. Even if I could have persuaded myself to meet with Khrushchev it would have been only wishful thinking to believe that the resolution of any outstanding issues could have resulted. Khrushchev, the acknowledged head of the Communist bloc, could have spoken authoritatively for his side, but I, as the head of only one nation (albeit the strongest) of the Free World could have made no significant commitment binding upon all. So, only on the highly improbable assumption that Khrushchev was prepared to make major concessions to the West could anything have been accomplished at such a meeting.

After much discussion with my advisers and some of my trusted friends among Free World leaders, I decided that we should try either to have the resolution withdrawn by its authors or, if this proved impossible, to make sure of its defeat.

My first move, therefore, was to address a communication to each of the co-signers, as individuals, explaining my views on the proposal.

In these identical letters, I said:

> The questions which are disrupting the world at the present time are of immediate and vital concern to other nations as well [in addition to the U.S.A. and the U.S.S.R.]. The importance of these matters is such as to go beyond personal or official relations between any two individuals. . . . I have many times personally pledged myself, regardless of every kind of personal consideration, to meet with anyone at anytime if there is any serious promise of productive results. There is nothing in the words or actions of the government of the Soviet Union which gives me any reason to believe that the meeting you suggest would hold any such promise. I would not wish to participate in a mere gesture which, in present circumstances, might convey a thoroughly misleading and unfortunate impression to the peoples of the world.
>
> If the Soviet Union seriously desires a reduction in tensions it can readily pave the way for useful negotiations by actions in the United Nations and elsewhere. If Soviet representatives should wish to discuss concrete measures to reduce tensions my representatives, including the Secretary of State, are always available for this purpose. Should such exploratory discussions reveal that the Soviet Union is prepared to return to the path of peaceful negotiation with some prospect of fruitful results, then I personally would be prepared to meet and negotiate with the representative of the Soviet government and with the heads of other governments as their interests were involved.

The "neutralist" resolution was eventually defeated, with the United States voting against it and the Soviet bloc abstaining. Mr. Khrushchev had helped us, however, by criticizing the resolution in public. Immediately, speculation began that our active role in defeating the resolution had cost us dearly in good will among many neutrals. Possibly, but it cost us a pittance compared to the impossible situation that would have developed from either my refusal to comply with an approved resolution of the United Nations or from the spectacle of my engaging in a fruitless diplomatic duel.

Fortunately, Mr. Khrushchev's public conduct negated the propaganda windfall that might have been his through the action of "the five." His attack on Saturday, October 1, including his expression of scorn for the resolution, had been a violent one. Yet, during his visits with various neutralist leaders in New York he seemed at times to be attempting to engender support for a meeting such as the five had proposed.

Khrushchev continued his bad manners to the last. A most spectacular exhibition was when he stood up and began interrupting an address by Prime Minister Macmillan. Harold handled the situation calmly. With immense dignity, British reserve in its finest flower, he simply paused long enough to ask for a translation of Khrushchev's insults. In an effort to outdo even this demonstration, Khrushchev later removed his shoe and brandished it at the other delegates, and then banged it on the desk to sound his disapproval during speeches by Western delegates. Trying to restore quiet, the General Assembly President, Frederick H. Boland of Ireland, beat his gavel so hard that it broke. With order completely gone, he called the General Assembly session to an abrupt end for the day.

On his last day in this country, Khrushchev addressed the General Assembly for two hours, then departed in the evening. Other leaders from the Communist bloc left with him or soon thereafter.

* * *

When Khrushchev departed, few indeed thought he had gained any propaganda advantage by the tragicomic sideshow he had put on in New York. His behavior could not but have shocked every serious-minded diplomat who had come to the meeting to participate, hopefully, in earnest and intelligent discussion. There was not a single vote that Khrushchev's side could carry. Had he decided to allow the resolution of the five neutrals to work for him, he could perhaps have caused the United States acute discomfort. Whatever his reasons for not doing do, the only cause he hurt was his own.

But his efforts to disrupt the proceedings of the United Nations General

Assembly held a lesson for all students of government. Khrushchev displayed poor manners, but he did nothing illegal. Once again it was demonstrated that human institutions involving orderly processes can operate successfully only when participants show self-restraint and a sense of responsibility. It has been said that freedom is merely the opportunity for self-discipline; when restraint is gone, so is the effectiveness of the democratic system.

CHAPTER XXV

Twilight

> In looking forward to the moment, which is intended to terminate the career of my public life, my feelings do not permit me to suspend the deep acknowledgment of that debt of gratitude which I owe to my beloved country.
>
> —*Washington, Farewell Address*

LATE in December of 1959, Governor Nelson Rockefeller of New York announced his withdrawal from the race for the 1960 Republican presidential nomination, assuring, at least at that time, the unopposed selection of Vice President Nixon. For some months it had been a foregone conclusion that the nomination was going to Nixon. Governor Rockefeller's wise decision promised the avoidance of divisive and costly struggles in the party.

My satisfaction did not imply any lack of appreciation of Nelson Rockefeller's abilities. He had worked loyally and effectively in my administration, and I had applauded his spectacular 1958 victory in the New York gubernatorial contest. Nevertheless, it was my conviction that Dick Nixon, by reason of his unique preparation for the Presidency, unmatched in our history, would be a worthy nominee of the Republican party. In addition to his earlier service in the House and Senate, his years in the Vice Presidency had given him extended opportunities to study the workings of the federal government, to meet world leaders, to gain an understanding of domestic and international conditions. He had traveled widely, knew our defenses, had shown an unusual grasp of foreign policy and economic affairs.

As I looked forward to the forthcoming campaign, I decided to write Nixon a confidential memorandum on the conduct of a campaign and on possible nominees for the Vice Presidency, which I did on January 13, 1960. Excerpts from that memo:

The man nominated for Vice President should, of course, have the qualifications to take over the Presidency whenever circumstances might compel him to do so, and should be able to speak from this broad base. Men who might qualify are, among others, [Robert] Anderson, Lodge, Mitchell, McElroy, Rockefeller, Rogers, Morton, Halleck, and, if he could be induced to go into political life, General Gruenther. (In this list, I have not tried to arrange names in any order of priority.)

To speak in the field of foreign affairs, likely selections would be Lodge, Dillon, Secretary of the Treasury Anderson, possibly [former Presidential Assistant] Dillon Anderson. (Herter not mentioned because of office). (a)

To discuss finance and the duties of the Secretary of the Treasury are such men as Anderson, Stans, Dillon, Hauge, [Under Secretary Julian] Baird, [Under Secretary Fred] Scribner, and George Humphrey.

In the field of Defense there are Gates, McElroy, Seaton, and Dillon Anderson. Possibly others could be added from among the civilians now holding appointive office in the Defense Department. Brucker might be good. (a)

(a) Speeches in these fields should never be strictly partisan, but they can properly extol Republican record and policies.

Post Office Department: Arthur Summerfield, Charlie Hook, Stans, [former Deputy Postmaster General Edson O.] Sessions.

Agriculture: The man who stands highest, so far as knowledge of this subject and integrity of purpose are concerned, is of course, Secretary Benson. Many Republicans think that any public appearance by him would be a detriment in the Middle West. Nevertheless it is possible that he could be used efficiently in the metropolitan areas because his viewpoint is that of the nation and not of the local voters. Individuals who would be listened to respectfully in the farm areas would include [former American Farm Bureau Federation President] Allan [B.] Kline, Dean W. I. Myers (Cornell), Congressman Les Arends, Congressman Charlie Hoeven and, if he could be induced to participate in the political campaign, Milton Eisenhower.

Attorney General: There might be Rogers, Brownell, [Deputy Attorney General Lawrence] Walsh, . . . Dewey, and others.

In Interior are: Seaton, Governor Hatfield, Walter Williams.

Commerce: Chuck Percy, Secretary Mueller, Hauge, Walter Williams, Harold Boeschenstein, Stephen Bechtel [the last two outstanding industrialists].

Labor: Jim Mitchell, [former Assistant Secretary of Labor] Rocco Siciliano, and selected members of the labor committees in both the Senate and the House.

H.E.W.: Flemming, Oveta Hobby, Chuck Percy, Hauge.

Two subjects not to be neglected are Housing and Budget. A number of men, in and out of public life, could meet the requirements. Housing could well be handled by [Housing and Home Finance Agency Administrator Norman P.] Mason and Aksel Nielsen [President of the Title Guaranty Company of Denver].

Each of the individuals named above is sufficiently well informed to talk on the whole general field of political philosophy, and in each talk his major theme should be the field assigned by the candidate. . . .

The Vice President, who had long since told me that he planned to make the race for the Presidency, really began his active campaign at the beginning of 1960. Then, in April, Governor Rockefeller, in a speech delivered in Philadelphia, seemed—from press extracts—to voice criticism of the administration and thus to imply a repudiation of his earlier decision not to seek the presidential nomination.

I was puzzled. Since the speech dealt especially with foreign affairs, I asked Douglas Dillon, Under Secretary of State, to find out what Rockefeller hoped to accomplish. Doug Dillon saw Nelson in New York and quickly reported: Nelson had suggested in his Philadelphia speech that the United States promote a western hemisphere economic union and also offer to place part of its nuclear weapons under NATO control. The text of the speech as a whole, Under Secretary Dillon felt, did not seem critical of the foreign policy of the administration, as the condensed press reports had suggested.

Subsequent correspondence with Nelson, however, did not eliminate all doubt about his political purposes. On June 8 he joined me for breakfast at the White House. Though avoiding any intimation of personal candidacy, he did say he was interested in learning more about Dick Nixon's attitudes on "certain issues." Our talk was quite general, but inherent in his comments was criticism of what he felt was Nixon's failure to make known his convictions on a number of problems. I deliberately took the role of audience.

After the meeting he promptly issued a statement to reporters which included a declaration of his personal position on specific foreign and domestic policies, and a demand that Nixon make known his views on all major public issues before, not after, the Republican Convention.[1] The circumstances and the setting assured him wide publicity, and caused me to feel that I had unwittingly been made a party to the quarrel.

The direct challenge to Dick Nixon was one thing. Quite another was

[1] Over the next six weeks Rockefeller and his staff put out a series of study papers recommending action on foreign policy, national defense, economic growth, civil rights, government reorganization, medical care for the aged, disarmament, education, and Latin American policy. This collection of papers was called by some a liberal Republican candidate's repudiation of a conservative Republican administration's performance. To me this was an oversimplification; I tried to look beyond the labels to find out what Nelson had on his mind.

that several features of Rockefeller's published opinions seemed to be based on flimsy evidence. At the legislative leaders' meeting the next day, I called attention to his recommendation for an increase in civil and military defense spending of $3½ billion, a figure which he had not mentioned at our breakfast conference. "I suspect that Nelson has been listening too closely to half-baked advisers," I said.

Nonetheless, I opposed any effort to silence Nelson. "I think he has a right to express his opinions—and he is a prominent Republican," I told the leaders. "In fact, the National Committee might well invite him to deliver a major address before the Convention."

That evening, in a telephone call to my secretary, Mrs. Whitman, Nelson said he wanted my judgment on whether or not he should become an avowed candidate. After several unsuccessful attempts, my return call finally reached him on the morning of June 11. I told him that his latest statement did not conform to what he had said to me personally. If I understood him, he was now contending that the administration had done a good job with the exception of defense, where he felt the budget was more than $3 billion too low.

As to his candidacy, I said candidly that if he announced now, after having definitely withdrawn earlier, people would say he was "off again, on again, gone again, Finnegan." I suggested that he could scarcely claim to be the only one in step in the party and told him frankly that in my judgment it would be a mistake for him to become a declared candidate. Should he decide otherwise, I added, three specific pieces of advice might help him: "Don't make any mistakes in a hurry; don't let anybody else write your speeches; and let the party know you'll support the nominee."

The next day he announced that, though his previous withdrawal from the race still stood, he would run if drafted.

* * *

On July 13 the delegates to the Democratic National Convention nominated John F. Kennedy on the first ballot. To balance the ticket he selected as his running mate the Majority Leader of the Senate, Lyndon B. Johnson.[2] It was a surprise political pairing; in the pre-convention period, Senator Johnson had insisted that his experience had

[2] Of the two men on this ticket I knew Lyndon Johnson better. Our friendship came of a birthstate in common and long personal acquaintance.

We had had our differences, especially in domestic and economic policy. I resented his role in the Senate's rejection of Lewis Strauss as Secretary of Commerce. Yet, when put in perspective, he was far more often helpful than obstructive in furthering the recommendations I sent to the Congress. The amount of legislative accomplishment that had been achieved during the six years that I had to work with an opposition Congress led in the Senate by Lyndon Johnson was impressive. For

made him a better presidential prospect than the junior senator from Massachusetts; some of his statements in that period were much more critical of Senator Kennedy than anything Dick Nixon later said in the campaign.

The degree of ideological balance in the 1960 Democratic ticket was suggested by the fact that, as Vice President Nixon later pointed out in a statement issued in the campaign, the two men had "flatly disagreed 264 times on roll call votes in the Congress. . . . They have disagreed on farm policy, disagreed on taxes, disagreed on civil rights, disagreed on foreign aid, disagreed on foreign policy, disagreed on defense. They have disagreed on labor issues, disagreed on public works, disagreed on housing, disagreed on Tidelands oil. Name it, and they have disagreed on it—from anti-trust, atomic energy, banking and controls to the national economy, education, clean elections, natural gas. They have disagreed on highways, mail rates, and loyalty oaths. They have even disagreed on fireworks." They had most recently disagreed over Senator Kennedy's judgment that to save the Paris summit conference after the U-2 incident, the United States should have apologized or expressed regret to Khrushchev.

* * *

Despite their differences—or perhaps because of them—the Kennedy-Johnson ticket struck some observers as a masterful coup. Shortly after news of this partnership reached the White House, one of my most respected advisers, Dr. Gabriel Hauge, sent me a note expressing his concern over what he deemed to be the new Democratic strength. In his view, shared by a number of others, there was just one answer: to persuade Nelson Rockefeller to run for the Vice Presidency. And, he concluded, "The only man who could persuade Nelson is you, Sir."

As soon as I read this note, I put in a call for Hauge, who was then in Chicago serving as Executive Secretary of the Republican National Convention's Platform Committee.

"Gabe, I have talked to Nelson two or three times," I said. "You've read in the papers what he's said publicly: that he would not run for the Vice Presidency 'even if the President asked me.'"[3]

---

this I was grateful and frequently told him so. We remain, on my part at least, good friends.

[3] Incidentally, I have never been able fully to understand the disdain that so many presidential hopefuls display toward the Vice Presidency. After all, Amendment XII to the Constitution declares that the qualifications for incumbents of both offices must be the same, a requirement that makes an election to the Vice Presidency an honor, in many respects, second only to that of election to the Presidency. Moreover, about 25 per cent of our Presidents have died in office.

This cooled Gabe's ardor a bit. I told him that Nixon was the only man who might persuade Nelson to accept the nomination as Vice President. Dick could succeed by promising to take himself out of the political picture in 1964 and leave the field to Rockefeller should they be successful in 1960, I suggested, only half-seriously. Nelson might accept such a proposal, but of course I could not imagine anyone of Nixon's relative youth ever making it.

On the evening of July 22 the Vice President unexpectedly flew to New York City for a meeting at Governor Rockefeller's home to discuss the second spot on the ticket and to establish a meeting of minds on the wording of specific planks in the platform. Rockefeller declared firmly that he did not want the vice presidential nomination. Then he and the Vice President hammered out a personal agreement on major public policies. It called for an accelerated rate of economic growth. On civil rights they very rightly said: "Our program for civil rights must assure aggressive action to remove the remaining vestiges of segregation or discrimination in all areas of national life—voting and housing, schools and jobs." On defense it declared that "the United States can afford and must provide the increased expenditures to implement fully this necessary program for strengthening our defense posture. There must be no price ceiling on America's security." That section seemed somewhat astonishing, coming as it did from two people who had long been in administration councils and who had never voiced any doubt—at least in my presence—of the adequacy of America's defenses.

At the end of the meeting, in the early hours of the following morning, Nixon and Rockefeller telephoned Charles Percy, Chairman of the Republican Platform Committee, and read to him the text of platform declarations on which they had agreed. Percy in turn gave these to Bob Merriam, my personal representative in the platform drafting sessions. That morning at eight o'clock Bob telephoned my office and spoke to Jim Hagerty. Jim showed me the wording on defense, then called Merriam back: "That section is unacceptable. We'll call you later with some changes."

Meanwhile Rockefeller made the original text public.

Senator Barry Goldwater and other conservatives saw a Nixon "surrender" to Rockefeller. Others particularly deplored the section on national defense. The members of the Platform Committee, who had been laboring for long days and nights, saw the document falling with heavy impact on their own draft.

Shortly after noon the Vice President telephoned to tell me about the meeting and of the suggestions it had produced for the platform. The next day, in another phone call, I informed him of reports I had been receiving of opposition among the members of the Platform Committee; the Nixon-Rockefeller statement, they said, contained large divergences from the convictions of the administration. I added that I had also received a number of telegrams urging me now to support Senator Goldwater. The Vice President said that the members of the committee were upset because they did not want to appear to be giving in to Rockefeller and because Rockefeller had put out the statement unilaterally.

"My only interest is to get a platform that is both sound and helpful to the Republican ticket," I said. But I left no doubt that it would be difficult for me to be enthusiastic about a platform which did not reflect a respect for the record of the Republican administration, and a purpose of building on this record.

The Vice President agreed. "What I'm trying to do," he said, "is to find some ground on which Nelson can be with us and not against us."[4] I understood Dick's problem. It is a unique one that faces anyone running for office or helping to write a platform whose party is then in power. The platform maker or the candidate must obviously support the administration and its record or lose the allegiance of a significant section of his party. On the other hand, he cannot be in the position of standing still—he must never forget the basic precept, biological, and political, that change is the law of life. To promise and pledge *new* effort, *new* programs, and *new* ideas without appearing to criticize the current party and administration—that is indeed an exercise in tightrope walking.

I made it plain to Dick that I was by no means advocating that we stand still on the programs and accomplishments of the past eight years. We should promise continued and, if possible, accelerated progress—and mean it. The Vice President agreed.

Later that same day Chairman Percy of the Platform Committee called me to say, "Mr. President, I'll give you $100 for every word in the platform that makes you unhappy."

The committee was proceeding to hammer out a platform acceptable to all. The defense plank incorporated my wording to the letter: "There *is* no price ceiling on America's security," it said in part. "The United States can and must provide whatever is necessary to insure its own security and that of the free world, to provide any necessary increased expenditures to meet new situations. . . . To provide more would be wasteful. To provide less would be catastrophic."

[4] A number of people during the campaign, and more particularly after the results of the election were known, complained that Nelson Rockefeller had not enthusiastically supported the national ticket. I believe this criticism to be unjustified. Although, of course, the loss of New York State was a tremendous disappointment, I think that Governor Rockefeller did his utmost to keep it in the Republican lineup.

In addressing the convention on the evening of July 26, my goal was to draw the party together and emphasize the base upon which its future could be created. So I said, "Though there is room for healthy argument within our party, you [delegates] have come to this Convention with a unity of basic conviction and philosophy unprecedented in the nation's political history." Despite normal platform compromises, they had. And it was, of course, part of my intention to encourage unity.

The speech detailed the nation's gains which had been realized under Republican programs. In the military field I referred to the increase in defense spending from less than $12 billion before the Korean War under the Democrats to more than $41 billion in 1960, and to the reshaping of our Air Force with new supersonic jets, and of our Navy with the revolutionary new submarine-borne Polaris missiles.

"In the successes of the past seven and a half years," I concluded, "you have a solid foundation on which to build toward new levels of attainment. But thank God there is no smugness or complacency about your accomplishments." And based on the platform episode, there certainly was not.

As his vice presidential running mate, Mr. Nixon selected UN Ambassador Henry Cabot Lodge of Massachusetts. I agreed with Mr. Nixon that Cabot Lodge had unusual qualifications for the Vice Presidency. His record in the Senate had been a distinguished one; he had been in the military service, and his seven and a half years' experience as our ambassador to the United Nations had been notable.

* * *

With the Republican convention having named a national ticket, my responsibility for determining the character and tone of Republican national campaigns naturally fell to other hands.

Early in August the Vice President and I agreed that I could do the most good by making a number of speeches around the country, before non-partisan audiences, in support of principles that had guided my administration. I believed with him that these would help the ticket more at the moment than partisan speeches under political sponsorship. No one wanted to see us win the election more than I. As I told Ben Fairless in a telephone conversation on August 19: "I'm going to make eight to ten appearances during the campaign. Motorcades kill me, but I'm going to do them to try to arouse enthusiasm." I said I would do any honorable thing to avoid turning the country over to the "big spending" type of Democrats.

Nixon's campaign was interrupted at its outset by circumstances beyond his control. Congress consumed tedious weeks in winding up its business, and Dick himself was confined for a painful period after the adjournment in Walter Reed Army Hospital. He had to cancel planned visits to New England, Alaska, Mississippi, and Louisiana; but on Monday, September 12, at Friendship International Airport in Baltimore, I saw him and Cabot off for the big weeks of the campaign. That they had a tough job ahead of them was evidenced by a Gallup Poll report on this question: "Which *party* would you like to see win the congressional elections in your state?" The Democrats were favored by 58 per cent, the Republicans by 42 per cent.

The Republican party's minority position was a serious problem for its candidates. Another was the quality of the Kennedy-Johnson campaign. At home, the Democrats claimed, the United States was standing still; abroad it was suffering from lowered prestige. "Last year," the Democratic presidential nominee declared, "the Soviet Union exceeded the growth of this country by three times." "Unemployment," he amplified elsewhere, capitalizing on a temporary increase during the month of October, "has doubled in this country since Mr. Eisenhower took office, while the number of jobs has grown only 15 per cent." He demanded that the United States Information Agency release a public opinion poll which, he alleged, showed that our prestige abroad had reached a new low.

Ignoring his earlier comparison of Castro to Simon Bolivar, Senator Kennedy announced that two Republican ambassadors to Cuba had warned that Castro was a Communist, and that the administration had done nothing about it. He also charged "Most of the equipment and arms and resources for Castro came from the United States, flowed out of Florida and other parts of the United States to Castro in the mountains. There isn't any doubt about that." (If the implication here was that the government backed Castro, it was totally untrue.) Discovering evidence of poverty or hunger or injustice or inadequate education in Asia, Africa, or Latin America, he somehow managed to leave the impression that the administration in Washington was to blame for all the ills of the world and that if the Democrats were elected the ills would disappear.

He almost made a habit of reversing himself, as on the defense of Quemoy and Matsu, on apologizing to Khrushchev, and on non-intervention in Cuba.

* * *

On September 26 came the first of the several television debates between the two candidates. In principle I had opposed them. But the decision had been made very early, with a commitment given at the end of the Republican National Convention in July.

I could not witness the first debate, for I was in New York City that evening, addressing the National Council of Catholic Charities.

Several days after the first debate Nelson Rockefeller wrote me an urgent letter asking me to plan to give a day to an appearance in New York State in the last week or ten days of the campaign; if I could do so, he said, the Republicans would have a "chance" of delivering the state's forty-five electoral votes to Nixon and Lodge. "Unfortunately," he added, "it is beginning to look as though (your appearance) might be a 'must.'"

Not only in New York but all over the country Republican workers were intensifying their efforts, particularly after the discouraging popular verdict on the first debate—that Senator Kennedy had scored an upset victory. On October 1 I wrote Dick, in a confidential letter:

> I rather think that your appearance at the closed circuit [Republican fund-raising] dinner on September 29th may mark the beginning of an upsurge in general enthusiasm for our national ticket. I thought, and I know many others who felt the same, that you rang the bell.
>
> Over past weeks there have come to me directly and indirectly expressions of hope that our campaign might produce more "zip" and that it should be more hardhitting—not necessarily in terms of personal attack but in urgent support of our own plans, programs and candidates.

The second debate, on October 7, made us feel much better. In the third, the two candidates argued at length on their differences over the defense of Formosa and the defensibility of Quemoy and Matsu. The Vice President's performance was improved. Kennedy, taking the "sophisticated" view—pull out of Quemoy and Matsu—was finding it hard to defend this untenable position.[5]

Meanwhile, I was busily engaged in other activities, including a series of speeches. To a large audience I had warmly endorsed Dick and Cabot at the September 29 closed-circuit fund-raising dinner. In a later address in San Francisco, I asked that we "not be misled by those who, inexplicably, seem so fond of deprecating the standing, condition, and performance of the entire nation.

"Surely we must avoid smugness and complacency. But when in the face of a bright record of progress and development, we hear some mis-

[5] I have serious doubts about the value of debates in a presidential election. They tend to be a test of reaction time rather than a genuine exposition of the participants' philosophies and programs. Further, in debate, candidates tend to overstate their views. In the 1960 situation I had a very practical objection: Nixon was widely known; Kennedy was not; dramatic debates would therefore help Kennedy.

guided people wail that the United States is stumbling into the status of a second-class power and that our prestige has slumped to an all-time low, we are simply listening to debasement of the truth."

On October 24 at Rice University in Houston I reminded the audience that nothing was more destructive of orderly progress than wild fluctuation between the extremes of panic and complacency. It had long been the aim of the administration to build steadily and soundly the economic and military strength we would need over the coming decades; ". . . this is not done," I said, "by hasty or ill-considered actions, crash programs [or] efforts that stop and go like traffic at a busy intersection."

Then on October 27 at Staunton, Virginia, in ceremonies honoring the memory of Woodrow Wilson, I cited his warnings against excessive centralization of government and remarked that Wilson "was not a man who believed in bruising the ears of his fellow men with shrill cries of alarm." By that time the ears of some Americans had been badly bruised, and as these quotes suggest, my temperature had been rising.

Earlier that week I had, after talking with Dick, announced a step-up in my schedule of political speeches. In a major nationwide telecast from Philadelphia on October 28, this time under Republican sponsorship, I emphasized the economic progress of the past eight years—the increase in personal income, earnings, savings, classrooms, homes, factories, highways. I declared our military strength "the most powerful on earth."

Then I turned to the Democratic candidates' attack: "Now in glib political oratory we have heard this progress called 'standing still.' If this is 'standing still,' America needs more of it.

"What qualities must the next President have?" I asked.

"Character; ability; responsibility; experience."

I extolled the virtues of the Republican ticket and in various ways tried to convey the conviction that our ticket was far abler than that of the Democratic party.

"We need a leader who will not, one day, say he would give up territory to the Communists, then change his mind on it a day or so later." This referred to Senator Kennedy's about face on the Taiwan situation. "Because, my friends, upon such decisions can hinge peace or war."

Finally I focused on "some statements in this campaign that have had world-wide circulation and have cruelly distorted the image of America"—allegations of the United States' low prestige, for example, and of our military weakness, talk which I labeled "an exercise in calculated confusion. . . .

". . . anyone who seeks to grasp the reins of world leadership should not spend all his time wringing his hands."

I called upon the opposition to spell out for the American people how they would pay for the many billions of additional federal spending pledged by their platform of glittering promises. I remarked that they could not pay for them with high hopes alone.

"But if they would pay for these programs by deficit spending, raising the debt of our children and grandchildren, and thereby debase our currency, let them so confess. . . ."

I said: "Of course 'America must move.' But forward—not backward. . . . I see no sense in America galloping in reverse to what has been called a New Frontier."[6]

Election day was November 8.

That night I watched the returns with John and Barbara and a friend of theirs, Dorothy Daniel. By 11 o'clock, when I went to bed, the results were not encouraging. The next morning, though the election had turned from an initial landslide into a horse race, no one held out much hope for the Republicans. At 12:25 in the afternoon the Vice President telephoned me from his headquarters at the Ambassador Hotel in Los Angeles.

"I still think we'll take California, Minnesota, and Illinois by the time the absentee ballots come in," he said. "But even so, we won't have enough. Therefore," he added, "I have conceded the election." (He had earlier refused to do so because of the inconclusiveness of the returns the night before.)

"I ran 7 per cent *ahead* of the other Republican candidates," he said. "Kennedy ran a little more than that behind other Democratic candidates." The final result, indeed, showed how close the Vice President had come to winning. Trailing by only 113,000 votes, he and Cabot Lodge polled 49.5 per cent of the total, against 49.7 per cent for Kennedy and Johnson. The Republican ticket had carried twenty-six states; Kennedy and Johnson had carried twenty-three.[7] A switch of fewer than 12,000 votes in five states would have reversed the result.

Later the Vice President recalled that during that conversation he had never heard me sound more depressed. He was right. As I wrote to a friend several weeks later, when I heard the outcome, I felt as though

[6] In ensuing months, many good Republicans said I had not made as many campaign speeches as I should—that by more strenuous effort I could have changed the national decision. I shall later discuss my afterthoughts on this, but here I only want to record the fact that I made far more speeches than the new leaders of the party had originally asked me to. I faced a dilemma: I would do anything reasonable to help Nixon win, but if I did too much I might create the feeling that Nixon was not a leader in his own right—that his election depended upon his "riding on coattails."

[7] Mississippi gave its vote to a slate of unpledged electors, who voted for Senator Harry Byrd.

"I had been hit in the solar plexus with a ball bat—" as though eight years of work had been for naught.

It was a low moment, and about all I remember of November 9 is that when I began debating whether to cancel my previously planned trip to Augusta, my staff—and my son in particular—objected violently, almost shoving me aboard the plane. At the moment I had little spirit to argue. (The doctors, I later learned, had been concerned in the last days that I had temporarily used up all my available cardiac reserves in the closing weeks of the campaign.)

To waste time mourning the loss of any contest is never profitable. Alibis, even if convincing, provide little comfort to losers. While I believe that an objective analysis of results in a political campaign can—or should—provide lessons for the future, the atmosphere immediately following an election is normally so charged with elation on the one side and disappointment on the other that objectivity is notable only for its absence.

I leave that argument to history. Nevertheless, the campaign illustrated several things to me. It showed the influence of television: for some reasons one man projects well, another does not. It showed again how much elections can be controlled by sentiment and emotion rather than by facts and experience. And it showed the importance of successful appeals to large special interest groups.

* * *

The days after the defeat were not without heartwarming messages. One that I prize highly came from Prime Minister Harold Macmillan:

> I feel I must write a few words to you on a purely personal basis at this time. The election of a new President has brought home to me the situation which of course I knew must come, that the period of our close cooperation together in so many fields is drawing to an end. When I look back on the first time we met in the Hotel St. George, nearly 20 years ago, I realize how long this friendship has been. I know that nothing will ever impair its strength or its usefulness to our two countries.
>
> As a soldier you had under your command the largest force that Britain has ever put into action by air, sea or land; as President you have done everything to maintain the close friendship of our two countries. I think you must have realized when you drove from London Airport last year what the British people feel about you.
>
> I can only assure you that I will try my best to keep our Governments and our countries on the same course. But I cannot of course ever hope to have anything to replace the sort of relations that we have had.

But now it was time to begin winding up our affairs and preparing to turn the reins of government over to my successor.

Even before the election, I had set up machinery for an orderly transfer of responsibilities and duties to the incoming President. Planning for this transfer went forward with efficiency and dispatch.

On the Sunday following the election Dick Nixon telephoned me to say that Senator Kennedy had, through his father and former President Hoover, suggested that he and Nixon meet. I agreed with the Vice President that he should accept. But I suggested that Dick withhold judgment on a key question likely to come up: whether any top Republicans should serve in the new administration. I opposed the practice, particularly for those who might be destined for party leadership. After Douglas Dillon was invited to become Secretary of the Treasury, I talked to him several times in an effort to discourage him and later sent out my negative conclusion in a letter.

* * *

On December 6, Senator Kennedy came to the White House, at my invitation, for a discussion on the transfer of responsibilities. Immediately after the meeting with Senator Kennedy I dictated a seven-page memorandum [see Appendix BB].

We talked at considerable length of organization, of financial problems, including the imbalance of payments, of Berlin, Cuba, and the Far East; of NATO, of the leading European personalities, and other matters of interest to him.

While meetings such as this can rarely serve as an indication of the future, I must confess to considerable gratification in this visit with the young man who was to be my successor. Throughout the entire proceedings he conducted himself with unusual good taste. Resisting any temptation to flood the White House with his own retinue, he came riding in the back seat of an automobile completely by himself. In our conversations I was struck by his pleasing personality, his concentrated interest and his receptiveness. There was complete understanding, of course, that my administration would carry full responsibility up to the last minute. How much more we still had to face in the next six weeks I would never have guessed.

* * *

While for some time much of our interest had been given to the election and its aftermath, there were important subjects demanding attention—in the international money markets, in Southeast Asia, and in the Caribbean.

"Free Gold Prices Spurt in Europe," a headline declared on the morning of October 21. For several reasons, including some never made public, the price of gold on the London market—ordinarily about $35 an ounce—had hit a peak the day before of $40.60. Although the price soon went down again, one reason for the buying spree had not disappeared. It was the continuing weakness of the United States' balance of payments.

From the end of World War II to 1957, while other countries were rebuilding their dollar reserves, and while the United States was supplying them with products to rebuild their factories, the regular annual outflow of dollars gave us little concern; in fact, the government had been striving to help our friends earn dollars. By 1957, however, the European countries and Japan had rebuilt their economies; with highly efficient new plants and low wage costs, they engaged us in trade competition. As a result, our export surpluses shrank, going from $6 billion in 1957 to a low point of $910 million in 1959. But the costs of our stationing military men abroad and of our programs for foreign assistance remained high. So did the net outflow of private capital—direct business investments, payments for stocks and bonds, loans, and deposits. In 1960 this outflow, mostly for short-term investments in Europe paying interest rates higher than those in the United States, may have totaled as much as $5 billion. Therefore, despite a continuing export surplus which reversed its earlier decline and more than quadrupled between 1959 and 1960, going to approximately $4.5 billion, American dollars were cascading overseas; our balance of payments deficit went to $3.5 billion in 1958 and $3.7 billion in 1959. A series of governmental measures were initiated in the fall of 1959 to increase American exports, to reduce government buying overseas, and to encourage other Free World countries to join us in assisting the underdeveloped peoples but in the third quarter of 1960 our deficit reached an annual rate of more than $4 billion.

More and more, as this balance of payments weakness continued, many people—reportedly including some Americans—were cashing their dollars in for gold in foreign markets: between 1958 and 1960, the United States lost approximately $5 billion worth. In part this loss of gold was due to fear of—or speculation against—a possible devaluation of the dollar. For one thing, the glittering promises of the Democrats in the campaign were reportedly convincing foreign bankers that the United States might embark on an orgy of fiscal irresponsibility. This fact made a chronically bad situation acute. "If the American dollar is going to be radically devalued," the foreign line of reasoning went, "we had better cash our dollars in for gold right now."

On the day after the election I met with Secretary Anderson, Under

Secretaries Dillon and Baird, Secretary Gates, Deputy Defense Secretary Douglas, General Lemnitzer, and Federal Reserve Board Chairman William McChesney Martin on the situation, which Secretary Anderson said required urgent steps.

"At this very moment," he said, "the United States holds $18.1 billion in gold. Tomorrow it will sell gold worth another $218 million. This means that on Friday we shall go below a reserve of $18 billion for the first time in many, many years. By law we must hold $12 billion of that to back up our own currency. That leaves less than $6 billion—and there are at this moment about $19 billion in instant demands against us, which could be presented at any time. Already many small countries are coming in to ask for their gold, of which they have about $2 billion worth in demand claims." He read off a list of about twenty small countries now asking the United States for gold.

"The problem they face," Anderson said, "is a real one; they could not stand the loss if the dollar were to decline in value."

We knew that overseas the dollar was the backing for other currencies, such as the franc or lira. If people all over the world lost confidence in the dollar and rushed to convert all their claims into gold, the Free World's monetary system could collapse.

"There are several things we can do," he continued. "We can raise our tariffs and tighten our customs barriers. If we do this we shall be reversing the trade policies we've followed for the past eight years." Other countries would retaliate, and the trouble would continue. "Second, we could ask Congress to reduce or remove the requirement that we keep a specified percentage of gold to back our own currency. This course would set off the biggest monetary debate in our history. In addition," he went on, "we could change the dollar price of gold, but others would do the same, and we'd gain nothing."

Finally he said, "We could put an embargo on the export of gold, which, though it would not destroy our own monetary system, would destroy the international gold standard in our lifetimes. Or we could prohibit Americans from holding gold abroad. If we did this, other countries would take it as a signal that we were going to devalue our dollar, and start a run on our gold stocks."

None of these possibilities looked especially attractive at the moment.[8]

There was another set of solutions we considered. First we could cut down the number of dependents of military and other governmental personnel abroad, reduce our troop strength overseas where practicable,

[8] In January of 1961, we did issue a regulation prohibiting Americans from foreign ownership of gold.

stop the procurement of foreign-made items for our post exchanges and commissaries, tie more of our loans to underdeveloped countries to purchases of American products, and of course do our utmost to balance the budget, add to our already voluminous exports, and get our allies to increase their foreign aid.

We concluded that this kind of program would be preferable, and I asked Secretary Anderson to serve as chairman of a group to prepare a plan of action. It was important to do something promptly to increase our foreign receipts, cut our foreign payments, or hopefully do both. We needed, by Spartan-like measures, to assure creditor nations that our government was determined to act effectively to correct its balance of payments position.

During the following week Secretary Anderson's group readied the draft of a presidential directive. On November 15, I met with him, Secretary Gates, and others to discuss it. We examined carefully a proposed reduction in military dependents overseas and the effect this might have on morale.

Secretary Gates felt that the military services would really be unhappy, particularly if they were to carry the whole—or nearly the whole—of the burden. "Moreover," he went on, "if it turns out to stir up a major issue, it will give our political critics a great advantage. It'll be like the bank holiday of 1933; the Democrats will be riding this white horse for the next twenty years, alleging that they had to unsnarl the mistakes of the Republicans." I largely discounted this political effect, believing that proper leadership in the armed services—and concern for the lower grades—could take care of most of the morale problem.

"We can't sit still and see our monetary system destroyed. People have to realize this fact," I said. "I'm willing to accept whatever criticism, and accept the responsibility for corrective measures as long as we're using common sense and setting reasonable policies."

Recognizing the need for governmental groups other than the military to do their part, too, I directed Jim Hagerty to make public the directive which, it was estimated, could cut the deficit by a billion dollars a year.[9]

At the close of the meeting I instructed General Persons to call Senator Kennedy's personal representative, Clark Clifford, and tell him I thought

[9] In addition to reducing the number of military dependents abroad from 484,000 to 200,000 (at 15,000 a month beginning January 1, 1961), it also ordered the Pentagon to cut its foreign procurement to the bone, directed the ICA and Development Loan Fund to "place primary emphasis on financing goods and services of United States origin in all of its activities," and directed every department of government to pull back as many as possible of its employees stationed overseas. The "hardship" foreign service tour, requiring the separation of families, was for thirteen months only.

it highly important that he see Secretary Anderson as soon as possible on this urgent question.

Late in November, Secretary Anderson and Under Secretary Dillon traveled to Germany to induce the Germans to share the burden of assistance to underdeveloped areas. As a prosperous nation—one which had built up its holdings of gold and dollars by an estimated $2 billion in the year ended September 30, 1960—that country, I thought, should in fairness participate in the program, and this would, of course, be helpful in solving our problem of imbalance of payments. On November 28 my emissaries returned and reported to me the results of their mission.

"On Monday," Secretary Anderson reported, "we met with Chancellor Adenauer. We described our gold problem, emphasized the necessity for defending the dollar, and reminded him that our troop support costs in Germany run to $600 million a year. Again and again, however, Chancellor Adenauer kept repeating that only one thing worried him; the possibility that we might redeploy some of our troops."

The Germans agreed to conduct a $1 billion foreign aid program in the coming year; they estimated that 20 per cent of this amount would buy goods in the United States. They also agreed to explore the possibility of buying some military equipment in the United States, about $250 million worth.

* * *

Though the balance of payments problem remains with us, the immediate crisis came to an end, in part because of the administration's obvious determination to prevent the deterioration of the dollar, through word and action.

As we strove to counter the threat to the dollar, we simultaneously worked to combat a Communist threat to Laos—a Southeast Asian kingdom with an area about twice that of Pennsylvania and with a population of about three million scattered throughout its mountains and dense forests. Despite its remoteness, we were determined to preserve the independence of Laos against a takeover backed by its neighbors to the north—Communist China and North Vietnam. For the fall of Laos to Communism could mean the subsequent fall—like a tumbling row of dominoes—of its still-free neighbors, Cambodia and South Vietnam and, in all probability, Thailand and Burma. Such a chain of events would open the way to Communist seizure of all Southeast Asia.[10]

Complicating this problem was the difficulty of determining, with rea-

[10] Map, "Pathet Lao Attacks on Laos, December 1960," appears following page 360.

sonable accuracy, what was going on in this mysterious Asian land. All through the fall of 1960 we studied intelligence reports day-by-day and sometimes hour-by-hour. Out of much confusion a cast of five principal characters appeared. The first two were Prince Souphanouvong, leader of the pro-Communist Pathet Lao organization located principally in two small northeastern provinces bordering North Vietnam and Red China, and his half-brother, Prince Souvanna Phouma, the neutralist Prime Minister.[11] Then there were a paratroop captain of obscure motives, named Kong Le, who in August of 1960 had staged a coup and thrown out the pro-Western government then in office; a former minister of defense named Phoumi Nosavan, who refused to acknowledge the new—and technically legal—government under Souvanna Phouma, and continued to lead forces in opposition to both it and to the rebel organization of Souphanouvong; and finally there was Prince Boun Oum, who in September announced that he would set up his own government to rival that of Souvanna Phouma—a government which quickly won Phoumi Nosavan's recognition and backing.

By October it appeared that Souvanna Phouma was either an accomplice or a captive of Captain Kong Le who, himself, was an accomplice of the Communist Pathet Lao. During the second week of October a special mission to Laos—Assistant Secretary of Defense John N. Irwin II, and Assistant Secretary of State J. Graham Parsons—failed, despite a great effort, to persuade Souvanna Phouma not to bring the Pathet Lao into his government. By the first of December the country was edging closer to all-out civil war, and the Soviet Union began airlifting supplies to the pro-Communist Laotian forces. Then on December 8 a newcomer, Colonel Kouprasith Abhay, an associate of Phoumi, executed a coup against Souvanna Phouma's government in Vientiane. Later that same day there was a second coup: Kong Le took over Vientiane. Souvanna Phouma fled to Cambodia.

On December 13 the forces of Phoumi and Kouprasith[12] together began a counterattack on Vientiane. As the fight went on, the King ap-

[11] Laos has a king who as head of state, Commander-in-Chief of the Army, and Supreme Religious Authority, reigns from the royal capital of Luang Prabang, population 8000. He appoints the Prime Minister, who is responsible to the National Assembly. This body is elected every five years by universal suffrage, and is located at the administrative capital of Vientiane (population then 100,000), farther south down the Mekong River. The national flag of Laos is colored red with a three-headed white elephant in the center, a fitting symbol for a country which from its birth had suffered from division.

[12] Thereafter Colonel Kouprasith disappeared from public view.

pointed Prince Boun Oum as head of a provisional government, one to which, at last, we could give open support.

As Phoumi proceeded to retake Vientiane, General Goodpaster reported the events to me. "Two points are giving us concern: the fact that Phoumi has not yet taken the airport at Vientiane, which is of great importance to the Soviets' airlift; and the fact that the pro-Communists are probably advancing on Luang Prabang—the royal capital."

He then posed several questions: "First, should we seek to have Thai aircraft transport supplies into the area? Second, if the Thais can't do the job, should we use United States aircraft? Third, should we suggest that Thai forces seize the airfield at Vientiane and hold the one at Luang Prabang? Finally, should we support reconnaissance of Laos by Thai aircraft and of North Vietnam by United States aircraft?"

Obviously this was a time to exploit success. We had a request for aid from a legally constituted government, and the SEATO Pact committed us to preserve the security of the area of Laos. I approved the use of Thai transport aircraft and United States aircraft as well. Answers to the other questions, I said, should await further developments, but I directed an immediate check on the feasibility of using high-altitude reconnaissance equipment to reconnoiter North Vietnam.

Boun Oum and Phoumi soon entered Vientiane in triumph, and Kong Le's forces retreated north from that city.

During the next two weeks the Soviet Union flew more than 180 sorties into Laos in support of Kong Le and the Pathet Lao; it was becoming apparent that the new anti-Communist government of Boun Oum would need a great measure of outside help if it was to survive.[13]

On December 31 we held a critical conference. General Charles Cabell, Deputy Director of the CIA, reported that about fifteen hundred to twenty-five hundred troops, organized in battalions, with mortars, were moving into Laos from the direction of North Vietnam, though their exact origin was still unknown. General Lemnitzer informed us that the attaché plane accredited to the Laotian government had taken pictures of the Soviets air-dropping supplies. Part of the Pathet Lao controlled a large area north of Vientiane, from which they were attacking eastward. Still another Pathet Lao force was driving westward from Sam Neua province toward Xieng Khouang. If these two forces joined, they would cut Laos in half. Finally, an attack from Phong Saly province was pushing

[13] Souvanna Phouma, at the moment, was still in Cambodia; it was possible that he would try to set up a Communist "national front" government.

southward into north-central Laos, and General Phoumi himself was commanding the defense against it.

This was disturbing news. Possibly we had another Lebanon on our hands. While we needed more information—such as indisputable proof of North Vietnamese or Red Chinese intervention—before taking overt action, I was resolved that we could not simply stand by. I thought we might be approaching the time when we should make active use of the Seventh Fleet, including landing parties.

I knew, however, that our allies, particularly the French, would hesitate to take decisive action to cooperate with us: from the outset the French had hoped that Souvanna Phouma's "neutralist" government would work; and they disliked Phoumi Nosavan.

"For the moment," I said finally, "here's what we must do: Induce Souvanna Phouma to resign as Prime Minister and if possible persuade him to leave Cambodia and depart for France. Get Boun Oum to allow the National Assembly to approve his government. Inform the British and French of our positions and moves and seek their support. Alert the SEATO Council, but for the moment, do not request specific overt action by the alliance. Redeploy our own forces to bring them within striking range in the event they have to intervene against the North Vietnamese. We then should make a serious approach to the Russians, telling Ambassador Thompson to let Khrushchev know that we view these events with grave concern, that we are moving our forces to assure, if necessary, that the legitimate government of Laos will not be destroyed, and that if a major war comes, the United States will not be caught napping."

As the group prepared to leave the room, I summarized: "We cannot let Laos fall to the Communists even if we have to fight"—adding, "with our allies or without them."[14]

The next day, New Year's Day 1961, the Boun Oum government reported that Communist forces had captured the Plaine des Jarres—a four-thousand-foot plateau north of Vientiane, of strategic importance because of its airstrip and its main highway connecting North Vietnam with Luang Prabang and Vientiane. The North Vietnamese were claiming the capture of the Plaine and the city of Xieng Khouang, halfway across the neck of Laos.

Emergency White House meetings again became routine. On January 2 General Lemnitzer reported that if we had to intervene, the current

[14] A letter from Prime Minister Macmillan, written on December 30, the day before the meeting just described, expressed views that, in reference to Laotian political affairs, were in conformity with ours. This letter found in Appendix CC.

plan called for our forces to hold the two main cities (Vientiane and Luang Prabang), leaving the protection of the countryside to the Laotians.

"It's my conviction," I interposed, "that if we ever have to resort to force, there's just one thing to do: clear up the problem completely." We should not allow a situation to develop, costly in both blood and treasure, without achieving our objectives.

Though we and the British were in general agreement, the French, Secretary Herter reported, were not backing our efforts to get Souvanna Phouma to resign, nor were they willing to recognize Boun Oum. I told the group that I would send a message to President de Gaulle right away. That message said in part:

> . . . The evidence is indisputable that the Soviets are conducting a massive airlift in support of the Pathet Lao and others in rebellion against the King of Laos. There is also growing evidence of substantial intervention of indeterminate proportion from North Vietnam. It is not my purpose to raise with you the legal niceties of the status of the Boun Oum government which, as you know, we have been urging to complete the final steps of applicable constitutional process. What I do want to tell you is that we take most seriously this evidence of an effort by the Soviet bloc to bring the Kingdom of Laos under its domination and control. The United States takes very seriously its obligation under the SEATO Treaty as we assume you and the other parties do likewise. It seems to me that this is a time when we should make clear to the other side that, whereas from time to time we may differ on tactics and methods, we are nevertheless at one and resolute in the face of any Sino-Soviet threat. I hope we can make this unity clear to the world.

On January 5, Ambassador Hervé Alphand delivered to me President de Gaulle's reply:

> It appears obvious to me, as to you, that Pathet Lao elements are operating in the north of the country, and doubtless also certain other elements associated with them at the moment are receiving considerable support in the form of matériel from the Communist countries, namely the Soviet Union and the Republic of North Vietnam. This state of affairs is in itself fraught with danger for the future of Laos and is most certainly contrary to the spirit and provisions of the Geneva agreements.
>
> The difficulties we have encountered in outlining and pursuing a joint Western policy are, unfortunately, partly responsible for the situation that has resulted in the disintegration of the Government of Prince Souvanna Phouma and the fighting in Vientiane. . . .

Obviously, General de Gaulle was not particularly disturbed by the situation in Laos itself; he was still more concerned with a tripartite approach to global problems, including this one.

* * *

In the final weeks of my administration, the situation remained cloudy and serious. The United States charged the Soviet Union and North Vietnam with an extensive part in the military operations in Laos. The Laotian parliament approved the Boun Oum government by a vote of 41–0, with 11 abstentions. That government announced it would launch a drive to retake the Plaine des Jarres and Xieng Khouang.

As the administration came to a close, we left a legacy of strife and confusion in Laos. This I regretted deeply. But we left also, I believe, a correct policy of supporting the Boun Oum government. We were ready to stand by it against aggression from the outside.[15]

* * *

Ever since the initial success of the Castro revolution, we had increasing trouble with that government.

By the end of September 1960 the United States was getting ready to shut down the governmentally owned Nicaro nickel processing plant and to abolish preferential tariffs for Cuban exports to the United States. We were speeding up the evacuation of American citizens. Other moves were imminent.

In October Secretary of Commerce Mueller and Under Secretary of State Dillon recommended a prohibition of all exports to Cuba except medical supplies and non-subsidized food products, on the ground that Cuba had failed to pay for imports from the United States. The plan was to deny Cuba items, particularly spare parts for American-made equipment, and thus cause costly shutdowns. This would in turn cause other shutdowns and have, it was believed, a snowballing effect.

Also in October I received a letter criticizing the government for not making clear that the United States would not allow Castro to capture our naval base at Guantanamo Bay. Wondering how anyone could have

[15] On March 11, 1961, the Pathet Lao launched a new major offensive. The new United States administration, in a statement put out March 23, implied it was changing the policy of its Republican predecessor: "If in the past there has been any possible ground for misunderstanding of our support for a truly *neutral* Laos, there should be none now." By June of 1962, we had a "truly neutral Laos"—a brand new government of National Union, headed by Souvanna Phouma, who held also the Ministry of Defense—a government including the Communist Souphanouvong (Economics Minister) and General Phoumi (Finance Minister).

As of this writing nearly four years later, the Pathet Lao have occupied most of Laos against the Souvanna Phouma government.

any doubts as to this point, I directed the issuance of a White House statement, asserting the United States would never permit the seizure of that base. Indeed, some days earlier, we had reinforced the base with Marines; now the Navy put mine fields around the base. The Cuban government hastily let it be known that it would never attack Guantanamo. I had often told my associates that the last thing that Castro would do was to give us such a clear reason to eliminate him.

Castroite groups were, however, threatening other Latin American countries. They began stirring up trouble against the government of President Betancourt of Venezuela, and a few weeks later we became concerned about possible Communist influence in the new government that had just seized power in El Salvador.

On November 13, Secretary Herter reported a revolt against the government in Guatemala, saying the situation there was not good. I decided that if we received a request from Guatemala for assistance, we would move in without delay.

At that moment, Cuban exiles were training in Guatemala, and we had to consider the possibility of Castro's sending forces of his own to attempt an overthrow of the Guatemalan government. To guard against this possibility, we agreed to that government's request for United States naval units to patrol Guatemala's Caribbean coast. Simultaneously, a similar request came from the government of Nicaragua, which claimed evidence of Cuban complicity in a recent revolt within its borders. Naval units were directed to remain on the alert in the area, and our aircraft were to conduct patrols. They were ordered to report promptly any evidence of a Castroite attempt to send supplies or reinforcements to the rebels, but would refrain from combat unless specifically authorized or unless necessary to bar a direct Communist invasion attempt. Three weeks later the emergency ended, and we recalled the patrol.

On January 2, 1961, Fidel Castro ordered the United States to cut its Embassy staff in Havana to eleven persons within forty-eight hours. The staff, he alleged, totaled three hundred, with 80 per cent of them spies. The truth was that the Embassy had only eighty-seven persons, of whom more than half were Cubans. But this message from Castro was the last straw. We broke off diplomatic relations with Cuba immediately.

Meanwhile, covert training of exiles[16] for any possible future operations against Castro was going forward. Units were growing steadily in strength and efficiency against the time when actual tactical planning could be undertaken. In December I suggested to the State Department that the time might now be propitious for organizing a "front" against

[16] The activity was still centered, principally, in Guatemala.

Castro among the refugees, with the United States recognizing the leader and his associates as the legal government of Cuba, with the proviso, however, that the exiles themselves would voluntarily select from their own number an acceptable "head of government." I added that if they could do so at once, "I'd like to see recognition accorded promptly—if possible, before January 20."

On the morning of January 10, the *New York Times* carried an article, with a map, describing the training of anti-Castro forces in Guatemala. Although some details in the article were inaccurate, it told most of the story. I decided that we should say nothing at all about this article. Believing that my successor might want some day to assist the refugee forces to move into Cuba, I considered that we were limited in what we could say about them.

So, to the incoming administration, we left units of Cuban refugees busily training and preparing hopefully for a return to their native land. Because they had as yet been unable to find the leader they wanted—a national leader known to be both anti-Castro and anti-Batista—it was impossible to make specific plans for a military invasion. However, their hatred of Castro, their patriotism, and their readiness to sacrifice for the restoration of freedom in Cuba could not be doubted.

* * *

The life of my administration was now measured in hours, and on the evening of January 17 I spoke in farewell to the American people:

> Three days from now, after half a century in the service of our country, I shall lay down the responsibilities of office as, in traditional and solemn ceremony, the authority of the Presidency is vested in my successor.
>
> This evening I come to you with a message of leave-taking and farewell, and to share a few final thoughts with you, my countrymen.
>
> Like every other citizen, I wish the new President, and all who will labor with him, Godspeed. I pray that the coming years will be blessed with peace and prosperity for all.

During the years of my Presidency, and especially the latter years, I began to feel more and more uneasiness about the effect on the nation of tremendous peacetime military expenditures. In the peaceful life-span of the United States, our practice had been to maintain a minimum defense establishment. For a time, we trusted to the protection of two vast oceans. We frequently indulged in a rather naïve belief that any American could be made into a competent soldier within a matter of weeks or days. Every one of our wars was followed by rapid, drastic demobilization in the assumption that the world had become too civilized to fight again. With victory in World War II we began to reduce our forces so precipitously that every year from 1947 to 1950—on the eve of the Korean War—our annual military budget never exceeded $12 billion.

But in mid-1953, after the end of the Korean War, I determined that we would not again become so weak militarily as to encourage aggression. This decision demanded a military budget that would establish, by its very size, a peacetime precedent.

None of us was blind to the possible consequences of this move. We knew that such immense expenditures were made necessary by the frictions of international politics and the growing costs of weaponry. The effects of these expenditures on the nation's economy would be serious. Some of these effects would surely be seen as beneficial. But their eventual influence on our national life, unless watched by an alert citizenry, could become almost overpowering.

To counter this caution, there are, of course, other interested parties. Many groups find much value to themselves in constant increases in defense expenditures. The military services, traditionally concerned with 100 per cent security, are rarely satisfied with the amounts allocated to them, out of an even generous budget.

The makers of the expensive munitions of war, to be sure, like the profits they receive, and the greater the expenditures the more lucrative the profits. Under the spur of profit potential, powerful lobbies spring up to argue for even larger munitions expenditures. And the web of special interest grows.

Each community in which a manufacturing plant or a military installation is located profits from the money spent and the jobs created in the area. This fact, of course, constantly presses on the community's political representatives—congressmen, senators, and others—to maintain the facility at maximum strength.

All of these forces, and more, tend, therefore, to override the convictions of responsible officials who are determined to have a defense structure of adequate size but are equally determined that it shall not grow beyond that level. In the long run, the combinations of pressures for growth can create an almost overpowering influence. Unjustified military spending is nothing more than a distorted use of the nation's resources.

In the making of every military budget, my associates and I were guided by these considerations. We did our best to achieve real security without surrendering to special interest.

The idea, then, of making a final address as President to the nation seemed to call on me to warn the nation, again, of the danger in these developments. I could think of no better way to emphasize this than to include a sobering message in what might otherwise have been a farewell of pleasantries.

The most quoted section of the speech came in these paragraphs:

> A vital element in keeping the peace is our military establishment. Our arms must be mighty, ready for instant action, so that no potential aggressor may be tempted to risk his own destruction.
>
> Our military organization today bears little relation to that known by any of my predecessors in peacetime, or indeed by the fighting men of World War II or Korea.
>
> Until the latest of our world conflicts, the United States had no armaments industry. American makers of plowshares could, with time and as required, make swords as well. But now we can no longer risk emergency improvisation of national defense; we have been compelled to create a permanent armaments industry of vast proportions. Added to this, three and a half million men and women are directly engaged in the defense establishment. We annually spend on military security more than the net income of all United States corporations.
>
> This conjunction of an immense military establishment and a large arms industry is new in the American experience. The total influence—economic, political, even spiritual—is felt in every city, every state house, every office of the federal government. We recognize the imperative need for this development. Yet we must not fail to comprehend its grave implications. Our toil, resources, and livelihood are all involved; so is the very structure of our society.
>
> In the councils of government we must guard against the acquisition of unwarranted influence, whether sought or unsought, by the military-industrial complex. The potential for the disastrous rise of misplaced power exists and will persist.
>
> We must never let the weight of this combination endanger our liberties or democratic processes. We should take nothing for granted. Only an alert and knowledgeable citizenry can compel the proper meshing of the huge industrial and military machinery of defense with our peaceful methods and goals, so that security and liberty may prosper together.

This was, at the end of my years in the White House, the most challenging message I could leave with the people of this country.

* * *

The next morning I held my final news conference. In the last question a reporter asked: ". . . would you sum up for us your idea of what kind of a United States you would like your grandchildren to live in?" My answer summed up all I'd been trying to do for eight years:

I hoped that they might live "in a peaceful world . . . enjoying all of the privileges and carrying forward all the responsibilities envisioned for

View of San Diego, California, from seventy thousand feet

"Proof of the [U-2] plane's capacity to produce photography of excellent definition was striking. I was shown photographs, taken from an altitude of seventy thousand feet, of some of our important cities. On these we could easily count the automobiles on the streets and even the lines marking the parking areas for individual cars. There was no doubt about the quality of the information to be obtained."

"Communist elements began urging violence to prevent my entry into [Japan]....My emissaries conducted themselves magnificently; one of the news pictures of the episode showed Jim Hagerty coolly taking photographs with a miniature camera of the howling crowd while they rocked his car."

Welcoming crowds in Seoul, South Korea

" 'The Communists, some time ago, reached the conclusion that these visits were of such positive value to the Free World as to obstruct Communist imperialism....Through their propaganda they bitterly opposed my entry into the Philippines...Taiwan...Okinawa ...Korea, and, of course, Japan.' "

"On Monday, July 25, Cabot Lodge gave the Security Council the facts of the entire flight. 'The American RB-47 plane was over international waters and at no time flew over Soviet territory, Soviet territorial waters, or Soviet airspace. The shooting down of this plane, as the Soviet government alleges, can only have been a deliberate and reckless attempt to create an international incident.'"

TURBULEN

Young political speaker
in Leopoldville

"In flood force, the spirit of nationalism had grown in all Africa. The determination of the peoples for self-rule, their own flag, and their own vote in the United Nations resembled a torrent overrunning everything in its path."

"Dr. Ralph Bunche was the representative on the spot of the Secretary-General."

UN Secretary-General
Dag Hammarskjold, far right
enters Katanga province with
Premier Moise Tshombe
(waving)

"...within a few weeks of the initial rioting, the whole sorry mess fell to the United Nations.... Speed was essential, and response was immediate."

UMMER

mier Nikita Khrushchev at
UN session in
v York, September 1960

Premier Fidel Castro

"Khrushchev's performance, together with the subsequent 4½-hour harangue by Fidel Castro, did much to reinforce the bad impression created by their boorish antics in public a couple of days earlier."

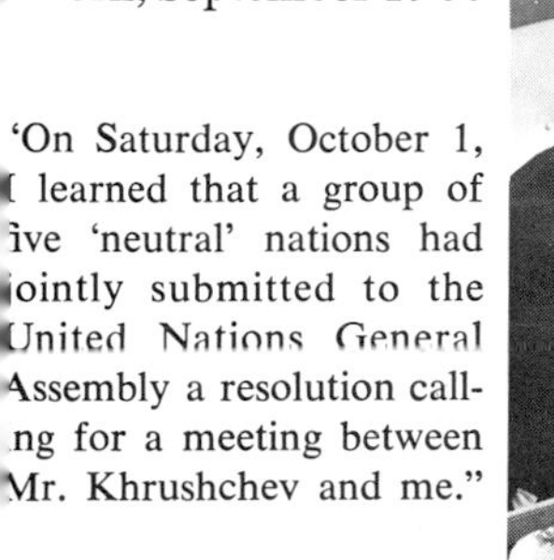

'On Saturday, October 1, [learned that a group of ive 'neutral' nations had iointly submitted to the United Nations General Assembly a resolution call- ng for a meeting between Mr. Khrushchev and me."

Prime Minister Nehru talks with President Josef Tito of Yugo- slavia, center

President Gamal Abdel Nasser, U.A.R., with President Sukarno of Indonesia *(right)*

resident
wame Nkrumah
f Ghana

President
Sylvanus Olympio
of Togo

"My schedule in New York included talks with only two leaders of tropical Africa, Kwame Nkrumah of Ghana and Sylvanus Olympio of Togo. In talking with them, my main objective was to advance the recommendation I had made in my United Nations address for the formation of regional groupings of nations."

"On September 26 came the first of the several television debates between the two candidates. In principle I had opposed them. But the decision had been made very early, with a commitment given at the end of the Republican National Convention in July."

"Even before the election, I had set up machinery for an orderly transfer of responsibilities and duties to the incoming President.... On December 6, Senator Kennedy came to the White House, at my invitation..."

"How much more we still had to face in the next six weeks I would never have guessed."

"As we strove to counter the threat to the dollar, we simultaneously worked to combat a Communist threat to Laos."

Pathet Lao forces on the march through Sam Neua province

Left to right: Colonel John S. D. Eisenhower, Barbara Anne, Barbara Eisenhower, David, the President, Mrs. (Mamie) Eisenhower with Mary Jean and Susan Elaine

the good citizen of the United States, and this means among other things the effort always to raise the standards of our people in their spiritual, . . . intellectual, . . . [and] economic strength. That's what I would like to see them have."

* * *

On January 19, the day before President-elect Kennedy's inauguration, I invited him to come to my office for a final briefing. When we had met before, on December 6, we had talked in terms of broad objectives and policies; today my purpose was more specific—to make him familiar with the immediate, split-second decisions he might be required to make as Commander-in-Chief after his inauguration only twenty-four hours away. I went over the major foreign and domestic problems which were most likely to require early decisions. His decisions, I said, would be made easier by well-established procedures and competent professional aides. But he had to know these procedures before he took the oath of office, not after; then there might not be time. He had to know, for example, the significance of the satchel filled with orders applicable to an emergency and carried by an unobtrusive man who would shadow the President for all his days in office. To give an example of the mechanical assistance he would have at his command in order to take a hurried trip of any kind, I pushed a button and said, "Send a chopper." In just six minutes a helicopter sat down on the lawn outside my oval office.

Mr. Kennedy seemed pleased. He took the briefing in good stride. But the conference was a sober one; neither of us apparently felt any impulse to minimize the significance of the transfer of immense responsibilities, now only hours away.

The evening of January 19, 1961, saw a deluge of snow dumped on Washington. For the first time in eight years many of the staff were unable to return home because of the blizzard. Some spent the night in the shelter in the basement of the White House, where they were made as comfortable as possible. Early in the evening Secretary Gates called to say he was turning out all possible troops from Fort Belvoir, Fort Myer, and other locations to assist the overwhelmed authorities in Washington to clear the streets and make the 1961 inauguration possible without delay.

JANUARY 20, 1961

"For an enemy," Maurice Stans remarked at one of our final meetings, "January 20 would be the ideal date for an attack on the United States."

A presidential inauguration could be a moment of practical dead center for the federal governmental mechanism. Further, an emergency, arising at home or abroad during the first twenty-four hours after a new President takes his oath of office, would demand decisions and actions which, by reason of the unfamiliarity of new officials with their duties and authority, might result in bewilderment and lack of intelligent reaction, with resultant damage to the United States.

I reflected on such possibilities as I attended the inauguration ceremonies of President Kennedy on January 20, 1961, and felt some satisfaction in the fact that we had spared nothing in assisting our successors in these matters. Moreover, I was thankful indeed that America's deterrent power was so formidable and our defense forces so alert as to insure that no recklessness in any capital of the world might try to take advantage of the moment.

So, after the now President Kennedy had repeated the traditional, "So help me God," Mamie and I, making our way toward a side exit, made a fantastic discovery. We were free—as only private citizens in a democratic nation can be free. This time as we left the Capitol, we were not solemnly accompanied by escorting committees of the Senate and the House or surrounded by the always loyal and helpful members of the Secret Service. Quietly avoiding the general flow of the crowd, we made our own way to a waiting car, interested, for the moment, only in arriving promptly at a post-inaugural luncheon to be given by Admiral and Mrs. Strauss, two of the ablest, most personable and dedicated persons who have ever graced the Washington scene. Their guests were members of the Cabinet, heads of other agencies of the government, our close friends and their wives. There, all of us found opportunity to reminisce, in a relaxed atmosphere, about the past eight years.

At the end of this happy but poignant affair, we said our adieus, and my wife and I started the eighty-mile trip to Gettysburg, where a small family reunion awaited us and our new life would begin.

We followed the route, now grown familiar to us, through the suburbs of northwest Washington, past Rockville, Frederick, Thurmont, and Emmitsburg. We talked of our years in the White House, which had been our home for a longer time than any other place in our forty-four years of married life and would always hold for us a wealth of pleasant memories. During those years three of our grandchildren left babyhood behind and learned to swim and ride and began their formal education. The youngest was born in Walter Reed Army Hospital and christened in the lovely Blue Room of the White House. We formed many new and enduring friendships, and every day we learned something new about our country and its people, and the great world about us.

During all the days of early January we had been busy saying our farewells to scores of our official family whom we had come to like and admire. Today we had left behind, also, the devoted people of the personal staff of the White House—the ushers, policemen, Secret Servicemen, housekeepers, waiters, doormen, carpenters, painters, engineers, florists, plumbers, gardeners, electricians, and others who had spent these eight years, never in the spotlight but always engaged in keeping the White House a fit shrine for the people of this nation and in making our daily lives pleasant, happy, and free of inconvenience and annoyance. To say good-bye to them had been truly difficult.

As we rolled through the countryside, we found that many of our fellow citizens had learned of our planned route and paused along the way to wave a friendly greeting. Approaching Emmitsburg, we were saluted once more, as in November of 1955, by the students and the sisters of St. Joseph College. Much had happened since that day, over five years before, when the College had paid us a similar compliment as Mamie and I were driving to Gettysburg for convalescence from my heart attack. Mamie was particularly excited, the more so because she was an honorary doctor of the College. On this day, standing in the fresh, deep snow, all the lovely young girls in their caps and gowns and the faculty of sisters lined the road to welcome us back to the region where we were establishing our new home.

* * *

And so we came to Gettysburg and to the farm we had bought eleven years earlier, where we expected to spend the remainder of our lives.

Afterthoughts

Hindsight is more accurate than foresight but less valuable.

NOW that the factual recital of my eight years in the Presidency is completed, I may in a questioning mood indulge for a while in the luxury of hindsight. As I look over my shoulder, the landscape of memory is dominated by the ridges and peaks of crises, which almost conceal the peaceful pastoral plains between them. But there were occasional calm and happy hours and I realize that in concentrating on the bold features of the whole I have written in these two volumes a somewhat distorted story. It is an account of a succession of events, decisions, and actions, but obviously it must fall to historians to sort out better than I have been able to do the important from the trivial, the interesting from the boring, the subjective from the coldly factual.

During the more than three years of writing, I have of necessity made a maximum and often tiresome use of documentary records to jog, fortify, or correct a sometimes untrustworthy memory. But it occurred to me that there might be value in setting down several ideas, lessons, or merely speculations that require no documentation, for they would be completely personal. A few of these are of such scope and complexity that a full analysis of them could command an entire book; others involve conclusions so unorthodox as to preclude quick acceptance. I shall not attempt the former or expect the latter. But, employing no special guideposts and no planned order of priority, I am disposed to discuss at random a few ideological, political, and organizational subjects in the hope that some may deem them to be worthy of consideration. And so doing, I confess I enjoy standing on the comfortable ground of retrospect.

THE COLD WAR

Because the cold war is the central fact of our time, it is natural that I should begin with observations that are based upon or related to the policies we pursued during my years of responsibility for the conduct of our foreign relations.

It is often said that the United States does not have a foreign policy; that, instead, it is constantly improvising to meet each new situation. There is a modicum of truth in such a remark, but it is also a statement of obvious untruth. A sudden *coup d'état* in a Middle East country can affect the means and methods we apply to further our basic purpose (to defend freedom in that region). It can create crisis in neighboring nations. No absolute pre-planning is feasible, no rigid policy can apply. One need is to confer promptly with America's interested friends and for all, if possible, to agree on a course of action. But the need for quick reaction in emergencies does not deny the requirement for a well-thought-out and applicable general policy.

A nation's global policy comprises the worldwide objectives of the government and the basic methods and programs developed for achieving them. It is therefore a mistake to think of foreign policy in the singular; it is scarcely too much to say that there must be a separate policy for our relations with every nation, for we obviously must take into account the special situation, aspirations, and problems of each. Needless to say, each of these special adaptations must conform to the abiding principles and objectives of our nation.

Fundamental objectives and basic methods of governments may and sometimes do change with the times. This is not peculiar to the United States. In the mid-nineteenth century the objectives of Prussia's Bismarck were the formation of the German Empire and making it the dominant power of Europe. His method, primarily, was military conquest, now as outmoded, among nations of the West, as the flintlock musket. Late in the nineteenth and early in the twentieth century the United States briefly succumbed to interventionism. But for some decades our purposes abroad have been the establishment of universal peace with justice, free choice for all peoples, rising levels of human well-being, and the development and maintenance of frank, friendly, and mutually helpful contacts with all nations willing to work for parallel objectives. The broad programs of the United States used toward these ends have been forged over a period of time, but once initiated they have changed little.

A principal step toward fundamental goals, taken while World War

II was still raging, was to help found the United Nations. Since 1945 the United States—despite manifold disappointments due to deplorable weaknesses in the international organization and the uncooperative attitude of nations dominated by the Communists—has been steadfast in its support of the Charter. Moreover, our country has been quick to participate in all the organization's efforts to settle international controversies by negotiation. Under four Presidents, these efforts have been one major aspect of our basic foreign policy.

A second important program—especially since the Korean aggression—has been to sustain security forces fully adequate to counter any hostile move against us. This marked a sharp break with America's traditional policy. After each of our wars—down to and including World War II—our unilateral disarmament reached embarrassing and dangerous levels. But when, in 1953, the Korean armistice was signed, our government embarked on a new program of peacetime military preparation, costly, it is true, but in my opinion, in view of the world situation, decidedly necessary. No free nation can disregard the persistently announced purpose of the Communist imperialists to dominate the globe and this threat, backed as it is by the material strength of the U.S.S.R., its satellites, and its allies, is one of the important factors influencing our global foreign policy.

The Communists know, as we do, that the security of a nation depends upon a balanced strength comprised of morale, economic productivity, and military power. The delicately balanced and complex problem constantly posed to us of the United States was, and still is, this: to sustain a national determination to defend freedom with all we have, to devise and maintain indefinitely a military posture of such effectiveness that the Communists will abandon any thought of all-out military attack against us or our allies, and to support this military capacity so prudently as to avoid undermining our economic soundness. We need an adequate defense, but every arms dollar we spend above adequacy has a long-term weakening effect upon the nation and its security.

A third part of our national security programing has been to aid through loans, grants, and exchanges others that share our love of liberty.[1] The purpose has been to make them stronger and more effective

[1] The "isolationist" has not gone from among us. Those that remain oppose American help to other friendly nations. Such people—unwittingly, perhaps—strengthen the possibility that weaker nations, feeling abandoned, will one by one fall under Communist domination. While I think that isolationists do not want us surrounded by a sea of Communism, and so have to turn ourselves into a garrison state, they should try to achieve a global view of the ideological struggle and not narrow their gaze to the undoubted mistakes that have too often marred the United States' effort to lead the Free World in achieving a genuine collective defense.

partners in the work of establishing a stable and peaceful world under the rule of law. The Truman Doctrine and the Marshall Plan were forerunners of the Mutual Security Program and of our current financial assistance in support of the less-developed nations. While this effort is not well understood by the public, there can be little doubt that without it our international situation would be much more dangerous than it now is. There can be even less doubt that it will have to be—hopefully with more cooperation from other industrialized nations—continued for a considerable time.

Unfortunately, mistakes in administering foreign aid have too frequently been made, and have been so highly publicized that they have created a distorted view among the uninformed. Further, after my brother Milton's investigations in Latin America, I became convinced we were making fundamental policy errors, in that continent. In the mid- and late fifties, as we markedly increased private and public aid to the nations of Latin America, the masses there intensified their criticism of us, for they felt that we were supporting and strengthening the prevailing social order, which in their view denied them simple justice. So, we began changing our programs, culminating in the Act of Bogota in 1960, and later in the Charter of Punta del Este. Under these international compacts, special aid was to be extended only if recipient nations carried out social reforms which truly promoted economic and political democracy. The program is still under trial, but from this and other lessons I have concluded that, save in exceptional circumstances, our foreign aid should be granted mainly to those countries where each maintains or is clearly moving toward a governmental system and social methods that command the respect and support of the vast majority of its own citizens. Otherwise, our aid, if it helps to sustain in power regimes which are oppressive, may actually become self-defeating. To be effective our assistance must be discriminating.

Another enduring policy through which we have pursued our basic objectives has been that of strengthening our own and the Free World's security through a system of alliances, developed under the provisions of the United Nations Charter. I believe these policies must be intelligently continued. In addition to our bilateral mutual security treaties, we have signed multilateral treaties with the members of NATO and SEATO, with Australia and New Zealand, and with the nations of Latin America.[2] A *sine qua non* for success in establishing "collective security" is the practice of good faith among all signatories, and in maintenance of close relations

[2] The United States, though not a treaty member, is a supporter of CENTO.

among the leaders of the participating governments. Unless we maintain this kind of relationship, misunderstandings will arise and Free World security will be weakened.

These few important features of our postwar foreign relations demonstrate that global policy reflects a worldwide situation and will change markedly only as that situation is revolutionized.

Operational policies and programs developed to meet unique situations are quite a different matter. In these two volumes I have described how we dealt, over a period of eight years, with problems involving Iran, Trieste, Guatemala, Korea, Suez, Lebanon, the Formosa Strait, Vietnam, Laos, Austria, Cuba, and other areas. Methods varied, but I believe history will recognize we adhered consistently to principle and that we dealt honestly and on the whole effectively with each of these troublesome problems.

The United States lost no foot of the Free World to Communist aggression, made certain that the Soviets and China understood the adequacy of our military power, and dealt with them firmly but not arrogantly. We regarded our friends as respected partners and valued partners and tried always to create mutual confidence and trust, well knowing that without these ingredients alliances would be of little enduring value.

* * *

Despite difficulties that have intermittenly arisen in recent history among free nations, the truly virulent problems in international affairs spring from the persistent, continuing struggle between freedom and Communism. Though that struggle has been dissected, discussed, and debated so long and so heatedly that additional words seem redundant, I am constrained to add still more words to the millions that have been devoted to the subject.

The conflict between liberty and slavery is as old as history, as new as the latest tick of the clock. It reflects the instinctive rebellion of men, descended from tribes that knew no law except the survival of the fittest, to resist every attempt by any of their fellows to subdue, regiment, and utilize them to further the ambitions of would-be rulers.

On the other hand, this conflict reflects the truisms that freedom must be earned and defended each day, and that there must be an orderly society because a maximum of personal liberty depends upon avoidance of transgression on the freedom and rights of others.

External forces, thirsting for power, are always ready to destroy freedom. Witness the fate of Austria and Ethiopia before the opening of

World War II, and Hungary, Poland, North Vietnam, Czechoslovakia, Bulgaria, and others since its close.

Freedom's destruction from within has, as its classical example, ancient Rome; a more modern one is Germany in the thirties. Only a sturdy and vigilant citizenry, deeply dedicated to liberty and alert to any external or internal encroachment, can sustain freedom. Where sturdiness and vigilance, where clarity of vision are weakened—as by the cloying effects of governmental subsidy and false promises of easy living—freedom comes face to face with its deadliest internal enemy, the misled and complacent citizen. "Experience," the late Justice Brandeis said, "should teach us to be more on our guard to protect liberty when the government's purposes are beneficent."

Communism, no matter how it may be described or disguised, requires dictatorship as a condition of its existence. Moreover, because the Communist leaders recognize that freedom appeals deeply to man's basic instincts while regimentation is abhorrent to his nature, they conclude that the perpetuation of their doctrine depends upon the total destruction of individual liberty. This eliminates freedom of choice between their own and other ideologies. This is the international expression of their "one party only" political system at home.

The cardinal democratic concept that men are created equal and endowed with certain inalienable rights has been developed out of a religious faith. Communists scorn religion, labeling it the opiate of the people; should they accept the doctrine of the equality of all in the sight of God they could then claim no right, except that of naked power, to dominate and rule the lives of others.[3]

Thus released from any restraint, morality, in the Communist view, is that which serves the Party's good. Communists embrace every kind of tactic to gain their fundamental objective, the domination of the earth's peoples. Whatever may seem to them at any moment to be the most advantageous direction of advance needs no other justification. They use force, the threat of force, economic pressure and penetration, deceit, blackmail, distortion, propaganda, bribery, and lies to attain their ends, all with the sanction of their doctrine. The fairer their words the more suspect they are. "By their deeds" you must know them. Only where any promise of theirs can be verified at every step may the Western

[3] Khrushchev was once an altar boy; he told me that as a youth he had won prizes for excellence in religious education and ritual. But to become a dedicated Communist he had to become an atheist, and though now, in conversation, he will often consciously or unconsciously call upon the Deity to confirm the truth of his statements, officially he has no belief or faith in a Supreme Being.

world be justified in agreeing to mutual concessions or restrictions. This truth must be taken to heart by all the free nations as a guide in every negotiation with Communists. Failure to do so is interpreted by them as stupidity and earns only their contempt.

One of the areas of intense disagreement between the West and the Communists is the fate of the so-called European satellites. In the turmoil and confusion of the closing stages of World War II and the succeeding months, the Soviets made good their control over the eastern tier of European nations, establishing during that period a group of miniature Soviet states. The possession of all these satellites, including East Germany, places Communism in a strong geographic position in central Europe. Not only does this deny to the West the additional strength that would be forthcoming from independent and Western-orientated peoples such as those of the Baltic States, Poland, Czechoslovakia, and others, but it greatly interferes with the traditional trade that in the past has been of mutual advantage to East and West Europe. By the same token the Kremlin has not hesitated to utilize all of the facilities and skills of the captive nations to improve and strengthen its own economic fabric.

It is important to appreciate, however, that the forced subjugation of these peoples has created a long-term weakness in the Communist hegemony, for the political situation in those states is universally recognized as surface obedience to the Kremlin. Majority opinion in none of them supports Communism; with bitter resentment seething underneath a quiescent exterior, the 1956 revolt in Hungary and that of 1953 in East Germany, to say nothing of postwar unrest in Poland and the building of the Berlin wall to check the mass flight of East Germans, have provided the unmistakable evidence. Soviet leaders in my opinion are quite well aware of this potential weakness in Eastern Europe, a situation that cannot fail to create some cautions in their counsels.

It has been the consistent policy of the United States to maintain contacts with the captive countries and in appropriate instances even to assist them with economic help. Basically we want to keep alive in these peoples the hope of eventual delivery from their Communist masters. We want to let them know that the Free World is still concerned about them.

It is well to remember, also, that the Russian people, like all others in the world, want to live full, peaceful, and, as far as possible, prosperous and happy lives. Unfortunately, they have never known freedom and have no yardstick by which to measure the comparative advantages of life under Communist rule and under systems of self-government. They are sternly denied any broad, genuine knowledge of the outside world. Because they have been permitted gradually to achieve since World War II, somewhat higher material standards of life than they endured in the early years of Bolshevism or under the Czars they have, understandably, become more content with their lot than they were in earlier years. Indeed, because they are allowed to learn nothing better, it is not strange that in general they now consider themselves fortunate. But this will not be so when they finally become exposed to the quality of life in the free areas of the civilized world, especially life in the more advanced nations.

As a consequence, it should always be a part of Free World policy to make available to all peoples, including those of the Iron Curtain nations, information about the history, achievements, attitudes, and aspirations of peoples of whom they now know little or nothing. That the Communists fear the coming of a day when such enlightenment may be gained is again proved by the rigidity with which they maintain a closed society, enforcing ignorance of the outside world as a policy. Advancing communication techniques will one day overcome this obstacle by making it impossible to "jam" broadcasts. In the meantime our support of the United States Information Agency and Radio Free Europe should be generous, and those organizations should be guided by persons selflessly dedicated to the promotion of freedom and the propagation of truth.

Manifestly we cannot counter Communist tactics with their own weapons; with free speech and a free press established in most of the important nations of the West, there is no possibility of employing the big lie, often repeated, as a means either of unifying our own people or influencing others. Any attempt to do so would be futile, foolish, and, for us, immoral, and the lies so employed would bewilder and divide the nations of the West. We must use truth and fairness in explaining ourselves and in seeking to inform peoples—Western, uncommitted, and Communist—of the shallowness and inhumanity of the Communist system. Credibility in our informational programs is the first essential, and it cannot be achieved by falsehood and hypocrisy, which would be promptly exposed by a free press. But we can and should dwell upon the human satisfactions to be realized in a society of individual freedom.

This worldwide educational policy should be tirelessly pursued; its implementation should be studied, revised, and perfected, both as to the content of our messages and the techniques of dissemination.

When the day comes that the Communist peoples are as well-informed as those of the free nations, then dissatisfaction, unrest, and smoldering resentment among hundreds of millions will eventually bring about either reforms in the governmental structure or violent destruction of Communist dictatorships.

The Communists believe, or pretend they do, that the world's democracies carry within themselves the seeds of their own destruction. They preach that economic competition, descending into conflict between classes, between special groups and between capitalist nations, will grow so fierce and debilitating that free systems will disappear under Communist pressures.

Yet just recently, in 1963, Russia, despite the vastness of her territory and her vaunted competence in productivity, was compelled to go to free nations to buy, on credit, much of the grain needed to feed her hungry people. The United States, following the lead of Canada, entered into an agreement to sell Russia wheat of the value of about a quarter of a billion dollars. Time will prove whether this was wise. Meanwhile it will be interesting to observe to what degree the peasants and workingmen of Russia learn that this wheat came from a "decadent capitalistic nation" and that the Kremlin boasts that the Soviet Union is the most powerful and productive nation in the world are little more than "sounding brass and tinkling cymbals."[4]

We hear much, from men of little understanding, about the United States losing the "initiative" in the cold war. The Communists, by virtue of their dictatorial system, can create, at will, incidents out of which new Free World anxieties are born, burgeoning at times into crises. For example, when in 1957 the Soviets began to create difficulties in the Middle East, their influence seemed to grow rapidly and many thought the region would soon be lost to the Free World. This trend was effectively blocked by the congressional support of the Middle East Resolution, by Allied cooperation in supporting legitimate governments, and by the necessary and successful American intervention with troops in Lebanon in 1958. Then, almost without pause, the Communists renewed threatening activities in the Formosa Strait. In both instances the United States, though not provocative, was firm in support of its friends and unyielding in fundamentals. The next Communist move was to rekindle the fires always smoldering around Berlin.

Troublemaking should not be confused with true initiative. Always hopeful of bringing significant parts of the Western or neutralist areas within their orbit, the Communists resort to advance—then retreat, then threat and then cajolery. Measured against the background of the world struggle, these forays and blustering threats do not mean that the Soviets

[4] In 1945 I visited a Moscow factory where I saw machine tools stamped with the names of an American firm in Akron, Ohio. Yet I was told by my interpreter that every workingman in the plant believed that the tools that saved so much labor had been produced within their own nation.

have and retain the initiative. However, should the Free World begin to accept and give way before these ventures, then indeed we should fear loss of the initiative. This was the real tragedy of the Berlin wall, which, built in late 1961 and in defiance of international agreements,[5] yet evoked no quick or effective response by the United Nations, the United States, or any of our allies.

The major portion of world power—moral, intellectual, economic, and military—still lies outside the Communist bloc. This the Soviets well know. They cannot gain the initiative unless they succeed in dividing us against ourselves. I confess I experience uneasy moments when I see major Free World nations disagreeing publicly and sharply among themselves in solving problems critical to their common future. The difficulties facing the Free World in Cuba, Vietnam, Berlin, and elsewhere *can* be handled with confidence and success if those who love freedom will work together in the knowledge that individual selfish interest must never prevail over the welfare of the total free community. The greatest single task facing the leaders of the major free nations is to weld their peoples into dependable, cooperative organizations, characterized by mutual respect and a willingness to share the responsibility of defeating each new Communist adventure, and in promoting the positive actions essential to building a world of peace, justice, and rising levels of living.

So long as we, the United States, and our stanch allies, deal summarily with every thrust of every kind against the Free World's rights and pursue together programs calculated to bring about, gradually, a better life for the world's multitudes, then the initiative will remain with us.

Communists think in terms of decades and generations, rather than merely in months or years. They hope that over the long term, selfishness, fear, or complacency will cause us to fail to sustain essential internal balance and dependable Free World cooperation, thus bringing about a deterioration of the strength and resolute leadership which now faces them. If this should occur, the consequences for us would be disastrous. We, therefore, must likewise think in terms of decades and generations. Long-sustained military power, economic health, moral and intellectual vitality, dependable Free World cooperation, eternal vigilance, and informed and resolute leadership—these are the ingredients of ultimate success.

[5] At the Council of Foreign Ministers in Paris in the spring of 1949, France, the U.K., the U.S.S.R., and the U.S. agreed to "take the measures necessary to insure the normal functioning and utilization of rail, water, and road transport for [the] movement of persons and goods and . . . communications [between] the Eastern zone and the Western zones and between the zones and Berlin."

ORGANIZATION

Having lived all my adult years with problems of organization, it was natural that in the White House I should give attention to the possibility of improving organization and management at higher governmental levels.

To the public there is nothing intriguing about government structure, operations, and systems of policy formation and execution. To the young the word "organization" has little meaning. Because hero worship is natural to them, they think not of organization but of leaders—particularly successful military commanders of the past—as individuals of much mental agility, personal magnetism, moral and physical courage—in short, of genius. Indeed, they easily identify themselves with their own favorite. In the martial dreams of almost every boy he finds himself in command of vast armies, which he maneuvers and directs across continents and through sanguinary battles with such precision, all-seeing eye, and infallible judgment that in moments he achieves victory, bows to the plaudits of the imaginary multitude, and goes on the next dream campaign. What does he need with organization?

In the approach of many older people to problems of organization and control there seems to be something of the child. To the adult mind "organization" seems to summon visions of rigidity and machine-like operation, with an inescapable deadly routine and stodginess in human affairs. Yet it is not the enemy of imagination or of any other attractive human characteristic. Its purpose is to simplify, clarify, expedite, and coordinate; it is a bulwark against chaos, confusion, delay, and failure.

Organization cannot of course make a successful leader out of a dunce, any more than it should make a decision for its chief. But it is effective in minimizing the chances of failure and in insuring that the right hand does, indeed, know what the left hand is doing.

Skillful and thorough organization of vast enterprises is essential to their successful operation. Certainly this applies to the United States government. In 1776, Americans flatly rejected the theory of government by an autocrat of vast powers, and eleven years later confirmed in our Constitution that we would be a union of self-governing people. Our fate would therefore depend upon the wisdom and the good sense of the millions, not the influence of the few; deliberately we established a nation that requires, respects, and places its faith *in organization,* determined and fixed by laws. Organization was our answer to the threat of tyranny. Through highly organized Legislative, Executive, and Judicial machinery our people make and implement their decisions.

Organization in the Executive branch provides the means for performing systematically, promptly, and accurately the research and related work essential to the orderly presentation to the President of all the pertinent facts and calculations which he must take into account in making a sound decision on any issue. Thereafter, it assures that his decision is communicated to and essential resulting action is coordinated among the appropriate agencies.

Good organization provides for the allocation of authority and fixing of responsibility in each echelon of the entire establishment. Inefficient functioning of governmental organization, bringing about indecision and untimely counterorders, was apparently part of the cause for the 1961 Bay of Pigs fiasco.

To describe satisfactory staff organization for the Presidency in terms of my own experience, one or two obvious generalizations are pertinent: For one thing, the Chief Executive must first select his principal assistants from among the ablest, most dedicated and experienced men and women he can find. An ideal organization can be of little help if personnel selections are badly made, either through honest error or employment of wrong standards. Conversely, if the principal assistants to the Executive are strong, understanding, and devoted individuals of integrity, they can make even a jerry-built organization function, at least haltingly. The ideal combination, of course, is to have capable personnel and a logical system.

No specific organization is sacrosanct in its details; it is established and used by humans and it can be changed by them. Indeed, at times this may be necessary because of changing conditions or even by the entry of a new personality. Thus, for example, my use of Vice President Nixon as a member of advisory bodies and as a personal representative in many affairs, both domestic and foreign, created an organizational precedent in American history. Traditionally the Vice President had been the forgotten man of the Washington scene; more than one man, because of his lack of respect for the office, has refused to be considered for nomination to the post. But Mr. Nixon's willingness to perform a variety of tasks, at my request, and his presence at all important policy meetings, assured that in the event of my death or disability, his own knowledge and understanding of the changing world and domestic situations would have no gaps.

* * *

From the beginning of our national life, Presidents have been assisted, in the performance of their necessary duties, by advisory groups, the oldest and, for many years the principal one, being the Cabinet. In modern times there are also the National Security Council, the Council of Economic Advisers, the Science Advisory Committee, and many ad hoc committees and commissions appointed for study of particular subjects. None of these bodies has any power of its own. Misapprehensions concerning this simple truth have been many and often expressed.

My assistant, General Goodpaster, once showed me, in a state of complete exasperation, a press account on the subject of presidential functioning that ran about as follows:

> . . . . one method is to turn to his subordinates—to his chiefs of staff and his Cabinet officers and Secretaries and so forth, getting them to argue out the issues and to bring him an agreed upon decision. On the whole, this is President Eisenhower's method.
>
> The other way is to sit like a judge at a hearing while the issues to be decided are debated. After hearing the debate, and examining the evidence, after he has heard the debaters cross-examine each other, after he has questioned them, he makes his decision.

Goodpaster was so perturbed at such a distortion of fact that I laughed aloud; "Andy," I said, "let's not worry about how decisions are made; let's just be sure they are right."

Of course, the ridiculous character of this particular report is obvious when it is realized that such a thing as unanimity in a meeting of men of strong convictions working on complex problems is often an impossibility. Could anyone imagine George Humphrey, Foster Dulles, Ezra Taft Benson, Harold Stassen, Arthur Summerfield, Herbert Brownell, Lewis Strauss, C. D. Jackson, and James Mitchell reaching a unanimous conclusion on the main features of a proposed test ban, a national tax and expenditure program, a labor crisis, or foreign aid? They would not. I never asked or expected them to do so; in fact, had they presented a unanimous conclusion I would have suspected that some important part of the subject was being overlooked, or that my subordinates had failed to study the subject.

Although no staff, council, or cabinet attempted to make decisions for me, yet every subordinate was always expected, within his own area of delegated authority and within the limits of established policy, to solve his own problems. Upon this I insisted; whenever I had to make a decision that properly belonged to a subordinate I admonished him once, but if he failed again it was time to begin looking for a replacement. This was a maxim of General George Marshall.

Yet recognizing that major decisions belong solely to the head of the government does not imply any endorsement of a personality cult. Whether that head is weak or strong, thoughtful or impulsive, knowledgeable or ignorant, his is the basic responsibility and he must give the final word on every major question—and that word must be respected.

The questions reaching a President's desk are great in volume and so varied in character as to defy clear-cut classification. But their nature does encourage a rough division between those things that pertain mainly to international affairs and those that belong principally to the domestic field. The dividing line is neither sharp nor constant, but this rough classification does explain the existence of the two permanent and most important advisory bodies that during the 1950s served with me: the Cabinet for domestic affairs, the National Security Council for all matters pertaining to the nation's security.

The steady expansion in governmental requirements throughout our history has led to an essential increase in the number of the President's immediate assistants. This group, housed in the Executive Offices, has to be supervised and coordinated either by the President himself or through delegated authority. My own experience clearly pointed to the need for a senior Presidential Staff Assistant, to whom was given the duty of daily coordination of the staff[6] to the end that all its parts became in effect an extension of the President's own faculties.

The White House staff was not, however, authorized to act as a buffer between me and principal subordinates; its duty was to help, not to isolate me. An intelligent and experienced head of such a staff—in my presidential years Governor Sherman Adams and then General Wilton B. Persons occupied this post—assured that all members had an understanding of their proper functions and that all such functions were properly coordinated.

The task of coordination among heads of Departments and Agencies divides itself into two vaguely defined parts. The first involves important policies and operations. These always required my personal decisions. The second, dealing with detailed tactics, within the framework of approved policies, was normally handled by the staff. Such staff coordination was a convenient device for keeping trivia out of the hands of important officials, not a means of multiplying the number of straw bosses who were authorized to communicate with Cabinet and other responsible officials. Moreover, my orders required that if any department or agency head found it necessary to see me for any purpose whatsoever, he was always free to do so, without interference or hindrance from anyone.

Between the categories of subjects to be handled by the President and

[6] Except those staff members who were principally involved in foreign relations.

by his staff respectively lies a shadow area. Some subjects or problems are of such significance as to preclude handling through routine staff operations; at the same time they could well be handled efficiently without the constant attention of the President. I found two functions of government that required this kind of intermediate supervision—certain features in foreign affairs and business procedures.

By the terms of the Constitution the President is responsible for the conduct of our foreign relations. For this function the Secretary of State is his principal and indispensable assistant but by no means is he the only official who bears some responsibility in the field. Defense forces are deployed abroad in peacetime in such a fashion as to fulfill national objectives; these are of concern to the Secretary of State and of course the operations of these forces are under the control of the Secretary of Defense. Daily coordination between the State and Defense Departments is imperative. The United States Information Agency, constantly purveying news to other nations, can operate effectively only in close coordination with all departments that have responsibilities abroad. Every governmental operation that requires expenditures abroad, most important of which are those of the military forces, is of concern to the Treasury Department. The Agriculture, Commerce, and Labor Departments maintain many representatives abroad. Other agencies have duties and responsibilities that affect our foreign relations.

Policy decisions affecting these far-flung operations were my responsibility, but for daily coordination, I early organized the Operations Coordinating Board (OCB). Its membership included important officials of agencies which were directly in charge of specific foreign operations. It functioned fairly well. However, I came finally to believe that this work could have been better done by a highly competent and trusted official with a small staff of his own, rather than by a committee whose members had to handle the task on a part-time basis.

If such a plan were adopted the individual needed would, of course, have to be knowledgeable in international affairs, capable as a leader, and intimately familiar with all activities of the relevant departments and agencies so as to achieve the maximum of willing and effective cooperation. He would become, in a practical sense, a Deputy Chairman of the National Security Council. During the intervals between the President's meetings with the Council such an assistant would be, day-by-day, engaged in the task of making sure that agencies having any connection with foreign problems were all working together to carry out the President's decisions.

This official, who might have a title such as Secretary for International Coordination or First Secretary, could perform other useful functions. In behalf of the President, he could keep under close scrutiny not only normal foreign policy operations, but also such ever-changing matters as trade relations, shipments abroad of subsidized products, foreign aid, balance of payments, and a myriad of similar matters. For example, he could, without denigrating the positions of other Cabinet officers, make certain that public addresses on various phases of international affairs by high officials conformed to the President's views. In short, he could help insure that the President's policies were scrupulously observed and that the actions of one department would not negate those of another.

We once made an agreement, largely at the instigation of the Secretary of Agriculture, to sell to India a quantity of wheat at reduced prices and for soft currency. The State Department concurred at a "low level." Much later I was plaintively told by U Nu, Prime Minister of Burma, that our action had seriously interfered with his nation's sales of rice to India, resulting in real damage to Burma's economy. Even though the sale may have been desirable in spite of this fact, we should have provided advance information and explanation to the Burmese in order to assure their understanding, if not their concurrence. It is this kind of error—and other far less or more important ones—that better organization can help avoid.

On the "business side" of government better coordination also seemed necessary. The United States conducts the greatest business operation in the world and it is desirable that the huge departments, each responsible for vast expenditures, should conduct their affairs with maximum efficiency. The Congress, recognizing in the early 1920s the need for orderliness in the conduct of governmental business, established the Bureau of the Budget. In the years since, this agency has given its attention primarily to the development and execution, under presidential supervision, of the detailed expenditure programs for the coming year, to certain matters of government organization, to review of departmental legislative proposals before they reach the President's desk, and to supervision of some of the statistical services.

Obviously there is much more to business management than this. With the advent of electronic computers, considerable improvements in the business affairs of the government have been made. Even so, overlappings, confusion, and duplications are often serious, causing unnecessary costs.

Just as the President cannot personally handle the day-by-day coordination of operating details in the foreign field, so too he cannot give constant personal attention to minutiae of governmental business matters. Should he attempt to do so, he would be compelled to neglect matters of much greater importance. So I concluded that either an additional Secretary was needed, or that the position and authority of the director of the Bureau of the Budget should be upgraded. He should supervise the across-the-board business practices of the government—seeking to increase standardization wherever possible—and take over the functions handled by the "Special Assistant for Personnel." He should organize an inspectional service and revamp the Bureau of the Budget so as to give equal status to all functions: budget formation, expenditure control, standardization and promotion of effective business operations, legislative clearance, personnel, inspection, and organizational studies. In such a position and with this authority he would be an invaluable assistant to the President in promoting good government at least cost. Also he could surely save the President a good deal of time.

These two problems, coordination of detailed international operations and better management, had bothered me from the beginning of my White House service and I frequently discussed them with my Advisory Committee on Government Organization[7] as well as with individual members of the Cabinet.

Other observers had noted deficiencies in these two fields, and some students of government had suggested corrective devices. Former President Hoover, testifying before a Senate committee, suggested for business coordination the creation by law of a new post in the Executive branch, to be filled by an "Administrative Vice President." With this I emphatically agreed except for the use of the title "Vice President." I believed that to refer to an official, other than the elected Vice President, by that title, even with limiting adjectives, would cause confusion, while by the same token Cabinet officers might feel they were being reduced in rank and importance. One of the most persuasive appeals available to the President when he asks outstanding men to take Cabinet or other independent posts, usually at some personal sacrifice, is the assurance that each in his own field is the direct and principal assistant of the President. I would not disturb this clearly understood and eminently proper relationship, not even in appearance.

What I sought was a Cabinet of equals, but with two additional members, each of whom on behalf of the President would perform certain functions affecting a number or even all of the other Cabinet officers. Clearly, I thought, the title of each of the new members would have to include the word "Secretary," so as to let all others know that they were not being downgraded. I came to believe that the two most satisfactory titles for these officials would, if authorized, be "Secretary for International Coordination" and "Secretary for Business Management."

[7] Nelson Rockefeller, Arthur Flemming, Milton Eisenhower.

When I began to discuss these possibilities with others, in 1955, I quickly learned that to obtain the adoption of the plan a great deal of educational work would have to be done, beginning with the Cabinet itself. Among those who initially objected to the concept of a "Secretary for International Coordination" was Foster Dulles. At that time it was inconceivable to him that anyone other than the Secretary of State could have any right to speak to or for the President on any matter involving international affairs, even though the matter might fall, legally, outside the purview of his own responsibility. He held firmly to this position even though I told him that he was the individual I wanted to be the "International" Secretary.

Later, however, he came to agree to the wisdom of such a plan. He said that he would like to give the bulk of his time to assisting in developing policy and making certain that the government moved as a unit in all its foreign relations. Instead of this, however, too much of his time and energy was devoted to participating in hearings before congressional committees, many of which he thought unnecessary, attending to the multitudinous personnel problems of the Department, and conferring with others whose activities touched upon his own in the effort to avoid misunderstandings between our government and others. He found it increasingly difficult, because of all his administrative duties, to find time to give comprehensive attention to all facets of international policy, planning, and diplomatic activity that pertained properly to his office.

In earlier and simpler days, all foreign affairs of our government were coordinated under the immediate supervision of the Secretary of State while the President, in fulfilling his constitutional responsibility for foreign relations, could work almost exclusively with the Secretary. Our popular concept of the President-Secretary of State relationship was formed then and still lingers, even though a host of informational, trade, financial, military, and other matters now affecting our relations abroad are not under the jurisdiction of the Secretary of State.

One other aspect of this problem merits consideration. A modern Secretary of State must be out of the country on vital missions much of the time, as must other Secretaries and agency heads, but the problem of helping the President carry on the coordinating responsibilities, as I have outlined them, exists every hour of every day. The Secretary for International Coordination would always be available for the purpose.

Other Cabinet officers initially voiced doubts about the need for a "business manager," and I decided that I would allow this idea to simmer until its newness would cease to shock them. Gradually, most of them accepted the idea as promising real improvement in the conduct of governmental business.

While there seems no point in reciting all the baffling obstacles, legislative and otherwise, that prevented me from submitting these reforms for congressional approval, I still believe firmly that they could be helpful to the President. But I repeat that organization and procedures, save where they are rigidly fixed by law, should conform to each President's experience, desires, and methods of work.

LOOKING TO THE HILL

Another subject that constantly intrigued me was the possibility of making changes that might improve the law-making process and increase the efficiency of representative government.

Some of the possibilities for improvement involve subjective judgments which can be verified or disproved only by actual test. Most provoke widely varying opinions. For example:

—Would it be desirable to extend the terms of members of the House of Representatives from two to four years?

—Should we seek to increase party unity and party responsibility in our government and, if so, what might we do to increase them?

—Does the adoption of the 22nd Amendment, limiting the President's tenure in his office, make it logical that a somewhat similar amendment should apply to the members of Congress?

—Should the President be given the power to veto any item in any appropriation bill or any part of legislation authorizing expenditures without vetoing those portions of the bill of which he approves?

—Would it be preferable to change the dates of national elections and of the inauguration of the President and Vice President so as to provide a reasonable period for a new President to study and familiarize himself with the specific governmental problems of the moment before he would be required to present to the Congress his legislative program in the State of the Union message and his fiscal and financial programs in the annual Budget Message and his Economic Report?

—Is any reform needed in our federal court system?

While I have formed at least tentative personal judgments on each of these matters, I am well aware that they would, if proposed without careful informational programs, encounter strenuous objections by affected individuals and groups.

It is clear that to incorporate into our system the changes alluded to in these questions, constitutional amendments would be required in some, if not all cases. What is not so obvious, perhaps, is that the adoption of the relevant amendments could not possibly be achieved through the customary procedures of amending the Constitution, which involve passage of each by two-thirds vote of both Houses of the Congress before submission to the states for approval. Some of the suggestions would make changes that in some fashion or other would be distasteful to the members of one or both Houses of the Congress; consequently, the only way to get them considered by the nation as a whole would be through a constitutional convention assembled under the alternative method of amendment prescribed in the Constitution.[8]

* * *

In considering the length of the term of a member of the House of Representatives, look first at certain pertinent circumstances that are vastly different today from those prevailing when the Constitution was written. In 1787 communications were slow and laborious. The fastest transportation was by horse or sailing ship. It was difficult for a congressman representing an area distant from the nation's capital, like Georgia or Massachusetts, to keep in close contact with his constituency while Congress was in session. Fortunately, the sessions were not so prolonged as they have tended to become in later years, and a representative could use the recess period to acquaint his constituents with his political beliefs and actions, and could explore public attitudes in his district. To make sure that these personal accountings were not neglected too long, the term of the representative was set at two years. The framers of the Constitution apparently believed that in this way the members of the House of Representatives, elected by popular vote, would remain "close to the people."

These circumstances have changed dramatically. Every congressman's vote on an important matter one day can bc known by his constituents that same evening. By newsletter, radio, televised and personal appearances, questionnaires, and telephone, a congresssman keeps constantly aware of changing political convictions in his own district. Usually he can reach his home and, no matter how remote it may be, return to his place in the Congress without missing more than one or two roll calls, if any. Most congressmen, someone once said, have become adept in keeping both ears to the ground. At the same time, sessions of Congress tend to become protracted as a constantly mounting volume and a widening variety of business needs to be considered.

Another point to be considered in frequent elections is that of expense. Because of the efficiency of communications, a congressman is, in effect,

[8] A constitutional convention must be called by the Congress if so requested by two-thirds of the states; any amendments therein recommended, if approved by three-fourths of the states, become part of our basic law.

running for office all the time. One congressman told me that, as an average, at least $100,000 is spent on his behalf for each re-election.

The major objection to changing the term of the congressman from two to four years would unquestionably come from the members of the Senate. Because the House member must be elected every two years, and cannot run for the two offices simultaneously, it is impossible for him to run for the Senate while retaining his seat in the House. But if his term were one of four years, it would be possible for him, in senatorial elections occurring in those years when he himself is not up for re-election, to challenge a senator for the nomination of his party, or to run in the national election without jeopardizing his own position. Most senators, sensitive to this possibility, will oppose lengthening of the term of the congressman to four years.

I suspect that almost every member of the House of Representatives would favor the extension; more important, I believe it would be to the advantage of the country.

One hoped-for advantage would be that of promoting the likelihood of "one-party responsibility" during any term of a President. Because representatives would be elected at the same time as the President, it would be more likely that the Executive branch and the House of Representatives would be of the same party.[9]

The desirability of single-party responsibility in directing the national government at any given time should be obvious, because only when the Legislative and Executive branches are controlled by the same party is it possible to fix responsibility. Our system, which cannot guarantee such an outcome, is at times unfavorably compared with the parliamentary form, used in most of the countries of Western Europe. There are, of course, advantages and disadvantages to be found in both of these widely used forms.[10]

The basic feature of the parliamentary system is that it combines in one body both Legislative and Executive functions. "Her Majesty's government" in Britain includes the Prime Minister, his Cabinet, and the agencies of government of which they are in charge. The Prime Minister is a member of the House of Commons and is the chosen head of the majority party; the members of his Cabinet are, except in the rare case of coalition government, all members of the same party. (The House of Lords has little official power but, at times, considerable influence in Britain.)

Whenever, in the British House of Commons, a significant segment

[9] The results of the 1956 election, in which the national ticket achieved an overwhelming popular majority, while my party did not succeed in regaining control of either House, was a historic exception.

[10] The current French system includes some features of both systems.

of the Prime Minister's party deserts him and his Cabinet on an important issue and, joining with the opposition, rejects the government's recommendations, an immediate general election in the nation is required. This means that each member of the House must at once seek re-election. Quite naturally he dislikes all the time, work, and expense involved, to say nothing of the danger of being defeated. As a consequence, it is only in exceptional circumstances that so many of the majority party desert the Prime Minister that a new election is required. The influence of this situation in promoting harmony within the party is apparent.

In our form of government, terms of office are for fixed periods. It follows that no matter what the size of the popular majority a President may enjoy during his tenure of office, no senator or representative suffers any specific and immediate penalty for voting against his party leader. There have been occasions when a President, even one enjoying a strong majority in the Congress, has not found it possible to obtain favorable action from the Congress. For example, President Franklin Roosevelt always had large majorities in both Houses, yet in a number of instances when he felt it necessary to veto bills of the Congress he could not find even the necessary one-third of the members present and voting in either House to sustain his veto.

While by no means would I like to see our own form of government so modified as to make the tenure of office of senators and the representatives dependent upon their regimented agreement with the Executive, I do believe that all citizens, including governmental officials, could and should do much to assure healthier party discipline. Unless we give more attention to party responsibility, elections will become even more meaningless than now, so far as party principles and pledges are concerned.[11]

[11] The parliamentary system has its important weaknesses. For example, in the handling of foreign relations, a parliamentary government can easily become almost powerless when a change of leadership occurs. During my years in the White House, French governments changed—though without compelling a general election, as in Britain—with bewildering frequency. We often found, in our dealings with the French, that proposed international conferences or meetings would be delayed for days until the French knew who would be responsible for the conduct of their government for the next few weeks.

At the end of World War II, when the Russian, American, and British heads of government were conferring in Potsdam, an unexpected result in a general election caused a change in the British government. Prime Minister Winston Churchill had to leave in the middle of the conference, yielding his place to the new Prime Minister, Clement Attlee. Under our system such an unexpected change could not happen. While the political complexion of the Congress can change at two-year intervals, this circumstance does not decisively affect Executive leadership.

The most recent French system confers upon the President greater power than is possessed by the President of the United States. The French system in my judgment places too much dependency upon one man, no matter how capable he may be.

One improvement in governmental operation that could be achieved is that of better cooperation between the Chief Executive and the members of the Congress. This cooperation, which must necessarily be initiated by the President because it is his programs that are to be passed or rejected, should be genuine. Nothing spurious or deceitful should be employed. It should be characterized by mutual respect and good faith.

In my case such cooperation was a necessity even had I preferred to rely on other methods such as the use of patronage or employing the social and economic influences inherent in the Presidency. For two years the Republican party enjoyed a meager majority in the Congress; for six I had to deal with one that was controlled by the opposition. Consequently, not only did I have weekly meetings with the leaders of my own party, but on every matter on which bipartisan interest could be generated—for example, on Mutual Security Appropriations, defense problems, and all types of foreign crises and programs—I made it a practice to bring to my office leaders of both parties to discuss the matter before final action was taken.

I cultivated personal as well as political friendships; I used direct and indirect contacts to convince legislators that the solutions we advocated were good for the country and therefore good for them. About the only threat which I ever employed—if it could be called that—was to warn that I would veto any bill that plainly ran counter to the basic tenets of my political philosophy. This must have had some effect, because of scores of bills I vetoed, only two were ever overridden.[12]

Even though I could wish that measures would be adopted—if not the one I propose, then others—to promote party unity, our system, as a whole, has served us well. I believe that it will continue to do so, even if at times it appears that too many are more concerned with personal gain than with the public good. The common sense of the American public will, in the long run, force political parties and political leaders to operate with some degree of caution even if not always with a high level of wisdom.

* * *

Would it be desirable to limit the length of time that a member of either House of Congress could serve?

The 22nd Amendment was added to the Constitution so that no President could be elected more than twice to that office. This leads one to

[12] On occasion I warned my fellow Republicans that I would not campaign for any who might oppose me on important internal efforts, especially the combating of unnecessary government expenditures.

ask: If this kind of limitation is good in the Presidency why should not the same kind of reasoning apply to congressional tenure?[13]

Should there now be adopted an amendment to limit congressional tenure there would be several notable effects. The change would reduce the influence of seniority in both Houses of the Congress. Henry Clay, at the age of thirty-four, was elected Speaker of the House. Today it is possible for mere endurance to elevate a man to the chairmanship of an important committee for which position he does not necessarily have noticeable qualifications, yet the aggregate influence of the chairmen in either House is indeed substantial. If a reasonable limitation were put on congressional tenure there would certainly be more attention paid than at present to merit and qualities of leadership in the allocation of important congressional posts. Since re-election for term after term would no longer be possible, a related advantage would be that members would probably give more attention to national good and less to their personal political fortunes.

If the terms of the House members were extended to four years with tenure limited to three elections with a maximum time of service of sixteen years (to cover interim appointments), and that of senators to two terms of six years, with a maximum service time of eighteen years, each man so serving would tend to think of his congressional career as an important and exciting interlude in his life, a period dedicated to the entire public rather than as a way of making a living or making a career of exercising continuous political power. Possibly each would spend less time in keeping his eyes on the next election and more in centering them on the good of the nation. A more rapid turnover of the membership in both Houses with its constant infusion of new blood would largely eliminate the "career" politician in Congress, but I can see little damage that would result from such a change except possibly to the personal ambitions of particular individuals.

Many argue for the value of long experience in Congress. Admittedly, experience may produce greater skill in political maneuvering in the legislative process, but does not necessarily produce better statesmen. One potential advantage of limited tenure would be its tendency to bring in people fresh from the world of business and professional affairs, with the possibility that congressional work would be expedited. If so, we would rarely see a session enduring more than six months.

If desired, this particular amendment could be made inapplicable to

[13] Incidentally, I originally thought the 22nd Amendment was unwise; but long before I left the Presidency I publicly stated that I had changed my mind and had come to believe, on balance, that the amendment was good for the nation.

any individual now a member of the Congress. Another clause might provide that the amendment would apply, initially, to only half the states, and four years later to the other half. This would assure that at no time would there be approached a 100 per cent turnover in the membership of either House. Again, an amendment of this kind could never achieve the blessing of Congress; it could be initiated only by the states.

* * *

Another matter of national importance is the desirability, suggested by several Presidents, of providing by law for the "item veto." Authority for vetoing, item by item, specific features of bills passed by state legislatures has long been in the hands of many of our state governors. If similar authority were possessed by the President respecting financial bills, he could improve economy and efficiency and, if he were so disposed, could prevent "pork barreling" in the Congress.

Probably the framers of our Constitution contemplated that each bill introduced into the Congress would have one major purpose only and would be passed, amended, or rejected on the basis of the Congress's conviction as to its special need and desirability. However, in practice, Congress often passes a bill whose main provisions are generally desirable, but included also may be wasteful or needless expenditure authorizations. Thus, the President is often in the position of approving expenditures he feels are undesirable because they are appended to legislation which he deems in the best interests of the nation. This situation is often encountered in bills authorizing the construction of public works. A number of such projects may have been properly surveyed by the appropriate federal agencies and found to be practical and beneficial to our economy; the President may have recommended their approval by the Congress. But in the same bill the Congress, without any semblance of justification except local greed or special interest, will often add one or more projects which have not been surveyed and for which the cost-benefit ratio has not been determined.

When a number of congressmen get together, each with a special local project, and mutually promise to vote for various individual projects so as to get all approved, the process is called "logrolling," the result a "pork barrel" bill. The practice has been so long continued that the Congress is startled and annoyed when a President, determined to stop this indefensible expenditure of public money for the benefit of local politicians, disapproves the entire bill. In the only two vetoes I had overriden by the Congress, both dealt with expenditures that I thought undesirable. The influence of appropriated money to promote political ambition was so strong that I could not, by veto, defeat it.

Sometimes "riders" to a money bill will deal with policy matters of importance. Thus the Congress once inserted in an agricultural appropriation bill, which I felt I had to sign, a rider that directed the Secretary of Agriculture to subsidize the export of American cotton to whatever extent was necessary for the United States to regain its historic share of the world cotton market. This was done without prior consultation with me, the Secretary of State, or the Secretary of Agriculture, and thus we were not able to cushion the shock experienced in friendly nations such as Mexico and Peru. They were injured by this measure. Had I possessed the item veto authority, I would have sent this rider back to the Congress and approved the remainder of the bill.

The item veto could legally be authorized without constitutional amendment. However, because many congressmen see political advantages for themselves in preserving the present system, they can never be expected to pass a law giving the President such power regardless of its value. An amendment, through a constitutional convention demanded by the states, would again be necessary.

Another change that could and, I think, should be included in this amendment is a provision that any congressional attempt to increase an expenditure above that recommended in the President's Budget would require a two-thirds vote in both Houses.

* * *

Still another suggestion for possible improvement of our current governmental practices is that we change dates for the quadrennial election and inauguration of the President and Vice President. If such a change were made it could apply also to the election of senators and congressmen.

At present the Congress convenes in early January and a few days later, in every fourth year, a President is inaugurated. A newly elected President must almost immediately either accept the specific recommendations made to the Congress by his predecessor or, with little opportunity for analysis, make significant changes in them. This applies to the State of the Union message, in which the year's legislative program is laid out; the Budget message, which prescribes the President's recommendations on expenditures for the year, and the Economic Report, which contains not only an analysis of the economic situation and progress during the year just past, but also recommendations on future economic policies. All of this occurs shortly after January 20. The difficulties become more acute when a President and his immediate predecessor are of different political parties.

Such a system has obvious defects. A President making his recommendations to the Congress for the first time should have more time to formulate his own decisions on expenditures and programs for the coming year. I believe we should make no change in the time of the annual convening of the regular congressional session, but I do believe that the date for the general election should be set at about September 20 and the inauguration date of new officials no later than November 1.

Opponents will argue that such a change would require the national conventions to meet by mid-July and that this fact might interfere with the congressional session. To this I would reply that if Congress will do its work efficiently it could easily accomplish everything needed for the nation in many weeks fewer than it presently consumes, except in times of emergency. The suggested new dates would allow more than nine weeks between the nominating conventions and election, which is ample time for candidates using modern communication media to discuss the issues and for the electorate to make judgments, both as to platforms and candidates.

In this connection I believe that each radio and television network and all other stations should be required in each presidential election to give, free of charge, to each national ticket of the two major parties, six hours of prime time; the six hours to be "managed" for each party by the presidential nominee thereof, and the hours so adjusted as to be fair to both parties.

The six weeks between election and inauguration would allow time for the incoming President to form his cabinet. The inauguration itself might call for a short special session of the Congress; but this could be called by the outgoing President. Thereafter the two and two-thirds months between inauguration and the convening of the next Congress would give to the new President a valuable opportunity to formulate his plans for the coming year, including his recommendations to the Congress.

Such a change, as I have said, is unlikely to be quickly adopted. But if several Presidents, in succession, should come to similar conclusions, I believe the effort should be made.

* * *

Should the terms of active service for federal judges be limited?

When the founders established the federal judiciary they had no conception of political parties as we now know them. While I believe that all Americans heartily approve the obvious effort of the Constitution's framers to assure immunity of the federal judiciary from political or other pressures, few would deny that, nowadays, appointments of judges are at times influenced by political considerations. The "court packing" attempt of three decades ago is pertinent evidence.

Life expectancy has been lengthened by many years since the Constitution was written in 1787. It could now become possible for the same Supreme Court, because of life tenure for its members, to function as an almost unchanged group for three or four decades. If, then, most of the members of the Court were definitely inclined toward a single political philosophy, the Court could, by a long series of decisions and orders gradually, but radically, change our system—even against the majority convictions of the electorate. Moreover, the dangers of senility cannot be overlooked.

Without disturbing any present arrangement for lifetime income for federal judges there might well be examined the usefulness and desirability of limiting the active careers of each to twenty years or to the age of seventy-two, whichever might be earlier. As at present, such "emeritus" judges could be utilized on a voluntary basis for appropriate duties as long as each was deemed mentally and physically capable of serving effectively.

A simple constitutional amendment would certainly have the effect of bringing fresh blood and fresh thinking to our courts.

The law of life is change.

* * *

Another matter, one that does not directly concern normal governmental functioning, but is urgently important, is that of devising satisfactory methods of governing presidential succession and the determination of "presidential disability." This subject concerned the nation intensely during the long illnesses of President Garfield and President Wilson and to lesser extent during the three I suffered in the mid-fifties. On each of these later occasions the length of the period during which the doctors prevented me from paying attention to important official business was short—the longest was no longer than a week. Nevertheless, had an emergency occurred during even this brief period the Vice President should have been assured of my recognition of his constitutional right and duty to act in my stead.

Concerning the order of succession, I had long favored the law that existed before 1947 over the one now controlling, but after reflection I have come to believe that a much better method for handling the matter should be adopted.

I believe that at any time a Vice President succeeds to the Presidency he should immediately nominate another individual as Vice President to fill the vacancy, with the nomination to be approved by both bodies of the Congress, rather than merely by the Senate.

Should such an event occur during recess of Congress, I think a special session should be promptly called so that there could be no question that public opinion, as represented by the Congress, approved the new President's nominee.

There is of course the bothersome possibility that some type of disaster might remove the President and the Vice President simultaneously. I believe that to cover this contingency we should return to the provisions of the law that governed succession before 1947, but with the proviso that if both President and Vice President should be lost, their successor should be considered only as an "acting President," and, unless the next regularly scheduled presidential election should occur in less than eighteen months, the Congress should provide for a special election of a President and a Vice President to serve out the presidential term then current.

I would heartily support a constitutional amendment authorizing action of this kind.

To determine the existence and nature of a presidential disability and recovery and the action to be taken seem to me to be more complicated. Many systems have been proposed, but each seems so cumbersome in character as to preclude prompt action in emergency. My personal conclusion is that the matter should be left primarily to the two individuals concerned, the President and the Vice President, subject possibly to a concurring majority opinion, whenever practicable, of the President's Cabinet.

Disabilities can be of different kinds, one caused by physical or mental illness, or another by an absence from the seat of government of such a character as to preclude presidential decisions and action in time of emergency. Wherever possible I believe that a President's disability should be acknowledged and announced by himself. If circumstances make this impossible I think the Vice President should voluntarily step forward, announce the disability, and assume the presidential responsibilities and duties. It should be made clear that in this case the Vice President would be merely an "acting President" and would require no new oath of office and would receive no presidential emoluments, unless and until he might succeed to the office.

The end of the disability would be determined by the President himself upon his declaration in writing that he was ready to resume his office. Should there be disagreement between the President and the Vice President as to whether the former was ready to resume his duties and the Cabinet should agree with the Vice President, then the Vice President should continue to serve for the time being. Since time would not now be a critical factor, the matter should then go to a commission comprising the three senior members of the Cabinet, the Speaker of the House, the President pro tem of the Senate, and the leader of the minority party in each House of the Congress. They should be advised by four medical personnel recognized by the American Medical Association as competent in their fields whose function it would be to examine the President and report to the other members of the commission. Each member of the medical portion of the commission should be selected and requested to serve by a majority vote of the Cabinet. Such a group of medical experts could serve throughout a presidential term if so desired.

I should add that the chance is very remote that such a dispute might occur, for the simple reason that we must assume that in these serious affairs the individuals concerned would be men of good will, concerned with the welfare of the nation as a whole. The only possibility to be feared is that a President might become so mentally deranged that his personal convictions regarding his recovery might be logically doubted by reasonable men, thus requiring a decision of the kind that a politically and medically competent commission could make. However, again recognizing the value of public opinion, I believe that the findings of the entire commission might well be submitted to both Houses of the Congress for approval.

There is no foolproof method covering every contingency and every possibility that could arise in the circumstances now under discussion. We must trust that patriotic men of common sense, operating within constitutional guidelines, will make decisions that will gain and hold the approval of those in the mainstream of American thinking.

In addition to the preceding suggestions there are some revisions of rules and customs that deserve attention but are not proper subjects for possible constitutional amendment; for example, "conflict of interest." The Senate, in confirming or rejecting a nominee for federal office, has made much of this matter. The phrase is used to describe a situation in which a nominee has economic interests that could be affected by an occupant of the federal office for which he has been recommended by the President.

There are definite possibilities of this kind and meticulous care should be used in making the necessary examination. But common sense should likewise be used in reaching a decision, because a habit of capricious rejection merely because a man has succeeded in accumulating savings through a lifetime of effort would eventually mean that the government would be manned by near-paupers, or would be asked to seek candidates among the "safely" impecunious. Moreover, and somewhat more than incidentally, it would appear that in each House of Congress a like examination should be made into the financial and economic affairs of each new member before he is seated.

Finally, I have a very few recommendations I should like to direct to the controlling officials in each of the states and in our major political parties. These have to do with the composition, conduct, and timing of the national conventions, held quadrennially, and of the selection of delegates for them.

Without presenting arguments, pro and con for each of my suggestions I will give, here, a few reasons behind each of my suggestions, and brief personal comments on the effect of their adoption.

First, I believe that since the advent of television and communications satallites with, soon, broadened facilities for bringing the proceedings of national conventions into every living room of the civilized world, we should have some concern about the "image" of the United States our conventions are helping to create. As of now the pictures carried are of inefficiency, confusion, near chaos, and inexcusably bad manners.

I would propose that no one be allowed on the convention floor except necessary pages and other officials and authorized delegates, these last to the number established by law for the Electoral College. (Alternates could sit in reserved balcony seats, to be called when needed.) All newspaper, radio, television, or other publicity personnel should occupy specific areas, but none on the floor itself. There should be in the convention enclosure no orchestras or bands except one (or an organ) authorized by the Chairman, and it could play only at times specified by him. No so-called spontaneous demonstrations in favor of any individual should be tolerated. The penalty for disobedience should be expulsion from the floor for that session, with alternates directed to take the places of those expelled. Applause for any person, event, or other reason should last no more than five minutes. Lack of decent decorum—such as obvious drinking, shouting, mingling of delegations and the like—should, after warning, bring upon the offender the penalty of expulsion.

The entire demeanor of delegates, speakers, officials, and visitors should be such as to demonstrate the seriousness of the convention's purposes; everything making it nothing more than a circus should be sternly repressed.

I believe that states in which primaries are held should, by compact among themselves, arrange for primaries to be held simultaneously, on any mutually convenient date in the spring of the election year. When delegates are chosen by convention both political parties in each state would, I hope, agree that they be held on the same day as the primaries in other states.

It is my conviction that through these and other revisions in current practice both parties would enhance their prestige, present a better and in fact more accurate picture both here and abroad of "self-government at work," improve the efficiency of the selective process, and make each of us prouder of party institutions than we now are.

LOOKING BACK

Anyone who pauses to look back on many incidents of his life—whether of yesterday or of childhood days—often feels or is likely to mournfully mutter, "I could certainly have done *that* better." No question is asked of me more often, either by myself or others, than "What were your greatest disappointments in the Presidency?" This is frequently accompanied by its natural corollary, "What do you consider was your greatest accomplishment or what provided your deepest satisfaction?" Curiously enough, this latter question I never ask myself; indeed, I have even given up attempts to reply to those who ask it. True, in this volume and its predecessor I have recorded decisions and actions in which, as President for eight years, I played a decisive part, and which I then thought correct else I would have acted otherwise. Some worked out to my definite satisfaction because I thought they promoted the best interests of the United States. But which success may have been the most important is a subject that does not interest me greatly. On the other hand, to analyze the reasons where or why something went wrong and to speculate on matters on which there is no proof of success or failure are mental exercises that intrigue me mightily.

In point of time, one of the questions of this latter kind to excite my retrospective examination involves the wisdom—or its lack—I exercised when I decided to stand for the Presidency.

By 1952 the United States sorely needed a change from one-party domination. Most thoughtful citizens would agree, I think, with De Tocqueville's conclusion that a change in party control in Democratic governments at reasonably spaced periods is advisable. By 1952 I fervently believed that the time was overdue. The Republicans had to win or abjectly accept the conclusion that a "centralized" power philosophy was permanently supplanting our once-proud tradition of depending for national progress upon individual initiative, self-reliance, and private, competitive enterprise. In addition, this kind of change was almost mandatory if we were to sustain our long-cherished two-party political system.

The real question that had then to be answered by the Republican party, was, "What individual, as the Republican nominee, would be the most likely to win and so give the nation a chance for reflection on current political trends and to experience a period of living under a more individualistic and decentralized philosophy of government?" In the first volume of this memoir I have adverted to many of the arguments used by friends to induce me to enter politics, but the political victory of 1952, while not answering definitely the question of what candidate might best have assured victory, was successful in effecting the change that I believe to be absolutely necessary. To that extent my judgment and that of my friends was vindicated.

In *Mandate for Change* I have also detailed the reasons that led me to accept the 1956 nomination. One of the goals I set for myself when I agreed to run again for the Presidency was to unify, and strengthen, the Republican party. My success was slight. Certainly I did not succeed in the hope of so increasing the party's appeal to the American electorate as to assure a few more years, after 1960, of Republican government.

Even now I wonder whether progress toward this objective might have been swifter if I had withdrawn from politics in 1956 and thus allowed Dick Nixon, or some other nominee, to carry on the campaign of that year as the Republican standard bearer.

At least I had been chagrined when, in spite of the great majority achieved by the national ticket I headed in 1956, the Republican party was unable to gain control of either House of the Congress. Had I been convinced that by personally stepping aside another Republican nominee could have been elected in 1956—thus, hopefully, increasing chances for another success in 1960—it would have been a great satisfaction for me to do so. But at the time Republican leaders, with few exceptions, were positive that my withdrawal would mean a 1956 defeat for the Republican party. They could have been wrong. So the question must remain unanswered.

* * *

My principal political disappointment was the defeat of Dick Nixon in 1960. I cannot ascribe any rational cause for the outcome, for I still believe, as I did then, that any objective comparison of the relative capacities and qualifications of the two opposing candidates would have resulted in an overwhelming judgment in Nixon's favor. But Senator Kennedy won by a paper-thin margin, and one of the questions that still haunts me is what more I personally might have done to achieve the right verdict. As of that time, I did what I thought best, and even more than the Vice President planned for. But I participated, on an intensively partisan basis, only in the final week of the campaign. I shall never cease to wonder whether a more extensive program of political speaking on my part might have had a favorable effect on the outcome.

One of my major regrets is that as we left the White House I had to admit to little success in making progress in global disarmament or in reducing the bitterness of the East-West struggle. I have already detailed our efforts toward these ends, and their negative results.

I think no one can justifiably charge the bleak record to any lack of striving on our part. We kept on trying even though we were familiar with the dreary history of earlier attempts and of the arrogant and belligerent attitudes of the Communists in approaching such problems. We believed that with the advent of weapons possessing an unimaginable destructiveness and of unmanned vehicles capable of carrying those weapons with a respectable degree of accuracy to any spot on the globe, all the more reason existed for men to understand that they must lay aside old concepts of expanding empires or furthering their interests by force. We hoped that contemplation of the dark prospects posed by a race in modern armaments would lead all to help in developing cooperative plans that would give to the strong and the weak, the rich and the poor, the highly industrialized and the more primitive societies a common conviction that the world had now to come under a rule of law.

The difficulty was the frozen position of hostility with which the Communists greeted every Western proposal for enforceable, mutual disarmament or for any removal of the causes of tensions that so plague the world. In spite of an agreement for a partial test ban on atomic explosions no dent in the Communist attitude has been made since. It seems incomprehensible that the men in the Kremlin can be ready to risk the destruction of their entire industrial fabric, their cities, their society, and their ambitions rather than to enter into practical treaties, including systems of mutual inspection, that would immeasurably enrich their lives and those of all nations in the world.

But though, in this, I suffered my greatest disappointment, it has not destroyed my faith that in the next generation, the next century, the next millennium these things will come to pass.

* * *

In evaluating contemporary events, policies, and personalities we are apt to resort, as I have, to the trite observation that history will have to make the final judgment; that only time can bring the current scene into perspective. But I think it is also true that the judgment of history, to some degree, will always be altered by the events that followed upon the life of the subject attracting the historian's interest, whether or not these events were directly related to the person under scrutiny.

Suppose that South Carolina's attempt at "nullification" in Jackson's time had been successful, or the outcome of the war between the states had been reversed. With either of these results standing as a precedent it is likely that a number of separate, stagnant, weak, and mutually jealous nations would occupy the territory of what is now a strong, prosperous, and still-growing Union. Had this come about, how would we now view George Washington, Jefferson, Hamilton, Tom Paine, or Benjamin Franklin?

They would still be known, of course, as gallant men of their time—but instead of revering them as the founders of a wonderful nation of power and influence with a practical system of self-government, present-day historians would likely classify them as disciples of a strange—possibly laudable—but impractical doctrine of equality of all before the law. In like manner writers of the future, concerned with the decade of the fifties, will be conditioned in their thinking to some extent by the events of the years separating those historians from us of today.

There will eventually be recorded, of course, the outcome of the arguments between the schools of thought that divide us, more or less, into two political parties and many more factions holding differing views respecting our economy and governmental responsibility.

If the nation should turn decisively, for instance, toward sound fiscal procedures in government, toward less intrusion into the business and individual lives of the nation, toward depending more, in pursuit of national objectives, upon the initiative and ambitions of its millions of citizens and localities and toward methods calculated to prevent further erosion in the value of our currency, then the future would hold encomiums for my administration as the first great break with the political philosophy of the decades beginning in 1933. The years of my two terms would be counted as some of the most meaningful during our national existence.

On the other hand, if the citizenry should adopt and the federal government should intensify its practice of the theories of recent Democratic administrations, then the growth of paternalism to the point of virtual regimentation would so condition the attitude of future historians that our time in office would be represented as only a slight impediment to the trend begun in 1933 under the New Deal. They would diminish all our Republican efforts to preserve the importance of the individual as against the state as one of the last gasps of old, obsolete, and shopworn ideas that had lost—according to their judgment—whatever validity they may once have had in a simpler, less sophisticated age.

Again, if, miraculously, the Communists should one day renounce and abandon their objectives of world revolution and world domination, a definite division in historical judgments would be created. We, who carried official responsibilities in America during the 1950s, might then be accused by some of delaying this development by policies that were too suspicious, untrusting, or hostile. Hopefully, however, other and more competent historians would argue that firm pursuit of these policies helped to bring about the Communist transformation.

In any case, we knew what we faced at the time and acted accordingly.

Many things have happened since the day I left the Presidency on January 20, 1961. Intensely interesting to me are those that bear some relation to, or were affected by, the decisions and actions of my two administrations.

Without delving extensively into political happenings and trends since I returned to private life—they may be the subject of other writings, perhaps—I cannot avoid some mention of problems, continuing or emerging, that cause me as deep concern as they did in the days when I bore the responsibilities of the Presidency. Most of these, it seems, revolve around one profound question: Will a great self-governing people such as ours—a people that in three and a half centuries converted a vast wilderness into the richest and most powerful political grouping on earth—continue to practice, in affluence, the pioneering virtues and be guided by the moral values that in leaner times brought us, by the middle of the twentieth century, to an unparalleled pinnacle of power?

To pose this question suggests another, possibly more meaningful one: Do we see signs, even now, that point to a weakening among our people of the qualities of moral courage, determination, self-reliance, venturesomeness, and ambitions to excel, so constantly noted by past writers of the American saga?

Communications media bring to us sickening and depressing accounts of deliberate lawlessness, arrogant selfishness, disloyalty, laxity in conduct, and all kinds of downright wickedness. Worse, when learning of these things, we seem to have lost some of our capacity for honesty and righteous indignation.

A reckless driver, personally responsible for a serious accident, has his license suspended for a few weeks. The number of divorces goes steadily upward. A movie star becomes a drug addict, another leads a loose and lascivious life, and both become "hotter" box office attractions than before.

The electorate of a city chooses as its mayor a man serving a jail sentence; churches and homes are bombed; innocent children pay with broken bodies, sometimes with their lives, for the hate and prejudice that lighted the fuses. Witnesses to a murder refuse to "get involved" either by assisting the victim or helping the police.

Such things would provide little cause for comment if they were isolated instances of the presence among us of individuals with psychopathic tendencies. When they are reported regularly as normal occurrences throughout the land, and we seemingly accept them as just "human nature," the situation has sinister implications.

The real question for each of us then becomes: "Am I doing my duty as a citizen?" For certain it is that if every decent person in this nation would arouse his own conscience, help elect to public office persons of proved courage and integrity, support vocally and morally his police force, his corps of teachers, the local judges and the lawmakers and their governors in state capitals, soon the numerous newspaper accounts of such crimes, delinquencies, and neglect would decline. And each of us would once again stand straight and proud, proud of himself, his children, and the community in which he lives.

One of the citizen's duties is to look clearly at the struggle of the Negro for his constitutional rights in America. The Supreme Court has, in innumerable decisions, declared the intent of the Constitution to be the assurance of equality before the law of all citizens, regardless of such irrelevant factors as race, color, or religion. Every good American has the moral as well as the legal obligation to make reality of these purposes. This is part of the unfinished business of our nation and to fail to accomplish this peacefully is to weaken ourselves at home and to distort the true meaning of America abroad.

LOOKING AHEAD

Our future is tied up not only with social, political, and economic developments in our own country but with the fate of the entire world and especially with that of all nations we refer to as having Western civilization.

The final nineteen years of my half-century in the public service found me deeply involved in the prosecution and the aftermath of World War II—the last civil war, we pray, to tear apart much of civilization. On a December day in 1941 I came to Washington to head the War Plans Division of the Army General Staff, and my involvement in European affairs began when I was given the responsibility of preparing for General Marshall an outline plan for the destruction of Hitlerism. That plan, approved in early 1942 by him and the governmental heads of the

United States and Great Britain, culminated in Operation OVERLORD, launched on June 6, 1944.

In the meantime, in mid-1942, I became the American Commander in Europe and, in succession, the Allied Commander-in-Chief in the Mediterranean and finally the Supreme Commander of the Allied Expeditionary Forces in Northern Europe.

My assignments after the war as Chief of Staff of the Army, then as informal Chairman of the Joint Chiefs of Staff, next as NATO Commander, serving in France, and finally for eight years as President of the United States, never permitted me, for any lengthy period, to divert my concern from problems involved in preserving and revitalizing Western Europe.

During those years I worked with some of the towering governmental figures of the West, among them Churchill, Hoover, Dulles, Marshall, Roosevelt, Truman, Adenauer, De Gaulle, Eden, Attlee, Macmillan, Baruch, Portal, Bevin, Tedder, Cunningham, Admiral King, Strauss, Bradley, Nimitz, and De Lattre de Tassigny. Theirs was a priceless company. All were products of Western culture—the finest yet to appear on earth, a culture holding the promise of unimaginable brilliance and achievement unless overtaken by complacency or major dissension in the Free World. That culture must either grow and spread or stand still and shrivel away.

Some observers have interpreted the dissolution of nineteenth-century colonialism and the postwar move toward nationalism among the less-developed nations as a decline in Western importance and leadership. I believe the opposite. I see the new relationships between former mother countries and the United States, on the one hand, and former colonies, on the other, as a giant step toward maturity and progress in the Free World community.

I believe that the breaking up of the ties of colonialism will have an effect in the future like that of waves caused by a sizable stone thrown into the center of a pond. The standards, the ethics, and the codes of the West have already begun pushing out from the original impact in a series of civilizing waves that are leaving their indelible wash upon all peoples. As former colonies, seeking advancement and stability, adopt some of the habits and coloration of the West, they will gradually satisfy the material, intellectual, aesthetic, and spiritual desires of their peoples and also spur other underdeveloped nations to further achievement.

In other words, I believe that the great ideas of the West will continue their outward journey in concentric circles until one day they cover the entire globe. Our cardinal concepts of human dignity, of free enterprise, and human liberty as codified and refined in Roman law, the Magna

Carta, the American Declaration of Independence and the Bill of Rights—and continuously enriched by the best thinking of other countries—will become so strong that as they crash against the conflicting currents of Communism, they will overcome and demolish dialectical materialism and the ideology of regimentation.

I never cease to be grateful for the privilege of having had a role in the revolutionary changes that have come about during these last two decades; I have unshakable faith that the ideals and the way of life that Western civilization has cherished and defended in bloody wars will flourish everywhere, to the infinite benefit of mankind.

At home we have a vast continent of natural resources, the inventiveness of our scientists is unexcelled, our level of education constantly rises, the indices by which we measure standards of living continue to go up, and opportunities and facilities for recreation and for engaging in artistic and intellectual activities are made ever more plentiful. Opportunities for the properly ambitious boy and girl increase daily. Prospects for the good life for the average American were never better, provided only that each continues to feel that he, himself, must earn and deserve these advantages.

Imbued with sense and spirit we will select future leaders who, proud of the character and riches bequeathed to us, will have the vision and selflessness to keep a firm, sure hand on the rudder of this splendid ship of state, guiding her, through future generations, to the great destiny for which she was created.

ACKNOWLEDGMENTS

My gratitude to three men in particular—as expressed in *Mandate for Change*—applies also to this book. Each rendered important and invaluable assistance, as spelled out in the acknowledgments in that earlier volume. The first two are my son, John S. D. Eisenhower, and my brother, Milton S. Eisenhower, both of whom brought not only family loyalty but typical family argument to our hundreds of conferences on the subject of this book. The third was the research chief for both volumes of *The White House Years,* Dr. William Bragg Ewald, Jr., to whom I am deeply obligated for the excellence of his work. Additionally, I must again express my appreciation to the International Business Machines Corporation for allowing him to remain with me through the completion of the project.

A number of people who were members of the 1953–1961 administration, and other interested and qualifed persons, have reviewed all or portions of this manuscript. For their assistance, which ranged from making small but vital points of fact to comprehensive comment on much of the text, I am deeply appreciative.

They include Bryce Harlow, who read and commented on every chapter, and those who helped on individual chapters: Sherman Adams, Robert Anderson, Herbert Brownell, Arthur F. Burns, Andrew J. Goodpaster, Gordon Gray, James C. Hagerty, Leonard Hall, Gabriel Hauge, Christian A. Herter, George Kistiakowsky, Fred Ladd, James P. Mitchell (now deceased), Malcolm Moos, Gerald D. Morgan, Maxwell M. Rabb, Roy Rubottom, Raymond J. Saulnier, Fred A. Seaton, Lewis L. Strauss, James Wadsworth, and Mrs. Ann C. Whitman. Kenneth R. McCormick read and followed the project with care and attention, and the editors of the *New York Times* submitted a number of helpful comments.

For their role in preparing the physical manuscript, in typing, proofreading, taking dictation, and checking innumerable details over the years, I want to thank my personal secretary, Miss Lillian Brown; and Mrs. Oscar Mehring, Miss Joyce Schwartz, Miss Elizabeth Beverly, and Miss Betty Shapian.

The readings, picture editing, copy editing, design, and other assistance rendered in New York by members of my publisher's staff have been of great value. Among many others, notable in this regard, have been Miss Elsa Anderson, Mr. Alex Gotfryd, Mr. James Leach, Mr. William Whipple, Mr. William Drennan, Miss Anne Hutchens, and Miss Lucia Staniels.

In both volumes, the maps of Rafael Palacios contribute in no small measure to whatever comprehension of the text the reader may achieve.

Finally, I must acknowledge the special services rendered by two members of Doubleday & Company, Inc. They are Douglas M. Black, past President of the organization, and Sam Vaughan, the editor assigned by the Company as my personal associate. The former was responsible for persuading me, in the first instance, to undertake the project; the latter worked with me constantly for four years in the effort to make the book more accurate, readable, and complete. In numberless ways they made my task easier—sometimes even enjoyable.

APPENDIXES

APPENDIX A

Press release of July 19, 1956

At the request of the Government of Egypt, the United States joined in December 1955 with the United Kingdom and with the World Bank in an offer to assist Egypt in the construction of a high dam on the Nile at Aswan. This project is one of great magnitude. It would require an estimated 12 to 16 years to complete at a total cost estimated at some $1,300,000,000, of which over $900,000,000 represents local currency requirements. It involves not merely the rights and interests of Egypt but of other states whose waters are contributory, including Sudan, Ethiopia, and Uganda.

The December offer contemplated an extension by the United States and United Kingdom of grant aid to help finance certain early phases of the work, the effects of which would be confined solely to Egypt, with the understanding that accomplishment of the project as a whole would require a satisfactory resolution of the question of Nile water rights. Another important consideration bearing upon the feasibility of the undertaking, and thus the practicability of American aid, was Egyptian readiness and ability to concentrate its economic resources upon this vast construction program.

Developments within the succeeding 7 months have not been favorable to the success of the project, and the U. S. Government has concluded that it is not feasible in present circumstances to participate in the project. Agreement by the riparian states has not been achieved, and the ability of Egypt to devote adequate resources to assure the project's success has become more uncertain than at the time the offer was made.

This decision in no way reflects or involves any alteration in the friendly relations of the Government and people of the United States toward the Government and people of Egypt.

The United States remains deeply interested in the welfare of the Egyptian people and in the development of the Nile. It is prepared to consider at an appropriate time and at the request of the riparian states what steps might be taken toward a more effective utilization of the water resources of the Nile for the benefit of the peoples of the region. Furthermore, the United States remains ready to assist Egypt in its effort to improve the economic condition of its people and is prepared, through its appropriate agencies, to discuss these matters within the context of funds appropriated by the Congress.

APPENDIX B

July 31, 1956

Dear Anthony:

From the moment that Nasser announced nationalization of the Suez Canal Company, my thoughts have been constantly with you. Grave problems are placed before both our governments, although for each of us they naturally differ in type and character. Until this morning, I was happy to feel that we were approaching decisions as to applicable procedures somewhat along parallel lines, even though there were, as would be expected, important differences as to detail. But early this morning I received the messages, communicated to me through Murphy from you and Harold Macmillan, telling me on a most secret basis of your decision to employ force without delay or attempting any intermediate and less drastic steps.

We recognize the transcendent worth of the Canal to the free world and the possibility that eventually the use of force might become necessary in order to protect international rights. But we have been hopeful that through a Conference in which would be represented the signatories to the Convention of 1888, as well as other maritime nations, there would be brought about such pressures on the Egyptian government that the efficient operation of the Canal could be assured for the future.

For my part, I cannot over-emphasize the strength of my conviction that some such method must be attempted before action such as you contemplate should be undertaken. If unfortunately the situation can finally be resolved only by drastic means, there should be no grounds for belief anywhere that corrective measues were undertaken merely to protect national or individual investors, or the legal rights of a sovereign nation were ruthlessly flouted. A conference, at the very least, should have a great educational effect throughout the world. Public opinion here and, I am convinced, in most of the world, would be outraged should there be a failure to make such efforts. Moreover, initial military successes might be easy, but the eventual price might become far too heavy.

I have given you my own personal conviction, as well as that of my associates, as to the unwisdom even of contemplating the use of military force at this moment. Assuming, however, that the whole situation continued to deteriorate to the point where such action would seem the only recourse, there are certain political facts to remember. As you realize, employment of United States forces is possible only through positive action on the part of the Congress, which is now adjourned but can be reconvened on my call for special reasons.

If those reasons should involve the issue of employing United States military strength abroad, there would have to be a showing that every peaceful means of resolving the difficulty had previously been exhausted. Without such a showing, there would be a reaction that could very seriously affect our peoples' feeling toward our Western Allies. I do not want to exaggerate, but I assure you that this could grow to such an intensity as to have the most far-reaching consequences.

I realize that the messages from both you and Harold stressed that the decision taken was already approved by the government and was firm and irrevocable. But I personally feel sure that the American reaction would be severe and that the great areas of the world would share that reaction. On the other hand, I believe we can marshal that opinion in support of a reasonable and conciliatory, but absolutely firm, position. So I hope that you will consent to reviewing this matter once more in its broadest aspects. It is for this reason that I have asked Foster to leave this afternoon to meet with your people tomorrow in London.

I have given you here only a few highlights in the chain of reasoning that compels us to conclude that the step you contemplate should not be undertaken until every peaceful means of protecting the rights and the livelihood of great portions of the world had been thoroughly explored and exhausted. Should these means fail, and I think it is erroneous to assume in advance that they needs must fail, then world opinion would understand how earnestly all of us had attempted to be just, fair and considerate, but that we simply could not accept a situation that would in the long run prove disastrous to the prosperity and living standards of every nation whose economy depends directly or indirectly upon East-West shipping.

With warm personal regard—and with earnest assurances of my continuing respect and friendship,

As ever,

DE

APPENDIX C

September 2, 1956

Dear Anthony:

I am grateful for your recent letter, and especially for your kind words on the role of the United States during the London Conference on the Suez Canal. I share your satisfaction at the large number of nations which thought as we do about the future operation of the Canal. In achieving this result we have set in motion a force which I feel will be very useful to us—the united and clearly expressed opinion of the majority users of the Suez waterway and of those nations most dependent upon it. This will exert a pressure which Nasser can scarcely ignore. From Foster I know that this accomplishment is due in no small measure to the expert leadership exhibited by Selwyn Lloyd as Chairman of the Conference, and to the guidance which he received from you.

As for the Russians, it is clear that they sought, at London, to impede the consolidation of a majority point of view, and to generate an atmosphere in the Near East which would make it impossible for Nasser to accept our proposals. I entirely agree with you that the underlying purpose of their policy in this problem is to undermine the Western position in the Near East and Africa, and to weaken the Western nations at home. We must never lose sight of this point.

Now that the London Conference is over, our efforts must be concentrated on the successful outcome of the conversations with Nasser. This delicate situation is going to require the highest skill, not only on the part of the five-nation Committee but also on the part of our Governments. I share your view that it is important that Nasser be under no misapprehension as to the firm interest of the nations primarily concerned with the Canal in safeguarding their rights in that waterway.

As to the possibility of later appeal to the United Nations, we can envisage a situation which would require UN consideration and of course there should be no thought of military action before the influences of the UN are fully explored. However, and most important, we believe that, before going to the UN, the Suez Committee of Five should first be given full opportunity to carry out the course of action agreed upon in London, and to gauge Nasser's intentions.

If the diplomatic front we present is united and is backed by the overwhelming sentiment of our several peoples, the chances should be greater that Nasser will give way without the need for any resort to force. This belief explains our policy at the Conference and also explains the statement which I gave out through Foster after I got back from San Francisco and had a chance to talk fully with him.

I am afraid, Anthony, that from this point onward our views on this situation diverge. As to the use of force or the threat of force at this juncture, I continue to feel as I expressed myself in the letter Foster carried to you some weeks ago. Even now military preparations and civilian evacuation exposed to public view seem to be solidifying support for Nasser which has been shaky in many important quarters. I regard it as indispensable that if we are to proceed solidly together to the solution of this problem, public opinion in our several countries must be overwhelming in its support. I must tell you frankly that American public opinion flatly rejects the thought of using force, particularly when it does not seem that every possible peaceful means of protecting our vital interests has been exhausted without result. Moreover, I gravely doubt we could here secure Congressional authority even for the lesser support measures for which you might have to look to us.

I really do not see how a successful result could be achieved by forcible means. The use of force would, it seems to me, vastly increase the area of jeopardy. I do not see how the economy of Western Europe can long survive the burden of prolonged military operations, as well as the denial of Near East oil. Also the peoples of the Near East and of North Africa and, to some extent, of all of Asia and all of Africa, would be consolidated against the West to a degree which, I fear, could not be overcome in a generation and, perhaps, not even in a century particularly having in mind the capacity of the Russians to make mischief. Before such action were undertaken, all our peoples should unitedly understand that there were no other means available to protect our vital rights and interests.

We have two problems, the first of which is the assurance of permanent and efficient operation of the Suez Canal with justice to all concerned. The second is to see that Nasser shall not grow as a menace to the peace and vital interests of the West. In my view, these two problems need not and possibly cannot be solved simultaneously and by the same methods, although we are exploring further means to this end. The first is the most important for the moment and must be solved in such a way as not to make the second more difficult. Above all, there must be no grounds for our several peoples to believe that anyone is using the Canal difficulty as an excuse to proceed forcibly against Nasser. And we have friends in the Middle East who tell us they would like to see Nasser's deflation brought about. But they seem unanimous in feeling that the Suez is not the issue on which to attempt to do this by force. Under those circumstances, because of the temper of their populations, they say they would have to support Nasser even against their better judgment.

Seldom, I think, have we been faced by so grave a problem. For the time being we must, I think, put our faith in the processes already at work to bring Nasser peacefully to accept the solution along the lines of the 18-nation proposal. I believe that even though this procedure may fail to give the setback to Nasser that he so much deserves, we can better retrieve our position subsequently than if military force were hastily invoked.

Of course, our departments are looking into the implications of all future developments. In this they will keep in close touch with appropriate officials of your Government, as is my wish.

With warm regard,

As ever,

D.E.

APPENDIX D

September 8, 1956

Dear Anthony:

Whenever, on any international question, I find myself differing even slightly from you, I feel a deep compulsion to re-examine my position instantly and carefully. But permit me to suggest that when you use phrases in connection with the Suez affair, like "ignoble end to our long history" in describing the possible future of your great country, you are making of Nasser a much more important figure than he is.

We have a grave problem confronting us in Nasser's reckless adventure with the Canal, and I do *not* differ from you in your estimate of his intentions and purposes. The place where we apparently do not agree is on the probable effects in the Arab world of the various possible reactions by the Western world.

You seem to believe that any long, drawn-out controversy either within the 18-nation group or in the United Nations will inevitably make Nasser an Arab hero and seriously damage the prestige of Western Europe, including the United Kingdom, and that of the United States. Further you apparently believe that there would soon result an upheaval in the Arab nations out of which Nasser would emerge as the acknowledged leader of Islam. This, I think, is a picture too dark and is severely distorted.

I shall try to give you a somewhat different appraisal of the situation. First, let me say that my own conclusions are based to some degree upon an understanding of current Arab feeling that differs somewhat from yours. I believe that as this quarrel now stands before the world, we can expect the Arabs to rally firmly to Nasser's support in either of two eventualities.

The first of these is that there should be a resort to force without thoroughly exploring and exhausting every possible peaceful means of settling the issue, regardless of the time consumed, and when there is no evidence before the world that Nasser intends to do more than to nationalize the Canal Company. Unless it can be shown to the world that he is an actual aggressor, then I think all Arabs would be forced to support him, even though some of the ruling monarchs might very much like to see him toppled.

The second would be what seemed like a capitulation to Nasser and complete acceptance of his rule of the Canal traffic.

The use of military force against Egypt under present circumstances might have consequences even more serious than causing the Arabs to support Nasser. It might cause a serious misunderstanding between our two countries because I must say frankly that there is as yet no public opinion in this country which is prepared to support such a move, and the most significant public opinion that there is seems to think that the United Nations was formed to prevent this very thing.

It is for reasons such as these that we have viewed with some misgivings your preparations for mounting a military expedition against Egypt. We believe that Nasser may try to go before the United Nations claiming that these actions imply a rejection of the peaceful machinery of settling the dispute, and therefore may ask the United Nations to brand these operations as aggression.

At the same time, we do not want any capitulation to Nasser. We want to stand firmly with you to deflate the ambitious pretensions of Nasser and to assure permanent free and effective use of the Suez waterway under the terms of the 1888 Treaty.

It seems to Foster and to me that the result that you and I both want can best be assured by slower and less dramatic processes than military force. There are many areas of endeavor which are not yet fully explored because exploration takes time.

We can, for example, promote a semi-permanent organization of the user governments to take over the greatest practical amount of the technical problems of the Canal, such as pilotage, the organization of the traffic patterns, and the collection of dues to cover actual expenses. This organization would be on the spot and in constant contact with Egypt and might work out a *de facto* "coexistence" which would give the users the rights which we want.

There are economic pressures which, if continued, will cause distress in Egypt.

There are Arab rivalries to be exploited and which can be exploited if we do not make Nasser an Arab hero.

There are alternatives to the present dependence upon the Canal and pipelines which should be developed perhaps by more tankers, a possible new pipeline to Turkey and some possible rerouting of oil, including perhaps more from this hemisphere, particularly to European countries which can afford to pay for it in dollars.

Nasser thrives on drama. If we let some of the drama go out of the situation and concentrate upon the task of deflating him through slower but sure processes such as I described, I believe the desired results can more probably be obtained. Gradually it seems to me we could isolate Nasser and gain a victory which would not only be bloodless, but would be more far-reaching in its ultimate consequences than could be anything brought about by force of arms. In addition, it would be less costly both now and in the future.

Of course, if during this process Nasser himself resorts to violence in clear disregard of the 1888 Treaty, then that would create a new situation and one in which he and not we would be violating the United Nations Charter.

I assure you we are not blind to the fact that eventually there may be no escape from the use of force. Our resolute purpose must be to create conditions of operation in which all users can have confidence. But to resort to military action when the world believes there are other means available for resolving the dispute would set in motion forces that could lead, in the years to come, to the most distressing results.

Obviously there are large areas of agreement between us. But in these exchanges directed toward differing methods I gain some clarification of the confusing and conflicting considerations that apply to this problem.

With warmest regard,

As ever your friend,

APPENDIX E

Thus, the Users Association, as we conceived it, was to secure pilots for convoys and to collect the tolls which had normally been paid to the now defunct Suez Canal Company. These tolls would then be utilized to defray expenses incurred in the pay of pilots and other administrative matters and would provide also a just compensation to the Egyptians.

The idea of paying tolls to a Users Association rather than to the Egyptian government directly might, at first blush, appear fantastic were it not for the fact that the Suez Canal itself is an open waterway, devoid of physical barriers anywhere along its route. Thus, if we should be compelled to operate the Canal with no Egyptians whatsoever it would be possible for a ship at anchor in either end of the Canal to house the necessary administrative personnel and pilots—indeed, everything necessary to assemble and conduct convoys—thus providing the means to transit the Canal. If such a scheme were adopted, and if a convoy were to head through the Canal under the auspices of a Users Association's pilots, the Egyptians would then have to resort to sunken vessels or warlike measures to prevent use of the Canal.

By no means did Foster and I, at that time, visualize this association as a mechanism to "take over" the Canal or as an infringement on Egyptian sovereignty. Rather, we hoped for utmost cooperation between the Users Association and Egypt, which would, of course, be the only nation to realize profit for use of the waterway. The idea of the Association was to take the problem of canal transit out of the hands of the "statesmen" and put it into the hands of the technicians on the spot.

In the event the Egyptians decided to use force to stop convoys from going through the Canal except under their own terms, then we felt that each shipper would have to decide for himself whether to accept Egyptian terms or to take the route around the Cape of Good Hope. For our own part, the United States would not, as circumstances as they then stood, attempt to "shoot our way through" the Canal, but would rather use the Cape route.

Foster and I were not particularly optimistic respecting the success of this scheme. We regarded it merely as an interim measure, even if accepted by the Egyptians. As I saw it, the maximum hope that we could harbor would be a *de facto* arrangement whereby technical representatives of the nations of the Users Association would deal on concrete matters directly with Egyptian experts on the spot. In a way this technical cooperation would have been a face-saver for Nasser, since one of the basic assumptions under which we worked at the time was that the Egyptians would find operating the Canal extremely difficult if not impossible without the benefit of the Western pilots who must soon surely leave.

If, however, these modest results could not be achieved, the Users Association, representing Asian countries as well as Western, would still be a powerful force to mobilize world opinion, particularly since Nasser would probably need to use force to stop our convoys. It would allow these eighteen nations, under a collective bargaining arrangement, to speak with one voice.

Initially the plan for the Users Association was received with considerable enthusiasm by influential portions of the British and French governments. The British foreign secretary, Selwyn Lloyd, told our ambassador on September 12 that the British government was particularly pleased with the plan because it constituted a "slap in the face" for Nasser and would be popular in Parliament for that reason. If the United States would join this club, he said, and would pay the Canal tolls to the association, the Prime Minister would then express approval of the plan in Parliament, after which the British government would ask for United Nations Security Council action requiring Nasser to implement the 1888 Convention on the basis of this plan. With our support he hoped this action would be approved by the Security Council by a vote of nine to two. Pineau and Mollet also told Ambassador Dillon of their feeling that the Users Association proposal fully satisfied the need for action on the part of Britain and France, and would be helpful in avoiding the dangers of hostilities. Indeed, at this meeting Pineau said he now saw a good chance of avoiding war unless Nasser should be guilty of further provocation.

It soon became apparent, however, that the United States on the one hand and Britain and France on the other hand had different understandings on its meaning. Anthony Eden implied when he first publicly proposed the scheme in a special session of Parliament on Wednesday, September 12, that the users organization would use force if necessary to secure entry to the Canal. His wording was, ". . . if the Egyptian Government should seek to interfere . . . that Government will once more be in breach of the convention of 1888 . . . Her Majesty's Government and others concerned will be free to take such further steps as seem to be required either through the United Nations, *or by other means for the assertion of their rights*" (italics mine). By this time the Labor party, whose leader, Hugh Gaitskell, had supported Eden strongly at the first blush of Nasser's internationalization of the Canal, now dissented. The words used by the Prime Minister before Parliament brought cries of "Resign! Resign!" from the Labor members present. In Washington the next day Foster issued a statement, which I had approved, describing the Users Association in these words:

"We are thus prepared to participate in a users' organization. . . . It is our thought that the users' association would, among other things, provide qualified pilots for the users' ships; would initially receive the dues from the ships of members of the association passing through the canal, which sums would be used to defray the expenses of the organization and to pay appropriate compensation to Egypt for its contribution to the maintenance of the Canal and the facilities of transit; and so far as practical arrange for the pattern of traffic of the member vessels through the Canal.

"It is our hope that perhaps practical on-the-spot arrangements for cooperation can be achieved without prejudice to the rights of anyone. This may provide a provisional *de facto* working arrangement until formal agreements can be reached."

He then went on in a masterful way to explain:

"I recall that at a press conference held here two or three weeks ago, I said that the great difficulty with this situation was not that the problems themselves were unsolvable, but that they became unsolvable in the context of great concepts such as 'sovereignty' and 'dignity' and 'grandeur' and the 'East versus the West,' and things of that sort. The problems should be solvable if you break them down to concrete things, such as who are going to be the pilots; where are they going to be; are they qualified pilots; do we have a right to pilots of our own choosing if they are qualified or has Egypt the right to impose upon our vessels pilots of its own choosing; what is the pattern of traffic?

". . . But perhaps—and this is our hope—if we get operating problems out of the hands of the diplomats, the statesmen, and get it down perhaps into a situation where practical ship operators are dealing with practical people on the part of Egypt, maybe some of these problems will be solvable.

"The idea that this is a program which is designed to impose some regime upon Egypt is fantastic. That is not at all the concept."

In addition he specifically denied that the Users Association was undertaking to *shoot its way* through the Canal.

On Friday, September 14, the Western pilots, apparently with Nasser's permission, walked off their jobs, now leaving the Canal to the complete management of the Egyptians.

As the next development Nasser denounced the Users Association as a "declaration of war," apparently in an effort to make it appear that the association was nothing but a device to lead all members down the path to war, for which the British and French were ostensibly preparing.

On Wednesday, September 19, the foreign ministers of the eighteen nations concerned met in London for what was temed the "Second London Conference." Governments were given a week or ten days to decide whether or not to join. Of course our great hope was that Iran, Pakistan, and Ethiopia would stay with us behind the leadership of Turkey despite Egyptian pressure. Foster described the Scandinavians as "lukewarm," however, and the Spanish "equivocal." A series of weak speeches induced him to present our position that afternoon in forceful terms.

The conference terminated on September 21. In the statement issued at the time the conferees issued a declaration providing for the establishment of a Suez Canal Users Association. This document, general in nature, stated that the Suez Canal Users Association should strive, "(1) To facilitate any steps which may lead to a final or provisional solution of the Suez Canal problem and to assist the members in the exercise of their rights as users of the Suez Canal in consonance with the 1888 Convention, with due regard for the rights of Egypt;

"(2) To promote safe, orderly, efficient, and economical transit of the Canal by vessels of any member nation desiring to avail themselves of the facilities of SCUA and to seek the cooperation of the competent Egyptian authorities for this purpose. . . .

"(4) To receive, hold and disburse the revenues accruing from dues and other sums which any user of the Canal may pay to SCUA, without prejudice to existing rights, pending a final settlement. . . .

"(6) To assist in dealing with any practical problems arising from the failure of the Suez Canal adequately to serve its customary and intended purpose and to study forthwith means that may render it feasible to reduce dependence on the Canal. . . ."

At the same time there were rumblings of a Cabinet crisis in France, caused by a feeling in the French Assembly that the Mollet government had not made good its pledge of a "severe riposte" against Nasser. The Users Association simultaneously was being criticized by the British press, though not publicly by its government. Ironically much of the most severe criticism of the statement and declaration came from the British Laborite press, which had so objected to Prime Minister Eden's implication nine days before concerning possible use of force; now they objected that the association was not sufficiently forceful. Said the Laborite *Daily Herald:* "The Dulles plan, hailed as a fiery sword at Nasser's head, turned out to be a blunt kitchen knife, safe but not particularly useful." The trouble with this criticism was that the plan was not a knife, it was a bunch of carrots for a hungry horse, and it provided means for supplying the carrots.

APPENDIX F

OCTOBER 15, 1956

MEMORANDUM FOR THE RECORD

The Secretary of State, accompanied by Mr. Hoover and Mr. Rountree of his office, came to see me about the deteriorating situation in the Israel-Jordan area.

It seems to be taken internationally as a foregone conclusion that Jordan is breaking up, and of course all the surrounding countries will be anxious to get their share of the wreckage, including Israel. In fact, there is some suspicion that the recent savage blows of the Israel border armies against the strong points within Jordan territory are intended to hasten this process of dissolution.

On the other side of the picture, there is some indication that Britain is really serious in her announced intention of honoring her Pact with Jordan, which requires her to help defend Jordan in the case of outside invasion.

Should this occur, we would have Britain in the curious position of helping to defend one of the Arab countries, while at the same time she is engaged in a quarrel—which sometimes threatens to break out into war—with Egypt over the Suez question.

All this brings to the fore one particular thing we must bear in mind. It is this: As of this moment we are dealing with the existing situation—that is, with Jordan enjoying the rights of a sovereign country. At the same time, in view of the possible disintegration of the Jordanian government, we must be ready to deal with the situation in which the people and territory of that country would be absorbed by others.

For the moment we can deal only with the first problem.

The Secretary of State is having a long conference with the Israeli Ambassador to this country, Mr. Eban. The Ambassador is about to return to his own country and is visiting Foster to discuss some of the factors in the above problem.

I have told the Secretary of State that he should make very clear to the Israelis that they must stop these attacks against the borders of Jordan. If they continue them, and particularly if they carry them on to the point of trying to take over and hold the territory west of the Jordan River, they will certainly be condemned by the United Nations, and not only Arab opinion but all world opinion will be brought to bear against this little country. Moreover, should there be a United Nations Resolution condemning Israel, there will be no brake or deterrent possible against any Soviet move into the area to help the Arab countries. They could bring considerable forces in under the guise that they were carrying out a United Nations mandate, the ultimate effect of which would be to Sovietize the whole region, including Israel.

There has been some disposition to believe that Ben-Gurion's obviously aggressive attitude is inspired, at this moment, by three things:

(a). His desire to take advantage of the gradual deterioration in Jordan and to be ready to occupy and lay claim to a goodly portion of the area of that nation;

(b). The preoccupation of Egypt and the Western powers in the Suez question, which would tend both to minimize the possibility that Egypt would enter a war against him promptly, while at the same time it would impede Britain's capability of reinforcing Jordan.

(c). His belief that the current political campaign in the United States will keep this government from taking a strong stand against any aggressive move he might make.

Secretary Dulles will warn the Ambassador that while, of course, we would hate to create misunderstandings and needless passion in this country over this question, at this moment he should inform his government that no considerations of partisan politics will keep this government from pursuing a course dictated by justice and international decency in the circumstances, and that it will remain true to its pledges under the United Nations.

Ben-Gurion should not make any grave mistakes based upon his belief that winning a domestic election is as important to us as preserving and protecting the interests of the United Nations and other nations of the free world in that region. The Secretary is to point out, moreover, that even if Ben-Gurion, in an aggressive move, should get an immediate advantage in the region, that on a long-term basis aggression on his part cannot fail to bring catastrophe and such friends as he would have left in the world, no matter how powerful, could not do anything about it.

Foster will make this attitude clear and unmistakable to Mr. Eban.

At the same time I have Foster's promise to have ready a policy or plan that would guide our action in the event that the dissolution of Jordan would actually take place and thus create a new situation in the world.

D.D.E.

Appendix:

It is believed that one of the recent Israeli raids against Jordan involved two or three battalions of infantry, artillery, and jet airplanes. Incidentally, our high-flying reconnaissance planes have shown that Israel has obtained some 60 of the French Mystère pursuit planes, when there had been reported the transfer of only 24. Jordan has no aviation.

D.D.E.

APPENDIX G

October 30, 1956

Dear Anthony:

I address you in this note not only as head of Her Majesty's Government but as my long-time friend who has, with me, believed in and worked for real Anglo-American understanding.

Last night I invited Mr. Coulson, currently your Washington representative, to come to my house to talk over the worsening situation in the Mid East. I have no doubt that the gist of our conversation has already been communicated to you. But it seemed to me desirable that I should give you my impressions concerning certain phases of this whole affair that are disturbing me very much.

Without bothering here to discuss the military movements themselves and their possible grave consequences, I should like to ask your help in clearing up my understanding as to exactly what is happening between us and our European allies—especially between us, the French and yourselves.

We have learned that the French had provided Israel with a considerable amount of equipment, including airplanes, in excess of the amounts of which we were officially informed. This action was, as you know, in violation of agreements now existing between our three countries. We know also that this process has continued in other items of equipment.

Quite naturally we began watching with increased interest the affairs in the Eastern Mediterranean. Late last week we became convinced that the Israel mobilization was proceeding to a point where something more than mere defense was contemplated, and found the situation serious enough to send a precautionary note to Ben-Gurion. On Sunday we repeated this note of caution and made a public statement of our actions, informing both you and the French of our concern. On that day we discovered that the volume of communication traffic between Paris and Tel Aviv jumped enormously, alerting us to the probability that France and Israel were concerting detailed plans of some kind.

When on Monday actual military moves began, we quickly decided that the matter had to go immediately to the United Nations, in view of our Agreement of May, 1950, subscribed to by our three governments.

Last evening our Ambassador to the United Nations met with your Ambassador, Pierson Dixon, to request him to join us in presenting the case to the United Nations this morning. We were astonished to find that he was completely unsympathetic, stating frankly that his government would not agree to any action whatsoever to be taken against Israel. He further argued that the tri-partite statement of May, 1950, was ancient history and without current validity.

Without arguing the point as to whether or not the tri-partite statement is or should be outmoded, I feel very seriously that whenever any agreement or pact of this kind is in spirit renounced by one of its signatories, it is only fair that the other signatories should be notified. Since the United States has continued to look upon that statement as representing the policies and determination of our three governments, I have not only publicly announced several times that it represents our policy, but many of our actions in the Mid East have been based upon it. For example, we have in the past denied arms both to Egypt and to Israel on the ground that the 1950 statement was their surest guarantee of national security. We have had no thought of repudiating that statement and we have none now.

All of this development, with its possible consequences, including the possible involvement of you and the French in a general Arab war, seems to me to leave your government and ours in a very sad state of confusion, so far as any possibility of unified understanding and action are concerned. It is true that Egypt has not yet formally asked this government for aid. But the fact is that if the United Nations finds Israel to be an aggressor, Egypt could very well ask the Soviets for help—and then the Mid East fat would really be in the fire. It is this latter possibility that has led us to insist that the West must ask for a United Nations examination and possible intervention, for we may shortly find ourselves not only at odds concerning what we should do, but confronted with a de facto situation that would make all our present troubles look puny indeed.

Because of all these possibilities, it seems to me of first importance that the UK and the US quickly and clearly lay out their present views and intentions before each other, and that, come what may, we find some way of concerting our ideas and plans so that we may not, in any real crisis, be powerless to act in concert because of misunderstanding of each other. I think it important that our two peoples, as well as the French, have this clear understanding of our common or several viewpoints.

With warm personal regard.

As ever,

Ike E.

APPENDIX H

November 27, 1956

Dear Winston:

I agree fully with the implication of your letter that . . . back of the difficulties that the free world is now experiencing lies one principal fact that none of us can afford to forget. The Soviets are the real enemy of the Western World, implacably hostile and seeking our destruction.

Many months ago it became clear that the Soviets were convinced that the mere building of mighty military machines would not necessarily accomplish their purposes, while at the same time their military effort was severely limiting their capacity for conquering the world by other means, especially economic. Unquestionably the greatest factor in turning their minds away from general war as a means of world conquest was their knowledge of America's and Britain's large and growing strength in nuclear and fission weapons.

Starting almost at the instant that Nasser took his high-handed action with respect to the Canal, I tried earnestly to keep Anthony informed of public opinion in this country and of the course that we would feel compelled to follow if there was any attempt to solve by force the problem presented to the free world through Nasser's action. I told him that we were committed to the United Nations and I particularly urged him, in a letter of July thirty-first, to avoid the use of force, at least until it had been proved to the world that the United Nations was incapable of handling the problem. My point was that since the struggle with Russia had obviously taken on a new tactical form, we had to be especially careful that any course of action we adopted should by its logic and justice command world respect, if not sympathy. I argued that to invade Egypt merely because that country had chosen to nationalize a company would be interpreted by the world as power politics and would raise a storm of resentment that, within the Arab States, would result in a long and dreary guerilla warfare; something on the order that the French are now experiencing in Algeria.

I have tried to make it clear that we share the opinion of the British . . . [and] others that . . . we would have to concert our actions in making certain that he [Nasser] did not grow to be a danger to our welfare. But for the reasons I have given above, I urged that the nationalization of the Canal Company was not the vehicle to choose for bringing about correction in this matter.

Sometime in the early part of October, all communication between ourselves on the one hand and the British and the French on the other suddenly ceased. Our intelligence showed the gradual buildup of Israeli military strength, finally reaching such a state of completion that I felt compelled on two successive days to warn that country that the United States would honor its part in the Tri-Partite Declaration of May, 1950—in short, that we would oppose clear aggression by any power in the Mid-East.

But so far as Britain and France were concerned, we felt that they had deliberately excluded us from their thinking; we had no choice but to do our best to be prepared for whatever might happen.

The first news we had of the attack and of British-French plans was gained from the newspapers and we had no recourse except to assert our readiness to support the United Nations, before which body, incidentally, the British Government had itself placed the whole Suez controversy.

Now I still believe that we must keep several facts clearly before us, the first one always being that the Soviets are the real enemy and all else must be viewed against the background of that truth. The second fact is that nothing would please this country more nor, in fact, could help us more, than to see British prestige and strength renewed and rejuvenated in the Mid-East. We want those countries to trust and lean toward the Western World, not Russia. A third fact is that we want to help Britain right now, particularly in its difficult fuel and financial situation, daily growing more serious.

All we have asked in order to come out openly has been a British statement that it would conform to the resolutions of the United Nations. The United Nations troops do not, in our opinion, have to be as strong as those of an invading force because any attack upon them will be an attack upon the whole United Nations and if such an act of folly were committed, I think that we could quickly settle the whole affair.

. . . I continue to believe that the safety of the western world depends in the final analysis upon the closest possible ties between Western Europe, the American hemisphere, and as many allies as we can induce to stand with us. If this incident has proved nothing else, it must have forcefully brought this truth home to us again. A chief factor in the union of the free world must be indestructible ties between the British Commonwealth and ourselves.

The only difficulty I have had in the particular instance is the fact that to me it seemed the action of the British Government was not only in violation of the basic principles by which this great combination of nations can be held together, but that even by the doctrine of expediency the invasion could not be judged as soundly conceived and skillfully executed.

So I hope that this one may be washed off the slate as soon as possible and that we can then together adopt other means of achieving our legitimate objectives in the Mid-East. Nothing saddens me more than the thought that I and my old friends of years have met a problem concerning which we do not see eye to eye. I shall never be happy until our old time closeness has been restored.

With warm regard and best wishes for your continued health.

As ever,

Ike E.

APPENDIX I

LETTER TO GOVERNOR JAMES F. BYRNES

August 14, 1953

Dear Jimmy:

As you know, I have been thinking of the whole field of equality of opportunity. Since our recent lunch together at which we discussed the pending "School Segregation" case, it has scarcely been absent from my mind.

I think that it is incumbent upon people who honestly believe in the power of leadership, education, example, and acceptance of clear official responsibility to show constant progress in the direction of complete justice. We who hold office not only must discharge the duties placed upon us by the constitution and by conscience, but also must, by constructive advances, prove to be mistaken those who insist that true reforms can come only through overriding Federal law and Federal police methods.

As I observed to you, I feel that my oath of office, as well as my own convictions, requires me to eliminate discrimination within the definite areas of Federal responsibility. You replied to the effect: "You can do no less."

There is one of these areas of Federal responsibility where my efforts may run counter to customs in some States. This is the area involved in the "non-discrimination" clauses in Federal contracts.

In presenting my views to you on this particular matter, I am keeping in mind the whole scope of our conversation. On the basis of that discussion, I am hopeful not only that we may reach fruitful understanding in this matter—but also that, in so doing, it can be shown that progress does not depend on Federal fiat.

This matter of compliance with the law and regulations in governmental contracts is being put into the hands of a Committee which I am appointing. I realize that if one should follow up the words "Federal contract" far enough—on an academic research job—one could get into a lot of secondary and auxiliary activity, conceivably causing a confusion that would make any attempt at enforcement most difficult. But I do believe that States should cooperate in, and never impede, the enforcement of Federal regulations *where the Federal Government has clear and exclusive responsibility in the case.*

Assume, for example, that we should have a Federal contract under execution in the Charleston Navy Yard: I feel that if there should be any trouble at the Yard in enforcing the non-discrimination regulations, you as Governor could instantly announce that, since this is clearly a Federal matter, beyond State jurisdiction, compliance should be complete and cheerful.

I sincerely believe that such cooperation would reassure those who seem to feel that the only alternative to stringent Federal action is no action at all.

I am, of course, dedicated to discharging the official responsibilities of my office, just as I am determined to respect the constitutional authority and responsibilities of others. In this particular case, I believe it is incumbent upon us to make constant and distinct progress toward eliminating those things that all of us would class as unjust and unfair. In this category there clearly falls, to my mind, the right to equal consideration in Federal employment, regardless of race or color.

If the above makes sense to you, than I should like you to communicate with your fellow Governors who feel generally as you do in these matters, and to whom you referred when we had our recent conversation.

With warm personal regard,

Sincerely,

APPENDIX J

Aide-mémoire handed to Israeli Ambassador Abba Eban on February 11, 1957, by Secretary Dulles:

The United Nations General Assembly has sought specifically, vigorously, and almost unanimously, the prompt withdrawal from Egypt of the armed forces of Britain, France and Israel. Britain and France have complied unconditionally. The forces of Israel have been withdrawn to a considerable extent but still hold Egyptian territory at Sharm el Shaikh at the entrance to the Gulf of Aqaba. They also occupy the Gaza Strip which is territory specified by the Armistice arrangements to be occupied by Egypt.

We understand that it is the position of Israel that (1) it will evacuate its military forces from the Gaza Strip provided Israel retains the civil administration and police in some relationship to the United Nations; and (2) it will withdraw from Sharm el Shaikh if continued freedom of passage through the Straits is assured.

With respect to (1) the Gaza Strip—it is the view of the United States that the United Nations General Assembly has no authority to require of either Egypt or Israel a substantial modification of the Armistice Agreement, which, as noted, now gives Egypt the right and responsibility of occupation. Accordingly, we believe that Israeli withdrawal from Gaza should be prompt and unconditional, leaving the future of the Gaza Strip to be worked out through the efforts and good offices of the United Nations.

We recognize that the area has been a source of armed infiltration and reprisals back and forth contrary to the Armistice Agreement and is a source of great potential danger because of the presence there of so large a number of Arab refugees—about 200,000. Accordingly, we believe that the United Nations General Assembly and the Secretary-General should seek that the United Nations Emergency Force, in the exercise of its mission, move into this area and be on the boundary between Israel and the Gaza Strip.

The United States will use its best efforts to help to assure this result, which we believe is contemplated by the Second Resolution of February 2, 1957.

With respect to (2) the Gulf of Aqaba and access thereto—the United States believes that the Gulf comprehends international waters and that no nation has the right to prevent free and innocent passage in the Gulf and through the Straits giving access thereto. We have in mind not only commercial usage, but the passage of pilgrims on religious missions, which should be fully respected.

The United States recalls that on January 28, 1950, the Egyptian Ministry of Foreign Affairs informed the United States that the Egyptian occupation of the two islands of Tiran and Sanafir at the entrance of the Gulf of Aqaba was only to protect the islands themselves against "possible damage or violation" and that "this occupation being in no way conceived in a spirit of obstructing in any way innocent passage through the stretch of water separating these two islands from the Egyptian coast of Sinai, it follows that this passage, the only practicable one, will remain free as in the past, in conformity with international practice and recognized principles of the law of nations."

In the absence of some overriding decision to the contrary, as by the International Court of Justice, the United States, on behalf of vessels of United States registry, is prepared to exercise the right of free and innocent passage and to join with others to secure general recognition of this right.

It is of course clear that the enjoyment of a right of free and innocent passage by Israel would depend upon its prior withdrawal in accordance with the United Nations Resolutions. The United States has no reason to assume that any littoral state would under these circumstances obstruct the right of free and innocent passage.

The United States believes that the United Nations General Assembly and the Secretary-General should, as a precautionary measure, seek that the United Nations Emergency Force move into the Straits area as the Israeli forces are withdrawn. This again we believe to be within the contemplation of the Second Resolution of February 2, 1957.

(3) The United States observes that the recent resolutions of the United Nations General Assembly call not only for the prompt and unconditional withdrawal of Israel behind the Armistice lines but call for other measures.

We believe, however, that the United Nations has properly established an order of events and an order of urgency and that the first requirement is that forces of invasion and occupation should withdraw.

The United States is prepared publicly to declare that it will use its influence, in concert with other United Nations members, to the end that, following Israel's withdrawal, these other measures will be implemented.

We believe that our views and purposes in this respect are shared by many other nations and that a tranquil future for Israel is best assured by reliance upon that fact, rather than by an occupation in defiance of the overwhelming judgment of the world community.

APPENDIX K

In April 1956, for example, I approved the establishment by the Atomic Energy Commission of the Enrico Fermi Award, which had been proposed to me by Chairman Strauss. This award consisted of a prize of $50,000 and a gold medal bearing the likeness of the great Italian-born scientist who had done so much to place the United States in a position of pre-eminence in the area of nuclear physics. He had built the first reactor in which the fission of uranium atoms was controllable, and he had also made a great number of contributions to theoretical physics. He stood in the front rank of those immigrants to our shores who had fled the intolerance and dictatorship of Fascism to find in the Free World and amidst our institutions the climate in which their genius could continue to flower. Later I presented the first Fermi Award to Dr. John von Neumann, the outstanding mathematician of the time, who was then in the terminal stages of his struggle with cancer. In September of the following year, I heartily approved the award of the Fermi Award to Dr. Ernest O. Lawrence, best known to the public as the inventor of the cyclotron, but who had also contributed largely to our technological achievements in World War II. The significance of the Fermi Award lay in the fact that it was the first considerable recognition of excellence in the area of science to be made by the government as distinct from private or academic honors. I have always believed in public recognition of very great service to the nation. It is true that we run a danger of debasement of such distinctions by an indiscriminate selection of recipients, based upon transient popularity or favoritism, but a system of honors founded upon real merit and awarded with discrimination to preserve the integrity of awards is an incentive to our youth and establishes standards more enduring and more commendable than mere material success.

APPENDIX L

November 22, 1957

Dear George:

This noon I took your letter home with me and read it thoroughly. My instant reaction is that if confidence in this country will be won only if we have a significant reduction in the budget, and damaged or even destroyed if the budget goes up, then there better be some looking for storm cellars.

There has been at least a 6 per cent rise in the cost of everything during the last two years, much of it in the last year. This factor alone destroys hope of any substantial reduction, particularly when you remember that Charlie and I, working on the military budget a year and a half ago, battled our way down to the 38 billion mark only with the greatest difficulty. Since 6 per cent of 38 billion is more than 2 billion, you can see what a bloody fight I have been waging in the current sessions.

I am making copies of your letter, and on a confidential basis furnishing it to Neil McElroy, Dr. Saulnier, Percy Brundage and Sinny Weeks. I am likewise giving a copy to Ezra Benson, but I am not giving one to Bob Anderson. Upon delivering your letter to me, he said he was thoroughly acquainted with its contents.

Over the past five years it seems to me that I have put in two-thirds of my time fighting increased expenditures in government, yet only this morning we had our mid-year review of the budget and we find that with the exception of one or two very unimportant agencies, the '57 expenditures for every single Department of government exceed comparable ones in the year '56. (I am talking calendar years here.) Every one of these increases has been brought about by law, except that of the Treasury Department where the extra amount is entirely for interest.

With warm regard,

As ever,

APPENDIX M

(*New York Times,* August 14, 1960, page 1)

Eye in the Sky

Discoverer XIII was designed as a reconnaissance satellite that eventually will carry into orbit cameras that will photograph the earth's surface either on impulses from the ground or internal timing devices. It is stabilized in space to present the same surface to the earth at all times. It is equipped with a detachable capsule in which exposed film would be returned to earth.

Since the first Discoverer was launched in February, 1959, seven of the satellites have achieved orbit. Each attempt to recover the capsules, however, failed. One landed in the vicinity of Spitzbergen Island and was lost. Another came down outside the Pacific target area and was never sighted. Malfunctions prevented proper ejection of the others.

Last Thursday, at 7:15 P.M. as Discoverer XIII was completing its seventeenth circuit on a polar orbit, its 300-pound capsule was ejected over the far northern Pacific, on radio command from earth. Rockets slowed it from its orbiting speed and it descended toward earth. Its path was followed by the Air Force by radio signals from its instruments. As it approached the earth's atmosphere, a switch activated by deceleration released a parachute. C-119 transport planes were in the recovery area near Hawaii but their attempts to catch the parachute failed. However, planes sighted the capsule and followed it to its landing. A Navy frogman, dropped from a hovering helicopter, attached a line and the capsule was taken aboard.

While nose cones and capsules from ballistic missiles have been shot into space and returned, this was the first time that an object that had been in orbit has been successfully recovered. This achievement is a necessary prelude to any attempt to send living creatures into space and back.

Of the two achievements, the return of the Discoverer's capsule is the more important in terms of the race into outer space. The next step will be to put into orbit and return small animals. Plans for such experiments are already in the works. A period of study would follow to determine the effects on living creatures of orbital flight. The objective, of course, is to prepare the way for space flight by humans. The U. S. Mercury project has set a target date of 1961 for the first attempt. The Russians are pointing at a similar goal, but there is as yet no indication that they have solved the problem of return. Thus there is still a question as to which will be the first to take this ultimate step.

APPENDIX N

July 25, 1958

Dear Mr. Chairman:

I have studied your letter of July twenty-third. I find in it apparent misunderstandings of the views expressed in my letter of July twenty-second, which I would request you to read again more carefully.

I then said that if, despite the facts established in the recent meetings of the Security Council, your Government still desires to allege that the situation in Lebanon constitutes an imminent danger to peace in the Middle East, the proper forum for appropriate discussion is the United Nations Security Council. I am glad that you now recognize the responsibility of the United Nations and have withdrawn your original proposal which would have gravely undermined the prestige and authority of the United Nations.

My letter pointed out that the Charter of the United Nations authorizes members of government, and that of course includes Heads of Government and Foreign Ministers, to represent a member nation at the Security Council and that if such a meeting were generally desired, the United States would join in following that orderly procedure. It is, of course, not yet certain that such a meeting is in fact "generally desired," although that may prove to be the case.

You now make specific suggestions dealing with the composition of the Security Council and the conditions under which nations other than members of the Council may participate in discussions of the Council. My letter to you of July twenty-second urged that one of the advantages of proceedings in the Security Council is that there are established rules on these matters and it is accordingly not necessary to rely on improvising. I pointed out that when rules of this kind are sought to be improvised there is raised a whole series of new problems, notably as to the participation and non-participation of various states. The United States will adhere, in these respects, to the Charter, which lays down the conditions under which nations which are not members of the Council may participate in the discussions of the Council.

As to the agenda, we agree that it should be limited to a discussion of the problems of the Middle East, including the causes of those problems. I would, however, be lacking in candor if I did not make clear that to put peace and security on a more stable basis in the Middle East requires far more than merely a consideration of Lebanon and Jordan. These situations are but isolated manifestations of far broader problems. In my opinion the instability of peace and security is in large measure due to the jeopardy in which small nations are placed. It would be the purpose of the United States to deal with the specific incidents you raise within that broad context. To do otherwise would be to be blind to the teaching of history.

You will recall, Mr. Chairman, that World War II was brought about by a series of acts of direct and indirect aggression against small nations. In March 1939 the then head of the Soviet Communist Party pointed out that the failure of non-aggressive nations, among which he named Britian and France, to check direct or indirect aggression against small countries meant "giving free rein to war and, consequently, transforming the war into a world war." That forecast unhappily proved true.

You will also recall the 1950 "Peace through Deeds" Resolution of the General Assembly, which condemns the "fomenting of civil strife in the interest of a foreign power" as among "the gravest of all crimes."

It is my earnest hope that through the United Nations Security Council steps can be taken in regard to the Middle East which, by making peace more secure there, will help promote it elsewhere.

In conclusion, I suggest that the Permanent Representatives of the members of the United Nations Security Council in New York should exchange views, under arrangements made by the Secretary-General, to ascertain that a meeting of the kind and under conditions I suggest is generally acceptable. If so they should also agree upon a date which would be generally satisfactory. The date of July twenty-eighth would be too early for us.

I am today authorizing our own Permanent Representative to act in this sense.

Sincerely,

APPENDIX O

MEMORANDUM RE FORMOSA STRAIT SITUATION

September 4, 1958

Events in the Taiwan Straits indicate that the Chicoms, with Soviet backing, have begun tentatively to put into operation a program, which has been prepared for over the past 3 years, designed initially to liquidate the Chinat positions in Taiwan and the offshore islands, and with probably even more far-reaching purposes.

The program has been begun by intense pressure on the weakest and most vulnerable of such positions, namely, the Chinat-held offshore islands of Quemoy and Matsu. It seems that the operation is designed to produce a cumulating rollback effect, first on the offshore islands, and then on Taiwan, the "liberation" of which is the announced purpose of the present phase. The "liberation," if it occurred, would have serious repercussions on the Philippines, Japan, and other friendly countries of the Far East and Southeast Asia.

The first phase of the operation—that involving Quemoy and/or Matsu—would be primarily military; for these initial obstacles cannot be overcome otherwise. The follow-up against Taiwan might be primarily subversive, taking advantage of the blow to the Republic of China involved in the loss of the offshore islands where it has virtually staked its future. However, armed Chicom attack against Taiwan is not to be excluded. This is, indeed, forecast by the current Chinese Communist broadcasts.

The taking over of Taiwan by the Communists would greatly enhance Communist influence and prestige throughout the free Asian world and depreciate that of the US.

The foregoing summary is based upon the following more specific estimates:

1) In the absence of US intervention, the Chicoms, by accepting heavy casualties, could take Quemoy by an amphibious assault supported by artillery and aerial bombardment. Such an assault could be staged with little advance notice. The operation once initiated might take from one to several days depending on the quality of the resistance.

2) If the Chicoms believe the US will not intervene, they can be expected to mount such an assault whenever they believe the defenders have been sufficiently "softened up."

3) If the Chicoms believe the US would actively intervene to throw back an assault, perhaps using nuclear weapons, it is probable there would be no

attempt to take Quemoy by assault and the situation might quiet down, as in 1955.

4) It is, however, also possible that if the Chicoms felt that the US would intervene only if there were a major assault, they might keep that assault as an overhanging menace but never an actuality, and meanwhile continue the type of pressures now being exerted, including bombardment and attempted blockade, on the theory that if this were prolonged, the defense would collapse due to deterioration of morale and lack of supply.

5) Under these conditions, and if interdiction were not broken, the morale and defense capability of the defenders would, in fact, deteriorate and might eventually collapse, particularly since the US would find it difficult to find new ways to support the morale. Indeed, the US would find it difficult to maintain in the area its present show of strength for any considerable period of time.

6) If Quemoy were lost either through assault or surrender, this would have a serious impact upon the authority and military capability of the anti-Communist, pro-US, government on Formosa. It would be exposed to subversive and/or military action which would probably bring about a government which would eventually advocate union with Communist China and the elimination of US positions on the island.

7) If the foregoing occurred, it would seriously jeopardize the anti-Communist barrier consisting of the insular and peninsular positions in the Western Pacific; e.g., Japan, Republic of Korea, Republic of China, Republic of the Philippines, Thailand and Vietnam. Other governments in Southeast Asia such as those of Indonesia, Malaya, Cambodia, Laos and Burma would probably come fully under Communist influence. US positions in this area, perhaps even Okinawa, would probably become untenable, or unusable, and Japan with its great industrial potential would probably fall within the Sino-Soviet orbit. These events would not happen all at once but would probably occur over a period of a few years. The consequences in the Far East would be even more far-reaching and catastrophic than those which followed when the United States allowed the Chinese mainland to be taken over by the Chinese Communists, aided and abetted by the Soviet Union.

8) The impact of these adverse developments in the Western Pacific and Southeast Asia would undoubtedly have serious, world-wide effects.

9) If the Communists, acting on the supposition that we will not actively intervene, seek to take Quemoy by assault and become increasingly committed, and if we then do intervene, there might be a period between the beginning of assault and irrevocable commitment when prompt and substantial US intervention with *conventional* weapons might lead the Chicoms to withhold or reverse their assault effort. Otherwise, our intervention would probably not be effective if it were limited to the use of conventional weapons.

10) US destroyers are cooperating with the Chinat sea supply operations within the limits of international waters, i.e., up to within three miles of Quemoy. There is thus a possibility of a deliberate or accidental hit by the Chicoms, which would have potential and unplanned reactions which might involve at least limited retaliation.

11) Once we intervened to save the offshore islands, we could not abandon that result without unacceptable damage to the safety of the free world and our influence in it.

If accomplishment of this result required the use of nuclear weapons, there would be a strong popular revulsion against the US in most of the world. It would be particularly intense in Asia and particularly harmful to us in Japan.

If relatively small detonations were used with only air bursts, so that there would be no appreciable fallout or large civilian casualties, and if the matter were quickly closed, the revulsion might not be long-lived or entail consequences as far-reaching and permanent as though there had occurred the series of political reversals indicated in Point 7 above. It is not certain, however, that the operation could be thus limited in scope or time, and the risk of a more extensive use of nuclear weapons, and even a risk of general war, would have to be accepted.

(References are here made to Quemoy as the most likely Communist target. If Matsu became the initial target, the situation would be substantially the same.)

APPENDIX P

The Department of State has taken note of the broadcast of the Fukien Command of the Chinese Communist Army, rebroadcast by Peiping Radio late yesterday (August 27), in which Peiping states, "The Chinese People's Liberation Army has determined to liberate Taiwan, a territory of the fatherland, as well as the offshore islands and the landing on Quemoy is imminent." The fact that the offshore islands are related intimately to Taiwan in this Peiping radio threat confirms what Secretary Dulles said in his recent letter to Mr. Morgan, Chairman of the House Foreign Affairs Committee. The Secretary pointed out that the ties between the offshore islands and Formosa have become closer, that their interdependence has increased, and that he believed that it would be "highly hazardous" for anyone to assume that if the Chinese Communists were to attempt to change the situation by force and now attack or seek to conquer these islands, that could be a limited operation.

This direct threat and the massive bombardment of Quemoy come as stark reminders of Peiping's . . . repeated professions of peaceful intentions.

APPENDIX Q

The United States was using the enormous quantity of 240 billion gallons of water a day. But we knew that in the succeeding two decades that figure could double or even triple. Our population, we knew, could expand from less than 175 million to 275 million by 1980, perhaps to 350 million by the end of the century. Moreover, we knew of the increasingly ravenous thirst of industry: to produce one ton of acetate, for example, a factory needs approximately a quarter of a million gallons of water. It takes more than a half million gallons to blast off an Atlas missile.

Although by 1958 Americans in many hundreds of communities had experienced water shortages (as I write these words the nearby town of Hanover, Pennsylvania has announced that it may have to close down its public schools because of a lack of water in the city reservoir), we still have not reached the limit of our fresh water supply. In the West we use only about one-third of all the water that falls, in the East only about one-eighth. Nonetheless with our heightening need must continue our varied efforts to conserve water—to "nail the raindrop where it falls" on lands far upstream in every water basin, to continue the construction of multiple-purpose dams to hold back water which would otherwise run unused to the ocean, to combat water pollution by such things as industrial and urban wastes, herbicides, and insecticides—and above all to pursue perhaps the most promising of all possibilities, the conversion of salt water into fresh water.

APPENDIX R

During the administration of President Andrew Johnson the United States had bought Alaska from Russia for $7,200,000—an amount which some Americans of 1867 called an unconscionable price to pay for Secretary of State Seward's "icebox."

Under an act of August 24, 1912, the Territory of Alaska came into existence, with an elective legislative assembly. On March 30, 1916, Judge James Wickersham, Delegate from Alaska, introduced the Territory's first statehood bill; since 1933 a similar bill had come before every Congress.

Hearings finally began in 1947, under the Republican 80th Congress. A bill passed the House in 1950, but the Senate failed to act. In 1952 the Senate voted to recommit a similar measure. There the cause stood when I took office.

The story of the struggle for Hawaiian statehood parallels that of Alaska. In 1898 the independent nation of Hawaii became part of the United States and, in 1900, was given the status of an incorporated territory. In 1919 its first statehood bill was introduced. In 1947 and 1950 the House passed such measures, but the Senate failed to act.

APPENDIX S

The purpose of the Foreign Minister's meeting should be to reach positive agreements over as wide a field as possible, and in any case to narrow the differences between the respective points of view and to prepare constructive proposals for consideration by a conference of Heads of Government later in the summer. On this understanding and as soon as developments in the Foreign Minister's meeting justify holding a Summit Conference, the United States Government would be ready to participate in such a conference. The date, place and agenda for such a conference would be proposed by the meeting of Foreign Ministers. The conference of Heads of Government could consider and if possible resolve some wider problems such as those referred to in the Soviet Government's note of March 2nd and in previous communications from the United States Government and where necessary establish machinery for further negotiation on these problems.

APPENDIX T

November 7, 1958

My dear friend:

I felt that I must write a word to you to say how much I am thinking about you and your many problems. You can rest assured that the affection which we all have for you in this country is in no way dependent upon the political fortunes of the Republican Party.

You are fortunate in having spent most of your life as a soldier. I, alas, have been for 35 years a politician. The ups and downs of politics are very strange and sometimes very bitter. But when one looks at them as a whole one realises that democracy is a strange animal and that all one can hope to do is to do our best. In my first constituency, in Tees-side, I fought six elections—I lost three and won three. I remember very well that when one lost one was apt to say how tiresome and foolish all this business of counting noses was: when one won, of course, one felt convinced of the soundness of public opinion.

The truth is that those who have reached positions like yours rest secure in their own sense of having done their duty. I remember well Churchill's feelings in 1945 when he was rejected by a people who had only survived through his leadership. I also remember my admiration for the way in which he accepted the facts and overcame them. If I may say so I think your position is not unlike his at that time. It was the Party that dragged Churchill down and not the opposite. Your record and reputation will remain untarnished by temporary reverses.

Ever yours,

/s/ Harold

APPENDIX U

ACTION ON PRESIDENT'S BUDGETS AS OF JULY 26, 1959

The President's budget for 1960 proposes a $70-million surplus. To date, House action turns this into a $814-million deficit. Senate action to date would create a deficit of $1272-million.

HOUSE OF REPRESENTATIVES:	*Effect on President's budgets (1959 and subsequent years)*
The President proposes that Congress enact motor fuel and aviation gas taxes and increase postal rates, all of which would provide $676-million. Congress has taken no action and the Democratic leadership indicates none is planned.	Denies $676-million in needed revenues.
The House has passed a voluntary pension plan for self-employed persons which would reduce receipts by $365-million.	Reduces Government's revenues by $365-million.

* * * * * *

On the other hand, the House has taken the following *spending* action:

Passed veterans' housing loan act for $100-million. (Status: Law)	$100-million more than President's budget.
Passed $126-million aid-to-airports bill. (Status: Law)	$6-million more than President's budget.
Extended temporary unemployment compensation for remainder of this fiscal year, adding $75-million to 1959 expenditures. (Status: Law)	$75-million more than President's budget.
Passed Federal Water Pollution Control Act. (Status: Senate Public Works Committee)	$840-million more than President's budget.

Passed veterans' pension bill. (Status: Senate Finance Committee)	$208-million more than President's budget.
Appropriation actions have reduced new obligational authority by $1015-million.	$1015-million less than requested.

* * * * * *

SENATE:	*Effect on President's budgets (1959 and subsequent years)*
Failure to act on President's proposed postal rate increase and certain tax increases.	Denies $676-million in needed revenues.
Passed aid-to-airports bill. (Status: Law)	$6-million more than President's budget.
Area redevelopment act. (Status: House Banking and Currency Committee)	$337-million more than President's budget.
Extended temporary unemployment compensation for remainder of this fiscal year, adding $75-million to 1959 expenditures. (Status: Law)	$75-million more than President's budget.
Passed grants to states for education TV. (Status: House Interstate and Foreign Commerce Committee)	$50-million more than President's budget.
Passed extension of school milk program for fiscal years 1960 and 1961. (Status: House Agriculture Committee)	$10-million more than President's budget.
International medical research: $50-million annually. (Status: House Interstate and Foreign Commerce Committee)	$50-million more than President's budget.
Passed veterans' housing loan act. (Status: Law)	$100-million more than President's budget.
Passed peacetime exservicemen's readjustment benefits—$100-million first year; $500-million by fourth year. (Status: House Veterans Affairs Committee)	$100-million more than President's budget.
Appropriation action has increased new obligational authority by $459-million.	$459-million more than requested.

* * * * * *

SUMMARY:

After seven months of this session of Congress, the House of Representatives has taken actions that increased the President's requests by $1,255-million.	+ $1,255-million
All Senate action to date has increased the President's requests by $1,863-million.	+ $1,863-million

NOTE: Excludes Housing Bill—vetoed by President—which was $565-million more than President's budget.

APPENDIX V

June 16, 1959

The Foreign Ministers of France, the United Kingdom, the United States and the Union of Soviet Socialist Republics have examined the question of Berlin in the desire to find mutually satisfactory solutions to the problems which have been raised and which derive essentially from the division of Berlin and of Germany. They agreed that the best solution for these problems would be the reunification of Germany. They recognized, however, that pending reunification, the existing situation and the Agreements at present in force can be modified in certain respects and have consequently agreed upon the following:

(a) The Soviet Foreign Minister has made known the decision of the Soviet Government no longer to maintain forces in Berlin.

The Foreign Ministers of France, the United Kingdom and the United States declare that it is the intention of their Governments to limit the combined total of their forces in Berlin to the present figure (approximately 11,000) and to continue to arm these forces only with conventional weapons as at present. The three Ministers further declare that their governments will from time to time consider the possibility of reducing such forces if developments in the situation permit.

(b) The Ministers agreed that there shall continue to be free and unrestricted access to West Berlin by land, by water and by air for all persons, goods and communications, including those of the French, United Kingdom and United States forces stationed in West Berlin. The procedures applicable shall be those in effect in April 1959. However, without prejudice to existing basic responsibilities, these procedures may where it is not already the case be carried out by German personnel.

June 19, 1959

The Ministers likewise reaffirmed that freedom of movement will continue to be maintained between East and West Berlin.

All disputes which might arise with respect to access will be raised and settled between the four Governments. The latter will establish a quadripartite Commission which will meet in Berlin to examine any difficulties arising out of the application of the present sub-paragraph and to facilitate their settlement. The Commission may make arrangements if necessary to consult German experts.

The Ministers consider that measures should be taken consistent with fundamental rights and liberties to avoid in both parts of Berlin activities which might either disturb public order or seriously affect the rights and interests, or amount to interference in the internal affairs, of others.

The Ministers agreed that unless subsequently modified by Four Power agreement these arrangements will continue in force until the reunification of Germany.

APPENDIX W

On July 30 Mr. Herter notified me that at least the three Western foreign ministers had made clear three major points. First, we insisted on continuation of all Allied rights in Berlin, whether or not a moratorium on the entire issue was arranged. The second was our determination to maintain the level of Allied strength in Berlin. The Soviets argued that because there would be no Soviet units in the city, the Allies should reduce their garrisons drastically. Their argument was palpably specious, because not only could East German forces substitute for the Russian, but the entire city would be still surrounded by Soviet units. Though we had already discussed the possibility of reducing the numerical strength of the Allied units, we rejected this proposal out of hand, having in mind the shock to the morale of West Berliners that would be caused by almost total removal of the Allied forces. The third point had to do with a Soviet proposal for an all-German committee, representing both sides of the Iron Curtain, to discuss reunification. To this, of course, Chancellor Adenauer would never agree. Our position was that a negotiating committee, if established, should come from the four occupying powers, with both East and West German advisers present.

I informed the Secretary of State that we should stand firm on the first and third points. If the British and French were willing, I went on, we would be prepared to issue a unilateral statement by the Western powers limiting forces to something like eight to ten thousand troops compared to the eleven thousand then on duty. This point was almost academic. While there was need for sizable Allied troop units as a living proof to West Berliners of Western sincerity in supporting their rights and liberties, there was no possibility that a Western garrison could be maintained at a strength that could provide an effective defense against all-out Soviet aggression. A reduction of some one or two thousand was of little consequence, but a reduction to a maximum of a few hundred would be interpreted by the West Berliners as surrender.

APPENDIX X

November 12, 1959

Dear Jim:

There appears frequently in the press speculation concerning the kind of labor-management laws that Congress will be proposing, considering and possibly passing in the event that the steel strike resumes after the eighty-day period of work required under the Taft-Hartley Act. Congressional activity of this kind would be much intensified if a resumed steel strike were accompanied by others, including the railroads, "Can" companies and so on.

Sometime back I requested that you, with the Attorney General, Secretary of Labor, Chairman of the Council of Economic Advisers and others study this whole field to see whether or not there was anything of a practical character that could be suggested and enacted into law *without* sooner or later starting a definite trend toward governmental control of the entire economy.

One thing that crossed my mind was inspired by some of the projects under study which look toward partial disposal of accumulated surpluses in stock piles of copper, aluminum, rubber and other commodities.

The Taft-Hartley Act can be invoked only when the continuation of a strike endangers or threatens to endanger the national security or health. What this means is that the Taft-Hartley injunctive process is presumably invoked when the strike becomes not merely an internecine warfare between labor and management, but which *really becomes an attack on the welfare of the entire nation.* On this basic assumption the government intervenes to protect the public.

Now, assume that the government had, as a matter of policy, acquired a considerable stock of inventories in the types of steel that are essential to the Defense Department and to those portions of the industry that necessarily satisfy the fundamental requirements of the public. A new law could provide that these inventories might be used under stated conditions prescribed by law and thus tend to make both parties more amenable to conciliation.

Inventories are, of course, of a fixed and static character and the point might be made that they would be useful for a matter of sixty days or something of that kind. The law might then provide that ten days after production in any essential industry had been stopped by strike, the government could authorize the lowering or elimination of tariffs on steel and invite an inflow of the kind of things we need.

Of course we realize that no industry in any country is geared up to a sudden increase of output. But if we had the authority of which I speak on the books, probably most of the steel exporting countries would somewhat enlarge their own inventories in the hope of making quick and large sales to the United States. Our cost and price structure in this country is such that whatever these companies throughout the world might have on hand would be immediately on the road toward our shores. The effect of this would probably be to lower prices here at home and both the steel companies and the unions would be on notice that their position could no longer be regarded as completely monopolistic. Of course it is possible that some companies using steel products brought in from abroad would be hit by secondary boycotts. In such cases the law should be so broad as to allow the tariff to be removed from . . . articles [similar to those] produced by that particular company from such steel products.

I realize that there would be many practical obstacles (and perhaps even more serious political ones) to getting such laws on the books, but I am quite sure that if such authority did exist, we might see a great diminution in the number of strikes. Certainly such a position would discourage the continuation of any long strike.

Of course any such authority would cease the moment the strike was settled. But foreign steel already contracted for and shipped would come in. Since I think there would be a great rush on the part of industrial nations to take advantage of our prices, the shipments could reach a considerable amount. Knowledge on the part of companies and unions would have a great influence in keeping domestic industry from attempting to become the master of the people. . . .

I think this is not too brilliant a thought. I have not even developed in my own mind anything that I could call a real idea. The only thing I am trying to say is that I am searching to see what kind of thing the United States can do to protect itself against these disruptive strikes brought about by the selfishness and stupidity of both sides and which at the same time [will not] violate our principles of free economic practices.

With warm regard,

As ever,

APPENDIX Y

1. The actual adverse effects of steel strikes on the economy have not been of serious magnitude. A major reason why steel strikes have had so little measurable impact is that when a strike approaches a critical stage, pressures upon the parties to settle become substantially irresistible.

2. Partial operation in the interest of national defense should be given far more serious attention than it has in the past.

3. Early intervention tends to frustrate and hinder the process of negotiation and has neither secured settlements nor avoided strikes. Late, informal, and mediatory intervention has produced settlements and appears to be least harmful in achieving a pattern of private agreement.

4. Minor modifications in the mechanism for handling national emergency disputes hold little promise for altering the above conclusion.

5. Collective bargaining settlements in steel have not been a predominant independent influence in establishing or modifying wage trends in the economy.

6. The wage and price effects of steel settlements, and industry decisions with respect to price policy, when realistically interpreted, have had a minimal effect upon the price level in the economy.

7. The increasingly stringent compulsions of competition provide important protection for steel users.

8. A major problem confronting the parties in collective bargaining is to adjust to the increasingly competitive environment in a manner best suited to protect their mutual longer-term interests.

9. The exaggerated interpretation of the national emergency dimension of steel strikes and resulting Government intervention have tended to reduce the compulsions for avoiding strikes relative to the pressures for ending them.

It is significant that the public interest has not been seriously harmed by strikes in steel, or by steel collective bargaining agreements despite common public opinion to the contrary. Minor changes in existing legislation will not provide demonstrably superior results in the avoidance of future steel strikes. Moreover, the problems involved do not seem to indicate the necessity for the more drastic forms of governmental intervention that are sometimes proposed. In the light of these conclusions it is hoped that the public and its representatives will be very cautious in approving legislative changes affecting the existing collective bargaining system.

APPENDIX Z

August 21, 1958

3. . . . The spacing between the control posts in continental aseismic areas would be about 1700 kilometres, and in seismic areas about 1000 kilometres. The spacing between the control posts in ocean areas would vary between 2000 and more than 3500 kilometres; the spacing between island control posts in seismic areas would be about 1000 kilometres. This would lead to the following approximate distribution of control posts over the globe (with a network including 110 continental posts): North America—24, Europe—6, Asia—37, Australia—7, South America—16, Africa—16, Antarctica—4; together with 60 control posts on islands and about 10 ships.

4. . . . In order to carry out the tasks required one might need for each control post about 30 persons with various qualifications and fields of specialization, and also some persons for the auxiliary servicing staff.

5. In addition to the basic network described, air sampling would be accomplished by aircraft carrying out regular flights along north–south routes over the oceans along the peripheries of the Atlantic and Pacific Oceans, and also over areas of the oceans which are remote from surface control posts. . . .

APPENDIX AA

December 19, 1959

Mr. Fisk (*United States of America*): I had hoped that we would not be called upon today to reargue our cases, particularly since I understand that the annexes to the report which we have submitted to you today are to be published, and particularly also because these questions have been so thoroughly covered in the verbatim records.

However, since Dr. [E. K.] Federov has read his incorrect, distorted, and misleading statement, I feel that the record would be lopsided if I did not make a few moderate comments on behalf of the United States delegation.

Mr. Federov has referred to a large number of very highly technical and complicated matters. I do not propose to comment on all of them, for the reasons that I have cited. There are, however, a few which deserve comment at this time.

Mr. Federov has returned once again to the argument which he has used persistently throughout our meetings—namely, the argument that the new data based on the Hardtack experiments are invalid because they in effect do not represent a test of the system recommended by the Geneva Conference of Experts. I should like to observe that that assertion is irrelevant. I would, furthermore, observe that the instruments which were used in the Hardtack experiments have been conclusively shown, in the course of the meetings of the Technical Working Group, to be superior to those which we understand were recommended by the Conference of Experts. Mr. Federov challenges us because not every one of the total number of seismographs used in the Hardtack experiments was used in every experiment. This has no essential bearing on the results. I would simply observe that sixteen seismographs, well calibrated and well placed, for any one of these underground explosions, are a rather unusually large number and the data from them are good, relevant, and complete.

Mr. Federov charges us with changing the source data as a matter of whim. I should like to remind him that the source data are the seismograms themselves. Many of them have been available to the Soviet delegation for a number of months. In the first few meetings of the Technical Working Group, 250 were made available to the Soviet delegation. Those are the source data. If the Soviet scientists are willing to do their own homework, they have available every bit of data that we have labored on for so long.

Mr. Federov says that we introduced new data at the nineteenth meeting of the Working Group. That is an absurd statement. I should like to observe that it was only at last, at that nineteenth meeting, that we could even bring Mr. Federov to discuss on a technical basis the very important question of first motion. Furthermore, what he calls new data were obtained by measuring the very seismograms that had been made available to the Soviet delegation earlier.

I should now like to make some remarks about the final report of the United States delegation concerning the work of the Technical Working Group.

In accordance with the Group's terms of reference, the United States delegation bases its report on all scientifically valid conclusions concerning the detection and identification of nuclear events based on new studies and data, whether such conclusions would lead to improvements of the system or would lead to an assessment which would make the system appear less effective. It is our view that mentioning only the potential improvements in the final conclusions on this subject would mislead the Conference on the Discontinuance of Nuclear Weapon Tests concerning the present technical status of the possible control system.

One of the important conclusions in the section of our report on new data deals with the so-called first motion problem—that is, the direction in which a seismic needle would swing as a first response to a seismic disturbance. This direction was considered by the Conference of Experts in 1958 to be the primary tool for discriminating between earthquakes and explosions. The conclusion drawn by the United States delegation, based on new data, is that this method of discrimination is much less effective than had been thought.

A further important conclusion in that section concerns the possibility of concealment of underground nuclear explosions by detonating such explosions in a very large cavity in salt or hard rock. It was shown theoretically that the seismic signal of a given explosion under these conditions could be reduced three hundredfold or more as compared to the signals produced in the Nevada tests. Consequently, explosions could be made to look smaller by this factor and thus be much harder to detect and locate.

Another item of the same section deals with a subject to which Mr. Federov has given such attention—that is, the estimate of the number of earthquakes which would be expected to be detected and located by the system. The conclusion is that the estimates of such a number are very uncertain but that about 15,000 earthquakes per year would be located by the system over the whole world, corresponding to earth movements produced by nuclear explosions of more than one kiloton. For larger explosions, such as 20 kilotons, the number of equivalent earthquakes is about 2,000 worldwide.

All delegations concurred in the section on seismic improvements, and I do not believe that it needs any further comment. However, much work and research must be done to make these new methods effective.

We then have a section on criteria based on objective instrument readings which could be used by the control organization in determining the eligibility of detected and located seismic events for inspection. Agreement was not reached on that section. It is the United States delegation's view that such criteria must be formulated so that a large number of explosions would not be classified as natural earthquakes and that the criteria must be based on well-established technical information. Unfortunately, the resulting criteria classify only a small fraction of the seismic events as natural earthquakes, leaving a large number eligible for inspection. It was the Soviet delegation's view that criteria must be specified by the Working Group which would remove a large fraction of the seismic events from eligibility for inspection by identifying them as natural earthquakes. However, it is the United States delegation's view that this is impossible within present technical knowledge. In fact, the criteria proposed by the Soviet delegation would have classified such events as the recent United States underground nuclear test explosions, which ranged up to 19 kilotons in yield, as natural earthquakes and thus would have made them ineligible for inspection. It is the United States delegation's view that as scientific knowledge progresses, more useful criteria can be formulated in the future.

We recognize that there is a great deal of additional seismic information available, as listed in a substantial section of our report, but that information is not sufficiently complete to be formulated into specific criteria. The United States delegation feels that such auxiliary information should be very useful if evaluated in a competent technical manner in connection with a particular seismic event.

The problem of the formulation of criteria is a strictly technical problem. If technical knowledge permits one to identify a large fraction of seismic events as earthquakes, then it is clearly a great advantage to the control system. If technical knowledge does not permit that, then seismic events must remain eligible for inspection. Determination of the means of selecting events to be inspected must be left for further consideration by the main Conference.

APPENDIX BB

ACCOUNT OF DECEMBER 6, 1960 MEETING WITH PRESIDENT-ELECT* KENNEDY

1. I arranged for an informal military parade in front of the White House to receive the President-elect. I met him on the north portico of the mansion. We immediately started talks in my office.

2. It quickly became apparent that any single meeting, no matter of what length, could do little more than hit the high spots in the problem of transferring Federal control from one Administration to another.

The agenda suggested in advance by Senator Kennedy had as its first three items: Berlin, the Far East and Cuba. He had previously been briefed by Allen Dulles a number of times and had some familiarity with the details of these three subjects. Even so, there was no point in trying to go deeply into the details of these subjects because a full morning could be easily devoted to the possibilities, both adverse and favorable, that lie before us.

3. The Senator was interested in the National Security setup and its operations. He suggested also that I give him any ideas I might have about improving the Pentagon operation.

I explained to him in detail the purpose and work habits of the Security Council, together with its two principal supporting agencies—the Planning Board and the Operations Coordinating Board. I said that the National Security Council had become the most important weekly meeting of the government; that we normally worked from an agenda, but that any member could present his frank opinion on any subject, even on those that were not on the formal agenda. I made clear to him that conferences in the White House are not conducted as Committee meetings in the Legislative Branch. There is no voting by members and each group has one purpose only—to advise the President on the facts of particular problems and to make to him such recommendations as each member may deem applicable. I described how "splits" in Planning Board papers were handled.

He, obviously, could not be expected to understand the operations of the Security Council from one short briefing, and I urged him to appoint, as soon as he possibly could, an individual that he would want to take over the duties, after January 20, of Gordon Gray. I stated that if he would do this,

* "President-designate" is the formal and proper term for the winning candidate before the Electoral College has met, I am told.

D.E., 1965.

Mr. Gray would make it his business to acquaint such an individual in detail with the operations of the National Security Council and with the general content of the files.

Regarding the Pentagon setup, the Senator mentioned a report he had just received from the so-called Symington Committee. From the papers I had learned something about the report and while I consider it so useless as to be ridiculous, I was careful to say nothing about the report as such.

I did urge him to avoid any reorganization *until he himself could become well acquainted with the problem.* (Incidentally, I made this same suggestion with respect to the White House staff, the National Security Council, and the Pentagon.) I told him that improvements could undoubtedly be made in the Pentagon and the command organization, but I also made it clear that the present organization and the improved functioning of the establishment had, during the past eight years, been brought about by patient study and long and drawn out negotiations with the Congress and the Armed Services. Much has been said about "streamlining" such an organization in the belief that too many advisers and assistants are impeding the making of wise and prompt decisions. I think that something along this line might possibly be done, but in a mechanism such as the Defense establishment, which spends something on the order of 42 billion dollars a year. I pointed out that the Secretary of Defense should be fortified with the finest military and civilian advisers he could get. I pointed out the value of our scientific experts and their counsel. The importance of scientific research is illustrated by the amount of money devoted to the designing, development and testing of any weapons, without placing a single one of them in the operational inventory. (Incidentally, this figure is 6½ billion dollars. Another 23½ billion dollars goes to pay for maintenance of personnel and equipment.) This emphasized, I told him, the need for earnest study and thinking before making radical changes.

4. I spent some time explaining the difference between the functions of the White House staff as an immediate supporting body to the President on the one hand, and the relations between the President and his Cabinet officers. These, both individually and collectively, are always in contact with the President on any important problem affecting one or more.

I told him that without a personal staff all the detailed problems that would arise, even after major policies had been approved, would come directly to the attention of the President—and all of this without any coordination among Departments.

I told him the divisions within the White House were the Military Aides on the one hand and the civilian staff on the other. This civilian staff comprehends a legal section, an economic section, a liaison section and a secretarial section. The records section is a somewhat separated organism, because it is not only manned and headed by civil service personnel, but is the only permanent body in the White House.

The Senator seemed to be a bit amazed when I told him about the great numbers of people that operate in the Signal Corps, Transportation and Evacuation activities, all under the Military Aides. I also described the functions of Camp David.

Within the civilian side, many minor problems arise at the staff level among the different Departments. To expect each Department head to take up each of these with the President or to hold special Cabinet meetings would be undesirable and indeed in the long run impossible. Consequently this coordination is achieved by the President's personal staff, operating under its chief, a man whom I have given the title "The Assistant to the President."

Aside from certain responsibilities of the President touching upon the Regulatory Commissions, there are ten statutory Departments, each headed by a Cabinet officer and, in addition to these, we have the Bureau of the Budget, the Atomic Energy Commission, the Office of Civil and Defense Mobilization, the Council of Economic Advisers, the General Services Administration, the Federal Aviation Agency, and the Veterans Administration.

In addition we have the Central Intelligence Agency, the Civil Service Commission and the United States Information Agency. The Assistant to the President, the Director of the Bureau of the Budget, and the Director of the Office of Civil and Defense Mobilization have been accorded Cabinet rank, as has the President's Representative to the United Nations.

With all these agencies officially and directly subordinate to the President only, and with every problem engaging the attention of any agency normally affecting others, it is easy to see that there is a vast volume of staff coordination required. All of this is done by the President's personal staff.

I said nothing to him about the ceremonies, making of engagements, confidential correspondence, and many other activities which of course are handled normally by the President directly with the responsible individual.

5. Senator Kennedy wanted to get my personal thinking about Macmillan, De Gaulle and Adenauer. I gave him my opinions concerning these people as I have formed them over many years of association with them. I told him that I did not believe that my own comments would mean too much. I did venture the opinion that if he would take the trouble to meet them and talk with them individually and collectively, he would be impressed by their ability and their integrity, even though there would be many instances where he would disagree with their stated opinions.

6. I voluntarily brought up the question of NATO and our ballistic missile proposal to that organization. I told him that De Gaulle has created a number of difficulties in the operation of NATO. I gave Senator Kennedy my opinion that it was the most important alliance to which we belong, one whose maintenance and strength was vital to our own security and prosperity.

In this context I brought up the subject of dealing more closely with our allies in the matter of atomic weapons. I told him that our hands were somewhat tied because the *Joint Committee of Congress dealing with atomic matters was formed and is operating under a law that was written at a time when we had a true monopoly of atomic manufacture.* Today the international club is growing and I think it is worse than silly to allow America's interests and responsibilities in this field to be handled by a Committee whose principal purpose is to stand watch over the *operations* of the Atomic Energy Commission —which is an operative and *not* a policy making organization. I told him that our relations with the Congress on this subject should be handled through the Foreign Relations Committees and the Defense Committees in both Houses. Frankly, I see no need for the continuance of the Joint Committee on Atomic Energy.

7. I talked to the Senator for some twenty minutes on the present situation and the Balance of Payments and foreign confidence in the dollar, and the way that confidence is affected by the balance or imbalance of budgets. I attach a copy of a short memorandum on the matter, but after I had talked to him Secretary Anderson gave him a much longer briefing on the whole matter, lasting some forty-five minutes. I pray that he understands it. Certainly his attitude was that of a serious, earnest seeker for information and the implication was that he will give full consideration to the facts and suggestions we presented.

Partly because of the outflow of gold caused by the great deployments we have abroad, but also because of other reasons, including my conviction that America is carrying far more than her share of free world defense, I told him that I was going to warn the NATO community of the U.S.'s intention of redeploying some of its troops from Europe unless other arrangements could, at the very least, stop this drain on our gold. I told him that I informed him of this so he would not be surprised, and the decision was made and the announcement would be made in such a way as to leave him a free hand in reversing this policy if he so chooses. I told him that while I believe thoroughly that the European nations, all of which have been so vastly strengthened by the billions we poured out through the Marshall Plan and since, were reaching a level of economic productivity that is for them unprecedented, they still seem to be unwilling to pick up what seemed to us to be their fair share of the defense burden. This government has pointed out to them often that we have taken the responsibility for the creation and maintenance of the free world's deterrent. We provide a vast portion of the navies and most of the bombing force in the free world. And we think that the European nations and Canada should be prepared to maintain a much larger proportion of the ground defense formations.

8. On the personal side, Senator Kennedy asked me whether I could be prepared, upon call from him, to serve the country in such areas and in such manner as may seem appropriate. I told him that, of course, the answer was obvious, but I did say that I thought I had the right, after many long years of service and in view of my age, to suggest that if he should request anything from me, it should be normally in terms of conferences and consultations on subjects on which I have had some experience, rather than errands which might necessitate frequent and lengthy travel. While I did not exclude the possibility of making some trip for some extraordinary reason, I did say that in the main I would like to have this restriction on my understanding.

9. Senator Kennedy was very much concerned with the activities of General Goodpaster, and said he would like to hold Goodpaster for two months into

the new Administration. I told him that I thought a better solution would be for him to appoint a man right now who could take Goodpaster's post (the duties of which I detailed at some length) and allow Goodpaster to leave with the rest of us on January 20th. He said he would be handicapped unless he had Goodpaster for a month or two, really favoring the second. Of course I had to say that he would soon be the Commander-in-Chief and he could *order* General Goodpaster to do anything, and those duties would be efficiently performed; but I told him, also, of Goodpaster's great desire to go to active line duty and that a particular spot was being held for him. I asked the Senator if he would assure me that that spot would be held.

(That evening I called General Decker and told him the details of this conversation and asked him, as a personal favor to me, to make it his business to protect Goodpaster's future to this extent. He said there would be no trouble about this.)

Later in the conversation with the three [service] Secretaries, Senator Kennedy repeated this promise, and I think there should be no difficulty in fulfilling it.

10. Finally, I told the Senator that this hurried description of his many functions and duties would possibly be confusing, but if he should like to come back at any time all he had to do was give my secretary a ring and we would set up an appointment promptly.

D.D.E.

APPENDIX CC

December 30, 1960

My dear Friend:

I am much disturbed at the trouble that we are both getting into over Laos. For the first time for many years it seems that our policies, although of the same strategic purpose, have been a little divergent on tactics. This we must surely remedy as soon as we can. As I see it there are two things that ought to be done in order to strengthen our joint position vis-à-vis not only the Communist Powers who send us legalistic Notes, but especially vis-à-vis the moderate and uncommitted countries who are watching what is happening.

The first would be somehow to persuade Phouma to resign. You will no doubt agree on this because you have always been sceptical as to Phouma's value, and anyway he has now left the country and can serve most usefully by resigning his office whatever might be the ultimate arrangements made.

Secondly, there is the question as to how we can strengthen and solidify in the eyes of the world Boun Oum's claim to be the proper government. Surely this can be done by his getting Parliamentary approval according to the rules of the Constitution. I am told that there should be no difficulty about this, for the Parliament is in the habit of supporting the government of the hour. Nevertheless, it would have a considerable advantage if the same processes which legitimised Phouma's government are carried out in the case of Boun Oum's and the present Constitutional set-up maintained. If there were any danger of the Parliament turning nasty, that would be another thing. But I am told that this should be within our power to handle.

Forgive me for this simple approach, but I am so worried about there being any divergence of method between us.

I have purposely left out of this message the question of the International Commission. That we should perhaps consider later and separately. I am sure we both agree that the first step is to get established a proper legitimate government.

With warm regard,

As ever,

Harold

Index

Index

E. stands for Eisenhower, Dwight D.

UNITED STATES

NEUTRAL

COMMUNIST BLOC

NATO Belgium, Canada, Denmark, France, West Germany, Greece, Iceland, Italy, Luxembourg, Netherlands, Norway, Portugal, Turkey, United States

CENTO Iran, Pakistan, Turkey, United Kingdom

SEATO Australia, France, New Zealand, Pakistan, Philippines, Thailand, United Kingdom, United States

ANZUS Australia, New Zealand, United States

RIO PACT Argentina, Bolivia, Brazil, Chile, Colombia, Costa Rica, Cuba, Dominican Republic, Ecuador, El Salvador, Guatemala, Haiti, Honduras, Mexico, Nicaragua, Panama, Paraguay, Peru, United States, Uruguay, Venezuela

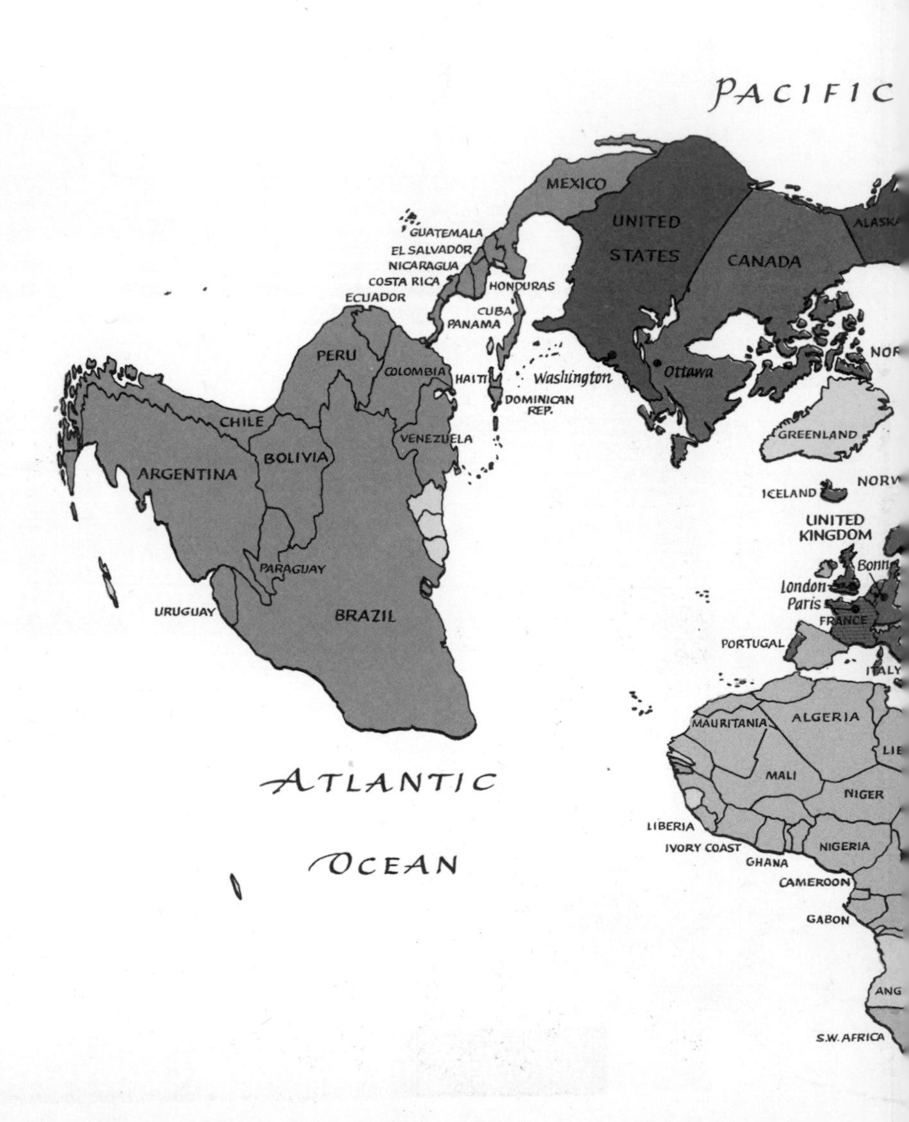

palacios